Presented to the

Library, Westmar College

by Wayne K. Detloff, M. D.

Class 1942

BOLLINGEN SERIES XX

THE COLLECTED WORKS

OF

C. G. JUNG

VOLUME 14

EDITORS

SIR HERBERT READ

MICHAEL FORDHAM, M.D., M.R.C.P.

GERHARD ADLER, PH.D.

WILLIAM MCGUIRE, *executive editor*

MYSTERIUM CONIUNCTIONIS

AN INQUIRY INTO THE SEPARATION AND SYNTHESIS

OF PSYCHIC OPPOSITES IN ALCHEMY

C. G. JUNG

SECOND EDITION

TRANSLATED BY R. F. C. HULL

BOLLINGEN SERIES XX

PRINCETON UNIVERSITY PRESS

Second printing, 1974
Third printing, 1976

Translated from *Mysterium Coniunctionis: Untersuchung über die Trennung
und Zusammensetzung der seelischen
Gegensätze in der Alchemie,* Parts I and
II, published by Rascher Verlag, Zurich,
1955 and 1956 (Vols. X and XI of *Psychologische Abhandlungen,* edited by
C. G. Jung)

LIBRARY OF CONGRESS CATALOGUE CARD NUMBER: 75-156
ISBN 0-691-09766-6
PRINTED IN THE UNITED STATES OF AMERICA

EDITORIAL NOTE *

Volume 14 of the Collected Works presents Jung's last great work, on which he was engaged for more than a decade, from 1941 to 1954. He finished it in his eightieth year. As is to be expected from its culminating position in his writings and from its subject matter, the book gives a final account of his lengthy researches into alchemy.

Jung's interest in the symbolical significance of alchemy for modern depth psychology first found expression, in 1929, in his commentary to *The Secret of the Golden Flower.* The theme was taken up again in his Eranos lectures of 1935 and 1936, which formed the basis of *Psychology and Alchemy,* originally published in 1944. Further researches led to the publication of essays now included in *Alchemical Studies,* Volume 13 of the Collected Works. A preliminary study of the special symbolism of the *coniunctio* in relation to psychotherapeutic problems appeared in *The Psychology of the Transference* (1946), while the connection between philosophical alchemy and Christianity was elaborated in *Aion* (1951). All these themes are brought together in *Mysterium Coniunctionis,* where Jung continues his work of interpretation by examining in detail a number of texts taken from the alchemical classics. The scope of the book is indicated in its subtitle: "An Inquiry into the Separation and Synthesis of Psychic Opposites in Alchemy." This process, summed up in the trenchant formula *solve et coagula*—"dissolve and coagulate"— underlies the *opus alchymicum* and may be symbolically understood as the process of psychic integration.

The focus of the book is on the symbolism of the *coniunctio* and the preceding stages of dissociation. These are known in alchemy as the *chaos* or *prima materia,* and they lead via the intermediate stages to a resolution of the conflict of opposites in the production of the *lapis philosophorum.* Fresh evidence is brought to bear upon Jung's thesis that the *lapis* is not only a

* Revised for the second edition (1970).

parallel of the Christ figure, but a symbolical prefiguration of psychic totality, or the self.

Jung's inquiry is of a highly advanced character and necessitates a wide knowledge of the concepts of analytical psychology in general and Jung's previous publications on alchemy in particular. The reader who follows Jung in his search for a deeper understanding of the *opus alchymicum* will not only discover in this book new and fascinating aspects of the history of the European mind but will also be rewarded by fresh insights into such basic psychological problems as the structure of the self and the ego and their relation to one another, the nature of transference and countertransference, and the process of active imagination. In many ways this book is the summing up of all Jung's later work.

*

The English edition differs from the Swiss in the following particulars. It comprises Volumes I and II of that version. Volume III is an edition and study by Marie-Louise von Franz of *Aurora Consurgens,* a thirteenth-century treatise traditionally attributed to Thomas Aquinas and rediscovered by Jung, which has been issued in English as a companion volume to *Mysterium Coniunctionis,* but outside the Collected Works. The paragraph numbers of the present work do not correspond to those in the two Swiss volumes, which run in separate sequence. Further, many of the longer paragraphs have been broken up, and in certain instances the material has been rearranged within the chapters to facilitate the exposition. The most important of these changes were made with the author's consent.

In order not to overload the footnotes, the Latin and Greek passages have been put into an appendix. An asterisk in a footnote indicates that the quotation translated there or in the main text will be found in the appendix under the corresponding footnote number of the chapter in question.

Two sections of this work were previously published: Chapter II, section 3, appeared as "Das Rätsel von Bologna" in *Beitrag zur Festschrift Albert Oeri* (Basel, 1945), pp. 265–79 (translated as "The Bologna Enigma," *Ambix,* London, II, 1946, 182–91); Chapter III, section 3, appeared as "De Sulphure" in *Nova Acta Paracelsica* (Einsiedeln), V (1948), 27–40.

For the second edition, numerous corrections and revisions have been made in cross-references to other volumes of the Collected Works now available, and likewise in the Bibliography.

The Gesammelte Werke edition of the present work appeared in 1968 as, in effect, a reprint of the 1955/1956 Swiss edition, retaining its textual arrangement and paragraph numbering. In order to facilitate cross-reference between the English and German text, a table has been added to this edition, correlating the paragraph numbers: see below, pp. 697ff.

One paragraph (183 in Vol. II, p. 124 of the Gesammelte Werke edition) was inadvertently omitted in the first edition of the present volume. It should follow paragraph 518 on page 368 and is translated here as paragraph 518a.

518a   The reader must pardon my use of metaphors that are linguistically analogous to dogmatic expressions. If you have conceptions of things you can have no conceptions of, then the conception and the thing appear to coincide. Nor can two different things you know nothing of be kept apart. I must therefore expressly emphasize that I do not go in for either metaphysics or theology, but am concerned with psychological facts on the borderline of the knowable. So if I make use of certain expressions that are reminiscent of the language of theology, this is due solely to the poverty of language, and not because I am of the opinion that the subject-matter of theology is the same as that of psychology. Psychology is very definitely not a theology; it is a natural science that seeks to describe experienceable psychic phenomena. In doing so it takes account of the way in which theology conceives and names them, because this hangs together with the phenomenology of the contents under discussion. But as empirical science it has neither the capacity nor the competence to decide on questions of truth and value, this being the prerogative of theology.

TRANSLATOR'S NOTE

Standard translations of Latin and Greek texts have been used where they conformed more or less to the author's own versions, and they are referred to in the footnotes. Where such translations were unsuitable or nonexistent, as is particularly the case with the texts in the appendix, an English version has been supplied by Mr. A. S. B. Glover. To him I would like to express my deepest thanks for his tireless help in preparing this book. My thanks are also due to Miss Barbara Hannah and Dr. Marie-Louise von Franz, for reading through the typescript and making many valuable suggestions.

TABLE OF CONTENTS

ix

LIST OF PLATES

The plates follow page 330

FOREWORD

This book—my last—was begun more than ten years ago. I first got the idea of writing it from C. Kerényi's essay on the Aegean Festival in Goethe's *Faust*.[1] The literary prototype of this festival is *The Chymical Wedding* of Christian Rosencreutz, itself a product of the traditional hierosgamos symbolism of alchemy. I felt tempted, at the time, to comment on Kerényi's essay from the standpoint of alchemy and psychology, but soon discovered that the theme was far too extensive to be dealt with in a couple of pages. Although the work was soon under way, more than ten years were to pass before I was able to collect and arrange all the material relevant to this central problem.

As may be known, I showed in my book *Psychology and Alchemy*, first published in 1944,[2] how certain archetypal motifs that are common in alchemy appear in the dreams of modern individuals who have no knowledge of alchemical literature. In that book the wealth of ideas and symbols that lie hidden in the neglected treatises of this much misunderstood "art" was hinted at rather than described in the detail it deserved; for my primary aim was to demonstrate that the world of alchemical symbols definitely does not belong to the rubbish heap of the past, but stands in a very real and living relationship to our most recent discoveries concerning the psychology of the unconscious. Not only does this modern psychological discipline give us the key to the secrets of alchemy, but, conversely, alchemy provides the psychology of the unconscious with a meaningful historical basis. This was hardly a popular subject, and for that reason it remained largely misunderstood. Not only was alchemy almost entirely unknown as a branch of natural philosophy and as a religious movement, but most people were unfamiliar with the modern discovery of the archetypes, or had at least misunderstood them. Indeed, there were not a few who regarded them as sheer fantasy, although the well-known example of whole

[1] *Das Aegäische Fest: Die Meergötterszene in Goethes Faust II.*
[2] [First Swiss edn., 1944, but the two chief component essays first appeared in *Eranos Jahrbuch 1935* and *1936.*—EDITORS.]

numbers, which also were discovered and not invented, might have taught them better, not to mention the "patterns of behaviour" in biology. Just as numbers and instinctual forms do exist, so there are many other natural configurations or types which are exemplified by Lévy-Bruhl's *représentations collectives*. They are not "metaphysical" speculations but, as we would expect, symptoms of the uniformity of *Homo sapiens*.

Today there is such a large and varied literature describing psychotherapeutic experiences and the psychology of the unconscious that everyone has had an opportunity to familiarize himself with the empirical findings and the prevailing theories about them. This is not true of alchemy, most accounts of which are vitiated by the erroneous assumption that it was merely the precursor of chemistry. Herbert Silberer [3] was the first to try to penetrate its much more important psychological aspect so far as his somewhat limited equipment allowed him to do so. Owing to the paucity of modern expositions and the comparative inaccessibility of the sources, it is difficult to form an adequate conception of the problems of philosophical alchemy. It is the aim of the present work to fill this gap.

As is indicated by the very name which he chose for it—the "spagyric" [4] art—or by the oft-repeated saying "solve et coagula" (dissolve and coagulate), the alchemist saw the essence of his art in separation and analysis on the one hand and synthesis and consolidation on the other. For him there was first of all an initial state in which opposite tendencies or forces were in conflict; secondly there was the great question of a procedure which would be capable of bringing the hostile elements and qualities, once they were separated, back to unity again. The initial state, named the *chaos,* was not given from the start but had to be sought for as the *prima materia*. And just as the beginning of the work was not self-evident, so to an even greater degree was its end. There are countless speculations on the nature of the endstate, all of them reflected in its designations. The commonest are the ideas of its permanence (prolongation of life, immortality, incorruptibility), its androgyny, its spirituality and corporeality, its human qualities and resemblance to man (homunculus), and its divinity.

[3] *Problems of Mysticism and Its Symbolism,* first pub. 1914.
[4] From σπάειν, 'rend, tear, stretch out', ἀγείρειν, 'bring or collect together'.

The obvious analogy, in the psychic sphere, to this problem of opposites is the dissociation of the personality brought about by the conflict of incompatible tendencies, resulting as a rule from an inharmonious disposition. The repression of one of the opposites leads only to a prolongation and extension of the conflict, in other words, to a neurosis. The therapist therefore confronts the opposites with one another and aims at uniting them permanently. The images of the goal which then appear in dreams often run parallel with the corresponding alchemical symbols. An instance of this is familiar to every analyst: the phenomenon of the transference, which corresponds to the motif of the "chymical wedding." To avoid overloading this book, I devoted a special study to the psychology of the transference,[5] using the alchemical parallels as a guiding thread. Similarly, the hints or representations of wholeness, or the self, which appear in the dreams also occur in alchemy as the numerous synonyms for the *lapis Philosophorum,* which the alchemists equated with Christ. Because of its great importance, this last relationship gave rise to a special study, *Aion.* Further offshoots from the theme of this book are my treatises "The Philosophical Tree," "Synchronicity: An Acausal Connecting Principle," and "Answer to Job."

The first and second parts of this work [6] are devoted to the theme of the opposites and their union. The third part is an account of, and commentary on, an alchemical text, which, evidently written by a cleric, probably dates from the thirteenth century and discloses a highly peculiar state of mind in which Christianity and alchemy interpenetrate. The author tries, with the help of the mysticism of the Song of Songs, to fuse apparently heterogeneous ideas, partly Christian and partly derived from natural philosophy, in the form of a hymnlike incantation. This text is called *Aurora consurgens* (also *Aurea hora*), and traditionally it is ascribed to St. Thomas Aquinas. It is hardly necessary to remark that Thomist historians have always reck-

[5] Cf. "Psychology of the Transference."

[6] [This refers to the Swiss edition, which was published in three parts, each a separate volume, the third being devoted to a contribution by M.-L. von Franz. Parts I and II constitute the present volume. Part III has appeared in English under the title *Aurora Consurgens: A Document Attributed to Thomas Aquinas on the Problem of Opposites in Alchemy* (Bollingen Series LXXVII, New York and London, 1966), as a companion volume to *Mysterium Coniunctionis* but outside the Collected Works.—EDITORS.]

oned it, or wanted to reckon it, among the spurious and false writings, no doubt because of the traditional depreciation of alchemy. This negative evaluation of alchemy was due, in the main, to ignorance. People did not know what it meant to its adepts because it was commonly regarded as mere gold-making. I hope I have shown in my book *Psychology and Alchemy* that, properly understood, it was nothing of the sort. Alchemy meant a very great deal to people like Albertus Magnus and Roger Bacon, and also to St. Thomas Aquinas. We have not only the early testimony of Zosimos of Panopolis from the third century, but that of Petrus Bonus of Ferrara from the beginning of the fourteenth century, which both point to the parallelism of the alchemical arcanum and the God-man. *Aurora consurgens* tries to amalgamate the Christian and alchemical view, and I have therefore chosen it as an example of how the spirit of medieval Christianity came to terms with alchemical philosophy, and as an illustration of the present account of the alchemical problem of opposites.[7]

Today, once again, we hear tendentious voices still contesting the hypothesis of the unconscious, declaring that it is nothing more than the personal prejudice of those who make use of this hypothesis. Remarkably enough, no consideration is given to the proofs that have been put forward; they are dismissed on the ground that all psychology is nothing more than a preconceived subjective opinion. It must be admitted that probably in no other field of work is there so great a danger of the investigator's falling a victim to his own subjective assumptions. He of all people must remain more than ever conscious of his "personal equation." But, young as the psychology of unconscious processes may be, it has nevertheless succeeded in establishing certain facts which are gradually gaining general acceptance. One of these is the polaristic structure of the psyche, which it shares with all natural processes. Natural processes are phenomena of energy, constantly arising out of a "less probable state" of polar tension. This formula is of special significance for psychology, because the conscious mind is usually reluctant to see or admit

[7] [The Swiss edition adds: "For Parts I and II I am responsible, while my co-worker, Dr. Marie-Louise von Franz, is responsible for Part III. We have brought the book out jointly, because each author has participated in the work of the other."]

the polarity of its own background, although it is precisely from there that it gets its energy.

The psychologist has only just begun to feel his way into this structure, and it now appears that the "alchemystical" philosophers made the opposites and their union one of the chief objects of their work. In their writings, certainly, they employed a symbolical terminology that frequently reminds us of the language of dreams, concerned as these often are with the problem of opposites. Since conscious thinking strives for clarity and demands unequivocal decisions, it has constantly to free itself from counterarguments and contrary tendencies, with the result that especially incompatible contents either remain totally unconscious or are habitually and assiduously overlooked. The more this is so, the more the unconscious will build up its counterposition. As the alchemists, with but few exceptions, did not know that they were bringing psychic structures to light but thought that they were explaining the transformations of matter, there were no psychological considerations to prevent them, for reasons of sensitiveness, from laying bare the background of the psyche, which a more conscious person would be nervous of doing. It is because of this that alchemy is of such absorbing interest to the psychologist. For this reason, too, it seemed necessary to my co-worker and myself to subject the alchemical conception of opposites, and their union or reconciliation, to a thoroughgoing investigation. However abstruse and strange the language and imagery of the alchemists may seem to the uninitiated, they become vivid and alive as soon as comparative research reveals the relationship of the symbols to processes in the unconscious. These may be the material of dreams, spontaneous fantasies, and delusional ideas on the one hand, and on the other hand they can be observed in works of creative imagination and in the figurative language of religion. The heterogeneous material adduced for comparison may seem in the highest degree baffling to the academically educated reader who has met these items only in an impersonal context—historical, ethnic, or geographical—but who does not know their psychological affinities with analogous formations, themselves derived from the most varied sources. He will naturally be taken aback, at first, if certain symbols in ancient Egyptian texts are brought into intimate relationship with modern findings concerning the popular religion of India and at the same time with the dreams of an unsuspecting European. But what is difficult for the historian and philologist to swallow is no obstacle for the physician. His biological training has left him with far too strong an impression of the comparability of all human activities for him to make any particular to-do about the similarity, indeed the fundamental sameness, of human beings and their psychic manifestations. If he is a psychiatrist, he will not be astonished at the essential similarity of psychotic contents, whether they come from the Middle Ages or from the present, from Europe or from Australia, from India or from the Americas. The processes underlying them are instinctive, therefore universal and uncommonly conservative. The weaver-bird builds his nest in his own peculiar fashion no matter where he may be, and just as we have no grounds for assuming that he built his nest differently three thousand years ago, so it is very improbable that he will alter his style in the next three thousand. Although contemporary man believes that he can change himself without limit, or be changed through external influences, the astounding, or rather the terrifying, fact remains that despite civilization and Christian education, he is still, morally, as much in bondage to his instincts as an animal, and can therefore fall victim at any moment to the beast within. This is a more universal truth than ever before, guaranteed independent of education, culture, language, tradition, race, and locality.

Investigation of alchemical symbolism, like a preoccupation with mythology, does not lead one away from life any more than a study of comparative anatomy leads away from the anatomy of the living man. On the contrary, alchemy affords us a veritable treasure-house of symbols, knowledge of which is extremely helpful for an understanding of neurotic and psychotic processes. This, in turn, enables us to apply the psychology of the unconscious to those regions in the history of the human mind which are concerned with symbolism. It is just here that questions arise whose urgency and vital intensity are even greater than the question of therapeutic application. Here there are many prejudices that still have to be overcome. Just as it is thought, for instance, that Mexican myths cannot possibly have anything to do with similar ideas found in Europe, so it is held to be a fantastic assumption that an uneducated modern man should dream of classical myth-motifs which are known only to a specialist. People still think that relationships like this are far-fetched and therefore improbable. But they forget that the structure and function of the bodily organs are everywhere more or less the same, including those of the brain. And as the psyche is to a large extent dependent on this organ, presumably it will—at least in principle—everywhere produce the same forms. In order to see this, however, one has to abandon the widespread prejudice that the psyche is identical with consciousness.

C. G. JUNG

October 1954

MYSTERIUM
CONIUNCTIONIS

AN INQUIRY

INTO THE SEPARATION AND SYNTHESIS

OF PSYCHIC OPPOSITES IN ALCHEMY

I

THE COMPONENTS OF THE CONIUNCTIO

1. THE OPPOSITES

1 The factors which come together in the coniunctio are conceived as opposites, either confronting one another in enmity or attracting one another in love.[1] To begin with they form a dualism; for instance the opposites are *humidum* (moist) / *siccum* (dry), *frigidum* (cold) / *calidum* (warm), *superiora* (upper, higher) / *inferiora* (lower), *spiritus–anima* (spirit–soul) / *corpus* (body), *coelum* (heaven) / *terra* (earth), *ignis* (fire) / *aqua* (water), bright / dark, *agens* (active) / *patiens* (passive), *volatile* (volatile, gaseous) / *fixum* (solid), *pretiosum* (precious, costly; also *carum*, dear) / *vile* (cheap, common), *bonum* (good) / *malum* (evil), *manifestum* (open) / *occultum* (occult; also *celatum*, hidden), *oriens* (East) / *occidens* (West), *vivum* (living) / *mortuum* (dead, inert), *masculus* (masculine) / *foemina* (feminine), Sol / Luna. Often the polarity is arranged as a quaternio (quaternity), with the two opposites crossing one another, as for instance the four elements or the four qualities (moist, dry, cold, warm), or the four directions and seasons,[2] thus producing the cross as an emblem of the four elements and symbol of the sublunary physical world.[3] This fourfold Physis, the cross, also appears in the

---

1 Ripley says: "The coniunctio is the uniting of separated qualities or an equalizing of principles." "Duodecim portarum axiomata philosophica," *Theatrum chemicum*, II, p. 128.

2 Cf. the representation of the *tetrameria* in Stolcius de Stolcenberg, *Viridarium chymicum*, Fig. XLII.

3 Cf. "Consilium coniugii," *Ars chemica*, p. 79: "In this stone are the four elements, and it is to be compared to the world and the composition of the world." * [For the Latin or Greek of the quotations marked with an asterisk, see the Appendix.—Editors.] Also Michael Maier, *De circulo physico quadrato*, p. 17: "Nature, I say, when she turned about the golden circle, by that movement made its four qualities equal, that is to say, she squared that homogeneous simplicity turning back on itself, or brought it into an equilateral rectangle, in such a way that contraries are bound together by contraries, and enemies by enemies, as if with everlasting bonds, and are held in mutual embrace." * Petrus Bonus says: "The elements are conjoined in the circle in true friendship" * (*Bibliotheca chemica*, II, p. 35).

signs for earth ♁, Venus ♀, Mercury ☿, Saturn ♄, and Jupiter ♃.[4]

2   The opposites and their symbols are so common in the texts that it is superfluous to cite evidence from the sources. On the other hand, in view of the ambiguity of the alchemists' language, which is "tam ethice quam physice" (as much ethical as physical), it is worth while to go rather more closely into the manner in which the texts treat of the opposites. Very often the masculine-feminine opposition is personified as King and Queen (in the *Rosarium philosophorum* also as Emperor and Empress), or as *servus* (slave) or *vir rubeus* (red man) and *mulier candida* (white woman);[5] in the "Visio Arislei" they appear as Gabricus (or Thabritius) and Beya, the King's son and daughter.[6] Theriomorphic symbols are equally common and are often found in the illustrations.[7] I would mention the eagle and toad ("the eagle flying through the air and the toad crawling on the ground"), which are the "emblem" of Avicenna in Michael Maier,[8] the eagle representing Luna "or Juno, Venus, Beya, who is fugitive and winged like the eagle, which flies up to the clouds and receives the rays of the sun in his eyes." The toad "is the opposite of air, it is a contrary element, namely earth, whereon alone it moves by slow steps, and does not trust itself to another element. Its head is very heavy and gazes at the earth. For this reason it denotes the philosophic earth, which cannot fly [i.e., cannot be sublimated], as it is firm and solid. Upon it as a foundation the golden house [9] is to be built. Were it not for the

---

[4] Cf. John Dee, "Monas hieroglyphica," *Theatr. chem.*, II, p. 220.

[5] Cf. "Consilium coniugii," *Ars chemica*, pp. 69f., and "Clangor buccinae," *Artis auriferae*, I, p. 484. In the Cabala the situation is reversed: red denotes the female, white (the left side) the male. Cf. Mueller, *Der Sohar und seine Lehre*, pp. 20f.

[6] "Aenigmata ex visione Arislei," *Art. aurif.*, I, pp. 146ff. Union of sun and moon: Petrus Bonus (ed. Lacinius), *Pretiosa margarita novella* (1546), p. 112. The archetype of the heavenly marriage plays a great role here. On a primitive level this motif can be found in shamanism. Cf. Eliade, *Shamanism*, p. 75.

[7] The most complete collection of the illustrations that appeared in printed works is Stolcius de Stolcenberg's *Viridarium chymicum figuris cupro incisis adornatum* (Frankfurt, 1624).

[8] *Symbola aureae mensae*, p. 192.*

[9] The "treasure-house" (*gazophylacium, domus thesauraria*) of philosophy, which is a synonym for the *aurum philosophorum*, or lapis. Cf. von Franz, *Aurora Consurgens*, pp. 101ff. The idea goes back to Alphidius (see "Consilium coniugii," *Ars chemica*, p. 108) and ultimately to Zosimos, who describes the lapis as a shining

4

earth in our work the air would fly away, neither would the fire have its nourishment, nor the water its vessel." [10]

3   Another favourite theriomorphic image is that of the two birds or two dragons, one of them winged, the other wingless. This allegory comes from an ancient text, *De Chemia Senioris antiquissimi philosophi libellus*.[11] The wingless bird or dragon prevents the other from flying. They stand for Sol and Luna, brother and sister, who are united by means of the art.[12] In Lambspringk's "Symbols" [13] they appear as the astrological Fishes which, swimming in opposite directions, symbolize the spirit / soul polarity. The water they swim in is *mare nostrum* (our sea) and is interpreted as the body.[14] The fishes are "without bones and cortex." [15] From them is produced a *mare immensum*, which is the *aqua permanens* (permanent water). Another symbol is the stag and unicorn meeting in the "forest." [16] The stag signifies the soul, the unicorn spirit, and the forest the body. The next two pictures in Lambspringk's "Symbols" show the lion and lioness,[17] or the wolf and dog, the latter

white temple of marble. Berthelot, *Collection des anciens alchimistes grecs*, III, i, 5.

10 *Symb. aur. mensae*, p. 200.

11 The printing is undated, but it probably comes from Samuel Emmel's press at Strasbourg and may be contemporaneous with *Ars chemica*, which was printed there in 1566 and matches our libellus as regards type, paper, and format. The author, Senior Zadith filius Hamuel, may perhaps have been one of the Harranites of the 10th cent., or at least have been influenced by them. If the *Clavis maioris sapientiae* mentioned by Stapleton ("Muhammad bin Umail: His Date, Writings, and Place in Alchemical History") is identical with the Latin treatise of the same name, traditionally ascribed to Artefius, this could be taken as proved, since that treatise contains a typical Harranite astral theory. Ruska ("Studien zu M. ibn Umail") groups Senior with the *Turba* literature that grew up on Egyptian soil.

12 Senior says: "I joined the two luminaries in marriage and it became as water having two lights" * (*De chemia*, pp. 15f.).

13 *Musaeum hermeticum*, p. 343. (Cf. Waite, *The Hermetic Museum Restored and Enlarged*, I, pp. 276f.)

14 *Corpus* (as *corpus nostrum*) usually means the chemical "body" or "substance," but morally it means the human body. "Sea" is a common symbol of the unconscious. In alchemy, therefore, the "body" would also symbolize the unconscious.

15 "Aenigmata philosophorum II," *Art. aurif.*, I, p. 149. Cf. *Aion*, pars. 195, 213 n. 51.

16 See *Psychology and Alchemy*, fig. 240.

17 They also appear in the "XI ˙Clavis" of Basilius Valentinus, *Chymische Schrifften*, p. 68, and in *Viridarium*, Figs. XI, LV, LXII. Variants are lion and snake (*Viridarium*, Fig. XII), lion and bird (Fig. LXXIV), lion and bear (Figs. XCIII and CVI).

5

two fighting; they too symbolize soul and spirit. In Figure VII the opposites are symbolized by two birds in a wood, one fledged, the other unfledged. Whereas in the earlier pictures the conflict seems to be between spirit and soul, the two birds signify the conflict between spirit and body, and in Figure VIII the two birds fighting do in fact represent that conflict, as the caption shows. The opposition between spirit and soul is due to the latter having a very fine substance. It is more akin to the "hylical" body and is *densior et crassior* (denser and grosser) than the spirit.

4   The elevation of the human figure to a king or a divinity, and on the other hand its representation in subhuman, theriomorphic form, are indications of the *transconscious character* of the pairs of opposites. They do not belong to the ego-personality but are supraordinate to it. The ego-personality occupies an intermediate position, like the "anima inter bona et mala sita" (soul placed between good and evil). The pairs of opposites constitute the phenomenology of the paradoxical *self*, man's totality. That is why their symbolism makes use of cosmic expressions like *coelum / terra*.[18] The intensity of the conflict is expressed in symbols like fire and water,[19] height and depth,[20] life and death.[21]

2. THE QUATERNIO AND THE MEDIATING ROLE OF MERCURIUS

5   The arrangement of the opposites in a quaternity is shown in an interesting illustration in Stolcenberg's *Viridarium chymicum* (Fig. XLII), which can also be found in the *Philosophia reformata* of Mylius (1622, p. 117). The goddesses represent the four seasons of the sun in the circle of the Zodiac (Aries, Cancer, Libra, Capricorn) and at the same time the four degrees of heat-

[18] Cf. Petrus Bonus, "Pretiosa margarita novella," *Theatr. chem.*, V, pp. 647f.: "Hermes: At the end of the world heaven and earth must be joined together, which is the philosophical word." * Also *Mus. herm.*, p. 803 (Waite, II, p. 263).

[19] Ms. Incipit: "Figurarum Aegyptiorum Secretarum." 18th cent. (Author's collection.)

[20] "Thus the height is hidden and the depth is made manifest" * (*Mus. herm.*, p. 652).

[21] Cf. the oft-repeated saying: "From the dead he makes the living" * (Mylius, *Philosophia reformata*, p. 191).

6

ing,[22] as well as the four elements "combined" around the circular table.[23] The synthesis of the elements is effected by means of the circular movement in time (*circulatio, rota*) of the sun through the houses of the Zodiac. As I have shown elsewhere,[24] the aim of the *circulatio* is the production (or rather, reproduction) of the Original Man, who was a sphere. Perhaps I may mention in this connection a remarkable quotation from Ostanes in Abu'l-Qasim, describing the intermediate position between two pairs of opposites constituting a quaternio:

> Ostanes said, Save me, O my God, for I stand between two exalted brilliancies known for their wickedness, and between two dim lights; each of them has reached me and I know not how to save myself from them. And it was said to me, Go up to Agathodaimon the Great and ask aid of him, and know that there is in thee somewhat of his nature, which will never be corrupted. . . . And when I ascended into the air he said to me, Take the child of the bird which is mixed with redness and spread for the gold its bed which comes forth from the glass, and place it in its vessel whence it has no power to come out except when thou desirest, and leave it until its moistness has departed.[25]

6   The quaternio in this case evidently consists of the two *malefici*, Mars and Saturn (Mars is the ruler of Aries, Saturn of Capricorn); the two "dim lights" would then be feminine ones, the moon (ruler of Cancer) and Venus (ruler of Libra). The opposites between which Ostanes stands are thus masculine / feminine on the one hand and good / evil on the other. The way he speaks of the four luminaries—he does not know how to save himself from them—suggests that he is subject to Heimarmene,

---

22 Mylius, p. 118. The fourth degree is the *coniunctio*, which would thus correspond to Capricorn.

23 Mylius remarks (p. 115): ". . . equality arises . . . from the four incompatibles mutually partaking in nature." * A similar ancient idea seems to be that of the ἡλιακὴ τράπεζα (solar table) in the Orphic mysteries. Cf. Proclus, *Commentaries on the Timaeus of Plato*, trans. by Taylor, II, p. 378: "And Orpheus knew indeed of the Crater of Bacchus, but he also establishes many others about the solar table." * Cf. also Herodotus, *The Histories*, III, 17–18 (trans. by de Selincourt, p. 181), and Pausanias, *Description of Greece*, VI, 26, 2 (trans. by Jones, III, pp. 156ff.).

24 Cf. *Psychology and Alchemy*, index, s.v. "rotundum," "sphere," "wheel," and especially (par. 469, n. 110) the wheel with twelve buckets for raising souls in the *Acta Archelai*.

25 Holmyard, *Kitāb al-'ilm al-muktasab*, p. 38.

the compulsion of the stars; that is, to a transconscious factor beyond the reach of the human will. Apart from this compulsion, the injurious effect of the four planets is due to the fact that each of them exerts its specific influence on man and makes him a diversity of persons, whereas he should be *one*.[26] It is presumably Hermes who points out to Ostanes that something incorruptible is in his nature which he shares with the Agathodaimon,[27] something divine, obviously the germ of unity. This

---

[26] The idea of uniting the Many into One is found not only in alchemy but also in Origen, *In Libr. I Reg.* [*I Sam.*] *Hom.*, I, 4 (Migne, *P.G.*, vol. 12, col. 998): "*There was one man.* We, who are still sinners, cannot obtain this title of praise, for each of us is not one but many . . . See how he who thinks himself one is not one, but seems to have as many personalities as he has moods, as also the Scripture says: A fool is changed as the moon." * In another homily, *In Ezech.*, 9, 1 (Migne, *P.G.*, vol. 13, col. 732) he says: "Where there are sins, there is multitude . . . but where virtue is, there is singleness, there is union." * Cf. *Porphyry the Philosopher to His Wife Marcella*, trans. by Zimmern, p. 61: "If thou wouldst practise to ascend into thyself, collecting together all the powers which the body hath scattered and broken up into a multitude of parts unlike their former unity . . ." Likewise the Gospel of Philip (cited from Epiphanius, *Panarium*, XXVI, 13): "I have taken knowledge (saith the soul) of myself, and have gathered myself together out of every quarter and have not begotten (sown) children unto the Ruler, but have rooted out his roots and gathered together the members that were scattered abroad. And I know thee who thou art, for I (she saith) am of them that are from above." (James, *The Apocryphal New Testament*, p. 12.) Cf. also *Panarium*, XXVI, 3: "I am thou, and thou art I, and wherever thou art, there I am, and I am scattered in all things, and from wherever thou wilt thou canst gather me, but in gathering me thou gatherest together thyself." The inner multiplicity of man reflects his microcosmic nature, which contains within it the stars and their (astrological) influences. Thus Origen (*In Lev. Hom.*, V, 2; Migne, *P.G.*, vol. 12, cols. 449–50) says: "Understand that thou hast within thyself herds of cattle . . . flocks of sheep and flocks of goats . . . Understand that the fowls of the air are also within thee. Marvel not if we say that these are within thee, but understand that thou thyself art another world in little, and hast within thee the sun and the moon, and also the stars . . . Thou seest that thou hast all those things which the world hath." * And Dorn ("De tenebris contra naturam," *Theatr. chem.* I, p. 533) says: "To the four less perfect planets in the heavens there correspond the four elements in our body, that is, earth to Saturn, water to Mercury [instead of the moon, see above], air to Venus, and fire to Mars. Of these it is built up, and it is weak on account of the imperfection of the parts. And so let a tree be planted from them, whose root is ascribed to Saturn," * etc., meaning the philosophical tree, symbol of the developmental process that results in the unity of the filius Philosophorum, or lapis. Cf. my "The Philosophical Tree," par. 409.

[27] The ἀγαθὸς δαίμων is a snakelike, chthonic fertility daemon akin to the "genius" of the hero. In Egypt as well it was a snakelike daemon giving life and healing power. In the Berlin Magic Papyrus it is the ἀγαθὸς γεωργός who fertilizes the earth. On Gnostic gems it appears together with Enoch, Enoch being an early

germ is the gold, the *aurum philosophorum*,[28] the bird of Hermes or the son of the bird, who is the same as the *filius philosophorum*.[29] He must be enclosed in the *vas Hermeticum* and heated until the "moistness" that still clings to him has departed, i.e., the *humidum radicale* (radical moisture), the prima materia, which is the original chaos and the sea (the unconscious). Some kind of coming to consciousness seems indicated. We know that the synthesis of the four was one of the main preoccupations of alchemy, as was, though to a lesser degree, the synthesis of the seven (metals, for instance). Thus in the same text Hermes says to the Sun:

... I cause to come out to thee the spirits of thy brethren [the planets], O Sun, and I make them for thee a crown the like of which was never seen; and I cause thee and them to be within me, and I will make thy kingdom vigorous.[30]

This refers to the synthesis of the planets or metals with the sun, to form a crown which will be "within" Hermes. The crown signifies the kingly totality; it stands for unity and is not subject to Heimarmene. This reminds us of the seven- or twelve-rayed crown of light which the Agathodaimon serpent wears on Gnostic gems,[31] and also of the crown of Wisdom in the *Aurora Consurgens*.[32]

7   In the "Consilium coniugii" there is a similar quaternio with the four qualities arranged as "combinations of two contraries,

parallel of Hermes. The Sabaeans who transmitted the Agathodaimon to the Middle Ages as the πνεῦμα πάρεδρον (familiar spirit) of the magical procedure, identified it with Hermes and Orpheus. (Chwolsohn, *Die Ssabier*, II, p. 624.) Olympiodorus (Berthelot, *Alch. grecs*, II, iv, 18) mentions it as the "more secret angel" (μυστικώτερον ἄγγελον), as the uroboros or "heaven," on which account it later became a synonym for Mercurius.

28 Cf. the Indian teachings concerning *hiranyagarbha*, 'golden germ,' and *purusha*. Also "The Psychology of Eastern Meditation," pars. 917f.

29 Cf. ὕλη τῆς ὀρνιθογονίας (the matter of the generation of the bird) in Zosimos (Berthelot, III, xliv, 1).

30 Holmyard, p. 37.

31 Cf. *Psychology and Alchemy*, figs. 203–5.

32 von Franz, pp. 53f. Cf. also Goodenough, "The Crown of Victory. . . ." Senior (*De chemia*, p. 41) calls the *terra alba foliata* "the crown of victory." In *Heliodori carmina*, v. 252 (ed. by Goldschmidt, p. 57) the soul, on returning to the body, brings it a νικητικὸν στέμμα, 'wreath of victory.' In the Cabala the highest Sefira (like the lowest) is called Kether, the Crown. In Christian allegory the crown signifies Christ's humanity: Rabanus Maurus, *Allegoriae in Sacram Scripturam* (Migne, *P.L.*, vol. 112, col. 909). In the Acts of John, §109 (James, *Apocryphal New Testament*, p. 268) Christ is called the diadem.

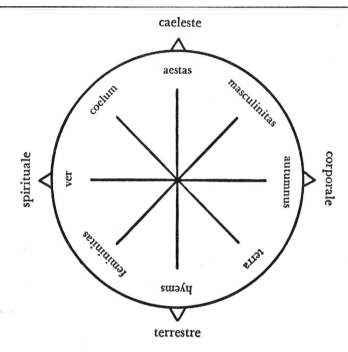

cold and moist, which are not friendly to heat and dryness." [33]
Other quaternions are: "The stone is first an old man, in the end
a youth, because the *albedo* comes at the beginning and the
rubedo at the end." [34] Similarly the elements are arranged as two
"manifesta" (water and earth), and two "occulta" (air and fire).[35]
A further quaternio is suggested by the saying of Bernardus
Trevisanus: "The upper has the nature of the lower, and the
ascending has the nature of the descending." [36] The following
combination is from the "Tractatus Micreris": "In it [the
Indian Ocean] [37] are images of heaven and earth, of summer,

[33] *Ars chemica*, p. 196.*

[34] "Opusculum autoris ignoti," *Art. aurif.*, I, p. 390. The author is generally cited
as "Rhasis." Cf. Ruska, *Turba Phil.*, pp. 161f. Also Ephraem Syrus, *Hymni et
Sermones* (ed. Lamy, I, col. 136): "Thy babe, O Virgin, is an old man; he is the
Ancient of Days and precedeth all time." *

[35] Dorn in "Physica Trismegisti," *Theatr. chem.*, I, p. 420. The division of the
elements into two higher "psychic" elements and two lower "somatic" elements
goes back to Aristotle. Cf. Lippmann, *Entstehung und Ausbreitung der Alchemie*,
I, p. 147.   [36] "Liber de alchemia," *Theatr. chem.*, I, p. 775.

[37] Sea is a synonym for the prima materia.

10

autumn, winter, and spring, male and female. If thou callest this spiritual, what thou doest is probable; if corporeal, thou sayest the truth; if heavenly, thou liest not; if earthly, thou hast well spoken." [38] Here we are dealing with a double quaternio having the structure shown in the diagram on page 10.

8   The double quaternio or ogdoad stands for a totality, for something that is at once heavenly and earthly, spiritual or corporeal, and is found in the "Indian Ocean," that is to say in the unconscious. It is without doubt the Microcosm, the mystical Adam and bisexual Original Man in his prenatal state, as it were, when he is identical with the unconscious. Hence in Gnosticism the "Father of All" is described not only as masculine and feminine (or neither), but as Bythos, the abyss. In the scholia to the "Tractatus aureus Hermetis" [39] there is a quaternio consisting of *superius / inferius, exterius / interius*. They are united into one thing by means of the circular distillation, named the Pelican: [40] "Let all be one in one circle or vessel." "For this vessel is the true philosophical Pelican, nor is any other to be sought after in all the world." The text gives the following diagram:

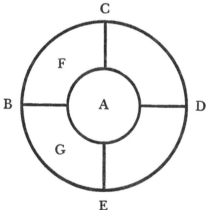

<hr/>

[38] *Theatr. chem.*, V, p. 111. This treatise (Micreris = Mercurius) is undoubtedly old and is probably of Arabic origin. The same saying is quoted by "Milvescindus" (Bonus, "Pretiosa marg. nov.," *Theatr. chem.*, V, pp. 662f.). In the *Turba* he is called "Mirnefindus."

[39] This treatise, of Arabic origin, is printed in *Bibliotheca chemica*, I, pp. 400ff.

[40] "For when she applies her beak to her breast, her whole neck with the beak is bent into the shape of a circle. . . . The blood flowing from her breast restores life to the dead fledglings." * Ibid., p. 442 b.

9   B C D E represent the outside, A is the inside, "as it were the origin and source from which the other letters flow, and likewise the final goal to which they flow back," [41] F G stands for Above and Below. "Together the letters A B C D E F G clearly signify the hidden magical Septenary." The central point A, the origin and goal, the "Ocean or great sea," is also called a *circulus exiguus,* very small circle, and a "mediator making peace between the enemies or elements, that they may love one another in a meet embrace." [42] This little inner circle corresponds to the Mercurial Fountain in the *Rosarium,* which I have described in my "Psychology of the Transference." The text calls it "the more spiritual, perfect, and nobler Mercurius," [43] the true arcane substance, a "spirit," and goes on:

For the spirit alone penetrates all things, even the most solid bodies.[44] Thus the catholicity of religion, or of the true Church, consists not in a visible and bodily gathering together of men, but in the invisible, spiritual concord and harmony of those who believe devoutly and truly in the one Jesus Christ. Whoever attaches himself to a particular church outside this King of Kings, who alone is the shepherd of the true spiritual church, is a sectarian, a schismatic, and a heretic. For the Kingdom of God cometh not with observation, but is within us, as our Saviour himself says in the seventeenth chapter of St. Luke.[45]

41 Ibid.*
42 Ibid., 408 b. Cf. the words of the "bride" in *Aurora Consurgens,* p. 143: "I am the mediatrix of the elements, making one to agree with another; that which is warm I make cold . . . that which is dry I make moist . . . that which is hard I soften, and the reverse." (Cf. Senior, *De chemia,* p. 34.)
43 *Bibl. chem.,* 408 a.
44 "It will penetrate every solid thing" * ("Tabula smaragdina"). The sentence "for the spirit alone penetrates all things, even the most solid bodies," is probably not without reference to "for the Spirit searcheth all things, yea, the deep things of God" in I Cor. 2:10 (AV). Likewise the Mercurius of the alchemists is a "spirit of truth," a *sapientia Dei,* but one who presses downward into the depths of matter, and whose acquisition is a *donum Spiritus Sancti.* He is the spirit who knows the secrets of matter, and to possess him brings illumination, in accordance with Paul's "even so the things of God knoweth no man, but the Spirit of God" (I Cor. 2:11).
45 Luke 17 : 21f. Recently, "within you" (*intra vos, ἐντὸς ὑμῶν*) has been translated as "among you," therefore, as our author says, "in the visible and bodily gathering together of men." This shows the modern tendency to replace man's inner co-

That the Ecclesia spiritualis is meant is clear from the text: "But you will ask, where then are those true Christians, who are free from all sectarian contagion?" They are "neither in Samaria, nor in Jerusalem, nor in Rome, nor in Geneva, nor in Leipzig," but are scattered everywhere through the world, "in Turkey, in Persia, Italy, Gaul, Germany, Poland, Bohemia, Moravia, England, America, and even in farthest India." The author continues: "God is Spirit,[46] and those who worship him must worship him in the spirit and in truth. After these examinations and avowals I leave it to each man to judge who is of the true Church, and who not." [47]

10   From this remarkable excursus we learn, first of all, that the "centre" unites the four and the seven into one.[48] The unifying agent is the spirit Mercurius, and this singular spirit then causes the author to confess himself a member of the Ecclesia spiritualis, for the spirit is God. This religious background is already apparent in the choice of the term "Pelican" for the circular process, since this bird is a well-known allegory of Christ.[49] The idea of Mercurius as a peacemaker, the mediator between the warring elements and producer of unity, probably goes back to Ephesians 2 : 13ff.:

---

hesion by outward community, as though anyone who had no communion with himself would be capable of any fellowship at all! It is this deplorable tendency that paves the way for mass-mindedness.

[46] Πνεῦμα ὁ Θεός. John 4 : 24.

[47] Bibl. chem., I, p. 443 a.

[48] In his "Speculativa philosophia" (Theatr. chem., I, p. 291) Dorn says of this union: "Such is the philosophical love between the parts of inanimate things, and the enmity also, as between the parts of men. [An allusion to projection!] But no more in the former than in the latter can there be a true union, unless the corruption of the said parts be removed before they are joined together; wherefore that which thou doest is for the sake of peace between enemies, that friends may come together in unity. In all imperfect bodies and those that fall short of their ultimate perfection friendship and enmity are both innate [an apt formulation of the coexistence of opposites in the unconscious "imperfect" state]; if the latter be removed by the work or effort of man, needs must the other return to its ultimate perfection through the art, which we have set forth in the union of man." * Cf. "The Spirit Mercurius," pars. 259ff.

[49] Cf. Honorius of Autun, Speculum de mysteriis ecclesiae (Migne, P.L., vol. 172, col. 936): "For it is said that the pelican so loves her young that she puts them to death with her claws. But on the third day for grief she wounds herself, and letting the blood from her body drip upon the fledglings she raises them from the

13

But now in Christ Jesus you who once were far off have been
brought near in the blood of Christ. For he is our peace, who has
made both one, and has broken down the dividing wall of hostility,
by abolishing in his flesh the law of commandments and ordinances,
that he might create in himself one new man in place of two, so
making peace, and might reconcile both to God in one body through
the cross, thereby bringing the hostility to an end. And he came and
preached peace to you who were far off and peace to those who were
near; for through him we both have access in one Spirit to the
Father. So then you are no longer strangers and sojourners, but you
are fellow citizens with the saints and members of the household of
God, built upon the foundation of the apostles and prophets, Christ
himself being the chief cornerstone, in whom the whole structure
is joined together and grows into a holy temple in the Lord; in
whom you are also built into it for a dwelling place of God in the
Spirit. [RSV] [50]

11 In elucidating the alchemical parallel we should note that
the author of the scholia to the "Tractatus aureus Hermetis"
prefaces his account of the union of opposites with the following
remark:

Finally, there will appear in the work that ardently desired blue or
cerulean colour, which does not darken or dull the eyes of the be-
holder by the healing power of its brilliance, as when we see the
splendour of the outward sun. Rather does it sharpen and strengthen
them, nor does he [Mercurius] slay a man with his glance like the
basilisk, but by the shedding of his own blood he calls back those
who are near to death, and restores to them unimpaired their former
life, like the pelican.[51]

Mercurius is conceived as "spiritual blood," [52] on the analogy

---

dead. The pelican signifies the Lord, who so loved the world that he gave his
only-begotten Son, whom on the third day he raised up, victor over death, and
exalted above every name." * Pelican is also the name of a retort, the spout of
which runs back into the belly of the vessel. [Cf. *Alchemical Studies,* fig. B7.]

50 Cf. the comment on II Cor. 3 : 6 ("for the letter killeth, but the spirit giveth
life") in Olympiodorus (Berthelot, II, iv, 41), where one with knowledge of the
hidden alchemical art is speaking: "How, then, do I understand the transformation
(μεταβολήν)? How are the water and the fire, hostile and opposed to one another
by nature, how are they come together in one, through harmony and friendship?"

51 *Bibl. chem.,* I, p. 442 b.

52 The *aqua permanens* "whose power is the spiritual blood, that is, the tincture.

of the blood of Christ. In Ephesians those who are separated "are brought near in the blood of Christ." He makes the two one and has broken down the dividing wall "in his flesh." *Caro* (flesh) [53] is a synonym for the prima materia and hence for Mercurius. The "one" is a "new man." He reconciles the two "in one body," [54] an idea which is figuratively represented in alchemy as the two-headed hermaphrodite. The two have one spirit, in alchemy they have one soul. Further, the lapis is frequently compared to Christ as the *lapis angularis* (cornerstone).[55] As we know, the temple built upon the foundation of the saints inspired in the *Shepherd of Hermas* a vision of the great building into which human beings, streaming from the four quarters, inserted themselves as living stones, melting into it "without seam." [56] The Church is built upon the rock that gave Peter his name (Matthew 16 : 18).

12   In addition, we learn from the scholia that the circle and the Hermetic vessel are one and the same, with the result that the mandala, which we find so often in the drawings of our patients,

---

. . . For the body incorporates the spirit through the tincture of the blood: for all that has Spirit, has also blood." * (Mylius, *Phil. ref.*, pp. 42f.) These quotations come from the *Turba* (ed. by Ruska, p. 129) and from the book al Habīb (quoted by Ruska, pp. 42f.). For the Greek alchemists gold was the "red blood of silver" (Berthelot, II, iv, 38 and 44). Cf. also Philo, *Quaestiones in Genesim*, II, 59: "But blood is the essence of the sensible and vital spirit; for he says in another place [Leviticus 17 : 14]: The spirit of all flesh is its blood." * Cf. Leisegang, *Der heilige Geist*, p. 97 n. and p. 94 n.

53 "Son, you must take of the fatter flesh." * (Quotation from Aristotle in *Rosarium philosophorum*, *Art. aurif.*, II, p. 318.) The prima materia "grows from flesh and blood." * ("Mahomet" in "Rosinus ad Sarratantam," *Art. aurif.*, I, p. 308.) "To take the egg in the flesh." * (Laurentius Ventura, *Theatr. chem.*, II, p. 274.) "Choose the tender flesh and you shall have the most excellent thing." * (Ibid., p. 292.) "Flesh and blood" correspond to the "inward and hidden fire." (Dorn, *Theatr. chem.*, I, p. 599.) For the patristic view see Augustine, *Quaestiones in Heptateuchum*, I, lx (Migne, *P.L.*, vol. 34, col. 616): "Perhaps he who was delivered for our transgressions [Christ] is signified by the flesh at evening." *

54 Cf. "Aenigmata phil.," *Art. aurif.*, I (1593), p. 151: "And then take the glass vessel with the bride and bridegroom and cast them into the furnace, and cause them to be roasted for three days, and then they will be two in one flesh." * (Cf. Gen. 2 : 24 and Matt. 19 : 5.)

55 "As Christ in the holy Scriptures is called the Stone rejected by the builders, so also doth the same befall the Stone of the Wise" * ("Epilogus Orthelii," *Theatr. chem.*, VI, p. 431).

56 "The Shepherd of Hermas," tr. by Lake, II, pp. 217ff., Similitude 9.

15

corresponds to the vessel of transformation. Consequently, the usual quaternary structure of the mandala[57] would coincide with the alchemists' quaternio of opposites. Lastly, there is the interesting statement that an Ecclesia spiritualis above all creeds and owing allegiance solely to Christ, the Anthropos, is the real aim of the alchemists' endeavours. Whereas the treatise of Hermes is, comparatively speaking, very old, and in place of the Christian Anthropos mystery[58] contains a peculiar paraphrase of it, or rather, its antique parallel,[59] the scholia cannot be dated earlier than the beginning of the seventeenth century.[60] The author seems to have been a Paracelsist physician. Mercurius corresponds to the Holy Ghost as well as to the Anthropos; he is, as Gerhard Dorn says, "the true hermaphroditic Adam and Microcosm":

Our Mercurius is therefore that same [Microcosm], who contains within him the perfections, virtues, and powers of Sol [in the dual sense of sun and gold], and who goes through the streets [*vicos*] and houses of all the planets, and in his regeneration has obtained the power of Above and Below, wherefore he is to be likened to their marriage, as is evident from the white and the red that are conjoined in him. The sages have affirmed in their wisdom that all creatures are to be brought to one united substance.[61]

Accordingly Mercurius, in the crude form of the prima materia, is in very truth the Original Man disseminated through the physical world, and in his sublimated form he is that reconstituted totality.[62] Altogether, he is very like the redeemer of the Basilidians, who mounts upward through the planetary spheres, conquering them or robbing them of their power. The remark

---

57 Cf. my "A Study in the Process of Individuation."

58 Cf. Schweitzer's view of Christian concepts as "late Jewish eschatology": *Geschichte der Leben-Jesu-Forschung*, p. 635.

59 The text is in *Psychology and Alchemy*, par. 454.

60 What would appear to be the first edition of the scholia, dated 1610, was published in Leipzig under the title *Hermetis Trismegisti Tractatus vere aureus de Lapidis philosophici secreto. Cum Scholiis Dominici Gnosii M.D.* The scholia are also printed in *Theatr. chem.*, IV, pp. 672ff., but there the author is said to be anonymous.

61 Dorn, "Congeries Paracelsicae chemicae," *Theatr. chem.*, I, p. 578.

62 In *Aurora Consurgens*, also (pp. 129f.), the Adam composed of the four elements is contrasted with the Adam "from pure elements," who, as the concluding sentence shows, is produced by the circulation of the four elements.

that he contains the powers of Sol reminds us of the above-mentioned passage in Abu'l-Qasim, where Hermes says that he unites the sun and the planets and causes them to be within him as a crown. This may be the origin of the designation of the lapis as the "crown of victory." [63] The "power of Above and Below" refers to that ancient authority the "Tabula smaragdina," which is of Alexandrian origin.[64] Besides this, our text contains allusions to the Song of Songs: "through the streets and houses of the planets" recalls Song of Songs 3 : 2: "I will . . . go about the city in the streets, and in the broad ways I will seek him whom my soul loveth." [65] The "white and red" of Mercurius refers to 5 : 10: "My beloved is white and ruddy." He is likened to the "matrimonium" or coniunctio; that is to say he *is* this marriage on account of his androgynous form.

3. THE ORPHAN, THE WIDOW, AND THE MOON

13   In the text cited at the end of the last section Dorn continues: "Hermes Trismegistus called the stone 'orphan'." [66] "Orphan" as the name of a precious stone is found in Albertus Magnus. The stone was called "orphan" because of its uniqueness—"it was never seen elsewhere"—and it was said to be in the Emperor's crown. It was "wine-coloured" and sometimes shone in the night, "but nowadays it does not shine [any more] in the darkness." [67] As Albertus Magnus was an authority on alchemy, he may have been the direct source both for Dorn and for Petrus Bonus (see n. 66). "Orphan" as the name of a gem may therefore mean something like the modern "solitaire"—a very apt name for the unique lapis Philosophorum. Apart from Dorn and Petrus Bonus, it seems that this name is found only in the

[63] Gratarolus, *Verae alchemiae*, II, p. 265.
[64] "He receives the power of the higher and the lower things. So shall you have the glory of the whole world." * "Tabula smaragdina," *De alchemia*, p. 363. Also Ruska, *Tabula Smaragdina*, p. 2.
[65] Cf. *Aurora Consurgens*, p. 135.
[66] *Theatr. chem.*, I, p. 578. * I do not know to which Hermes text Dorn is referring here. The orphan first appears in the *Pretiosa margarita novella* of Petrus Bonus: "This Orphan stone has no proper name" * (*Theatr. chem.*, V. p. 663). It is also in the edition of Janus Lacinius, 1546, p. 54r.
[67] Du Cange, *Glossarium*, s.v. "Orphanus."

17

Carmina Heliodori.[68] There it refers to the ὀρφανὸς ἔξοικος (homeless orphan) who is slain at the beginning of the work for purposes of transformation.

14   The terms "son of the widow" and "children of the widow" appear to be of Manichaean origin. The Manichaeans themselves were called "children of the widow." [69] The "orphan" referred to by Hermes must therefore have for his counterpart a *vidua* (widow) as the prima materia. For this there are synonyms such as *mater, matrix,* Venus, *regina, femina, virgo, puella praegnans,* "virgin in the centre of the earth," [70] Luna,[71] *meretrix* (whore), *vetula* (old woman), more specifically *vetula extenuata* (enfeebled, exhausted),[72] Mater Alchimia, "who is dropsical in the lower limbs and paralysed from the knees down," [73] and finally virago. All these synonyms allude to the virginal or maternal quality of the prima materia, which exists without a man [74] and yet is the "matter of all things." [75] Above all, the prima materia is the mother of the lapis, the *filius philosophorum.* Michael Maier [76] mentions the treatise of an anonymous author Delphinas, which he dates to some time before

68 Ed. by Goldschmidt, I, vv. 112–14, p. 29. Heliodorus was a Byzantine of the 8th cent. (Goldschmidt, p. 2: "In 716–17, in the reign of Theodosius [III].") Cassel (*Aus Literatur und Symbolik,* p. 248) gives Arnold (Arnaldus?), cited in Lesser's *Litho-theologie,* p. 1161, as the source for "Orphanus." I was unable to verify this statement.

69 It is said that in the Book of Secrets, Mani spoke of "the son of the widow," Jesus (Schaeder, *Urform und Fortbildungen des manichäischen Systems,* p. 75 n.). Bousset (*The Antichrist Legend,* p. 70) mentions the reign of a widow who will precede the Antichrist (according to a Greek and Armenian Apocalypse of Daniel, p. 68). Freemasons are also reckoned among the "children of the widow" (Eckert, *Die Mysterien der Heidenkirche, erhalten und fortgebildet im Bunde der alten und neuen Kinder der Wittwe*). "Widow" in the Cabala is a designation for Malchuth. Knorr von Rosenroth, *Kabbala denudata,* I, p. 118.

70 Mylius, *Phil. ref.,* p. 173.

71 Gratarolus, *Verae alch.,* II, p. 265.

72 This expression appears for the first time in *Aurora consurgens,* Part II, *Art. aurif.,* I, p. 201. Mylius (*Phil. ref.*), copies it. The "vieille exténuée" mentioned in Pernety (*Dictionnaire mytho-hermétique,* p. 280) goes back to the same source. Cf. also "a mistress of about a hundred years of age" in "Aureum saeculum redivivum," *Mus. herm.,* p. 64 (Waite, I, p. 59).

73 *Aurora consurgens* II, *Art. aurif.,* I, p. 196.

74 In *Aurora Consurgens,* p. 77, seven women seek one husband.

75 Cf. the "matrices of all things" in Rulandus, *Lexicon of Alchemy,* p. 226.

76 *Symb. aur. mensae,* p. 344.

1447.[77] He stresses that this author insisted particularly on the mother-son incest. Maier even constructs a genealogical tree showing the origin of the seven metals. At the top of the tree is the lapis. Its father is "Gabritius," who in turn was born of Isis and Osiris. After the death of Osiris Isis married their son Gabritius;[78] she is identified with Beya—"the widow marries her son." The widow appears here as the classical figure of the mourning Isis. To this event Maier devotes a special "Epithalamium in Honour of the Nuptials of the Mother Beya and Her Son Gabritius."[79] "But this marriage, which was begun with the expression of great joyfulness, ended in the bitterness of mourning," says Maier, adding the verses:

Within the flower itself there grows the gnawing canker:
Where honey is, there gall, where swelling breast, the chancre.[80]

For, "when the son sleeps with the mother, she kills him with the stroke of a viper" (*viperino conatu*). This viciousness recalls the murderous role of Isis,[81] who laid the "noble worm" in the path of the heavenly Father, Ra.[82] Isis, however, is also the healer, for she not only cured Ra of the poisoning but put together the dismembered Osiris. As such she personifies that arcane substance, be it dew [83] or the *aqua permanens*,[84] which unites the hostile

[77] Printed in *Theatr. chem.*, III, pp. 871ff. under the title "Antiqui Philosophi Galli Delphinati anonymi Liber Secreti Maximi totius mundanae gloriae."

[78] Gabritius therefore corresponds to Horus. In ancient Egypt Horus had long been equated with Osiris. Cf. Brugsch, *Religion und Mythologie der alten Ägypter*, p. 406. The Papyrus Mimaut has: "Do the terrible deed to me, the orphan of the honoured widow." * Preisendanz relates the "widow" to Isis and the "orphan" to Horus, with whom the magician identifies himself (*Papyri Graecae Magicae*, I, pp. 54f). We find the "medicine of the widow" in the treatise "Isis to Horus," Berthelot, *Alch. grecs*, I, xiii, 16.

[79] *Symb. aur. mensae*, p. 515. The epithalamium begins with the words: "When the mother is joined with the son in the covenant of marriage, count it not as incest. For so doth nature ordain, so doth the holy law of fate require, and the thing is not unpleasing to God." *

[80] "Est quod in ipsis floribus angat,
    Et ubi mel, ibi fel, ubi uber, ibi tuber."

[81] In Greco-Roman times Isis was represented as a human-headed snake. Cf. illustration in Erman, *Religion der Ägypter*, p. 391. For Isis as δράκων see Reitzenstein, *Poimandres*, p. 31.

[82] Erman, p. 301. The text derives from the time of the New Kingdom.

[83] Preisendanz, *Papyri Graec. Magicae*, II, p. 74: "I am Isis who am called dew." *

[84] Synonymous with *aqua vitae*. The relation of the "soul-comforting" water of the Nile to Isis is indicated on a bas-relief (illustrated in Eisler, *Weltenmantel und*

elements into one. This synthesis is described in the myth of Isis, "who collected the scattered limbs of his body and bathed them with her tears and laid them in a secret grave beneath the bank of the Nile." [85] The cognomen of Isis was χημεία, the Black One.[86] Apuleius stresses the blackness of her robe (*palla niger-rima*, 'robe of deepest black'),[87] and since ancient times she was reputed to possess the elixir of life [88] as well as being adept in sundry magical arts.[89] She was also called the Old One,[90] and she was rated a pupil of Hermes,[91] or even his daughter.[92] She appears as a teacher of alchemy in the treatise "Isis the Prophetess to her Son Horus." [93] She is mentioned in the role of a whore in Epiphanius, where she is said to have prostituted herself in Tyre.[94] She signifies earth, according to Firmicus Maternus,[95] and was equated with Sophia.[96] She is μυριώνυμος, 'thousand-named', the vessel and the matter (χώρα καὶ ὕλη) of good and evil.[97] She is the moon.[98] An inscription invokes her as "the One, who art All." [99] She is named σώτειρα, the redemptrix.[100] In

---

Himmelszelt, I. p. 70) in the Vatican, of a priestess of Isis bearing the *situla* (water-vessel). The two great parallels are the cup of water in the Early Christian communion, and the water vessel of Amitabha. For the Christian cup of water see "Transformation Symbolism in the Mass," pars. 311ff.; for the holy water in the worship of Amitabha, see Hastings, *Encyclopaedia*, I, p. 386 b, "Amitayus."

85 Latin MS, 18th cent., "Figurarum Aegyptiorum secretarum." (Author's possession.)

86 Eisler, II, p. 328, n. 1.

87 The Golden Ass, XI, 3 (trans. Adlington and Gaselee, p. 543): "utterly dark cloak." Cf. Hippolytus, *Elenchos*, I, 8.

88 Diodorus, *Bibliotheke Historike*, I, 25: τὸ τῆς ἀθανασίας φάρμακον.

89 She tried to make the child of the king of Phoenicia immortal by holding him in the fire. Plutarch, "Isis and Osiris," 16, *Moralia* (trans. by Babbitt, V, pp. 40f.).

90 Diodorus, I, § 11.

91 Ibid., I, 27.

92 The great Paris Magic Papyrus, line 2290. Preisendanz, *Papyri Graec. Mag.*, I, p. 143.

93 Berthelot, *Alch. grecs*, I, xiii. Ἴσις προφῆτις τῷ υἱῷ Ὥρῳ.

94 *Ancoratus* (ed. by Holl), c. 104, I, p. 126.

95 *Liber de errore profanarum religionum* (ed. by Halm), II, 6: "The earth is the body of Isis." * Cf. Plutarch, "Isis and Osiris," 38, pp. 92f.

96 Reitzenstein, *Zwei religionsgeschichtliche Fragen*, p. 108, and *Poimandres*, p. 44.

97 Plutarch, 53, pp. 130f.

98 Reitzenstein, *Poimandres*, p. 270.

99 *Corpus Inscriptionum Latinarum*, X, No. 3800 (= 3580), from Capua: "TE TIBI / UNA QUAE / ES OMNIA / DEA ISIS / ARRIUS BAL / BINUS V.C." (Now in Naples Museum.)

100 Reitzenstein, *Die hellenistischen Mysterienreligionen* (1927), pp. 27ff.

Athenagoras she is "the nature of the Aeon, whence all things grew and by which all things are."[101]

15   All these statements apply just as well to the prima materia in its feminine aspect: it is the moon, the mother of all things, the vessel, it consists of opposites, has a thousand names, is an old woman and a whore, as Mater Alchimia it is wisdom and teaches wisdom, it contains the elixir of life in potentia and is the mother of the Saviour and of the *filius Macrocosmi*, it is the earth and the serpent hidden in the earth, the blackness and the dew and the miraculous water which brings together all that is divided. The water is therefore called "mother," "my mother who is my enemy," but who also "gathers together all my divided and scattered limbs."[102] The *Turba* says (Sermo LIX):

Nevertheless the Philosophers have put to death the woman who slays her husbands, for the body of that woman is full of weapons and poison. Let a grave be dug for that dragon, and let that woman be buried with him, he being chained fast to that woman; and the more he winds and coils himself about her, the more will he be cut to pieces by the female weapons which are fashioned in the body of the woman. And when he sees that he is mingled with the limbs of the woman, he will be certain of death, and will be changed wholly into blood. But when the Philosophers see him changed into blood, they leave him a few days in the sun, until his softness is consumed, and the blood dries, and they find that poison. What then appears, is the hidden wind.[103]

The coniunctio can therefore take more gruesome forms than the relatively harmless one depicted in the *Rosarium*.[104]

16   It is clear from these parallels that Maier was fully justified in giving the name Isis to the prima materia or feminine transformative substance.[105] As Kerényi has brilliantly shown, using

---

[101] Athenagoras, *Legatio pro Christianis*, 22 (Migne, P.G., vol. 6, col. 939f.).

[102] *Ros. phil., Art. aurif.* (1572), II, p. 413. From the so-called "Dicta Belini" (Apollonius of Tyana), "Allegoriae sapientum," Distinctio 28, *Theatr. chem.*, V. p. 97.

[103] Ruska, *Turba philosophorum*, p. 247. The wind is the pneuma hidden in the prima materia. The final illustration in Maier's *Scrutinium chymicum* shows this burial.

[104] Cf. also the μάχη θηλεία (female combat) in *Carmen Archelai*, one of the *Carmina Heliodori* (p. 56, IV, lines 230f.) (ed. by Goldschmidt), where the materia flees under the rain of projectiles and ends up as a "corpse" in the grave.

[105] The corresponding masculine substance is red sulphur, the *vir* or *servus rubeus*, whose redness relates him to Typhon. In a "dirge for Gabricus who died after recently celebrating his marriage," Maier (*Symb. aur. mensae*, p. 518) does in fact

21

the example of Medea,[106] there is in that myth a typical combination of various motifs: love, trickery, cruelty, motherliness, murder of relatives and children, magic, rejuvenation, and—gold.[107] This same combination appears in Isis and in the prima materia and forms the core of the drama instigated by the mother-world, without which no union seems possible.

17   In Christian tradition the widow signifies the Church; in St. Gregory [108] the analogy is the story of the widow's cruse of oil (II Kings 4). St. Augustine says: "The whole Church is one widow, desolate in this world." [109] She "lacketh a husband, lacketh a man," for her bridegroom has not yet come. So too the soul is "destitute in the world." "But," Augustine continues, "thou art not an orphan, thou art not reckoned as a widow . . . Thou hast a friend . . . Thou art God's orphan, God's widow." [110]

18   Another tradition to be considered in regard to the widow is the Cabala. There the abandoned Malchuth is the widow, as Knorr von Rosenroth says: "[Almanah] Widow. This is Malchuth, when Tifereth is not with her." [111] Tifereth [112] is the son [113] and is interpreted by Reuchlin as the Microcosm. Malchuth [114] is Domina, the Mistress.[115] She is also called Shekinah,[116] the "indwelling" (of God), and virago.[117] The Sefira

mention Typhon as a possible cause of his death. He begins by saying: "She who was the cause of your life is also the cause of your death," but he then adds: "Three there seem to be who may have caused your death: Typhon, your mother, and Mulciber's [Vulcan's] furnace. He [Typhon] scatters the limbs of your body; it may be your mother alone, instead of your brother. But your mother feigns innocence." It is clear that Maier suspects the mother in particular, and wants to make Typhon, the red slave, only a "causa ministerialis."

106 Kerényi, *Töchter der Sonne*, pp. 92ff.

107 For this reason, the story of Medea's murder of Creon, her father-in-law, was also interpreted as an alchemical arcanum. Cf. Petrus Bonus, *Theatr. chem.*, V, p. 686.

108 *Super Ezechielem Hom.*, III (Migne, *P.L.*, vol. 76, col. 808).

109 *Expositions of the Book of Psalms*, Ps. 131, 23, vol. 6, p. 105.*

110 Ibid., Ps. 145, 18f., vol. 6, p. 356.

111 *Kabbala denudata*, I, 1, p. 118.* Knorr's source is Moses Cordovero, *Pardes Rimmonim*, ch. 23.

112 *Tifereth* means 'beauty.'   113 *Kabbala denudata*, p. 202.

114 *Malchuth* means 'kingdom, dominion.'   115 *Kabbala denudata*, p. 528.

116 She is called moon (p. 456), earth (p. 156), bride (p. 477), matron, queen of heaven, fish-pool (p. 215), sea, well, tree of knowledge of good and evil, hind of loves ("so is Malchuth especially called because of the mystery of the new moon," p. 77), belly (p. 192), etc.*   117 *Kabbala denudata*, p. 163.

Tifereth is the King, and in the usual arrangement of the Sefiroth he occupies the second place:

> Kether
> Tifereth
> Yesod
> Malchuth.

Kether, the Crown, corresponds to the upward-growing root of the Tree of the Sefiroth.[118] Yesod [119] signifies the genital region of the Original Man, whose head is Kether. Malchuth, conforming to the archetypal pattern, is the underlying feminine principle.[120] In this wicked world ruled by evil Tifereth is *not* united with Malchuth.[121] But the coming Messiah will reunite the King with the Queen, and this mating will restore to God his original unity.[122] The Cabala develops an elaborate hierosgamos fantasy which expatiates on the union of the soul with the Sefiroth of the worlds of light and darkness, "for the desire of the upper world for the God-fearing man is as the loving desire of a man for his wife, when he woos her." [123] Conversely, the Shekinah is present in the sexual act:

[118] According to some authorities, Sefira is derived from σφαίρα. Cf. Hastings, *Encyclopedia*, VII, p. 625 b, "Kabbala." According to a more recent view the word is derived from the root *sfr*, 'primordial number.' Cf. Scholem, *Major Trends in Jewish Mysticism*, pp. 76ff. For the Tree of the Sefiroth see "The Philosophical Tree," par. 411, and Scholem, pp. 214ff.

[119] *Yesod* means 'foundation.' In the MS in the Bibliothèque Nationale, Fr. 14765, pl. 8, Yesod is depicted like the Son of Man in Revelation 1 : 12 ff., with the seven stars in his right hand, the sword issuing from his mouth, and standing between the seven candlesticks. See infra, our Plate 3.

[120] Cf. *Kabbala denudata*, I, p. 240, 4: ". . . for Malchuth shall be called a watered garden, Isaiah 58 : 11, when Yesod is in her, and fills her, and waters her with waters from on high." * P. 477: "When Malchuth receives the inflowing from the fifty gates through Yesod, then is she called bride." * For Yesod as *membrum genitale*, ibid., p. 22. Cf. also Scholem, pp. 227f., and Hurwitz, *Archetypische Motive in der chassidischen Mystik*, pp. 123ff.

[121] Cf. the legend of Father Okeanos and Mother Tethys, who could no longer come together in a conjugal embrace. *Iliad*, XIV, ll. 300 ff. (trans. by Rieu), p. 265, and Roscher, *Lexikon*, V, col. 394 B, lines 30ff. This reference points only to the similarity of the motif, not to an equivalence of meaning.

[122] Cf. the cohabitation of Gabricus and Beya brought about by the intervention of the philosophers.

[123] *Der Sohar* (ed. by Mueller), p. 234. There is a parallel to this in the psychotic experiences of Schreber (*Memoirs of My Nervous Illness*), where the "rays of God" longingly seek to enter into him.

The *absconditus sponsus* enters into the body of the woman and is joined with the *abscondita sponsa*. This is true also on the reverse side of the process, so that two spirits are melted together and are interchanged constantly between body and body. . . . In the indistinguishable state which arises it may be said almost that the male is with the female, neither male nor female,[124] at least they are both or either. So is man affirmed to be composed of the world above, which is male, and of the female world below. The same is true of woman.[125]

19   The Cabala also speaks of the *thalamus* (bride chamber) or nuptial canopy beneath which sponsus and sponsa are consecrated, Yesod acting as *paranymphus* (best man).[126] Directly or indirectly the Cabala was assimilated into alchemy. Relationships must have existed between them at a very early date, though it is difficult to trace them in the sources. Late in the sixteenth century we come upon direct quotations from the *Zohar*, for instance in the treatise "De igne et sale" by Blasius Vigenerus.[127] One passage in this treatise is of especial interest to us as it concerns the mythologem of the coniunctio:

[The Sefiroth] end in Malchuth or the moon, who is the last to descend and the first to ascend from the elemental world. For the moon is the way to heaven, so much so that the Pythagoreans named her the heavenly earth and the earthly heaven or star,[128] because in the elemental world all inferior nature in respect to the heavenly, and the heavenly in respect to the intelligible world, is, as the Zohar says, feminine and passive, and is as the moon to the sun. In the same measure as [the moon] withdraws from the sun, until she is in opposition to him, so does her light increase in relation to us in this lower world, but diminishes on the side that looks upwards. Contrariwise, in her conjunction, when she is totally darkened for us, she is fully illuminated on that side which faces the sun. This should teach us that the more our intellect descends to the things

124 Cf. the parallel in the Gospel according to the Egyptians (James, *Apocryphal New Testament*, p. 11): "When the two become one and the male with the female is neither male nor female."
125 Waite, *The Holy Kabbalah*, p. 381.
126 *Kabbala denudata*, I, p. 338.
127 *Theatr. chem.*, VI, pp. 1ff. Blaise de Vigenère or Vigenaire (1523–96) was a learned scholar of Hebrew. He was secretary to the Duc de Nevers and then to Henry III of France.
128 Cf. Proclus, *Commentaries on the Timaeus of Plato*, where he says that Orpheus called the moon the heavenly earth (41 e), and the Pythagoreans the aetheric earth (32 b).

of sense, the more it is turned away from intelligible things, and the reverse likewise.[129]

The identification of Malchuth with Luna forms a link with alchemy, and is another example of the process by which the patristic symbolism of sponsus and sponsa had been assimilated much earlier. At the same time, it is a repetition of the way the originally pagan hierosgamos was absorbed into the figurative language of the Church Fathers. But Vigenerus adds something that seems to be lacking in patristic allegory, namely the darkening of the other half of the moon during her opposition. When the moon turns upon us her fullest radiance, her other side is in complete darkness. This strict application of the Sol-Luna allegory might have been an embarrassment to the Church, although the idea of the "dying" Church does take account, to a certain extent, of the transience of all created things.[130] I do not mention this fact in order to criticize the significance of the ecclesiastical Sol-Luna allegory. On the contrary I want to emphasize it, because the moon, standing on the borders of the sublunary world ruled by evil, has a share not only in the world of light but also in the daemonic world of darkness, as our author clearly hints. That is why her changefulness is so significant symbolically: she is duplex and mutable like Mercurius, and is like him a mediator; hence their identification in alchemy.[131] Though Mercurius has a bright side concerning whose spirituality alchemy leaves us in no doubt, he also has a dark side, and its roots go deep.

20   The quotation from Vigenerus bears no little resemblance to a long passage on the phases of the moon in Augustine.[132] Speaking of the unfavourable aspect of the moon, which is her changeability, he paraphrases Ecclesiasticus 27 : 12 with the words: "The wise man remaineth stable as the sun, but a fool is

[129] *Theatr. chem.*, VI, p. 17. Malchuth is also called moon (*Kabb. denud.* I, 1, pp. 195 and 501). Other cognomens are house and night, and in Joseph Gikatila *(Shaare ora)* fountain, sea, stone, sapphire, tree of knowledge, land of life. (This information was supplied by Dr. S. Hurwitz.) Malchuth is the "kingdom of God," described in the *Zohar* as Kenesseth Israel, "the mystical archetype of the community of Israel" (Scholem, p. 213).

[130] Cf. Rahner, "Mysterium Lunae," pp. 313ff.

[131] Jung, "The Spirit Mercurius," par. 273.

[132] Epistola LV, 7f. (*CSEL*, XXXIV, pp. 176f.)

changed as the moon," [133] and poses the question: "Who then is that fool who changeth as the moon, but Adam, in whom all have sinned?" [134] For Augustine, therefore, the moon is manifestly an ally of corruptible creatures, reflecting their folly and inconstancy. Since, for the men of antiquity and the Middle Ages, comparison with the stars or planets tacitly presupposes astrological causality, the sun causes constancy and wisdom, while the moon is the cause of change and folly (including lunacy).[135] Augustine attaches to his remarks about the moon a moral observation concerning the relationship of man to the spiritual sun,[136] just as Vigenerus did, who was obviously acquainted with Augustine's epistles. He also mentions (Epistola LV, 10) the Church as Luna, and he connects the moon with the wounding by an arrow: "Whence it is said: They have made ready their arrows in the quiver, to shoot in the *darkness of the moon* at the upright of heart." [137] It is clear that Augustine did not understand the wounding as the activity of the new moon herself but, in accordance with the principle "omne malum ab homine," as the result of man's wickedness. All the same, the addition "in obscura luna," for which there is no warrant in the original text, shows how much the new moon is involved. This hint of the admitted dangerousness of the moon is confirmed

---

133 The Vulgate has: "Homo sanctus in sapientia manet sicut sol, nam stultus sicut luna mutatur" (DV: "A holy man continueth in wisdom as the sun, but a fool is changed as the moon").

134 "Quis ergo est ille stultus, qui tamquam luna mutatur, nisi Adam, in quo omnes peccaverunt?"

135 Sol corresponds to the conscious man, Luna to the unconscious one, i.e., to his anima.

136 "For man's soul, when it turns away from the sun of righteousness, that is, from inward contemplation of the unchangeable truth, turns all its strength to earthly things, and thereby is darkened more and more in its inward and higher parts; but when it begins to return to that unchangeable wisdom, the more it draws nigh thereto in loving affection, the more is the outward man corrupted, but the inward man is renewed from day to day; and all that light of natural disposition, which was turned towards lower things, is directed to the higher, and in a certain wise is taken away from things of earth, that it may die more and more to this world and its life be hid with Christ in God." * (*CSEL*, XXXIV, p. 178.)

137 "Unde est illud: Paraverunt sagittas suas in pharetra, ut sagittent *in obscura luna* rectos corde." The Vulgate, Psalm 10 : 3, has only "in obscuro" (DV: "For behold, the wicked bend their bow, they fit the arrow to the string, to shoot in the darkness at the upright of heart"). Cf. the "arrows drunk with blood" in *Aurora Consurgens*, p. 67.

26

when Augustine, a few sentences later on, cites Psalm 71 : 7: "In his days justice shall flourish, and abundance of peace, until the moon shall be destroyed." [138] Instead of the strong "interficiatur" the Vulgate has the milder "auferatur"—shall be taken away or fail.[139] The violent way in which the moon is removed is explained by the interpretation that immediately follows: "That is, the abundance of peace shall grow until it consumes all changefulness of mortality." From this it is evident that the moon's nature expressly partakes of the "changefulness of mortality," which is equivalent to death, and therefore the text continues: "For then the last enemy, death, shall be destroyed, and whatever resists us on account of the weakness of the flesh shall be utterly consumed." Here the destruction of the moon is manifestly equivalent to the destruction of death.[140] The moon and death significantly reveal their affinity. Death came into the world through original sin and the seductiveness of woman (= moon), and mutability led to corruptibility.[141] To eliminate the moon from Creation is therefore as desirable as the elimination of death. This negative assessment of the moon takes full account of her dark side. The "dying" of the Church is also connected with the mystery of the moon's darkness.[142] Augustine's cautious and perhaps not altogether unconscious disguising of the sinister aspect of the moon would be sufficiently explained by his respect for the Ecclesia-Luna equation.

21   All the more ruthlessly, therefore, does alchemy insist on the dangerousness of the new moon. Luna is on the one hand the brilliant whiteness of the full moon, on the other hand she is the blackness of the new moon, and especially the blackness of the eclipse, when the sun is darkened. Indeed, what she does to

138 "Orietur, inquit, in diebus eius justitia et abundantia pacis, quoad usque *interficiatur luna*."

139 DV: "In his days justice shall flourish, and abundance of peace, until the moon shall fail."

140 Augustine further remarks that the name "Jericho" means "moon" in Hebrew, and that the walls of this city, the "walls of mortal life," collapsed (*Epist.,* LV, 10).

141 According to Origen, the sun and the moon were involved in the Fall (*Peri Archon*, I, 7, 4). Cited in Rahner, "Mysterium Lunae," p. 327.

142 Rahner (p. 314) speaks very aptly of the "mystical darkness of its (the moon's, i.e., the Church's) union with Christ" at the time of the new moon, the latter signifying the "dying" Church.

the sun comes from her own dark nature. The "Consilium coniugii" [143] tells us very clearly what the alchemists thought about Luna:

The lion, the lower sun,[144] grows corrupt through the flesh. [His flesh is weak because he suffers from "quartan fever." [145]] Thus is the lion [146] corrupted in his nature through his flesh, which follows the times of the moon,[147] and is eclipsed. For the moon is the *shadow of the sun,* and with corruptible bodies she is consumed, and through her corruption is the lion eclipsed with the help of the moisture of Mercurius,[148] yet his eclipse is changed to usefulness and to a better nature, and one more perfect than the first.

The changefulness of the moon and her ability to grow dark are interpreted as her corruptibility, and this negative quality can even darken the sun. The text continues:

During the increase, that is during the fullness of the blackness of the lead, which is our ore, my light [149] is absent, and my splendour is put out.

Then comes a passage which may have inspired the picture of the death of the royal pair in the *Rosarium,* but which is also significant as regards the dark side of the conjunction of Sol and Luna: [150]

---

143 First printing in *Ars chemica* (1566), p. 136.

144 The text has "id est Sol inferius," and so has the later printing of 1622 (*Theatr. chem.,* V, p. 515) as well as Manget's *Bibl. chem.* (II, p. 248a). It could therefore mean "the sun below." This would presumably be a "subterranean sun" equivalent to the *Sol niger* (Mylius, *Phil. ref.,* p. 19, and Ripley, *Chymische Schrifften,* p. 51).

145 The quartan fever occurs every fourth day. The text has here: "For on every fourth day he naturally suffers from a quartan fever." *

146 Leo, as the *domicilium solis,* stands for the sun, i.e., for the active (red) Mercurius.

147 "Per carnem suam sibi contemporaneam Lunarem vilescit." The original Arabic text of Senior (*De chemia,* p. 9) has "canem" instead of "carnem." The dog is Hecate's animal and pertains to the moon (pars. 174ff.). In Manichaeism it is said of the Original Man and his sons, who descended into matter, that "consciousness was taken from them, and they became like one who is bitten by a mad dog or a snake" (Theodore bar Konai, cited in Reitzenstein and Schaeder, *Studien zum antiken Synkretismus aus Iran und Griechenland,* p. 343).

148 The *aqua permanens.*

149 Sol is speaking.

150 "Consilium coniugii," pp. 141f.*

After this [151] is completed, you will know that you have the substance which penetrates all substances, and the nature which contains nature, and the nature which rejoices in nature.[152] It is named the Tyriac [153] of the Philosophers, and it is also called the poisonous serpent, because, like this, it bites off the head of the male in the lustful heat of conception, and giving birth it dies and is divided through the midst. So also the moisture of the moon,[154] when she receives his light, slays the sun, and at the birth of the child of the Philosophers she dies likewise, and at death the two parents yield up their souls to the son, and die and pass away. *And the parents are the food of the son . . .*

22   In this psychologem all the implications of the Sol-Luna allegory are carried to their logical conclusion. The daemonic quality which is connected with the dark side of the moon, or with her position midway between heaven and the sublunary world,[155] displays its full effect. Sun and moon reveal their antithetical nature, which in the Christian Sol-Luna relationship is so obscured as to be unrecognizable, and the two opposites cancel each other out, their impact resulting—in accordance with the laws of energetics—in the birth of a third and new thing, a son who resolves the antagonisms of the parents and is himself a "united double nature." The unknown author of the "Consilium" [156] was not conscious of the close connection of his psy-

---

151 The preceding passage runs: ". . . let the residual body, which is called earth, be reduced to ashes, from which the tincture is extracted by means of water . . . Then join it to its head and tail." * This refers to the production of the uroboros as the arcane substance that changes the natures.

152 This is the well-known formula of Democritus. Berthelot, *Alch. grecs*, II, i, 3: "Nature rejoices in nature, nature subdues nature, nature rules over nature." *

153 *Tyria tinctura* or *Tyrius color* (*Turba*, Sermo XIV), *lapis tyrii coloris* (Sermo XXI, XXVII). "Thus we call our Tyrian (colour) at each step of the procedure by the name of its colour" * (Sermo LXII). "This is the red sulphur, shining in the darkness; and it is the red jacinth, and the fiery and death-dealing poison, and the conquering Lion, and the evil-doer, and the cleaving sword, and the Tyrian (tincture) which heals all infirmities" * (*Theatr. chem.*, V, p. 705). *Tyriaca* is identical with *Theriaca*, which is none other than the arcane substance.

154 Luna sends the dew.

155 Where the aerial realm of the demons and Satan begins.

156 Schmieder (*Geschichte der Alchemie*, p. 106) thinks the author was an Arab of the 13th cent. The fact that the author took over *carnem* / *canem*, a mistake possible only in Latin, shows, however, that he must have been one of the early Latinists.

chologem with the process of transubstantiation, although the last sentence of the text contains clearly enough the motif of *teoqualo*, the "god-eating" of the Aztecs.[157] This motif is also found in ancient Egypt. The Pyramid text of Unas (Vth dynasty) says: "Unas rising as a soul, like a god who liveth upon his fathers and feedeth upon his mothers."[158] It should be noted how alchemy put in the place of the Christian sponsus and sponsa an image of totality that on the one hand was material, and on the other was spiritual and corresponded to the Paraclete. In addition, there was a certain trend in the direction of an Ecclesia spiritualis. The alchemical equivalent of the God-Man and the Son of God was Mercurius, who as an hermaphrodite contained in himself both the feminine element, Sapientia and matter, and the masculine, the Holy Ghost and the devil. There are relations in alchemy with the Holy Ghost Movement which flourished in the thirteenth and fourteenth centuries and was chiefly connected with the name of Joachim of Flora (1145–1202), who expected the imminent coming of the "third kingdom," namely that of the Holy Ghost.[159]

23   The alchemists also represented the "eclipse" as the descent of the sun into the (feminine) Mercurial Fountain,[160] or as the disappearance of Gabricus in the body of Beya. Again, the sun in the embrace of the new moon is treacherously slain by the snake-bite (*conatu viperino*) of the mother-beloved, or pierced by the *telum passionis*, Cupid's arrow.[161] These ideas explain the strange picture in Reusner's *Pandora*,[162] showing Christ being pierced with a lance by a crowned virgin whose body ends in a

[157] Cf. Bernardino de Sahagún, *General History of the Things of New Spain*, Book 3: *The Origin of the Gods* (trans. by Anderson and Dibble), pp. 5f.; also "Transformation Symbolism in the Mass," p. 224.

[158] Wallis Budge, *The Gods of the Egyptians*, I, p. 45.

[159] Cf. my account in *Aion*, pars. 137ff., 232ff.

[160] Cf. the Koran, Sura 18 (trans. by Dawood, p. 96), "the sun setting in a pool of black mud."

[161] Ripley, *Opera omnia*, p. 423. "Consilium coniugii," *Ars chemica*, p. 186: "He slew himself with his own dart." "Rosinus ad Sarrat.," *Art. aurif.*, I, p. 293: "Who with an arrow from our quiver bound together, that is, joined in one body, wretched me, that is, I who possess the matter of Mercury and the Moon . . . and my beloved, that is, the fatness of the Sun with the moisture of the Moon." *

[162] 1588 edn., p. 249. The picture is reproduced in my "Paracelsus as a Spiritual Phenomenon," fig. B4.

serpent's tail.[163] The oldest reference to the mermaid in alchemy is a quotation from Hermes in Olympiodorus: "The virginal earth is found in the tail of the virgin." [164] On the analogy of the wounded Christ, Adam is shown in the Codex Ashburnham pierced in the side by an arrow.[165]

24   This motif of wounding is taken up by Honorius of Autun in his commentary on the Song of Songs.[166] "Thou hast wounded my heart, my sister, my spouse; thou hast wounded my heart with one of thy eyes, and with one hair of thy neck" (DV).[167] The sponsa says (1 : 4): "I am black, but comely," and (1 : 5) "Look not upon me because I am black, because the sun hath scorched me." This allusion to the *nigredo* was not missed by the alchemists.[168] But there is another and more dangerous reference to the bride in 6 : 4f.: "Thou art beautiful, O my love, as Tirzah, comely as Jerusalem, terrible as an army with banners. Turn away thine eyes from me, for they have overcome me . . . 10: Who is this that looketh forth as the rising dawn [*quasi aurora consurgens*],[169] fair as the moon, bright as the sun, terrible as an army with banners?" [170] The bride is not only lovely

163 The drawing of this tail is certainly odd, and one wonders whether it represents water (?) or steam (?). The prototype of the picture can be found in the so-called *Drivaltigkeitsbuch*, fol. 2r. (Codex Germanicus Monacensis 598, 15th cent.) as well as in the Codex Germ. Alch. Vad., 16th cent. There she has a proper snake's tail. One text describes the vapours as arrows ("Consil. coniug.," p. 127). Cf. the eagles armed with arrows in the picture of Hermes Trismegistus from Senior (*Psychology and Alchemy*, fig. 128).

164 Berthelot, *Alch. grecs*, II, iv, 24.*

165 Cf. *Psychology and Alchemy*, fig. 131.

166 Migne, *P.L.*, vol. 172, col. 419.

167 "Vulnerasti cor meum soror mea sponsa. Vulnerasti cor meum in uno oculorum tuorum et in uno crine colli tui." The correct translation is [as in AV]: "Thou hast ravished my heart, my sister, my spouse; thou hast ravished my heart with one of thine eyes, with one chain of thy neck."

168 Cf. *Aurora Consurgens*, p. 133.

169 Here is, significantly enough, the source of the title of that mysterious treatise discussed in von Franz, *Aurora Consurgens*, which complements the present work.

170 AV mod.* A more exact translation of the original text would be "terrible as a host of armies." The Hebrew word *nidgālōt* is read by recent commentators as *nirgālōt*, plural of Nirgal or Nergal. The Babylonian Nergal was the god of war and the underworld, the Lord of spirits, and the god of the midday heat of summer. Wittekindt (*Das Hohe Lied und seine Beziehungen zum Ištarkult*, p. 8) therefore translates "terrible as the planets." "Evidently the opposites in the figure of Istar are meant. . . . She is the gracious goddess of love and beauty, but she is also warlike, a slayer of men" (p. 9). On account of his magic, even greater con-

and innocent, but witch-like and terrible, like the side of Selene that is related to Hecate. Like her, Luna is "all-seeing," an "all-knowing" eye.[171] Like Hecate she sends madness, epilepsy, and other sicknesses. Her special field is love magic, and magic in general, in which the new moon, the full moon, and the moon's darkness play a great part. The animals assigned to her—stag, lion, and cock [172]—are also symbols of her male partner in alchemy. As the chthonic Persephone her animals, according to Pythagoras, are dogs,[173] i.e., the planets. In alchemy Luna herself appears as the "Armenian bitch." [174] The sinister side of the moon plays a considerable role in classical tradition.

25   The sponsa is the dark new moon—in Christian interpretation the Church in the nuptial embrace [175]—and this union is at the same time a wounding of the sponsus, Sol or Christ. Honorius comments on "Thou hast wounded my heart" as follows:

By heart is signified love, which is said to be in the heart, and the container is put in the place of the contained; and this metaphor is taken from the lover who loves his beloved exceeding much, so that his heart is wounded with love. So was Christ upon the cross wounded for love of his Church: [176] "Thou didst first wound my heart when I was scourged for thy love, that I might make thee my sister. . . . Again thou didst wound my heart with one of thine

---

siration should be given to the underworld aspect of Nergal as the Lord of spirits. Cf. Morris Jastrow, *Die Religion Babyloniens und Assyriens*, I, pp. 361, 467. The reading *nirgālōt* is also accepted by Haller (*Das Hohe Lied*, p. 40). Hebrew *d* and *r* are very easily confused.

171 Roscher, *Lexikon*, II, col. 3138.

172 Ibid., col. 3185.

173 Ibid.

174 Cf. infra, par. 174; also "The Psychology of the Transference," par. 458, n. 4.

175 In Cabalistic interpretation she is Israel, bride of the Lord. Thus the *Zohar* says: "And when is he (God) called One? Only at that hour when the *matrona* (= Malchuth) will pair with the King, and 'the kingdom will belong to God,' as is said. What is meant by kingdom? It is the children of Israel, for the King unites himself with her, as is said: 'On that day God is known . . . as One.'"

176 Augustine (*Sermo suppositus*, 120, 8) says: "Like a bridegroom Christ went forth from his chamber, he went out with a presage of his nuptials into the field of the world. . . . He came to the marriage bed of the cross, and there, in mounting it, he consummated his marriage. And when he perceived the sighs of the creature, he lovingly gave himself up to the torment in the place of his bride, . . . and he joined the woman to himself for ever." *

eyes [177] when, hanging upon the cross, I was wounded for love of thee, that I might make thee my bride to share my glory." [178]

26   The moment of the eclipse and mystic marriage is death on the cross. In the Middle Ages the cross was therefore logically understood as the mother. Thus in the Middle English "Dispute between Mary and the Cross," the cross is a "false tree" that destroyed Mary's fruit with a deadly drink. She laments: "My sonys stepmodir I thee calle." Sancta Crux replies:

> Lady, to thee I owe honour . . .
> Thi fruyt me florysschith in blood colour. [179]

27   The motif of wounding in alchemy goes back to Zosimos (3rd cent.) and his visions of a sacrificial drama. [180] The motif does not occur in such complete form again. One next meets it in the *Turba:* "The dew is joined to him who is wounded and given over to death." [181] The dew comes from the moon, and he who is wounded is the sun. [182] In the treatise of Philaletha, "Introitus apertus ad occlusum Regis palatium," [183] the wounding is caused

[177] It is remarkable that in ancient Egypt as well the eye is connected with the hierosgamos of the gods. The first day of autumn (i.e., of the dwindling sun) is celebrated in the Heliopolitan inscriptions as the "feast day of the goddess Yusasit," as the "arrival of the sister who makes ready to unite herself with her father." On that day "the goddess Mehnit completes her work, so that the god Osiris may enter into the left eye." Brugsch, *Religion und Mythologie der alten Aegypter,* p. 286.

[178] Honorius, loc. cit.* The wounding of the Redeemer by love is an idea that gave rise to some curious images among the later mystic writers. The following is from a *Libellus Desideriorum Joannis Amati:* "I have learnt an art, and have become an archer, good intention is my bow and the ceaseless desires of my soul are the arrows. The bow is spanned continually by the hand of God's gracious help, and the Holy Ghost teaches me to shoot the arrows straight to heaven. God grant that I may learn to shoot better, and one day hit the Lord Jesus." Held, *Angelus Silesius: Sämtliche Poetische Werke,* I, p. 141.

[179] Morris, *Legends of the Holy Rood,* pp. 197ff.

[180] Berthelot, *Alch. grecs,* III, i–vi. The aspect of killing is discussed in my "The Visions of Zosimos," pars. 91ff., and the sacrificial death in "Transformation Symbolism in the Mass," pars. 376ff.

[181] Ruska, *Turba,* Sermo 58, p. 161.*

[182] Hg (the alchemical "dew") "penetrates" the gold (sun) by amalgamation.

[183] The treatise is supposed to have been written in 1645. Printed in *Mus. herm.,* pp. 647ff. (Waite, II, pp. 165ff.). The name of the author, Eirenaeus Philaletha, is a pseudonym ("peaceful lover of truth"); the real author is conjectured to be the English alchemist Thomas Vaughan (1621–65)—incorrectly, it seems to me. See Waite, *The Works of Thomas Vaughan,* pp. xivff., and Ferguson, *Bibliotheca Chemica,* II, p. 194.

by the bite of the rabid "Corascene" dog,[184] in consequence of which the hermaphrodite child suffered from hydrophobia.[185] Dorn, in his "De tenebris contra naturam," associates the motif of wounding and the poisonous snake-bite with Genesis 3: "For the sickness introduced into nature by the serpent, and the deadly wound she inflicted, a remedy is to be sought."[186] Accordingly it is the task of alchemy to root out the original sin, and this is accomplished with the aid of the *balsamum vitae* (balsam of life), which is "a true mixture of the natural heat with its radical moisture." "The life of the world is the light of nature and the celestial sulphur,[187] whose substance is the aetheric moisture and heat of the firmament, like to the sun and moon."[188] The conjunction of the moist (= moon) and the hot (= sun) thus produces the balsam, which is the "original and incorrupt" life of the world. Genesis 3 : 15, "he shall bruise your head, and you shall bruise his heel" (RSV), was generally taken as a prefiguration of the Redeemer. But since Christ was free from the stain of sin the wiles of the serpent could not touch him, though of course mankind was poisoned. Whereas the Christian belief is that man is freed from sin by the redemptory act of Christ, the alchemist was evidently of the opinion that the "restitution to the likeness of original and incorrupt nature" had still to be accomplished by the art, and this can only mean that Christ's work of redemption was regarded as incomplete. In

184 See infra, par. 174.

185 *Mus. herm.*, p. 658: "This is the infant Hermaphrodite, who from his very cradle has been bitten by the mad Corascene dog, wherefore he rages in madness with perpetual fear of water (hydrophobia)." * (See infra, pars. 176f.) The "rabid black dog" is chased away "with water and blows," and "thus will the darkness be dispelled." From this it can be seen that the mad dog represents the nigredo and thus, indirectly, the dark new moon, which eclipses the sun (cf. Senior, *De chemia*, p. 9: "Leo decays, weakened by the dog [flesh]").* The "infant" would correspond to the raging Attis, κατηφὲς ἄκουσμα 'Ρέας, "the dark rumour of Rhea," "whom the Assyrians call thrice-desired Adonis," the son-lover who dies young (Hippolytus, *Elenchos*, V, 9, 8). According to the legend of Pessinus, Agdistis (Cybele), the mother of Attis, was herself hermaphroditic at first but was castrated by the gods. She drove Attis mad, so that he did the same thing to himself at his wedding. Zeus made his body incorruptible, and this forms the parallel to the *incorruptibilitas* of the alchemical "infant." Cf. Pausanias, *Description of Greece*, VII, 17 (Frazer trans., III, pp. 266f.).

186 *Theatr. chem.*, I, p. 518.*

187 *Lux naturae* and *caeleste sulphur* are to be understood as identical.

188 *Theatr. chem.*, I, p. 518.*

view of the wickednesses which the "Prince of this world," [189] undeterred, goes on perpetrating as liberally as before, one cannot withhold all sympathy from such an opinion. For an alchemist who professed allegiance to the Ecclesia spiritualis it was naturally of supreme importance to make himself an "unspotted vessel" of the Paraclete and thus to realize the idea "Christ" on a plane far transcending a mere imitation of him. It is tragic to see how this tremendous thought got bogged down again and again in the welter of human folly. A shattering example of this is afforded not only by the history of the Church, but above all by alchemy itself, which richly merited its own condemnation —in ironical fulfilment of the dictum "In sterquiliniis invenitur" (it is found in cesspools). Agrippa von Nettesheim was not far wrong when he opined that "Chymists are of all men the most perverse." [190]

28   In his "Mysterium Lunae," an extremely valuable study for the history of alchemical symbolism, Rahner [191] mentions that the "waxing and waning" of the bride (Luna, Ecclesia) is based on the *kenosis* [192] of the bridegroom, in accordance with the words of St. Ambrose: [193]

Luna is diminished that she may fill the elements. Therefore is this a great mystery. To her it was given by him who confers grace upon all things. He emptied her that he might fill her, as he also emptied himself that he might fill all things. He emptied himself that he might come down to us. He came down to us that he might rise again for all. . . . Thus has Luna proclaimed the mystery of Christ.[194]

---

[189] John 12 : 31.   [190] *The Vanity of Arts and Sciences* (anon. trans.), p. 315.*
[191] *Zeitschrift für kath. Theol.,* LXIII, p. 431.
[192] = emptying. See next paragraph.
[193] *Hexameron,* IV, 8, 32 (Migne, P.L., vol. 14, col. 204).*
[194] Prof. Rahner was kind enough to send me the following explanation: "The fundamental idea of the theologians is always this: the earthly fate of the Church as the body of Christ is modelled on the earthly fate of Christ himself. That is to say the Church, in the course of her history, moves towards a death, as well in her individual members (here is the connecting-link with the doctrine of 'mortification') as in her destiny as a whole, until the last day when, after fulfilling her earthly task, she becomes 'unnecessary' and 'dies,' as is indicated in Psalm 71 : 7: 'until the moon shall fail.' These ideas were expressed in the symbolism of Luna as the Church. Just as the *kenosis* of Christ was fulfilled in death, even death on the cross (Phil. 2 : 8), and out of this death the 'glory' of the divine nature (2 : 9f.) was bestowed on Christ's 'form as a servant' (2 : 7), whence this whole process can be compared with the setting (death) of the sun and its rising anew (glory), even so it is with the parallel *kenosis* of Ecclesia-Luna. The closer Luna approaches to

29   Thus the changefulness of the moon is paralleled by the transformation of the pre-existent Christ from a divine into a human figure through the "emptying," that passage in Philippians (2 : 6) which has aroused so much comment: ". . . who, though he was in the form of God, did not count equality with God a thing to be clung to, but emptied himself, taking the form of a servant, being born in the likeness of men" (RSV / DV).[195] Even the most tortuous explanations of theology have never improved on the lapidary paradox of St. Hilary: "Deus homo, immortalis mortuus, aeternus sepultus" (God-man, immortal-dead, eternal-buried).[196] According to Ephraem Syrus, the *kenosis* had the reverse effect of unburdening Creation: "Because the creatures were weary of bearing the prefigurations of his glory, he disburdened them of those prefigurations, even as he had disburdened the womb that bore him." [197]

the sun, the more is she darkened until, at the conjunction of the new moon, all her light is 'emptied' into Christ, the sun. (It is well worth noting that just at this point Augustine speaks of the strange speculations of the Manichaeans about the two 'light-ships,' when the ship of Luna pours out its light into the ship of the sun, *Epistola* 55, iv, 6.) Augustine now applies this to the individual Christians of whom the Ecclesia is composed. The remarkable paradox of Luna, that she is darkest when nearest the sun, is a symbol of Christian asceticism: 'The more the inward man draws nigh to the sun, the more is the outward man destroyed, but the inward man is renewed from day to day' (a variation of II Cor. 4 : 16). That is, the Christian dies like Luna and his life is 'hid with Christ in God' (Coloss. 3 : 3). All this Augustine says in *Epistola* 55, v, 8. Afterwards he applies it to the Church and her destiny (*Epistola* 55, vi, 10): she will vanish into Christ, the sun, at the end of time: 'donec interficiatur Luna.' Augustine here translates the ἀνταναιρεθῇ of Psalm 71 : 7 by 'interficiatur'; in his *Enarratio in Ps. 71* (Migne, *P.L.*, vol. 36, cols. 907f.) he expatiates on the translation of this Greek word and there renders it by 'tollatur' (is removed) and 'auferatur' (taken away). The doctrine implied in all these passages is that the Church in her future glory ceases her work of salvation, which is destined only for the earth, and that she is totally eclipsed by the splendour of Christ the sun, because (and this again is a strange paradox) in the resurrection of the flesh she herself has become the 'full moon,' and indeed the 'sun.' 'Permanebit cum Sole,' she 'shall live while the sun endures,' as Ps. 71 : 5 (RSV 72 : 5) says."

195 Ὃς ἐν μορφῇ θεοῦ ὑπάρχων οὐχ ἁρπαγμὸν ἡγήσατο τὸ εἶναι ἴσα θεῷ ἀλλὰ ἑαυτὸν ἐκένωσεν μορφὴν δούλου λαβών.

196 *De trinitate*, I, 13 (Migne, *P.L.*, vol. 10, col. 35). The passage says literally: "Hence, just as the truths that God became man, that the Immortal died, that the Eternal was buried, do not belong to the order of the rational intellect but are an exceptional work of power, so it is an effect not of intellect but of omnipotence that he who is man is likewise God, that he who died is immortal, that he who was buried is eternal." *   197 *Hymni et Sermones* (ed. Lamy), II, col. 802.*

36

30   St. Ambrose's reference to the *kenosis* makes the changing of the moon causally dependent on the transformation of the bridegroom. The darkening of Luna then depends on the sponsus, Sol, and here the alchemists could refer to the darkening of the beloved's countenance in Song of Songs 1 : 4–5. The sun, too, is equipped with darts and arrows. Indeed, the secret poisoning that otherwise emanates from the coldness and moisture of the moon is occasionally attributed to the "cold dragon," who contains a "volatile fiery spirit" and "spits flames." Thus in Emblem L of the *Scrutinium* [198] he is given a masculine role: he wraps the woman in the grave in a deadly embrace. The same thought occurs again in Emblem V, where a toad is laid on the breast of the woman so that she, suckling it, may die as it grows.[199] The toad is a cold and damp animal like the dragon. It "empties" the woman as though the moon were pouring herself into the sun.[200]

4. ALCHEMY AND MANICHAEISM

31   At the beginning of the last section I mentioned the term "orphan" for the lapis. Here the motif of the unknown or absent father seems to be of special importance. Mani is the best-known example of the "son of the widow." His original name was said to be Κούβρικος (Cubricus); later he changed it to Manes, a Babylonian word meaning "vessel." [201] As a four-year-old boy he was sold as a slave to a rich widow. She came to love him, and later adopted him and made him her heir. Together with her wealth he inherited the "serpent's poison" of his doctrine—the four books of Scythianos, the original master of his adoptive father Terebinthos, named "Budda." [202] Of this Scythianos there is a

198 Maier, *Scrut. chymicum*, p. 148.
199 Ibid., p. 13, from "Tractatulus Aristotelis," *Art. aurif.*, I, p. 369.
200 Cf. the Manichaean idea of the moon emptying her "soul-content" into the sun.
201 Epiphanius, *Panarium*, LXVI, 1 (ed. by Holl), III, pp. 14f.; Hegemonius, *Acta Archelai* (ed. by Beeson), LXII; Socrates Scholasticus, *The Ecclesiastical History*, I, 22; Theodoret, *Haereticarum fabularum compendium*, I, 26 (Migne, *P.G.*, vol. 83, col. 378).
202 This might be a reference to Buddhism. The Manichaean theory of metempsychosis may possibly come from the same source. Scythianos is said to have travelled to India. According to Suidas, *Lexikon* (ed. by Adler, part 3, p. 318), Scythianos-Manes was a Βραχμάνης (Brahman). Cf. also Cedrenus, *Historiarum compendium*, I, 456 (Migne, *P.G.*, vol. 121, col. 498).

legendary biography which equates him with Simon Magus; [203] like him, he is said to have come to Jerusalem at the time of the apostles. He propounded a dualistic doctrine which, according to Epiphanius,[204] was concerned with pairs of opposites: "white and black, yellow and green, moist and dry, heaven and earth, night and day, soul and body, good and evil, right and wrong." From these books Mani concocted his pernicious heresy which poisoned the nations. "Cubricus" is very like the alchemical Kybrius,[205] Gabricus,[206] Kibrich,[207] Kybrich, Kibric,[208] Kybrig, Kebrick,[209] Alkibric,[210] Kibrit,[211] Kibrith,[212] Gabricius, Gabrius,[213] Thabritius, Thabritis,[214] and so on.[215] The Arabic word *kibrit* means sulphur.

32   In the *Aurora consurgens* "sulphur nigrum" stands side by side with "vetula," the first being a synonym for spirit and the second for soul. Together they form a pair roughly comparable to the devil and his grandmother. This relationship also occurs in Rosencreutz's *Chymical Wedding*,[216] where a black king sits beside a veiled old woman. The "black sulphur" is a pejorative name for the active, masculine substance of Mercurius and points to its dark, saturnine nature, which is evil.[217] This is the wicked Moorish king of the *Chymical Wedding*, who makes the king's daughter his concubine (*meretrix*), the "Ethiopian" of other treatises,[218] analogous to the "Egyptian" in the "Passio

203 Cyril of Jerusalem, *Katechesis*, VI, 21 (*Opera*, ed. by Reischl, I, p. 185).

204 *Panarium*, LXVI, 2 (ed. by Holl, III, p. 18).

205 Rulandus, *Lexicon*, p. 187.   206 *Art. aurif.*, II, p. 246.

207 "Maria Prophetissa," *Art. aurif.*, I, p. 321.

208 "Scala philosophorum," ibid., II, p. 116.

209 Reusner, *Pandora*, p. 297, interpreted as "arsenic," i.e., the active masculine element, from ἄρρην or ἄρσην.

210 Petrus de Silento, "Opus," *Theatr. chem.*, IV, p. 1114.

211 Anthonius de Abbatia, *Epistolae duae*, in Roth-Scholtz, *Deutsches Theatrum Chemicum*, III, p. 703.   212 Pernety, *Dict. mytho-hermétique*, p. 233.

213 Ibid., p. 179.   214 "Visio Arislei," *Art. aurif.*, I, pp. 147f.

215 The name "Cubricus" for Mani has so far not been satisfactorily explained. Cf. Schaeder, *Urform und Fortbildungen des manich. Systems*, pp. 88f, n.

216 Trans. by Foxcroft, p. 162.

217 Cf. my "Spirit Mercurius," pars. 271, 276.

218 Cf. *Psychology and Alchemy*, par. 484. Also *Aurora Consurgens*, p. 57: ". . . the shadow of death, for a tempest hath overwhelmed me; then before me shall the Ethiopians fall down and my enemies shall lick my earth." * Cf. Origen, *De oratione*, 27, 12 (Migne, *P.G.*, vol. 11, cols. 514f.): "He who participates in 'the

Perpetuae,"[219] who from the Christian point of view is the devil. He is the activated darkness of matter, the *umbra Solis* (shadow of the sun), which represents the virginal-maternal *prima materia*. When the doctrine of the "Increatum"[220] began to play a role in alchemy during the sixteenth century, it gave rise to a dualism which might be compared with the Manichaean teaching.[221]

33   In the Manichaean system matter (*hyle*) is personified by the dark, fluid, human body of the evil principle. As St. Augustine says, the substance of evil "had its own hideous and formless bulk, either gross which they called earth, or thin and tenuous like the air; for they imagine it to be some malignant mind creeping over the earth."[222] The Manichaean doctrine of the Anthropos shares the dual form of its Christ figure with alchemy, in so far as the latter also has a dualistic redeemer: Christ as saviour of man (Microcosm), and the lapis Philosophorum as saviour of the Macrocosm. The doctrine presupposes on the one hand a Christ incapable of suffering (*impatibilis*), who takes care of souls, and on the other hand a Christ capable of suffering (*patibilis*),[223] whose role is something like that of a *spiritus vegetativus*, or of Mercurius.[224] This spirit is imprisoned in the body of the princes of darkness and is freed as follows by angelic beings who dwell in the sun and moon: assuming alternately male and female form they excite the desires of the wicked and cause them to break out in a sweat of fear, which falls upon the

dragon' is none other than 'the Ethiopian' spiritually, himself changed into a serpent." * (*Alexandrian Christianity*, trans. by Oulton and Chadwick, p. 301). Epiphanius, *Panarium*, XXVI, 16 (ed. by Holl, I, p. 296) speaks of the "Aethiopes denigrati peccato" (Ethiopians blackened by sin).

219 *Passio SS. Perpetuae et Felicitas*, ed. by van Beek, pp. 26f. Cf. also M.-L. von Franz's "Passio Perpetuae," in *Aion* (Swiss edn., pp. 389ff.).

220 Cf. Paracelsus, "Philosophia ad Athenienses" (Sudhoff, XIII, pp. 390f.); Dorn, "Physica genesis," *Theatr. chem.*, I, p. 380, and *Psychology and Alchemy*, pars. 430ff.

221 Cf. "the unbegotten father, the unbegotten earth, and the unbegotten air" of the Manichaeans (Augustine, *De Actis cum Felice*, I, 18; Migne, *P.L.*, vol. 42, col. 532), mentioned by Bardesanes and Marinus (Bousset, *Hauptprobleme der Gnosis*, p. 97) and by Hermogenes: "God created all things from coexistent and ungenerated matter." * (Hippolytus, *Elenchos*, VIII, 17, 1.)

222 *Confessions*, V, 10 (trans. by Sheed, p. 75).

223 Augustine, *Reply to Faustus*, XX, 2 (trans. by Stothert and others, p. 253).

224 Walch, *Entwurf einer vollständigen Historie der Ketzereien*, I, p. 753.

earth and fertilizes the vegetation.[225] In this manner the heavenly light-material is freed from the dark bodies and passes into plant form.[226]

34   The inflammation by desire has its analogy in the alchemist's gradual warming of the substances that contain the arcanum. Here the symbol of the sweat-bath plays an important role, as the illustrations show.[227] Just as for the Manichaeans the sweat of the archons signified rain,[228] so for the alchemists sweat meant dew.[229] In this connection we should also mention the

225 Augustine, "The Nature of the Good," 44 (*Earlier Writings*, trans. by Burleigh, p. 344).

226 Cf. *Faust* II, the angel scene at Faust's death. Mephistopheles is addressing the angels:

> "Us spirits you call damned, and look askance.
> Witch-masters, you, par excellence;
> For men and maid you lead astray.
> What an adventure curst and dire!
> Is this love's elemental game?"
>   (*Faust, Part Two,* trans. by Wayne, p. 277.)

227 Maier, *Scrut. chymicum,* pp. 82ff. Laurentius Ventura, "De ratione conficiendi Lapidis," *Theatr. chem.,* II, p. 293: "The stone . . . begins to sweat because of the narrowness of its prison." *

228 Hegemonius, *Acta Archelai,* IX: "This prince sweats because of his tribulation, and his sweat is rain." * Christensen ("Les Types du premier Homme et du premier Roi dans l'histoire légendaire des Iraniens," p. 16) quotes from the Bundahisn (3, 19) that Ormuzd fashioned a "shining youth" from his sweat and that the first men were made from the sweat of Ymir (p. 35). According to Arabic tradition, Ormuzd sweated because of his "doubting thought" (cf. my "Answer to Job," par. 579); from this doubting thought came Ahriman, and from his sweat Gayomart. In ancient Egypt, the gods of the seasons brought forth the harvest with the sweat of Osiris' hands (Budge, *Coptic Apocrypha in the Dialect of Upper Egypt,* Intro., pp. lxviif.). Dorn ("Congeries Paracelsicae," *Theatr. chem.,* I, p. 584) has the following remarkable passage on the lapis: "In its last operations . . . a dark liquid, ruddy like blood, drips from the matter and its vessel; whence they predicted that in the last days there would come upon the earth a most pure man, through whom would be brought about the liberation of the world, and that he would give forth drops of blood of a rose-red hue, whereby the world would be redeemed from the fall." * Cf. my "The Philosophical Tree," pars. 383ff.

229 "And Marcus says, They conceive in the baths, signifying the gentle and damp heat of the baths in which the stone sweats when it begins to dissolve" * ("Consil. coniugii," *Ars chemica,* p. 167.) This passage is a commentary on Senior, *De chemia,* p. 79. The "Epistola ad Hermannum," *Theatr. chem.,* V, p. 894, says: "Then the most perfect body is taken and applied to the fire of the Philosophers; then . . . that body becomes moist, and gives forth a kind of bloody sweat after the putrefaction and mortification, that is, a Heavenly Dew, and this dew is called the Mercury of the Philosophers, or Aqua Permanens." * Cf. the Creator making

strange legend reported in the *Acta Archelai,* concerning the apparatus which the "son of the living Father" invented to save human souls. He constructed a great wheel with twelve buckets which, as they revolved, scooped up the souls from the deep and deposited them on the moon-ship.[230] In alchemy the *rota* is the symbol of the *opus circulatorium.* Like the alchemists, the Manichaeans had a "virago," the male virgin Joel,[231] who gave Eve a certain amount of the light-substance.[232] The role she plays in regard to the princes of darkness corresponds to that of Mercurius duplex, who like her sets free the secret hidden in matter, the "light above all lights," the *filius philosophorum.* I would not venture to decide how much in these parallels is to be ascribed directly to Manichaean tradition, how much to indirect influence, and how much to spontaneous revival.

35   Our starting-point for these remarks was the designation of the lapis as "orphan," which Dorn mentions apparently out of the blue when discussing the union of opposites. The material we have adduced shows what an archetypal drama of death and rebirth lies hidden in the coniunctio, and what immemorial human emotions clash together in this problem. It is the moral task of alchemy to bring the feminine, maternal background of the masculine psyche, seething with passions, into harmony with the principle of the spirit—truly a labour of Hercules! In Dorn's words:

Learn therefore, O Mind, to practise sympathetic love in regard to thine own body, by restraining its vain appetites, that it may be apt with thee in all things. To this end I shall labour, that it may drink with thee from the fountain of strength,[233] and, when the two are made one, that ye find peace in their union. Draw nigh, O Body, to this fountain, that with thy Mind thou mayest drink to satiety and hereafter thirst no more after vanities. O wondrous efficacy of this fount, which maketh one of two, and peace between enemies! The fount of love can make *mind* out of spirit and soul, but this maketh *one man* of mind and body.[234]

---

the first men out of sweat in Eliade (*Shamanism,* p. 334 n.), who mentions this in connection with the sweat-bath.

230 Text in *Psychology and Alchemy,* par. 469, n. 110.   231 A parallel to Barbelo.

232 "And when it appears, it is as a comely woman to men, but to women it has the appearance of a beautiful and desirable youth." * (*Acta Archelai,* IX.)

233 "Est hominum virtus fides vera" (the strength of man is true faith). Dorn, "Speculativa philosophia," *Theatr. chem.,* I, p. 298.   234 Ibid., p. 229.

II

THE PARADOXA

1. THE ARCANE SUBSTANCE AND THE POINT

[36]   The tremendous role which the opposites and their union play in alchemy helps us to understand why the alchemists were so fond of paradoxes. In order to attain this union, they tried not only to visualize the opposites together but to express them in the same breath.[1] Characteristically, the paradoxes cluster most thickly round the arcane substance, which was believed to contain the opposites in uncombined form as the prima materia, and to amalgamate them as the lapis Philosophorum. Thus the lapis [2] is called on the one hand base, cheap, immature, volatile, and on the other hand precious, perfect, and solid; or the prima materia is base and noble,[3] or precious and *parvi momenti* (of little moment). The materia is visible to all eyes, the whole world sees it, touches it, loves it, and yet no one knows it.[4] "This

---

[1] Cf. Bonus, "Pretiosa margarita novella," *Theatr. chem.*, V, pp. 66of.: "The philosophers of old saw that this stone in its birth and sublimation . . . could be compared in parables . . . with all things that are in the world, whether bodily or intellectual. Wherefore whatever they are able to say and declare concerning virtues and vices, concerning the heavens and all things corporeal or incorporeal, the creation of the world . . . and of all the elements . . . and concerning corruptible and incorruptible, visible and invisible things, spirit and soul and body . . . and concerning life and death, good and evil, truth and falsehood, unity and multiplicity, poverty and riches, that which flies and that which flies not, war and peace, conqueror and conquered, toil and repose, sleep and waking, conception and birth, childhood and old age, male and female, strong and weak, white and red and all colours, hell and the pit and their darkness and their sulphurous fires, and also concerning paradise and its sublimity, its light and beauty, and its inestimable glory, and in short concerning those things that are and those that are not, those which may be spoken of and those which may not be spoken of, all these things they are able to say of this worshipful stone." *

[2] By "lapis" is meant both the initial material, the prima materia, and the end-product of the opus, the lapis in its strict sense.

[3] Or again, the filius is "vilis et carior" (base and more dear). "Consil. coniugii," *Ars chemica*, p. 150. Cf. Senior, *De chemia*, p. 11.

[4] "Tractatus aureus," *Mus. herm.*, p. 10 (Waite, I, p. 13).

stone therefore is no stone," [5] says the *Turba*, "that thing is cheap and costly, dark, hidden, and known to everyone, having one name and many names." [6] The stone is "thousand-named" like the gods of the mystery religions, the arcane substance is "One and All" (ἓν τὸ πᾶν). In the treatise of Komarios, where "the philosopher Komarios teaches the Philosophy to Cleopatra," it is said: "He showed with his hand the unity of the whole." [7] Pelagios asks: "Why speak ye of the manifold matter? The substance of natural things is one, and of one nature that which conquers all." [8]

37   Further paradoxes: "I am the black of the white and the red of the white and the yellow of the red"; [9] or "The principle of the art is the raven, who flies without wings in the blackness of night and in the brightness of day." [10] The stone is "cold and moist in its manifest part, and in its hidden part is hot and dry." [11] "In lead is the dead life," [12] or "Burn in water and wash in fire." [13] The "Allegoriae sapientum" speak of two figures, one of which is "white and lacking a shadow, the other red and lacking the redness." [14] A quotation from "Socrates" runs: "Seek the coldness of the moon and ye shall find the heat of the sun." [15] The opus is said to be "a running without running, moving without motion." [16] "Make mercury with mercury." [17] The philosophical tree has its roots in the air [18] (this is probably a reference to the tree of the Sefiroth). That paradox and ambivalence are the keynotes of the whole work is shown by *The Chymical Wedding:* over the main portal of the castle two words are written: "Congratulor, Condoleo." [19]

38   The paradoxical qualities of Mercurius have already been discussed in a separate study.[20] As Mercurius is the principal

5 Cf. the "body that is not a body," in "Rosinus ad Euthiciam," *Art. aurif.*, I, p. 249.

6 Sermo XIII, Ruska, p. 122.*

7 Berthelot, *Alch. grecs*, IV, xx, 3. (MS. 2252, Bibl. Nat., Paris.)

8 Ibid., IV, i. 7.*   9 *Ros. phil., Art. aurif.*, II, p. 258.

10 "Tractatus aureus," *Ars chemica*, p. 12.   11 *Ros. phil., Art. aurif.*, II, p. 259.

12 Mylius, *Phil. ref.*, p. 269.   13 *Ros. phil.*, p. 269.

14 *Theatr. chem.*, V, p. 67.   15 Ibid., p. 87.

16 "Tractatus Aristotelis," *Theatr. chem.*, V, p. 886.*

17 Khunrath, *Von hylealischen Chaos*, p. 224, and others.*

18 "Gloria mundi," *Mus. herm.*, p. 270 (Waite, I, p. 218).

19 Trans. by Foxcroft, p. 30.

20 "The Spirit Mercurius," pars. 255ff.

name for the arcane substance, he deserves mention here as the paradox *par excellence*. What is said of him is obviously true of the lapis, which is merely another synonym for the "thousand-named" arcane substance. As the "Tractatus aureus de Lapide" says: "Our matter has as many names as there are things in the world." [21] The arcane substance is also synonymous with the Monad and the Son of Man mentioned in Hippolytus:

Monoïmos . . . thinks that there is some such Man of whom the poet speaks as Oceanus, when he says: Oceanus, origin of gods and origin of men.[22] Putting this into other words, he says that the Man is all, the source of the universe, unbegotten, incorruptible, everlasting; and that there is a Son of the aforesaid Man, who is begotten and capable of suffering, and whose birth is outside time, neither willed nor predetermined. . . .[23] This Man is a single Monad, uncompounded and indivisible, yet compounded and divisible; loving and at peace with all things yet warring with all things and at war with itself in all things; unlike and like itself, as it were a musical harmony containing all things; . . . showing forth all things and giving birth to all things. It is its own mother, its own father, the two immortal names. The emblem of the whole man ($\tau\epsilon\lambda\epsilon\acute{\iota}ov$ $\dot{a}v\theta\rho\acute{\omega}\pi ov$), says Monoïmos, is the jot or tittle.[24] This one tittle is the uncompounded, simple, unmixed Monad, having its composition from nothing whatsoever, yet composed of many forms, of many parts. That single, undivided jot is the many-faced, thousand-eyed, and thousand-named jot of the iota. This is the emblem of that perfect and invisible Man. . . . The Son of the Man is the one iota, the one jot flowing from on high, full and filling all things, containing in himself everything that is in the Man, the Father of the Son of the Man.[25]

---

21 *Mus. herm.*, p. 10 (Waite, I, p. 13).*

22 A condensation of the Iliad, XIV, 201 and 246: "I am going to the ends of the fruitful earth to visit Ocean, the forbear of the gods, and Mother Tethys . . . even Ocean Stream himself, who is the forbear of them all." (Trans. by Rieu, pp. 262f.)

23 *Elenchos* VIII, 12, 2ff. (Cf. Legge trans., *Philosophumena*, II, p. 107.)

24 The iota, the smallest Greek character, corresponding to our "dot" (which did not exist in Greek). Cf. Luke 16 : 17: "And it is easier for heaven and earth to pass than one tittle of the law to fall." *

25 *Elenchos* VIII, 12, 5ff. (Legge, II, pp. 107f.). All this is a Gnostic paraphrase of John 1 and at the same time a meaningful exposition of the psychological self. In Jewish tradition Adam signifies, not a letter, but only the small hook at the top of the Yod ( ). (*Shaare Kedusha*, III, 1, cited in *Encycl. Judaica*, s.v. "Adam Kadmon.")

39   The alchemists seem to have visualized their lapis or prima materia in a similar manner. At any rate they were able to cap the paradoxes of Monoïmos. Thus they said of Mercurius: "This spirit is generated from the substances of the sea [26] and calls himself moist, dry, and fiery," [27] in close agreement with the invocation to Hermes in the magic papyrus entitled "The Secret Inscription," where Hermes is addressed as a "damp-fiery-cold spirit" (ὑγροπυρινοψυχρὸν πνεῦμα).[28]

40   The mystery of the smallest written sign, the point, is also known to alchemy. The point is the symbol of a mysterious creative centre in nature. The author of the "Novum lumen" [29] admonishes his reader:

> But you, dear reader, you will have above all to consider the point in nature . . . and you need nothing else, but take care lest you seek that point in the vulgar metals, where it is not. For these metals, the common gold more especially, are dead. But our metals are alive, they have a spirit, and they are the ones you must take. For know that fire is the life of the metals.

The point is identical with the prima materia of the metals, which is a "fatty water" (aqua pinguis), the latter being a product of the moist and the hot.

41   John Dee (1527–1607) speculates as follows: "It is not unreasonable to suppose, that by the four straight lines which run in opposite directions from a single, individual point, the mystery of the four elements is indicated." According to him, the quaternity consists of four straight lines meeting in a right angle. "Things and beings have their first origin in the point and the monad." [30] The centre of nature is "the point originated by God," [31] the "sun-point" in the egg.[32] This, a commentary on the

---

[26] Pernety (Dict. mytho-hermétique, p. 293, s.v. "mer") says of the "sea" of the alchemists: "Their sea is found everywhere, and the sages navigate it with a calmness which is not altered by winds or tempests. Their sea in general is the four elements, in particular it is their mercury." Cf. Psychology and Alchemy, par. 57, n. 1, and par. 265. For the "man from the sea" cf. II Esdras (Apoc.) 11 and 13, fifth and sixth visions.

[27] Mylius, Phil. ref., p. 192.*

[28] Pap. IV, lines 1115ff. Preisendanz, Pap. Graec. Magicae, I, p. 110.

[29] Mus. herm., p. 559 (Waite, II, p. 89).

[30] "Monas hieroglyphica," Theatr. chem., II, p. 218.*

[31] Mus. herm., p. 59.

[32] "Consil. coniugii," Ars chemica, pp. 95 and 125: "Punctus Solis in medio rubeus"

Turba says, is the "germ of the egg in the yolk."[33] Out of this little point, says Dorn in his "Physica Genesis," the wisdom of God made with the creative Word the "huge machine" of the world.[34] The "Consilium coniugii" remarks that the point is the chick (*pullus*).[35] Mylius adds that this is the bird of Hermes,[36] or the spirit Mercurius. The same author places the soul in the "midpoint of the heart" together with the spirit, which he compares with the angel who was "infused with the soul at this point" (i.e., in the womb).[37] Paracelsus says that the "anima iliastri" dwells in the fire in the heart. It is "incapable of suffering," whereas the "anima cagastris" is capable of suffering and is located in the water of the pericardium.[38] Just as earth corresponds to the triangle and water to the line, so fire corresponds

(the sun-point in the midst of the yolk). Yolk corresponds to fire. "In the midst of the yolk" is the *quintum elementum*, the quintessence, from which will grow the chick. Cf. Mylius, *Phil. ref.*, p. 145.

[33] "The sun-point is the germ of the egg, which is in the yolk, and that germ is set in motion by the hen's warmth." * Codex Berolinensis Latinus 532, fol. 154ᵛ. Ruska, *Turba*, p. 94.

[34] *Theatr. chem.*, I, p. 382: "O wondrous wisdom, which by a word alone was able to bring into being every part of the vast and weighty mass of this huge machine that hath been made since the creation." *

[35] *Ars chemica*, p. 95.

[36] Mylius, *Phil. ref.*, p. 131.

[37] P. 21. Here Mylius mentions the "crime of the spirit," from an anonymous treatise ("Liber de arte chymica incerti authoris," *Art. aurif.*, I, pp. 613f.). The crime of the spirit was that the spirit brought about the fall of the soul. It says to the soul: "I will bring thee to eternal death, to hell and the house of darkness. To whom the soul: My spirit, why dost thou not return me to that breast wherefrom by flattery thou didst take me? I thought thou wert bound to me by necessity. But I am thy friend, and I will conduct thee to eternal glory." * "I will do so indeed, but alas, I am compelled to go away, though I will set thee above all precious stones and make thee blessed. Wherefore I beseech thee, when thou comest to the throne of thy kingdom, be mindful sometimes of me." * This passage points fairly clearly to Luke 23 : 42: "Remember me when thou comest into thy kingdom." Accordingly the soul, as the *lapis pretiosissimus*, has the significance of a redeemer. The spirit, on the other hand, plays the role of the Gnostic *Naas*, the serpent who brought about the fall of our first parents. The text even says of it: "But if that spirit remaineth with the soul and body, there is perpetual corruption there." * For this remarkable aspect of the spirit see my "Phenomenology of the Spirit in Fairytales," sec. 3, and "The Spirit Mercurius," pars. 264ff., also Aniela Jaffé's comments on "Phosphorus" in "Bilder und Symbole aus E. T. A. Hoffmanns Märchen 'Der Goldene Topf.'" Here the spirit obviously plays the role of a "Luciferian" (light-bringing) *principium individuationis*.

[38] Cf. my "Paracelsus as a Spiritual Phenomenon," par. 201.

to the point.[39] Democritus stresses that fire consists of "fiery globules." [40] Light, too, has this round form, hence the designation "sun-point." This point is on the one hand the world's centre, "the salt-point in the midst of the great fabric of the whole world," as Khunrath calls it (salt = Sapientia). Yet it is "not only the bond but also the destroyer of all destructible things." Hence this "world-egg is the ancient Saturn, the . . . most secret lead of the sages," and the "ambisexual Philosophic Man of the Philosophers, the Catholick Androgyne of the Sophists," the Rebis, etc.[41] The most perfect form is round, because it is modelled on the point. The sun is round and so is fire, since it is composed of the "fiery globules" of Democritus. God fashioned the sphere of light round himself. "God is an intelligible sphere whose centre is everywhere and whose circumference is nowhere." [42] The point symbolizes light and fire, also the Godhead in so far as light is an "image of God" or an "exemplar of the Deity." This spherical light modelled on the point is also the "shining or illuminating body" that dwells in the heart of man. The light of nature is the "radical moisture" (*humidum radicale*) which, as "balsam," works from the heart, like the sun in the macrocosm and, we must conclude, like God in the "supracelestial world." Thus does Steeb describe the δεύτερος θεός, the "second God" in man.[43] The same author derives the gold from the dew or supracelestial balsam sinking into the earth. Here he is probably referring to the older formulations of Maier,[44] where the sun generates the gold in the earth. Hence the gold, as Maier says, obtains a "simplicity" approaching that of the circle (symbol of eternity) and the indivisible point. The gold has a "circular form." [45] "This is the line which runs back upon itself, like the snake that with its head bites its own tail, wherein that supreme and eternal painter and potter, God, may rightly be discerned." [46] The gold is a "twice-bisected circle," i.e., one divided into four quadrants and therefore a quaternity, a division made by nature "that contraries may be bound together by contraries." [47] It can therefore, he says, be compared

39 Steeb, *Coelum Sephiroticum,* p. 19.   40 Cf. Aristotle, *De anima,* I, 2.
41 *Von Hylealischen Chaos,* pp. 194ff.
42 Cf. St. Bonaventure, *Itinerarium,* 5 (trans. by James, p. 60).*
43 *Coel. Sephir.,* pp. 19, 33, 35ff., 117.   44 *De circulo quadrato,* p. 29.
45 Ibid., p. 15.   46 p. 16.   47 Ibid., p. 41.

to the "sacred city," Jerusalem [48] (cf. Revelation 21 : 1off.). It is "a golden castle engirt with a triple wall," [49] "a visible image of eternity." [50] "Though gold be mute so far as sound or voice is concerned, yet by virtue of its essence it proclaims and everywhere bears witness to God." And just as God is "one in essence," so the gold is "one homogeneous substance." [51] For Dorn the unity of God,[52] the "unarius," is the "centre of the ternarius," the latter corresponding to the circle drawn round the centre.[53] The point as the centre of the quaternio of the elements is the place where Mercurius "digests and perfects." [54]

2. THE SCINTILLA

42   The point is identical with the $\sigma\pi\iota\nu\theta\dot\eta\rho$,[55] scintilla, the "little soul-spark" of Meister Eckhart.[56] We find it already in the teachings of Saturninus.[57] Similarly Heraclitus, "the physicist," is said to have conceived the soul as a "spark of stellar essence." [58] Hippolytus says that in the doctrine of the Sethians the darkness

[48] "And therefore it represents the idea of the heavenly Jerusalem," p. 38. Cf. the heavenly Jerusalem as "bride" in *Aurora Consurgens*, pp. 53f., and as the *domus thesauraria* (treasure-house) of the *Sapientia Dei*, pp. 101ff.

[49] * Cf. the Anthropos symbolism in the Codex Brucianus, *Psychology and Alchemy*, pars. 138f.

[50] *De circ. quad.*, pp. 42f.*

[51] Ibid., pp. 45f.*

[52] Nelken reports ("Analytische Beobachtungen über Phantasien eines Schizophrenen," p. 536) on an insane patient with Gnosticist delusions who stated that God the Father had shrunk to a small point owing to the continual emission of his semen. The semen was lured from him by a "cosmic whore," who sprang from his blood when it mixed with the darkness. This is a pathological version of the "vir a foemina circumdatus" ("A woman shall compass a man": Jeremiah 31 : 22).

[53] "Congeries Paracelsicae," *Theatr. chem.*, I, pp. 545ff. Dorn is an opponent of the quaternity. Cf. "Psychology and Religion," par. 104 and n. 47.

[54] Anonymous scholia to the "Tractatus aureus" in *Theatr. chem.*, IV, p. 691.

[55] Bousset (*Hauptprobleme der Gnosis*, p. 321) says: "The Gnostics believed that human beings, or at any rate some human beings, carry within them from the beginning a higher element (the $\sigma\pi\iota\nu\theta\dot\eta\rho$) deriving from the world of light, which enables them to rise above the world of the Seven into the upper world of light, where dwell the unknown Father and the heavenly Mother."

[56] Meerpohl, "Meister Eckhardts Lehre vom Seelenfünklein."

[57] Irenaeus, *Adv. haer.*, I, 24. The *pneumatikoi* have in them a little bit of the Pleroma (II, 19). Cf. the teaching of Satorneilos in Hippolytus, *Elenchos*, VII, 28, 3 (Legge, II, pp. 80f.).

[58] Macrobius, *In somnium Scipionis*, I, cap. xiv, 19.

"held the brightness and the spark of light in thrall," [59] and that this "smallest of sparks" was finely mingled in the dark waters [60] below.[61] Simon Magus [62] likewise teaches that in semen and milk there is a very small spark which "increases and becomes a power [63] boundless and immutable." [64]

43   Alchemy, too, has its doctrine of the scintilla. In the first place it is the fiery centre of the earth, where the four elements "project their seed in ceaseless movement." "For all things have their origin in this source, and nothing in the whole world is born save from this source." In the centre dwells the Archaeus, "the servant of nature," whom Paracelsus also calls Vulcan, identifying him with the Adech, the "great man." [65] The Archaeus, the creative centre of the earth, is hermaphroditic like the Protanthropos, as is clear from the epilogue to the "Novum lumen" of Sendivogius: "When a man is illuminated by the light of nature, the mist vanishes from his eyes, and without difficulty he may behold the point of our magnet, which corresponds to both centres of the rays, that is, those of the sun and the earth." This cryptic sentence is elucidated by the following example: When you place a twelve-year-old boy side by side with a girl of the same age, and dressed the same, you cannot distinguish between them. But take their clothes off [66] and the difference will become apparent.[67] According to this, the centre consists in a conjunction of male and female. This is confirmed in a text by Abraham

---

[59] *Elenchos*, V, 19, 7 (Legge, I, p. 162).*

[60] This idea occurs in alchemy in numerous variations. Cf. Maier, *Symb. aur. mensae*, p. 380, and *Scrut. chymicum*, Emblema XXXI, p. 91: "The king swimming in the sea, crying with a loud voice: Whoso shall deliver me shall have a great reward." * Likewise *Aurora Consurgens*, p. 57: "Who is the man that liveth, knowing and understanding, to deliver my soul from the hand of hell?" * and beginning of ch. 8.

[61] *Elenchos*, V, 21, 1.

[62] Cf. "Transformation Symbolism in the Mass," par. 359.

[63] Cf. *Aion*, par. 344, n. 147 for a parallel in Frances G. Wickes, *The Inner World of Man*, p. 245.

[64] *Elenchos*, VI, 17, 7.

[65] *Von den dreyen ersten Principiis oder essentiis*, ch. IX. (Sudhoff, III, p. 11.) Cf. "Paracelsus the Physician," par. 39, n. 56; "Paracelsus as a Spiritual Phenomenon," pars. 168, 209, 226.

[66] The motif of undressing goes back to the Song of Songs 5 : 7: "The keepers of the walls took away my veil from me," and 5 : 3: "I have put off my coat, how shall I put it on?" The undressing symbolizes the extraction of the soul.

[67] *Mus. herm.*, p. 579 (Waite, II, p. 106).

Eleazar,[68] where the arcane substance laments being in the state of *nigredo:*

Through Cham,[69] the Egyptian, I must pass. . . . Noah must wash me . . . in the deepest sea, that my blackness may depart. . . . I must be fixed to this black cross, and must be cleansed therefrom with wretchedness and vinegar, and made white, that . . . my heart may shine like a carbuncle, and the old Adam come forth from me again. O! Adam Kadmon, how beautiful art thou! . . . Like Kedar I am black henceforth, ah! how long! O come, my Mesech,[70] and disrobe me, that mine inner beauty may be revealed. . . . O Shulamite, afflicted within and without, the watchmen of the great city will find thee and wound thee, and rob thee of thy garments . . . and take away thy veil. Who then will lead me out from Edom, from thy stout wall? . . . Yet shall I be blissful again when I am delivered from the poison wherewith I am accursed, and my inmost seed and first birth comes forth. . . . For its father is the sun, and its mother the moon.[71]

44   It is clear from this text that the "hidden" thing, the invisible centre, is Adam Kadmon, the Original Man of Jewish gnosis. It is he who laments in the "prisons" of the darkness,[72]

---

68 I have subjected this text to a detailed interpretation in Ch. v, pars. 591ff.

69 "Cham" (Ham) means the blackness. The Egyptian is the same as the Ethiopian. (von Franz, "Passio Perpetuae," pp. 464ff.)

70 *Mesech* means 'mixed drink.'

71 *Uraltes Chymisches Werck*, Part II, pp. 51f. This is supposed to be the book of Abraham the Jew which plays a great role in the biography of Nicholas Flamel.

72 A MS (*Incipit:* "Figurarum aegyptiorum," 18th cent., in my possession) gives another version of this motif: "There was a certain man, who was of use for nothing, and could not be kept under guard: for he broke out of all prisons, nay more, he made light of all punishments; yet a certain simple, humble, and sincere man was found, who well understood his nature, and counselled that he be deprived of all his garments and made naked." * According to the text (fol. 21r), the undressing signifies putrefaction. Cf. Trevisanus, *Theatr. chem.*, I, pp. 799ff. For the prison cf. *Aurora consurgens* I, Parable 3: "Of the Gate of Brass and Bar of Iron of the Babylonish Captivity." Similarly, in the *Carmina Heliodori* (Goldschmidt, p. 55), the *nigredo* is called a "wall like the blackness of darkness," or a "robe of destruction" (p. 56). This goes back to the ancient idea of σῶμα / σῆμα (body / sign). Cf. *Corpus Hermeticum* (ed. Scott, I, p. 172f.): "But first you must tear off this garment which you wear—this cloak of darkness, this web of ignorance, this [prop] of evil, this bond of corruption—this living death, this conscious corpse, this tomb you carry about with you." The *nigredo* is also represented as the "garment of darkness." Cf. *Aurora Consurgens*, p. 59: "He shall not deride my garment," and the parable in the "Aureum Saeculum Redivivum" of Madathanus, *Mus. herm.*, p. 61 (Waite, I, p. 58): "Her garments, which were rancid, ill-savoured,

and who is personified by the black Shulamite of the Song of Songs. He is the product of the conjunction of sun and moon.

45   The scintillae often appear as "golden and silver," and are found in multiple form in the earth.[73] They are then called "oculi piscium" (fishes' eyes).[74] The fishes' eyes are frequently mentioned by the authors, probably first by Morienus Romanus [75] and in the "Tractatus Aristotelis," [76] and then by many later ones.[77] In Manget there is a symbol, ascribed to the "philosopher Malus," [78] which shows eyes in the stars, in the clouds, in the water and in the earth. The caption says: "This stone is under you, and near you, and above you, and around you." [79] The eyes indicate that the lapis is in the process of evolution and grows from these ubiquitous eyes.[80] Ripley remarks that at the "desiccation of the sea" a substance is left over that "shines like a fish's eye." [81] According to Dorn, this shining eye is the sun,[82] which plunges the "centre of its eye" into the heart of man, "as if it were the secret of warmth and illumination." The fish's eye is always open, like the eye of God.[83] Something of the sort must have been in the mind of the alchemists, as is evi-

and poisonous, lay at her feet, whither she had cast them; and at length she broke forth in these words: 'I have put off my coat; how shall I put it on?' " * (Cf. Song of Songs 5 : 3).

[73] Mylius, *Phil. ref.*, p. 149. Similarly Morienus, "De transmut. metallica," *Art. aurif.*, II, p. 45.

[74] Morienus, ibid., p. 32, and Lagneus, "Harmonia chemica," *Theatr. chem.*, IV, p. 870.

[75] *Art. aurif.*, II, p. 32. They are bubbles of steam that rise up in the solution.

[76] *Theatr. chem.*, V, p. 884: "Until the earth shines like fishes' eyes." *

[77] "Granular bodies like fishes' eyes," * "Aquarium sapientum," *Mus. herm.*, p. 91 (Waite, I, p. 83). "At the beginning . . . like red grains and when they coagulate, like fishes' eyes." * Mylius, *Phil. ref.*, p. 193. The same in Penotus, "Regulae et Canones," *Theatr. chem.*, II, pp. 153f. "When they shine in it like fishes' eyes," * Ventura, "De ratione confic. lap.," *Theatr. chem.*, II, p. 333.

[78] *Bibliotheca chemica*, II, Tab. IX, Fig. 4. Malus, conjectured to be Magus, mentioned in Ruska (*Turba*) as an Arabian author. Cf. "The Spirit Mercurius," par. 287.

[79] A free version of "Rosinus ad Sarrat.," *Art. aurif.*, I, p. 310.*

[80] Evidently Dorn ("Congeries Paracelsicae," *Theatr. chem.*, I, p. 607) means the same thing when he says of the Phoenix as the transforming substance: "Its fledglings with their beaks pull out their mother's eyes." *

[81] *Opera*, p. 159.

[82] "Physica Trismegisti," *Theatr. chem.*, I, p. 423.

[83] Scheftelowitz, "Das Fischsymbol im Judentum und Christentum," p. 383.

denced by the fact that Eirenaeus Orandus [84] used as a motto for his edition of Nicolas Flamel [85] the words of Zechariah 4 : 10: "And they shall rejoice and see the plummet [*lapidem stanneum*] in the hand of Zorobabel. These are the seven eyes of the Lord that run to and fro through the whole earth." 3 : 9 is also relevant: "Upon one stone there are seven eyes" (DV). Firmicus Maternus may be referring to the latter passage when he says: [86] "The sign of one profane sacrament is θεὸς ἐκ πέτρας . . . [god from the rock].[87] The other is the stone which God promised to send to strengthen the foundations of the promised Jerusalem.[88] Christ is signified to us by the venerable stone." [89] Just as the "one stone" meant, for the alchemists, the lapis,[90] so the fishes' eyes meant the seven eyes or the one eye of God, which is the sun.

46   The Egyptians held that the eye is the seat of the soul; for example, Osiris is hidden in the eye of Horus.[91] In alchemy the eye is the *coelum* (heaven): "It is like an eye and a seeing of the soul, whereby the state of the soul and her intentions are ofttimes made known to us, and through the rays and the glance [of heaven] all things take form." [92] In Steeb's view, which agrees with that of Marsilius Ficinus,[93] the "coelum" is a "virtus,"

---

84 Pseudonym of an unknown author.

85 Nicholas Flamel, *His Exposition of the Hieroglyphicall Figures*.

86 *Liber de errore profanarum religionum*, 20, 1.*

87 A reference to the birth of Mithras from a rock.

88 The heavenly Jerusalem of the Apocalypse.

89 This reference is valid if the "stone with seven eyes" is taken not as the keystone but as the foundation stone of the temple. The first reference is to the *lapis angularis*, whose parallel in the Eastertide consecration of the fire is the *silex* (firestone), from which the spark springs forth. Cf. the first Collect for Easter Eve: "O God, who through thy Son, who is called the cornerstone, hast brought the fire of thy light to the faithful, make holy for our future use this new fire struck from the firestone."

90 Cf. what is said in "Adam and Eve," pars. 568f., below, about the Cabalistic stone, and particularly about the stone as Malchuth.

91 Campbell, *The Miraculous Birth of King Amon-Hotep III*, p. 67. According to Plutarch ("Isis and Osiris," 55, pp. 134f.), Typhon, the wicked brother-shadow of Osiris, wounded or tore out the eye of Horus, and this is to be interpreted as referring to the new moon. For the relation between the eye and "Chemia" see the important passage in Plutarch (33, pp. 82f.): "Egypt moreover, which has the blackest of soils, they call by the same name as the black portion of the eye, 'Chemia,' and compare it to a heart." *

92 Steeb, *Coelum Sephiroticum*, p. 47.*   93 *Opera*, II, pp. 1447f.

indeed a "certain perfect, living being." [94] Hence the alchemists called their *quinta essentia* "coelum." The idea of a *virtus* is borne out by the description of the Holy Ghost as an eye,[95] a parallel to the invocation to Hermes: "Hermes . . . the eye of heaven." [96] The eye of God emits power and light,[97] likewise the fishes' eyes are tiny soul-sparks from which the shining figure of the filius is put together. They correspond to the particles of light imprisoned in the dark Physis, whose reconstitution was one of the chief aims of Gnosticism and Manichaeism. There is a similar nexus of ideas in the *siddhaśila* of Jainism: "The *loka* [world] is held in the middle of the *aloka* [void], in the form of the trunk of a man, with *siddhaśila* at the top, the place where the head should be. This *siddhaśila* is the abode of the omniscient souls, and may be called the spiritual eye of the universe." [98]

47   The eye, like the sun, is a symbol as well as an allegory of consciousness.[99] In alchemy the *scintillulae* are put together to form the gold (Sol), in the Gnostic systems the atoms of light are reintegrated. Psychologically, this doctrine testifies to the personality- or ego-character of psychic complexes: just as the distinguishing mark of the ego-complex is consciousness, so it is possible that other, "unconscious" complexes may possess, as splinter psyches, a certain luminosity of their own.[100] From these atoms is produced the Monad (and the lapis in its various significations), in agreement with the teachings of Epicurus, who held that the concourse of atoms even produced God.[101]

48   In his chapter on knowledge,[102] Dorn uses the concept of the

94 On the authority of Leone Ebreo, *Philosophy of Love.*

95 Garnerus de S. Victore, *Gregorianum* (Migne, *P.L.*, vol. 193, col. 166).

96 Papyrus XLVI, British Museum. Cf. Preisendanz, *Pap. Graec. Magicae,* I, p. 194, li. 401.

97 Diodorus, *Bibliotheke Historike,* I, 11: "Osiris means many-eyed . . . for in shedding his rays in every direction he surveys with many eyes" * (Loeb edn., I, pp. 38f.).   98 Radhakrishnan, *Indian Philosophy,* I, p. 333.

99 Cf. Rabanus Maurus, *Allegoriae in Sacram Script.* (Migne, *P.L.*, vol. 112, col. 1009: "The eye is . . . clarity of intellect.")

100 Cf. my "Complex Theory," pars. 203f., and "Nature of the Psyche," pars. 388ff.

101 Hippolytus, *Elenchos,* I, 22, 2 (Legge, I, p. 58): "And that from the concourse of the atoms both God and all the elements came into being and that in them were all animals and other things." *

102 "Speculativa philosophia," *Theatr. chem.,* I, p. 275.

scintillae in moral form: "Let every man consider diligently in his heart what has been said above, and thus little by little he will come to see with his mental eyes a number of sparks shining day by day and more and more and growing into such a great light that thereafter all things needful to him will be made known." This light is the "light of nature." As Dorn says in his "Philosophia meditativa":

What madness deludes you? For in you, and not proceeding from you, he wills all this to be found, which you seek outside you and not within yourselves. Such is the vice of the common man, to despise everything his own, and always to lust after the strange. . . . The life, the light of men, shineth in us, albeit dimly, and as though in darkness.[103] It is not to be sought as proceeding from us, though it is in us and not of us,[104] but of Him to Whom it belongeth, Who hath deigned to make us his dwelling place. . . . He hath implanted that light in us that we may see in its light the light of Him who dwelleth in light inaccessible, and that we may excel his other creatures. In this especially we are made like unto Him, that He hath given us a spark of His light. Thus the truth is to be sought not in ourselves, but in the image of God [105] which is within us.[106]

49   In Dorn's view there is in man an "invisible sun," which he identifies with the Archeus.[107] This sun is identical with the "sun in the earth" (in agreement with the passage from "Novum lumen," supra, par. 43). The invisible sun enkindles an elemental fire which consumes man's substance [108] and reduces his body to the prima materia. It is also compared with "salt" or "natural balsam," "which has in itself corruption and protection against corruption." This paradoxical aspect is borne out by a curious saying: "Man is the bait, wherein the sparks struck by the flint,

103 John 1 : 4f: "In him was life, and the life was the light of men. And the light shineth in the darkness . . ."

104 "If a man knows how to transmute things in the greater world . . . how much more shall he know how to do in the microcosm, that is, in himself, the same that he is able to do outside himself, if he but know that the greatest treasure of man dwells within him and not outside him." * Dorn, "Spec. phil.," *Theatr. chem.*, I, p. 307.

105 *Imago Dei* is 'God-image' in the sense both of a "reflection" and an archetype.

106 *Theatr. chem.*, I, p. 460. Cf. *Aion*, pp. 37ff.

107 "The Archeus in man naturally practises the chymic art." * "Spec. phil.," p. 308. This agrees with Paracelsus.

108 "Because man is engendered in corruption, his own substance pursues him with hatred." * Ibid., p. 308.

i.e., Mercurius, and by the steel,[109] i.e., heaven, seize upon the tinder and show their power." [110] Mercurius as the "flint" is evidently thought of here in his feminine, chthonic form, and "heaven" stands for his masculine, spiritual quintessence. From the (nuptial) impact between the two the spark is struck, the Archeus, which is a "corrupter of the body," just as the "chemist" is a "corrupter of metals." This negative aspect of the scintilla is remarkable, but it agrees very well with the alchemists' less optimistic, medico-scientific view of the world.[111] For them the dark side of the world and of life had not been conquered, and this was the task they set themselves in their work. In their eyes the fire-point, the divine centre in man, was something dangerous, a powerful poison which required very careful handling if it was to be changed into the panacea. The process of individuation, likewise, has its own specific dangers. Dorn expresses the standpoint of the alchemists in his fine saying: "There is nothing in nature that does not contain as much evil as good." [112]

50   In Khunrath [113] the scintilla is the same as the elixir: "Now the elixir is well and truly called a shining splendour, or perfect scintilla of him who alone is the Mighty and Strong. . . . It is the true Aqua Permanens, eternally living." [114] The "radical moisture" is "animated . . . by a fiery spark of the World-Soul, for the spirit of the Lord filleth the whole world." [115] He also speaks of a plurality of sparks: "There are . . . fiery sparks of the World-Soul, that is of the light of nature, dispersed or scattered at God's command in and through the fabric of the great world into all fruits of the elements everywhere." [116] The scin-

---

109 Here *chalybs* means 'steel,' but as *chalybs Sendivogii* it is an arcane substance which is the "secret Salmiac." This is Sal Armoniacus, the "dissolved stone" (Ruland, *Lexicon*, p. 281). Elsewhere Ruland says: "Sal ammoniac is the star" * (Latin edn., p. 71). Mylius (*Phil. ref.*, p. 314) says of the miraculous aqua: "That is the best, which is extracted by the force of our chalybs which is found in the Ram's belly . . . before it is suitably cooked it is a deadly poison." * The ruler of Aries is Mars (= iron). Cf. "Ares" in Paracelsus ("Paracelsus as a Spiritual Phenomenon," pars. 176f.)   110 "Spec. phil.," p. 308.*

111 Cf. the "crime of the spirit" in n. 37.   112 "Spec. phil.," p. 307.*

113 Born in 1560, studied medicine, took his degree 1588 in Basel, and died 1605 in Leipzig.   114 *Von hylealischen Chaos*, pp. 54f.

115 P. 63. Cf. *Aurora Consurgens*, p. 97.

116 P. 94. The filling of the world with scintillae is probably a projection of the multiple luminosity of the unconscious. Cf. "Nature of the Psyche," pars. 388ff.

tilla is associated with the doctrine of the Anthropos: "The Son of the Great World . . . is filled, animated and impregnated . . . with a fiery spark of Ruach Elohim, the spirit, breath, wind or blowing of the triune God, from . . . the Body, Spirit, and Soul of the World, or . . . Sulphur and Salt, Mercury and the universal fiery spark of the light of nature." [117] The "fiery sparks of the World-Soul" were already in the chaos, the prima materia, at the beginning of the world.[118] Khunrath rises to Gnostic heights when he exclaims: "And our Catholick Mercury, by virtue of his universal fiery spark of the light of nature, is beyond doubt Proteus, the sea god of the ancient pagan sages, who hath the key to the sea and . . . power over all things: son of Oceanos and Tethys." [119] Many centuries lie between Monoïmos and Khunrath. The teachings of Monoïmos were completely unknown in the Middle Ages,[120] and yet Khunrath hit upon very similar thoughts which can hardly be ascribed to tradition.

3. THE ENIGMA OF BOLOGNA [121]

51   These paradoxes culminate in an allegedly ancient "monument," an epitaph said to have been found in Bologna, known as the Aelia-Laelia-Crispis Inscription. It was appropriated by the alchemists, who claimed, in the words of Michael Maier, that "it was set up by an artificer of old to the honour of God and in praise of the chymic art." [122] I will first give the text of this highly remarkable inscription:

D. M.	D. M.
Aelia Laelia Crispis, nec mulier, nec androgyna, nec puella, nec iuvenis, nec anus, nec casta, nec meretrix, nec pudica, sed omnia.	*Aelia Laelia Crispis,* neither man nor woman, nor mongrel, nor maid, nor boy, nor crone, nor chaste, nor whore, nor virtuous, but all.

117 Pp. 170f.

118 P. 217.

119 There are numerous other synonyms for the scintilla on pp. 220f. and 263f.

120 They were preserved only in Hippolytus, whose *Elenchos* was not discovered until the middle of the 19th cent., on Mount Athos. The passage about the iota (cf. Matthew 5 : 18) in Irenaeus (*Adv. haer.,* I, 3, 2) can hardly have given rise to a tradition.

121 Originally a contribution to the memorial volume for Albert Oeri (pp. 265ff.).

122 *Symb. aur. mensae,* p. 169.

Sublata neque fame, nec ferro, nec veneno, sed omnibus.—Nec coelo, nec aquis, nec terris, sed ubique iacet.	Carried away neither by hunger, nor by sword, nor by poison, but by all.—Neither in heaven, nor in earth, nor in water, but everywhere is her resting place.
Lucius Agatho Priscius, nec maritus, nec amator, nec necessarius, neque moerens, neque gaudens, neque flens, hanc neque molem, nec pyramidem, nec sepulchrum, sed omnia.	*Lucius Agatho Priscius,* neither husband, nor lover, nor kinsman, neither mourning, nor rejoicing, nor weeping, (raised up) neither mound, nor pyramid, nor tomb, but all.
Scit et nescit, (quid) cui posuerit.	He knows and knows not (what)[123] he raised up to whom.
(Hoc est sepulchrum, intus cadaver non habens.	(This is a tomb that has no body in it.
Hoc est cadaver, sepulchrum extra non habens.	This is a body that has no tomb round it.
Sed cadaver idem est et sepulchrum sibi.)	But body and tomb are the same.)

52   Let it be said at once: this epitaph is sheer nonsense, a joke,[124] but one that for centuries brilliantly fulfilled its function as a flypaper for every conceivable projection that buzzed in the human mind. It gave rise to a "cause célèbre," a regular psychological "affair" that lasted for the greater part of two centuries and produced a spate of commentaries, finally coming to an inglorious end as one of the spurious texts of the *Corpus Inscriptionum Latinarum,* and thereafter passing into oblivion. The reason why I am digging up this curiosity again in the twentieth century is that it serves as a paradigm for that peculiar attitude of mind which made it possible for the men of the Middle Ages to write hundreds of treatises about something that did not exist and was therefore completely unknowable. The interesting thing is not this futile stalking-horse but the projec-

---

123 See par. 67.

124 This was recognized very early. Thus Jacob Spon says in his *Voyage d'Italie, de Dalmatie, de Grèce et du Levant fait aux années 1675 et 1676,* I, p. 53: "I claim only that whoever composed it did not understand the principles of Latin names; for Aelia and Laelia are two different families, and Agatho and Priscus are two surnames that have no family connection." And on p. 351: "If any melancholy dreamer chooses to amuse himself by explaining it to pass the time, let him; myself I have already said that I do not believe it to be ancient, and would not put myself to the bother of investigating its riddle."

tions it aroused. There is revealed in them an extraordinary propensity to come out with the wildest fantasies and speculations —a psychic condition which is met with today, in a correspondingly erudite milieu, only as an isolated pathological phenomenon. In such cases one always finds that the unconscious is under some kind of pressure and is charged with highly affective contents. Sometimes a differential diagnosis as between tomfoolery and creativity is difficult to make, and it happens again and again that the two are confused.

53   Such phenomena, whether historical or individual, cannot be explained by causality alone, but must also be considered from the point of view of what happened afterwards. Everything psychic is pregnant with the future. The sixteenth and seventeenth centuries were a time of transition from a world founded on metaphysics to an era of immanentist explanatory principles, the motto no longer being "omne animal a Deo" but "omne vivum ex ovo." What was then brewing in the unconscious came to fruition in the tremendous development of the natural sciences, whose youngest sister is empirical psychology. Everything that was naïvely presumed to be a knowledge of transcendental and divine things, which human beings can never know with certainty, and everything that seemed to be irretrievably lost with the decline of the Middle Ages, rose up again with the discovery of the psyche. This premonition of future discoveries in the psychic sphere expressed itself in the phantasmagoric speculations of philosophers who, until then, had appeared to be the arch-pedlars of sterile verbiage.

54   However nonsensical and insipid the Aelia-Laelia epitaph may look, it becomes significant when we regard it as a question which no less than two centuries have asked themselves: What is it that you do not understand and can only be expressed in unfathomable paradoxes?

55   Naturally I do not lay this question at the door of that unknown humorist who perpetrated this "practical joke." It existed long before him in alchemy. Nor would he ever have dreamt that his joke would become a *cause célèbre*, or that it would lead his contemporaries and successors to question the nature of the psychic background—a question which, in the distant future, was to replace the certainties of revealed truth. He was only a *causa instrumentalis*, and his victims, as naïve and

innocent as himself, made their first, involuntary steps as psychologists.

56   It seems that the first report of the Aelia-Laelia inscription appeared in the treatise of a certain Marius L. Michael Angelus, of Venice, in the year 1548, and as early as 1683 [125] Caesar Malvasius [126] had collected no less than forty-five [127] attempts at interpretation. In alchemical literature, the treatise of the physician Nicholas Barnaud, of Crest (Dauphiné), who lived in the second half of the sixteenth century, has been preserved. He gave an alchemical interpretation of the inscription in, it appears, 1597.[128] To begin with, I shall keep to his interpretation and that of the learned Michael Maier.

57   Maier maintains that Aelia and Laelia represent two persons who are united in a single subject, named Crispis. Barnaud calls Aelia "solar," presumably a derivation from ἀέλιος, 'sun.' Laelia he interprets as "lunar." Crispis (curly-haired), thinks Maier, comes from the curly hairs which are converted into a "very fine powder." [129] Maier obviously has in mind the tincture, the arcane substance. Barnaud on the other hand says that "our materia" is "obvoluta, intricata," therefore curly. These two persons, says Maier, *are* neither man nor woman, but they once *were;* similarly, the subject *was* in the beginning an hermaphrodite but no longer *is* so, because though the arcane substance is composed of sponsus and sponsa, and is thus as it were

125 The inscription is also mentioned in Toniola, *Basilea sepulta retecta continuata* (1661), p. 101 of Appendix, "Exotica monumenta."

126 *Aelia Laelia Crispis Non Nata Resurgens* (1683). Among the commentators Reusner (author of *Pandora*), Barnaud, Turrius, and Vitus are cited, but not Michael Maier.

127 Ferguson (*Bibliotheca chemica*, I, p. 6) mentions 43 commentators. But there are two others in Malvasius, presumably friends of the author, who are introduced as "Aldrovandus Ulisses of Bologna and his comrade our Achilles" (p. 29). Thus, by 1683, the number of known commentators had risen to 48 (including Maier). Ulysses Aldrovandus, of Bologna, lived from 1522 to 1605. He was a famous doctor and philosopher. "Our Achilles" may be identical with Achilles Volta. His name is mentioned as one of the commentators in Schwartz, *Acta eruditorum*, p. 333. Unfortunately I have no access to his treatise. The total number of commentators is, however, larger than 48.

128 Cf. Ferguson, s.v. Barnaud and Aelia Laelia. Barnaud's "Commentarium" is printed in *Theatr. chem.*, III, pp. 836ff., and also in Manget, *Bibl. chem.*, II, pp. 713ff.

129 According to Ruland (*Lexicon*, p. 91), "capilli" is a name for the *lapis Rebis*. It was also conjectured that the prima materia might be found in hair.

bisexual, as a third thing it is new and unique. Neither is the subject a maid or virgin, because she would be "intact." In the opus, however, the virgin is called a mother although she has remained a virgin. Nor is the subject a boy, because the consummation of the coniunctio contradicts this, nor a crone,[130] because it still retains its full strength, nor a whore,[131] because it has nothing to do with money, nor is it virtuous, because the virgin has cohabited with a man. The subject, he says, is a man and a woman, because they have completed the conjugal act, and an hermaphrodite because two bodies are united in one. It is a girl because it is not yet old, and a youth because it is in full possession of its powers. It is an old woman because it outlasts all time (i.e., is incorruptible). It is a whore because Beya [132] prostituted herself to Gabritius before marriage. It is virtuous because the subsequent marriage gave absolution.[133]

58 "But all" is the real explanation of the enigma: all these designations refer to qualities of the *one thing,* and these were thought of as existing, but they are not entities in themselves. The same is true of the "Carried away" passage. The substance (uroboros) devours itself and thus suffers no hunger; it does not die by the sword but "slays itself with its own dart," like the scorpion, which is another synonym for the arcane substance.[134] It is not killed by poison because, as Barnaud says, it is a "good poison," a panacea with which it brings itself to life again.[135] At the same time it is killed by all three: by hunger for itself, by

130 Cf. supra, par. 14, "vetula" and "vidua."

131 "Nec casta" (not chaste) is missing in Maier.

132 From Arab. *al-baida,* 'the White One'.

133 "For marriage, like a cloak, covers and hides whatever is vicious." * *Symb. aur. mensae,* pp. 170f.

134 "Scorpion, i.e., poison. Because it kills itself and brings itself to life again." * Mylius, *Phil. ref.,* p. 256, and *Ros. phil., Art. aurif.,* II, p. 272. "Euoi, two-horned one, twin-formed one! This god of yours is not twin-formed, but multiform . . . he is the basilisk and the scorpion . . . he is the crafty serpent . . . he is the many-coiled dragon, who is taken with a hook . . . this god of yours is decked with the hairs of the Lernaean snake." * Firmicus Maternus, *Lib. de err. prof. relig.,* 21, 2 (ed. Halm, *Corp. script. lat.,* II).

135 "(The divine water) makes natures come forth from their natures, and it quickens the dead." Djabir, "Livre du Mercure oriental" (Berthelot, *Chimie au moyen âge,* III, 213). Cf. "Komarios to Cleopatra" (Berthelot, *Alch. grecs,* IV, xx, 15): "Stand up from the grave . . . and the medicament of life has entered into you." * "The tincturing spirit and the metallic water that is poured out over the body, bringing it to life." * *Aurora consurgens* II, in *Art. aurif.,* I, p. 229.

the sword of Mercurius,[136] and by its own poison as snake or scorpion. "By all" again points to the arcane substance, as Barnaud says: "This is everything, it has within itself everything needful for its completion, everything can be predicated of it, and it of everything." [137] "For the One is the whole, as the greatest Chymist saith: because [of the One] everything is, and if the whole had not the whole [in itself], the whole would not be." [138]

59   That the arcanum is neither in heaven, nor on earth, nor in water is explained by Maier as a reference to the lapis, which "is found everywhere." It is found in all the elements and not only in one of them. Here Barnaud is rather more subtle, for he equates heaven with the soul, earth with the body, and water with the spirit,[139] and thus arrives at the idea of the wholeness of a living organism. "Our material," he says, "is simultaneously in heaven, on earth, and in the water, as if wholly in the whole and wholly in each part; so that those parts, though otherwise divisible, can no longer be separated from one another after they are made one: the whole Law and Prophets of alchemy seem to depend upon this." [140]

60   Barnaud explains the name of him who raised the tomb, Lucius Agatho Priscius, as follows: Lucius is "lucid," "endowed with the most lucid intellect"; [141] Agatho is "good-natured" (Gk. ἀγαθός, 'good'), "upright"; Priscius is "priscus" (pristine), "senior" (of ancient time), "reckoned among those upright Philosophers of old." Maier maintains that these names "signified the chief requisite necessary for the fulfilment of the art."

61   "Neither husband nor lover" etc. means that Aelia Laelia drew him to herself "as the magnet the iron" and changed him into her "nebulous and black nature." In the coniunctio he became her husband, and was "necessary" [142] to the work. But Maier does not tell us to what extent he was *not* the husband etc.

---

136 With regard to "the piercing sword, the dividing blade of Mercurius" see "The Visions of Zosimos," pars. 86, 109f.

137 "Commentarium," *Theatr. chem.*, III, p. 844.*

138 * Cf. Berthelot, *Alch. grecs*, III, xviii, 1.* Barnaud seems to have known the Paris MS No. 2327 (Berthelot, p. ix).

139 He adds "which is accustomed to bear away the spirit." Cf. the "crime of the spirit," supra, n. 37.   140 *Theatr. chem.*, III, p. 845.*

141 Barnaud calls him "adorned with both natural and divine light" (p. 840).

142 Maier does not take *necessarius* here as meaning "kinsman."

Barnaud says: "These are the chief causes, namely marriage, love, and consanguinity, which move a man to raise a column to the dead in the temple of memory, and none of these can here be considered." Lucius had another purpose in mind: he wished the art, "which teaches everything, which is of all things the most precious and is concealed under this enigma, to appear upon the scene," so that the investigators might "apply themselves to the art and true science, which surpasses all else in worth." True, he makes an exception of "that holiest investigation [*agnitionem*] of God and Christ, whereon our salvation depends," [143] a proviso we often meet in the texts.

62 Maier ignores the negative in "neither mourning" etc. just as he did in "neither husband." "In truth," he says, "all this can as well be said positively of Lucius and not negatively." On the other hand Barnaud remarks that it draws a picture of an "intrepid philosopher, smooth and rounded." [144] "Neither mound" etc. is again explained positively by Maier: Aelia is herself the mound, which endures as something firm and immovable. This is a reference to the incorruptibility which the opus sought to achieve. He says the pyramid signifies a "flame to eternal remembrance," and this was Aelia herself. She was buried because Lucius "did everything he had to do in her name." He takes her place, as it were, just as the *filius philosophorum* takes the place of the maternal prima materia, which till then had been the only effective arcane substance. Barnaud declares that though Lucius is a building, it does not fulfil its purpose (since it is a symbol). "But all" he refers to the "Tabula smaragdina," because the epitaph as a whole points to the "medicina summa et catholica."

63 By "He knows and knows not" Maier thinks that Lucius knew it at first but no longer knew it afterwards, because he himself was ungratefully forgotten. It is not clear to me what this is intended to mean. Barnaud takes the monument as an allegory of the lapis, of which Lucius knew. He explains the "quid" as "quantum," for Lucius probably did not know how

143 *Theatr. chem.*, III, p. 846.
144 The "wise man, whole, smoothed and rounded" is an Horatian figure, meaning a man who is not dependent on earthly things. Cf. *Satires*, lib. II, vii, 83f.: "Who then is free? The wise man, who is lord over himself, whom neither poverty nor death nor bonds affright, who bravely defies his passions, and scorns ambition, who in himself is a whole, smoothed and rounded." * Horace, *Satires, Epistles, and Ars Poetica* (trans. by Fairclough), p. 231.

much the stone weighed. Neither, of course, did he know for what future discoverer he had made the inscription. Barnaud's explanation of "quid" is decidedly feeble. It would be more to the point to remember that the lapis is a fabulous entity of cosmic dimensions which surpasses human understanding. Consideration for the prestige of the alchemist may have prevented him from indulging this suggestive thought, for as an alchemist he could not very well admit that the artifex himself did not know what he was producing with his art. Had he been a modern psychologist he might have realized, with a little effort, that man's totality, the self, is by definition [145] beyond the bounds of knowledge.

64   With "This is a tomb" etc. we reach the first *positive* statement (barring the names) of the inscription. Maier's opinion is that this has nothing to do with the tomb, which was no tomb, but that Aelia herself is meant. "For she herself is the container, converting into herself the contained; and thus she is a tomb or receptacle that has no body or content in it, as was said of Lot's wife, who was her own tomb without a body, and a body without a tomb." [146] He is evidently alluding to the second version of the "Arisleus Vision," which says: "With so much love did Beya embrace Gabricus that she absorbed him wholly into her own nature and dissolved him into indivisible particles." [147] Ripley says that at the death of the king all his limbs were torn into "atoms." [148] This is the motif of dismemberment which is

[145] In so far as it is the sum of conscious and unconscious processes.

[146] *Symb. aur. mensae*, p. 173.*

[147] *Ros. phil., Art. aurif.*, II, p. 246. The empirical model for this is the amalgamization of gold with mercury. Hence the saying: "The whole work lies in the solution" (i.e., of sun and moon in mercury). Ibid., p. 270.

[148] *Opera*, p. 351. He says there arises a "thickening of the air [i.e., a concretizing of the spirit] and all the limbs are torn to atoms." * The "mangled King" refers to Osiris, well known to the alchemists, and his dismemberment. Thus Olympiodorus (Berthelot, II, iv, 42) mentions Osiris as the "straitened tomb (ἡ ταφὴ ἐσφιγμένη) which hides all his limbs." He is the moist principle (in agreement with Plutarch, "Isis and Osiris," c. 33, trans. by Babbitt, V, pp. 80f.) and "has bound together (συνέσφιγξεν) the whole of the lead," obviously as its "soul." Typhon sealed the coffin of Osiris with lead. (Plutarch, ibid.) Osiris and Isis together form the androgynous prima materia (Maier, *Symb. aur. mensae*, pp. 343f., and Pernety, *Dict. mytho-hermétique*, p. 359). He has affinities with the "sick" or "imprisoned" King, the *Rex marinus* of the "Visio Arislei." He is "many-eyed" (*oculi piscium!*) in Diodorus, I, 11 (Loeb edn., I, pp. 38f.) and "many-formed" like Attis (or the "self-transforming" Mercurius). In the hymn to Attis (Hippolytus, *Elenchos*, V, 9, 8) he

well known in alchemy.[149] The atoms are or become "white sparks" shining in the *terra foetida*.[150] They are also called the "fishes' eyes." [151]

65   The explanation of Aelia herself as the "tomb" would naturally appeal to an alchemist, as this motif plays a considerable role in the literature. He called his vessel a "tomb," [152] or, as in the *Rosarium,* a "red tumulus of rock." The *Turba* says that a tomb must be dug for the dragon and the woman.[153] Interment is identical with the *nigredo*.[154] A Greek treatise describes the alchemical process as the "eight graves." [155] Alexander found the "tomb of Hermes" when he discovered the secret of the art.[156] The "king" is buried in Saturn,[157] an analogy of the buried Osiris.[158] "While the *nigredo* of the burial endures, the woman rules," [159] referring to the eclipse of the sun or the conjunction with the new moon.

is said to be "a corpse, or a god, or the unfruitful one." * He must be freed from his grave or prison. Cf. the daily rite of the king in cutting out the sacrificial victim's eye in memory of the eye of Horus, which contained the soul of Osiris. (Campbell, *The Miraculous Birth of King Amon-Hotep III*, p. 67.) On the first day of Phamenoth (beginning of spring) Osiris enters the new moon. This is his conjunction with Isis (Plutarch, p. 83). "And as at the beginning the sun is hidden in the moon, so, hidden at the end, it is extracted from the moon." * Ventura, "De ratione confic. lapidis," *Theatr. chem.*, II, p. 276.

149 Cf. "Transformation Symbolism in the Mass," pars. 345ff., 400, 410f.

150 The bad smell is the "stench of the graves." "For its [the dead body's] smell is evil, and like the stench of the graves." * Maier, *Symb. aur. mensae,* and Morienus, "De transmut. metallica," *Art. aurif.*, II, p. 33. The stench of the underworld is an idea that dates back to ancient Egypt. Cf. the "Book of Gates," cited by Wallis Budge, *Coptic Apocrypha in the Dialect of Upper Egypt,* p. lxvi.

151 "The pure lato is cooked until it begins to shine like fishes' eyes." * Morienus in *Art. aurif.*, II, p. 32.

152 "This One being placed in its spherical tomb." * ("Tract. Aristot.," *Theatr. chem.*, V, p. 886.) "The vessel is also called the tomb." * (Hoghelande, "De alchemiae diffic.," *Theatr. chem.*, I, p. 199.) *Vas* = 'tomb, prison.' (Ventura, "De ratione confic. lap.," *Theatr. chem.*, II, p. 289.) In *Aurora Consurgens*, p. 135, the stone is to be removed "from the door of my sepulchre."

153 Ruska, *Turba,* Sermo LIX, p. 162.

154 Dorn, "Physica Trismegisti," *Theatr. chem.*, I (1659), p. 436.

155 Berthelot, *Alch. grecs*, IV, xxiii.

156 Albertus Magnus, "Super arborem Aristot.," *Theatr. chem.*, II, p. 527.

157 "The tomb in which our king is buried is called . . . Saturn" * (Waite, *Herm. Mus.*, II, p. 189).

158 Firmicus Maternus, *De err. prof. rel.*, 2, 3: "In their shrines they have the idol of Osiris buried." *

159 "Liber Alze," *Mus. herm.*, p. 332 (Waite, I, p. 267).* Cf. "Ludus puerorum,"

66   Thus, concludes Maier, tomb and body are the same. Barnaud says:

> Bury, they say, each thing in the grave of the other. For when Sulphur, Sal and Aqua, or Sol, Luna and Mercurius, are in our material, they must be extracted, conjoined, buried and mortified, and turned into ashes. Thus it comes to pass that the nest of the birds becomes their grave, and conversely, the birds absorb the nest and unite themselves firmly with it. This comes to pass, I say, that soul, spirit and body, man and woman, active and passive, in one and the same subject, when placed in the vessel, heated with their own fire and sustained by the outward magistery of the art, may in due time escape [to freedom].[160]

In these words the whole secret of the union of opposites is revealed, the *summa medicina,* which heals not only the body but the spirit. The word "escape" presupposes a state of imprisonment which is brought to an end by the union of opposites. The Hindus described this as *nirdvandva,* "free from the opposites," a conception that, in this form at least, is alien to the Christian West because it relativizes the opposites and is intended to mitigate, or even heal, the irreconcilable conflict in the militant Christian attitude.[161]

67   The interpretation here given of this enigmatic inscription should be taken for what it is: a testament to the alchemical way of thinking, which in this instance reveals more about itself than the epitaph would seem to warrant. But here we must tread carefully, for a good many other explanations are possible and have, in fact, been given.[162] Above all, we have to consider the gen-

---

Art. aurif., II, p. 189: "Therefore Avicenna says: So long as the *nigredo* is manifest, the dark woman prevails, and that is the first strength of our stone." *

160 "Commentarium," *Theatr. chem.,* III, pp. 847f.

161 Cf. *Psychology and Alchemy,* pars. 23ff. The fact that the alchemists, in their attempts to solve the Enigma, immediately thought of the most significant thing they knew, namely the secret of their art, is understandable at a time when there were enigmas even concerning God, the holy scriptures, etc. Cf. Lorichius, *Aenigmatum libri* III (fol. 23r), which also contains the riddle of the hermaphrodite: "When my pregnant mother bore me," etc. (see infra, par. 89.)

162 Athanasius Kircher's interpretation in his *Oedipus Aegyptiacus* (II, ch. 6, p. 418) is purely alchemical and not distinguished by any originality. He calls the inscription "the prime chymic enigma," mentioning that Wilhelmus Baroldus the Englishman made a Cabalistic interpretation. The monument is mentioned in Drexelius, *Opera* (I, p. 69): "There is at Bologna an ancient epitaph which has puzzled the wits of many. . . . Some interpret it as referring to man's soul, others

uineness of the monument and its origin. None of the three authors so far mentioned actually saw the inscription. At the time of Malvasius, in 1683, there were apparently only two original transcripts of it, one in Bologna, the other in Milan. The one in Bologna ends with the words "cui posuerit." The other, in Milan, adds "Hoc est sepulcrum" etc., and also a "quid" to the "Scit et nescit" of the Bologna version. Further, at the head of the Milan version there is an unelucidated "A.M.P.P.D." in place of the "D.M." (Diis Manibus) at the head of the other. Malvasius states that the monument was destroyed,[163] but he cites eyewitnesses who claimed to have seen the inscription and copied it, in particular Joannes Turrius of Bruges, who in January 1567 wrote a letter to Richardus Vitus (Richard White of Basingstoke) saying that he had "read the epitaph with his own eyes" in the villa of Marcus Antonius de la Volta, "at the first milestone outside the Porta Mascharella," Bologna. It was, as the eyewitness and commentator Joannes Casparius Gevartius reports, let into the wall joining the villa to the church. A few of the chiselled letters were "worn with time and corroded by a kind of rust," which, he says, testified to its antiquity.[164] Malvasius endeavoured to prove its genuineness with the help of numerous other Roman epitaphs,[165] and advanced the following theory:

The inscription speaks of a daughter who is to be born to Laelius and who is destined for Agatho as a bride; but she is neither daughter nor bride, because, though conceived, she is not born, and not born, because she miscarried. Therefore Agatho, long chosen as the husband, disappointed in such great hope and betrayed by fate, rightly mocks himself, or pretends to mock himself, with this enigmatic inscription.[166]

68   Malvasius goes out of his way to be fair to the author of the epitaph. He calls Agatho "very skilled in this science and that";[167] indeed he compares him, as being a "pre-eminent wor-

---

to the water from the clouds, others to Niobe changed into a rock, others in yet other ways." *

163 All this is in Malvasius, *Aelia Laelia*, p. 55.

164 P. 103.

165 Prof. Felix Staehelin has informed me that the inscription is cited in *Corp. inscr. lat.*, XI, Part I, p. 15*, No. 88*, under the spurious ones. [These asterisks are part of the refs. in the *Corp.*]   166 P. 40.*   167 P. 90.

shipper of the exceedingly auspicious number Three," [168] to Hermes Trismegistus, and calls him "Thrice-Greatest," an allusion to the concluding sentence of the "Tabula smaragdina." [169] He does this because the inscription is divided into three parts,[170] to which he devotes a long dissertation. Here he gets into difficulties with the four elements and the four qualities, and, like all the alchemists, flounders about in his attempts to interpret the axiom of Maria.[171] His idea of a miscarriage likewise comes within the sphere of alchemy (not to mention Gnosticism),[172] for we read in the "Tractatus Aristotelis": [173] "This serpent is impetuous, seeking the issue [death] before birth, wishing to lose the foetus and desiring a miscarriage." [174] This refers, of course, to the Mercurial serpent or prima materia, which, the treatise maintains,[175] strives to pass quickly through the transformation process and to force the light-seeds of the *anima mundi* hidden within it into flower.

69   Of the numerous interpretations made by the commentators I would like to mention one which seems to me worth rescuing from oblivion. This is the view expressed by the two friends of Malvasius (see n. 127), namely that Lucius Agatho was a real person, but that Aelia was a "fictitious woman," or perhaps an "evil genius" in female form or an "ungodly spirit," who in the opinion of one of them "flies about in the air," and according to the other dwells in the earth and was "enclosed and affixed

168 "Auspicatissimi . . . Ternarii Cultorem eximium."
169 "Therefore I am called Hermes Trismegistus, as having three parts of the philosophy of the whole world." *
170 "God prefers odd numbers." *
171 Cf. *Psychology and Alchemy*, pars. 26, 209.
172 Cf. the Phibionites, Stratiotics, etc., in Epiphanius, *Panarium*, XXVI, 5 (ed. Holl, I, p. 281). The same idea occurs in Manichaeism: Reitzenstein and Schaeder, *Studien zum antiken Synkretismus aus Iran und Griechenland*, p. 346. For alchemy the so-called third sonship of Basilides is particularly important (cf. *Aion*, pars. 118ff.). The sonship (υἱότης) left below in the "universal seed-bed" (πανσπερμία) was "left behind in formlessness like an early birth" (ἐν τῇ ἀμορφίᾳ καταλελειμμένη οἱονεὶ ἐκτρώματι)(Hippolytus, *Elenchos*, VII, 26, 7). Cf. Paul (I Cor. 15 : 8): "Last of all, as to one untimely born, he appeared also to me" (RSV).
173 This treatise derives from the old Latinists, or from the "Arabists," whose connection with Arabic tradition is uncertain.
174 *Theatr. chem.*, V, p. 881.*
175 "The subtlety of nature . . . provided the cause of growth and life, and restored itself in the most perfect natures." * "This Serpent . . . swells like a coal-black Toad, and . . . begs to be freed from its misery." *

in a Junonian oak"; a "sylvan sprite, nymph, or hamadryad" who, when the oak was cut down and burnt, was obliged to seek another dwelling-place and so was found, "as if dead, in this sarcophagus." Thus it was that she was "praised, described, and commemorated by the loved and loving Agatho." [176]

70   According to this interpretation, Aelia is Agatho's anima, projected into a "Junonian oak." The oak is the tree of Jupiter, but it is also sacred to Juno.[177] In a metaphorical sense, as the feminine carrier of the anima projection, it is Jupiter's spouse and Agatho's beloved. Mythologically, nymphs, dryads, etc. are nature- and tree-numina, but psychologically they are anima projections,[178] so far as masculine statements are concerned.

71   This interpretation can be found in the *Dendrologia* of one of the above-mentioned friends, Ulysses Aldrovandus:

> I maintain that Aelia Laelia Crispis was one of the Hamadryads
> . . . who was tied to an oak in the neighbourhood of the city of
> Bologna, or shut up inside it. She appeared to him both in the
> tenderest and in the harshest form, and while for some two thousand
> years she had made a show of inconstant looks like a Proteus, she
> bedevilled the love of Lucius Agatho Priscius, then a citizen of
> Bologna, with anxious cares and sorrows, which assuredly were con-
> jured up from chaos, or from what Plato calls Agathonian con-
> fusion.[179]

One can hardly imagine a better description of the feminine archetype that typifies a man's unconscious than the figure of this "most hazardous beloved" (*incertissima amasia*), who pursues him like a teasing sprite amid the stillness of the "groves and springs." It is clear from the text of the inscription that it gives no ground for interpreting Aelia as a wood nymph. Aldrovandus tells us, however, that the Porta Mascharella in Bologna, near which the inscription was alleged to have been found, was called "Junonia" in Roman times, from which he concludes that Juno was obviously the spiritus loci. In support of his hypothesis

---

[176] *Aelia Laelia*, p. 29.
[177] On the Capitoline Hill there was an ancient oak sacred to the Capitol. For "Junonia" see Plutarch, "Quaestiones Romanae," 92, *Moralia* (ed. Babbitt), IV, pp. 138f.
[178] Cf. *Psychology and Alchemy*, par. 116, and "Paracelsus as a Spiritual Phenomenon," pars. 179f., 214ff.
[179] *Dendrologia*, I, p. 211.*

68

that Aelia was a dryad, the learned humanist cites a Roman epitaph that was found in this region:

CLODIA PLAVTILLA
SIBI ET
QVERCONIO AGATHONI
MARITO OPTIMO

This epitaph does in fact occur in the *Corpus Inscriptionum
Latinarum*,[180] but there the operative words are:

Q. VERCONIO AGATHONI

So Quintus Verconius must suffer his name to be changed to
Querconius to suit the author.

72   Aldrovandus explains the puzzling "hoc est sepulcrum" by
saying that the oak supplied the necessary building material for
the tomb! In substantiation of this he adds that there was in that
locality a village with the name of "Casaralta," [181] which he
analyses into *casa* (house), *ara* (altar), *alta* (high).

73   As a further contribution he quotes an Italian poem about a
great oak, "representing," he says, "the world of the elements,
planted as it were in a heavenly garden, where Sun and Moon
are spread out like two flowers." [182] This allusion to the world-
oak of Pherecydes leads us straight to the sun-and-moon tree of
alchemy, to the red and white lily,[183] the red slave and the white
woman (or white dove),[184] and the four-hued blossoms of the

---

180 *Corp. inscr. lat.*, XI, 1, pp. 163, 884: MVTINA.

181 I must leave to the author the responsibility for the correctness of this statement.   182 *Dendrologia*, I, p. 215.*

183 Concerning white and red see *The Zohar* (trans. by Sperling and Simon), I, p. 3:
"As the lily among thorns [Song of Songs 2 : 1] is tinged with red and white, so
the community of Israel is visited now with justice and now with mercy." In contrast to alchemy, red is co-ordinated with the feminine, and white with the masculine, side of the Sefiroth system.

184 Cf. the doves in the "grove of Diana," *Mus. herm.*, p. 659 (Waite, II, p. 170).
The dove symbol may be derived directly from Christian allegory. Here we must
consider the maternal significance of the dove, since Mary is called the *columba
mystica*. (Godefridus, *Homiliae Dominicales*, Migne, *P.L.*, vol. 174, col. 38.) Cf.
further the "hidden mother" designated as a dove in the Acts of Thomas (James,
Apocryphal New Testament, p. 388) and the dove symbolism of the Paraclete in
Philo ("Who is the Heir of Divine Things?" Loeb edn., IV, pp. 398f.). Nelken
describes the vision an insane patient had of "God the Father": on his breast he
bore a tree of life with red and white fruit, and on it was sitting a dove. ("Analytische Beobachtungen," p. 541.)

69

Tree in the Western Land.[185] Reusner's *Pandora* portrays the tree as a torch-bearing woman, its top sprouting out of her crowned head.[186] Here the tree is personified by its feminine numen.

74   Aldrovandus's interpretation is essentially alchemical, as we can see from the treatise of Bernardus Trevisanus (Count of the March and Trevis, 1406–90).[187] He tells the parable [188] of an adept who finds a clear spring set about with the finest stone and "secured to the trunk of an oak-tree," the whole surrounded by a wall. This is the King's bath in which he seeks renewal. An old man, Hermes the mystagogue, explains how the King had this bath built: he placed in it an old oak, "cloven in the midst." [189] The fountain was surrounded by a thick wall, and "first it was enclosed in hard, bright stone, then in a hollow oak." [190]

75   The point of the parable, evidently, is to bring the oak into connection with the bath. Usually this is the nuptial bath of the royal pair. But here the Queen is missing, for it is only the King who is renewed. This unusual version [191] of the motif suggests that the oak, as the feminine numen, has taken the place of the Queen. If this assumption is correct, it is particularly significant that the oak is first said to be "cloven" and later to be "hollow." Now it seems to be the upright trunk or "stock" of the fountain,[192] now a living tree casting a shadow, now the trough of the fountain. This ambiguity refers to the different aspects of the tree: as the "stock," the oak is the source of the fountain, so to speak; as the trough it is the vessel, and as the

185 Abu'l-Qasim Muhammad, *Kitāb al-'ilm al-muktasab,* ed. by Holmyard, p. 23.
186 *Psychology and Alchemy,* fig. 231. Cf. Sapientia Dei as the tree of life in *Aurora Consurgens,* p. 35.
187 "De chemico miraculo," *Theatr. chem.,* I, pp. 773ff.
188 P. 799.
189 "He inserted an old oak, cloven in the midst, which is protected from the rays of the sun, casting a shadow" * (p. 800).
190 P. 800.*
191 Usually the king is alone only when he is sitting in the sweat-bath.
192 ["Brunnenstock." The fountain described here is of a type commonly found in rural parts of central Europe. Shaped like a flattened "L," it consists of an upright block of wood, the "stock," from which the waterpipe projects over a long trough hollowed out of a tree-trunk.—TRANS.]

protecting tree it is the mother.[193] From ancient times the tree was man's birthplace;[194] it is therefore a source of life. The alchemists called both the vessel and the bath the "womb."[195] The cloven or hollow trunk bears out this interpretation.[196] The King's bath is itself a matrix, the tree serving as an attribute of the latter. Often, as in the Ripley Scrowle,[197] the tree stands in the nuptial bath, either as a pillar or directly as a tree in whose branches the numen appears in the shape of a mermaid (= anima) with a snake's tail.[198] The analogy with the Tree of

[193] The text is ambiguous on this point: "Petii rursum utrum fonti Rex esset amicus et fons ipsi? Qui ait, mirum in modum sese vicissim amant, fons Regem attràhit et non Rex fontem: *nam Regi velut mater est*" p. 801). (I asked again whether the King was friendly to the fount, and the fount to him. And he replied, they are wonderfully fond of each other. The fount attracts the King, and not the King the fount: *for it is like a mother to the King.*) There is a similar association in Cyril of Jerusalem, *Catecheses Mystagogicae*, II, 4 (*Opera*, ed. Reischl, II, p. 361): "And that saving water is made both a tomb and a mother to you." * Cf. Usener, *Das Weihnachtsfest*, p. 173.

[194] Cf. Ovid, *Metamorphoses*, VII (trans. by Miller, I, p. 386f.): "Before my eyes the same oak-tree seemed to stand, with just as many branches and just as many creatures on its branches." Isidore states that the "winged oak" (ὑπόπτερος δρῦς) of Pherecydes was wrapped in a hood (φᾶρος) like a woman. (Diels, *Vorsokratiker*, I, p. 47.) The "veiling" is an attribute of Artemis Chitone, and particularly of Ishtar: she is *tashmetu*, the Veiled One, Situri-Sabitu, who sits on the throne of the sea, "covered in a veil." (Wittekindt, *Das Hohe Lied*, p. 15.) The constant attribute of Ishtar is the palm. According to the Koran, Sura 19, Mary was born under a palm-tree, just as Leto gave birth under a palm-tree in Delos. Maya gave birth to the Buddha with the assistance of a willow. Human beings are said to be born of oaks (Pauly-Wissowa, *Realencyclopädie*, s.v. "Drys"). Further material in my "The Philosophical Tree," pars. 418f., 458ff.

[195] This is also the liturgical name for the font. See the Preface in the Benedictio Fontis: "May he fecundate this water for the regeneration of man," etc. Cf. "Consil. coniugii," *Ars chemica*, p. 204: "By matrix he means the root of the gourd." * "The spagyric vessel is to be constructed in the likeness of the natural vessel" * (Dorn, "Physica Trismeg.," *Theatr. chem.*, I, p. 430). The "natural vessel" is the uterus. (*Aurora consurgens* II, in *Art. aurif.*, I, p. 203.)

[196] "The place of gestation, even though it is artificial, yet imitates the natural place, since it is concave and closed." * ("Consil. coniugii," p. 147.)

[197] Cf. *Psychology and Alchemy*, fig. 257.

[198] There is a widespread idea that souls and numina appear as snakes (for instance the numen of the hero, Cecrops, Erechtheus, etc.). Cf. John Chrysostom, *Homilia XXVI (alias XXV) in Joannem* (Migne, *P.G.*, vol. 59, col. 155): "For what the mother is to the unborn child, that water is to the believer. For in water he is moulded and formed. Of old it was said: Let the water bring forth creeping things with a living soul. But since the Lord entered the streams of the Jordan,

71

Knowledge is obvious.[199] The Dodonian oak was the abode of an oracle, the anima here playing the role of prophetess.[200] The snake-like Mercurius appears as a tree numen in Grimm's fairytale of "The Spirit in the Bottle." [201]

76   The tree has a remarkable relation to the old man in the *Turba:*

Take that white tree and build around it a round dark house covered with dew, and place in it [202] a man of great age, a hundred years old, and close the house upon them and make it fast, so that no wind or dust can get in. Then leave them for one hundred and eighty days in their house. I say that that old man ceases not to eat of the fruits of that tree until the completion of that number [180], and that old man becomes a youth. O what wondrous natures, which have changed the soul of that old man into a youthful body, and the father is become the son.[203]

77   In this context we may perhaps cite a rather obscure text from Senior: [204]

Likewise Marchos [205] said, It is time for this child to be born, and he related the following parable: We shall build him a house, which

---

the water beareth no longer creeping things with living souls, but reasonable souls bearing the Holy Spirit." *

[199] According to Hegemonius (*Acta Archelai*, p. 18), Jesus was the paradisal tree, indeed the Tree of Knowledge, in Manichaean tradition: "The trees which are [in paradise] are the lusts and other temptations that corrupt the thoughts of men. But that tree in paradise whereby good is known is Jesus, and the knowledge of him which is in the world: and he who receives this discerns good from evil." * Here the Tree of Knowledge is regarded as a remedy for concupiscence, though outwardly it is not to be distinguished from the other (corrupting) trees.

[200] Cf. *Psychology and Alchemy*, figs. 8 and 19.

[201] Cf. "The Spirit Mercurius," pars. 239, 247f.

[202] "Impone ei" could refer to the tree, as "imponere" also means to "put on." The tree can be a birthplace. Cf. the ancient motif of tree-birth.

[203] Sermo 58.

[204] *De chemia*, p. 78.*

[205] Probably identical with Marcus Graecus, author of the so-called "Book of Fire." He is difficult to date. (Cf. Lippmann, *Entstehung und Ausbreitung der Alchemie*, I, pp. 477ff.) The fact that he is mentioned by Senior, whose Arabic writings are extant, may date him before the 10th cent. In Berthelot (*Chimie au moyen âge*, III, p. 124) there is a dialogue between Marqûsh, king of Egypt, and Safanjā, king of Saïd. Cf. M. T. Ali, ed., "Three Arabic Treatises on Alchemy by Muhammad Bin Umail" (10th cent.), and the excursus by H. E. Stapleton and M. H. Husain ("M. b. Umail: His Date, Writings, and Place in Alchemical History," p. 175).

is called the grave of Sihoka. He [or Mariyah] [206] said, There is an earth [207] near us, which is called 'tormos,' [208] where there are serpents [or witches] [209] that eat the darkness [210] out of the burning stones, and on these stones they drink the blood of black goats.[211] While they remain in the darkness, they conceive in the baths [212] and give birth [213] in the air, and they stride on the sea,[214] and they inhabit vaults and sepulchres, and the serpent fights with the male, and the male continues forty nights in the grave, and forty nights in the little house.[215]

78   The Latin translation "serpent" for "witch" is connected with the widespread primitive idea that the spirits of the dead are snakes. This fits in with the offering of goat's blood, since the sacrifice of black animals to the chthonic numina was quite customary. In the Arabic text the "witches" refer to the female demons of the desert, the jinn. The grave-haunting numen is likewise a widespread idea that has lingered on into Christian

206 Stapleton and Husain (p. 177, n. 12) have here: "It is a house, which is called the grave (*qabr*) of Sahafa. She said (*qālat*) etc. Possibly the name Māriyah has been omitted."

207 Or 'region'?

208 τόρμος = 'hole'? The Arabic text has *tūmtī*.

209 The Arabic word for "reptile" really means 'witch'. Cf. Stapleton and Husain (p. 177, n. 14): "The Arabic word properly means witches who consume the livers [*iecora* instead of *opaca*] of children and drink the milk of black goats." Stapleton rejects "reptile."

210 In the Arabic text, "liver."

211 This makes one think of an altar fire and a goat sacrifice. Cf. "the blood of a most fine buck goat" (von Franz, *Aurora Consurgens*, p. 103). In Pibechios (Berthelot, *Alch. grecs*, III, xxv, 3) goat's blood is a synonym for the divine water. Here the blood is used to feed the shades, as in the Nekyia, when Odysseus sacrifices black sheep, and, for Tiresias in particular, a black ram: ". . . the dark blood poured in. And now the souls of the dead who had gone below came swarming up from Erebus" (Rieu trans., p. 172).

212 This may refer to the "dissolved" state in the liquid medium.

213 Reading "pariunt" for "pereunt."

214 In the form of *volatilia* and *vapores*.

215 This shows traces of Christian influence. The "Aquarium sapientum" (*Mus. herm.*, p. 117) says on this score: "Christ fasted in the wilderness for forty days and forty nights, as also he preached and worked miracles for forty months on earth, and lay for forty hours in the tomb. For forty days, between his rising from the dead and his ascension into heaven, he conversed with his disciples and showed himself alive to them." * "Forty" is a prefiguration of the length of the opus. According to Genesis 50 : 3, forty days are required for embalming. Forty seems to be a magic multiple of four, 10 (the *denarius*) × 4.

73

legend. I have even met it in the dream of a twenty-two-year-old theological student, and I give this dream again so that those of my readers who are familiar with the language of dreams will be able to see the full scope of the problem we are discussing.[216]

79   *The dreamer was standing in the presence of a handsome old man dressed entirely in* black. *He knew it was the* white *magician. This personage had just addressed him at considerable length, but the dreamer could no longer remember what it was about. He recalled only the closing words: "And for this we need the help of the* black *magician." At that moment the door opened and in came another old man exactly like the first, except that he was dressed in* white. *He said to the white magician, "I need your advice," but threw a sidelong, questioning glance at the dreamer, whereupon the white magician answered: "You can speak freely, he is an innocent." The white-clad black magician then related his story. He had come from a distant land where something extraordinary had happened. The country was ruled by an old king who felt his death near and had therefore sought out a worthy tomb for himself. There were in that land a great number of tombs from ancient times, and the king had chosen the finest for himself. According to legend, it was the tomb of a virgin who had died long ago. The king caused it to be opened, in order to get it ready for use. But when the bones were exposed to the light of day they suddenly took on life and changed into a black horse, which galloped away into the desert. The black magician had heard this story and immediately set forth in pursuit of the horse. After a journey of many days through the desert he reached the grasslands on the other side. There he met the horse grazing, and there also he came upon the find on account of which he now needed the advice of the white magician. For he had found the lost keys of paradise, and he did not know what to do with them.* Here the dream ended.

80   The tomb was obviously haunted by the spirit of the virgin, who played the part of the king's anima. Like the nymph in Malvasius, she was forced to leave her old dwelling-place. Her

216 I have mentioned this dream several times, for instance in "Archetypes of the Collective Unconscious," par. 71, "The Phenomenology of the Spirit," par. 398, "Analytical Psychology and Education," par. 208, and "The Relations between the Ego and the Unconscious," par. 287.

chthonic and sombre nature is shown by her transformation into a black horse, a kind of demon of the desert. We have here the widespread conception of the anima as horsewoman and night-mare, a real "ungodly spirit," and at the same time the well-known fairytale motif of the aging king whose vitality is at an end. As a *sous-entendu* a magical, life-renewing marriage with the nymph seems to be planned (somewhat in the manner of the immortal Merlin's marriage with his fairy), for in paradise, the garden of love with the apple-tree, all opposites are united. As Isaiah says:

He will make her wilderness like Eden, and her desert like the garden of the Lord [51 : 3].

There the wolf shall dwell with the lamb, and the leopard shall lie down with the kid; and the calf and the young lion and the fatling together; and a little child shall lead them. And the cow and the bear shall feed; their young ones shall lie down together; and the lion shall eat straw like the ox. And the suckling child shall play on the hole of the asp, and the weaned child shall put his hand on the cockatrice's den [11 : 6f.].

There white and black come together in kingly marriage, "as a bridegroom decketh himself with ornaments, and as a bride adorneth herself with her jewels" (61 : 10). The two antithetical magicians are obviously making ready the work of union, and what this must mean for a young theologian can be conceived only as that colossal problem whose solution was considered by the more speculative alchemists to be their chief task. Therefore the Senior text continues:

He [the male] will be roused,[217] like the white doves,[218] and his step shall rejoice, and he shall cast his seed upon the marble [219] into the

217 Cf. Stapleton and Husain, p. 178.

218 The love-birds of Astarte.

219 Here marble is the female substance, the so-called Saturnia (or Luna, Eva, Beya, etc.) which dissolves the sun. "Sparkling marble is the elixir for the whitening" * (Mylius, *Phil. ref.*, p. 234.) "Et de là changea sa forme noire et devint comme marbre blanc et le soleil était le plus haut" (MS. 3022, Bibl. de l'Arsenal, Paris). For the meridional position of the sun see "The Visions of Zosimos," pars. 86 (III, v bis), 95, 107f. "Marble" is also a name for the "water like to itself," i.e., Mercurius duplex. (Philaletha in *Mus. herm.*, p. 770.) This Senior passage is commented on in "Consil. coniugii": "And let them cast their seed on the marble of the statues [?], and into the deifying water like to itself, and flying ravens will come and fall upon that statue. By ravens . . . he means the

image [or spirit that dwells in the marble], and the ravens will come flying, and will fall upon it and gather it up. Then they will fly to the tops of the mountains, whither none can climb, and they will become white,[220] and multiply. . . . Likewise no man hath known this, unless he himself hath conceived it in his head.

81   This text describes the resurrection after death, and if we are not deceived, it takes the form of a coniunctio, a coming together of the white (dove) and the black (raven), the latter being the spirit that dwells in the tombstone (see n. 219). Since, as often happens, theriomorphic symbols (snakes and doves) are used for the male and female elements, this points to the union of unconscious factors.[221] The ravens that gather up the seed (or the product of the union?) and then fly with it to the tops of

nigredo." * The Consilium seems to point to what was known in alchemy as the "statua." The origin of this idea is to be found in the treatise of Komarios (Berthelot, IV, xx, 14f.), where the soul, after the dark shadow has been removed from the body, awakens the now shining body from Hades, that it may rise from the grave, since it is clothed in spirituality and divinity. (For the exact text see "The Statue," infra, par. 559.) In *Aurora consurgens* II (*Art. aurif.*, I, p. 196) *mater Alchimia* is likewise a statue, but one consisting of different metals. So, too, do the seven statues in Raymond Lully (Norton's "Ordinall," *Theatr. chem. Brit.*, ch. 1, p. 21). In Mylius (*Phil. ref.*, p. 19) it is said: "It is a great mystery to create souls, and to mould the lifeless body into a living statue." * According to the teaching of the Mandaeans (Bousset, *Hauptprobleme der Gnosis*, p. 34) and of the Naassenes (Hippolytus, *Elenchos*, V, 7; Legge, I, p. 122), Adam was a "corporeal" or "lifeless" statue. Similarly in Hegemonius (*Acta Archelai*, VIII) the "perfect man" was a "pillar of light," referred to also in *Act. Arch.*, XIII: "But then shall these things be, when the statue shall come." * We must bear these ideas in mind in reading Lully (*Codicillus*, ch. 49, p. 88): "Always extract oil [= soul] from the heart of the statues; for the soul in parable is fire, and a hidden fire." * Senior (*De chemia*, p. 65) says: "We warm its water, which is extracted from the hearts of statues of stone." * And in *Ros. phil.* (*Art. aurif.*, II, p. 335) we read: ". . . Venerate the souls in statues: for their dwelling is in them." * Cf. the statue of the hermaphrodite, erected in the form of a cross, which "sweats," in Bardesanes (Schultz, *Dokumente der Gnosis*, p. lv). The statue or pillar has affinities with the tree of light and tree of fire, as well as with the world's axis. Cf. the pillar erected to Adonai Sabaoth in Book II of the Sibylline Oracles (ed. Geffcken, p. 39). Further material in "The Philosophical Tree," pars. 421ff.
220 The Arabic text says "they will lay eggs."
221 A woman patient who was much concerned with the problem of opposites dreamt that *"on the shore of a lake* [i.e., the edge of the unconscious] *two ring-snakes as thick as an arm, with pale human heads, were copulating."* About six months later came the following dream: *"A snow-white snake with a black belly was growing out of my breast. I felt a deep love for it."*

the mountains [222] represent the helpful spirits or familiars who complete the work when the skill of the artifex has failed him. They are not, as in *Faust*, beautiful angels but dark messengers of heaven, who at this point themselves become white.[223] Even in *Faust* the angels are not entirely innocent of the arts of seduction,[224] and the angels' inability to sin is, as we know, to be taken so relatively that women have to keep their heads covered in church on account of the moral frailty of these winged messengers, which has more than once proved disastrous in ancient times (e.g., Genesis 6 : 2).

82   Similar motifs occur in modern dreams, and can be found in persons who have never been remotely concerned with alchemy. For instance, a patient had the following dream: *"A large pile of wood was burning at the foot of a high wall of rock; the flames shot up with clouds of smoke. It was a lonely and romantic spot. High in the air, a flock of great black birds circled round the fire. From time to time one of the birds plunged straight into the blaze and was joyfully burnt to death, turning white in the process."* [225] As the dreamer himself remarked, the dream had a numinous quality, and this is quite understandable in view of its meaning: it repeats the miracle of the phoenix, of transformation and rebirth (the transformation of the *nigredo* into the *albedo,* of unconsciousness into "illumination") as described in the verses from the *Rosarium philosophorum:*

> Two eagles fly up with feathers aflame,
> Naked they fall to earth again.
> Yet in full feather they rise up soon . . .[226]

83   After this digression on transformation and resurrection, let us turn back to the motif of the oak-tree, whose discussion was started by the commentators on the Enigma.

84   We come across the oak in yet another alchemical treatise, the "Introitus apertus" of Philaletha.[227] There he says: "Learn,

[222] Birds flying up and down appear frequently in the literature and symbolize the ascending vapours. The "heaven" to which they ascend is the alembic or *capitelum* (helmet), which was placed over the cooking-vessel to catch the steam as it condensed.

[223] At any rate this is the interpretation of the Latin translator.

[224] See ch. I, n. 226.

[225] I have to thank Dr. C. A. Meier for this dream.

[226] *Art. aurif.,* II, p. 293. Cf. "Psychology of the Transference," par. 528.

[227] *Mus. herm.,* pp. 652ff. (Waite, II, p. 166).

then, who are the companions of Cadmus; who is the serpent that devoured them; and what the hollow oak to which Cadmus spitted the serpent."

85   In order to clarify this passage, I must go back to the myth of Cadmus, a kinsman of the Pelasgian Hermes Ithyphallikos.[228] The hero set out to find his lost sister Europa, whom Zeus had carried away with him after turning himself into a bull. Cadmus, however, received the divine command to give up the search, and instead to follow a cow, with moon markings on both her sides, until she lay down, and there to found the city of Thebes. At the same time he was promised Harmonia, the *daughter* of Ares and Aphrodite as a wife. When the cow had lain down, he wanted to sacrifice her, and he sent his companions to fetch water. They found it in a grove sacred to Ares, which was guarded by a dragon, the *son* of Ares. The dragon killed most of the companions, and Cadmus, enraged, slew it and sowed the dragon's teeth. Immediately armed men sprang up, who fell to fighting among themselves until only five remained. Cadmus was then given Harmonia to wife. The spitting of the snake (dragon) to the oak seems to be an addition of Philaletha's. It represents the banishment of the dangerous daemon into the oak,[229] a point made not only by the commentary on the Aelia inscription in Malvasius but by the fairytale of "The Spirit in the Bottle."

86   The psychological meaning of the myth is clear: Cadmus has lost his sister-anima because she has flown with the supreme deity into the realm of the suprahuman and the subhuman, the unconscious. At the divine command he is not to regress to the incest situation, and for this reason he is promised a wife. His sister-anima, acting as a psychopomp in the shape of a cow (to correspond with the bull of Zeus), leads him to his destiny as a dragon-slayer, for the transition from the brother-sister relationship to an exogamous one is not so simple. But when he succeeds in this, he wins "Harmonia," who is the *dragon's sister*. The dragon is obviously "disharmony," as the armed men sprung

228 From the 3rd cent. B.C., Cadmus, as a culture hero, was identified with Hermes Kadmilos.

229 Like the hamadryads, snakes are tree numina. A snake guarded the apples of the Hesperides and the oak of Ares in Colchis. Melampus received the gift of second sight from snakes which he found in a hollow oak.

from its teeth prove. These kill one another off as though exemplifying the maxim of Pseudo-Democritus, "nature subdues nature," which is nothing less than the *uroboros* conceptually formulated. Cadmus holds fast to Harmonia while the opposites in projected form slaughter one another. This image is a representation of the way in which a split-off conflict behaves: it is its own battle-ground. By and large this is also true of yang and yin in classical Chinese philosophy. Hand in hand with this self-contained conflict there goes an unconsciousness of the moral problem of opposites. Only with Christianity did the "metaphysical" opposites begin to percolate into man's consciousness, and then in the form of an almost dualistic opposition that reached its zenith in Manichaeism. This heresy forced the Church to take an important step: the formulation of the doctrine of the *privatio boni,* by means of which she established the identity of "good" and "being." Evil as a μὴ ὄν (something that does not exist) was laid at man's door—*omne bonum a Deo, omne malum ab homine.*[230] This idea together with that of original sin formed the foundation of a moral consciousness which was a novel development in human history: one half of the polarity, till then essentially metaphysical, was reduced to a psychic factor, which meant that the devil had lost the game if he could not pick on some moral weakness in man. Good, however, remained a metaphysical substance that originated with God and not with man. Original sin had corrupted a creature originally good. As interpreted by dogma, therefore, good is still wholly projected but evil only partly so, since the passions of men are its main source. Alchemical speculation continued this process of integrating metaphysical projections in so far as it began to dawn on the adept that both opposites were of a psychic nature. They expressed themselves first of all in the duplicity of Mercurius, which, however, was cancelled out in the unity of the stone. The lapis was—*Deo concedente*—made by the adept and was recognized as an equivalent of the *homo totus.* This development was extremely important, because it was an attempt to integrate opposites that were previously projected.

87   Cadmus is interpreted alchemically as Mercurius in his masculine form (Sol). He seeks his feminine counterpart, the quicksilver, which is his sister (Luna), but she meets him in the shape

---

230 Cf. *Aion,* pars. 8off.

of the Mercurial serpent, which he must first kill because it contains the furious conflict of warring elements (the chaos). From this arises the harmony of the elements, and the coniunctio can now take place. The spoils of the struggle, in this case the dragon's skin, are, according to ancient custom, offered to the hollow oak, the mother, who is the representative of the sacred grove and the fount. In other words, it is offered up to the unconscious as the source of life, which produces harmony out of disharmony.[231] Out of the hostility of the elements there arises the bond of friendship between them, sealed in the stone, and this bond guarantees the indissolubility and incorruptibility of the lapis. This piece of alchemical logic is borne out by the fact that, according to the myth, Cadmus and Harmonia *turned to stone* (evidently because of an *embarras de richesse:* perfect harmony is a dead end). In another version, they turn into *snakes,* "and even into a basilisk," Dom Pernety[232] remarks, "for the end-product of the work, incorporated with its like, acquires the power ascribed to the basilisk, so the philosophers say." For this fanciful author Harmonia is naturally the prima materia, and the marriage of Cadmus,[233] which took place with all the gods assisting, is the coniunctio of Sol and Luna, followed by the production of the tincture or lapis. Pernety's interpretation of Harmonia would be correct only if she were still allied with the dragon. But since she lost the reptile, she had logically to change herself and her husband into snakes.

88   Thus Malvasius, as well as the more interesting of the commentators, remain within the magic circle of alchemical mythologems. This is not surprising, since Hermetic philosophy, in the form it then took, was the only intellectual instrument that could help fill the dark gaps in the continuity of understanding.

231 Musical ideas are sounded in alchemy since there are also alchemical "compositions" in existence. Michael Maier tried his hand at this art in his *Atalanta fugiens.* Examples are printed in Read, *Prelude to Chemistry,* pp. 281ff. For the parallel between alchemy and music see Berthelot, III, xliv, 1 and VI, xv, 2ff.

232 *Les Fables égyptiennes et grecques,* II, p. 121.

233 Pernety derives Cadmia from Cadmus. Ruland takes Cadmia as cobalt (which means "kobold"). Cadmia seems to have been zinc oxide and other zinc compounds. (Lippmann, *Entstehung und Ausbreitung der Alchemie,* II, p. 24.) Cadmus is connected with alchemy because he invented the art of mining and working gold. Cadmia is included in Galen's pharmacopoeia as a means for drying deep ulcers. (*De simplicium medicamentorum facultatibus,* IX, pp. 599ff.) It was also known to Pliny. (*Hist. nat.,* XXXII, ch. 7, and XXXIII, ch. 5.)

The Enigma of Bologna and its commentaries are, in fact, a perfect paradigm of the method of alchemy in general. It had exactly the same effect as the unintelligibility of chemical processes: the philosopher stared at the paradoxes of the Aelia inscription, just as he stared at the retort, until the archetypal structures of the collective unconscious began to illuminate the darkness.[234] And, unless we are completely deluded, the inscription itself seems to be a fantasy sprung from that same paradoxical *massa confusa* of the collective unconscious. The contradictoriness of the unconscious is resolved by the archetype of the nuptial coniunctio, by which the chaos becomes ordered. Any attempt to determine the nature of the unconscious state runs up against the same difficulties as atomic physics: the very act of observation alters the object observed. Consequently, there is at present no way of objectively determining the real nature of the unconscious.

89   If we are not, as Malvasius was, convinced of the antiquity of the Aelia inscription, we must look round in the medieval literature for possible sources or at least analogies. Here the motif of the triple prediction, or triple cause, of death might put us on the right trail.[235] This motif occurs in the "Vita Merlini" in the old French romance *Merlin,* as well as in its later imitations in the Spanish and English literature of the fifteenth century. But the most important item, it seems to me, is the so-called "Epigram of the Hermaphrodite," attributed to Mathieu de Vendôme (ca. 1150):

> When my pregnant mother bore me in her womb,
>   they said she asked the gods what she would bear.
> A boy, said Phoebus, a girl, said Mars, neither, said Juno.
>   And when I was born, I was a hermaphrodite.
> Asked how I was to meet my end, the goddess replied: By arms;
>   Mars: On the cross; Phoebus: By water. All were right.
> A tree overshadowed the waters, I climbed it;
>   the sword I had with me slipped, and I with it.
> My foot caught in the branches, my head hung down in the
>   stream;

234 Rather like the marriage-dance of the dancing couples in Kékulé's vision of the benzol ring. Cf. "The Psychology of the Transference," par. 353.
235 Cf. Wickersham Crawford, "El Horoscopo del Hijo del Rey Alcaraz en el 'Libro de Buen Amor,'" pp. 184ff.

And I—male, female, and neither—suffered by water, weapon, and cross.[236]

90   Another parallel, but dating from late antiquity, is mentioned by Maier. It is one of the "Platonic Riddles" and runs: "A man that was not a man, seeing yet not seeing, in a tree that was not a tree, smote but did not smite with a stone that was not a stone a bird that was not a bird, sitting yet not sitting."[237] The solution is: A one-eyed eunuch grazed with a pumice-stone a bat hanging from a bush.[238] This joke was, of course, too obvious to lend itself to alchemical evaluation. Similarly, the Epigram of the Hermaphrodite was not, so far as I know, taken up by the alchemists, though it might have been a more suitable subject for exegesis. This kind of jest probably underlies the Aelia inscription. The seriousness with which the alchemists took it, however, is justified not only because there is something serious in every joke, but because paradox is the natural medium for expressing transconscious facts. Hindu philosophy, which likewise struggled to formulate transcendental concepts, often comes very near to the paradoxes so beloved of the alchemists, as the following example shows: "I am not a man, neither am I a god, a goblin, a Brahmin, a warrior, a merchant, a shudra, nor disciple of a Brahmin, nor householder, nor hermit of the forest, nor yet mendicant pilgrim: Awakener to Myself is my name."[239]

91   Another source that needs seriously considering is mentioned by Richard White of Basingstoke.[240] He maintains that Aelia Laelia is "Niobe transformed," and he supports this interpretation by referring to an epigram attributed to Agathias Scholasticus, a Byzantine historian:[241]

236 Lorichius, *Aenigmatum libri* III, fol. 23r.*

237 *Symbola aureae mensae*, p. 171.*

238 The riddle refers to Plato's remark in the *Republic* (V, 479 B-C): " 'They are ambiguous like the puzzles you hear at parties,' he replied, 'or the children's riddle about the eunuch hitting the bat and what he threw at it and what it was sitting on.' " (Lee trans., p. 243.) The scholium then gives the "Vir non vir" cited above. It is cited in another form as the riddle of Panarkes (Athenaeus, *Deipnosophists*, X, 452): "A man that was not a man hit a bird that was not a bird, perched on wood that was not wood, with a stone that was not a stone. The answer to these things is, severally, eunuch, bat, fennel, and pumice." * (Gulick trans., IV, pp. 550f.)

239 Zimmer, *Der Weg zum Selbst*, p. 54.

240 Richardus Vitus Basinstochius, *Aelia Laelia Crispis Epitaphium Antiquuum*, etc.

241 Whether Agathias was the author is uncertain. He was in Byzantium in 577

This tomb has no body in it.
This body has no tomb round it.
But it is itself body and tomb.[242]

White, convinced that the monument was genuine, thinks that
Agathias wrote his epigram in imitation of it, whereas in fact
the epigram must be its predecessor or at least have derived from
the same source on which the unknown author of the Aelia
inscription drew.

92   Niobe seems to have an anima-character for Richard White,
for, continuing his interpretation, he takes Aelia (or Haelia, as
he calls her) to be the soul, saying with Virgil: "Fiery is her
strength, and heavenly her origin. From this Haelia takes her
name." [243] She was called Laelia, he says, on account of Luna,
who exerts a hidden influence on the souls of men. The human
soul is "androgynous," "because a girl has a masculine and a
man a feminine soul." [244] To this remarkable psychological
insight he adds another: the soul is also called an "old woman,"
because the spirit of young people is weak. This aptly expresses
the psychological fact that, in people with an all too youthful
attitude of consciousness, the anima is often represented in
dreams as an old woman.

93   It is clear that Richard White points even more plainly to
the anima in the psychological sense than Aldrovandus. But
whereas the latter stressed her mythological aspect, White
stresses her philosophical aspect. In his letter of February 1567
to Johannes Turrius, he writes that the soul is an idea "of such
great power that she creates the forms and things themselves,"
also "she has within herself the 'selfness' of all mankind." [245]

---

and 582. Among other things he wrote a Κύκλος τῶν νέων ἐπιγραμμάτων (Cycle of
New Epigrams), much of which is preserved in the *Anthologia palatina et
planudea,* including the above epigram. (Cf. *Anthologia Graeca Epigrammatum,*
ed. Stadtmueller, II, Part 1, p. 210, No. 311.) Eustathius Macrembolites (*Aenigmata,*
p. 209, 8 H) cites the above-mentioned interpretation of Holobolus, that the
epigram refers to Lot's wife.

242 Richardus Vitus, p. 11.*

243 Cf. *Aeneid,* VI, 730: "These life seeds have a fiery strength and heavenly origin." *

244 This psychological insight, which was rediscovered only in the 20th century,
seems to have been a commonplace among the alchemists from the middle of the
16th century on.

245 "She has so to speak the identity (selfness: αὐτότητα) of all mankind in herself." * Vitus, p. 48.

She transcends all individual differences. "Thus, if the soul would know herself, she must contemplate herself, and gaze into that place where the power of the soul, Wisdom, dwells." [246] This is just what happened to the interpreters of the Bolognese inscription: in the darkness of the enigma, the psyche gazed at herself and perceived the wisdom immanent in her structure— the wisdom that is her strength. And, he adds, "man is nothing other than his soul." [247] It should be noted that he describes this soul quite differently from the way it would be described by a biological or personalistic psychology today: it is devoid of all individual differences, it contains the "selfness of all mankind," it even creates the objective world by the power of its wisdom. This description is far better suited, one would think, to the *anima mundi* than to the *anima vagula* of the personal man, unless he means that enigmatic background of everything psychic, the collective unconscious. White comes to the conclusion that the inscription means nothing less than the soul, the form imprinted on and bound to matter.[248] This, again, is what happened to the interpreters: they formulated the baffling inscription in accordance with the imprint set upon it by the psyche.

94   White's interpretation is not only original but profoundly psychological. His deserts are certainly not diminished by his having, so it would seem, arrived at his deeper view only after he received Turrius's letter of January 1567. Turrius was of the opinion that "Aelia and Laelia" stood for "form and matter." He interprets "neither in heaven, nor on earth, nor in water" as follows: "Since the prima materia is *nothing*, but is conceived solely by the imagination, it cannot be contained in any of these places." [249] It is not an object of the senses, but is "conceived solely by the intellect," therefore we cannot know how this material is constituted. It is evident that Turrius's interpretation likewise describes the projection of the psyche and its contents, with the result that his secondary explanations are a *petitio principii*.

95   As is clear from the title of his book, *Allegoria peripatetica de generatione, amicitia, et privatione in Aristotelicum Aenigma*

---

246 P. 50.*   247 P. 50.*
248 "In this Epitaph the soul is described as an idea" * (p. 46).
249 P. 40.*

Elia Lelia Crispis,[250] Fortunius Licetus reads the whole philosophy of Aristotle into the monument. He mentions the report that it was "sculptured in stone, formerly set in a high position on the walls of St. Peter's," but he does not say that he saw it with his own eyes, for in his day it was no longer in existence, if ever it existed at all. He thinks the inscription contains the summation of a serious philosophical theory about the origin of mundane things, a theory that was "scientifico-moralis" or "ethico-physica." "It is the author's intention to combine in a way to be marvelled at the attributes of generation, friendship, and privation." [251] That is why, he says, the monument is a true treasure-house.

96   After reviewing a number of earlier authors who had devoted themselves to the same theme, Licetus mentions the work of Joannes Casparius Gevartius,[252] who propounded the theory that the inscription described the nature of Love. This author cites the comic poet Alexis in Athenaeus:

> I think that the painters, or, to put it more concisely, all who make images of this god, are unacquainted with Eros. For he is neither female nor male; again, neither god nor man, neither stupid nor yet wise, but rather composed of elements from everywhere, and bearing many qualities under a single form. For his audacity is that of a man, his timidity a woman's; his folly argues madness, his reasoning good sense; his impetuosity is that of an animal, his persistence that of adamant, his love of honour that of a god.[253]

97   Unfortunately I was unable to get hold of the original treatise of Gevartius. But there is a later author, Caietanus Felix Veranius, who takes up the Eros theory apparently as his own discovery in his book, *Pantheon argenteae Elocutionis*.[254] He mentions a number of earlier commentators, amongst whom Gevartius is conspicuously absent. As Gevartius is named in the earlier lists, it is scarcely likely that Veranius was unacquainted with him. The suspicion of plagiarism is almost unescapable. Veranius defends his thesis with a good deal of skill, though considering the undeniable paradoxicality of Eros the task he sets

---

250 Padua, 1630.
251 *Allegoria peripatetica,* pp. 166f.*
252 *Electorum libri* III, Bk. III, cap. I, pp. 81ff.
253 *Deipnosophists,* XIII, 562 (trans. by Gulick), VI, pp. 36f.
254 Vol. II, p. 215.

himself is not too difficult. I will mention only one of his arguments, concerning the end of the inscription. "The inscription ends," he says, "with 'scit et nescit quid cui posuerit,' because though the author of this enigmatic inscription knows that he has dedicated it to Love, he does not know what Love really is, since it is expressed by so many contradictions and riddles. Therefore he knows and does not know know to whom he dedicated it."

98   I mention the interpretation of Veranius mainly because it is the forerunner of a theory which was very popular at the end of the nineteenth and the beginning of the twentieth century, namely Freud's sexual theory of the unconscious. Veranius even goes so far as to conjecture that Aelia Laelia had a special talent for eroticism (therein anticipating Aldrovandus). He says: "Laelia was a whore; Crispis comes from 'curly-haired,' because curly-haired people are frailer than others and more prone to the allurements of Love." Here he quotes Martial: "Who's that curly-headed fellow who's always running round with your wife, Marianus? Who *is* that curly-headed fellow?" [255]

99   Now it is, as a matter of fact, true that apart from the personal striving for power, or *superbia*, love, in the sense of *concupiscentia*, is the dynamism that most infallibly brings the unconscious to light. And if our author was of the type whose besetting sin is concupiscence, he would never dream that there is any other power in heaven or earth that could be the source of his conflicts and confusions. Accordingly, he will cling to his prejudice as if it were a universal theory, and the more wrong he is the more fanatically he will be convinced of its truth. But what can love mean to a man with a hunger for power! That is why we always find two main causes of psychic catastrophes: on the one hand a disappointment in love and on the other hand a thwarting of the striving for power.

100   The last interpretation I shall mention is one of the most recent. It dates from 1727, and though its argument is the stupidest its content is the most significant. How it can be both is explained by the fact that the discovery of significance is not always coupled with intelligence. The spirit bloweth where it listeth. . . . Despite the inadequacy of his equipment, the author, C. Schwartz,[256] managed to get hold of a brilliant idea

255 Lib. V, epigram 61.*   256 *Acta eruditorum* (1727), p. 332.

whose import, however, entirely escaped him. His view was that Lucius Agatho Priscius meant his monument to be understood as the *Church*. Schwartz therefore regards the inscription as being not of classical but of Christian origin, and in this, as compared with the others, he is undoubtedly right. His arguments, however, are threadbare—to take but one example, he tries to twist "D.M." into "Deo Magno." Although his interpretation is not in the least convincing, it nevertheless remains a significant fact that the symbol of the Church in part expresses and in part substitutes for all the secrets of the soul which the humanistic philosophers projected into the Aelia inscription. In order not to repeat myself, I must refer the reader to what I said about the protective function of the Church in "Psychology and Religion." [257]

101   The interpretive projections we have been examining are, with the exception of the last, identical with the psychic contents that dropped out of their dogmatic framework at the time of the Renaissance and the Great Schism, and since then have continued in a state of secularization where they were at the mercy of the "immanentist" principle of explanation, that is, a naturalistic and personalistic interpretation. The discovery of the collective unconscious did something to alter this situation, for, within the limits of psychic experience, the collective unconscious takes the place of the Platonic realm of eternal ideas. Instead of these models giving form to created things, the collective unconscious, through its archetypes, provides the *a priori* condition for the assignment of meaning.

102   In conclusion, I would like to mention one more document that seems relevant to our context, and that is the anecdote about Meister Eckhart's "daughter":

A daughter came to the Dominican convent asking for Meister Eckhart. The porter said, Who shall I tell him? She answered, I do not know. Why do you not know? he inquired. Because, she said, I am neither virgin nor spouse, nor man nor wife nor widow nor lady nor lord nor wench nor thrall. The porter went off to Meister Eckhart. Do come out, he said, to the strangest wight that ever I heard, and let me come too and put your head out and say, Who is asking for me? He did so. She said to him what she had said to the porter. Quoth he, My child, thou hast a shrewd and ready tongue, I prithee

257 Pars. 32ff.

now thy meaning? An I were a virgin, she replied, I were in my first innocence; spouse, I were bearing the eternal word within my soul unceasingly; were I a man I should grapple with my faults; wife, should be faithful to my husband. Were I a widow I should be ever yearning for my one and only love; as lady I should render fearful homage; as wench I should be living in meek servitude to God and to all creatures; and as thrall I should be working hard, doing my best tamely to serve my master. Of all these things I am no single one, and am the one thing and the other running thither. The Master went away and told his pupils, I have been listening to the most perfect person I ween I ever met.[258]

103   This story is more than two hundred years older than the earliest reference to the Aelia inscription, and therefore, if there is any literary influence at all, it could at most be derived from Mathieu de Vendôme, which seems to me just as unlikely as that Meister Eckhart's vision of the "naked boy" was derived from the classical *puer aeternus*. In both cases we are confronted with a significant archetype, in the first that of the divine maiden (anima)), in the second that of the divine child (the self).[259] As we know, these primordial images can rise up anywhere at any time quite spontaneously, without the least evidence of any external tradition. This story could just as well have been a visionary rumour as a fantasy of Meister Eckhart or of one of his pupils. It is, however, rather too peculiar to have been a real happening. But occasionally reality is quite as archetypal as human fantasy, and sometimes the soul seems to "imagine things outside the body," [260] where they fall to playing, as they do in our dreams.

258 Evans, *Meister Eckhart,* I, p. 438.
259 Cf. my "The Psychology of the Child Archetype" and "The Psychological Aspects of the Kore."
260 "De sulphure," *Mus. herm.,* p. 617: "(The soul) imagines very many profound things outside the body, and by this is made like unto God." *

III

THE PERSONIFICATION OF THE OPPOSITES

1. INTRODUCTION

The alchemist's endeavours to unite the opposites culminate in the "chymical marriage," the supreme act of union in which the work reaches its consummation. After the hostility of the four elements has been overcome, there still remains the last and most formidable opposition, which the alchemist expressed very aptly as the relationship between male and female. We are inclined to think of this primarily as the power of love, of passion, which drives the two opposite poles together, forgetting that such a vehement attraction is needed only when an equally strong resistance keeps them apart. Although enmity was put only between the serpent and the woman (Genesis 3 : 15), this curse nevertheless fell upon the relationship of the sexes in general. Eve was told: "Thy desire shall be to thy husband, and he shall rule over thee." And Adam was told: "Cursed is the ground for thy sake . . . because thou hast hearkened unto the voice of thy wife" (3 : 16f.). Primal guilt lies between them, an *interrupted state of enmity,* and this appears unreasonable only to our rational mind but not to our psychic nature. Our reason is often influenced far too much by purely physical considerations, so that the union of the sexes seems to it the only sensible thing and the urge for union the most sensible instinct of all. But if we conceive of nature in the higher sense as the totality of all phenomena, then the physical is only one of her aspects, the other is pneumatic or spiritual. The first has always been regarded as feminine, the second as masculine. The goal of the one is union, the goal of the other is discrimination. Because it overvalues the physical, our contemporary reason lacks spiritual orientation, that is, pneuma. The alchemists seem to have had an inkling of this, for how otherwise could they have come upon that strange myth of the country of the King of the Sea, where

89

only like pairs with like and the land is unfruitful? [1] It was obviously a realm of innocent friendship, a kind of paradise or golden age, to which the "Philosophers," the representatives of the physical, felt obliged to put an end with their good advice. But what happened was not by any means a natural union of the sexes; on the contrary it was a "royal" incest, a sinful deed that immediately led to imprisonment and death and only afterwards restored the fertility of the country. As a parable the myth is certainly ambiguous; like alchemy in general, it can be understood spiritually as well as physically, "tam moralis quam chymica." [2] The physical goal of alchemy was gold, the panacea, the elixir of life; the spiritual one was the rebirth of the (spiritual) light from the darkness of Physis: healing self-knowledge and the deliverance of the pneumatic body from the corruption of the flesh.

105   A subtle feature of the "Visio Arislei" is that the very one who is meditating a pairing of the sexes is king of the land of innocence. Thus the *rex marinus* says: "Truly I have a son and a daughter, and therefore I am king over my subjects, because they possess nothing of these things. Yet I have borne a son and a daughter in my brain." [3] Hence the king is a potential traitor to the paradisal state of innocence because he can generate "in his head," and he is king precisely because he is capable of this sin against the previous state of innocence. Since he can be different from them he is *more* than any of his subjects and therefore rightly their king, although, from the physical standpoint, he is counted a bad ruler. [4]

106   Here again we see the contrast between alchemy and the prevailing Christian ideal of attempting to restore the original state of innocence by monasticism and, later, by the celibacy of the priesthood. The conflict between worldliness and spirituality, latent in the love-myth of Mother and Son, was elevated by Christianity to the mystic marriage of sponsus (Christ) and sponsa (Church), whereas the alchemists transposed it to the physical plane as the coniunctio of Sol and Luna. The Christian solution of the conflict is purely pneumatic, the physical rela-

[1] "Visio Arislei," *Art. aurif.,* I, pp. 146ff.
[2] Maier, *Symb. aur. mensae,* p. 156.   [3] "Visio Arislei," p. 147.
[4] The philosophers say to him: "Lord, king you may be, but you rule and govern badly." *

tions of the sexes being turned into an allegory or—quite illegitimately—into a sin that perpetuates and even intensifies the original one in the Garden. Alchemy, on the other hand, exalted the most heinous transgression of the law, namely incest, into a symbol of the union of opposites, hoping in this way to bring back the golden age. For both trends the solution lay in extrapolating the union of sexes into another medium: the one projected it into the spirit, the other into matter. But neither of them located the problem in the place where it arose—the soul of man.

07   No doubt it would be tempting to assume that it was more convenient to shift such a supremely difficult question on to another plane and then represent it as having been solved. But this explanation is too facile, and is psychologically false because it supposes that the problem was asked consciously, found to be painful, and consequently moved on to another plane. This stratagem accords with our modern way of thinking but not with the spirit of the past, and there are no historical proofs of any such neurotic operation. Rather does all the evidence suggest that the problem has always seemed to lie outside the psyche as known to us. Incest was the hierosgamos of the gods, the mystic prerogative of kings, a priestly rite, etc. In all these cases we are dealing with an archetype of the collective unconscious which, as consciousness increased, exerted an ever greater influence on conscious life. It certainly seems today as if the ecclesiastical allegories of the bridegroom and bride, not to mention the now completely obsolete alchemical coniunctio, had become so faded that one meets with incest only in criminology and the psychopathology of sex. Freud's discovery of the Oedipus complex, a special instance of the incest problem in general, and its universal incidence have, however, reactivated this ancient problem, though mostly only for doctors interested in psychology. Even though laymen know very little about certain medical anomalies or have a wrong idea of them, this does not alter the facts any more than does the layman's ignorance of the actual percentage of cases of tuberculosis or psychosis.

108   Today the medical man knows that the incest problem is practically universal and that it immediately comes to the surface when the customary illusions are cleared away from the foreground. But mostly he knows only its pathological side and

leaves it steeped in the odium of its name, without learning the lesson of history that the painful secret of the consulting-room is merely the embryonic form of a perennial problem which, in the suprapersonal sphere of ecclesiastical allegory and in the early phases of natural science, created a symbolism of the utmost importance. Generally he sees only the "materia vilis et in via eiecta" from the pathological side and has no idea of its spiritual implications. If he saw this, he could also perceive how the spirit that has disappeared returns in each of us in unseemly, indeed reprehensible guise, and in certain predisposed cases causes endless confusion and destruction in great things as in small. The psychopathological problem of incest is the aberrant, natural form of the union of opposites, a union which has either never been made conscious at all as a psychic task or, if it was conscious, has once more disappeared from view.

109   The persons who enact the drama of this problem are man and woman, in alchemy King and Queen, Sol and Luna. In what follows I shall give an account of the way in which alchemy describes the symbolic protagonists of the supreme opposition.

2. SOL

110   In alchemy, the sun signifies first of all gold, whose sign it shares. But just as the "philosophical" gold is not the "common" gold,[5] so the sun is neither just the metallic gold [6] nor the heavenly orb.[7] Sometimes the sun is an active substance hidden in the gold and is extracted as the *tinctura rubea* (red tincture). Sometimes, as the heavenly body, it is the possessor of magically effective and transformative rays. As gold and a heavenly body [8]

---

[5] Senior, *De chemia*, p. 92.*

[6] "Gold and silver in their metallic form are not the matter of our stone." * "Tractatus aureus," *Mus. herm.*, p. 32 (Waite, I, p. 33).

[7] Because gold is not subject to oxidization, Sol is an arcanum described in the "Consilium coniugii" as follows: "A substance equal, permanent, fixed for the length of eternity" * (*Ars chemica*, p. 58). "For Sol is the root of incorruption." * "Verily there is no other foundation of the Art than the sun and its shadow" * (ibid., p. 138).

[8] Rupescissa, *La Vertu et la propriété de la quinte essence*, p. 19: "Jceluy soleil est vray or. . . . L'or de Dieu est appelé par les Philosophes, Soleil; car il est fils du Soleil du Ciel, et est engendré par les influences du Soleil ès entrailles et veines de la terre."

it contains an active sulphur of a red colour, hot and dry.[9] Because of this red sulphur the alchemical sun, like the corresponding gold, is red.[10] As every alchemist knew, gold owes its red colour to the admixture of Cu (copper), which he interpreted as Kypris (the Cyprian, Venus), mentioned in Greek alchemy as the transformative substance.[11] Redness, heat, and dryness are the classical qualities of the Egyptian Set (Gk. Typhon), the evil principle which, like the alchemical sulphur, is closely connected with the devil. And just as Typhon has his kingdom in the forbidden sea, so the sun, as *sol centralis,* has its sea, its "crude perceptible water," and as *sol coelestis* its "subtle imperceptible water." This sea water *(aqua pontica)* is extracted from sun and moon. Unlike the Typhonian sea, the life-giving power of this water is praised, though this does not mean that it is invariably good.[12] It is the equivalent of the two-faced Mercurius, whose poisonous nature is often mentioned. The Typhonian aspect of the active sun-substance, of the red sulphur, of the water "that does not make the hands wet," [13] and of the "sea water" should not be left out of account. The author of the "Novum lumen chemicum" cannot suppress a reference to the latter's paradoxical nature: "Do not be disturbed because you sometimes find contradictions in my treatises, after the custom of the philosophers; these are necessary, if you understand that no rose is found without thorns." [14]

111   The active sun-substance also has favourable effects. As the so-called "balsam" it drips from the sun and produces lemons, oranges, wine, and, in the mineral kingdom, gold.[15] In man the

9 Sulphur is even identical with fire. Cf. "Consil. coniugii" (*Ars chemica,* p. 217): "Know therefore that sulphur is fire, that is, Sol." * In Mylius (*Phil. ref.,* p. 185) Sol is identical with sulphur, i.e., the alchemical Sol signifies the active substance of the sun or of the gold.

10 "Our Sol is ruddy and burning." * (Zacharius, "Opusculum," *Theatr. chem.,* I, p. 840.) Bernardus Trevisanus goes so far as to say: "Sol is nothing other than sulphur and quicksilver." * (Ibid., Flamel's annotations, p. 860.)

11 Olympiodorus (Berthelot, *Alch. grecs,* II, iv, 43): "Smear [with it] the leaves of the shining goddess, the red Cyprian."

12 Cf. the sulphur parable (infra par. 144), where the water is "most dangerous."

13 Hoghelande, *Theatr. chem.,* I, p. 181.

14 *Mus. herm.,* pp. 581f. (Waite, II, p. 107).

15 Steeb, *Coelum sephiroticum,* p. 50. Paracelsus, in "De natura rerum" (Sudhoff, XI, p. 330), says: "Now the life of man is none other than an astral balsam, a balsamic impression, a heavenly and invisible fire, an enclosed air." *De Vita longa*

balsam forms the "radical moisture, from the sphere of the supracelestial waters"; it is the "shining" or "lucent body" which "from man's birth enkindles the inner warmth, and from which come all the motions of the will and the principle of all appetition." It is a "vital spirit," and it has "its seat in the brain and its governance in the heart." [16]

112   In the "Liber Platonis Quartorum," a Sabaean treatise, the *spiritus animalis* or solar sulphur is still a πνεῦμα πάρεδρον, a ministering spirit or familiar who can be conjured up by magical invocations to help with the work.[17]

113   From what has been said about the active sun-substance it should be clear that Sol in alchemy is much less a definite chemical substance than a "virtus," a mysterious power [18] believed to have a generative [19] and transformative effect. Just as the physical sun lightens and warms the universe, so, in the human body, there is in the heart a sunlike arcanum from which life and warmth stream forth.[20] "Therefore Sol," says Dorn, "is rightly named the first after God, and the father and begetter of all,[21] because in him the seminal and formal virtue of all things whatsoever lies hid." [22] This power is called "sulphur." [23] It is a hot, daemonic principle of life, having the closest affinities with the sun in the earth, the "central fire" or "ignis gehennalis" (fire of

(ed. Bodenstein, fol. c 7v): "(Treating of a certain invisible virtue) he calls it balsam, surpassing all bodily nature, which preserves the two bodies by conjunction, and upholds the celestial body together with the four elements." *

16 Steeb, p. 117. The moon draws "universal form and natural life" from the sun. (Dorn, "Physica genesis," *Theatr. chem.*, I, p. 397.)

17 *Theatr. chem.*, V. p. 130.

18 "It were vain to believe, as many do, that the sun is merely a heavenly fire." * (Dorn, "Physica Trismegisti," *Theatr. chem.*, I, p. 423.)

19 The alchemists still believed with Proclus that the sun generates the gold. Cf. Proclus, *Commentaries on the Timaeus of Plato* 18 B (trans. by Taylor), I, p. 36.

20 Dorn ("Phys. Trismeg.," p. 423) says: "As the fount of life of the human body, it is the centre of man's heart, or rather that secret thing which lies hid within it, wherein the natural heat is active." *

21 Zosimos (Berthelot, *Alch. grecs*, III, xxi, 3) cites the saying of Hermes: "The sun is the maker of all things." *

22 "Phys. Trismeg.," p. 423.* The Codex Berol. Lat. 532 (fol. 154v) says of the germ-cell of the egg: "The sun-point, that is, the germ of the egg, which is in the yolk." *

23 "The first and most powerful male and universal seed is, by its nature, sulphur, the first and most powerful cause of all generation. Wherefore Paracelsus says that the sun and man through man generate man." * (Dorn, ibid.)

hell). Hence there is also a *Sol niger*, a black sun, which coincides with the *nigredo* and *putrefactio,* the state of death.[24] Like Mercurius, Sol in alchemy is ambivalent.

114   The miraculous power of the sun, says Dorn, is due to the fact that "all the simple elements are contained in it, as they are in heaven and in the other heavenly bodies." "We say that the sun is a single element," he continues, tacitly identifying it with the quintessence. This view is explained by a remarkable passage from the "Consilium coniugii": "The Philosophers maintained that the father of the gold and silver is the animating principle [*animal*] of earth and water, or man or part of a man, such as hair, blood, menstruum, etc." [25] The idea at the back of this is that primitive conception of a universal power of growth, healing, magic, and prestige,[26] which is to be found as much in the sun as in men and plants, so that not only the sun but man too, and especially the enlightened man, the adept, can generate the gold by virtue of this universal power. It was clear to Dorn (and to other alchemists as well) that the gold was not made by the usual chemical procedures,[27] for which reason he called gold-making (chrysopoeia) a "miracle." The miracle was performed by a *natura abscondita* (hidden nature), a metaphysical entity "perceived not with the outward eyes, but solely by the mind." [28] It was "infused from heaven,[29] provided that the adept had approached as closely as possible to things divine and

24 Cf. infra, p. 98. The alchemical sun also rises out of the darkness of the earth, as in *Aurora Consurgens*, pp. 125f.: "This earth made the moon . . . then the sun arose . . . after the darkness which thou hast appointed therein before the sunrise." *

25 *Ars chemica*, p. 158. On a primitive level, blood is the seat of the soul. Hair signifies strength and divine power. (Judges 13 : 5 and 16 : 17ff.)

26 Cf. the works of Lehmann, Preuss, and Röhr. A collection of mana-concepts can be found in my "On Psychic Energy," pars. 114ff.

27 Cf. Bonus, "Pretiosa margarita novella," *Theatr. chem.*, V, p. 648: "And in this wise Alchemy is supernatural, and is divine. And in this stone is all the difficulty of the Art, nor can any sufficient natural reason be adduced why this should be so. And thus it is when the intellect cannot comprehend this nor satisfy itself, but must yet believe it, as in miraculous divine matters; even as the foundation of the Christian faith, being supernatural, must first be taken as true by unbelievers, because its end is attained miraculously and supernaturally. Therefore God alone is the operator, nature taking no part in the work." *

28 "Spec. phil.," *Theatr. chem.*, I, p. 298; also "Phil. chemica," p. 497.

29 Cf. *Aurora Consurgens*, p. 111: "For I could not wonder enough at the great virtue of the thing, which is bestowed upon and infused into it from heaven." *

at the same time had extracted from the substances the subtlest powers "fit for the miraculous act." "There is in the human body a certain aethereal substance, which preserves its other elemental parts and causes them to continue," [30] he says. This substance or virtue is hindered in its operations by the "corruption of the body"; but "the Philosophers, through a kind of divine inspiration, knew that this virtue and heavenly vigour can be freed from its fetters, not by its contrary . . . but by its like." [31] Dorn calls it "veritas." "It is the supreme power, an unconquerable fortress, which hath but very few friends, and is besieged by innumerable enemies." It is "defended by the immaculate Lamb," and signifies the heavenly Jerusalem in the inner man. "In this fortress is the true and indubitable treasure, which is not eaten into by moths, nor dug out by thieves, but remaineth for ever, and is taken hence after death." [32]

115   For Dorn, then, the spark of divine fire implanted in man becomes what Goethe in his original version of *Faust* called Faust's "entelechy," which was carried away by the angels. This supreme treasure "the animal man understandeth not. . . . We are made like stones, having eyes and seeing not." [33]

116   After all this, we can say that the alchemical Sol, as a "certain luminosity" (*quaedam luminositas*), is in many respects equal to the *lumen naturae*. This was the real source of illumination in alchemy, and from alchemy Paracelsus borrowed this same source in order to illuminate the art of medicine. Thus the concept of Sol has not a little to do with the growth of modern consciousness, which in the last two centuries has relied more and more on the observation and experience of natural objects. Sol therefore seems to denote an important psychological fact. Consequently, it is well while delineating its peculiarities in greater detail on the basis of the very extensive literature.

117   Generally Sol is regarded as the masculine and active half of Mercurius, a supraordinate concept whose psychology I have discussed in a separate study.[34] Since, in his alchemical form,

30 "Phil. meditativa," *Theatr. chem.*, I, p. 456. There is a similar passage on p. 457: "Further, in the human body is concealed a certain substance of heavenly nature, known to very few, which needeth no medicament, being itself the incorrupt medicament." *   31 P. 457.
32 P. 458. See also "Spec. phil.," p. 266.
33 P. 459.*
34 "The Spirit Mercurius."

Mercurius does not exist in reality, he must be an unconscious projection, and because he is an absolutely fundamental concept in alchemy he must signify the unconscious itself. He is by his very nature the unconscious, where nothing can be differentiated; but, as a *spiritus vegetativus* (living spirit), he is an active principle and so must always appear in reality in differentiated form. He is therefore fittingly called "duplex," both active and passive. The "ascending," active part of him is called Sol, and it is only through this that the passive part can be perceived. The passive part therefore bears the name of Luna, because she borrows her light from the sun.[35] Mercurius demonstrably corresponds to the cosmic Nous of the classical philosophers. The human mind is a derivative of this and so, likewise, is the diurnal life of the psyche, which we call consciousness.[36] Consciousness requires as its necessary counterpart a dark, latent, non-manifest side, the unconscious, whose presence can be known only by the light of consciousness.[37] Just as the day-star rises out of the nocturnal sea, so, ontogenetically and phylogenetically, consciousness is born of unconsciousness and sinks back every night to this primal condition. This duality of our psychic life is the prototype and archetype of the Sol-Luna symbolism. So much did the alchemist sense the duality of his unconscious assumptions that, in the face of all astronomical evidence, he equipped the sun with a shadow: "The sun and its shadow bring the work to perfection." [38] Michael Maier, from whom this saying is taken, avoids the onus of explanation by substituting the shadow of the earth for the shadow of the sun in the forty-fifth discourse of his *Scrutinium*. Evidently he could

---

35 Cf. the ancient idea that the sun corresponds to the right eye and the moon to the left. (Olympiodorus in Berthelot, *Alch. grecs*, II, iv, 51.)

36 Just as for the natural philosophers of the Middle Ages the sun was the god of the physical world, so the "little god of the world" is consciousness.

37 Consciousness, like the sun, is an "eye of the world." (Cf. Pico della Mirandola, "Disputationes adversus astrologos," lib. III, cap. X, p. 88r.) In his *Heptaplus* (Expositio 7, cap. IV, p. 11r) he says: "Since Plato calls the Sun . . . the visible son of God, why do we not understand that we are the image of the invisible son? And if he is the true light enlightening every mind, he hath as his most express image this Sun, which is the light of the image enlightening every body." *

38 This idea occurs already in the *Turba* (ed. by Ruska, p. 130): "But he who hath tinged the poison of the sages with the sun and its shadow, hath attained to the greatest secret." * Mylius (*Phil. ref.*, p. 22) says: "In the shadow of the sun is the heat of the moon." *

97

not wholly shut his eyes to astronomical reality. But then he cites the classical saying of Hermes: "Son, extract from the ray its shadow," [39] thus giving us clearly to understand that the shadow is contained in the sun's rays and hence could be extracted from them (whatever that might mean). Closely related to this saying is the alchemical idea of a black sun, often mentioned in the literature.[40] This notion is supported by the self-evident fact that without light there is no shadow, so that, in a sense, the shadow too is emitted by the sun. For this physics requires a dark object interposed between the sun and the observer, a condition that does not apply to the alchemical Sol, since occasionally it appears as black itself. It contains both light and darkness. "For what, in the end," asks Maier, "is this sun without a shadow? The same as a bell without a clapper." While Sol is the most precious thing, its shadow is *res vilissima* or *quid vilius alga* (more worthless than seaweed). The antinomian thinking of alchemy counters every position with a negation and vice versa. "Outwardly they are bodily things, but inwardly they are spiritual," says Senior.[41] This view is true of all alchemical qualities, and each thing bears in itself its opposite.[42]

118   To the alchemical way of thinking the shadow is no mere *privatio lucis;* just as the bell and its clapper are of a tangible substantiality, so too are light and shadow. Only thus can the saying of Hermes be understood. In its entirety it runs: "Son,

[39] From ch. II of the "Tractatus aureus," *Ars chemica,* p. 15.*
[40] Cf. Mylius, *Phil. ref.,* p. 19. Here the *sol niger* is synonymous with the *caput corvi* and denotes the *anima media natura* in the state of *nigredo,* which appears when the "earth of the gold is dissolved by its own proper spirit." * Psychologically, this means a provisional extinction of the conscious standpoint owing to an invasion from the unconscious. Mylius refers to the "ancient philosophers" as a source for the *sol niger.* A similar passage occurs on p. 118: "The sun is obscured at its birth. And this denigration is the beginning of the work, the sign of putrefaction, and the sure beginning of the commixture." * This *nigredo* is the "changing darkness of purgatory." Ripley (*Chymische Schrifften,* p. 51) speaks of a "dark" sun, adding: "You must go through the gate of the blackness if you would gain the light of Paradise in the whiteness." Cf. *Turba,* p. 145: "nigredo solis."
[41] *De chemia,* p. 91.*
[42] The *sol niger* is a "counter-sun," just as there is an invisible sun enclosed in the centre of the earth. (See Agnostus, *Prodromus Rhodostauroticus,* 1620, Vr.) A similar idea is found in Ventura (*Theatr. chem.,* II, p. 276): "And as at the beginning the sun is hidden in the Moon, so, hidden at the end, it is extracted from the moon." *

extract from the ray its shadow, and the corruption that arises from the mists which gather about it, befoul it and veil its light; for it is consumed by necessity and by its redness." [43] Here the shadow is thought of quite concretely; it is a mist that is capable not only of obscuring the sun but of befouling it ("coinquinare" —a strong expression). The redness (rubedo) of the sun's light is a reference to the red sulphur in it, the active burning principle, destructive in its effects. In man the "natural sulphur," Dorn says, is identical with an "elemental fire" which is the "cause of corruption," and this fire is "enkindled by an invisible sun unknown to many, that is, the sun of the Philosophers." The natural sulphur tends to revert to its first nature, so that the body becomes "sulphurous" and fitted to receive the fire that "corrupts man back to his first essence." [44] The sun is evidently an instrument in the physiological and psychological drama of return to the prima materia, the death that must be undergone if man is to get back to the original condition of the simple elements and attain the incorrupt nature of the pre-worldly paradise. For Dorn this process was spiritual and moral as well as physical.

119   Sol appears here in a dubious, indeed a "sulphurous" light: it corrupts, obviously because of the sulphur it contains.[45]

120   Accordingly, Sol is the transformative substance, the prima materia as well as the gold tincture. The anonymous treatise "De arte chymica" distinguishes two parts or stages of the lapis. The first part is called the sol terrenus (earthly sun). "Without

---

43 "Tractatus aureus," Ars chemica, p. 15.

44 Dorn, "Spec. phil.," Theatr. chem., I, p. 308. He conceives it in the first place as a physiologically destructive action which turns the salts in the body into chalk, so that the body becomes "sulphurous." But this medical observation is introduced by the remark: "Because man is engendered in corruption, his own substance pursues him with hatred." By this he means original sin and the corruption resulting therefrom.

45 I am not forgetting that the dangerous quality of Sol may also be due to the fact that his rays contain the miraculous water "which by the power of the magnet is extracted from the rays of the sun and moon." * This water is a putrefying agent, because "before it is properly cooked it is a deadly poison." Mylius, Phil. ref., p. 314. This aqua permanens is the ὕδωρ θεῖον (divine water), the "divinity" being sulphur. It was called "sulphur water" (τὸ θεῖον also means sulphur) and is the same as mercury. Θεῖον or θήϊον in Homer was believed to possess apotropaic powers, and this may be the reason why it was called "divine."

the earthly sun, the work is not perfected." [46] In the second part of the work Sol is joined with Mercurius.

On earth these stones are dead, and they do nothing unless the activity of man is applied to them. [Consider] [47] the profound analogy of the gold: the aethereal heaven was locked to all men, so that all men had to descend into the underworld, where they were imprisoned for ever. But Christ Jesus unlocked the gate of the heavenly Olympus and threw open the realm of Pluto, that the souls might be freed, when the Virgin Mary, with the cooperation of the Holy Ghost in an unutterable mystery and deepest sacrament, conceived in her virgin womb that which was most excellent in heaven and upon earth, and finally bore for us the Redeemer of the whole world, who by his overflowing goodness shall save all who are given up to sin, if only the sinner shall turn to him. But the Virgin remained incorrupt and inviolate: therefore not without good reason is Mercurius made equal [aequiparatur] to the most glorious and worshipful Virgin Mary.[48]

It is evident from this that the coniunctio of Sol and Mercurius is a hierosgamos, with Mercurius playing the role of bride. If one does not find this analogy too offensive, one may ask oneself with equanimity whether the arcanum of the opus alchymicum, as understood by the old masters, may not indeed be considered an equivalent of the dogmatic mystery. For the psychologist the decisive thing here is the subjective attitude of the alchemist. As I have shown in *Psychology and Alchemy*, such a profession of faith is by no means unique.[49]

121   The metaphorical designation of Christ as Sol [50] in the language of the Church Fathers was taken quite literally by the alchemists and applied to their *sol terrenus*. When we remember that the alchemical Sol corresponds psychologically to consciousness, the diurnal side of the psyche, we must add the Christ analogy to this symbolism. Christ appears essentially as the *son*—the son of his mother-bride. The role of the son does in fact devolve upon ego-consciousness since it is the offspring of the maternal

[46] *Art. aurif.*, I, p. 58ff.*

[47] The text only has "auri similitudinem profundam," without a verb.

[48] *Art. aurif.*, I, pp. 58off.   [49] "The Lapis-Christ Parallel."

[50] Especially as "sol iustitiae" (sun of justice), Malachi 4 : 2. Cf. Honorius of Autun, *Speculum de mysteriis Ecclesiae* (Migne, *P.L.*, vol. 172, col. 921): "For, like to the sun beneath a cloud, so did the sun of justice lie concealed under human flesh." * Correspondingly, the Gnostic Anthropos is identical with the sun. (Cf. Reitzenstein, *Poimandres*, p. 280.)

unconscious. Now according to the arch authority, the "Tabula smaragdina," Sol is the father of Mercurius, who in the above quotation appears as feminine and as the mother-bride. In that capacity Mercurius is identical with Luna, and—via the Luna-Mary-Ecclesia symbolism—is equated with the Virgin. Thus the treatise "Exercitationes in Turbam" says: "As blood is the origin of flesh, so is Mercurius the origin of Sol . . . and thus Mercurius is Sol and Sol is Mercurius." [51] Sol is therefore father and son at once, and his feminine counterpart is mother and daughter in one person; furthermore, Sol and Luna are merely aspects of the same substance that is simultaneously the cause and the product of both, namely Mercurius duplex, of whom the philosophers say that he contains everything that is sought by the wise. This train of thought is based on a quaternity:

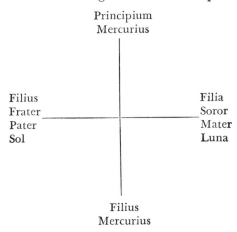

Principium
Mercurius

Filius
Frater
Pater
Sol

Filia
Soror
Mater
Luna

Filius
Mercurius

122   Although the Sol symbolism is reminiscent of the dogmatic models, its basic schema is very different; for the dogmatic schema is a Trinity embracing only the Deity but not the universe.[52] The alchemical schema appears to embrace only the material world, yet, on account of its quaternary character, it comes near to being a representation of totality as exemplified in the symbol of the cross erected between heaven and earth. The cross is by implication the Christian totality symbol: as an instrument of torture it expresses the sufferings on earth of the

51 *Art. aurif.*, I, p. 155.
52 The alchemical equivalent of the Trinity is the three-headed serpent (**Mercurius**). See *Psychology and Alchemy*, fig. 54.

incarnate God, and as a quaternity it expresses the universe, which also includes the material world. If we now add to this cruciform schema the four protagonists of the divine world-drama—the Father as *auctor rerum,* the Son, his counterpart the Devil (to fight whom he became man), and the Holy Ghost, we get the following quaternity:

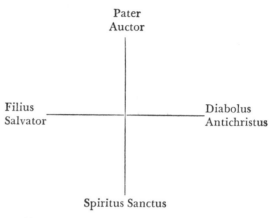

123   I will not discuss the various aspects of this quaternity more closely here, as I have already done so in a separate study.[53] I mention it only for comparison with the alchemical one. Quaternities such as these are logical characteristics of Gnostic thinking, which Koepgen has aptly called "circular." [54] We have

[53] Cf. my "Psychological Approach to the Dogma of the Trinity," pars. 243ff. Though some may find it objectionable, the opposition between Christ and the devil in the above schema presupposes an inner relationship (regarded by the Ebionites, says Epiphanius, as that between two brothers). Angelus Silesius seems to have felt something of the sort, too:

> "Were from the Devil all his His-ness gone,
> You'd see the Devil sitting in God's throne."

Cherubinischer Wandersmann, I, No. 143 (Cf. Flitch version, p. 144). By "His-ness" Angelus Silesius means the "selfhood which damns," as is incontestably true of all selfhood that does not acknowledge its identity with God.

[54] The thinking in the Psalms and of the prophets is "circular. Even the Apocalypse consists of spiral images . . . One of the main characteristics of Gnostic thinking is circularity." (Koepgen, *Gnosis des Christentums,* p. 149.) Koepgen gives an example from Ephraem Syrus: "Make glad the body through the soul, but give the soul back to the body, that both may be glad that after the separation they are joined again" (p. 151). An alchemist could have said the same of the uroboros, since this is the primal symbol of alchemical truth. Koepgen also describes dogma as "circular": it is "round in the sense of a living reality. . . . Dogmas are con-

already met similar figures in our account of the opposites, which were often arranged in quaternities. The rhythm of both schemas is divided into three steps:

Alchemical: {Beginning / Origin / Mercurius} — {Development / Sol / Luna} — {Goal / Filius / Mercurius}

Christian: {Auctor / Pater} — {Development of Conflict / Salvator / Diabolus} — {Paraclete / Holy Ghost / Church or Kingdom of God}

124   The alchemical drama leads from below upwards, from the darkness of the earth to the winged, spiritual *filius macrocosmi* and to the *lux moderna;* the Christian drama, on the other hand, represents the descent of the Kingdom of Heaven to earth. One has the impression of a mirror-world, as if the God-man coming down from above—as in the Gnostic legend—were reflected in the dark waters of Physis. The relation of the unconscious to the conscious mind is to a certain extent complementary, as elementary psychogenic symptoms and dreams caused by simple somatic stimuli prove.[55] (Hence the strange idea, taught for instance by Rudolf Steiner, that the Hereafter possesses qualities complementary to those of this world.) Careful observation and analysis show, however, that not all dreams can be regarded mechanically as mere complementary devices but must be interpreted rather as attempts at *compensation,* though this does not prevent very many dreams from having, on a superficial view, a distinct complementary character. Similarly, we could regard the alchemical movement as a reflection of the Christian one.[56]

cerned with the religious reality, and this is circular" (p. 52). He calls attention to the "fact of not knowing and not recognizing, which lies at the core of the dogma itself" (p. 51). This remark indicates the reason or one of the reasons for the "roundness": dogmas are approximative concepts for a fact that exists yet cannot be described, and can only be approached by circumambulation. At the same time, these facts are "spheres" of indeterminable extent, since they represent *principles.* Psychologically they correspond to the archetypes. Overlapping and interpenetration are an essential part of their nature. "Roundness" is a peculiarity not only of dogmas, but, in especial degree, of alchemical thought.

55 Particularly dreams about hunger, thirst, pain, and sex. Another complementary factor is the feminine nature of the unconscious in a man.

56 For the compensatory aspect of this "reflection" see *Psychology and Alchemy,* pars. 26ff.

Koepgen makes a significant distinction between two aspects of Christ: the descending, incarnate God, and the ascending, Gnostic Christ who returns to the Father. We cannot regard the latter as the same as the alchemical *filius regius,* although Koepgen's schema offers an exact parallel to the alchemical situation.[57] The redeemer figure of alchemy is not commensurable with Christ. Whereas Christ is God and is begotten by the Father, the *filius regius* is the soul of nature, born of the world-creating Logos, of the Sapientia Dei sunk in matter. The *filius regius* is also a son of God, though of more distant descent and not begotten in the womb of the Virgin Mary but in the womb of Mother Nature: he is a "third sonship" in the Basilidian sense.[58] No traditional influences should be invoked in considering the conceptual structure of this filius; he is more an autochthonous product deriving from an unconscious, logical development of trends which had already reached the field of consciousness in the early Christian era, impelled by the same unconscious necessity as produced the later development of ideas. For, as our modern experience has shown, the collective unconscious is a living process that follows its own inner laws and gushes up like a spring at the appointed time. That it did so in alchemy in such an obscure and complicated way was due essentially to the great psychological difficulties of antinomian thinking, which continually came up against the demand for the logical consistency of the metaphysical figures, and for their emotional absoluteness. The "bonum superexcedens" of God allows no integration of evil. Although Nicholas Cusanus ventured the bold thought of the *coincidentia oppositorum,* its logical consequence—the relativity of the God-concept—proved disastrous for

[57] Koepgen, p. 112.

[58] Cf. "The Spirit Mercurius," pars. 282f. In another respect, also, the *filius philosophorum* is a "third" when we consider the development in the concept of the devil among the Ebionites (Epiphanius, *Panarium,* XXX). They spoke of two figures begotten by God, one of them Christ, the other the devil. The latter, according to Psellus, was called by the Euchites Satanaël, the elder brother of Christ. (Cf. *Aion,* par. 229, and "The Spirit Mercurius," pars. 271f. In relation to these two the *filius regius*—as *donum Spiritus Sancti* and son of the prima materia—is a "third sonship," which, in common with the prima materia, can trace its descent—though a more distant one—from God. For the threefold sonship see Hippolytus, *Elenchos,* VII, 22, 7f. (Legge, II, pp. 71f.) and *Aion,* pars. 118f. The "sonships" come from the "true light" (John 1 : 9), from the Logos, the *sapientia Patris.* Hippolytus, VII, 22, 4 (Legge, II, pp. 68f.).

Angelus Silesius, and only the withered laurels of the poet lie on his grave. He had drunk with Jacob Boehme at the fount of Mater Alchimia. The alchemists, too, became choked in their own confusions.

125   Once again, therefore, it is the medical investigators of nature who, equipped with new means of knowledge, have rescued these tangled problems from projection by making them the proper subject of psychology. This could never have happened before, for the simple reason that there was no psychology of the unconscious. But the medical investigator, thanks to his knowledge of archetypal processes, is in the fortunate position of being able to recognize in the abstruse and grotesque-looking symbolisms of alchemy the nearest relatives of those serial fantasies which underlie the delusions of paranoid schizophrenia as well as the healing processes at work in the psychogenic neuroses. The overweening contempt which other departments of science have for the apparently negligible psychic processes of "pathological individuals" should not deter the doctor in his task of helping and healing the sick. But he can help the sick psyche only when he meets it as the unique psyche of that particular individual, and when he knows its earthly and unearthly darknesses. He should also consider it just as important a task to defend the standpoint of consciousness, clarity, "reason," and an acknowledged and proven good against the raging torrent that flows for all eternity in the darkness of the psyche—a πάντα ῥεῖ that leaves nothing unaltered and ceaselessly creates a past that can never be retrieved. He knows that there is nothing purely good in the realm of human experience, but also that for many people it is better to be convinced of an absolute good and to listen to the voice of those who espouse the superiority of consciousness and unambiguous thinking. He may solace himself with the thought that one who can join the shadow to the light is the possessor of the greater riches. But he will not fall into the temptation of playing the law-giver, nor will he pretend to be a prophet of the truth: for he knows that the sick, suffering, or helpless patient standing before him is not the public but is Mr or Mrs X, and that the doctor has to put something tangible and helpful on the table or he is no doctor. His duty is always to the individual, and he is persuaded that nothing has happened if this individual has not been helped. He is answerable

to the individual in the first place and to society only in the second. If he therefore prefers individual treatment to collective ameliorations, this accords with the experience that social and collective influences usually produce only a mass intoxication, and that only man's action upon man can bring about a real transformation.[59]

126   It cannot have escaped the alchemists that their Sol had something to do with man. Thus Dorn says: "From the beginning man was sulphur." Sulphur is a destructive fire "enkindled by the invisible sun," and this sun is the Sol Philosophorum,[60] which is the much sought-after and highly praised philosophic gold, indeed the goal of the whole work.[61] In spite of the fact that Dorn regards the sun and its sulphur as a kind of physiological component of the human body, it is clear that we are dealing with a piece of physiological mythology, i.e., a projection.

127   In the course of our inquiry we have often seen that, despite the complete absence of any psychology, the alchemical projections sketch a picture of certain fundamental psychological facts and, as it were, reflect them in matter. One of these fundamental facts is the primary pair of opposites, consciousness and unconsciousness, whose symbols are Sol and Luna.

128   We know well enough that the unconscious appears personified: mostly it is the anima [62] who in singular or plural form represents the collective unconscious. The personal unconscious is personified by the shadow.[63] More rarely, the collective unconscious is personified as a Wise Old Man.[64] (I am speaking here

---

[59] In psychotherapy the situation is no different from what it is in somatic medicine, where surgery is performed on the *individual*. I mention this fact because of the modern tendency to treat the psyche by group analysis, as if it were a collective phenomenon. The psyche as an individual factor is thereby eliminated.
[60] "Spec. phil.," *Theatr. chem.*, I, p. 308.
[61] Ripley, *Chymische Schrifften*, p. 34: "For then your Work will obtain the perfect whiteness. Then turn from the East towards midday, there it should rest at a fiery place, for that is the harvest or end of the Work. . . . Thereupon the sun will shine pure red in its circle and will triumph after the darkness."
[62] Cf. "Concerning the Archetypes, with Special Reference to the Anima Concept." An example of the anima in plural form is given in *Psychology and Alchemy*, pars. 58ff.
[63] Examples of both archetypes are to be found ibid., Part II. Cf. also *Aion*, chs. 2 and 3. Another problem is the *shadow of the self*, which is not considered here.
[64] Cf. *Psychology and Alchemy*, par. 159.

only of masculine psychology, which alone can be compared with that of the alchemists.) It is still rarer for Luna to represent the nocturnal side of the psyche in dreams. But in the products of active imagination the symbol of the moon appears much more often, as also does the sun, which represents the luminous realm of the psyche and our diurnal consciousness. The modern unconscious has little use for sun and moon as dream-symbols.[65] Illumination ("a light dawns," "it is becoming clear," etc.) can be expressed just as well or even better in modern dreams by switching on the electric light.

129   It is therefore not surprising if the unconscious appears in projected and symbolized form, as there is no other way by which it might be perceived. But this is apparently not the case with consciousness. Consciousness, as the essence of all conscious contents, seems to lack the basic requirements for a projection. Properly understood, projection is not a voluntary happening; it is something that approaches the conscious mind from "outside," a kind of sheen on the object, while all the time the subject remains unaware that he himself is the source of light which causes the cat's eye of the projection to shine. Luna is therefore conceivable as a projection; but Sol as a projection, since it symbolizes consciousness, seems at first glance a contradiction in terms, yet Sol is no less a projection than Luna. For just as we perceive nothing of the real sun but light and heat and, apart from that, can know its physical constitution only by inference, so our consciousness issues from a dark body, the ego, which is the indispensable condition for all consciousness, the latter being nothing but the association of an object or a content with the ego. The ego, ostensibly the thing we know most about, is in fact a highly complex affair full of unfathomable obscurities. Indeed, one could even define it as a *relatively constant personification of the unconscious itself,* or as the Schopenhauerian mirror in which the unconscious becomes aware of its own face.[66] All the worlds that have ever existed before man were

65 Examples of the sun and moon dreams are given ibid., p. 135.

66 Here the concept of the *self* can be mentioned only in passing. (For a detailed discussion see *Aion,* ch. 4.) The self is the hypothetical summation of an indescribable totality, one half of which is constituted by ego-consciousness, the other by the shadow. The latter, so far as it can be established empirically, usually presents itself as the inferior or negative personality. It comprises that part of the collective unconscious which intrudes into the personal sphere, there forming the so-called

physically *there*. But they were a nameless happening, not a definite actuality, for there did not yet exist that minimal concentration of the psychic factor, which was also present, to speak the word that outweighed the whole of Creation: That is the world, and this is I! That was the first morning of the world, the first sunrise after the primal darkness, when that inchoately conscious complex, the ego, the son of the darkness, knowingly sundered subject and object, and thus precipitated the world and itself into definite existence,[67] giving it and itself a voice and a name. The refulgent body of the sun is the ego and its field of consciousness—*Sol et eius umbra:* light without and darkness within. In the source of light there is darkness enough for any amount of projections, for the ego grows out of the darkness of the psyche.

130   In view of the supreme importance of the ego in bringing reality to light, we can understand why this infinitesimal speck in the universe was personified as the sun, with all the attributes that this image implies. As the medieval mind was incomparably more alive than ours to the divine quality of the sun, we may assume that the totality character of the sun-image was implicit in all its allegorical or symbolic applications. Among the sig-

---

personal unconscious. The shadow forms, as it were, the bridge to the figure of the anima, who is only partly personal, and through her to the impersonal figures of the collective unconscious. The concept of the self is essentially intuitive and embraces ego-consciousness, shadow, anima, and collective unconscious in indeterminable extension. As a totality, the self is a coincidentia oppositorum; it is therefore bright and dark and yet neither.

If we hypostatize the self and derive from it (as from a kind of pre-existent personality) the ego and the shadow, then these would appear as the empirical aspects of the opposites that are preformed in the self. Since I have no wish to construct a world of speculative concepts, which leads merely to the barren hair-splitting of philosophical discussion, I set no particular store by these reflections. If such concepts provisionally serve to put the empirical material in order, they will have fulfilled their purpose. The empiricist has nothing to say about the concepts self and God in themselves, and how they are related to one another.

67 Genesis 1 : 1–7 is a projection of this process. The coming of consciousness is described as an objective event, the active subject of which is not the ego but Elohim. Since primitive people very often do not feel themselves the subject of their thinking, it is possible that in the distant past consciousness appeared as an outside event that happened to the ego, and that it was integrated with the subject only in later times. Illumination and inspiration, which in reality are sudden expansions of consciousness, still seem to have, even for us, a subject that is not the ego. Cf. Neumann, *The Origins and History of Consciousness*, pp. 102ff.

nifications of the sun as totality the most important was its frequent use as a God-image, not only in pagan times but in the sphere of Christianity as well.

131   Although the alchemists came very close to realizing that the ego was the mysteriously elusive arcane substance and the longed-for lapis, they were not aware that with their sun symbol they were establishing an intimate connection between God and the ego. As already remarked, projection is not a voluntary act; it is a natural phenomenon beyond the interference of the conscious mind and peculiar to the nature of the human psyche. If, therefore, it is this nature that produces the sun symbol, nature herself is expressing an identity of God and ego. In that case only unconscious nature can be accused of blasphemy, but not the man who is its victim. It is the rooted conviction of the West that God and the ego are worlds apart. In India, on the other hand, their identity was taken as self-evident. It was the nature of the Indian mind to become aware of the world-creating significance of the consciousness [68] manifested in man.[69] The West, on the contrary, has always emphasized the littleness, weakness, and sinfulness of the ego, despite the fact that it elevated one man to the status of divinity. The alchemists at least suspected man's hidden godlikeness, and the intuition of Angelus Silesius finally expressed it without disguise.

132   The East resolves these confusing and contradictory aspects by merging the ego, the personal atman, with the universal atman and thus explaining the ego as the veil of Maya. The Western alchemist was not consciously aware of these problems. But when his unspoken assumptions and his symbols reached the plane of conscious gnosis, as was the case with Angelus

[68] I use the word "consciousness" here as being equivalent to "ego," since in my view they are aspects of the same phenomenon. Surely there can be no consciousness without a knowing subject, and vice versa.

[69] Cf. Rig-Veda, X, 31, 6 (trans. from Deussen, *Geschichte der Philosophie*, I, 1, p. 140):

> "And this prayer of the singer, continually expanding,
> Became a cow that was there before the world was,
> The gods are foster-children of the same brood,
> Dwelling together in the womb of this god."

Vajasaneyi-samhita, 34, 3 (trans. from Deussen, *Die Geheimlehre des Veda*, p. 17):

> "He who as consciousness, thought, decision,
> Dwells as immortal light within man."

Silesius, it was precisely the littleness and lowliness of the ego [70] that impelled him to recognize its identity with its extreme opposite.[71] It was not the arbitrary opinions of deranged minds that gave rise to such insights, but rather the nature of the psyche itself, which, in East and West alike, expresses these truths either directly or clothed in transparent metaphors. This is understandable when we realize that a world-creating quality attaches to human consciousness as such. In saying this we violate no religious convictions, for the religious believer is at liberty to regard man's consciousness (through which, as it were, a second world-creation was enacted) as a divine instrument.

133   I must point out to the reader that these remarks on the significance of the ego might easily prompt him to charge me with grossly contradicting myself. He will perhaps remember that he has come across a very similar argument in my other writings. Only there it was not a question of ego but of the *self*, or rather, of the personal atman in contradistinction and in relation to the suprapersonal atman. I have defined the self as the totality of the conscious and the unconscious psyche, and the ego as the central reference-point of consciousness. It is an essential part of the self, and can be used *pars pro toto* when the significance of consciousness is borne in mind. But when we want to lay emphasis on the psychic totality it is better to use the term "self." There is no question of a contradictory definition, but merely of a difference of standpoint.

3. SULPHUR [72]

134   Because of the singular role it plays in alchemy, sulphur deserves to be examined rather more closely. The first point of

70 "Save as a child, one goes not in where all
   God's children are: the door is much too small."
                                        Cherubinischer Wandersmann, I, No. 153.
71 "I am God's child and son, and he is mine.
   How comes it that we both can both combine?" (I, 256)
   "God is my centre when I close him in;
   And my circumference when I melt in him." (III, 148)
   "God, infinite, more present is in me
   Than if a sponge should soak up all the sea." (IV, 156)
   "The hen contains the egg, the egg the hen,
   The twain in one, and yet the one in twain." (IV, 163)
   "God becomes 'I' and takes my manhood on:
   Because I was before him was that done!" (IV, 259)
72 Part of this section appeared in *Nova Acta Paracelsica,* 1948, pp. 27ff.

interest, which we have already touched on, is its relation to Sol: it was called the prima materia of Sol, Sol being naturally understood as the gold. As a matter of fact, sulphur was sometimes identified with gold.[73] Sol therefore derives from sulphur. The close connection between them explains the view that sulphur was the "companion of Luna." [74] When the gold (Sol) and his bride (Luna) are united, "the coagulating sulphur, which in the corporal gold was turned outwards [*extraversum*], is turned inwards" (i.e., introverted).[75] This remark indicates the psychic double nature of sulphur (*sulphur duplex*); there is a red and a white sulphur, the white being the active substance of the moon, the red that of the sun.[76] The specific "virtue" of sulphur is said to be greater in the red variety.[77] But its duplicity also has another meaning: on the one hand it is the prima materia, and in this form it is burning and corrosive (*adurens*), and "hostile" to the matter of the stone; on the other hand, when "cleansed of all impurities, it is the matter of our stone." [78] Altogether, sulphur is one of the innumerable synonyms for the prima materia [79] in its dual aspect, i.e., as both the initial material and the end-product. At the beginning it is "crude" or "common" sulphur, at the end it is a sublimation product of the process.[80] Its fiery nature is unanimously stressed,[81] though

[73] Laurentius Ventura, "De ratione confic. lap.," *Theatr. chem.*, II, pp. 334f.

[74] "Figurarum Aegyptiorum," MS, 18th cent. Author's possession.

[75] "Introitus apertus," *Mus. herm.*, p. 652 (Waite, II, p. 165).

[76] "Tractatus aureus," *Mus. herm.*, p. 33 (Waite, I, p. 34); Mylius, *Phil. ref.*, p. 54.

[77] Ventura, *Theatr. chem.*, II, p. 342.

[78] "Tract. aureus," *Mus. herm.*, p. 24 (Waite, I, p. 26).

[79] Ibid., pp. 11 and 21 (Waite, I, pp. 14 and 23); Aegidius de Vadis, "Dialogus," *Theatr. chem.*, II, p. 100; Ripley, "Axiomata philosophica," *Theatr. chem.*, II, p. 125.

[80] Ripley, *Theatr. chem.*, II, p. 125. As *sulphur incremabile*, it is an end-product in *Theatr. chem.*, II, p. 302, and also in "De sulphure," *Mus. herm.*, p. 622 (Waite, II, p. 142).

[81] "Consil. coniug.," *Ars chemica*, p. 217. In Paracelsus (ed. Huser, II, p. 521) sulphur is one of the three primary fires ("fire is the body of souls"). In his *Vita longa* (ed. Bodenstein, fol. a 6ᵛ) he says: "Sulphur is everything that burns, and nothing catches fire save by reason of sulphur." * Trevisanus ("De chemico miraculo," *Theatr. chem.*, I, p. 793) says: "For sulphur is none other than the pure fire hidden in the mercury." * In Mylius (*Phil. ref.*, p. 50) the philosophical sulphur is "simple living fire, quickening other dead bodies [or: inert substances]." * Cf. also Penotus, "Regulae et canones," *Theatr. chem.*, II, p. 150. Sulphur as "magna flamma" is a danger to the little life-flame of the alchemists ("De sulphure," *Mus. herm.*, p. 637).

this fieriness does not consist merely in its combustibility but
in its occult fiery nature. As always, an allusion to occult qualities means that the material in question was the focus of projections which lent it a numinous significance.

135   In keeping with its dual nature sulphur is on the one hand
corporal and earthly,[82] and on the other an occult, spiritual
principle. As an earthly substance it comes from the "fatness of
the earth," [83] by which was meant the radical moisture as prima
materia. Occasionally it is called "cinis extractus a cinere" (ash
extracted from ash).[84] "Ash" is an inclusive term for the scoriae
left over from burning, the substance that "remains below"—a
strong reminder of the chthonic nature of sulphur. The red
variety is thought of as masculine,[85] and under this aspect it
represents the gold or Sol.[86] As a chthonic being it has close
affinities with the dragon, which is called "our secret sulphur." [87]
In that form it is also the *aqua divina,* symbolized by the uroboros.[88] These analogies often make it difficult to distinguish
between sulphur and Mercurius, since the same thing is said
of both. "This is our natural, most sure fire, our Mercurius,
our sulphur," says the "Tractatus aureus de lapide." [89] In the
Turba quicksilver is a fiery body that behaves in exactly the
same way as sulphur.[90] For Paracelsus sulphur, together with
Sal (salt), is the begetter of Mercurius, who is born of the sun
and moon.[91] Or it is found "in the depths of the nature of Mercurius," [92] or it is "of the nature of Mercurius," [93] or sulphur
and Mercurius are "brother and sister." [94] Sulphur is credited

82 Ripley, *Opera omnia,* p. 150.

83 "Tract. aureus," *Mus. herm.,* p. 24 (Waite, I, p. 26).

84 *Aurora consurgens* II, in *Art. aurif.,* I, p. 229.

85 In the Symbolic Table of Penotus (*Theatr. chem.,* II, p. 123) sulphur is co-ordinated with "virilitas prima" and "Dii caelestes." The further co-ordination of
sulphur with lion, dragon, and unicorn is the direct opposite of the heavenly.

86 "Consil. coniug.," *Ars chemica,* p. 217, and "Epistola ad Hermannum," *Theatr.
chem.,* V, p. 893.

87 Mylius, *Phil. ref.,* p. 104; Zacharius, "Opusculum," *Theatr. chem.,* I, p. 859.

88 Mylius, p. 179; *Mus. herm.,* p. 37 (Waite, I, p. 37).   89 *Mus. herm.,* p. 39.

90 *Turba,* p. 149, lines 21ff. "Consil. coniug." (p. 66) says: "All quicksilver is sulphur" (a quotation attributed to Plato). On p. 202 there is a similar quotation
from Geber.   91 *De pestilitate,* lib. 1 (ed. Sudhoff, XIV, p. 597).

92 Quotation from Geber in Trevisanus, *Theatr. chem.,* I, p. 793.

93 Quotation from Morienus, ibid.

94 Ripley, *Chymische Schrifften,* p. 31. For Mercurius as the "wife" of sulphur,
who "receives from him the impregnation of the fruit," see ibid., pp. 10f.

with Mercurius' "power to dissolve, kill, and bring metals to life." [95]

136   This intimate connection with Mercurius makes it evident that sulphur is a spiritual or psychic substance of universal import, of which nearly everything may be said that is said of Mercurius. Thus sulphur is the soul not only of metals but of all living things; in the "Tractatus aureus" it is equated with "nostra anima" (our soul).[96] The *Turba* says: "The sulphurs are souls that were hidden in the four bodies." [97] Paracelsus likewise calls sulphur the soul.[98] In Mylius sulphur produces the "ferment" or "soul which gives life to the imperfect body." [99] The "Tractatus Micreris" says: ". . . until the green son appears, who is its [100] soul, which the Philosophers have called the green bird and bronze and sulphur." [101] The soul is also described as the "hidden part [*occultum*] of the sulphur." [102]

137   In the sphere of Christian psychology, green has a spermatic, procreative quality, and for this reason it is the colour attributed to the Holy Ghost as the creative principle.[103] Accordingly Dorn says: "The male and universal seed, the first and most potent, is the solar sulphur, the first part and most potent cause of all generation." [104] It is the life-spirit itself. In his "De tenebris contra naturam" Dorn says: "We have said before that the life of the world is the light of nature and the celestial sulphur, whose substrate [*subiectum*] is the aetheric moisture and the

95 "De sulphure," *Mus. herm.*, p. 626 (Waite, II, p. 145).

96 *Mus. herm.*, p. 39 (Waite, I, p. 39). "Our," of course, means: how we, the alchemists, understand it. Similarly in the *Turba*, p. 123, lines 17f.

97 *Turba*, p. 149.* The "four bodies" refer to the ancient *tetrasomia*, consisting of four metals. Dorn ("Congeries Paracelsicae," *Theatr. chem.*, I, p. 622) accuses the Greeks of having turned the number four (i.e., the *tetrasomia*) into a monarchy of devilish idols, ruled over by Saturn, Venus, Mars, and Mercury.

98 *De natura rerum*, lib. 1 ("De Generatione rerum naturalium"). (Sudhoff, **XI**, p. 318; Huser, 1590, VI, p. 265.)

99 *Phil. ref.*, p. 202.

100 Referring to a "Sol" mentioned earlier.

101 *Theatr. chem.*, V, p. 103.*

102 Hoghelande, "Liber de alchimiae diff.," *Theatr. chem.*, I, p. 171.

103 God is equated with greenness in the *Cherubinischer Wandersmann* (I, 190):
      "God is my sap: the leaves and buds I show,
        They are his Holy Ghost, by whom I grow."

104 "Physica Trismegisti," *Theatr. chem.*, I, p. 423. Hoghelande (*Theatr. chem.*, I, p. 172) quotes from Lully: "The father and the male seed," and from Aquinas: "The substance of sulphur is like to the paternal seed, active and formative." *

heat of the firmament, namely Sol and Luna." [105] Sulphur has here attained cosmic significance and is equated with the light of nature, the supreme source of knowledge for the natural philosophers. But this light does not shine unhindered, says Dorn. It is obscured by the darkness of the elements in the human body. For him, therefore, sulphur is a shining, heavenly being. Though this sulphur is a "son who comes from imperfect bodies," he is "ready to put on the white and purple garments." [106] In Ripley he is a "spirit of generative power, who works in the moisture." [107] In the treatise "De sulphure" he is the "virtue of all things" and the source of illumination and of all knowledge.[108] He knows, in fact, everything.[109]

138   In view of the significance of sulphur it is worth our while to take a look at its effects as described by the alchemists. Above all, it burns and consumes: "The little power of this sulphur is sufficient to consume a strong body." [110] The "strong body" is the sun, as is clear from the saying: "Sulphur blackens the sun and consumes it." Then, it causes or signifies the putrefactio, "which in our day was never seen," says the *Rosarium*.[111] A third capacity is that of coagulating,[112] and a fourth and fifth those of tincturing (*tingere, colorare*) and maturing (*maturare*).[113] Its "putrefying" effect is also understood as its ability to "corrupt." Sulphur is the "cause of imperfection in all metals," the "corrupter of perfection," "causing the blackness in every operation"; "too much sulphurousness is the cause of corruption," it is "bad and not well mixed," of an "evil, stinking odour and of feeble strength." Its substance is dense and tough,

105 *Theatr. chem.*, I, p. 518.
106 "Phil. chemica," ibid., p. 482.
107 *Chymische Schrifften*, p. 10.
108 "But what is more, in his Kingdom there is a mirror in which the whole World is to be seen. Whosoever looks into this mirror, can see and learn therein the parts of the wisdom of the whole World, and so departs fully knowledgeable in these Three Kingdoms." * *Mus. herm.*, p. 635 (Waite, II, p. 151).
109 Cf. the conversation between the alchemist and a "voice" in *Mus. herm.*, p. 637: "Master, doth Sulphur know aught concerning the metals? Voice: I have told thee that he knoweth all things, and of the metals even much more than of other things." * "He is the heart of all things" * (p. 634).
110 *Turba*, p. 125, line 10.
111 *Art. aurif.*, II, p. 229.
112 Zacharius, "Opusculum," *Theatr. chem.*, I, p. 842.
113 "De sulphure," *Mus. herm.*, p. 632 (Waite, II, p. 149).

and its corruptive action is due on the one hand to its combustibility and on the other to its "earthy feculence." "It hinders perfection in all its works." [114]

139   These unfavourable accounts evidently impressed one of the adepts so much that, in a marginal note, he added "diabolus" to the *causae corruptionis*.[115] This remark is illuminating: it forms the counterpoint to the luminous role of sulphur, for sulphur is a "Lucifer" or "Phosphorus" (light-bringer), from the most beautiful star in the chymic firmament down to the *candelulae,* "little bits of sulphurous tow such as old women sell for lighting fires." [116] In addition to so many other qualities, sulphur shares this extreme paradox with Mercurius, besides having like him a connection with Venus, though here the allusion is veiled and more discreet: "Our Venus is not the common sulphur, which burns and is consumed with the combustion of the fire and of the corruption; but the whiteness of the Venus of the Sages is consumed with the combustion of the white and the red [*albedinis et rubedinis*], and this combustion is the entire whitening [*dealbatio*] of the whole work. Therefore two sulphurs are mentioned and two quicksilvers,[117] and these the Philosophers have named one and one,[118] and they rejoice in one another,[119] and the one contains the other." [120]

140   Another allusion to Venus occurs in one of the parables in "De sulphure," [121] about an alchemist who is seeking the sulphur. His quest leads him to the grove of Venus, and there he learns through a voice, which later turns out to be Saturn's, that Sulphur is held a prisoner at the command of his own mother. He is praised as the "artificer of a thousand things," as the heart

114 Mylius, *Phil. ref.,* pp. 61ff.

115 In my copy of *Phil. ref.,* p. 62. In Glauber (*De natura salium,* pp. 41 and 43) sulphur is the "exceeding black devil of hell" who quarrels with the salt.

116 "De sulphure," *Mus. herm.,* p. 640 (Waite, II, p. 155).* *Candelulae* are "Elychnia of Sulphur, in which threads or morsels of wood are inserted." * (Ruland, *Lexicon,* Latin edn., p. 457.)

117 The higher and the lower, the subtle and the coarse, the spiritual and the material.

118 They are one and the same, however. As above so below, and vice versa. Cf. "Tabula smaragdina."

119 "Nature rejoices in nature," according to the axiom of Democritus.

120 An allusion to the uroboros. The text of this passage is in "Rosinus ad Sarratantam," *Art. aurif.,* I, p. 302.

121 *Mus. herm.,* p. 633ff. (Waite, II, pp. 149ff.).

of all things, as that which endows living things with understanding, as the begetter of every flower and blossom on herb
and tree, and finally as the "painter of all colours." [122] This
might well be a description of Eros. In addition we learn that
he was imprisoned because in the view of the alchemists he had
shown himself too obliging towards his mother. Although we
are not told who his mother was, we may conjecture that it was
Venus herself who shut up her naughty Cupid.[123] This interpretation is corroborated by the fact, firstly, that Sulphur, unknown
to the alchemist, was in the grove of Venus [124] (woods, like trees,
have a maternal significance); secondly, that Saturn introduced
himself as the "governor of the prison," and all alchemists with
knowledge of astrology would have been familiar with the secret
nature of Saturn; [125] thirdly, that after the disappearance of the
voice the alchemist, falling asleep, saw in the same grove a fountain and near it the personified Sulphur; and, finally, that the
vision ends with the chymical "embrace in the bath." Here
Venus is undoubtedly the *amor sapientiae* who puts a check on
Sulphur's roving charms. The latter may well derive from the
fact that his seat in the Uroboros is in the tail of the dragon.[126]
Sulphur is the masculine element par excellence, the "sperma

122 A patient dreamt: *"Animals were being hunted. The devil, their patron saint,
appeared. Suddenly all the colours appeared in his dark-brown face, and then a
vermilion spot in his cheek."*
123 The only other figure who could be the mother is Luna. She, too, appears later
in the parable, but in the form of Diana, i.e., in the role of daughter-sister.
124 The green colour attributed to Sulphur he has in common with Venus, as the
verses in the *Gemma gemmarum* show. Venus says:

> "Transparent / green / and fair to view
> I am commixt of every hue /
> Yet in me's a Red Spirit hid /
> No name I know by which he's bid /
> And he did from my husband come /
> The noble Mars, full quarrelsome."

The "red spirit" is our Sulphur—"painter of all colours."
125 The "Occulta chemicorum philosophia," printed in the 1611 edn. of Basilius
Valentinus' *Triumphwagen Antimonii* (pp. 579ff.), mentions an astrological characteristic of Saturn: he is "supreme tester," and Sol and Luna (who "only exist
through him"), warm his cold body "better than a young woman" (p. 583). Already
in the pre-Ptolemaic tradition Saturn was connected with dubious love-affairs
(Bouché-Leclercq, *L'Astrologie grecque*, p. 436, n. 1). *Mus. herm.*, p. 623 (Waite,
II, p. 143) mentions the "infernal prisons where Sulphur lies bound."
126 "Sulphur is his [the dragon's] tail." (*Ars chemica*, p. 140.)

homogeneum";[127] and since the dragon is said to "impregnate himself," his tail is the masculine and his mouth the feminine organ. Like Beya,[128] who engulfed her brother in her own body and dissolved him into atoms, the dragon devours himself from the tail upwards until his whole body has been swallowed into his head.[129] Being the inner fire of Mercurius,[130] Sulphur obviously partakes of his most dangerous and most evil nature, his violence being personified in the dragon and the lion, and his concupiscence in Hermes Kyllenios.[131] The dragon whose nature sulphur shares is often spoken of as the "dragon of Babel" or, more accurately, the "dragon's head" (*caput draconis*), which is a "most pernicious poison," a poisonous vapour breathed out by the flying dragon. The dragon's head "comes with great swiftness from Babylon." However, the "winged dragon" that stands for quicksilver becomes a poison-breathing monster only after its union with the "wingless dragon," which corresponds to sulphur.[132] Sulphur here plays an evil role that accords well with the sinful "Babel." Furthermore, this dragon is equated with the human-headed serpent of paradise, which had the "imago et similitudo Dei" in its head, this being the deeper reason why the dragon devours its hated body. "His head lives in eternity, and therefore it is called glorious life, and the angels serve him." [133] This is a reference to Matthew 4 : 11: "Then the devil leaveth him, and behold, angels came and ministered unto him."

141   Hence we get the parallel of the dragon's head with Christ, corresponding to the Gnostic view that the son of the highest divinity took on the form of the serpent in paradise in order to teach our first parents the faculty of discrimination, so that they should see that the work of the demiurge was imperfect. As the

127 Johannes à Mehung (Jean de Meung) in "Demonstratio naturae," *Mus. herm.,* p. 162 (Waite, I, p. 135). Jean de Meung lived *c.* 1250–1305.
128 In the second version of the Vision of Arisleus in *Ros. phil., Art. aurif.,* II (1572), p. 246.
129 Albertus Magnus, "Super arborem Aristotelis," *Theatr. chem.,* II, pp. 526f.
130 "The whole arcanum lies hidden in the sulphur of the Philosophers, which is also contained in the inmost part of their mercury." * *Mus. herm.,* p. 643 (Waite, II, p. 157).
131 Regarding Hermes Kyllenios see "The Spirit Mercurius," par. 278.
132 Flamel, "Summarium philosophicum," *Mus. herm.,* p. 173 (Waite, I, p. 142).
133 Albertus Magnus, p. 525.*

son of the seven planets the dragon is clearly the *filius macrocosmi* and, as such, a parallel figure to Christ and at the same time his rival.[134] The dragon's head contains the precious stone, which means that consciousness contains the symbolic image of the self, and just as the lapis unites the opposites so the self assimilates contents of consciousness and the unconscious. This interpretation fully accords with the traditional significance of the dragon's head as a favourable omen.

142   From what has been said it should be evident that sulphur is the essence of an active substance. It is the "spirit of the metals," [135] forming with quicksilver, the other "spirit of nature," the two principles and the matter of the metals, since these two principles are themselves metals *in potentia*.[136] Together with Mercurius it also forms the lapis.[137] In fact, it is the "heart of all things" [138] and the "virtue of all things." [139] Enumerating, along with water and moisture, the synonyms for the lapis as the "whole secret and life of all things whatsoever," the "Consilium coniugii" says: "The oil that takes up the colour, that is, the radiance of the sun, is itself sulphur." [140] Mylius compares it to the rainbow: "The sulphur shines like the rainbow above the waters . . . the bow of Isis stands half on the pure, liquid, and flowing water and half on the earth . . . hence the whole property of sulphur and its natural likeness are expressed by the rainbow." Thus sulphur, so far as it is symbolized by the rainbow, is a "divine and wonderful experience." A few lines further on, after mentioning sulphur as one of the components of the water, Mylius writes that Mercurius (i.e., the water) must be cleansed by distillation "from all foulness of the earth, and then Lucifer, the impurity and the accursed earth, will fall from the golden heaven." [141] Lucifer, the most beautiful of the angels,

134 Cf. *Psychology and Alchemy*, par. 26.
135 Mylius, *Phil. ref.*, p. 185.
136 Ventura, *Theatr. chem.*, II, p. 262.
137 Ibid., p. 276.
138 *Mus. herm.*, p. 634.
139 Ibid., p. 635.
140 *Ars chemica*, p. 66. The oil is described as resembling the *anima media natura* in "Aphorismi Basiliani" (*Theatr. chem.*, IV, p. 368): "But the quickening power, like that which holds the world together, is midway between spirit and body, and the bond of them both, especially in the sulphur of a certain rubeous and transparent oil . . ." *
141 *Phil. ref.*, p. 18.* An older source is "De arte chymica," *Art. aurif.*, I, p. 608.

becomes the devil, and sulphur is "of the earth's foulness."
Here, as in the case of the dragon's head, the highest and the
lowest are close together. Although a personification of evil, sulphur shines above earth and water with the splendour of the
rainbow, a "natural vessel" [142] of divine transformation.

143   From all this it is apparent that for the alchemists sulphur
was one of the many synonyms for the mysterious transformative substance.[143] This is expressed most plainly in the *Turba:* [144]
"Therefore roast it for seven days, until it becomes shining like
marble, because, when it does, it is a very great secret [*arcanum*],
since sulphur has been mixed with sulphur; and thereby is the
greatest work accomplished, by mutual affinity, because natures
meeting their nature mutually rejoice." [145] It is a characteristic
of the arcane substance to have "everything it needs"; it is a
fully autonomous being, like the dragon that begets, reproduces,
slays, and devours itself. It is questionable whether the alchemists, who were anything but consistent thinkers, ever became
fully conscious of what they were saying when they used such
images. If we take their words literally, they would refer to an
"Increatum," a being without beginning or end, and in need
of "no second." Such a thing can by definition only be God
himself, but a God, we must add, seen in the mirror of physical
nature and distorted past recognition. The "One" for which the
alchemists strove corresponds to the *res simplex,* which the
"Liber quartorum" defines as God.[146] This reference, however,
is unique, and in view of the corrupt state of the text I would
not like to labour its significance, although Dorn's speculations
about the "One" and the "unarius" are closely analogous. The
Turba continues: "And yet they are not different natures, nor

142 So named by Lully. Cf. Hoghelande, *Theatr. chem.,* I, p. 199.
143 This is consistently so in Khunrath; cf. *Von Hylealischen Chaos,* p. 264. In
"Rosinus ad Euthiciam," *Art. aurif.,* I, p. 252, it is the "name of the divine water."
In Zacharius (*Theatr. chem.,* I, p. 831) sulphur is the "fatness in the caverns of the
earth." * Cf. Ruland, *Lexicon,* p. 305. Pernety (*Dict. mytho-herm.,* pp. 148f.) says:
"On voit le mot de soufre attribué à bien des matières même très opposées entre
elles . . . Les Philosophes ont donné à ce soufre une infinité de noms."
144 P. 192.
145 An allusion to the axiom of Democritus.
146 "That from which things have their being is God the invisible and unmoved,
whose will created the intelligence; from the will and intelligence is produced the
simple soul; but the soul gives rise to the discriminated natures from which the
composite natures are produced," etc.* (*Theatr. chem.,* V, p. 145.)

several, but a single one, which unites their powers in itself, through which it prevails over the other things. See you not that the Master has begun with the One and ended with the One? For he has named those unities the water of the sulphur, which conquers the whole of nature." [147] The peculiarity of sulphur is also expressed in the paradox that it is "incremabile" (incombustible), "ash extracted from ash." [148] Its effects as *aqua sulfurea* are infinite.[149] The "Consilium coniugii" says: "Our sulphur is not the common sulphur," [150] which is usually said of the philosophical gold. Paracelsus, in his "Liber Azoth," describes sulphur as "lignum" (wood), the "linea vitae" (line of life), and "fourfold" (to correspond with the four elements); the spirit of life is renewed from it.[151] Of the philosophical sulphur Mylius says that such a thing is not to be found on earth except in Sol and Luna, and it is known to no man unless revealed to him by God.[152] Dorn calls it the "son begotten of the imperfect bodies," who, when sublimated, changes into the "highly esteemed salt of four colours." In the "Tractatus Micreris" it is even called the "treasure of God." [153]

144   These references to sulphur as the arcane and transformative substance must suffice. I would only like to stress Paracelsus' remark about its fourfold nature, and that of his pupil Dorn about the four colours as symbols of totality. The psychic factor which appears in projection in all similarly characterized arcane substances is the unconscious self. It is on this account that the well-known Christ-lapis [154] parallel reappears again and again, as for instance in the above-mentioned parable of the adept's adventure in the grove of Venus. As we saw, he fell asleep after having a long and instructive conversation with the voice of Saturn. In his dream he beholds the figures of two men by the

147 P. 255.

148 *Aurora consurgens* II, in *Art. aurif.*, I, p. 229. In "Consil. coniug." it is called "incombustible" (p. 149).

149 "It has no end to its action, for it goes on tincturing for ever." * (Ibid., p. 164.)

150 Ibid., p. 199.

151 In Huser, II, p. 525; in Sudhoff, XIV, p. 555, ϕ is used for sulphur; here as in Mylius associated with the rainbow. Sudhoff, without stating any reasons, textual or otherwise, reckons the *Liber Azoth* among the spurious treatises. I cannot agree with this view.

152 *Phil. ref.*, p. 50.

153 *Theatr. chem.*, V, p. 106.

154 For a detailed discussion see *Psychology and Alchemy*, Part III, ch. 5.

fountain in the grove, one of them Sulphur, the other Sal. A quarrel arises, and Sal gives Sulphur an "incurable wound." Blood pours from it in the form of "whitest milk." As the adept sinks deeper into sleep, it changes into a river. Diana emerges from the grove and bathes in the miraculous water. A prince (Sol), passing by, espies her, they are inflamed for love of one another, and she falls down in a swoon and sinks beneath the surface. The prince's retinue refuse to rescue her for fear of the perilous water,[155] whereupon the prince plunges in and is dragged down by her to the depths. Immediately their souls appear above the water and explain to the adept that they will not go back into "bodies so polluted," and are glad to be quit of them. They would remain afloat until the "fogs and clouds" have disappeared. At this point the adept returns to his former dream, and with many other alchemists he finds the corpse of Sulphur by the fountain. Each of them takes a piece and operates with it, but without success.[156] We learn, further, that Sulphur is not only the "medicina" but also the "medicus"—the wounded physician.[157] Sulphur suffers the same fate as the body

[155] The stream, though small, is "most dangerous." The servants say they have once tried to cross it, but "we scarcely escaped the peril of eternal death." They add: "We know too that our predecessors perished here." The servants are the alchemists, and the stream or its water symbolizes the danger threatening them, which is clearly the danger of drowning. The psychic danger of the opus is the irruption of the unconscious and the "loss of soul" caused thereby. I have in my possession an alchemical MS. of the 17th cent., showing an invasion of the unconscious in a series of pictures. The images produced bear all the marks of schizophrenia.

[156] "De sulphure," *Mus. herm.*, pp. 639f.

[157] Prof. C. Kerényi has kindly lent me the MS. of his work on Asklepios [trans. *Asklepios: Archetypal Image of the Physician's Existence*, 1959], which is of the greatest interest to all doctors. He describes the primordial physician as the "wounded wounder" (Chiron, Machaon, etc.). But, curiously enough, there are other parallels too. In our treatise the Prince is called "vir fortis," the strong man. He is without doubt the sun, and he surprises Diana while bathing. The birth-myth of Asklepios states that the sun-god Apollo surprised Coronis (the "crow maiden") while she was bathing in Lake Boibeis [ibid., pp. 93ff.]. Coronis, being black, is associated with the new moon ($\sigma\acute{v}vo\delta os$ ·*solis et lunae*), and her dangerousness is shown in the name of her father Phlegyas ("the incendiary"). Her brother or uncle was Ixion, rapist and murderer. The connection of Coronis with the moon is also explained by the fact that Phoebe (moon) was her ancestress. When Coronis was already pregnant with Apollo's son, Asklepios, she had intercourse with the chthonic Ischys ($\iota\sigma\chi\acute{v}s$ = strong, the "vir fortis") and as a punishment was slain by Artemis. The child was rescued from the body of its mother, on the funeral

that is pierced by the lance of Mercurius. In Reusner's *Pandora* [158] the body is symbolized as Christ, the second Adam, pierced by the lance of a mermaid, or a Lilith or Edem.[159]

145   This analogy shows that sulphur as the arcane substance was set on a par with Christ, so that for the alchemists it must have meant something very similar. We would turn away in disgust from such an absurdity were it not obvious that this analogy, sometimes in clear and sometimes in veiled form, was thrust upon them by the unconscious. Certainly there could be no greater disparity than that between the holiest conception known to man's consciousness and sulphur with its evil-smelling compounds. The analogy therefore is in no sense evidential but can only have arisen through intense and passionate preoccupation with the chemical substance, which gradually formed a *tertium comparationis* in the alchemist's mind and forced it upon him with the utmost insistence. The common denominator of these two utterly incommensurable conceptions is the self, the image of the whole man, which reached its finest and most significant development in the "Ecce Homo," and on the other hand appears as the meanest, most contemptible, and most insignificant thing, and manifests itself to consciousness precisely in that guise. As it is a concept of human totality, the self is by definition greater than the ego-conscious personality, embracing besides this the personal shadow and the collective

---

pyre, by Apollo. Kerényi supposes an identity between the bright Apollo and the dark Ischys. (A similar identity would be that of Asklepios and Trophonios.) The wounds of the physicians were usually caused by arrows, and the same fate was suffered by Asklepios: he was struck with the thunderbolt of Zeus because of an excess of zeal and skill, for he had not only healed the sick but called back the dead, and this was too much for Pluto. (Cf. Wilamowitz-Moellendorff, "Isyllos von Epidauros," pp. 44ff.) The "Novum lumen chemicum" gives an "Aenigma coronidis" (*Mus. herm.*, pp. 585ff.; Waite, II, pp. 111ff.), but this, except for the miraculous "water at times manifested to thee in sleep," contains nothing that would point to the myth of Asklepios. Dom Pernety (*Fables égyptiennes et grecques*, II, p. 152) correctly interprets Coronis as *putrefactio, nigredo, caput corvi*, and the myth as an opus. This is surprisingly apt, since alchemy, although the alchemists did not know it, was a child of this mythology, or of the matrix from which the classical myth sprang as an elder brother.

158 Reproduced in "Paracelsus as a Spiritual Phenomenon" (fig. B4).

159 Cf. *Psychology and Alchemy*, fig. 150, where one "telum passionis" bears the sign of Mercurius, the other the sign of sulphur.

unconscious. Conversely, the entire phenomenon of the unconscious appears so unimportant to ego-consciousness that we would rather explain it as a *privatio lucis* [160] than allow it an autonomous existence. In addition, the conscious mind is critical and mistrustful of everything hailing from the unconscious, convinced that it is suspect and somehow dirty. Hence the psychic phenomenology of the self is as full of paradoxes as the Hindu conception of the atman, which on the one hand embraces the universe and on the other dwells "no bigger than a thumb" in the heart. The Eastern idea of atman-purusha corresponds psychologically to the Western figure of Christ, who is the second Person of the Trinity and God himself, but, so far as his human existence is concerned, conforms exactly to the suffering servant of God in Isaiah [161]—from his birth in a stable among the animals to his shameful death on the cross between two thieves.

146   The contrast is even sharper in the Naassene picture of the Redeemer, as reported by Hippolytus: [162] " 'Lift up your heads, O ye gates, and be ye lift up, ye everlasting doors, and the King of glory shall come in.' [163] This is the wonder of wonders. 'For who,' saith he [the Naassene], 'is this King of glory? A worm and no man, a reproach of men, and despised of the people; [164] this same is the King, and mighty in battle.' " But the battle, say the Naassenes, refers to the warring elements in the body. This association of the passage from the Psalms with the idea of conflict is no accident, for psychological experience shows that the symbols of the self appear in dreams and in active imagination at moments of violent collision between two opposite points of

160 As is evident in the very word *un*-conscious.
161 Isaiah 52 : 14: "As many were astonished at him—his appearance was so marred, beyond human semblance, and his form beyond that of the sons of men." 53 : 2f.: "For he grew up before [us] like a young plant, and like a root out of dry ground; he had no form or comeliness that we should look at him, and no beauty that we should desire him. He was despised and rejected of men; a man of sorrows, and acquainted with grief; and as one from whom men hide their faces he was despised, and we esteemed him not." [RSV. In the last verse, alternative readings for "sorrows" and "grief" are "pains" and "sickness"; cf. *Schmerzen* and *Krankheit* in the Zürcher Bibel, quoted by the author.—Trans.]
162 *Elenchos*, V, 8, 18 (Legge, I, p. 134).
163 Psalm 24 : 7.
164 Psalm 22 : 6.

view, as compensatory attempts to mitigate the conflict and "make enemies friends." Therefore the lapis, which is born of the dragon, is extolled as a saviour and mediator since it represents the equivalent of a redeemer sprung from the unconscious. The Christ-lapis parallel vacillates between mere analogy and far-reaching identity, but in general it is not thought out to its logical conclusion, so that the dual focus remains. This is not surprising since even today most of us have not got round to understanding Christ as the psychic reality of an archetype, regardless of his historicity. I do not doubt the historical reality of Jesus of Nazareth, but the figure of the Son of Man and of Christ the Redeemer has archetypal antecedents. It is these that form the basis of the alchemical analogies.

147   As investigators of nature the alchemists showed their Christian attitude by their "pistis" in the object of their science, and it was not their fault if in many cases the psyche proved stronger than the chemical substance and its well-guarded secrets by distorting the results. It was only the acuter powers of observation in modern man which showed that weighing and measuring provided the key to the locked doors of chemical combination, after the intuition of the alchemists had stressed for centuries the importance of "measure, number, and weight." [165] The prime and most immediate experience of matter was that it is animated, which for medieval man was self-evident; indeed every Mass, every rite of the Church, and the miraculous effect of relics all demonstrated for him this natural and obvious fact. The French Enlightenment and the shattering of the metaphysical view of the world were needed before a scientist like Lavoisier had the courage finally to reach out for the scales. To begin with, however, the alchemists were fascinated by the soul of matter, which, unknown to them, it had received from the human psyche by way of projection. For all their intensive preoccupation with matter as a concrete fact they followed this psychic trail, which was to lead them into a region that, to our way of thinking, had not the remotest connection with chemistry. Their mental labours consisted in a predominantly intuitive apprehension of psychic facts, the intellect playing only the

[165] "Mensura, numerus et pondus." Cf. von Franz, *Aurora Consurgens*, Parable 4 (p. 83).

modest role of a famulus. The results of this curious method of
research proved, however, to be beyond the grasp of any psychology for several centuries. If one does not understand a person,
one tends to regard him as a fool. The misfortune of the alchemists was that they themselves did not know what they were
talking about. Nevertheless, we possess witnesses enough to the
high esteem in which they held their science and to the wonder-
ment which the mystery of matter instilled into them. For they
discovered—to keep to sulphur as our example—in this substance, which was one of the customary attributes of hell and the
devil, as well as in the poisonous, crafty, and treacherous Mercurius, an analogy with the most sacrosanct figure of their religion. They therefore imbued this arcanum with symbols intended to characterize its malicious, dangerous, and uncanny
nature, choosing precisely those which in the positive sense were
used for Christ in the patristic literature. These were the snake,
the lion, the eagle, fire, cloud, shadow, fish, stone, the unicorn
and the rhinoceros, the dragon, the night-raven, the man encompassed by a woman, the hen, water, and many others. This
strange usage is explained by the fact that the majority of the
patristic allegories have in addition to their positive meaning a
negative one. Thus in St. Eucherius [166] the rapacious wolf "in
its good part" signifies the apostle Paul, but "in its bad part"
the devil.

148   From this we would have to conclude that the alchemists had
discovered the psychological existence of a shadow which op-
poses and compensates the conscious, positive figure. For them
the shadow was in no sense a *privatio lucis;* it was so real that
they even thought they could discern its material density, and
this concretism led them to attribute to it the dignity of being
the matrix of an incorruptible and eternal substance. In the religious sphere this psychological discovery is reflected in the
historical fact that only with the rise of Christianity did the
devil, the "eternal counterpart of Christ," assume his true form,
and that the figure of Antichrist appears on the scene already
in the New Testament. It would have been natural for the alchemists to suppose that they had lured the devil out of the darkness
of matter. There were indeed indications of this, as we have

[166] *Liber formularum spiritalis intelligentiae*, V (Migne, *P.L.*, vol. 50, col. 751).

seen, but they are exceptions. Far more prevalent and truly characteristic of alchemy was the optimistic notion that this creature of darkness was destined to be the *medicina,* as is proved by the use of the term "medicina et medicus" for the untrustworthy sulphur. The very same appellation appears as an allegory of Christ in St. Ambrose.[167] The Greek word φάρμακον (poison and antidote) is indicative of this ambivalence. In our parable of the sulphur the river of "most dangerous" water, which caused so many deaths, is analogous to the water from the side of Christ and the streams that flowed from his belly. What in one place is a river of grace is a deadly poison in another—harbouring within it, however, the potentialities of healing.

149   This is not mere euphemism or propitiatory optimism, but rather an intuitive perception of the compensating effect of the counter-position in the unconscious, which should not be understood dualistically as an absolute opposite but as a helpful though nonetheless dangerous complement to the conscious position. Medical experience shows that the unconscious is indeed actuated by a compensatory tendency, at any rate in normal individuals. In the domain of pathology I believe I have observed cases where the tendency of the unconscious would have to be regarded, by all human standards, as essentially destructive. But it may not be out of place to reflect that the self-destruction of what is hopelessly inefficient or evil can be understood in a higher sense as another attempt at compensation. There are murderers who feel that their execution is condign punishment, and suicides who go to their death in triumph.

150   So, although the alchemists failed to discover the hidden structure of matter, they did discover that of the psyche, even if they were scarcely conscious of what this discovery meant. Their naïve Christ-lapis parallel is at once a symbolization of the chemical arcanum and of the figure of Christ. The identification or paralleling of Christ with a chemical factor, which was in essence a pure projection from the unconscious, has a reactive effect on the interpretation of the Redeemer. For if A (Christ) = B (lapis), and B = C (an unconscious content), then

[167] *Explanatio Psalmorum XII,* ed. Petschenig, pp. 139, 256.

A = C. Such conclusions need not be drawn consciously in order to be made effective. Given the initial impulse, as provided for instance by the Christ-lapis parallel, the conclusion will draw itself even though it does not reach consciousness, and it will remain the unspoken, spiritual property of the school of thought that first hit upon the equation. Not only that, it will be handed down to the heirs of that school as an integral part of their mental equipment, in this case the natural scientists. The equation had the effect of channelling the religious numen into physical nature and ultimately into matter itself, which in its turn had the chance to become a self-subsistent "metaphysical" principle. In following up their basic thoughts the alchemists, as I have shown in *Psychology and Alchemy,* logically opposed to the son of the spirit a son of the earth and of the stars (or metals), and to the Son of Man or *filius microcosmi* a *filius macrocosmi,* thus unwittingly revealing that in alchemy there was an autonomous principle which, while it did not replace the spirit, nevertheless existed in its own right. Although the alchemists were more or less aware that their insights and truths were of divine origin, they knew they were not sacred revelations but were vouchsafed by individual inspiration or by the *lumen naturae,* the *sapientia Dei* hidden in nature. The autonomy of their insights showed itself in the emancipation of science from the domination of faith. Human intolerance and shortsightedness are to blame for the open conflict that ultimately broke out between faith and knowledge. Conflict or comparison between incommensurables is impossible. The only possible attitude is one of mutual toleration, for neither can deprive the other of its validity. Existing religious beliefs have, besides their supernatural foundation, a basis in psychological facts whose existence is as valid as those of the empirical sciences. If this is not understood on one side or the other it makes no difference to the facts, for these exist whether man understands them or not, and whoever does not have the facts on his side will sooner or later have to pay the price.

151   With this I would like to conclude my remarks on sulphur. This arcane substance has provided occasion for some general reflections, which are not altogether fortuitous in that sulphur represents the active substance of the sun or, in psychological

language, the *motive factor in consciousness:* on the one hand the will, which can best be regarded as a dynamism subordinated to consciousness, and on the other hand compulsion, an involuntary motivation or impulse ranging from mere interest to possession proper. The unconscious dynamism would correspond to sulphur, for compulsion is the great mystery of human life. It is the thwarting of our conscious will and of our reason by an inflammable element within us, appearing now as a consuming fire and now as life-giving warmth.

152   The *causa efficiens et finalis* of this lack of freedom lies in the unconscious and forms that part of the personality which still has to be added to the conscious man in order to make him whole. At first sight it is but an insignificant fragment—a *lapis exilis, in via eiectus,* and often inconvenient and repellent because it stands for something that demonstrates quite plainly our secret inferiority. This aspect is responsible for our resistance to psychology in general and to the unconscious in particular. But together with this fragment, which could round out our consciousness into a whole, there is in the unconscious an already existing wholeness, the "homo totus" of the Western and the *Chên-yên* (true man) of Chinese alchemy, the round primordial being who represents the greater man within, the Anthropos, who is akin to God. This inner man is of necessity partly unconscious, because consciousness is only part of a man and cannot comprehend the whole. But the whole man is always present, for the fragmentation of the phenomenon "Man" is nothing but an effect of consciousness, which consists only of supraliminal ideas. No psychic content can become conscious unless it possesses a certain energy-charge. If this falls, the content sinks below the threshold and becomes unconscious. The possible contents of consciousness are then sorted out, as the energy-charge separates those capable of becoming conscious from those that are not. This separation gives rise on the one hand to consciousness, whose symbol is the sun, and on the other hand to the shadow, corresponding to the *umbra solis.*

153   Compulsion, therefore, has two sources: the shadow and the Anthropos. This is sufficient to explain the paradoxical nature of sulphur: as the "corrupter" it has affinities with the devil, while on the other hand it appears as a parallel of Christ.

4. LUNA

a. The Significance of the Moon

154   Luna, as we have seen, is the counterpart of Sol, cold,[168] moist, feebly shining or dark, feminine, corporeal, passive. Accordingly her most significant role is that of a partner in the coniunctio. As a feminine deity her radiance is mild; she is the lover. Pliny calls her a "womanly and gentle star." She is the sister and bride, mother and spouse of the sun.[169] To illustrate the sun-moon relationship the alchemists often made use of the Song of Songs (Canticles),[170] as in the "confabulation of the lover with the beloved" in *Aurora Consurgens.*[171] In Athens the day of the new moon was considered favourable for celebrating marriages, and it still is an Arabian custom to marry on this day; sun and moon are marriage partners who embrace on the twenty-eighth day of the month.[172] According to these ancient ideas the moon is a vessel of the sun: she is a universal receptacle, of the sun in particular [173]; and she was called "infundibulum terrae" (the funnel of the earth), because she "receives and pours out" [174] the powers of heaven. Again, it is said that the "moisture of the moon" (*lunaris humor*) takes up the sunlight,[175] or that Luna draws near to the sun in order to "extract from him,

168 "Gloria mundi," *Mus. herm.,* p. 275 (Waite, I, p. 221).

169 Dorn, "Physica Trismeg.," *Theatr. chem.,* I, p. 424.

170 "This union the Philosophers have declared in various ways, and likened it, for instance, to the wedlock of a bride and bridegroom (as in the Song of Solomon)." * *Mus. herm.,* p. 90 (Waite, I, p. 82).

171 The immediate model for this was probably Senior's "Epistola solis ad lunam crescentem" (*De chemia,* pp. 7f.), but it may also have been inspired by Cicero's *De natura deorum,* III, 11: ". . . unless indeed we hold that the sun holds conversation with the moon, when their courses approximate" (trans. Rackham, pp. 312ff.). Luna was identified with the wife *par excellence,* Juno: ". . . considering the moon and Juno to be the same" (Macrobius, *Saturnalia,* lib. I, cap. XV).

172 Wittekindt, *Das Hohe Lied und seine Beziehungen zum Ištarkult,* pp. 13 and 23. Further material in Eisler, *Weltenmantel und Himmelszelt,* I, pp. 122ff.; II, pp. 370, 435, 602.

173 Penotus, *Theatr. chem.,* I, p. 681.

174 Steeb, *Coelum sephiroticum,* p. 138. The original idea is in Plutarch, "Isis and Osiris," 43: "She [Selene] is receptive and made pregnant by the sun, but she in turn emits and disseminates into the air generative principles." (*Moralia,* trans. Babbitt, V, pp. 104f.).

175 "Consilium coniugii," *Ars chemica,* pp. 141f.

as from a fountain, universal form and natural life"; [176] she also brings about the conception of the "universal seed of the sun" in the quintessence, in the "belly and womb of nature." [177] In this respect there is a certain analogy between the moon and the earth, as stated in Plutarch and Macrobius.[178] *Aurora Consurgens* says that "the earth made the moon," [178a] and here we should remember that Luna also signifies silver. But the statements of the alchemists about Luna are so complex that one could just as well say that silver is yet another synonym or symbol for the arcanum "Luna." Even so, a remark like the one just quoted may have been a reference to the way in which ore was supposed to have been formed in the earth: the earth "receives" the powers of the stars, and in it the sun generates the gold, etc. The *Aurora consurgens* therefore equates the earth with the bride: "I am that land of the holy promise," [179] or at any rate it is in the earth that the hierosgamos takes place.[180] Earth and moon coincide in the *albedo,* for on the one hand the sublimated or calcined earth appears as *terra alba foliata,* the "sought-for good, like whitest snow," [181] and on the other hand Luna, as mistress

---

176 Dorn, "Physica genesis," *Theatr. chem.,* I, p. 397. As early as Firmicus Maternus (*Matheseos,* I, 4, 9) we find the idea that the moon undergoes a kind of rebirth from the sun. This idea reached its highest development in the patristic parallel between the moon and the Church. Cf. Rahner, "Mysterium Lunae."

177 Dorn, "Phys. Trismeg.," *Theatr. chem.,* I, p. 426. For the Stoics the moon was the mediatrix between the world of eternal stars and the lower, earthly realm; similarly in Macrobius (*In somnium Scipionis,* I, 21) the moon stands midway between things divine and things corruptible. Mennens, in his "Aureum vellus" (*Theatr. chem.,* V, p. 321) says: "But the Moon, being the lowest of the planets, is said to conceive like a womb the virtues of all the stars, and then to bestow them on sublunary things . . . The moon implants all the virtues of the stars for the generation of all things, and especially their seeds." * The moon also has a life-giving influence on minerals, "fashioning and preserving in its [the earth's] bowels the various species of stones, metals, nay more, of living things." *

178 Plutarch, "The Face on the Moon," 21 (XII, p. 139); Macrobius, *In somn. Scip.,* I, 11, and Orphic fragment 81: ἄλλη γαῖα, 'another earth.' See Eisler, *Weltenmantel,* II, p. 657.   178a P. 125.   179 P. 141.

180 "He desires to lie with his mother in the midst of the earth." * ("Allegoriae sapientum," *Theatr. chem.,* V, p. 69.) Vigenerus ("De igne et sale," *Theatr. chem.,* VI, p. 98) says: "And the heaven of incorruptible bodies and the seat and vessel of things that change not is the Moon, which rules over moisture and represents water and earth." *

181 *Ros. phil.,* in *Art. aurif.,* II, pp. 338f.: ". . . when thou seest the earth as whitest snow . . . the ash is extracted from ash and earth, sublimed and honoured . . . the white foliated earth is the good that is sought." *

of the *albedo*,[182] is the *femina alba* of the coniunctio [183] and the "mediatrix of the whitening." [184] The lunar sulphur is white, as already mentioned. The *plenilunium* (full moon) appears to be especially important: When the moon shines in her fulness the "rabid dog", the danger that threatens the divine child,[185] is chased away. In Senior the full moon is the arcane substance.

155   In ancient tradition Luna is the giver of moisture and ruler of the water-sign Cancer (♋). Maier says that the *umbra solis* cannot be destroyed unless the sun enters the sign of Cancer, but that Cancer is the "house of Luna, and Luna is the ruler of the moisture" [186] (juice, sap, etc.). According to *Aurora consurgens* II, she is herself the water,[187] the "bountiful nurse of the dew." [188] Rahner, in his "Mysterium Lunae," shows the extensive use which the Church Fathers made of the allegory of the moon-dew in explaining the effects of grace in the ecclesiastical sacraments. Here again the patristic symbolism exerted a very strong influence on the alchemical allegories. Luna secretes the dew or sap of life. "This Luna is the sap of the water of life, which is hidden in Mercurius." [189] Even the Greek alchemists supposed there was a principle in the moon (τὴν τῆς σελήνης οὐσίαν),

182 "For the first work is towards the whitening, in the house of the Moon." * (D'Espagnet, *Arcanum Hermeticae philosophiae opus*, p. 82.)
183 The *servus rubicundus* (red slave) and the *femina alba* (white woman) form the traditional pair. The "whiteness" occurs also in Chinese alchemy and is likened to a virgin: "The white lives inside like a virgin." (Wei Po-yang, "An Ancient Chinese Treatise on Alchemy," p. 238.) For the whiteness of the moon cf. Wittekindt's translation of Song of Songs 6 : 10: "Who is that, rising like the moon, beautiful as the whiteness?" (*Das Hohe Lied*, p. 8.) *Lebānā* = whiteness, a designation for the moon in Isaiah 24 : 23 and 30 : 26.
184 Ripley, *Opera omnia*, p. 362. The same in "Gloria mundi," *Mus. herm.*, p. 217 (Waite, I, p. 176), and "Fons chymicae veritatis," *Mus. herm.*, p. 809 (Waite, II, p. 267).
185 Philaletha, "Introitus apertus," *Mus. herm.*, p. 659 (Waite, II, p. 170). See infra, pars. 182ff.
186 *Symb. aur. mensae*, p. 378.
187 *Art. aurif.*, I, p. 191.
188 "Consil. coniug.," *Ars chemica*, p. 57. Similarly "Rosinus ad Sarrat." (*Art. aurif.*, I, p. 301): "Moisture . . . from the dominion of the Moon." Macrobius says: "But there is a certain property . . . and nature in the light that flows from it, which moistens bodies and bathes them as with a hidden dew." * (*Saturnalia*, lib. VII, cap. XVI.)
189 *Mus. herm.*, p. 809 (Waite, II, p. 267).

which Christianos [190] calls the "ichor of the philosopher" (τά ὑγρὰ τοῦ φιλοσόφου).[191] The relation of the moon to the soul, much stressed in antiquity,[192] also occurs in alchemy though with a different nuance. Usually it is said that from the moon comes the dew, but the moon is also the *aqua mirifica* [193] that extracts the souls from the bodies or gives the bodies life and soul. Together with Mercurius, Luna sprinkles the dismembered dragon with her moisture and brings him to life again, "makes him live, walk, and run about, and change his colour to the nature of blood." [194] As the water of ablution, the dew falls from heaven, purifies the body, and makes it ready to receive the soul; [195] in other words, it brings about the *albedo,* the white state of innocence, which like the moon and a bride awaits the bridegroom.

156   As the alchemists were often physicians, Galen's views must surely have influenced their ideas about the moon and its effects. Galen calls Luna the "princeps" who "rightly governs this earthly realm, surpassing the other planets not in potency, but in proximity." He also makes the moon responsible for all physical changes in sickness and health, and regards its aspects as decisive for prognosis.

157   The age-old belief that the moon promotes the growth of plants led in alchemy not only to similar statements but also to the curious idea that the moon is itself a plant. Thus the *Rosarium* says that Sol is called a "great animal" whereas Luna

190 Ὁ Χριστιανός is not a proper name but only the designation by which an anonymous "Christian philosopher" was known. He was said to have been a contemporary of Stephen of Alexandria, and would thus have lived in the reign of the Emperor Heraclius, at the turn of the 6th cent.

191 He compares it to the "ever-flowing fount of Paradise." * (Berthelot, *Alch. grecs,* VI, i, 2.) In Macrobius (*In somn. scip.,* I, 11) Luna is the "author and creator of mortal bodies," * and (I, 19) "the vegetative principle, that is, growth, comes to us from the roundness of the moon." *

192 The moon receives the souls of the dead (Hegemonius, *Acta Archelai,* ed. Beeson, p. 11). The soul comes from the moon: "The moon produces the soul . . . for man's generation." * (Plutarch, "The Face on the Moon," 28, pp. 198f.) Further material in Capelle, *De luna stellis lacteo orbe animarum sedibus.*

193 "Mercurial water of the moon" and "fount of the mother." Cf. "Rosinus ad Sarrat.," *Art. aurif.,* I, p. 299.

194 Albertus Magnus, "Super arborem Aristotelis," *Theatr. chem.,* II, p. 525.

195 *Ros. phil.,* in *Art. aurif.,* II, pp. 275ff.

is a "plant." [196] In the alchemical pictures there are numerous sun-and-moon trees.[197] In the "Super arborem Aristotelis," the "circle of the moon" perches in the form of a stork on a wonder-working tree by the grave of Hermes.[198] Galen [199] explains the *arbor philosophica* as follows: "There is a certain herb or plant, named Lunatica or Berissa,[200] whose roots are metallic earth, whose stem is red, veined with black, and whose flowers are like those of the marjoram; there are thirty of them, corresponding to the age of the moon in its waxing and waning. Their colour is yellow." [201] Another name for Lunatica is Lunaria, whose flowers Dorn mentions, attributing to them miraculous powers.[202] Khunrath says: "From this little salty fountain grows also the tree of the sun and moon, the red and white coral-tree of our sea," which is that same Lunaria and whose "salt" is called "Luna Philosophorum et dulcedo sapientum" (sweetness of the sages).[203] The "Allegoriae super librum Turbae" describe the

196 Ibid., p. 243.

197 See *Psychology and Alchemy*, figs. 116 and 188. Cf. also the sun-and-moon trees of the "House of the Sun" in the *Romance of Alexander:* "Perhaps you would like to see the most holy trees of the Sun and Moon, which will declare the future to you." * (Hilka, *Der altfranzösische Prosa-Alexanderroman*, pp. 203f.)

198 *Theatr. chem.*, II, p. 527.

199 Naturally an alchemistic pseudo-Galen. Galen is credited with having written a *Liber Secretorum*, to which unfortunately I have no access.

200 Du Cange (*Glossarium ad scriptores mediae et infimae Graecitatis*, Appendix, p. 38) gives: "βήρσσα, τὸ μῶλυ, molix." The herbal of Tabernaemontanus (*Kräuterbuch*, I, p. 408) mentions "βμσασᾱ = ἄρμαλα = πήγανον ἄγριον, *Peganum sylvestre*, called μῶλυ by Galen, *Hermelraute*, often confused with hemlock. A cure for epilepsy and melancholic fantasies, makes sleepy and drunken like wine, is used in love-potions." Dioscorides (*De medica materia*, lib. III, cap. 46, p. 349) says that *Ruta sylvestris* "is called *moly* in Cappadocia and Galatia, neighboring regions of Asia." Galen (*De simplicium medicamentorum facultatibus*, lib. VII, p. 491) states: "Moly, *Ruta sylvestris*, has a black root and a milk-white flower." For "moly" see Rahner, "Die seelenheilende Blume: Moly und Mandragora in antiker und christlicher Symbolik."

201 *Aurora consurgens* II, in *Art. aurif.*, I, p. 222. The "yellow flowers" are reminiscent of the "Cheyri," the miraculous herb of Paracelsus. Cf. infra, par. 698, and "Paracelsus as a Spiritual Phenomenon," par. 171 and n. 7. In his *Labyrinthus medicorum* (Sudhoff, XI, p. 205) Paracelsus mentions the Lunatica: "Thus there is in the Lunatica the course of the whole moon, not visible, but in spirit."

202 He calls the flowers "most familiar to the philosophers." "Congeries Paracelsicae," *Theatr. chem.*, I, p. 581.

203 *Von hylealischen Chaos*, p. 270.

moon-plant thus: "In the lunar sea [204] there is a sponge planted, having blood and sentience [*sensum*],[205] in the manner of a tree that is rooted in the sea and moveth not from its place. If thou wouldst handle the plant, take a sickle to cut it with, but have good care that the blood floweth not out, for it is the poison of the Philosophers." [206]

158   From all this it would seem that the moon-plant is a kind of mandrake and has nothing to do with the botanical Lunaria (honesty). In the herbal of Tabernaemontanus, in which all the magico-medicinal properties of plants are carefully listed, there is no mention of the alchemical Lunatica or Lunaria. On the other hand it is evident that the Lunatica is closely connected with the "tree of the sea" in Arabian alchemy [207] and hence with the *arbor philosophica*,[208] which in turn has parallels with the

204 * I have not been able to find a parallel for "maris Luna." "Sea" always signifies the solvent, i.e., the *aqua permanens*. In it Sol bathes, is immersed or drowned, often alone. The parallel to Luna in the bath, as we have shown above (n. 157), is Diana. But she never drowns in her bath, because she is the water itself.

205 "Spongia" means not only sponge but also pumice-stone, which has the same porous structure. Thus the "Liber quartorum" (*Theatr. chem.*, V, p. 190) says: "But that which is a vapour or subtlety in those parts is retained only by a hard body . . . and whenever there is a stone which surrounds the substances like a sponge." * Possibly referring to this passage Mylius (*Phil. ref.*, p. 107) writes: "The Sun and Moon are calcined philosophically with the first water, that the bodies may be opened and become spongy and subtle, and the second water enter more easily." * Ruland (*Lexicon*, p. 300) takes over from Dioscorides (*De medica materia*, lib. V, cap. 96, p. 625) the differentiation of sponges into male (one species of which is called *tragos*, 'goat') and female. Their ashes were used as a styptic. Ruland adds, from Avicenna, that sponges "have souls," by which he probably meant the vapours they produce when they are warmed. But then, for the alchemists, "anima" always had a special meaning which Avicenna formulates as follows: "The higher part is the soul, which quickens the whole stone and makes it live again." * Ruland stresses that sponges have "understanding" (*intellectum*) because they contract when they hear a noise or are touched. He regards the sponge as "a zoophyte, neither animal nor vegetable, but having a third nature." *

206 *Art. aurif.*, I, p. 141.

207 Cf. *Psychology and Alchemy*, par. 537, where the text of Abu'l-Qāsim (*Kitāb al-'ilm al-muktasab*) is cited in Holmyard's translation.

208 See *Psychology and Alchemy*, figs. 122, 131, 135, 186, 188. Ventura: "The roots of its ores are in the air and its summits in the earth. And when they are torn from their places, a horrible sound is heard and there follows a great fear. Wherefore go quickly, for they quickly vanish." * (*Theatr. chem.*, II, p. 257.) This obviously refers to the mandragora, which shrieks when it is pulled out. See "The Philosophical Tree," par. 380, n. 4, and pars. 410ff.

Cabalistic tree of the Sefiroth [209] and with the tree of Christian mysticism [210] and Hindu philosophy.[211]

159   Ruland's remark that the sponge "has understanding" (see n. 205) and Khunrath's that the essence of the Lunaria is the "sweetness of the sages" point to the general idea that the moon has some secret connection with the human mind.[212] The alchemists have a great deal to say about this, and this is the more interesting as we know that the moon is a favourite symbol for certain aspects of the unconscious—though only, of course, in a man. In a woman the moon corresponds to consciousness and the sun to the unconscious. This is due to the contrasexual archetype in the unconscious: anima in a man, animus in a woman.

209 Here the tree is God himself: "The purpose of the Creation was, that God should be known as Lord and Ruler; He, the stem and root of the world." (*Zohar* I, fol. 11b, as cited by Hamburger, *Encyclopädie der Judentums*, II.) Joseph Gikatila says: "Know that the holy names of God found in the Scriptures are all dependent on the four-letter name YHVH. Should you object that the name Ehyeh is the ground and the source, know that the four-letter name may be likened to the trunk of a tree, whereas the name Ehyeh is the root of this tree. From it, further roots and branches extend in every direction." (Winter and Wünsche, *Die Jüdische Literatur seit Abschluss des Kanons*, III, p. 267.) Of the "crown" (Kether) it is said: "It is the source which makes the tree fruitful and drives the sap through all its arms and branches. For You, Lord of the worlds, You who are the ground of all grounds, the cause of all causes, You water the tree from that source, which, like the soul in the body, spreads life everywhere." (*Tikkune Zohar*, as cited by Joel, *Die Religionsphilosophie des Sohar*, pp. 308f., and Bischoff, *Elemente der Kabbalah*, I, p. 82.)

210 John of Ruysbroeck (1294–1381) says of the tree of Zacchaeus (Luke 19): "And he must climb up into the tree of faith, which grows from above downwards, for its roots are in the Godhead. This tree has twelve branches, which are the twelve articles of faith. The lower speak of the Divine Humanity, and of those things which belong to our salvation of soul and of body. The upper part of the tree tells of the Godhead, of the Trinity of Persons, and of the Unity of the Nature of God. And the man must cling to that unity, in the highest part of the tree; for there it is that Jesus must pass with all his gifts." (*The Adornment of the Spiritual Marriage*, trans. by Wynschenk Dom, pp. 47f.)

211 *Katha Upanishad*, II, 6, 1 (SBE, XV, p. 21): "There is that ancient tree, whose roots grow upward and whose branches grow downward—that indeed is called the Bright, that is called Brahman, that alone is called the Immortal. All worlds are contained in it, and no one goes beyond."

212 The Sanskrit word *manas* means 'mind'. It includes all intellectual as well as emotional processes, and can therefore mean, on the one hand, understanding, intellect, reflection, thought, etc., and, on the other, soul, heart, conscience, desire, will, etc. *Manas* is an organ of the inner "soul," or *atman*. (MacDonell, *A Sanskrit-*

160   In the gnosis of Simon Magus, Helen (Selene) is πρώτη ἔννοια,[213] sapientia,[214] and ἐπίνοια.[215] The last designation also occurs in Hippolytus: "For Epinoia herself dwelt in Helen at that time." [216] In his Ἀπόφασις μεγάλη ("Great Explanation"), Simon says:

> There are two offshoots from all the Aeons, having neither beginning nor end, from one root, and this root is a certain Power [δύναμις], an invisible and incomprehensible Silence [σιγή]. One of them appears on high and is a great power, the mind of the whole [νοῦς τῶν ὅλων], who rules all things and is a male; the other below is a great Thought [ἐπίνοια μεγάλη], a female giving birth to all things. Standing opposite one another, they pair together and cause to arise in the space between them an incomprehensible Air, without beginning or end; but in it is a Father who upholds all things and nourishes that which has beginning and end. This is he who stood, stands, and shall stand, a masculo-feminine Power after the likeness of the pre-existing boundless Power which has neither beginning nor end, abiding in solitude [μονότητι].[217]

161   This passage is remarkable for several reasons. It describes a *coniunctio Solis et Lunae* which Simon, it seems, concretized in his own life with Helen, the harlot of Tyre, in her role as Ishtar. As a result of the pairing with the *soror* or *filia mystica*, there was begotten a masculo-feminine pneuma, curiously designated "Air." Since pneuma, like spirit, originally meant air in motion, this designation sounds archaic or else deliberately physicistic. It is evident, however, that air is used here in the

---

English Dictionary, s.v. *manas*). Rig-veda, X, 90, 13 (trans. by Griffith, II, p. 519) says: "The Moon was gendered from his mind, and from his eye the Sun had birth." This refers to the two eyes of Purusha, the macrocosmic Primordial Man (Anthropos), who created the world by transforming himself into it—a very primitive concept which perhaps underlies the "generation by adaptation" mentioned in the "Tabula smaragdina" (infra, par. 162). *Brihadaranyaka Upanishad* (I, 3, 16) says: "When the mind had become freed from death, it became the moon" (trans. by Max Müller, II, p. 81).

213 Bousset, *Hauptprobleme der Gnosis*, p. 78. Ἔννοια means 'thought, conception, reflection, view', also 'meaning', and, as contrasted with ἄνοια (thoughtlessness), could be translated by the modern terms 'insight' and 'consciousness', while ἄνοια is in certain places (for instance in the *Corpus Hermeticum*) fittingly rendered by 'unconsciousness'. In Orphism, Selene is the "all-wise maiden."

214 Clement of Rome, *Recognitiones* (Migne, P.G., vol. 1, col. 1254).

215 'Notion, invention, purpose, design'.   216 *Elenchos*, VI, 19, 2.

217 Ibid., 18, 2. (Cf. Legge, II, p. 13.)

spiritual sense of pneuma since its progenitors bear names—
νοῦς, ἔννοια, ἐπίνοια—which have a noetic character and thus pertain
to the spiritual sphere. Of these three names Nous is the most
general concept, and in Simon's day it was used indiscriminately
with pneuma. Ennoia and Epinoia mean nothing that could not
be rendered just as well by Nous; they differ from the latter
only in their special character, emphasizing the more specific
contents of the inclusive term Nous. Further, they are both of
the feminine gender required in this context, whereas Nous is
masculine. All three indicate the essential similarity of the
components of the syzygy and their "spiritual" nature.

162   Anyone familiar with alchemy will be struck by the resemblance between Simon's views and the passage in the "Tabula
smaragdina":

And as all things proceed from the One, through the meditation
of the One, so all things proceed from this one thing, by adaptation.[218]

Its father is the Sun, its mother the Moon; the wind hath carried
it in his belly.[219]

163   Since "all things" proceed from the meditation of the One,
this is true also of Sol and Luna, who are thus endowed with an
originally pneumatic character. They stand for the primordial
images of the spirit, and their mating produces the *filius macrocosmi*. Sol and Luna in later alchemy are undoubtedly arcane
substances and volatilia, i.e., spirits.[220]

164   We will now see what the texts have to say about Luna's
noetic aspect. The yield is astonishingly small; nevertheless there
is the following passage in the *Rosarium:*

218 Ruska rightly rejects "adoptione" as a variant. By "things" the alchemists understood "substances." The "adaptation" process is reminiscent of the notion,
found especially among the Australian aborigines, that the Original Being changed
himself into the things and creatures of this world. The striking use of the neuter
pronoun "illud" is easily explained by the hermaphroditism of the product, which
is constantly stressed.

219 Ruska, *Tabula Smaragdina*, p. 2.* Senior says of this text (*De chemia*, p. 30f.):
"Air is a mediator between fire (= Sol) and water (= Luna) by reason of its heat
and moisture." "Air is the life of everything." "The son of wisdom is born in the
air." *

220 Cf. Senior, p. 20: ". . . spirit and soul, when they shall have been boiled down
in the repetition of the distillation, will be mixed together in a universal mixture,
and the one will retain the other and they will become one. One in subtlety and
spirituality . . ." *

Unless ye slay me, your understanding will not be perfect, and in my sister the moon the degree of your wisdom increases, and not with another of my servants, even if ye know my secret.[221]

Mylius copies out this sentence uncritically in his *Philosophia reformata*.[222] Both he and the *Rosarium* give the source as the "Metaphora Belini de sole.". [223] The "Dicta Belini" are included in the "Allegoriae sapientum," but there the passage runs:

I announce therefore to all you sages, that unless ye slay me, ye cannot be called sages. But if ye slay me, your understanding will be perfect, and it increases in my sister the moon according to the degree of our wisdom, and not with another of my servants, even if ye know my secret.[224]

Belinus, as Ruska is probably right in conjecturing, is the same as Apollonius of Tyana,[225] to whom some of the sermons in the *Turba* are attributed. In Sermo 32, "Bonellus" discusses the problem of death and transformation, likewise touched on in our text. The other sermons of Bonellus have nothing to do with our text, however, nor does the motif of resurrection, on account of its ubiquity, signify much, so that the "Dicta" in all probability have no connection with the *Turba*. A more likely source for the "Dicta" would be the (Harranite?) treatise of Artefius, "Clavis maioris sapientiae": [226] "Our master, the philosopher Belenius, said, Set your light in a vessel of clear glass, and observe that all the wisdom of this world revolves round the following three . . ." [227] And again: "But one day my master, the philosopher Bolemus, called me and said, Eh! my son, I hope

---

221 "Nisi me interfeceritis, intellectus vester non erit perfectus, et in sorore mea Luna crescit gradus sapientiae vestrae, et non cum alio ex servis meis, etsi sciretis secretum meum." *Art. aurif.*, II, p. 380. The "servants" refer to the planets, or to the corresponding metals.

222 P. 175. Here he cites this sentence as coming from the "Epistola Solis ad Lunam," which is in Senior, *De chemia*, pp. 7ff., but it does not occur there.

223 Mylius, *Phil. ref.*, p. 309, and *Ros. phil.*, in *Art. aurif.*, II, p. 378.

224 "Nuncio ergo vobis omnibus sapientibus, quod nisi me interficiatis, non potestis sapientes nuncupari. Si vero me interfeceritis, intellectus vester erit perfectus, et in sorore mea crescit luna, secundum gradum sapientiae nostrae et non cum alio ex servis meis, etsi sciretis secretum meum." (*Theatr. chem.*, V, pp. 96ff.)

225 Other corruptions of the name are Bolemus, Belenius, Balinas, Bellus, Bonellus.

226 *Theatr. chem.*, IV, p. 221.

227 * The "three" refers to the three ways of combining souls: in the body, in the soul, in the spirit.

that thou art a man of spiritual understanding and canst attain to the highest degree of wisdom." [228] Then follows an explanation about how two contrary natures, active and passive, arose from the first simple substance. In the beginning God said "without uttering a word," "Let there be such a creature," and thereupon the simple (*simplex*) was there. Then God created nature or the prima materia, "the first passive or receptive [principle], in which everything was present in principle and in potency." In order to end this state of suspension God created the "*causa agens,* like to the circle of heaven, which he resolved to call Light. But this Light received a certain sphere, the first creature, within its hollowness." The properties of this sphere were heat and motion. It was evidently the sun, whereas the cold and passive principle would correspond to the moon.[229]

165   It seems to me not unlikely that the "Dicta Belini" are connected with this passage from Artefius rather than with the *Turba,* since they have nothing to do with the sermons of Apollonius. They may therefore represent a tradition independent of the *Turba,* and this is the more likely since Artefius seems to have been a very ancient author of Arabic provenance.[230] He shares the doctrine of the "simplex" with the "Liber quartorum," [231] which too is probably of Harranite origin. I mention his theory of the creation here despite the fact that it has no parallels in the "Dicta." It seemed to me worth noting because of its inner connection with the "Apophasis megale" of Simon Magus. The "Dicta" are not concerned with the original separa-

228 *

229 I cannot refrain from pointing out the remarkable analogy that exists between Simon of Gitta and Pseudo-Apollonius on the one hand, and Lao-tzu on the other, with regard to the *principia mundi.* The components of *tao* are the masculine *yang* and the feminine *yin,* the one hot, bright, and dry like the sun, the other cold, dark, and moist like the (new) moon. The *Tao Teh Ching* (ch. 25) says of the Original Being:

> "There was something formless yet complete
> that existed before heaven and earth;
> Without sound, without substance,
> Dependent on nothing, unchanging,
> All pervading, unfailing.
> One may think of it as the mother of all things under heaven."
>
> (*The Way and Its Power,* trans. Waley, p. 174.)

230 He may even be identical with Senior. Cf. Stapleton and Husain, "Muhammad bin Umail," p. 126, n. 2.   231 *Theatr. chem.,* V, pp. 114ff.

tion of the natures but rather with the synthesis which bears much the same relation to the sublimation of the human mind (*exaltatio intellectus*) as the procedures of the "Liber quartorum." [232]

166   Besides the connection between Luna and intellect we must also consider their relation to Mercurius, for in astrology and mythology Mercurius is the divine factor that has most to do with Epinoia. The connections between them in alchemy have classical antecedents. Leaving aside the relation of Hermes to the Nous, I will only mention that in Plutarch Hermes sits in the moon and goes round with it (just as Heracles does in the sun).[233] In the magic papyri, Hermes is invoked as follows: "O Hermes, ruler of the world, thou who dwellest in the heart, circle of the moon, round and square." [234]

167   In alchemy Mercurius is the rotundum *par excellence*. Luna is formed of his cold and moist nature, and Sol of the hot and dry; [235] alternatively she is called "the proper substance of Mercurius." [236] From Luna comes the *aqua Mercurialis* or *aqua permanens;* [237] with her moisture, like Mercurius, she brings the slain dragon to life.[238] As we have seen, the circle of the moon is mentioned in the "Super arborem Aristotelis," where "a stork, as it were calling itself the circle of the moon," sits on a tree that is green within instead of without.[239] Here it is worth pointing out that the soul, whose connection with the moon has already been discussed, was also believed to be round. Thus Caesarius of Heisterbach says that the soul has a "spherical nature," "after the likeness of the globe of the moon." [240]

232 Cf. *Psychology and Alchemy*, pars. 366ff.

233 "Isis and Osiris," cap. 41, *Moralia* (trans. Babbitt), V, pp. 100f.

234 Preisendanz, *Pap. Graec. Mag.,* II, p. 139.*

235 "Gloria mundi," *Mus. herm.,* p. 266 (Waite, I, p. 215).

236 Mylius, *Phil. ref.,* p. 185; similarly in "Epist. ad Hermannum," *Theatr. chem.,* V, p. 893.   237 "Rosinus ad Sarrat." *Art. aurif.,* I, p. 299.

238 *Theatr. chem.,* II, p. 525.

239 Ibid., p. 527. Concerning the significance of the stork the "Aureum vellus" (*Theatr. chem.,* V, p. 446) says: "The stork devours serpents, and its flesh is profitable against all poisons." * The stork is therefore a dragon-killer and a symbol of the demon-conquering moon. This symbol is also an attribute of the Church.

240 *Dialogue on Miracles*, IV, 39 (trans. by Scott and Bland, I, p. 236). The moon is related to the soul by the further fact that it is the "receptacle of souls." Cf. Hegemonius, *Acta Archelai,* VIII.

168   Let us now turn back to the question raised by the quotation in the *Rosarium* from the "Dicta Belini." It is one of those approximate quotations which are typical of the *Rosarium*.[241] In considering the quotation as a whole it should be noted that it is not clear who the speaker is. The *Rosarium* supposes that it is Sol. But it can easily be shown from the context of the "Dicta" that the speaker could just as well be the filius Philosophorum, since the woman is sometimes called "soror," sometimes "mater," and sometimes "uxor." This strange relationship is explained by the primitive fact that the son stands for the reborn father, a motif familiar to us from the Christian tradition. The speaker is therefore the father-son, whose mother is the son's sister-wife. "According to the degree of our wisdom" is contrasted with "your understanding;" it therefore refers to the wisdom of the *Sol redivivus,* and presumably also to his sister the moon, hence "our" and not "my" wisdom. "The degree" is not only plausible but is a concept peculiar to the opus, since Sol passes through various stages of transformation from the dragon, lion, and eagle [242] to the hermaphrodite. Each of these stages stands for a new degree of insight, wisdom, and initiation, just as the Mithraic eagles, lions, and sun-messengers signify grades of initiation. "Unless ye slay me" usually refers to the slaying of the dragon, the *mortificatio* of the first, dangerous, poisonous stage of the anima ($=$ Mercurius), freed from her imprisonment in the prima materia.[243] This anima is also identified with Sol.[244] Sol is frequently called Rex, and there is a picture showing him being killed by ten men.[245] He thus suffers the same *mortificatio* as the dragon, with the difference that it is never a suicide. For Sol, in so far as the dragon is a preliminary form of the *filius Solis,* is in a sense the father of the dragon, although the latter is expressly said to beget itself and

241 Cf. *Psychology and Alchemy,* par. 140, n. 17, par. 220, n. 108, par. 385, n. 87.

242 Cf. Kalid, "Liber trium verborum," ch. VI, *Art. aurif.,* I (1593), pp. 357f.

243 "The dragon is born in the blackness and . . . kills itself." * *Ros. phil.,* in *Art. aurif.,* II, p. 230. The "soul in chains" occurs as early as the treatise of Sophe, the Egyptian: "the divine soul bound in the elements." Berthelot, III, xlii, 1, line 17.

244 "We place the soul of the world especially in the sun." * Mylius, *Phil. ref.,* p. 10.

245 See Fig. 8 in Mylius, p. 359, and Figura CI in Stolcenberg, *Viridarium chymicum.*

is thus an increatum.[246] At the same time Sol, being his own son, is also the dragon. Accordingly there is a *coniugium* of the dragon and the woman, who can only be Luna or the lunar (feminine) half of Mercurius.[247] As much as Sol, therefore, Luna (as the mother) must be contained in the dragon. To my knowledge there is never any question of her *mortificatio* in the sense of a slaying. Nevertheless she is included with Sol in the death of the dragon, as the *Rosarium* hints: "The dragon dieth not, except with his brother and his sister."[248]

169   The idea that the dragon or Sol must die is an essential part of the mystery of transformation. The *mortificatio,* this time only in the form of a mutilation, is also performed on the lion, whose paws are cut off,[249] and on the bird, whose wings are clipped.[250] It signifies the overcoming of the old and obsolete as well as of the dangerous preliminary stages which are characterized by animal-symbols.

170   In interpreting the words "your understanding increases in my sister," etc., it is well to remember that a philosophical interpretation of myths had already grown up among the Stoics, which today we should not hesitate to describe as psychological. This work of interpretation was not interrupted by the development of Christianity but continued to be assiduously practised in a rather different form, namely in the hermeneutics of the Church Fathers, which was to have a decided influence on alchemical symbolism. The Johannine interpretation of Christ as the pre-worldly Logos is an early attempt of this kind to put into other words the "meaning" of Christ's essence. The later medievalists, and in particular the natural philosophers, made the Sapientia Dei the nucleus of their interpretation of nature and thus created a new nature-myth. In this they were very much influenced by the writings of the Arabs and of the Harranites, the last exponents of Greek philosophy and gnosis, whose chief representative was Tabit ibn Qurra in the tenth century. One of these writings, the "Liber Platonis quartorum," is a dialogue in which Thebed (Tabit) speaks in person. In this

246 Cf. *Psychology and Alchemy*, pars. 430f.

247 See the final Emblema in Maier's *Scrutinium chymicum*, p. 148.

248 *Art. aurif.,* II, p. 224.* The passage occurs again on p. 241, with the added words: "That is, with Sol and Luna."

249 As in the frontispiece of *Le Songe de Poliphile* (*Psychology and Alchemy,* fig. 4).   250 Senior, *De chemia,* p. 15.

treatise the intellect as a tool of natural philosophy plays a role that we do not meet again until the sixteenth century, in Gerhard Dorn. Pico della Mirandola appeals to the psychological interpretation of the ancients and mentions that the "Greek Platonists" described Sol as διάνοια [251] and Luna as δόξα,[252] terms that are reminiscent of Simon's Nous and Epinoia.[253] Pico himself defines the difference as that between "scientia" and "opinio." [254] He thinks that the mind (*animus*), turning towards the spirit (*spiritus*) of God, shines and is therefore called Sol. The spirit of God corresponds to the *aquae superiores,* the "waters above the firmament" (Gen. 1 : 7). But in so far as the human mind turns towards the "waters under the firmament" (*aquae inferiores*), it concerns itself with the "sensuales potentiae," "whence it contracts the stain of infection" and is called Luna.[255] In both cases it is clearly the human spirit or psyche, both of which have, however, a double aspect, one facing upwards to the light, the other downwards to the darkness ruled by the moon ("The sun to rule the day, the moon also to govern the night"). "And while," says Pico, "we wander far from our fatherland and abide in this night and darkness of our present life, we make most use of that which turns us aside to the senses, for which reason we think many things rather than know them," [256]—a pessimistic but no doubt accurate view that fully accords with the spiritual benightedness and sinful darkness of this sublunary world, which is so black that the moon herself is tarnished by it.

171   The moon appears to be in a disadvantageous position compared with the sun. The sun is a concentrated luminary: "The day is lit by a single sun." The moon, on the other hand—"as if less powerful"—needs the help of the stars when it comes to the task of "composition and separation, rational reflection, definition," etc.[257] The appetites, as "potentiae sensuales," pertain to

---

251 'Thought, intellect, mind'.

252 'Opinion, view, notion'. Pico adds: "According to the principles of their teaching." "Heptaplus," *Opera omnia,* Lib. IV, cap. IV, p. 32.

253 In the same place Pico mentions that Plato and "certain younger" philosophers interpreted Sol as "active intellect, but the Moon [as] potential intellect." *

254 Ibid.   255 Ibid.   256 Ibid.

257 Ibid. Cf. the idea of the "inner firmament" as a symbol of the unconscious. "Nature of the Psyche," pars. 390f., and "Paracelsus the Physician," pars. 29ff.

the sphere of the moon; they are anger (*ira*) and desire (*libido*) or, in a word, *concupiscentia*. The passions are designated by animals because we have these things in common with them, and, "what is more unfortunate, they often drive us into leading a bestial life." [258] According to Pico, Luna "has an affinity with Venus, as is particularly to be seen from the fact that she is sublimated in Taurus, the House of Venus, so much that she nowhere else appears more auspicious and more beneficent." [259] Taurus is the house of the hierogamy of Sol and Luna.[260] Indeed, Pico declares that the moon is "the lowest earth and the most ignoble of all the stars," [261] an opinion which recalls Aristotle's comparison of the moon with the earth. The moon, says Pico, is inferior to all the other planets.[262] The novilunium is especially unfavourable, as it robs growing bodies of their nourishment and in this way injures them.[263]

172   Psychologically, this means that the union of consciousness (Sol) with its feminine counterpart the unconscious (Luna) has undesirable results to begin with: it produces poisonous animals such as the dragon, serpent, scorpion, basilisk, and toad; [264] then the lion, bear, wolf, dog,[265] and finally the eagle [266] and the

258 Cap. V. Pico adds: "Hence this saying of the Chaldees: The beasts of the earth inhabit thy vessel, and in Plato's Republic we learn that we have at home divers kinds of brutes." * Cf. the text from Origen supra, par. 6, n. 26. The English mystic John Pordage speaks in his *Sophia* (p. 108 of the Dutch edn., 1699) of the "horrible people" in the soul.

259 "Heptaplus," Lib. II, cap. III, p. 20.

260 Cf. Dee, "Monas hieroglyphica," *Theatr. chem.*, II, p. 219: "And when the semi-circle of the moon was brought to be the complement of the sun, there was evening and there was morning, one day. Be that (day) therefore the first, on which was made the light of the Philosophers." * The union of ⊙ and ☽ gives the sign for Taurus, ♉, ruler of the house of Venus. The marriage of day (sun) and night (moon) is the reason for the rather rare designation of the lapis as the "filius unius diei" (son of one day). See infra, pars. 472ff.

261 "We hold therefore the moon to be the lowest earth and the most ignoble of all stars, as is the earth, very like to it by the opacity of all its elements, and by its blemishes." * ("Heptaplus," Lib. II, cap. II, p. 18.)

262 "And we know the moon to be inferior to all." * ("In Astrologiam," X, iv, *Opera omnia*, I, p. 685.)

263 Ibid., III, v, p. 461f.

264 A milder form of these is the salamander.

265 Often mentioned as the "Corascene dog" (sun) and the "Armenian bitch" (moon). See infra, section B.

266 Said to devour its own wings or feathers. The eagle is therefore a variant of the uroboros.

raven. The first to appear are the cold-blooded animals, then warm-blooded predators, and lastly birds of prey or ill-omened scavengers. The first progeny of the *matrimonium luminarium* are all, therefore, rather unpleasant. But that is only because there is an evil darkness in both parents which comes to light in the children, as indeed often happens in real life. I remember, for instance, the case of a twenty-year-old bank clerk who embezzled several hundred francs. His old father, the chief cashier at the same bank, was much pitied, because for forty years he had discharged his highly responsible duties with exemplary loyalty. Two days after the arrest of his son he decamped to South America with a million. So there must have been "something in the family." We have seen in the case of Sol that he either possesses a shadow or is even a *Sol niger*. As to the position of Luna, we have already been told what this is when we discussed the new moon. In the "Epistola Solis ad Lunam crescentem" [267] Sol cautiously says: "If you do me no hurt, O moon." [268] Luna has promised him complete dissolution while she herself "coagulates," i.e., becomes firm, and is clothed with his blackness (*induta fuero nigredine tua*).[269] She assumes in the friendliest manner that her blackness comes from *him*. The matrimonial wrangle has already begun. Luna is the "shadow of the sun, and with corruptible bodies she is consumed, and through her corruption . . . is the Lion eclipsed." [270]

173   According to the ancient view, the moon stands on the border-line between the eternal, aethereal things and the ephemeral phenomena of the earthly, sublunar realm.[271] Macrobius says: "The realm of the perishable begins with the moon and goes downwards. Souls coming into this region begin to be subject to the numbering of days and to time. . . . There is no doubt that the moon is the author and contriver of mortal bodies." [272] Because of her moist nature, the moon is also the cause of

---

267 Senior, *De chemia,* p. 9.

268 Sol is mindful of the dangerous role of Luna: "No one torments me but my sister." ("Exercitationes in Turbam," *Art. aurif.,* I, p. 173.)

269 Song of Songs 1 : 5: "I am black, but comely," and 1 : 6: ". . . I am black because the sun has burnt me" is sometimes quoted.

270 "Consil. coniugii," *Ars chemica,* p. 136.*

271 *Commentary on the Dream of Scipio,* I, xxi, p. 181: "The moon, being the boundary of ether and air, is also the demarcation between the divine and the mortal." *   272 Ibid., I, xi, p. 131.*

decay.[273] The loveliness of the new moon, hymned by the poets and Church Fathers, veils her dark side, which however could not remain hidden from the fact-finding eye of the empiricist.[274] The moon, as the star nearest to the earth, partakes of the earth and its sufferings, and her analogy with the Church and the Virgin Mary as mediators has the same meaning.[275] She partakes not only of the earth's sufferings but of its daemonic darkness as well.[276]

b. The Dog

174   This dark side of the moon is hinted at in the ancient invocation to Selene as the "dog" or "bitch" (κυών), in the Magic Papyri.[277] There it is also said that in the second hour Helios appears as a dog.[278] This statement is of interest in so far as the "symbolizatio" [279] by the dog [280] entered Western alchemy

273 The heat and dew of the moon "turn flesh rotten." Macrobius, *Saturnalia*, lib. VII, cap. XVI.

274 The empirical method of physicians is a heresy, according to Isidore of Seville (*Liber etymologiarum*, IV, cap. IV, fol. xxir). There are three medical heresies, and of this one he says: "The second empirical method, the method of trial and error, was discovered by Aesculapius." *

275 Cf. Rahner, "Das christliche Mysterium von Sonne und Mond," p. 400.

276 The mediating position of the moon and the Church is mentioned by the alchemist William Mennens ("Aureum vellus," *Theatr. chem.*, V, p. 460): "[This] comes about when the light of the Moon begins to increase up to its fifteenth day and then to decrease until its thirtieth, returning then into the horns, until no light at all appears in it. According to this view, the Moon in allegory . . . signifies the Church, which is bright on its spiritual side, but dark on its carnal." * Note the due emphasis he lays on the two aspects of the Moon. This is the spirit of scientific truth as contrasted with the retouchings of the kerygmatic point of view, which plays such an unfortunate role in the two great Christian confessions.

277 Preisendanz, *Pap. Graec. Mag.*, I, p. 142, Pap. IV, line 2280. It is also said that Selene has the voice of a dog. (Pap. IV line 2810, p. 162, and IV, line 2550, p. 152.) Her confusion with Hecate naturally makes this attribute all the stronger. (Cf. Siecke, *Beiträge zur genauen Kenntnis der Mondgottheit bei den Griechen*, pp. 14f.) In the Iliad, VI, 344 Helen calls herself a "nasty, mean-minded bitch" (κυνὸς κακομηχάνου ὀκρυοέσσης). Κύνες are the pert, wanton maids of Penelope.

278 Line 1695, p. 126. In the twelfth hour he appears as a crocodile. Cf. the "dragon-son of the sun."

279 This term occurs in ch. 9 of the "Dialogus philosophiae" of Aegidius de Vadis (*Theatr. chem.*, II, p. 107). "Symbolizatio" is the drawing of parallels and analogies —in brief, an amplification, described by Clement of Alexandria (*Stromata*, V, 46, trans. Wilson, II, p. 248) as "symbolic interpretation."

280 In the history of symbols the dog is distinguished by an uncommonly wide range of associations, which I will not attempt to exhaust here. The Gnostic

through Kalid's "Liber secretorum," originally, perhaps, an Arabic treatise. All similar passages that I could find go back, directly or indirectly, to Kalid.[281] The original passage runs:

> Hermes [282] said, My son, take a Corascene dog and an Armenian bitch, join them together, and they will beget a dog of celestial hue, and if ever he is thirsty, give him sea water to drink: for he will guard your friend, and he will guard you from your enemy, and he will help you wherever you may be, always being with you, in this world and in the next. And by dog and bitch, Hermes meant things which preserve bodies from burning and from the heat of the fire.[283]

Some of the quotations are taken from the original text, others from the variant in the *Rosarium*, which runs:

> Hali, philosopher and king of Arabia, says in his Secret: Take a Coetenean [284] dog and an Armenian bitch, join them together, and they two will beget for you a puppy [*filius canis*] of celestial hue: and that puppy will guard you in your house from the beginning, in this world and in the next.[285]

As explanatory parallels, the *Rosarium* mentions the union of the white and red, and cites Senior: "The red slave has wedded the white woman." It is clear that the mating must refer to the royal marriage of Sol and Luna.

175   The theriomorphic form of Sol as a lion and dog and of Luna as a bitch shows that there is an aspect of both luminaries which justifies the need for a "symbolizatio" in animal form. That is to

---

parallel *Logos / canis* is reflected in the Christian one, *Christus / canis*, handed down in the formula "gentle to the elect, terrible to the reprobate," a "true pastor." * St. Gregory says: "Or what others are called the watch-dogs of this flock, save the holy doctors?" * (*Moralia in Job*, XX, vi, 15; Migne, *P.L.*, vol. 76, col. 145.) Also to be borne in mind is the "Indian dog," a quadruped on the earth but a fish in water. This ability to change its shape makes it an allegory of St. Paul. (All this and more can be found in Picinellus, *Mundus symbolicus*, I, pp. 352ff., s.v. *canis*.) In the *Hieroglyphics of Horapollo* (Boas trans., No. 39, p. 77) emphasis is laid on the dog's power to spread infection, especially rabies and diseases of the spleen. Because of its rich symbolic context the dog is an apt synonym for the transforming substance.

281 Khalid ibn Jazid (c. 700), an Omayyad prince. The "Liber secretorum" is ascribed to him. The text is quoted in *Theatr. chem.*, IV, p. 859.

282 One of the many Hermes quotations whose origins are obscure.

283 *Art. aurif.*, I, pp. 340f.*

284 Cf. "Psychology of the Transference," par. 353, n. 1.

285 *Art. aurif.*, II, p. 248.* This passage is cited in *Theatr. chem.*, IV, p. 832.

say the two luminaries are, in a sense, animals or appetites, although, as we have seen, the "potentiae sensuales" are ascribed only to Luna. There is, however, also a *Sol niger,* who, significantly enough, is contrasted with the day-time sun and clearly distinguished from it. This advantage is not shared by Luna, because she is obviously sometimes bright and sometimes dark. Psychologically, this means that consciousness by its very nature distinguishes itself from its shadow, whereas the unconscious is not only contaminated with its own negative side but is burdened with the shadow cast off by the conscious mind. Although the solar animals, the lion and the eagle, are nobler than the bitch, they are nevertheless animals and beasts of prey at that, which means that even our sun-like consciousness has its dangerous animals. Or, if Sol is the spirit and Luna the body, the spirit too may be corrupted by pride or concupiscence, a fact which we are inclined to overlook in our one-sided admiration of the "spirit."

176   Kalid's "son of the dog" is the same as the much extolled "son of the philosophers." The ambiguity of this figure is thus stressed: it is at once bright as day and dark as night, a perfect *coincidentia oppositorum* expressing the divine nature of the self. This thought, which seems an impossible one for our Christian feelings, is nevertheless so logical and so irresistible that, by however strange and devious a route, it forced its way into alchemy. And because it is a natural truth it is not at all surprising that it became articulate very much earlier. We are told in the *Elenchos* of Hippolytus that, according to Aratus,

Cynosura [286] is the [little] Bear, the Second Creation, the small, narrow way,[287] and not the great Bear [ἡ ἐλίκη]. For it leads not backward, but guides those who follow it forward to the straight way, being the tail of the Dog. *For the Logos is a dog* [κύων γαρ ὁ λόγος] who guards and protects the sheep against the wiles of the wolves, and chases the wild beasts from Creation and slays them, and begets all things. For Cyon [κύων], they say, means the Begetter.[288]

[286] Κυνόσουρα means 'dog's tail' and denotes the constellation of the Little Bear.
[287] Perhaps a reference to Matthew 7 : 14: ". . . strait is the gate, and narrow is the way, which leadeth unto life."
[288] *Elenchos,* IV, 48, 10 (cf. Legge, I, p. 112). Κύειν means 'to be pregnant', also 'beget'. The related verb κυνεῖν means 'to kiss'.

Aratus associates the Dog with the growth of plants, and continues:

> But with the rising of the Dog-star, the living are distinguished by the Dog from the dead, for in truth everything withers that has not taken root. *This Dog, they say, being a certain divine Logos,* has been established judge of the quick and the dead, and as the Dog is seen to be the star of the plants, so is the Logos, they say, in respect of the heavenly plants, which are men. For this reason the Second Creation Cynosura stands in heaven as an image of the rational creature [λογικῆς κτίσεως]. But between the two Creations stretches the Dragon, hindering anything of the Great Creation from entering the lesser, and watching over everything that exists [τὰ καθεστη-κότα] in the Great Creation, like the Kneeler,[289] observing how and in what manner each thing exists [καθέστηκε] in the Lesser Creation.

177   Kalid's *filius canis* [290] is "of celestial hue," an indication of its heavenly origin from the great luminaries. The blue colour or likeness to a dog [291] is also attributed to the woman who in Hippolytus is described as περεηφικόλα,[292] and who is pursued by a grey-haired, winged, ithyphallic old man (πρεσβύτης). He is named φάος ῥυέντης, Flowing Light, and she is ἡ φικόλα, "which means Dark Water" (τὸ σκοτεινὸν ὕδωρ).[293] Behind these figures may be discerned a *coniunctio Solis et Lunae,* both the sun and the new moon appearing in their unfavourable aspect. Here too there arises between them the "harmony" of an intermediary spirit (πνεῦματος), roughly corresponding to the position of the *filius philosophorum.*[293a] Kalid's *filius* plays the role of a guiding spirit or familiar whose invocation by magic is so typical of the Harranite texts. A parallel to the dog-spirit is the poodle in *Faust,* out of whom Mephistopheles emerges as the familiar of Faust the alchemist.

178   In this connection I would like to mention the incest dream of a woman patient: *Two dogs were copulating. The male went head first into the female and disappeared in her belly.*[294] The-

---

289 Ὁ ἐγγόνασι, the Kneeler, is the constellation of Hercules. Cf. *Elenchos,* V, 16, 16.
290 For "canis" as synonym for the lapis see Lagneus, "Harmonia chemica," *Theatr. chem.,* IV, p. 822.   291 Wendland has "κυνοειδῆ". "Κυανοειδῆ" is a conjecture.
292 One conjecture is "Περσεφόνη Φλυά."   293 *Elenchos,* V, 20, 6f.
293a Cf. pars. 160f.
294 The motif of disappearance occurs in the second version of the Gabricus / Beya myth (*Ros. phil., Art. aurif.,* 1593, II, p. 263) and in the submersion of the sun (p. 333).

riomorphic symbolism is always an indication of a psychic process occurring on an animal level, i.e., in the instinctual sphere. The dream depicts a reversed birth as the goal of a sexual act. This archetypal situation underlies the incest motif in general and was present in modern man long before any consciousness of it. The archetype of incest is also at the back of the primitive notion that the father is reborn in the son, and of the heirosgamos of mother and son in its pagan and Christian form; [295] it signifies the highest and the lowest, the brightest and the darkest, the best and the most detestable. It represents the pattern of renewal and rebirth, the endless creation and disappearance of symbolic figures.

179 The motif of the dog is a necessary counterbalance to the excessively praised "light-nature" of the stone. Apart from the saying of Kalid there is still another aspect of the dog, of which, however, we find only sporadic hints in the literature. One such passage occurs in the "De ratione conficiendi lapidis philosophici" of Laurentius Ventura: [296]

Therefore pull down the house, destroy the walls, extract therefrom the purest juice [297] with the blood, and cook that thou mayest eat. Wherefore Arnaldus saith in the Book of Secrets: [298] Purify the stone, grind the door to powder, tear the bitch to pieces, choose the tender flesh, and thou wilt have the best thing. In the one thing are hidden all parts, in it all metals shine. Of these [parts], two are the artificers, two the vessels, two the times, two the fruits, two the ends, and one the salvation.[299]

180 This text abounds in obscurities. In the preceding section Ventura discusses the unity of the lapis and the medicina, mentioning the axioms "Introduce nothing alien" and "Nothing from outside" [300] with quotations from Geber, the *Turba,* and the "Thesaurus thesaurorum" of Arnaldus.[301] Then he turns to

[295] The same archetype forms the background to the Nicodemus dialogue in John 3.   [296] A Venetian physician of the 16th cent.
[297] The text has "succu." It could therefore mean 'extract the most pure with the juice and blood.'
[298] Schmieder (*Geschichte der Alchemie,* p. 153) mentions a MS of Arnaldus de Villanova, "De secretis naturae," and so does Du Fresnoy, *Histoire de la philosophie hermétique,* III, p. 325.
[299] *Theatr. chem.,* II, pp. 292f.*
[300] "Noli alienum introducere" and "nihil extraneum," an oft-repeated saying.
[301] *Art. aurif.,* II, pp. 385ff.

the "superfluities to be removed." [302] The lapis, he says, is "by nature most pure." It is therefore sufficiently purified when it is "led out of its proper house and enclosed in an alien house." The text continues:

In the proper house the flying bird is begotten, and in the alien house [303] the tincturing stone. The two flying birds [304] hop on to the tables and heads of the kings,[305] because both, the feathered bird and the plucked,[306] have given [us] this visible art [307] and cannot relinquish the society of men.[308] The father [309] of [the art] urges the indolent to work, its mother [310] nourishes the sons who are ex-

302 "Superflua removenda," an equally popular phrase.
303 The idea of the "house" may have derived originally from astrology. Here the house (as *domus propria*) means the matrix of the substance, but as *domus aliena* it means the chemical vessel (for instance the *domus vitrea*, 'house of glass'). The "flying bird" is a gas that issues from the matrix. The stone, on the other hand, signifies the substance, which does not leave its house like the gas, but must be transferred to another vessel. The gas (spirit) is invisible and feminine by nature, and therefore belongs to the unconscious sphere, whereas the substance is visible and tangible—"more real," as it were. It is masculine and belongs to the conscious sphere (in a man). Accordingly the *domus aliena* could be interpreted as consciousness, and the *domus propria* as the unconscious.
304 In the "separatio" one of the birds can fly, the other not. The "unio" produces the winged hermaphrodite.
305 Perhaps the only parallel to this * is in Senior (*De chemia*, p. 78): "And the ravens will come flying and fall upon it." * The idea is, obviously, that the birds share the king's meal, a possible influence here being the marriage of the king's son (Matthew 22 : 2ff.) and the marriage of the Lamb (Revelation 19 : 9ff.). Rex always signifies the sun, while the king's table signifies the bright world of day, i.e., consciousness, in and by which the contents of the unconscious (the birds) are recognized. These are the "fishes and birds" that bring the stone. (Cf. *Aion*, par. 224.)
306 Variants of the "bird flying and without wings" (Senior, *De chemia*, p. 37.) For the plucked bird see "Allegoriae super turbam," *Art. aurif.*, I, p. 140: "Take a cock crowned with a red comb and pluck it alive." *
307 The two birds are the two luminaries, Sol and Luna, or their spirits. One bird is male and without wings, the other female and winged. When bound together as "colligatae" they represent the coniunctio. They are the parents of the lapis, which is practically identical with "Ars nostra" since it is an "artificium" (artefact).
308 "Hominum consortia relinquere nescit." In other words, they remain with men, which reminds us of Kalid's "always being with you" (par. 174). The birds are personified contents of the unconscious which, once they are made conscious, cannot become unconscious again. As we know, an essential if not decisive part of any analytical treatment is based on the fact that conscious realization generally brings about a psychic change.
309 Sol as the day-star.
310 Luna as the mother of the living and mistress of the night.

hausted by their labours, and quickens and adorns their weary limbs.

Then follows the passage "Therefore pull down the house," etc. If the reader has perused the foregoing passage with the footnotes he will see that these instructions are the typical alchemical procedure for extracting the spirit or soul, and thus for bringing unconscious contents to consciousness. During the *solutio, separatio,* and *extractio* the *succus lunariae* (juice of the moon-plant), blood, or *aqua permanens* is either applied or extracted. This "liquid" comes from the unconscious but is not always an authentic content of it; often it is more an effect of the unconscious on the conscious mind. The psychiatrist knows it as the indirect effect of constellated unconscious contents which attracts or diverts attention to the unconscious and causes it to be assimilated. This process can be observed not only in the gradual formation of hypochondriac obsessions, phobias, and delusions, but also in dreams, fantasies, and creative activities when an unconscious content enforces the application of attention. This is the *succus vitae*,[311] the blood, the vital participation which the patient unconsciously forces on the analyst too, and without which no real therapeutic effect can be achieved. The attention given to the unconscious has the effect of incubation, a brooding [312] over the slow fire needed in the initial stages of the work; [313] hence the frequent use of the terms *decoctio, digestio, putrefactio, solutio.* It is really as if attention warmed the unconscious and activated it, thereby breaking down the barriers that separate it from consciousness.

181   In order to set free the contents hidden in the "house" [314] of

[311] The *succus vitae* is once more the *aqua permanens,* which remarkably enough is also designated "dog," as a passage in the "Opus praeclarum" of Valentinus (*Theatr. chem.,* IV, p. 1069) shows: ". . . of the water . . . which is called Dog of the balsam, or virgin's milk, or our quicksilver, or soul, or wind, or the dragon's tail." *

[312] The arcane substance is frequently likened to an egg. Cf. the treatise "Concerning the Egg" (περὶ τοῦ ᾠοῦ. Berthelot, *Alch. grecs,* I, iii), where the equivalents are the brain-stone (οἱ δὲ λίθον ἐγκέφαλον), the stone that is no stone (ἕτεροι λίθον οὐ λίθον), and the image of the world (ἕτεροι τὸ τοῦ κόσμου μίμημα), as in the *Turba* (ed. Ruska, p. 112) and numerous other places.

[313] Cf. the frequent direction "on a slow fire."

[314] As stated above, the term "domus" is often used. *Domus thesauraria* (treasurehouse) denotes the place where the arcanum is found, or else it is the chemical vessel (*domus vitrea*) or furnace. Cf. "Visio Arislei," *Art. aurif.,* I, p. 148.

the unconscious (*anima in compedibus!*) the "matrix" must be opened. This matrix is the "canicula," the moon-bitch, who carries in her belly that part of the personality which is felt to be essential, just as Beya did Gabricus. She is the vessel which must be broken asunder in order to extract the precious content, the "tender flesh," [315] for this is the "one thing" on which the whole work turns. In this one thing all parts of the work are contained.[316] Of these parts two are the artificers, who in the symbolical realm are Sol and Luna, in the human the adept and his *soror mystica*,[317] and in the psychological realm the masculine

315 *Caro* (flesh) is a name for the arcane substance, especially when it is "vivified." The "Consil. coniug." says (*Ars chemica*, p. 234): "That globe receives the flesh, i.e., the coagulation, and the blood, i.e., the tincture." * Dorn reveals the reason for this in his "Spec. phil." (*Theatr. chem.*, I, p. 300): "Hence we can understand the philosophical transmutations: do we not know that the pure substance of bread and wine is transformed into flesh and blood?" * Trevisanus ("De chemico miraculo," *Theatr. chem.*, I, p. 802) is equally clear when he says of the "king": "And now he gives his red and bleeding flesh to be eaten by us all." * In "Congeries Paracelsicae" (*Theatr. chem.*, I, p. 599) Dorn says that the medicament "can be made more than perfect through its own flesh and blood," in agreement with the above quotation from the "Consilium." A quotation from Malchamech in *Ros. phil.* (*Art. aurif.*, II, p. 238) says of the lapis: "It grows from flesh and blood." Often we come across the "fat flesh," as in a quotation from Pseudo-Aristotle in Mylius (*Phil. ref.*, p. 277): "Son, you must take of the fatter flesh," and (p. 70): "Eat a morsel of the fat flesh," a quotation from Arnaldus de Villanova ("Thesaurus thesaurorum," *Art. aurif.*, II, p. 406). "Caro" is an allusion to the "fleshly" nature of man, which is tinctured by the opus. The "Liber Platonis quartorum" (*Theatr. chem.*, V, p. 144) emphasizes this, and also the importance of "having knowledge of the gross, disordered, fleshly body, which is the burden of nature and reaches to the simple soul." * The "animam simplicem" comes close to Plato's "eternal Idea."

316 Arnaldus de Villanova (p. 397) lays stress on the oneness of the stone: "For there is one stone, one medicine, to which nothing from outside is added, nor is it diminished, save that the superfluities are removed." * *Ros. phil.* (*Art. aurif.*, II, p. 206) is even more emphatic: "One the stone, one the medicament, one the vessel, one the procedure, and one the disposition." *

317 Classic pairs are Simon Magus and Helen, Zosimos and Theosebeia, Nicholas Flamel and Peronelle, Mr. South and his daughter (Mrs. Atwood, author of *A Suggestive Enquiry into the Hermetic Mystery*). A good account of Flamel's career can be found in Larguier, *Le Faiseur d'or Nicolas Flamel*. The *Mutus liber* of Altus, recently reprinted, represents the *Mysterium Solis et Lunae* as an alchemical operation between man and wife, in a series of pictures. That such an abstruse and, aesthetically speaking, far from commendable book should be reprinted in the 20th century is proof of the psyche's secret and quite irrational participation in its own mysterium. I have attempted to describe the psychology of these relationships in my "Psychology of the Transference."

consciousness and the feminine unconscious (anima). The two vessels are again Sol and Luna,[318] the two times are probably the two main divisions of the work, the *opus ad album et ad rubeum*.[319] The former is the *opus Lunae,* the latter the *opus Solis*.[320] Psychologically they correspond to the constellation of unconscious contents in the first part of the analytical process and to the integration of these contents in actual life. The two fruits [321] are the fruit of the sun-and-moon tree,[322] gold and silver, or the reborn and sublimated Sol and Luna. The psychological parallel is the transformation of both the unconscious

[318] Cf. the illustrations in the *Mutus liber,* where this motif is well represented.

[319] The opus is to be performed at certain fixed, symbolical times. For example, the *Arcanum hermeticae Philosophiae opus* (p. 82) says: "For the first work towards the whiteness must be brought to an end in the house of the Moon, and the second in the second house of Mercury. The first work towards the redness [should end] in the second house of Venus; the latter terminates in the second royal throne of Jove, wherefrom our most mighty King receives his crown adorned with precious stones." * Besides this time co-ordination there are a number of others. The "Consilium coniugii" (*Ars chemica,* p. 65) says: "The white [stone] begins to appear at sunset on the face of the waters, hiding itself until midnight, and thereafter it inclines towards the deep. But the red works contrariwise, for it begins to rise above the waters at sunrise and thereafter descends into the deep." *

[320] Cf. Senior, *De chemia,* pp. 26ff. His account is not altogether clear on this point—which, as he himself admits, is due to the obscurities of the whole procedure. On p. 28 he says: "And the second work is the albefaction and the rubefaction, and the sages have brought these two works together in one. For when they speak of the one, they speak of the other also, and hence their writings seem to the readers to be contradictory." *

[321] The result of the opus is often called its "fruit," as in the *Turba,* Sermo LVIII (Ruska, p. 161): "Why hast thou ceased to speak of the tree, of the fruit whereof he that eateth shall never hunger?" * (This passage is probably not without reference to John 6 : 35: ". . . he that cometh to me shall never hunger, and he that believeth on me shall never thirst.") The *Turba* continues: "I say that old man ceases not to eat of the fruits of that tree . . . until that old man becomes a youth . . . and the father is become the son." * It is questionable whether this is a Christian interpolation.

[322] There are many pictures of the *arbor philosophica.* In patristic language it is "the fruitful tree which is to be nourished in our hearts" (Gregory the Great, *Super Cantica Canticorum,* 2 : 3; Migne, *P.L.,* vol. 79, col. 495), like the vine in the Eastern Church: "Thou, prophet of God, art seen as a mighty vine, filling the whole world with divine words as with fruits" * (Theodore the Studite, *Hymnus de S. Ephrem,* in Pitra, *Analecta Sacra,* I, p. 341). "[I am] the fruitful vine" (*Aurora Consurgens,* p. 139). Aurora II likewise refers to John 15 : 1 and 5: "Know ye not that all holy writing is in parables? For Christ followed the same practice and said: I am the true vine." * (*Art. aurif.,* I, p. 186). Cf. also "The Philosophical Tree," par. 359, n. 5, par. 458 and n. 5.

and the conscious, a fact known to everyone who methodically "has it out" with his unconscious. The two ends or goals are these transformations. But the salvation is one, just as the thing is one: it is the same thing at the beginning as at the end, it was always there and yet it appears only at the end. This thing is the self, the indescribable totality, which though it is inconceivable and "irrepresentable" is none the less necessary as an intuitive concept. Empirically we can establish no more than that the ego is surrounded on all sides by an unconscious factor. Proof of this is afforded by the association experiment, which gives a graphic demonstration of the frequent failure of the ego and its will. The psyche is an equation that cannot be "solved" without the factor of the unconscious; it is a totality which includes both the empirical ego and its transconscious foundation.

182   There is still another function of the dog in alchemy which has to be considered. In the "Introitus apertus" of Philaletha we find the following passage:

This Chamaeleon is the infant hermaphrodite, who is infected from his very cradle by the bite of the rabid Corascene dog, whereby he is maddened and rages with perpetual hydrophobia; nay, though of all natural things water is the closest to him, yet he is terrified of it and flees from it. O fate! Yet in the grove of Diana there is a pair of doves, which assuage his raving madness. Then will the impatient, swarthy, rabid dog, that he may suffer no return of his hydrophobia and perish drowned in the waters, come to the surface half suffocated; but do thou chase him off with pails of water and blows, and keep him at a distance, and the darkness will disappear. When the moon is at the full, give him wings and he will fly away as an eagle, leaving Diana's birds dead behind him.[323]

183   Here the connection with the moon tells us that the dark, dangerous, rabid dog changes into an eagle at the time of the plenilunium. His darkness disappears and he becomes a solar animal. We may therefore assume that his sickness was at its worst at the novilunium. It is clear that this refers to a psychic disturbance [324] which at one stage also infected the "infant hermaphrodite." Probably that too occurred at the novilu-

323 *Mus. herm.*, pp. 658f. (Waite, II, p. 171).
324 "The Spagyrics . . . extract from the moon itself an oil against falling-sickness and all affections of the brain." * Penotus, *Theatr. chem.*, I, p. 714.

nium,[325] i.e., the stage of *nigredo*. Just how the mad dog with its terror of water got into the water at all is not clear, unless perhaps it was in the *aquae inferiores* from the beginning. The text is preceded by the remark: "Whence will come the Chamaeleon or our Chaos, in which all secrets are hid in their potential state." The chaos as prima materia is identical with the "waters" of the beginning. According to Olympiodorus lead (also the prima materia) contains a demon that drives the adept mad.[326] Curiously enough, Wei Po-yang, a Chinese alchemist of the second century, compares lead to a madman clothed in rags.[327] Elsewhere Olympiodorus speaks of the "one cursed by God" who dwells in the "black earth." This is the mole, which, as Olympiodorus relates from a Hermetic book, had once been a man who divulged the mysteries of the sun and was therefore cursed by God and made blind. He "knew the shape of the sun, as it was." [328]

184   It is not difficult to discern in these allusions the dangers, real or imaginary, which are connected with the unconscious. In this respect the unconscious has a bad reputation, not so much because it is dangerous in itself as because there are cases of latent psychosis which need only a slight stimulus to break out in all their catastrophic manifestations. An anamnesis or the touching of a complex may be sufficient for this. But the unconscious is also feared by those whose conscious attitude is at odds with their true nature. Naturally their dreams will then assume an unpleasant and threatening form, for if nature is violated she takes her revenge. In itself the unconscious is neutral, and its normal function is to compensate the conscious position. In it the opposites slumber side by side; they are wrenched apart only by the activity of the conscious mind, and the more one-

325 Not only does Luna cause moon-sickness, she herself is sick or ailing. One sickness is the "combustible sulphur" which prevents her from staying in the mixture, the other is "excessive coldness and dampness." Hollandus, *Theatr. chem.*, III, p. 365.

326 "They fall into madness through ignorance." * Berthelot, *Alch. grecs*, II, iv, 46.

327 *Isis*, XVIII, p. 237. On p. 238 Wei Po-yang describes the madness that attacks the adept. Cf. "The Philosophical Tree," pars. 432ff.

328 Berthelot, II, iv, 52. An alchemist would say that he knew the secret of gold-making. Psychologically it would mean that he knew about the transformation of consciousness, but that it was abortive, so that instead of being illuminated he fell into deeper darkness.

sided and cramped the conscious standpoint is, the more painful or dangerous will be the unconscious reaction. There is no danger from this sphere if conscious life has a solid foundation. But if consciousness is cramped and obstinately one-sided, and there is also a weakness of judgment, then the approach or invasion of the unconscious can cause confusion and panic or a dangerous inflation, for one of the most obvious dangers is that of identifying with the figures in the unconscious. For anyone with an unstable disposition this may amount to a psychosis.

185 The raving madness of the infected "infant" is assuaged (we should really say "with caresses," for that is the meaning of "mulcere") by the doves of Diana. These doves form a pair—a love pair, for doves are the birds of Astarte.[329] In alchemy they represent, like all winged creatures, spirits or souls, or, in technical terms, the *aqua*, the extracted transformative substance.[330] The appearance of a pair of doves points to the imminent marriage of the filius regius and to the dissolution of the opposites as a result of the union. The filius is merely infected by the evil, but the evil itself, the mad dog, is sublimated and changed into an eagle at the plenilunium. In the treatise of Abraham Eleazar, the lapis in its dark, feminine form appears instead of the dog and is compared to the Shulamite in the Song of Songs. The lapis says: "But I must be like a dove." [331]

186 There is another passage in the "Introitus apertus" which is relevant in this context:

If thou knowest how to moisten this dry earth with its own water, thou wilt loosen the pores of the earth, and this thief from outside will be cast out with the workers of wickedness, and the water, by an admixture of the true Sulphur, will be cleansed from the leprous filth and from the superfluous dropsical fluid, and thou wilt have in

329 "In the philosophical sublimation or first preparation of Mercury a Herculean task confronts the worker . . . The threshold is guarded by horned beasts . . . naught will assuage their ferocity save the tokens of Diana and the doves of Venus, if the fates call thee" * (D'Espagnet, "Arcanum hermeticae philos.," XLII, *Bibliotheca chemica*, II, p. 653). The doves themselves were originally the "chicks of crows" (p. 655). The priestesses of Ishtar were called doves (Wittekindt, *Das Hohe Lied*, p. 12), just as the priestesses of the goddess of Asia Minor were called πελειάδες, 'wild doves' (Eisler, *Weltenmantel und Himmelszelt*, p. 158). The dove is also the attribute of the mother-goddess of the Hittites, who is depicted in an obscene position (Wittekindt, p. 50).

330 Eleazar, *Uraltes Chymisches Werck*, I, p. 34.

331 Ibid., p. 52. See infra, par. 624.

thy power the fount of the Knight of Treviso, whose waters are right-fully dedicated to the maiden Diana. Worthless is this thief, armed with the malignity of arsenic, from whom the winged youth fleeth, shuddering. And though the central water is his bride, yet dare he not display his most ardent love towards her, because of the snares of the thief, whose machinations are in truth unavoidable. Here may Diana be propitious to thee, who knoweth how to tame wild beasts, and whose twin doves will temper the malignity of the air with their wings, so that the youth easily entereth in through the pores, and instantly shaketh the foundations of the earth,[332] and raises up a dark cloud. But thou wilt lead the waters up even to the brightness of the moon, and the darkness that was upon the face of the deep shall be scattered by the spirit moving over the waters. Thus by God's command shall the Light appear.[333]

187   It is evident that this passage is a variation on the theme of the preceding text. Instead of the infant hermaphrodite we have the winged youth, whose bride is the fountain of Diana (Luna as a nymph). The parallel to the mad dog is the thief or ne'er-do-well who is armed with the "malignity of arsenic." His malignity is assuaged by the wings of the doves, just as the dog's rabies was. The youth's wings are a token of his aerial nature; he is a pneuma that penetrates through the pores of the earth and activates it—which means nothing less than the connubium of the living spirit with the "dry, virgin earth," or of the wind with the waters dedicated to the maiden Diana. The winged youth is described as the "spirit moving over the waters," and this may be a reference not only to Genesis but to the angel that troubled the pool of Bethesda.[334] His enemy, the thief who lies in wait for him, is, we are told earlier, the "outward burning vaporous sulphur," in other words *sulphur vulgi,* who is armed with the evil spirit, the devil, or is held captive by him in hell,[335] and is thus the equivalent of the dog choked in the water. That the dog

---

[332] The text is corrupt here: "concutit statim pero ledos." I read "terrae sedes." It refers to the resurrection of the lapis out of the earth, which it penetrated as the "aer sophorum" (air of the sages), one of the many allusions to the coniunctio. The birth of the lapis has its parallel in Christ's resurrection, hence the reference to the earthquake. (Cf. Matthew 28 : 2: "And behold, there was a great earth-quake . . .")

[333] Philaletha, *Mus. herm.,* p. 657 (Waite, II, p. 169).

[334] John 5 : 2ff.

[335] "He has the key to the infernal prison house where sulphur lies bound." * "De sulphure," *Mus. herm.,* p. 623 (Waite, II, p. 143).

and the thief are identical is clear from the remark that Diana knows how to tame wild beasts. The two doves do in fact turn out to be the pair of lovers who appear in the love-story of Diana and the shepherd Endymion. This legend originally referred to Selene.

188   The appearance of Diana necessarily brings with it her hunting animal the dog, who represents her dark side. Her darkness shows itself in the fact that she is also a goddess of destruction and death, whose arrows never miss. She changed the hunter Actaeon, when he secretly watched her bathing, into a stag, and his own hounds, not recognizing him, thereupon tore him to pieces. This myth may have given rise first to the designation of the lapis as the *cervus fugitivus* (fugitive stag),[336] and then to the rabid dog, who is none other than the vindictive and treacherous aspect of Diana as the new moon. The parable we discussed in the chapter on sulphur likewise contains the motif of the "surprise in the bath." But there it is Helios himself who espies her, and the relationship is a brother-sister incest that ends with their both being drowned. This catastrophe is inherent in the incest, for through incest the royal pair is produced

[336] "Servus fugitivus" (fugitive slave) is more common. "Cervus" occurs in Agrippa von Nettesheim (*The Vanity of Arts and Sciences*, p. 315): ". . . foolish Mysteries of this Art, and empty Riddles, of the Green Lion, the fugitive Hart." There is a picture of Diana and Actaeon on the title-page of *Mus. herm.*, 1678 (reproduced in Bernoulli, "Spiritual Development as Reflected in Alchemy"). In the Table of Figures in Manget (*Bibl. chem.*, II, Plate IX, Fig. 13) the stag appears as the emblem of "Mahomet Philosophus." It is a symbol of self-rejuvenation in Honorius of Autun, *Sermo in Epiphania Domini* (Migne, *P.L.*, vol. 172, col. 847), where it is said that the stag, when he has swallowed a poisonous snake, drinks water "that he may eject the poison, and then cast his horns and his hair and so take new"; we likewise should "put aside the horns of pride and the hair of worldly superfluity." In the legend of the Grail it is related that Christ sometimes appeared to his disciples as a white stag with four lions (= the four evangelists). (Cf. "Nature of Dreams," par. 559, n. 9, and the frontispiece to Vol. 8 of these *Coll. Works*.) Here too it is stated that the stag can renew itself (*Le Saint Graal*, III, pp. 219 and 224). Ruland (*Lexicon*, p. 96) mentions only that "*Cerviculae Spiritus* is a bone of the heart of the stag." Dom Pernety (*Dict. mytho-hermétique*, p. 72) says of the "cerveau ou cœur de cerf": "C'est la matière des Philosophes." The *Livre des Secrez de Nature* says: "The stag is a well-known beast, which renews itself when it feels it is growing old and weak. It goes to an ant-hill and digs at the foot thereof and brings forth thence a serpent, on which it tramples with its feet and afterwards eats; it then swells up, and so renews itself. Wherefore it lives for 900 years, as we find in scripture . . ." (Delatte, *Textes Latins et Vieux Français relatifs aux Cyranides*, p. 346.)

after animals have been killed or have killed one another.[337] The animals (dragon, lion, snake, etc.) stand for evil passions that finally take the form of incest. They are destroyed by their own ravenous nature, just as are Sol and Luna, whose supreme desire culminates apparently in incest. But since "all that passes is but a parable," incest, as we have said before, is nothing but a preliminary form of the unio oppositorum.[338] Out of chaos, darkness, and wickedness there rises up a new light once death has atoned for the "unavoidable machinations" of the Evil One.

c. An Alchemical Allegory

189   The newcomer to the psychology of the unconscious will probably find the two texts about the mad dog and the thief very weird and abstruse. Actually they are no more so than the dreams which are the daily fare of the psychotherapist; and, like dreams, they can be translated into rational speech. In order to interpret dreams we need some knowledge of the dreamer's personal situation, and to understand alchemical parables we must know something about the symbolic assumptions of the alchemists. We amplify dreams by the personal history of the patient, and the parables by the statements found in the text. Armed with this knowledge, it is not too difficult in either case to discern a meaning that seems sufficient for our needs. An interpretation can hardly ever be convincingly proved. Generally it shows itself to be correct only when it has proved its value as a heuristic hypothesis. I would therefore like to take the second of Philaletha's texts, which is rather clearer than the first, and try to interpret it as if it were a dream.

Tu si aridam hanc Terram, aqua sui generis rigare sciveris, poros Terrae laxabis,	If thou knowest how to moisten this dry earth with its own water, thou wilt loosen the pores of the earth,

190   If you will contemplate your lack of fantasy, of inspiration and inner aliveness, which you feel as sheer stagnation and a

[337] Since a psychic transformation is involved, the obscure passage in the Naassene hymn (Hippolytus, *Elenchos*, V, 10, 2), describing the sufferings of the soul, might be relevant here: "The soul . . . veiled in the form of a stag, wearies, overpowered by the pains of death." * But the text is so uncertain that it has little documentary value.   [338] Cf. "Psychology of the Transference,' pars. 419ff.

barren wilderness, and impregnate it with the interest born of alarm at your inner death, then something can take shape in you, for your inner emptiness conceals just as great a fulness if only you will allow it to penetrate into you. If you prove receptive to this "call of the wild," the longing for fulfilment will quicken the sterile wilderness of your soul as rain quickens the dry earth. (Thus the Soul to the Laborant, staring glumly at his stove and scratching himself behind the ear because he has no more ideas.)

| et externus hic fur cum Operatoribus nequitiae foras projicietur, | and this thief from outside will be cast out with the workers of wickedness, |

191   You are so sterile because, without your knowledge, something like an evil spirit has stopped up the source of your fantasy, the fountain of your soul. The enemy is your own crude sulphur, which burns you with the hellish fire of desirousness, or *concupiscentia*. You would like to make gold because "poverty is the greatest plague, wealth the highest good." [339] You wish to have results that flatter your pride, you expect something useful, but there can be no question of that as you have realized with a shock. Because of this you no longer even *want* to be fruitful, as it would only be for God's sake but unfortunately not for your own.

| purgabitur aqua per additamentum Sulphuris veri a sorde leprosa, et ab humore hydropico superfluo | and the water, by an admixture of the true Sulphur, will be cleansed from the leprous filth and from the superfluous dropsical fluid, |

192   Therefore away with your crude and vulgar desirousness, which childishly and shortsightedly sees only goals within its own narrow horizon. Admittedly sulphur is a vital spirit, a "Yetser Ha-ra," [340] an evil spirit of passion, though like this an active element; useful as it is at times, it is an obstacle between you and your goal. The water of your interest is not pure, it is poisoned by the leprosy of desirousness which is the common ill. You too are infected with this collective sickness. Therefore

339 Goethe, "Der Schatzgräber."
340 So in Rueckert's well-known poem. Hebrew *Yetser ha-ra* means "instinct of evil."

bethink you for once, "extrahe cogitationem," and consider: What is behind all this desirousness? A thirsting for the eternal, which as you see can never be satisfied with the best because it is "Hades" in whose honour the desirous "go mad and rave." [341] The more you cling to that which all the world desires, the more you are Everyman, who has not yet discovered himself and stumbles through the world like a blind man leading the blind with somnambulistic certainty into the ditch. Everyman is always a multitude. Cleanse your interest of that collective sulphur which clings to all like a leprosy. For desire only burns in order to burn itself out, and in and from this fire arises the true living spirit which generates life according to its own laws, and is not blinded by the shortsightedness of our intentions or the crude presumption of our superstitious belief in the will. Goethe says . . .

> That livingness I praise
> Which longs for flaming death. [342]

This means burning in your own fire and not being like a comet or a flashing beacon, showing others the right way but not knowing it yourself. The unconscious demands your interest for its own sake and wants to be accepted for what it is. Once the existence of this opposite is accepted, the ego can and should come to terms with its demands. Unless the content given you by the unconscious is acknowledged, its compensatory effect is not only nullified [343] but actually changes into its opposite, as it then tries to realize itself literally and concretely.

| habebisque in posse Comitis a Trevis Fontinam, cujus Aquae sunt proprie Dianae Virgini dicatae. | and thou wilt have in thy power the Fount of the Knight of Treviso, whose waters are rightfully dedicated to the maiden Diana. |

193   The fountain of Bernardus Trevisanus is the bath of renewal that was mentioned earlier. The ever-flowing fountain expresses a continual flow of interest toward the unconscious, a kind of constant attention or "religio," which might also be called devotion. The crossing of unconscious contents into consciousness is

341 Cf. Heraclitus, R. P. 49, in Burnet, *Early Greek Philosophy,* p. 141.
342 *West-östlicher Diwan.*
343 Naturally, this is true only during the process of coming to terms with the unconscious.

thus made considerably easier, and this is bound to benefit the psychic balance in the long run. Diana as the numen and nymph of this spring is an excellent formulation of the figure we know as the anima. If attention is directed to the unconscious, the unconscious will yield up its contents, and these in turn will fructify the conscious like a fountain of living water. For consciousness is just as arid as the unconscious if the two halves of our psychic life are separated.

Hic fur est nequam arsenicali malignitate armatus, quem juvenis alatus horret et fugit.	Worthless is this thief, armed with the malignity of arsenic, from whom the winged youth fleeth, shuddering.

194   It is evidently a difficult thing, this "cleansing from leprous filth"; indeed, d'Espagnet calls it a labour of Hercules. That is why the text turns back to the "thief" at this point. The thief, as we saw, personifies a kind of self-robbery. He is not easily shaken off, as it comes from a habit of thinking supported by tradition and milieu alike: anything that cannot be exploited in some way is uninteresting—hence the devaluation of the psyche. A further reason is the habitual depreciation of everything one cannot touch with the hands or does not understand. In this respect our conventional system of education—necessary as it was—is not entirely free from the blame of having helped to give the empirical psyche a bad name. In recent times this traditional error has been made even worse by an allegedly biological point of view which sees man as being no further advanced than a herd-animal and fails to understand any of his motivations outside the categories of hunger, power, and sex. We think in terms of thousands and millions of units, and then naturally there are no questions more important than whom the herd belongs to, where it pastures, whether enough calves are born and sufficient quantities of milk and meat are produced. In the face of huge numbers every thought of individuality pales, for statistics obliterate everything unique. Contemplating such overwhelming might and misery the individual is embarrassed to exist at all. Yet the real carrier of life is the individual. He alone feels happiness, he alone has virtue and responsibility and any ethics whatever. The masses and the state have nothing of the kind. Only man as an individual human being lives; the

state is just a system, a mere machine for sorting and tabulating the masses. Anyone, therefore, who thinks in terms of men minus the individual, in huge numbers, atomizes himself and becomes a thief and a robber to himself. He is infected with the leprosy of collective thinking and has become an inmate of that insalubrious stud-farm called the totalitarian State. Our time contains and produces more than enough of that "crude sulphur" which with "arsenical malignity" prevents man from discovering his true self.

195   I was tempted to translate *arsenicalis* as 'poisonous'. But this translation would be too modern. Not everything that the alchemists called "arsenic" was really the chemical element As. "Arsenic" originally meant 'masculine, manly, strong' (ἄρσην) and was essentially an arcanum, as Ruland's *Lexicon* shows. There arsenic is defined as an "hermaphrodite, the means whereby Sulphur and Mercury are united. It has communion with both natures and is therefore called Sun and Moon." [344] Or arsenic is "Luna, our Venus, Sulphur's companion" and the "soul." Here arsenic is no longer the masculine aspect of the arcane substance but is hermaphroditic and even feminine. This brings it dangerously close to the moon and the crude sulphur, so that arsenic loses its solar affinity. As "Sulphur's companion" it is poisonous and corrosive. Because the arcane substance always points to the principal unconscious content, its peculiar nature shows in what relation that content stands to consciousness. If the conscious mind has accepted it, it has a positive form, if not, a negative one. If on the other hand the arcane substance is split into two figures, this means that the content has been partly accepted and partly rejected; it is seen under two different, incompatible aspects and is therefore taken to be two different things.

196   This is what has happened in our text: the thief is contrasted with the winged youth, who represents the other aspect, or personifies the "true sulphur," the spirit of inner truth which measures man not by his relation to the mass but by his relation to the mystery of the psyche. This winged youth (the spiritual Mercurius) is obviously aware of his own weakness and flees "shuddering" from the crude sulphur. The standpoint of the

[344] P. 49.

inner man is the more threatened the more overpowering that of the outer man is. Sometimes only his invisibility saves him. He is so small that no one would miss him if he were not the *sine qua non* of inner peace and happiness.[345] In the last resort it is neither the "eighty-million-strong nation" nor the State that feels peace and happiness, but the individual. Nobody can ever get round the simple computation that a million noughts in a row do not add up to 1, just as the loudest talk can never abolish the simple psychological fact that the larger the mass the more nugatory is the individual.

197   The shy and delicate youth stands for everything that is winged in the psyche or that would like to sprout wings. But it dies from the poison of organizational thinking and mass statistics; the individual succumbs to the madness that sooner or later overtakes every mass—the death-instinct of the lemmings. In the political sphere the name for this is war.

Et licet Aqua centralis sit hujus Sponsa, tamen Amorem suum erga illam ardentissimum non audet exerere, ob latronis insidias, cujus technae sunt vere inevitabiles.	And though the central Water is his bride, yet dare he not display his most ardent love towards her, because of the snares of the thief, whose machinations are in truth unavoidable.

198   The goal of the winged youth is a higher one than the fulfilment of collective ideals, which are all nothing but makeshifts and conditions for bare existence. Since this is the absolute foundation, nobody will deny their importance, but collective ideals are not by a long way the breath of life which a man needs in order to live. If his soul does not live nothing can save him from stultification. His life is the soil in which his soul can and must develop. He has only the mystery of his living soul to set against the overwhelming might and brutality of collective convictions.

345 "In outward forms thou'lt not find unity,
       Thine eye must ever introverted be.
       Canst thou forget thyself, to all forlorn,
       Thou'lt feel God in thee, well and truly One."
(Tersteegen, *Geistliches Blumengärtlein inniger Seelen*, No. 102, p. 24.)
       "When I seek him outside, God makes me bad:
       Only within is salvation to be had."
(Angelus Silesius, *Sämtliche Poetische Werke*, ed. Held, I, p. 162.)

199   It is the age-old drama of opposites, no matter what they are called, which is fought out in every human life. In our text it is obviously the struggle between the good and the evil spirit, expressed in alchemical language just as today we express it in conflicting ideologies. The text comes close to the mystical language of the Baroque—the language of Jacob Boehme (1575–1624), Abraham of Franckenberg (1593–1652), and Angelus Silesius (1624–1677).

200   We learn that the winged youth is espoused to the "central Water." This is the fountain of the soul or the fount of wisdom,[346] from which the inner life wells up. The nymph of the spring is in the last analysis Luna, the mother-beloved, from which it follows that the winged youth is Sol, the *filius solis, lapis, aurum philosophicum, lumen luminum, medicina catholica, una salus*, etc. He is the best, the highest, the most precious *in potentia*. But he will become real only if he can unite with Luna, the "mother of mortal bodies." If not, he is threatened with the fate of the puer aeternus in *Faust*, who goes up in smoke three times.[347] The adept must therefore always take care to keep the Hermetic vessel well sealed, in order to prevent what is in it from flying away. The content becomes "fixed" through the mystery of the coniunctio, in which the extreme opposites unite, night is wedded with day, and "the two shall be one, and the outside as the inside, and the male with the female neither male nor female." [348] This apocryphal saying of Jesus from the beginning of the second century is indeed a paradigm for the alchemical union of opposites. Obviously this problem is an eschatological one, but, aside from the somewhat tortuous language of the times, it cannot be called abstruse since it has universal validity, from the *tao* of Lao-tzu to the *coincidentia oppositorum* of Cusanus. The same idea penetrated into Christianity in the form of the apocalyptic marriage of the Lamb (Rev. 22 : 9ff.), and we seldom find a high point of religious feeling where this eternal image of the royal marriage does not appear.

---

[346] Book of Enoch 48 : 1: ". . . fountains of wisdom; and all the thirsty drank of them." (Charles, *Apocrypha and Pseudepigrapha*, II, p. 216).
[347] Boy Charioteer, Homunculus, and Euphorion.
[348] Clement of Rome, Second Epistle to the Corinthians, 12 (*The Apostolic Fathers*, trans. Lake, I, p. 147).

201   I can do no more than demonstrate the existence of this image and its phenomenology. What the union of opposites really "means" transcends human imagination. Therefore the worldly-wise can dismiss such a "fantasy" without further ado, for it is perfectly clear: *tertium non datur*. But that doesn't help us much, for we are dealing with an eternal image, an archetype, from which man can turn away his mind for a time but never permanently.[349] Whenever this image is obscured his life loses its proper meaning and consequently its balance. So long as he knows that he is the carrier of life and that it is therefore important for him to live, then the mystery of his soul lives also—no matter whether he is conscious of it or not. But if he no longer sees the meaning of his life in its fulfilment, and no longer believes in man's eternal right to this fulfilment, then he has betrayed and lost his soul, substituting for it a madness which leads to destruction, as our time demonstrates all too clearly.

202   The "machinations of the thief," our text says, are "unavoidable." They are an integral part of the fateful drama of opposites, just as the shadow belongs to the light. Reason, however, cannot turn this into a convenient recipe, for inevitability does not diminish the guilt of what is evil any more than the merit of what is good. Minus remains minus, and guilt, as ever, has to be avenged. "Evil follows after wrong," says the Capuchin friar in Wallenstein's camp—a banal truth that is too readily forgotten, and because of this the winged youth cannot lead his bride home as quickly as he would wish. Evil cannot be eradicated once and for all; it is an inevitable component of life and is not to be had without paying for it. The thief whom the police do not catch has, nonetheless, robbed himself, and the murderer is his own executioner.

203   The thief in our text is armed with all evil, but in reality it is merely the ego with its shadow where the abysmal depths of

349 This has been shown once again in our own day by the solemn promulgation of the dogma of the Assumption. A Catholic author aptly remarks: "There seems to be some strange rightness in the portrayal of this reunion in splendour of Son and Mother, Father and Daughter, Spirit and Matter." (Victor White, "The Scandal of the Assumption," *Life of the Spirit*, V, p. 199.) In this connection it is worth recalling the words of Pope Pius XII's Apostolic Constitution, *Munificentissimus Deus:* "On this day the Virgin Mother was taken up to her heavenly bridal chamber" (English trans., p. 15). Cf. Antony of Padua, "Sermo in Assumptione S. Mariae Virginis," *Sermones*, III, p. 730.

human nature begin to appear. Increasing psychological insight hinders the projection of the shadow, and this gain in knowledge logically leads to the problem of the union of opposites. One realizes, first of all, that one cannot project one's shadow on to others, and next that there is no advantage in insisting on their guilt, as it is so much more important to know and possess one's own, because it is part of one's own self and a necessary factor without which nothing in this sublunary world can be realized. Though it is not said that Luna personifies the dark side, there is as we have seen something very suspicious about the new moon. Nevertheless the winged youth loves his moon-bride and hence the darkness to which she belongs, for the opposites not only flee one another but also attract one another. We all know that evil, especially if it is not scrutinized too closely, can be very attractive, and most of all when it appears in idealistic garb. Ostensibly it is the wicked thief that hinders the youth in his love for the chaste Diana, but in reality the evil is already lurking in the ideal youth and in the darkness of the new moon, and his chief fear is that he might discover himself in the role of the common sulphur. This role is so shocking that the noble-minded youth cannot see himself in it and puts the blame on the wiles of the enemy. It is as if he dared not know himself because he is not adult enough to accept the fact that one must be thankful if one comes across an apple without a worm in it and a plate of soup without a hair.

Esto hic tibi Diana propitia, quae feras domare novit,	Here may Diana be propitious to thee, who knoweth how to tame wild beasts,

204   The darkness which is opposed to the light is the unbridled instinctuality of nature that asserts itself despite all consciousness. Anyone who seeks to unite the opposites certainly needs Diana to be propitious to him, for she is being considered as a bride and it has yet to be seen what she has to present in the way of wild animals. Possibly the thief will appear quite insignificant by comparison.

cujus binae columbae pennis suis aeris malignitatem temperabunt,	and whose twin doves will temper the malignity of the air with their wings,

205   The tender pair of doves is an obviously harmless aspect of the same instinctuality, though in itself the theriomorphic symbol would be capable of an "interpretation from above downwards." Nonetheless, it should not be interpreted in this sense because the aspect of untamed animality and evil is represented in the previous quotation by the mad dog and in this one by the thief. In contrast to this, the doves are emblems of innocence and of marital love as well as of the Holy Ghost and Sapientia, of Christ and his Virgin Mother.[350] From this context we can see what the dove is intended to represent: it is the exact counterpart to the malignity of the thief. Together they represent the attack, first from one side and then from the other, of a dualistic being on the more restricted consciousness of man. The purpose or result of this assault is the widening of consciousness, which has always, it seems, followed the pattern laid down in Genesis 3 : 4f.: "Ye shall not surely die, for God doth know that in the day ye eat thereof, then your eyes shall be opened, and ye shall be as gods, knowing good and evil."

206   It is obviously a moment of supreme possibilities both for good and for evil. Usually, however, it is first one and then the other: the good man succumbs to evil, the sinner is converted to good, and that, to an uncritical eye, is the end of the matter. But those endowed with a finer moral sense or deeper insight cannot deny that this seeming one-after-another is in reality a happening of events side-by-side, and perhaps no one has realized this more clearly than St. Paul, who knew that he bore a thorn in the flesh and that the messenger of Satan smote him in the face lest he be "exalted above measure." [351] The one-after-another is a bearable prelude to the deeper knowledge of the side-by-side, for this is an incomparably more difficult problem. Again, the view that good and evil are spiritual forces outside us, and that man is caught in the conflict between

---

350 Also of gentleness, tameness, peacefulness (dove of Noah), simplicity ("simplices sicut columbae," Matthew 10 : 16; DV: "guileless as doves"). Christ, too, is called a dove: "The Lord Jesus was a dove . . . saying Peace be unto you. . . . Behold the dove, behold the green olive-branch in its mouth." * (Fernandius, cited in Picinellus, *Mundus Symbolicus*, p. 283.) Picinellus calls Mary the "most pure dove." The "Aureum vellus" (Mennens, *Theatr. chem.*, V, p. 311) interprets the dove as follows: "Wherefore the Prophet crieth: Who will give me wings like a dove, that is to say, spotless and simple thoughts and contemplations?" *
351 II Corinthians 12 : 7.

them, is more bearable by far than the insight that the opposites are the ineradicable and indispensable preconditions of all psychic life, so much so that life itself is guilt. Even a life dedicated to God is still lived by an ego, which speaks of an ego and asserts an ego in God's despite, which does not instantly merge itself with God but reserves for itself a freedom and a will which it sets up outside God and' against him. How *can* it do this against the overwhelming might of God? Only through self-assertion, which is as sure of its free will as Lucifer. All distinction from God is separation, estrangement, a falling away. The Fall was inevitable even in paradise. Therefore Christ is "without the stain of sin," because he stands for the whole of the Godhead and is not distinct from it by reason of his manhood.[352] Man, however, is branded by the stain of separation from God. This state of things would be insupportable if there were nothing to set against evil but the law and the Decalogue, as in pre-Christian Judaism—until the reformer and rabbi Jesus tried to introduce the more advanced and psychologically more correct view that not fidelity to the law but love and kindness are the antithesis of evil. The wings of the dove temper the malignity of the air, the wickedness of the aerial spirit ("the prince of the power of the air"—Ephesians 2 : 2), and they alone have this effect.

quod per poros facile ingreditur adolescens, concutit statim (terrae sedes), nubemque tetricam suscitat.	so that the youth easily entereth in through the pores, and instantly shaketh the foundations of the earth,[353] and raiseth up a dark cloud.

207   Once the malignity is tempered, sinfulness and its evil consequences are mitigated too, and that which has wings can embrace the earth. For now we come to the consummation of the hierosgamos, the "earthing" of the spirit and the spiritualizing of the earth, the union of opposites and reconciliation· of the divided (Ephesians 2 : 14),[354] in a word the longed-for act of redemption whereby the sinfulness of existence, the original

[352] A paradox which, like the *kenosis* doctrine (Philippians 2 : 6f.), is a slap in the face for reason.   [353] My conjecture. See supra, n. 332.

[354] An idea echoed in the dogma of the Assumption, which lays particular emphasis on the incorruptibility of the body, likening it, as the earthly vessel of divinity, to the ark of the covenant: "In the ark of the covenant, built of incorruptible wood and placed in the temple of God, they perceive an image of the

dissociation, will be annulled in God. The earthquake is on the one hand an allusion to Christ's descent into hell and his resurrection, and on the other hand a shaking of the humdrum earthly existence of man, into whose life and soul meaning has at last penetrated, and by which he is at once threatened and uplifted.

208   This is always an intuitive experience that is felt as a concrete reality. It is the prefiguration and anticipation of a future condition, a glimmering of an unspoken, half-conscious union of ego and non-ego. Rightly called a *unio mystica,* it is the fundamental experience of all religions that have any life in them and have not yet degenerated into confessionalism; that have safeguarded the mystery of which the others know only the rites it produced—empty bags from which the gold has long since vanished.

209   The earthquake sends up a dark cloud: consciousness, because of the revolution of its former standpoint, is shrouded in darkness, just as the earth was at Christ's death, which was followed by a resurrection. This image tells us that the widening of consciousness is at first upheaval and darkness, then a broadening out of man to the whole man. This "Man," being indescribable, is an intuitive or "mystical" experience, and the name "Anthropos" is therefore very apt because it demonstrates the continuity of this idea over the millennia.

tu undas superinduces ad Lunae usque candorem,	But thou wilt lead the waters up even to the brightness of the moon,

210   As we have seen, water here has the meaning of "fructifying interest," and its leading upwards means that it now turns towards the plenilunium, the gracious and serene complement of the sinister new moon and its perils.

atque ita Tenebrae, quae supra abyssi faciem erant, per spiritum se in aquis moventem discutientur. Sic jubente Deo Lux apparebit.	and the darkness that was upon the face of the deep shall be scattered by the spirit moving over the waters. Thus by God's command shall the Light appear.

most pure body of the Virgin Mary, preserved free from all corruption of the tomb." (*Munificentissimus Deus,* English trans., p. 13.) The coexistence in heaven of the real earthly body with the soul is expressed unequivocally in the words of the definition: ". . . was taken up . . . body and soul . . ."

211   The eye that hitherto saw only the darkness and danger of evil turns towards the circle of the moon, where the ethereal realm of the immortals begins, and the gloomy deep can be left to its own devices, for the spirit now moves it from within, convulses and transforms it. When consciousness draws near to the unconscious not only does *it* receive a devastating shock but something of its light penetrates into the darkness of the unconscious. The result is that the unconscious is no longer so remote and strange and terrifying, and this paves the way for an eventual union. Naturally the "illumination" of the unconscious does not mean that from now on the unconscious is less unconscious. Far from it. What happens is that its contents cross over into consciousness more easily than before. The "light" that shines at the end is the *lux moderna* of the alchemists, the new widening of consciousness, a further step in the realization of the Anthropos, and every one of these steps signifies a rebirth of the deity.

212   Herewith we end our contemplation of the text. The question now arises: Did the alchemists really have such thoughts and conceal them in their ornate metaphors? In other words, did Philaletha, the pseudonymous author of our text, have anything like the thoughts and ideas which I have put forward by way of interpretation? I regard this as out of the question, and yet I believe that these authors invariably said the best, most apposite, and clearest thing they could about the matter in hand. For our taste and our intellectual requirements this performance is, however, so unsatisfactory that we ourselves feel compelled to make a renewed attempt to say the same thing in still clearer words. It seems obvious to us that what we think about it was never thought by the alchemists, for if it had been it would doubtless have come out long ago. The "philosophers" took the greatest pains to unearth and reveal the secret of the stone, accusing the ancients of having written too copiously and too obscurely. If they, on their own admission, wrote "typice, symbolice, metaphorice," this was the best they could do, and it is thanks to their labours that we are today in a position to say anything at all about the secrets of alchemy.

213   All understanding that is not directly of a mathematical nature (which, incidentally, understands nothing but merely formulates) is conditioned by its time. Fundamental to alchemy

is a true and genuine mystery which since the seventeenth century has been understood unequivocally as psychic. Nor can we moderns conceive it to be anything except a psychic product whose meaning may be elicited by the methods and empirical experience of our twentieth century medical psychology. But I do not imagine for a moment that the psychological interpretation of a mystery must necessarily be the last word. If it is a mystery it must have still other aspects. Certainly I believe that psychology can unravel the secrets of alchemy, but it will not lay bare the secret of these secrets. We may therefore expect that at some time in the future our attempt at explanation will be felt to be just as "metaphorical and symbolical" as we have found the alchemical one to be, and that the mystery of the stone, or of the self, will then develop an aspect which, though still unconscious to us today, is nevertheless foreshadowed in our formulations, though in so veiled a form that the investigator of the future will ask himself, just as we do, whether we knew what we meant.

d. The Moon-Nature

214   We have treated at some length of the sinister and dangerous aspect of the new moon. In this phase the climax of the moon's waning, which in folklore is not always considered auspicious, is reached. The new moon is dangerous at childbirth and weddings. If a father dies at the waning moon, this brings the children bad luck. One also has to bow to the sickle moon or it will bring bad luck. Even the light of the moon is dangerous as it causes the moon-sickness, which comes from the "moon-wolf." The marriage bed, pregnant women, and small children should be protected from the moonlight. Whoever sews by moonlight sews the winding-sheet, and so on.[355]

215   The passage on the moon in Paracelsus' "De pestilitate" (III, 95) catches very aptly the atmosphere which hangs round the pale moonlight:

Now mark this: Wherever there is a disheartened and timid man in whom imagination has created the great fear and impressed it on him, the moon in heaven aided by her stars is the *corpus* to bring

[355] Baechtold and Stäubli, *Handwörterbuch des deutschen Aberglaubens*, VI, s.v. "Mond."

this about. When such a disheartened timid man looks at the moon under the full sway of his imagination, he looks into the *speculum venenosum magnum naturae* [great poisonous mirror of nature], and the sidereal spirit and *magnes hominis* [magnet of man] will thus be poisoned by the stars and the moon. But we shall expound this more clearly to you as follows. Through his imagination the timid man has made his eyes basilisk-like, and he infects the mirror, the moon, and the stars, through himself at the start, and later on so that the moon is infected by the imagining man; this will happen soon and easily, by dint of the magnetic power which the sidereal body and spirit exerts upon the celestial bodies [viz.] the moon and the stars in great Nature [viz., the Macrocosm]. Thus man in turn will be poisoned by this mirror of the moon and the stars which he has looked at; and this because (for, as you can see, it happens quite naturally) a pregnant woman at the time of menstruation similarly stains and damages the mirror by looking into it. For at such a time she is poisonous and has basilisk's eyes *ex causa menstrui et venenosi sanguinis* [because of the menstrual and poisonous blood] which lies hidden in her body and nowhere more strongly than in her eyes. For there the sidereal spirit of the stained body lies open and naked to the sidereal magnet. *Quia ex menstruo et venenoso sanguine mulieris causatur et nascitur basiliscus, ita luna in coelo est oculus basilisci coeli* [Because as the basilisk is caused and born from the menstrual and poisonous blood of a woman, thus the moon in the sky is the eye of the basilisk of heaven]. And as the mirror is defiled by the woman, thus conversely the eyes, the sidereal spirit, and the body of man are being defiled by the moon, for the reason that at such time the eyes of the timid imagining man are weak and dull, and the sidereal spirit and body draw poison out of the mirror of the moon into which you have looked. But not so that only one human being has the power thus to poison the moon with his sight, no; hence I say that, mostly, menstruating women do poison the moon and the stars much more readily and also more intensely than any man, easily so. Because as you see that they poison and stain the mirror made of metallic material—and what is even more, the glass mirror —much more and sooner they defile the moon and the stars at such a time. And even if at such time the moon only shines on water and the woman looks at the water, the moon will be poisoned, and by still many more means, but it would not do to reveal all this clearly. And such poisoning of the moon happens for this reason: it is the naked eye of the spirit and of the sidereal body and it often grows new and young as you can see. Just as a young child who looks into a mirror which was looked at by a menstruating woman will become long-sighted and cross-eyed and his eyes will be poisoned, stained, and ruined, as the mirror was stained by the menstruating woman; and so also the moon, and also the human being, is poisoned. And as the moon, when it grows new and young, is of a poisonous kind, this you shall notice in two ways, namely in the element of water and also in wood, loam, etc.: as this, when it is gathered at the wrong time will not burn well, but be worm-eaten, poisonous, bad, and putrid, so is also the moon, and that is why it can be poisoned so easily by merely looking at it and the moon with its light is the *humidum ignis* [moisture of fire], of a cold nature, for which reason it is capable of receiving the poison easily.[356]

216   In the Table of Correspondences in Penotus [357] the following are said to pertain to the moon: the snake, the tiger, the Manes, the Lemurs, and the *dei infernales*. These correlations show clearly how Penotus was struck by the underworld nature of the moon.[358] His "heretical" empiricism led him beyond the patristic allegories to a recognition of the moon's dark side, an aspect no longer suited to serve as an allegory of the beauteous bride of Christ. And just as the bitch was forgotten in the lunar allegory of the Church, so too our masculine judgment is apt to forget it when dealing with an over-valued woman. We should not deceive ourselves about the sinister "tail" of the undoubtedly desirable "head": the baying of Hecate is always there, whether it sound from near or from far. This is true of everything feminine and not least of a man's anima. The mythology of the moon is an object lesson in female psychology.[359]

217   The moon with her antithetical nature is, in a sense, a prototype of individuation, a prefiguration of the self: she is the "mother and spouse of the sun, who carries in the wind and the air the spagyric embryo conceived by the sun in her womb and

356 Sudhoff, XIV, pp. 651ff.

357 Pseudonym Bernardus à Portu Aquitanus, *Theatr. chem.*, II, p. 123.

358 The moon also has a relation to Saturn, the astrological maleficus. In the "Dicta Belini" Saturn is, as it were, the "father-mother" of the moon: "I am the light of all things that are mine and I cause the moon to appear openly from within my father Saturn, even from the regnant mother, who is at enmity with me." * ("Allegoriae sapientum," *Theatr. chem.*, V, p. 97.) Saturn plays the role of Typhon: dismemberment.

359 Medical psychologists would profit from Esther Harding's account of moon psychology in her book *Woman's Mysteries*. See especially ch. 12, "The Inner Meaning of the Moon Cycle."

belly." [360] This image corresponds to the psychologem of the pregnant anima, whose child is the self, or is marked by the attributes of the hero. Just as the anima represents and personifies the collective unconscious, so Luna represents the six planets or spirits of the metals. Dorn says:

From Saturn, Mercury, Jupiter, Mars and Venus nothing and no other metal can arise except Luna [i.e., silver]. . . . For Luna consists of the six spiritual metals and their powers, of which each has two. . . . From the planet Mercury, from Aquarius and Gemini, or from Aquarius and Pisces, Luna has her liquidity [*liquatio*] and her white brightness . . . , from Jupiter, Sagittarius, and Taurus her white colour and her great stability in the fire . . . , from Mars, Cancer, and Aries her hardness and fine resonance . . . , from Venus, Gemini, and Libra her degree of solidity [*coagulationis*] and malleability . . . , from Sol, Leo, and Virgo her true purity and great endurance against the strength of the fire . . . , from Saturn, Virgo, and Scorpio, or from Capricorn, her homogeneous body, her pure cleanness [*puram munditiem*], and steadfastness against the force of the fire.[361]

218   Luna is thus the sum and essence of the metals' natures, which are all taken up in her shimmering whiteness. She is multi-natured, whereas Sol has an exceptional nature as the "seventh from the six spiritual metals." He is "in himself nothing other than pure fire." [362] This role of Luna devolves upon the anima, as she personifies the plurality of archetypes, and also upon the Church and the Blessed Virgin, who, both of lunar nature, gather the many under their protection and plead for them before the *Sol iustitiae*. Luna is the "universal receptacle of all things," the "first gateway of heaven," [363] and William Mennens [364] says that she gathers the powers of all the stars in herself as in a womb, so as then to bestow them on sublunary creatures.[365] This quality seems to explain her alleged effect in the *opus ad Lunam*, when she gives the tincture the character and powers of all the stars. The "Fragment from the Persian

360 Dorn, "Phys. Trismeg.," *Theatr. chem.*, I, p. 424.* An allusion to "Tabula Smaragdina," *De Alchemia*, p. 363: "The wind hath borne it in his belly."
361 "Congeries Paracelsicae," *Theatr. chem.*, I, pp. 641f.
362 Ibid., p. 642.
363 Penotus in "De medicament. chem.," *Theatr. chem.*, I, p. 681.
364 "Aurei velleris Libri tres," *Theatr. chem.*, V, p. 321.
365 A parallel to the Maria Mediatrix of the Church, who dispenses grace.

Philosophers" says: "With this tincture all the dead are revived, so that they live for ever, and this tincture is the first-created ferment,[366] namely that 'to the moon,' [367] and it is the light of all lights and the flower and fruit of all lights,[368] which lighteth all things." [369]

219 This almost hymn-like paean to the *materia lapidis* or the tincture refers in the first instance to Luna, for it is during her work of whitening that the illumination takes place. She is the "mother in this art." In her water "Sol is hidden like a fire" [370] —a parallel to the conception of Selene as the μήτηρ τοῦ κόσμου in Plutarch. On the first day of the month of Phamenoth, Osiris enters into Selene, and this is evidently equivalent to the synodos in the spring. "Thus they make the power of Osiris to be fixed in the moon." [371] Selene, Plutarch says, is male-female and is impregnated by Helios. I mention these statements because they show that the moon has a double light, outside a feminine one but inside a masculine one which is hidden in it as a fire. Luna is really the mother of the sun, which means, psychologically, that the unconscious is pregnant with consciousness and gives birth to it. It is the night, which is older than the day:

> Part of the darkness which gave birth to light,
> That proud light which is struggling to usurp
> The ancient rank and realm of Mother Night.[372]

220 From the darkness of the unconscious comes the light of illumination, the *albedo*. The opposites are contained in it *in potentia*, hence the hermaphroditism of the unconscious, its capacity for spontaneous and autochthonous reproduction. This idea is reflected in the "Father-Mother" of the Gnostics,[373] as

366 Presumably aether as the *quinta essentia.*
367 The "opus ad Lunam" is the whitening (*albedo*), which is compared with sunrise.
368 That is, of all luminaries, i.e., stars.
369 *Art. aurif.,* I, p. 398.*
370 "Gloria mundi," *Mus. herm.,* p. 280 (Waite, I, p. 225).*
371 "Isis and Osiris," 43, *Moralia* (trans. by Babbitt, V, pp. 104f.).
372 Goethe, *Faust* (trans. by MacNeice), p. 48 (mod.).
373 For instance in Marcus the Gnostic. Cf. Hippolytus, *Elenchos,* VI, 42, 2 (Legge, II, p. 44).

well as in the naïve vision of Brother Klaus [374] and the modern vision of Maitland,[375] the biographer of Anna Kingsford.

221   Finally, I would like to say a few words about the psychology of the moon, which is none too simple. The alchemical texts were written exclusively by men, and their statements about the moon are therefore the product of masculine psychology. Nevertheless women did play a role in alchemy, as I have mentioned before, and this makes it possible that the "symbolization" will show occasional traces of their influence. Generally the proximity as well as the absence of women has a specifically constellating effect on the unconscious of a man. When a woman is absent or unattainable the unconscious produces in him a certain femininity which expresses itself in a variety of ways and gives rise to numerous conflicts. The more one-sided his conscious, masculine, spiritual attitude the more inferior, banal, vulgar, and biological will be the compensating femininity of the unconscious. He will, perhaps, not be conscious at all of its dark manifestations, because they have been so overlaid with saccharine sentimentality that he not only believes the humbug himself but enjoys putting it over on other people. An avowedly biological or coarse-minded attitude to women produces an excessively lofty valuation of femininity in the unconscious, where it is pleased to take the form of Sophia or of the Virgin. Frequently, however, it gets distorted by everything that misogyny can possibly devise to protect the masculine consciousness from the influence of women, so that the man succumbs instead to unpredictable moods and insensate resentments.

222   Statements by men on the subject of female psychology suffer principally from the fact that the projection of unconscious femininity is always strongest where critical judgment is most needed, that is, where a man is involved emotionally. In the metaphorical descriptions of the alchemists, Luna is primarily a reflection of a man's unconscious femininity, but she is also the principle of the feminine psyche, in the sense that Sol is the principle of a man's. This is particularly obvious in the astrological interpretation of sun and moon, not to mention the age-

374 Cf. "Brother Klaus," pars. 485f.
375 *Anna Kingsford: Her Life, Letters, Diary, and Work*, I, p. 130. I have quoted this vision at some length in my "Commentary on *The Secret of the Golden Flower*," par. 40.

old assumptions of mythology. Alchemy is inconceivable without the influence of her elder sister astrology, and the statements of these three disciplines must be taken into account in any psychological evaluation of the luminaries. If, then, Luna characterizes the feminine psyche and Sol the masculine, consciousness would be an exclusively masculine affair, which is obviously not the case since woman possesses consciousness too. But as we have previously identified Sol with consciousness and Luna with the unconscious, we would now be driven to the conclusion that a woman cannot possess a consciousness.

223 The error in our formulation lies in the fact, firstly, that we equated the moon with the unconscious as such, whereas the equation is true chiefly of the unconscious of a man; and secondly, that we overlooked the fact that the moon is not only dark but is also a giver of light and can therefore represent consciousness. This is indeed so in the case of woman: her consciousness has a lunar rather than a solar character. Its light is the "mild" light of the moon, which merges things together rather than separates them. It does not show up objects in all their pitiless discreteness and separateness, like the harsh, glaring light of day, but blends in a deceptive shimmer the near and the far, magically transforming little things into big things, high into low, softening all colour into a bluish haze, and blending the nocturnal landscape into an unsuspected unity.

224 For purely psychological reasons I have, in other of my writings, tried to equate the masculine consciousness with the concept of Logos and the feminine with that of Eros. By Logos I meant discrimination, judgment, insight, and by Eros I meant the capacity to relate. I regarded both concepts as intuitive ideas which cannot be defined accurately or exhaustively. From the scientific point of view this is regrettable, but from a practical one it has its value, since the two concepts mark out a field of experience which it is equally difficult to define.

225 As we can hardly ever make a psychological proposition without immediately having to reverse it, instances to the contrary leap to the eye at once: men who care nothing for discrimination, judgment, and insight, and women who display an almost excessively masculine proficiency in this respect. I would like to describe such cases as the regular exceptions. They demonstrate, to my mind, the common occurrence of a psychically predomi-

nant contrasexuality. Wherever this exists we find a forcible intrusion of the unconscious, a corresponding exclusion of the consciousness specific to either sex, predominance of the shadow and of contrasexuality, and to a certain extent even the presence of symptoms of possession (such as compulsions, phobias, obsessions, automatisms, exaggerated affects, etc.). This inversion of roles is probably the chief psychological source for the alchemical concept of the hermaphrodite. In a man it is the lunar anima, in a woman the solar animus, that influences consciousness in the highest degree. Even if a man is often unaware of his own anima-possession, he has, understandably enough, all the more vivid an impression of the animus-possession of his wife, and vice versa.

226   Logos and Eros are intellectually formulated intuitive equivalents of the archetypal images of Sol and Luna. In my view the two luminaries are so descriptive and so superlatively graphic in their implications that I would prefer them to the more pedestrian terms Logos and Eros, although the latter do pin down certain psychological peculiarities more aptly than the rather indefinite "Sol and Luna." The use of these images requires at any rate an alert and lively fantasy, and this is not an attribute of those who are inclined by temperament to purely intellectual concepts. These offer us something finished and complete, whereas an archetypal image has nothing but its naked fullness, which seems inapprehensible by the intellect. Concepts are coined and negotiable values; images are life.

227   If our formula regarding the lunar nature of feminine consciousness is correct—and in view of the *consensus omnium* in this matter it is difficult to see how it should not be—we must conclude that this consciousness is of a darker, more nocturnal quality, and because of its lower luminosity can easily overlook differences which to a man's consciousness are self-evident stumbling-blocks. It needs a very moon-like consciousness indeed to hold a large family together regardless of all the differences, and to talk and act in such a way that the harmonious relation of the parts to the whole is not only not disturbed but is actually enhanced. And where the ditch is too deep, a ray of moonlight smoothes it over. A classic example of this is the conciliatory proposal of St. Catherine of Alexandria in Anatole France's *Penguin Island*. The heavenly council had come to a

deadlock over the question of baptism, since although the penguins were animals they had been baptized by St. Maël. Therefore she says: "That is why, Lord, I entreat you to give old Maël's penguins a human head and breast so that they can praise you worthily. And grant them also an immortal soul—but only a little one!" [376]

228   This "lunatic" logic can drive the rational mind to the white heat of frenzy. Fortunately it operates mostly in the dark or cloaks itself in the shimmer of innocence. The moon-nature is its own best camouflage, as at once becomes apparent when a woman's unconscious masculinity breaks through into her consciousness and thrusts her Eros aside. Then it is all up with her charm and the mitigating half-darkness; she takes a stand on some point or other and captiously defends it, although each barbed remark tears her own flesh, and with brutal short-sightedness she jeopardizes everything that is the dearest goal of womanhood. And then, for unfathomable reasons—or perhaps simply because it is time—the picture changes completely: the new moon has once more been vanquished.

229   The Sol who personifies the feminine unconscious is not the sun of the day but corresponds rather to the *Sol niger*. It is not the real *Sol niger* of masculine psychology, the alter ego, the Brother Medardus of E. T. A. Hoffmann's story "The Devil's Elixir," or the crass identity of opposites which we meet with in Jekyll and Hyde. The unconscious Sol of woman may be dark, but it is not "coal black" (ἀνθρακώδης), as was said of the moon; it is more like a chronic eclipse of the sun, which in any case is seldom total. Normally a woman's consciousness emits as much darkness as light, so that, if her consciousness cannot be entirely light, her unconscious cannot be entirely dark either. At any rate, when the lunar phases are repressed on account of too powerful solar influences, her consciousness takes on an overbright solar character, while on the other hand her unconscious becomes darker and darker—*nigrum nigrius nigro*—and both are unendurable for both in the long run.

230   Her *Sol niger* is as void of light and charm as the gentling moonlight is all heavenly peace and magic. It protests too much that it is a light, because it is no light, and a great truth, because it invariably misses the mark, and a high authority, which never-

[376] Cf. *Penguin Island* (trans. by Evans), p. 30.

theless is always wrong, or is only as right as the blind tom-cat who tried to catch imaginary bats in broad daylight, but one day caught a real one by mistake and thereafter became completely unteachable. I do not want to be unfair, but that is what the feminine Sol is like when it obtrudes too much. (And it has to obtrude a bit if the man is to understand it!)

231   As a man normally gets to know his anima only in projected form, so too a woman in the case of her dark sun. When her Eros is functioning properly her sun will not be too dark, and the carrier of the projection may even produce some useful compensation. But if things are not right with her Eros (in which case she is being unfaithful to Love itself), the darkness of her sun will transfer itself to a man who is anima-possessed and who dispenses inferior spirit, which as we know is as intoxicating as the strongest alcohol.

232   The dark sun of feminine psychology is connected with the father-imago, since the father is the first carrier of the animus-image. He endows this virtual image with substance and form, for on account of his Logos he is the source of "spirit" for the daughter. Unfortunately this source is often sullied just where we would expect clean water. For the spirit that benefits a woman is not mere intellect, it is far more: it is an attitude, the spirit by which a man lives.[377] Even a so-called "ideal" spirit is not always the best if it does not understand how to deal adequately with nature, that is, with the animal man. This really would be ideal. Hence every father is given the opportunity to corrupt, in one way or another, his daughter's nature, and the educator, husband, or psychiatrist then has to face the music. For "what has been spoiled by the father"[378] can only be made good by a father, just as "what has been spoiled by the mother" can only be repaired by a mother. The disastrous repetition of the family pattern could be described as the psychological original sin, or as the curse of the Atrides running through the generations. But in judging these things one should not be too certain either of good or of evil. The two are about equally balanced. It should, however, have begun to dawn on our cultural

377 "Spirit and Life," pars. 629ff.
378 Cf. *I Ching, or the Book of Changes* (trans. Wilhelm and Baynes), I, p. 80, Hexagram 18: "Work on What Has Been Spoiled."

optimists that the forces of good are not sufficient to produce either a rational world-order or the faultless ethical behaviour of the individual, whereas the forces of evil are so strong that they imperil any order at all and can imprison the individual in a devilish system that commits the most fearful crimes, so that even if he is ethical-minded he must finally forget his moral responsibility in order to go on living. The "malignity" of collective man has shown itself in more terrifying form today than ever before in history, and it is by this objective standard that the greater and the lesser sins should be measured. We need more casuistic subtlety, because it is no longer a question of extirpating evil but of the difficult art of putting a lesser evil in place of a greater one. The time for the "sweeping statements" so dear to the evangelizing moralist, which lighten his task in the most agreeable way, is long past. Nor can the conflict be escaped by a denial of moral values. The very idea of this is foreign to our instincts and contrary to nature. Every human group that is not actually sitting in prison will follow its accustomed paths according to the measure of its freedom. Whatever the intellectual definition and evaluation of good and evil may be, the conflict between them can never be eradicated, for no one can ever forget it. Even the Christian who feels himself delivered from evil will, when the first rapture is over, remember the thorn in the flesh, which even St. Paul could not pluck out.

233   These hints may suffice to make clear what kind of spirit it is that the daughter needs. They are the truths which speak to the soul, which are not too loud and do not insist too much, but reach the individual in stillness—the individual who constitutes the meaning of the world. It is this knowledge that the daughter needs, in order to pass it on to her son.

5. SAL

a. Salt as the Arcane Substance

234   In this section I shall discuss not only salt but a number of symbolisms that are closely connected with it, such as the "bitterness" of the sea, sea-water and its baptismal quality, which in turn relates it to the "Red Sea." I have included the latter in the scope of my observations but not the symbol of the sea

as such. Since Luna symbolizes the unconscious, Sal, as one of its attributes, is a special instance of the lunar symbolism. This explains the length of the present entire chapter: extensive digressions are necessary in order to do justice to the various aspects of the unconscious that are expressed by salt, and at the same time to explain their psychological meaning.

235   Owing to the theory of "correspondentia," regarded as axiomatic in the Middle Ages, the principles of each of the four worlds—the intelligible or divine, the heavenly, the earthly, and the infernal [379]—corresponded to each other. Usually, however, there was a division into three worlds to correspond with the Trinity: heaven, earth, hell.[380] Triads were also known in alchemy. From the time of Paracelsus the most important triad was Sulphur-Mercurius-Sal, which was held to correspond with the Trinity. Georg von Welling, the plagiarist of Johann Rudolf Glauber, still thought in 1735 that his triad of fire, sun, and salt [381] was "in its root entirely one thing." [382] The use of the Trinity formula in alchemy is so common that further documentation is unnecessary. A subtle feature of the Sulphur-Mercurius-Sal formula is that the central figure, Mercurius, is by nature androgynous and thus partakes both of the masculine red sulphur and of the lunar salt.[383] His equivalent in the celestial realm is the planetary pair Sol and Luna, and in the "intelligible" realm Christ in his mystical androgyny, the "man en-

379 Vigenerus ("De igne et sale," *Theatr. chem.*, V, pp. 32f.) speaks of three worlds. The fire on earth corresponds to the sun in heaven, and this to the Spiritus Sanctus "in the intelligible world." But on p. 39 he suddenly remembers the fourth, forgotten world: "The fourth is infernal, opposed to the intelligible, glowing and burning without any light." * He also distinguishes four kinds of fire. (Cf. *Aion*, pars. 203, 393, and n. 81.)

380 Heaven, earth, hell (like sulphur, mercurius, sal) is a false triad: earth is dual, consisting of the light-world above and the shadow-world below.

381 Fire = sulphur, Sol = Mercurius (as the mother and son of Sol).

382 *Opus Mago-Cabbalisticum et Theosophicum*, p. 30.

383 A quotation from Hermes in *Rosarium phil.* (*Art. aurif.*, II, p. 244) mentions "Sal nostrae lunariae" (the salt of our moon-plant). "Our salt is found in a certain precious Salt, and in all things. On this account the ancient Philosophers called it the common moon" * (*Mus. herm.*, p. 217; Waite, I, p. 177). The salt from the Polar Sea is "lunar" (feminine), and the salt from the Equatorial Sea is "solar" (masculine): Welling, p. 17. Glauber (*De signatura salium, metallorum et planetarum*, p. 12) calls salt feminine and gives Eve as a parallel.

compassed by the woman,[384] i.e., sponsus and sponsa (Ecclesia). Like the Trinity, the alchemical "triunity" is a quaternity in disguise owing to the duplicity of the central figure: Mercurius is not only split into a masculine and a feminine half, but is the poisonous dragon and at the same time the heavenly lapis. This makes it clear that the dragon is analogous to the devil and the lapis to Christ, in accordance with the ecclesiastical view of the devil as an autonomous counterpart of Christ. Furthermore, not only the dragon but the negative aspect of sulphur, namely *sulphur comburens,* is identical with the devil, as Glauber says: "Verily, sulphur is the true black devil of hell, who can be conquered by no element save by salt alone." [385] Salt by contrast is a "light" substance, similar to the lapis, as we shall see.

236   From all this we get the following schema:

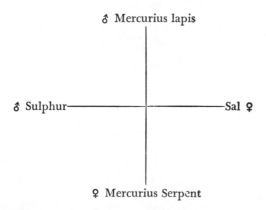

237   Here we have another of those well-known quaternities of opposites which are usually masked as a triad, just as the Christian Trinity is able to maintain itself as such only by eliminat-

384 St. Gregory, *In primum Regum expositiones,* I, i, 1 (Migne, *P.L.,* vol. 79, col. 23). This idea is developed in literal form, in both Tibetan and Bengali Tantrism, as Shiva in the embrace of Shakti, the maker of Maya. We find the same idea in alchemy. Mylius (*Phil. ref.,* pp. 8f.) says: "[God has] love all round him. Others have declared him to be an intellectual and fiery spirit, having no form, but transforming himself into whatsoever he wills and making himself equal to all things. . . . Whence, by a kind of similitude to the nature of the soul, we give to God, or the power of God which sustains all things, the name of Anima media natura or soul of the World." * The concluding words are a quotation from "De arte chymica," *Art. aurif.,* I, p. 608.
385 *De natura salium,* pp. 41ff.

ing the fourth protagonist of the divine drama. If he were included there would be, not a Trinity, but a Christian Quaternity. For a long time there had been a psychological need for this, as is evident from the medieval pictures of the Assumption and Coronation of the Virgin; it was also responsible for elevating her to the position of mediatrix, corresponding to Christ's position as the mediator, with the difference that Mary only transmits grace but does not generate it. The recent promulgation of the dogma of the Assumption emphasizes the taking up not only of the soul but of the body of Mary into the Trinity, thus making a dogmatic reality of those medieval representations of the quaternity which are constructed on the following pattern:

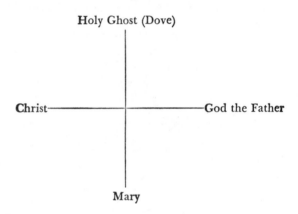

Holy Ghost (Dove)

Christ————————————God the Father

Mary

Only in 1950, after the teaching authority in the Church had long deferred it, and almost a century after the declaration of the dogma of the Immaculate Conception, did the Pope, moved by a growing wave of popular petitions,[386] feel compelled to declare the Assumption as a revealed truth. All the evidence shows that the dogmatization was motivated chiefly by the religious need of the Catholic masses. Behind this stands the archetypal numen of feminine deity,[387] who, at the Council of

386 "In the course of time these requests and petitions, so far from decreasing, grew daily more numerous and more insistent." *Munificentissimus Deus*, p. 5.
387 A Catholic writer says of the Assumption: "Nor, would it seem, is the underlying motif itself even peculiarly Christian; rather would it seem to be but one expression of a universal archetypal pattern, which somehow responds to some deep and widespread human need, and which finds other similar expressions in

Ephesus in 431, imperiously announced her claim to the title of "Theotokos" (God-bearer), as distinct from that of a mere "Anthropotokos" (man-bearer) accorded to her by the Nestorian rationalists.

238   The taking up of the body had long been emphasized as an historical and material event, and the alchemists could therefore make use of the representations of the Assumption in describing the glorification of matter in the opus. The illustration of this process in Reusner's *Pandora* [388] shows, underneath the coronation scene, a kind of shield between the emblems of Matthew and Luke, on which is depicted the extraction of Mercurius from the prima materia. The extracted spirit appears in monstrous form: the head is surrounded by a halo, and reminds us of the traditional head of Christ, but the arms are snakes and the lower half of the body resembles a stylized fish's tail. [389] This is without doubt the *anima mundi* who has been freed from the shackles of matter, the *filius macrocosmi* or Mercurius-Anthropos, who, because of his double nature, is not only spiritual and physical but unites in himself the morally highest and lowest. [390] The illustration in *Pandora* points to the great secret which the alchemists dimly felt was implicit in the Assumption. The proverbial darkness of sublunary matter has always been associated with the "prince of this world," the devil. He is the metaphysical figure who is excluded from the Trinity but who, as the counterpart of Christ, is the *sine qua non* of the drama of redemption. [391] His equivalent in alchemy is the dark side of Mercurius duplex and, as we saw, the active sulphur. He also conceals himself in the poisonous dragon, the preliminary, chthonic form of the *lapis aethereus*. To the natural philosophers of the Middle Ages, and to Dorn in particular, it was per-

---

countless myths and rituals, poems and pictures, practices and even philosophies, all over the globe." Victor White, "The Scandal of the Assumption," *Life of the Spirit*, V, p. 200.

388 (Basel, 1588), p. 253. Cf. *Psychology and Alchemy*, Fig. 232.

389 Cf. the man with a fish's tail in the mosaic on the floor of the cathedral of Pesaro, 6th cent., with the inscription: "Est homo non totus medius sed piscis ab imo." (This man is not complete, but half fish from the deep.) Becker, *Die Darstellung Jesu Christi unter dem Bilde des Fisches*, p. 127.

390 Cf. "The Spirit Mercurius," pars. 267ff.; also the arcane teaching of Paracelsus in "Paracelsus as a Spiritual Phenomenon," pars. 159ff.

391 Cf. "Dogma of the Trinity," pars. 248f., 252ff.

fectly clear that the triad must be complemented by a fourth, as the lapis had always been regarded as a quaternity of elements. It did not disturb them that this would necessarily involve the evil spirit. On the contrary, the dismemberment and self-devouring of the dragon probably seemed to them a commendable operation. Dorn, however, saw in the quaternity the absolute opposite of the Trinity, namely the female principle, which seemed to him "of the devil," for which reason he called the devil the "four-horned serpent." This insight must have given him a glimpse into the core of the problem.[392] In his refutation he identified woman with the devil because of the number two, which is characteristic of both. The devil, he thought, was the binarius itself, since it was created on the second day of Creation, on Monday, the day of the moon, on which God failed to express his pleasure, this being the day of "doubt" and separation.[393] Dorn puts into words what is merely hinted at in the *Pandora* illustration.

239   If we compare this train of thought with the Christian quaternity which the new dogma has virtually produced (but has not defined as such), it will immediately be apparent that we have here an "upper" quaternio which is supraordinate to man's wholeness and is psychologically comparable to the Moses quaternio of the Gnostics.[394] Man and the dark abyss of the world, the *deus absconditus,* have not yet been taken up into it. Alchemy, however, is the herald of a still-unconscious drive for maximal integration which seems to be reserved for a distant future, even though it originated with Origen's doubt concerning the ultimate fate of the devil.[395]

240   In philosophical alchemy, salt is a cosmic principle. According to its position in the quaternity, it is correlated with the feminine, lunar side and with the upper, light half. It is therefore not surprising that Sal is one of the many designations for the arcane substance. This connotation seems to have developed

392 For a closer discussion see "Psychology and Religion," pars. 104ff.
393 "De Tenebris contra Naturam," *Theatr. chem.,* I, p. 527. Cf. "Psychology and Religion," pars. 104, n. 47, 120, n. 11, and "Dogma of the Trinity," par. 262.
394 For details see *Aion,* pars. 359ff.
395 Ibid., par. 171, n. 29.

in the early Middle Ages under Arabic influence. The oldest
traces of it can be found in the *Turba*, where salt-water and sea-
water are synonyms for the *aqua permanens*,[396] and in Senior,
who says that Mercurius is made from salt.[397] His treatise is one
of the earliest authorities in Latin alchemy. Here "Sal Alkali"
also plays the role of the arcane substance, and Senior mentions
that the *dealbatio* was called "salsatura" (marination).[398] In the
almost equally old "Allegoriae sapientum" the lapis is described
as "salsus" (salty).[399] Arnaldus de Villanova (1235?–1313) says:
"Whoever possesses the salt that can be melted, and the oil that
cannot be burned, may praise God." [400] It is clear from this that
salt is an arcane substance. The *Rosarium*, which leans very
heavily on the old Latin sources, remarks that the "whole secret
lies in the prepared common salt," [401] and that the "root of the
art is the soap of the sages" (*sapo sapientum*), which is the "mineral" of all salts and is called the "bitter salt" (*sal amarum*).[402]
Whoever knows the salt knows the secret of the old sages.[403]
"Salts and alums are the helpers of the stone." [404] Isaac Hollandus calls salt the medium between the *terra sulphurea* and
the water. "God poured a certain salt into them in order to unite
them, and the sages named this salt the salt of the wise." [405]

241   Among later writers, salt is even more clearly the arcane substance. For Mylius it is synonymous with the tincture; [406] it is
the earth-dragon who eats his own tail, and the "ash," the

396 P. 283.

397 "First comes the ash, then the salt, and from that salt by divers operations the
Mercury of the Philosophers." * Quoted in *Ros. phil.* (*Art. aurif.*, II, p. 210) and in
"Clangor buccinae" (*Art. aurif.*, I, p. 488).

398 "De chemia," *Theatr. chem.*, V, p. 231. For "salsatura" see *Aurora consurgens*
II, in *Art. aurif.*, I, p. 205.

399 *Theatr. chem.*, V, p. 77.

400 Cited in *Ros. phil.*, p. 244.

401 Ibid.

402 Ibid., p. 222. The same on p. 225, where the salt is also called the "key that
closes and opens." In Parable VII of *Aurora Consurgens* (p. 141), the bride calls
herself the "key" (*clavicula*).

403 *Ros. phil.*, p. 244.

404 Ibid., p. 269. The text adds: "He who tastes not the savour of the salts, shall
never come to the desired ferment of the ferment." *

405 "Opera mineralia," *Theatr. chem.*, III, p. 411.

406 *Phil. ref.*, p. 189.

"diadem of thy heart." [407] The "salt of the metals" is the lapis.[408] Basilius Valentinus speaks of a "sal spirituale." [409] It is the seat of the virtue which makes the "art" possible,[410] the "most noble treasury," [411] the "good and noble salt," which "though it has not the form of salt from the beginning, is nevertheless called salt"; it "becomes impure and pure of itself, it dissolves and coagulates itself, or, as the sages say, locks and unlocks itself"; [412] it is the "quintessence, above all things and in all creatures." [413] "The whole magistery lies in the salt and its solution." [414] The "permanent radical moisture" consists of salt.[415] It is synonymous with the "incombustible oil," [416] and is altogether a mystery to be concealed.[417]

242   As the arcane substance, it is identified with various synonyms for the latter. Above all it is an "ens centrale." For Khunrath salt is the "physical centre of the earth." [418] For Vigenerus it is a component of "that virginal and pure earth which is contained in the centre of all composite elementals, or in the depths of the same." [419] Glauber calls salt the "concentrated centre of the elements." [420]

243   Although the arcane substance is usually identified with Mercurius, the relation of salt to Mercurius is seldom men-

---

407 Ibid., p. 195.

408 Ibid., p. 222. Also in *Ros. phil.*, p. 208; Khunrath, *Amphitheatrum sapientiae*, p. 194, and *Mus. herm.*, p. 20 (Waite, I, p. 22).

409 Cited in "Tract. aureus," *Mus. herm.*, p. 31 (Waite, I, p. 32). The writings of Basilius Valentinus do not date from the 15th cent. but are a 17th-cent. forgery.

410 "Alexander the Great, King of Macedonia, in his Philosophy has the following words: . . . Blessed be God in heaven who has created this art in the Salt." * "Gloria mundi," *Mus. herm.*, p. 217 (Waite, I, p. 176).

411 Ibid., p. 218 (Waite, I, p. 177).

412 Ibid., p. 216.

413 Ibid., p. 217. It is also described as the "balsam of nature" (Khunrath, *Hyl. Chaos*, p. 258) and as the "fifth element" (sea). Vigenerus, "De igne et sale," *Theatr. chem.*, VI, p. 122.

414 *Hyl. Chaos*, p. 256.

415 Ibid., p. 257.

416 Ibid., p. 260.

417 *Amphitheatrum*, p. 194.

418 *Hyl. Chaos*, p. 257.

419 "De igne et sale," p. 44.

420 *De natura salium*, p. 44. Glauber adds the verse: "In the salt and fire / Lies the treasure so dear."

tioned. Senior, as we noted, says that "by divers operations" Mercurius is made from salt,[421] and Khunrath identifies Mercurius with common salt.[422] The rarity of the identification strikes us just because the "salt of the wise" really implies its relation to Mercurius. I can explain this only on the supposition that salt did not acquire its significance until later times and then at once appeared as an independent figure in the Sulphur-Mercurius-Sal triad.

244   Salt also has an obvious relation to the earth, not to the earth as such, but to "our earth," by which is naturally meant the arcane substance.[423] This is evident from the aforementioned identification of salt with the earth-dragon. The full text of Mylius runs:

What remains below in the retort is our salt, that is, our earth, and it is of a black colour, a dragon that eats his own tail. For the dragon is the matter that remains behind after the distillation of water from it, and this water is called the dragon's tail, and the dragon is its blackness, and the dragon is saturated with his water and coagulated, and so he eats his tail.[424]

The rarely mentioned relation of salt to the *nigredo* [425] is worth noting here, for because of its proverbial whiteness salt is constantly associated with the *albedo*. On the other hand we would expect the close connection between salt and water, which is in fact already implicit in the sea-water. The *aqua pontica* plays an important role as a synonym for the *aqua permanens,* as also does "mare" (sea). That salt, as well as Luna, is an essential component of this is clear from Vigenerus: "There is nothing wherein the moisture lasts longer, or is wetter, than salt, of which the sea for the most part consists. Neither is there anything wherein the moon displays her motion more clearly than

---

421 *Art. aurif.,* I, p. 210. In the *Turba* salt-water and sea-water are synonyms for Mercurius.

422 *Hyl. chaos,* p. 257.

423 "Our salt, that is to say, our earth." "Tract. aureus," *Mus. herm.,* p. 20 (Waite, I, p. 22). Cf. also "Clangor buccinae," *Art. aurif.,* I, p. 488, and "Scala philosophorum," *Art. aurif.,* II, p. 107.

424 *Phil. ref.,* p. 195.

425 One place is in "Gloria mundi," *Mus. herm.,* p. 216 (Waite, I, p. 176): "(In the beginning) it is mostly black and evil-smelling." *

the sea, as can be seen . . . from its ebb and flow." Salt, he says, has an "inexterminable humidity," and "that is the reason why the sea cannot be dried up." [426] Khunrath identifies the *femina alba* or *candida* with the "crystalline salt," and this with the white water.[427] "Our water" cannot be made without salt,[428] and without salt the opus will not succeed.[429] According to Rupescissa (ca. 1350), salt is "water, which the dryness of the fire has coagulated." [430]

b. The Bitterness

245   Inseparable from salt and sea is the quality of *amaritudo*, 'bitterness'. The etymology of Isidore of Seville was accepted all through the Middle Ages: "Mare ab amaro." [431] Among the alchemists the bitterness became a kind of technical term. Thus, in the treatise "Rosinus ad Euthiciam," [432] there is the following dialogue between Zosimos and Theosebeia: "This is the stone that hath in it glory and colour. And she: Whence cometh its colour? He replied: From its exceeding strong bitterness. And she: Whence cometh its bitterness and intensity? He answered: From the impurity of its metal." The treatise "Rosinus ad Sarratantam episcopum" [433] says: "Take the stone that is black, white, red, and yellow, and is a wonderful bird that flies without wings in the blackness of the night and the brightness of the day: in the bitterness that is in its throat the colouring will be found." "Each thing in its first matter is corrupt and bitter," says Ripley. "The bitterness is a tincturing poison." [434] And Mylius: "Our stone is endowed with the strongest spirit, bitter

[426] "De igne et sale," *Theatr. chem.*, VI, p. 98.
[427] *Hyl. Chaos,* pp. 197f.
[428] Ibid., p. 229.
[429] Ibid., p. 254.
[430] "De confectione lapidis," *Theatr. chem.*, III, p. 199.
[431] *Liber etymologiarum,* XIII, 14, fol. lxviiiv.
[432] A corrupt version of "Zosimos ad Theosebeiam," owing to Arabic-Latin transmission. *Art. aurif.*, I, p. 264.
[433] *Art. aurif.,* I, p. 316. Cf. also *Ros. phil., Art. aurif.,* II, p. 258; Mylius, *Phil. ref.,* p. 249; "Tract. aureus," *Ars chemica,* pp. 11f.
[434] *Chymische Schrifften,* p. 100.

and brazen (*aeneus*)"; [435] and the *Rosarium* mentions that salt is bitter because it comes from the "mineral of the sea." [436] The "Liber Alze" [437] says: "O nature of this wondrous thing, which transforms the body into spirit! . . . When it is found alone it conquers all things, and is an excellent, harsh, and bitter acid, which transmutes gold into pure spirit." [438]

246   These quotations clearly allude to the sharp taste of salt and sea-water. The reason why the taste is described as bitter and not simply as salt may lie first of all in the inexactness of the language, since *amarus* also means 'sharp', 'biting', 'harsh', and is used metaphorically for acrimonious speech or a wounding joke. Besides this, the language of the Vulgate had an important influence as it was one of the main sources for medieval Latin. The moral use which the Vulgate consistently makes of *amarus* and *amaritudo* gives them, in alchemy as well, a nuance that cannot be passed over. This comes out clearly in Ripley's remark that "each thing in its first matter is corrupt and bitter." The juxtaposition of these two attributes indicates the inner connection between them: corruption and bitterness are on the same footing, they denote the state of imperfect bodies, the initial state of the prima materia. Among the best known synonyms for the latter are the "chaos" and the "sea," in the classical, mythological sense denoting the beginning of the world, the sea in particular being conceived as the παμμήτηρ, 'matrix of all creatures'.[439] The prima materia is often called *aqua pontica*. The salt that "comes from the mineral of the sea" is by its very nature bitter, but the bitterness is due also to the impurity of the imperfect body. This apparent contradiction is explained by the report of Plutarch that the Egyptians regarded the sea as something impure and untrustworthy (μηδὲ σύμφυλον αὐτῆς), and as the domain of Typhon (Set); they called salt the "spume of Typhon." [440] In his *Philosophia reformata*, Mylius mentions "sea-spume" together with the "purged or purified" sea, rock-salt, the bird, and Luna as equiva-

435 *Phil. ref.*, p. 244. The same in *Ros. phil.*, p. 248.
436 P. 222.
437 *Mus. herm.*, p. 328 (Waite, I, pp. 263f.).
438 A *Turba* quotation from Sermo XV of Flritis (or Fictes = Socrates). See Ruska, *Turba philosophorum*, pp. 124f.
439 Cf. *Psychology and Alchemy*, pars. 56f., 476.
440 "Isis and Osiris," 32, *Moralia* (trans. Babbitt) V, pp. 78f.

lent synonyms for the *lapis occultus*.[441] Here the impurity of the sea is indirectly indicated by the epithets "purged" or "purified." The sea-spume is on a par with the salt and—of particular interest—with the bird, naturally the bird of Hermes, and this throws a sudden light on the above passage from Rosinus, about the bird with bitterness in its throat. The bird is a parallel of salt because salt is a spirit,[442] a volatile substance, which the alchemists were wont to conceive as a bird.

247 As the expulsion of the spirit was effected by various kinds of burning (*combustio, adustio, calcinatio, assatio, sublimatio, incineratio,* etc.), it was natural to call the end-product "ash" —again in a double sense as *scoria, faex,* etc., and as the spirit or bird of Hermes. Thus the *Rosarium* says: "Sublime with fire, until the spirit which thou wilt find in it [the substance] goeth forth from it, and it is named the bird or the ash of Hermes. Therefore saith Morienus: Despise not the ashes, for they are the diadem of thy heart, and the ash of things that endure." [443] In other words, the ash is the spirit that dwells in the glorified body.

248 This bird or spirit is associated with various colours. At first the bird is black, then it grows white feathers, which finally become coloured.[444] The Chinese cousin of the *avis Hermetis,* the "scarlet bird," moults in a similar way.[445] We are told in the treatise of Wei Po-yang: "The fluttering Chu-niao flies the five colours." [446] They are arranged as follows:

441 The text is a poem which Mylius cites from an older source. The most important passages are the following:
    "There is a secret stone, hidden in a deep well
    Worthless and rejected, concealed in dung or filth . . .
    And this stone is a bird, and neither stone nor bird . . .
    . . . now sea-spume or vinegar,
    . . . .
    Now again the gem of salt, Almisadir the common salt . . .
    . . . .
    Now the sea, cleansed and purged with sulphur." *
Phil. ref., p. 305. At that time *gemma* simply meant "stone." Cf. Ruland, *Lexicon,* pp. 241f.
442 Cf. supra, par. 245: "Our stone is endowed with the strongest spirit."
443 *Art. aurif.,* II, pp. 282f.
444 Cf. Rosencreutz, *Chymical Wedding* (trans. by Foxcroft), p. 155.
445 The phoenix, the Western equivalent of this wonder-bird, is described by Maier as very colourful: "His neck is surrounded with a golden brightness, and the rest of his body by feathers of purple hue." * *Symb. aur. mens.,* p. 598.
446 *Isis,* XVIII, pp. 218, 258.

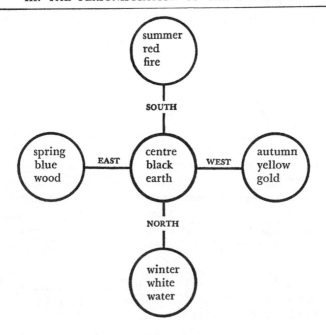

249   Earth occupies the central position as the fifth element, though it is not the quintessence and goal of the work but rather its basis, corresponding to terra as the arcane substance in Western alchemy.[447]

250   As regards the origin and meaning of the *avis Hermetis,* I would like to mention the report of Aelian that the ibis is "dear to Hermes, the father of words, since in its form it resembles the nature of the Logos; for its blackness and swift flight could be compared to the silent and introverted [ἔνδον ἐπιστρεφομένῳ] Logos, but its whiteness to the Logos already uttered and heard, which is the servant and messenger of the inner word." [448]

251   It is not easy for a modern mind to conceive salt, a cold-damp, lunar-terrestrial substance, as a bird and a spirit. Spirit, as the Chinese conceive it, is yang, the fiery and dry element, and this accords with the views of Heraclitus as well as with the Christian concept of the Holy Ghost as tongues of fire. Luna, we have seen,

447 It is strange that the editors of Wei Po-yang are of the opinion that no fundamental analogy obtains between Chinese and Western alchemy. The similarity is, on the contrary, amazing. [Cf. "Concerning Mandala Symbolism," pars. 630ff. (figs. 1–3).—EDs.]

448 *De natura animalium,* X, 29 (ed. Hercher, I, p. 257).

is unquestionably connected with *mens, manas,* mind, etc. But these connections are of a somewhat ambiguous nature. Although the earth can boast of an earth-spirit and other daemons, they are after all "spirits" and not "spirit." The "cold" side of nature is not lacking in spirit, but it is a spirit of a special kind, which Christianity regarded as demonic and which therefore found no acclaim except in the realm of the magical arts and sciences. This spirit is the snake-like Nous or Agathodaimon, which in Hellenistic syncretism merges together with Hermes. Christian allegory and iconography also took possession of it on the basis of John 3 : 14: "And as Moses lifted up the serpent in the wilderness, even so must the Son of man be lifted up." The mercurial serpent or "spirit Mercurius" is the personification and living continuation of the spirit who, in the prayer entitled the "Secret Inscription" in the Great Magic Papyrus of Paris, is invoked as follows:

Greetings, entire edifice of the Spirit of the air, greetings, Spirit that penetratest from heaven to earth, and from earth, which abideth in the midst of the universe, to the uttermost bounds of the abyss, greetings, Spirit that penetratest into me, and shakest me. . . . Greetings, beginning and end of irremovable Nature, greetings, thou who revolvest the elements that untiringly render service, greetings, brightly shining sun, whose radiance ministereth to the world, greetings, moon shining by night with disc of fickle brilliance, greetings, all ye spirits of the demons of the air. . . . O great, greatest, incomprehensible fabric of the world, formed in a circle! . . . dwelling in the aether, having the form of water, of earth, of fire, of wind, of light, of darkness, star-glittering, damp-fiery-cold Spirit! [ὑγροπυρινοψυχρὸν πνεῦμα].[449]

252   Here is a magnificent description of a spirit that is apparently the exact opposite of the Christian pneuma. This antique spirit is also the spirit of alchemy, which today we can interpret as the unconscious projected into heavenly space and external objects. Although declared to be the devil by the early Christians, it should not be identified outright with evil; it merely has the uncomfortable quality of being beyond good and evil, and it gives this perilous quality to anyone who identifies with it, as we can see from the eloquent case of Nietzsche and the psychic epidemic that came after him. This spirit that is "beyond good and

449 Preisendanz, *Pap. Graec. Mag.,* I, pp. 110ff. Pap. IV, 1115–66.

evil" is not the same as being "six thousand feet above good and evil," but rather the same distance below it, or better, before it. It is the spirit of the chaotic waters of the beginning, before the second day of Creation, before the separation of the opposites and hence before the advent of consciousness. That is why it leads those whom it overcomes neither upwards nor beyond, but back into chaos. This spirit corresponds to that part of the psyche which has not been assimilated to consciousness and whose transformation and integration are the outcome of a long and wearisome opus. The artifex was, in his way, conscious enough of the dangers of the work, and for this reason his operations consisted largely of precautions whose equivalents are the rites of the Church.

253   The alchemists understood the return to chaos as an essential part of the opus. It was the stage of the *nigredo* and *mortificatio,* which was then followed by the "purgatorial fire" and the *albedo*. The spirit of chaos is indispensable to the work, and it cannot be distinguished from the "gift of the Holy Ghost" any more than the Satan of the Old Testament can be distinguished from Yahweh. The unconscious is both good and evil and yet neither, the matrix of all potentialities.

254   After these remarks—which seemed to me necessary—on the "salt-spirit," as Khunrath calls it, let us turn back to the *amaritudo*. As the bitter salt comes from the impure sea, it is understandable that the "Gloria mundi" should call it "mostly black and evil-smelling in the beginning." [450] The blackness and bad smell, described by the alchemists as the "stench of the graves," pertain to the underworld and to the sphere of moral darkness. This impure quality is common also to the *corruptio,* which, as we saw, Ripley equates with bitterness. Vigenerus describes salt as "corruptible," in the sense that the body is subject to corruption and decay and does not have the fiery and incorruptible nature of the spirit. [451]

255   The moral use of qualities that were originally physical is clearly dependent, particularly in the case of a cleric like Ripley, on ecclesiastical language. About this I can be brief, as I can rely on Rahner's valuable "Antenna Crucis II: Das Meer der

450 *Mus. herm.,* p. 216 (Waite, I, p. 176).
451 "To the spiritual [body] is referred fire, to the corruptible [body], Salt." * "De igne et sale," *Theatr. chem.,* VI, p. 7.

Welt." Here Rahner brings together all the patristic allegories
that are needed to understand the alchemical symbolism. The
patristic use of "mare" is defined by St. Augustine: "Mare
saeculum est" (the sea is the world).[452] It is the "essence of the
world, as the element . . . subject to the devil." St. Hilary says:
"By the depths of the sea is meant the seat of hell." [453] The sea
is the "gloomy abyss," the remains of the original pit,[454] and
hence of the chaos that covered the earth. For St. Augustine
this abyss is the realm of power allotted to the devil and
demons after their fall.[455] It is on the one hand a "deep that
cannot be reached or comprehended" [456] and on the other the
"depths of sin." [457] For Gregory the Great the sea is the "depths
of eternal death." [458] Since ancient times it was the "abode of
water-demons." [459] There dwells Leviathan (Job 3 : 8),[460] who
in the language of the Fathers signifies the devil. Rahner documents the patristic equations: *diabolus = draco* = Leviathan =
cetus magnus = aspis (adder, asp) = *draco*.[461] St. Jerome says:
"The devil surrounds the seas and the ocean on all sides." [462]
The bitterness of salt-water is relevant in this connection, as it is
one of the peculiarities of hell and damnation which must be
fully tasted by the meditant in Loyola's *Exercises*. Point 4 of
Exercise V says he must, in imagination, "taste with the taste
bitter things, as tears, sadness, and the worm of conscience." [463]
This is expressed even more colourfully in the Spiritual Exercises of the Jesuit Sebastian Izquierdo (1686): "Fourthly, the
taste will be tormented with a rabid hunger and thirst, with no
hope of alleviation; and its food will be bitter wormwood, and
its drink water of gall." [464]

[452] *Expositions of the Book of Psalms:* Ps. 92 : 7, IV, p. 340.
[453] *Tractatus super Psalmos*, 68, 28 (Migne, *P.L.*, vol. 9, col. 487).*
[454] Rahner, "Antennae Crucis II," p. 105.
[455] *Expositions:* Ps. 148 : 9, VI, p. 424 (Migne, *P.L.*, vol. 36, col. 1943).
[456] Ibid., II, p. 193: "Profunditas aquarum impenetrabilis."
[457] Ibid., I, p. 412: "Profunditas peccatorum."
[458] *Homiliae in Evangelia*, 11, 4 (Migne, *P.L.*, vol. 76, col. 1116): "Aeternae mortis
profunda."   [459] Abt, *Die Apologie des Apuleius*, p. 257 (183).
[460] The Septuagint has μέγα κῆτος (great whale) for Leviathan.
[461] "Antennae Crucis, II," p. 108.
[462] *Epistula II ad Theodosium*, p. 12, in *Opera*, Sectio I, Pars I, Epistolarum
Pars I.*   [463] *Spiritual Exercises* (trans. by Rickaby), p. 41.*
[464] *Pratica di alcuni esercitij Spirituali di S. Ignatio*, "Esercitio dell'Inferno," H,
p. 6.* The concluding words are reminiscent of Jeremiah 23 : 15: "Behold, I will
feed them with wormwood [*absynthio*], and make them drink the water of gall."

c. The Red Sea

256   It might almost be one of the alchemical paradoxes that the Red Sea, in contrast to the significance ordinarily attached to "mare," is a term for the healing and transforming baptismal water,[465] and is thus an equivalent of the alchemical *aqua pontica*. St. Augustine says, "The Red Sea signifies baptism"; [466] and, according to Honorius of Autun, "the Red Sea is the baptism reddened by the blood of Christ, in which our enemies, namely our sins, are drowned." [467]

257   We must also mention the Peratic interpretation of the Red Sea. The Red Sea drowned the Egyptians, but the Egyptians were all "non-knowers" (οἱ ἀγνοοῦντες). The exodus from Egypt signifies the exodus from the body, which is Egypt in miniature, being the incarnation of sinfulness, and the crossing (περᾶσαι) [468] of the Red Sea is the crossing of the water of corruption, which is Kronos. The other side of the Red Sea is the other side of Creation. The arrival in the desert is a "genesis outside of generation" (ἔξω γενέσεως γενέσθαι). There the "gods of destruction" and the "god of salvation" are all together.[469] The Red Sea is a water of death for those that are "unconscious," but for those that are "conscious" it is a baptismal water of rebirth and transcendence.[470] By "unconscious" are meant those who have no gnosis, i.e., are not enlightened as to the nature and destiny of man in the cosmos. In modern language it would be those who have no knowledge of the contents of the personal and collective unconscious. The personal unconscious is the shadow and the inferior function,[471] in Gnostic terms the sinfulness and impurity that must be washed away by baptism. The collective unconscious expresses itself in the mythological teachings, character-

---

465 Doelger, *Antike und Christentum*, II, pp. 63ff.

466 *Tractates on the Gospel of St. John*, XXV, 9 (trans. by Innes), II, p. 80.*

467 *Speculum de mysteriis ecclesiae*, Migne, *P.L.*, vol. 172, col. 921.*

468 Whence the designation "Peratics," a Gnostic sect. (Cf. *Aion*, pp. 185f.) They were the "trans-scendentalists."

469 Hippolytus, *Elenchos*, V, 16, 4f.

470 There exists a level or threshold of consciousness which is characteristic of a definite time-period or stratum of society, and which might be compared to a water-level. The unconscious level rises whenever the conscious level falls, and vice versa. Anything that is not in the conscious field of vision remains invisible and forms a content of the unconscious.

471 Cf. *Psychological Types*, def. 30.

istic of most mystery religions, which reveal the secret knowledge concerning the origin of all things and the way to salvation. "Unconscious" people who attempt to cross the sea without being purified and without the guidance of enlightenment are drowned; they get stuck in the unconscious and suffer a spiritual death in so far as they cannot get beyond their one-sidedness. To do this they would have to be more conscious of what is unconscious to them and their age, above all of the inner opposite, namely those contents to which the prevailing views are in any way opposed. This continual process of getting to know the counterposition in the unconscious I have called the "transcendent function," [472] because the confrontation of conscious (rational) data with those that are unconscious (irrational) necessarily results in a modification of standpoint. But an alteration is possible only if the existence of the "other" is admitted, at least to the point of taking conscious cognizance of it. A Christian of today, for instance, no longer ought to cling obstinately to a one-sided credo, but should face the fact that Christianity has been in a state of schism for four hundred years, with the result that every single Christian has a split in his psyche. Naturally this lesion cannot be treated or healed if everyone insists on his own standpoint. Behind those barriers he can rejoice in his absolute and consistent convictions and deem himself above the conflict, but outside them he keeps the conflict alive by his intransigence and continues to deplore the pig-headedness and stiff-neckedness of everybody else. It seems as if Christianity had been from the outset the religion of chronic squabblers, and even now it does everything in its power never to let the squabbles rest. Remarkably enough, it never stops preaching the gospel of neighbourly love.

258 We should get along a lot better if we realized that the majority views of "others" are condoned by a minority in ourselves. Armed with this psychological insight, which today no longer has the character of revelation since common sense can grasp it, we could set out on the road to the union of the opposites and would then, as in the Peratic doctrine, come to the place where the "gods of destruction and the god of salvation are together." By this is obviously meant the destructive and

[472] Ibid., def. 51 (especially par. 828). See also my "The Transcendent Function."

constructive powers of the unconscious. This *coincidentia oppositorum* forms a parallel to the Messianic state of fulfilment described in Isaiah 11 : 6ff. and 35 : 5ff., though with one important difference: the place of "genesis outside of generation"—presumably an *opus contra naturam*—is clearly not paradise but ἡ ἔρημος, the desert and the wilderness. Everyone who becomes conscious of even a fraction of his unconscious gets outside his own time and social stratum into a kind of solitude, as our text remarks. But only there is it possible to meet the "god of salvation." Light is manifest in the darkness, and out of danger the rescue comes. In his sermon on Luke 19 : 12 Meister Eckhart says: "And who can be nobler than the man who is born half of the highest and best the world has to offer, and half of the innermost ground of God's nature and God's loneliness? Therefore the Lord speaks in the prophet Hosea: I will lead the noble souls into the wilderness, and speak into their hearts. One with the One, One from the One, and in the One itself the One, eternally!" [473]

259   I have gone into this Hippolytus text at some length because the Red Sea was of special significance to the alchemists. Sermo LXII of the *Turba* mentions the "Tyrian dye, which is extracted from our most pure Red Sea." It is the parallel of the *tinctura philosophorum,* which is described as black and is extracted "from the sea." [474] The old treatise "Rosinus ad Euthiciam" says: "And know that our Red Sea is more tincturing than all seas, and that the poison,[475] when it is cooked and becomes foul and discoloured, penetrates all bodies." [476] The tincture is the "dip" and the baptismal water of the alchemists, here asserted to come from the Red Sea. This idea is understandable in view of the patristic and Gnostic interpretation of the Red Sea as the blood of Christ in which we are baptized; hence the paralleling of the tincture, salt, and *aqua pontica* with blood.[477]

260   The Red Sea appears in a very peculiar manner in the "Tractatus Aristotelis ad Alexandrum Magnum," where a recipe says:

473 Cf. Evans trans., II, p. 86. This passage refers to Hosea 13 : 5: "I did know thee in the wilderness, and in the land of great drought."
474 *Turba,* ed. Ruska, p. 164.
475 *Venenum* or φάρμακον is a synonym for the tincture.   476 *Art. aurif.,* I, p. 272.
477 "Gloria mundi," *Mus. herm.,* p. 216: "In the work it becomes like unto blood."

Take the serpent, and place it in the chariot with four wheels, and let it be turned about on the earth until it is immersed in the depths of the sea, and nothing more is visible but the blackest dead sea. And there let the chariot with the wheels remain, until so many fumes rise up from the serpent that the whole surface [*planities*] becomes dry, and by desiccation sandy and black. All that is the earth which is no earth, but a stone lacking all weight. . . . [And when the fumes are precipitated in the form of rain,] you should bring the chariot from the water to dry land, and then you have placed the four wheels upon the chariot, and will obtain the result if you will advance further to the Red Sea, running without running, moving without motion [*currens sine cursu, movens sine motu*].[478]

261   This curious text requires a little elucidation. The serpent is the prima materia, the Serpens Hermetis, "which he [Hermes] sent to King Antiochus, that he might do battle with thee [Alexander] and thine army." [479] The serpent is placed "in the chariot of its vessel and is led hither and thither by the fourfold rotation of the natures, but it should be securely enclosed." The wheels are the "wheels of the elements." The vessel or vehicle is the "spherical tomb" of the serpent.[480] The fourfold rotation of the natures corresponds to the ancient tetrameria of the opus (its division into four parts), i.e., transformation through the four elements, from earth to fire. This symbolism describes in abbreviated form the essentials of the opus: the serpent of Hermes or the Agathodaimon, the Nous that animates the cold part of nature—that is, the unconscious—is enclosed in the spherical vessel of diaphanous glass which, on the alchemical view, represents the world and the soul.[481] The psychologist would see it rather as the psychic reflection of the world, namely, *consciousness* of the world and the psyche.[482] The transformation cor-

478 The rest of the title is: "olim conscriptus et a quodam Christiano Philosopho collectus" (Written of old and gathered together by a certain Christian Philosopher). *Theatr. chem.*, V, pp. 88off.

479 Here the author adds (p. 886): "It is better to take pleasure in the opus than in riches or in works of virtuosity (*virtuoso labore*)." * The rare "virtuosus" is equivalent to the Greek ἐνάρετος.

480 Ibid., p. 885.

481 In his sermon on the "vessel of beaten gold" (Ecclesiasticus 50 : 9) Meister Eckhart says: "I have spoken a word which could be spoken of Saint Augustine or of any virtuous soul, such being likened to a golden vessel, massive and firm, adorned with every precious stone." Cf. Evans, I, p. 50.

482 Not only the vessel must be round, but the "fimarium" it is heated in. The "fimarium" is made of *fimus equinus* (horse-dung). *Theatr. chem.*, V, p. 887.

responds to the psychic process of assimilation and integration by means of the transcendent function.[483] This function unites the pairs of opposites, which, as alchemy shows, are arranged in a quaternio when they represent a totality. The totality appears in quaternary form only when it is not just an unconscious fact but a conscious and differentiated totality; for instance, when the horizon is thought of not simply as a circle that can be divided into any number of parts but as consisting of four clearly defined points. Accordingly, one's given personality could be represented by a continuous circle, whereas the conscious personality would be a circle divided up in a definite way, and this generally turns out to be a quaternity. The quaternity of basic functions of consciousness meets this requirement. It is therefore only to be expected that the chariot should have four wheels,[484] to correspond with the four elements or natures. The chariot as a spherical vessel and as consciousness rests on the four elements or basic functions,[485] just as the floating island where Apollo was born, Delos, rested on the four supports which Poseidon made for it. The wheels, naturally, are on the outside of the chariot and are its motor organs, just as the functions of consciousness facilitate the relation of the psyche to its environment. It must, however, be stressed that what we today call the schema of functions is archetypally prefigured by one of the oldest patterns of order known to man, namely the quaternity, which always represents a consciously reflected and differentiated totality. Quite apart from its almost universal incidence it also appears spontaneously in dreams as an expression of the total personality. The "chariot of Aristotle" can be understood in this sense as a symbol of the self.

262   The recipe goes on to say that this symbolic vehicle should be immersed in the sea of the unconscious for the purpose of heating and incubation,[486] corresponding to the state of *tapas*,[487]

---

[483] Cf. *Psychological Types*, def. 29 and par. 828, and "The Transcendent Function."
[484] Cf. *Psychology and Alchemy*, par. 469.
[485] Cf. *Two Essays on Analytical Psychology*, par. 367.
[486] Cf. the heating and incubation of the Philosophers in the triple glass-house at the bottom of the sea in the Arisleus Vision. (Ruska, "Die Vision des Arisleus," *Historische Studien und Skizzen zu Natur- und Heilwissenschaft*, pp. 22ff.; cf. the "Psychology of the Transference," par. 455 and n. 22.)
[487] *Tapas* is a technical term, meaning 'self-incubation' ('brooding') in the *dhyana* state.

incubation by means of "self-heating." By this is obviously meant a state of introversion in which the unconscious content is brooded over and digested. During this operation all relations with the outside world are broken off; the feelers of perception and intuition, discrimination and valuation are withdrawn. The four wheels are "placed upon the chariot": outside everything is quiet and still, but deep inside the psyche the wheels go on turning, performing those cyclic evolutions which bring the mandala of the total personality,[488] the ground-plan of the self, closer to consciousness. But so long as consciousness has not completed the process of integration it is covered by the "blackest dead sea," darkened by unconsciousness and oppressed by heat, as was the hero in the belly of the whale during the night sea journey.[489] Through the incubation the snake-like content is vapourized, literally "sublimated," which amounts to saying that it is recognized and made an object of conscious discrimination.

263 The "evaporatio" is followed by the "desiccation of the surface," which then appears "sandy and black." Here the imagery changes: the allusion to the subsiding flood means psychologically that the black blanket of unconsciousness hiding the nascent symbol is drawn away. "Arena" (sand) is defined as the "pure substance of the stone," [490] and accordingly the text describes the regenerated earth as a "stone lacking all weight." The text does not explain just why it is weightless, but it is evident that nothing material, which alone has weight, is left over, and all that remains is the psychic content of the projection.

264 The opus is far from having come to an end at this point, for the *nigredo (terra nigra)* still prevails and the substance of the stone is still black. It is therefore necessary for the "fumes" (*evaporationes*) to precipitate and wash off the blackness, "whence the whole earth becomes white." The rain now falls so copiously that the earth is almost turned into a sea. Hence the direction that the chariot should be brought to dry land. This

488 For the psychology of the mandala see my "Commentary on *The Secret of the Golden Flower*," pars. 31ff., *Psychology and Alchemy*, pars. 122ff., "A Study in the Process of Individuation," and "Concerning Mandala Symbolism."
489 Cf. *Symbols of Transformation*, pars. 308ff., and the Arisleus vision, which seems to be the prototype of the motif of the king in the sweat-bath.
490 Ruland, *Lexicon*, p. 37.

is clearly another allusion to Noah's Ark and the flood.[491] With the coming of the flood the previous state of chaos would be restored, and the result of the opus would again be swamped by unconsciousness. This motif recurs in the form of the dragon that pursued Leto and the woman crowned with stars (Rev. 12 : 1f.).

265   If the chariot reaches dry land, this obviously means that the content has become visible and remains conscious, "and then," says the text, "you have placed the wheels upon the chariot." [492] The four natures or elements are gathered together and are contained in the spherical vessel, i.e., the four aspects or functions are integrated with consciousness, so that the state of totality has almost been attained. Had it really been attained the opus would be consummated at this point, but the "result" (*effectus*) is obtained only by advancing further. The "result" therefore means something more than integration of the four natures. If we take the loading of the chariot as the conscious realization of the four functions, this does in fact denote only the possibility of remaining conscious of the whole previous material, that is, of the principal aspects of the psyche. The question then arises as to how all these divergent factors, previously kept apart by apparently insuperable incompatibilities, will behave, and what the ego is going to do about it.

266   The singular image of the Nous-serpent enthroned on a chariot reminds us of the chariot-driving, snake-shaped gods of southern India, for instance on the immense black temple at Puri, which is itself a chariot of stone. I certainly don't want to suggest that there is any direct Indian influence in our text, for there is another model closer to hand, and that is Ezekiel's vision of the four creatures, with the faces respectively of a man, a lion, an ox, and an eagle. These four figures are associated with four wheels, "their construction being as it were a wheel within a wheel. When they went, they went in any of their four direc-

---

491 Remarkably enough, a 12th-cent. representation of the four-wheeled chariot (see below) bears the inscription: "Foederis ex arca Christi cruce sistitur ara" (Out of the ark of the covenant an altar is built by the cross of Christ).

492 "Plaustrum" also denotes the "chariot" in the sky, Charles' Wain (Ursa Major or Big Dipper). This constellation marks the celestial Pole, which was of great significance in the history of symbols. It is a model of the structure of the self.

tions without turning as they went." [493] Together they formed the moving throne of a figure having "the appearance of a man." In the Cabala this chariot (Merkabah) plays an important role as the vehicle on which the believers mount up to God and the human soul unites with the world-soul.

267   An interpretation of the four wheels as the *quadriga* and vehicle of divinity is found in a window medallion by Suger, the twelfth-century maker of stained glass for the Abbey of Saint-Denis.[494] The chariot which is depicted bears the inscription "QUADRIGE AMINADAB," referring to the Song of Songs 6 : 11 (DV): "My soul troubled me for the chariots of Aminadab." [495] God the Father stands on a four-wheeled chariot holding the crucifix before him. In the corners of the medallion are the four emblems of the evangelists, the Christian continuation of Ezekiel's winged creatures. The four gospels form, as it were, a quaternary podium on which the Redeemer stands.

268   Still another source might be Honorius of Autun. In his commentary on Song of Songs 6 : 11, he says that his "animalis vita" was troubled because the chariot signified the four evangelists. It was this chariot that the apostles and their followers had driven through the world. For Christ had said in the gospels: "Except ye repent, ye shall all likewise perish" (Luke 13 : 3). And it was to him, Honorius, that the words were addressed: "Return, return, O Shulamite" (Song of Songs 6 : 13).[496]

269   Psychologically the vision of Ezekiel is a symbol of the self consisting of four individual creatures and wheels, i.e., of differ-

---

[493] Ezekiel 1 : 16f. There is a similar vision in Zechariah 6 : 1: ". . . and behold, four chariots came out from between two mountains . . ." The first chariot had red horses, the second black, the third white, and the fourth dappled grey (RSV. Vulgate: *"varii et fortes"*; DV: "grisled and strong.") The horses "went forth to the four winds of heaven." For a remarkable parallel vision see Neihardt, *Black Elk Speaks, being the Life Story of a Holy Man of the Ogalala Sioux,* p. 23. In Black Elk's vision twelve black horses stand in the west, twelve white horses in the north, twelve bays in the east, and in the south twelve greys.
[494] Mâle, *L'Art religieux du XIIème siècle en France,* p. 182.
[495] The passage is corrupt. The Hebrew original text has only: "My soul set me — chariots of Aminadab." There are many different interpretations and conjectures, of which I will mention only Riwkah Schärf's: Merkābāh can also be the sun-chariot (2 Kings 23 : 11); Aminadab is a king's name, from Ammon, 'Amm, 'Ammī, a Semitic god, here possibly transferred to the sun-chariot.
[496] For Honorius this naturally has the moral meaning of "turn again." See his *Expositio in Cantica Cant.,* Migne, *P.L.,* vol. 172, col. 462.

ent functions. Three of the faces are theriomorphic and only one anthropomorphic, which presumably means that only one function has reached the human level, whereas the others are still in an unconscious or animal state. The problem of three and four (trinity and quaternity) plays a great role in alchemy as the "axiom of Maria" [497] and, like the vision of Ezekiel, is concerned with the God-image. The symbols of the self are as a rule symbols of totality, but this is only occasionally true of God-images. In the former the circle and the quaternity predominate, in the latter the circle and the trinity—and this, moreover, only in the case of abstract representations, which are not the only ones to occur.

270   These hints may throw a little light on the strange idea of the serpent-chariot. It is a symbol of the arcane substance and the quintessence, of the aether that contains all four elements, and at the same time a God-image or, to be more accurate, an image of the *anima mundi*. This is indicated by the Mercurial serpent, which in its turn was interpreted by the alchemists as the "spirit of life that was in the wheels" (DV).[498] We should also mention that according to Ezekiel 1 : 18 the inter-revolving wheels "were full of eyes round about." The old illustrators therefore produced something like an astrolabe in their attempts to depict the vision. The notion of wheels is naturally connected with movement in all directions, for the "eyes of the Lord run to and fro through the whole earth" (Zech. 4 : 10). It is said of the horses, too, that they "walk to and fro through the earth" (Zech. 6 : 7). Eyes are round and in common speech are likened to "cart-wheels." They also seem to be a typical symbol for what I have called the "multiple luminosities of the unconscious." By this I mean the seeming possibility that complexes possess a kind of consciousness, a luminosity of their own, which, I conjecture, expresses itself in the symbol of the soul-spark, multiple eyes (*polyophthalmia*), and the starry heaven.[499]

271   By reason of its "solar" nature the eye is a symbol of consciousness, and accordingly multiple eyes would indicate a mul-

[497] In this connection the alchemists also mentioned the three men in the fiery furnace, Daniel 3 : 20ff.
[498] Vulgate: "Quia spiritus vitae erat in rotis" Ezekiel 1 : 20. Cf. *Psychology and Alchemy*, par. 471.
[499] Cf. "On the Nature of the Psyche," pars. 395f.

tiplicity of conscious centres which are co-ordinated into a unity like the many-faceted eye of an insect. As Ezekiel's vision can be interpreted psychologically as a symbol of the self, we may also mention in this connection the Hindu definition of the self—here *hiranyagarbha*—as the "collective aggregate of all individual souls." [500]

272   Ezekiel's vision is of psychological importance because the quaternity embodied in it is the vehicle or throne of him who had the "appearance of a man." Together with the "spirit of life" in the wheels it represents the empirical self, the totality of the four functions. These four are only partly conscious. The auxiliary functions are partly, and the "inferior" or subliminal function is wholly, autonomous; they cannot be put to conscious use and they reach consciousness only indirectly as a *fait accompli,* through their sometimes disturbing effects. Their specific energy adds itself to the normal energy of the unconscious and thereby gives it an impulse that enables it to irrupt spontaneously into consciousness. As we know, these invasions can be observed systematically in the association experiment. [501]

273   The quaternity of the self appears in Ezekiel's vision as the true psychological foundation of the God-concept. God uses it as his vehicle. It is possible for the psychologist to verify the structure of this foundation, but beyond that the theologian has the last word. In order to clear up any misunderstandings, especially from the theological side, I would like to emphasize yet again that it is not the business of science to draw conclusions which go beyond the bounds of our empirical knowledge. I do not feel the slightest need to put the self in place of God, as short-sighted critics have often accused me of doing. If Indian philosophers equate the atman with the concept of God and many Westerners copy them, this is simply their subjective opinion and not science. A *consensus generalis* on this point would in itself be yet another fact which, for the empirical psychologist, is as well worth considering as the remarkable view of many theologians that religious statements have nothing to do with the psyche. Similarly, it is characteristic of the mystical philosophy of the alchemists that the Mercurial serpent is enthroned on the chariot. He is a living spirit who uses as his chariot the body

500 Ramanuja's commentary to the Vedanta-Sutras (SBE, XLVIII), p. 578.
501 Cf. my "Analysis of the Associations of an Epileptic."

that consists of the four elements. In this sense the chariot is the symbol of earthly life. A Georgian fairytale closes with the verses:

> I have dragged a cart up the mountain,
> It has become like a mountain.
> Summon me from this life
> Over to eternity.[502]

274   As I have said, the process of transformation does not come to an end with the production of the quaternity symbol. The continuation of the opus leads to the dangerous crossing of the Red Sea, signifying death and rebirth. It is very remarkable that our author, by his paradox "running without running, moving without motion," introduces a coincidence of opposites just at this point, and that the Hippolytus text speaks, equally paradoxically, of the "gods of destruction and the god of salvation" being together. The quaternity, as we have seen, is a quaternio of opposites, a synthesis of the four originally divergent functions. Their synthesis is here achieved in an image, but in psychic reality becoming conscious of the whole psyche [503] faces us with a highly problematical situation. We can indicate its scope in a single question: What am I to do with the unconscious?

275   For this, unfortunately, there are no recipes or general rules. I have tried to present the main outlines of what the psychotherapist can observe of this wearisome and all too familiar process in my study "The Relations between the Ego and the Unconscious." For the layman these experiences are a *terra incognita* which is not made any more accessible by broad generalizations. Even the imagination of the alchemists, otherwise so fertile, fails us completely here. Only a thorough investigation of the texts could shed a little light on this question. The same task challenges our endeavours in the field of psychotherapy. Here too are thousands of images, symbols, dreams, fantasies, and visions that still await comparative research. The only thing that can be said with some certainty at present is that there is a gradual process of approximation whereby the two positions,

---

502 "The Bald-headed Gooseherd." Cf. Dirr, *Kaukasische Märchen*, pp. 47ff.
503 "Whole" is meant here only in a relative sense, implying merely the most important aspects of the individual psyche and of the collective unconscious.

the conscious and the unconscious, are both modified. Differences in individual cases, however, are just as great as they were among the alchemists.

d. *The Fourth of the Three*

276   In the course of his mystic peregrination [504] Maier reached the Red ("Erythraean") Sea, and in the following way: he journeyed to the four directions, to the north (Europe), to the west (America), to the east (Asia).[505] Leaving Asia and turning south to Africa, he found a statue of Mercury, made of silver, and with a golden head. The statue pointed to Paradise, which he espied far off. Now because of its four rivers, and because it was the abode of the originally androgynous Primordial Man (Adam), the Garden of Eden was a favourite mandala in Christian iconography, and is therefore a symbol of totality and—from the psychological point of view—of the self. If we take the four directions and the four elements (see note 505) as a symbolical equivalent of the four basic functions of consciousness, we can say that Maier had become conscious of three of them by the time he reached Asia. This brings him to the fourth and last, the "inferior" function, which is the darkest and the most unconscious of all. "Africa" is not a bad image for this. But just as Maier was about to direct his steps thither, he had a vision of paradise as the primordial image of wholeness, which showed him that the goal of his journey lay in the attainment of this wholeness. By the time he reached Africa, he says, the sun was in its house, Leo, and the moon was in Cancer, "the moon having Cancer for the roof of its house". The proximity of the two houses indicates a *coniunctio Solis et Lunae,* the union of supreme opposites, and this is the crowning of the opus and the goal of the peregrination. He adds: "And this gave me great hope of the best augury."

277   The fourth function has its seat in the unconscious. In mythology the unconscious is portrayed as a great animal, for instance Leviathan, or as a whale, wolf, or dragon. We know from the myth of the sun-hero that it is so hot in the belly of the

504 *Symb. aur. mensae,* pp. 568ff.
505 Maier makes the following equations: Europe = earth, America = water, Asia = air, Africa = fire.

whale that his hair falls out.[506] Arisleus and his companions like-wise suffer from the great heat of their prison under the sea.[507] The alchemists were fond of comparing their fire to the "fire of hell" or the flames of purgatory. Maier gives a description of Africa which is very like a description of hell: "uncultivated, torrid, parched,[508] sterile and empty." [509] He says there are so few springs that animals of the most varied species assemble at the drinking-places and mingle with one another, "whence new births and animals of a novel appearance are born," which explained the saying "Always something new out of Africa." Pans dwelt there, and satyrs, dog-headed baboons, and half-men, "besides innumerable species of wild animals." According to certain modern views, this could hardly be bettered as a descrip-tion of the unconscious. Maier further reports that in the region of the Red Sea an animal is found with the name of "Ortus" (rising, origin). It had a red head with streaks of gold reaching to its neck, black eyes, a white face, white forepaws, and black hindpaws. He derived the idea of this animal from the remark of Avicenna: "That thing whose head is red, its eyes black and its feet white, is the magistery." [510] He was convinced that the legend of this creature referred to the phoenix, which was like-wise found in that region. While he was making inquiries about the phoenix he "heard a rumour" that not far off a prophetess, known as the Erythraean Sibyl, dwelt in a cave. This was the sibyl who was alleged to have foretold the coming of Christ. Maier is probably referring here not to the eighth book of the Sibylline Oracles, verse 217, at which point thirty-four verses begin with the following letters: ΙΗΣΟΥΣ ΧΡΕΙΣΤΟΣ ΘΕΟΥ ΥΙΟΣ ΣΩΤΗΡ ΣΤΑΥΡΟΣ,[511] but to the report of St. Augustine in *De*

---

[506] Frobenius, *Das Zeitalter des Sonnengottes*, p. 82 and note.

[507] "In the intense heat of summer." *Art. aurif.*, I, p. 148.

[508] "Sitibundus" means one who is parched with thirst on the sea. "Sitibundi in medio Oceani gurgite" (thirsting in the mid flood of Ocean).

[509] *Symb. aur. mensae*, p. 594. Maier completes the picture of hell by citing the legend of the oryx: "There the Oryx, thirsting in the great heat of summer, is said to curse the heat of the sun with the shedding of tears and repeated groanings." *

[510] Ibid., p. 199.* From Avicenna's *Liber de anima artis*, to which unfortunately I have no access. The saying is cited as an "Aenigma" in cap. X of the "Rosarius" of Arnaldus de Villanova (Gratarolus, *Verae alchemiae*, I, Part 2, p. 42).

[511] "The cross of Jesus Christ the Son of God, Saviour."

civitate dei,[512] which was well known in the Middle Ages. He also cites the passage about the sibyl in the *Constantini Oratio* of Eusebius and emphasizes that the sibylline prophecy referred to the "coming of Christ in the flesh." [512a]

278   We have seen earlier that the "Erythraean Sea" is a mysterious place, but here we meet with some noteworthy details. To begin with, our author reaches this sea just when he has completed the journey through the three continents and is about to enter the critical fourth region. We know from the Axiom of Maria and from *Faust* the crucial importance of that seemingly innocent question at the beginning of the *Timaeus:*

> SOCRATES: One, two, three—but where, my dear Timaeus, is the fourth of those guests of yesterday who were to entertain me today?
> TIMAEUS: He suddenly felt unwell, Socrates; he would not have failed to join our company if he could have helped it.[513]

279   The transition from three to four is a problem [514] on which the ambiguous formulation of Maria does not shed very much light.[515] We come across the dilemma of three and four in any number of guises, and in Maier's *Symbola aureae mensae* as well the step from three to four proves to be an important development presaged by the vision of paradise. The region of the Red Sea is proverbially hot, and Maier reached it at the end of July, "in the intense heat of summer." He was, in fact, "getting hot," uncommonly hot, as hot as hell, for he was approaching that region of the psyche which was not unjustly said to be inhabited by "Pans, Satyrs, dog-headed baboons, and half-men." It is not difficult to see that this region is the animal soul in man. For just as a man has a body which is no different in principle from that of an animal, so also his psychology has a whole series of lower storeys in which the spectres from humanity's past epochs

---

512 *The City of God,* II, p. 196. Cf. Geffcken, *Die Oracula Sibyllina,* pp. 153f.

512a Migne, *P.G.,* vol. 20, col. 1302.   513 *Plato's Cosmology* (trans. by Cornford), p. 9.

514 There are two Armenian legends concerning Alexander, of which the first runs as follows: "When Alexander came into the world, he at once ran about the room. But when he came to the fourth corner, an angel struck him down and gave him to understand that he would conquer only three-quarters of the world." In the second legend Alexander does conquer three-quarters of the world, but not the fourth, which is called that of the "righteous poor." A sea surrounds it and cuts it off from other parts of the earth. Dirr, *Kaukasische Märchen,* p. 259.

515 Cf. *Psychology and Alchemy,* pars. 209. Concerning the problem in the *Timaeus* see "A Psychological Approach to the Dogma of the Trinity," pars. 181ff.

still dwell, then the animal souls from the age of Pithecan-
thropus and the hominids, then the "psyche" of the cold-blooded
saurians, and, deepest down of all, the transcendental mystery
and paradox of the sympathetic and parasympathetic psychoid
processes.

280   So it is not surprising that our world-voyager felt that he
had landed in the hottest place—he was in Arabia Felix—in the
sweltering heat of summer! He was painfully aware that he was
risking his skin: "It's your concern when your neighbour's wall
is on fire." [516] He was the banquet-giver and the guest, the eater
and the eaten in one person.

281   "The innumerable species of animals" begin to show up
already by the Red Sea, headed by the fabulous four-footed
"Ortus," which combines in itself the four alchemical colours,
black, white, red, and yellow [517] (the gold streaks on head and
neck). Maier does not hesitate to identify the Ortus with the
phoenix, the other legendary inhabitant of Arabia Felix,[518] less
perhaps on account of its appearance than on account of its
name; for the phoenix, too, after consuming itself in the land of
Egypt, each time rose renewed, like the reborn sun in Heliopolis.

282   The Ortus is the alchemical "animal" which represents the
living quaternity in its first synthesis. In order to become the
ever-living bird of the spirit it needs the transforming fire,
which is found in "Africa," that is, in the encounter with and
investigation of the fourth function and the animal soul represented by the Ortus. By interpreting it as the phoenix, Maier
gave it a far-reaching change of meaning, as we shall see. For
besides his animal soul he also discovered in its vicinity a kind
of feminine soul, a virgin, to whom he at first appeared like an
importunate guest.[519] This was the sibyl who foretold the coming
of Christ. Thus, by the Red Sea, he met the animal soul in the
form of a monstrous quaternity, symbolizing, so to speak, the
prima materia of the self and, as the phoenix, rebirth. The mys-

516 Horace, *Epistolae,* I, xviii, 84.*
517 Corresponding to the *xanthesis, citrinitas,* or yellowing.
518 Isidore of Seville, *Liber etymologiarum* (XII, ch. 7, fol. lxv^v): "The phoenix, a
biru of Arabia, so called because it has a purple colour and is singular and unique
in all the world." *
519 "Whom, says she, seekest thou here, stranger? It is not lawful for a man to
approach a virgin." * The Sibyl pardons him, however, because he is "very desirous
of learning."

tery alluded to here is not only the encounter with the animal soul but, at the same time and in the same place, the meeting with the anima, a feminine psychopomp who showed him the way to Mercurius and also how to find the phoenix.[520]

283   It is worth noting that the animal is the symbolic carrier of the self. This hint in Maier is borne out by modern individuals who have no notion of alchemy.[521] It expresses the fact that the structure of wholeness was always present but was buried in profound unconsciousness, where it can always be found again if one is willing to risk one's skin to attain the greatest possible range of consciousness through the greatest possible self-knowledge—a "harsh and bitter drink" usually reserved for hell. The throne of God seems to be no unworthy reward for such trials. For self-knowledge—in the total meaning of the word—is not a one-sided intellectual pastime but a journey through the four continents, where one is exposed to all the dangers of land, sea, air, and fire. Any total act of recognition worthy of the name embraces the four—or 360!—aspects of existence. Nothing may be "disregarded." When Ignatius Loyola recommended "imagination through the five senses" [522] to the meditant, and told him to imitate Christ "by use of his senses," [523] what he had in mind was the fullest possible "realization" of the object of contemplation. Quite apart from the moral or other effects of this kind of meditation, its chief effect is the training of consciousness, of the capacity for concentration, and of attention and clarity of thought. The corresponding forms of Yoga have similar effects. But in contrast to these traditional modes of realization, where the meditant projects himself into some prescribed form, the self-knowledge alluded to by Maier is a projection into the empirical self as it actually is. It is not the "self" we like to imagine ourselves to be after carefully removing all the blemishes, but the empirical ego just as it is, with everything that it does and everything that happens to it. Everybody would like to be quit of this odious adjunct, which is precisely why in the East the ego is explained as illusion and why in the West it is offered up in sacrifice to the Christ figure.

---

520 For the anima in this role see *Psychology and Alchemy*, pars. 73f.
521 Namely in the form of symbolic animals which appear in dreams as prefigurations of the self.
522 *Spiritual Exercises* (trans. by Rickaby), p. 41.   523 Ibid., p. 215.

284   By contrast, the aim of the mystical peregrination is to understand all parts of the world, to achieve the greatest possible extension of consciousness, as though its guiding principle were the Carpocratic [524] idea that one is delivered from no sin which one has not committed. Not a turning away from its empirical "so-ness," but the fullest possible experience of the ego as reflected in the "ten thousand things"—that is the goal of the peregrination.[525] This follows logically from the psychological recognition that God cannot be experienced at all unless this futile and ridiculous ego offers a modest vessel in which to catch the effluence of the Most High and name it with his name. The significance of the vas-symbol in alchemy shows how concerned the artifex was to have the right vessel for the right content: "One is the lapis, one the medicament, one the vessel, one the procedure, and one the disposition." The *aqua nostra,* the transformative substance, is even its own vessel.[526] From this it is but a step to the paradoxical statement of Angelus Silesius:

> God is my centre when I close him in,
> And my circumference when I melt in him.[527]

285   Maier's Erythraean quadruped, the Ortus, corresponds to the four-wheeled chariot of Pseudo-Aristotle. The tetramorph, too, is a product of early medieval iconography,[528] combining the four winged creatures of Ezekiel's vision into a four-footed monster. The interpretation of the Ortus as the phoenix connects it with Christ, whose coming was prophesied by the Sibyl; for the phoenix is a well-known allegory of the resurrection of Christ and of the dead in general.[529] It is the symbol of transformation *par excellence.* In view of this well-known interpre-

---

524 Cf. "Psychology and Religion," par. 133.

525 Angelus Silesius says, however:

> "Turn inward for your voyage! For all your arts
> You will not find the Stone in foreign parts."

Cherubinischer Wandersmann, III, No. 118. All the same, no one has yet discovered himself without the world.   526 Mylius, *Phil. ref.,* pp. 33 and 245.

527 *Cher. Wand.,* III, No. 148.   528 See *Psychology and Alchemy,* fig. 53.

529 St. Ambrose says: "Let this bird teach us by his example to believe in the resurrection." * Epiphanius: "Why therefore did the wicked Jews not believe in the resurrection of our Lord Jesus Christ on the third day, when a bird brings himself to life again in the space of three days?" * Both cited in Picinellus, *Mundus symbolicus,* I, pp. 575, 576, 578.

tation of the phoenix and of the Erythraean oracle, it is amazing that any author at the beginning of the seventeenth century should dare to ask the sibyl, not to show him the way to Christ, but to tell him where he could find Mercurius! This passage offers another striking proof of the parallelism between Mercurius and Christ. Nor does the phoenix appear here as a Christ allegory but as the bearer and birthplace of the universal medicine, the "remedy against wrath and pain." As the sibyl once foretold the coming of the Lord, so now she is to point the way to Mercurius. Christ is the Anthropos, the Primordial Man; Mercurius has the same meaning, and the Primordial Man stands for the round, original wholeness, long ago made captive by the powers of this world. In Christ's case the victory and liberation of the Primordial Man were said to be complete, so that the labours of the alchemists would seem to be superfluous. We can only assume that the alchemists were of a different opinion, and that they sought their remedy against wrath and pain in order to complete what they considered to be Christ's unfinished work of redemption.

286   It is characteristic of Maier's views that the idea of most importance is not Mercurius, who elsewhere appears strongly personified, but a substance brought by the phoenix, the bird of the spirit. It is this inorganic substance, and not a living being, which is used as a symbol of wholeness, or as a means towards wholeness, a desideratum apparently not fulfilled by the Christ-symbol.[530] Involuntarily one asks oneself whether the intense personalization of the divine figures, as is customary in Christianity and quite particularly in Protestantism,[531] is not in the

[530] If the iconographic symbols spontaneously produced by modern people are examined in this respect, we seldom find a human being as the central figure (in a mandala, for instance), but, much more frequently, an impersonal abstract sign which is meant to express totality. Occasionally there is a face or head, but this only enhances the analogy with alchemy. (Cf. *Psychology and Alchemy*, par. 530, and "Transformation Symbolism in the Mass," pars. 363ff.) The most extreme expression of the abstract and impersonal in alchemy is the lapis. I have already drawn attention to the peculiar nature of these central figures in "Psychology and Religion," pars. 156ff.

[531] An exception to this is the third Person of the Trinity, the Holy Ghost, who is "breathed" by Father and Son (active and passive spiration: cf. my "Dogma of the Trinity," pars. 235ff. and n. 10). He is, as the usual representations show, the most "depersonalized" of the figures. I have already mentioned the alchemists' preference for the Holy Ghost. (See also *Aion*, pars. 141ff.)

end compensated, and to some extent mitigated, by a more objective point of view emanating from the unconscious.

e. Ascent and Descent

287   In his quest for wholeness so far, Michael Maier, besides crossing three continents and travelling in three directions, has discovered a statue of Mercurius pointing the way to paradise; he has glimpsed paradise from afar, he has found the animal soul and the sibylline anima, who now counsels him to journey to the seven mouths of the Nile (Ostia Nili), in order to seek for Mercurius. The continuation of his pilgrimage recalls the flight of the phoenix from Arabia, where it lives, to Egypt, where it dies and arises anew. We may therefore expect that something similar will befall the author. We are not told anything of his crossing of the Red Sea and of his recapitulation, in the reverse direction, of the miraculous wanderings of the children of Israel. We do, however, soon learn that something like a rebirth mystery is to take place, because Maier compares the seven mouths of the Nile to the seven planets. He first reaches the Canopic Gate, the western mouth of the delta, where he finds Saturn domiciled. Of the remaining planets we can recognize only Mars with certainty, as the description of the cities where the others dwell is not very clear. Amid innumerable hazards he traverses the seven regions without meeting Mercurius. He does not find him even in his own city. Finally he has to turn back and retrace his steps until he reaches the Canopic Gate, where this time he finds Mercurius. Although he learns from him all sorts of secrets, he fails to find the phoenix. Later, he will return again in order to discover the panacea. In his "Epigramma ad Phoenicem" he begs the wonderful bird to give the wise man its feathers,[532] and in his epigram to the "Medicina Phoeniciae" he rates it above "riches and gold, and he who does not think so is not a man but a beast." [533]

288   The experience of the fourth quarter, the region of fire (i.e., the inferior function), is described by Maier as an ascent and descent through the seven planetary spheres. Even if the peregrination up to this point was not an allegory of the opus

532 *Symb. aur. mens.*, p. 606.*
533 Ibid., p. 607.*

alchymicum, from now on it certainly is. The opus is a "transitus," a πέρασις in the Gnostic sense, a "transcension" and transformation whose subject and object is the elusive Mercurius. I will not discuss the nature of the transitus here in any great detail, as this would be the proper concern of an account of the opus itself. One aspect of the transitus, however, is the ascent and descent through the planetary spheres, and to this we must devote a few words. As the "Tabula smaragdina" shows, the purpose of the ascent and descent is to unite the powers of Above and Below. A feature worthy of special notice is that in the opus there is an ascent followed by a descent, whereas the probable Gnostic-Christian prototype depicts first the descent and then the ascent. There are numerous evidences of this in the literature and I do not need to cite them here. I will quote only the words of one of the great Greek Fathers, St. Basil, who says in his explanation of Psalm 17 : 10 [534] ("And he bowed the heavens and came down, and a black cloud was under his feet"): "David says here: God came down from heaven to help me and to chastise his enemies. But he clearly prophesies the incarnation [ἐνανθρώπησις] of Christ when he says: He bowed the heavens and came down. For he did not break through the heavens and did not make the mystery manifest, but came down to earth secretly, like rain upon the fleece,[535] because the incarnation was secret and unknown, and his coming into the world-order [ἐν τῇ οἰκονομίᾳ] was hidden." [536] Commenting on the next verse ("And he was borne upon the cherubim, and he flew"), Basil says: "For in ascending he rose above the Cherubim, whom David named also the wings of the wind, on account of their winged and stormy nature. By the wings of the wind is also meant the cloud which took him up." [537] Irenaeus sums up the mystery in the lapidary saying: "For it is He who descended and ascended for the salvation of men." [538]

[534] DV; AV, 18 : 9.

[535] πόκος = 'wool, fleece' (L. vellus). The passage refers to Psalm 71 : 6 (Vulgate): "Descendet sicut pluvia in vellus" (DV: "He shall come down like rains upon the fleece"), and Judges 6 : 37: "Ponam hoc vellus lanae in aera" (DV: "I will put this fleece of wool on the floor").

[536] Pitra, *Analecta sacra*, V, pp. 85f.

[537] Refers to Acts 1 : 9: ". . . and a cloud received him out of their sight."

[538] *Adv. haer.*, III, VI, 2 (*The Writings of Irenaeus*, I, p. 270).

289   In contrast to this, in alchemy the ascent comes first and then the descent. I would mention the ascent and descent of the soul in the *Rosarium* illustrations [539] and above all the exordium in the "Tabula smaragdina," whose authority held sway throughout the Middle Ages:

IV. Its father is the sun, its mother the moon; the wind hath carried it in his belly; its nurse is the earth.
VI. Its power is complete when it is turned towards the earth.
VIII. It ascendeth from the earth to heaven, and descendeth again to the earth, and receiveth the power of the higher and lower things. So wilt thou have the glory of the whole world.[540]

290   These articles (whose subject is sometimes masculine and sometimes neuter) describe the "sun-moon child" who is laid in the cradle of the four elements, attains full power through them and the earth, rises to heaven and receives the power of the upper world, and then returns to earth, accomplishing, it seems, a triumph of wholeness ("gloria totius mundi"). The words "So wilt thou have" are evidently addressed to the Philosopher, for he is the artifex of the *filius philosophorum*. If he succeeds in transforming the arcane substance he will simultaneously accomplish his own wholeness, which will manifest itself as the glory of the whole world.

291   There can be no doubt that the arcane substance, whether in neuter or personified form, rises from the earth, unites the opposites, and then returns to earth, thereby achieving its own transformation into the elixir. "He riseth up and goeth down in the tree of the sun," till he becomes the elixir, says the "Consilium coniugii." [541] The text continues:

Someone hath said,[542] And when I rise naked to heaven, then shall I come clothed upon the earth, and shall perfect all minerals.[543] And if we are baptized in the fountain of gold and silver, and the spirit of our body [i.e., the arcane substance] ascends into heaven with the father and the son, and descends again, then shall our souls

---

539 Reproduced in my "Psychology of the Transference," figs. 7 and 9.
540 Cf. "Tabula smaragdina" (ed. Ruska), p. 2.*
541 *Ars chemica,* p. 118.
542 This "someone," as is clear from the later text (in *Bibliotheca chemica*), is the "beloved" in the Song of Songs, i.e., Luna. She speaks here to Sol.
543 Possibly an allusion to the "Tabula smaragdina."

revive, and my animal body will remain white, that is, [the body] of the moon.[544]

292   Here the union of opposites consists in an ascent to heaven and a descent to earth in the bath of the tincture. The earthly effect is first a perfection of minerals, then a resuscitation of souls and a transfiguration of the animal body, which before was dark. A parallel passage in the "Consilium" runs:

His soul rises up from it [545] and is exalted to the heavens, that is, to the spirit, and becomes the rising sun (that is, red), in the waxing moon, and of solar nature.[546] And then the lantern with two lights,[547] which is the water of life, will return to its origin, that is, to earth. And it becomes of low estate, is humbled and decays, and is joined to its beloved,[548] the terrestrial sulphur.[549]

293   This text describes the ascent of the soul of the arcane substance, the incombustible sulphur. The soul as Luna attains its plenilunium, its sunlike brilliance, then wanes into the novilunium and sinks down into the embrace of the terrestrial sulphur, which here signifies death and corruption. We are reminded of the gruesome conjunction at the new moon in Maier's *Scrutinium chymicum,* where the woman and the dragon embrace in the grave.[550] The description Dorn gives in his "Physica Trismegisti" is also to the point: "In the end it will come to pass that this earthly, spagyric birth clothes itself with heavenly nature by its ascent, and then by its descent visibly puts on the nature of the centre of the earth, but nonetheless the nature of the heavenly centre which it acquired by the ascent is secretly preserved." [551] This "birth" (*foetura*) conquers the "subtile and spiritual sickness in the human mind and also all

544 "Consil. coniug.," p. 128; or remain "in the golden tree," p. 211. There may be a reference here to John 3 : 13: "And no one has ascended into heaven except him who has descended from heaven" (DV).
545 I.e., from the "sulphur nostrum" previously referred to.
546 "In Luna crescente, in naturam solarem." This could also be translated: "waxing in Luna into the nature of the sun."
547 The light of sun *and* moon.
548 The 1566 edn. has "figitur amanti eum." I read "eam."
549 Consil. coniug.," p. 165 (commentary in Senior, *De chemia,* p. 15). Cf. the "transposition of the lights" in the Cabala.
550 Emblema L, p. 148: "The dragon slays the woman and she him, and together they are bespattered with blood." *
551 *Theatr. chem.*, I, p. 409.

bodily defects, within as well as without." The medicament is produced "in the same way as the world was created." Elsewhere Dorn remarks that the "foetus spagyricus" is forced by the fire to rise up to heaven (*caelum*), by which he means from the bottom of the vessel to the top, and from there it descends again after attaining the necessary degree of ripeness, and returns to earth: "This spirit becomes corporeal again, after having become spirit from a body." [552]

294   As if in contradiction to the "Tabula smaragdina," whose authority he follows here, Dorn writes in his "Philosophia speculativa": "No one ascends into the heaven which ye seek, unless he who descends from the heaven which ye do not seek, enlighten him." [553] Dorn was perhaps the first alchemist to find certain statements of his "art" problematical,[554] and it was for this reason that he provided his *foetus spagyricus,* who behaves in an all too Basilidian manner, with a Christian alibi. At the same time he was conscious that the artifex was indissolubly one with the opus.[555] His speculations are not to be taken lightly as they are occasionally of the greatest psychological interest, e.g.: "The descent to the four and the ascent to the monad are simultaneous." [556] The "four" are the four elements and the monad is the original unity which reappears in the "denarius" (the

---

552 Ibid., p. 431. Dorn adds: "It was hidden of old by the Philosophers in the riddle: Make the fixed, said they, volatile, and the volatile fixed, and you will have the whole magistery." *

553 "Spec. phil.," *Theatr. chem.,* I, p. 276.* Here the allusion to John 3 : 13 is even clearer.

554 Cf. supra, n. 393.

555 He says, for instance: "Learn from within thyself to know all that is in heaven and on earth, that thou mayest be wise in all things. Knowest thou not that heaven and the elements were formerly one, and were separated from one another by divine artifice, that they might bring forth thee and all things? If thou knowest this, the rest cannot escape thee, or thou lackest all sense. Again, in every generation such a separation is necessary, as I have said above, and needs to be effected of thyself, before thou settest sail towards the true philosophy. Thou wilt never make from others the One which thou seekest, except first there be made one thing of thyself." * "Spec. phil.," p. 276. The stages of the ascent are: (1) devotion to the faith, (2) knowledge of God by faith, (3) love from the knowledge of God. ("Physica Trithemii," *Theatr. chem.,* I, p. 449.)

556 * A similar view is suggested in the "Congeries Paracelsicae chemicae," *Theatr. chem.,* I, p. 589: "Therefore it must be boiled, roasted, and melted; it ascends and descends, and all these operations are one single operation performed by the fire alone." *

number 10), the goal of the opus; it is the unity of the personality projected into the unity of the stone. The descent is analytic, a separation into the four components of wholeness; the ascent synthetic, a putting together of the denarius. This speculation accords with the psychological fact that the confrontation of conscious and unconscious produces a dissolution of the personality and at the same time regroups it into a whole. This can be seen very clearly in moments of psychic crisis, for it is just in these moments that the symbol of unity, for instance the mandala, occurs in a dream. "Where danger is, there / Arises salvation also," says Hölderlin.

295   While the older authors keep strictly to the "Tabula smaragdina," [557] the more modern ones, under the leadership of Dorn, tend to present the process the other way round. For instance, Mylius says that the earth cannot ascend unless heaven comes down first. And even then the earth can be sublimated to heaven only if it is "dissolved in its own spirit [558] and becomes one substance therewith." [559] The Paracelsist Penotus is even more emphatic. Speaking of Mercurius, he says:

As to how the son of man [*filius hominis*] is generated by the philosopher and the fruit of the virgin is produced, it is necessary that he be exalted from the earth and cleansed of all earthliness; then he rises as a whole into the air and is changed into spirit. Thus the word of the philosopher is fulfilled: He ascends from earth to heaven and puts on the power of Above and Below, and lays aside his earthly and uncleanly nature." [560]

[557] The *Rosarium phil.* formulates the ascent and descent as follows: "Our stone passes into earth, earth into water, water into air, air into fire, and there it stays, but on the other hand it descends." * *Art. aurif.*, II, p. 250.
[558] The water in which the earth is dissolved is the earth's soul or spirit, of which Senior says: "This divine water is the king descending from heaven." Before that, the "king" was in the earth. Cf. *Ros. phil.*, p. 283.
[559] *Phil. ref.*, p. 20. This idea derives from "De arte chymica" (*Art. aurif.*, I, p. 612). Here the descent is identical with God's incarnation. Our passage is followed by the text: "I will content thee with this parable: The Son of God coming down into the Virgin and there clothed with flesh is born as a man, who, after showing us the way of truth for our salvation, suffering and dying for us, after his resurrection returned to heaven, where the earth, that is, mankind, is exalted above all the circles of the world and set in the intellectual heaven of the most holy Trinity." *
[560] "De vera praep. medicament. chem.," *Theatr. chem.*, I, p. 681.

This complete identification of the lapis with the "son of man" must obviously end with its ascension. But that contradicts the original and widespread conception of the lapis as the tincture or medicine, which has meaning and value only if it applies itself to the base substances of the lower world. The upper world is in need of no medicine, since it is incorruptible anyway. A redeemer who proceeds from matter and returns to matter gradually became unthinkable. Those who identified the lapis absolutely with Christ stopped working in the laboratory, and those who preferred laboratory work slowly gave up their mystic language.

296   Ascent and descent, above and below, up and down, represent an emotional realization of opposites, and this realization gradually leads, or should lead, to their equilibrium. This motif occurs very frequently in dreams, in the form of going up- and downhill, climbing stairs, going up or down in a lift, balloon, aeroplane, etc.[561] It corresponds to the struggle between the winged and the wingless dragon, i.e., the uroboros. Dorn describes it also as the "circular distillation"[562] and as the "spagyric vessel" which has to be constructed after the likeness of the natural vessel, i.e., in the form of a sphere. As Dorn interprets it, this vacillating between the opposites and being tossed back and forth means being contained *in* the opposites. They become a vessel in which what was previously now one thing and now another floats vibrating, so that the painful suspension between opposites gradually changes into the bilateral activity of the point in the centre.[563] This is the "liberation from opposites," the *nirdvandva* of Hindu philosophy, though it is not really a philosophical but rather a psychological development. The "Aurelia occulta" puts this thought in the words of the dragon: "Many from one and one from many, issue of a famous line, I rise from the lowest to the highest. The nethermost power of the whole earth is united with the highest. I therefore am the One and the Many within me."[564] In these words

561 Cf. *Psychology and Alchemy*, pars. 64ff., 78f.
562 "Phys. Trismeg.," *Theatr. chem.*, I, p. 430.
563 This motif is not uncommon in mandalas drawn by patients, the centre being represented either by a fluttering bird, or a pulsing cyst or heart. (In pathology we speak of an "auricular flutter.") The same motif appears in the form of concentric rings (see "A Study in the Process of Individuation," Picture 8), or of waves surrounding a centre (Picture 3).   564 *Theatr. chem.*, IV, p. 575.

the dragon makes it clear that he is the chthonic forerunner of the self.

f. *The Journey through the Planetary Houses*

297   Returning now to Michael Maier's journey to the seven mouths of the Nile, which signify the seven planets, we bring to this theme a deepened understanding of what the alchemists meant by ascent and descent. It was the freeing of the soul from the shackles of darkness, or unconsciousness; its ascent to heaven, the widening of consciousness; and finally its return to earth, to hard reality, in the form of the tincture or healing drink, endowed with the powers of the Above. What this means psychologically could be seen very clearly from the *Hypnerotomachia* [565] were its meaning not overlaid by a mass of ornate detail. It should therefore be pointed out that the whole first part of the book is a description of the dreamer's ascent to a world of gods and heroes, of his initiation into a Venus mystery, followed by the illumination and semi-apotheosis of Poliphilo and his Polia. In the second, smaller part this leads to disenchantment and the cooling off of the lovers, culminating in the knowledge that it was all only a dream. It is a descent to earth, to the reality of daily life, and it is not altogether clear whether the hero managed to "preserve in secret the nature of the heavenly centre which he acquired by the ascent." [566] One rather doubts it. Nevertheless, his exciting adventure has left us a psychological document which is a perfect example of the course and the symbolism of the individuation process. The spirit, if not the language, of alchemy breathes through it and sheds light even on the darkest enigmas and riddles of the Masters. [567]

298   Maier's journey through the planetary houses begins with Saturn, who is the coldest, heaviest, and most distant of the planets, the maleficus and abode of evil, the mysterious and sinister Senex (Old Man), and from there he ascends to the region of the sun, to look for the Boy Mercurius, the longed-for and long-sought goal of the adept. It is an ascent ever nearer to the

---

[565] Colonna, *Hypnerotomachia Poliphili* (1499).
[566] Dorn, "Phys. Trismeg.," *Theatr. chem.*, I, p. 409.
[567] For a thorough psychological analysis of the text see Fierz-David, *The Dream of Poliphilo*, pp. 57ff.

sun, from darkness and cold to light and warmth, from old age to youth, from death to rebirth. But he has to go back along the way he came, for Mercurius is not to be found in the region of the sun but at the point from which he originally started. This sounds very psychological, and in fact life never goes forward except at the place where it has come to a standstill.[568] The sought-for Mercurius is the *spiritus vegetativus,* a living spirit, whose nature it is to run through all the houses of the planets, i.e., the entire Zodiac. We could just as well say through the entire horoscope, or, since the horoscope is the chronometric equivalent of individual character, through all the character-ological components of the personality. Individual character is, on the old view, the curse or blessing which the gods bestowed on the child at its birth in the form of favourable or unfavour-able astrological aspects. The horoscope is like the "chirog-raphum," the "handwriting of the ordinances against us . . . which Christ blotted out; and he took it out of the way, nailing it to his cross. And after having disarmed the principalities and powers he made a show of them openly, and triumphed over them." [569]

299   This very ancient idea of what we might call an inborn bill of debt to fate is the Western version of a prenatal karma. It is the archons, the seven rulers of the planets, who imprint its fate upon the soul. Thus Priscillian (d. *c.* 385) says that the soul, on its descent to birth, passes through "certain circles" where it is made captive by evil powers, "and in accordance with the will of the victorious prince is forced into divers bodies, and his handwriting inscribed upon it." [570] Presumably this means that the soul is imprinted with the influences of the various planetary spheres. The descent of the soul through the planetary houses corresponds to its passage through the gates of the planets as described by Origen: the first gate is of lead and is correlated with Saturn,[571] from which it is clear that Maier is following an old tradition.[572] His peregrinatio chymica repeats the old

568 A psychological statement which, like all such, only becomes entirely true when it can be reversed.   569 Colossians 2 : 14f. (AV, mod.).

570 Orosius, *Ad Aurelium Augustinum commonitorium (CSEL.,* XVIII, p. 153).*

571 *Contra Celsum,* VI, 22 (trans. by Chadwick), p. 334. (Migne, *P.G.,* vol. 9, col. 1324.)

572 Usually the series seems to begin with Saturn. Cf. Bousset, "Die Himmelsreise der Seele."

"heavenly journey of the soul," an idea which seems to have been developed more particularly in Persia.

300   I shall not go more closely here into the transitus through the planetary houses;[573] it is sufficient to know that Michael Maier, like Mercurius, passes through them on his mystic journey.[574] This journey is reminiscent of the voyage of the hero, one motif of which becomes evident in the archetypal meeting at the critical place (the "ford") with the Ortus, its head showing the four colours. There are other motifs too. Where there is a monster a beautiful maiden is not far away, for they have, as we know, a secret understanding so that the one is seldom found without the other. The sibyl, the guide of souls, shows the hero the way to Mercurius, who in this case is Hermes Trismegistus, the supreme mystagogue.

301   In the *Shepherd of Hermas* it is related that the hero, while travelling along the Via Campana, met a monster resembling a dragon of the sea ($\kappa\tilde{\eta}\tau os$):

And the beast had on its head four colours, black, then the colour of flame and blood, then golden, then white. After I had passed the beast by and had gone about thirty feet further, lo! a maiden met me, 'adorned as if coming forth from the bridal chamber,' all in white and with white sandals, veiled to the forehead, and a turban for a head-dress, but her hair was white.[575]

302   The similarity between the two stories is so complete that one is tempted to assume that Maier had read the *Shepherd of Hermas*. This is not very likely. Though he had a good education in the humanities I can see in his writings no evidence that he was familiar with the patristic literature, and in his references to the writings of Albertus and Thomas Aquinas[576] he might easily have let slip a remark of this kind. But one finds nothing, and it does not seem very probable, either, that Maier had direct knowledge of the New Testament Apocrypha.

[573] The interested reader is referred to Cumont, *Textes et Monuments relatifs aux Mystères de Mithra*, I, pp. 36ff.; Bousset, "Himmelsreise"; and Reitzenstein, "Himmelswanderung und Drachenkampf."

[574] Cf. the journey motif in *Psychology and Alchemy*, pars. 304f., 457 and n. 75. Concerning Mercurius see the *puer-senex* motif in Curtius, *European Literature and the Latin Middle Ages*, pp. 98ff.

[575] *Shepherd of Hermas*, IV, 1, 10-2, 1 (trans. by Lake), p. 63.

[576] In his *Symbola aureae mensae*.

303   Hermas interprets the maiden as the Church, and Maier, fifteen hundred years later, as the Erythraean Sibyl, which only goes to show once more that the newer is the older. The "supreme mistress" led Hermas to the kingdom of the triune God, but Maier she leads to Hermes Trismegistus and Trisomatos, the triadic Mercurius, who would reveal to him the secret of the phoenix's resurrection.[577] He can find Mercurius only through the rite of the ascent and descent, the "circular distillation," beginning with the black lead, with the darkness, coldness, and malignity of the malefic Saturn; then ascending through the other planets to the fiery Sol, where the gold is heated in the hottest fire and cleansed of all impurities; and finally returning to Saturn, where this time he meets Mercurius and receives some useful teachings from him. Saturn has here changed from a star of ill omen into a "domus barbae" (House of the Beard), where the "wisest of all," Thrice-Greatest Hermes, imparts wisdom.[578] Hermas too begins with the blackness; his mistress gives him the following explanation:

The black is this world in which you are living; the colour of fire and blood means that this world must be destroyed in blood and fire. The golden part is you, who have fled from this world, for even as gold is tried in the fire and becomes valuable, so also you who live among them are tried. . . . The white part is the world to come, in which the elect of God shall dwell; for those who have been chosen by God for eternal life will be without spot and pure.[579]

304   In alchemy the fire purifies, but it also melts the opposites into a unity. He who ascends unites the powers of Above and Below and shows his full power when he returns again to earth.[580] By this is to be understood the production on the one hand of the panacea or Medicina Catholica, and on the other, of

577 I would also draw attention to the maiden and the dragon and the triadic symbolism in *The Dream of Poliphilo* (ed. by Fierz-David), especially the encounter with the triple-tongued dragon and the black prism in the realm of Queen Eleuterilida (pp. 73ff. and 90ff.). For the Erythraean Sibyl see Curtius, pp. 101ff.
578 "Therefore I am called Hermes Trismegistos, as having three parts of the Philosophy of the whole world." * "Tabula smaragdina," *De alchemia* (1541), cap. 12. "Domus barbae" comes from Arab *al-birba*, 'pyramid', where Hermes was said to be buried.
579 *Shepherd of Hermas*, IV, 3, 2–3, 5 (Lake, p. 67).
580 "Its power is complete when it is turned towards the earth." * "Tabula smaragdina," *De alchemia* (1541), cap. 6.

a living being with a human form, the *filius philosophorum*, who is often depicted as a youth or hermaphrodite or child. He is a parallel of the Gnostic Anthropos, but he also appears as an Anthroparion, a kind of goblin, a familiar who stands by the adept in his work and helps the physician to heal.[581] This being ascends and descends and unites Below with Above, gaining a new power which carries its effect over into everyday life. His mistress gives Hermas this advice: "Therefore do not cease to speak to the ears of the saints" [582]—in other words, work among your fellow men by spreading the news of the Risen.

305   Just as Maier on his return met Mercurius, so Hermas in his next vision met the Poimen, the shepherd, "a white fleece round his shoulders, a knapsack on his back, and a staff in his hand." Hermas recognized that "it was he to whom I was handed over," [583] namely the shepherd of the lamb, which was himself. In iconography the good shepherd has the closest connections with Hermes Kriophoros (the lamb-bearer); thus even in antiquity these two saviour figures coalesced. Whereas Hermas is "handed over" to his shepherd, Hermes hands over his art and wisdom to his pupil Maier and thus equips him to do something himself and to work with the aid of the magic caduceus. This, for a physician who was an alchemist, took the place of the staff of Asklepios, which had only one snake. The sacred snake of the Asklepieion signified: The god heals; but the caduceus, or Mercurius in the form of the coniunctio in the retort, means: In the hands of the physician lie the magic remedies granted by God.[584]

[581] As, for example, Asklepios and his cabir, Telesphoros. Cf. Kerényi, *Asklepios*, pp. 58, 88, and C.A. Meier, *Antike Inkubation und moderne Psychotherapie*, pp. 47f.

[582] *Shepherd of Hermas*, IV, 3, 6 (Lake, p. 67).

[583] Ibid., V, 1–4 (p. 69).

[584] For the interpretation of the caduceus see Servius, *In Vergilii Carmina commentarii* (ed. by Thilo and Hagen), I, p. 508: "For the serpents have heads which look inward, in order to signify that ambassadors ought to discuss and agree among themselves. . . . For which reason . . . ambassadors of peace are called Caduceatores . . . and to those Caducei are added two apples, one of the Sun and one of the Moon. . . . Mercury causes these two fierce animals to agree, so surely we also ought to agree with one another." "Others say that the Latins call Mercury by that name as if he were Medicurrius, the mid-runner, because he is always passing between heaven and the lower regions . . . and that the Caduceus is assigned to him because he brings enemies together in friendship by mediating confidence." ✱ (Ibid. II, p. 220.) The medieval writer Pierius says of the caduceus: "He will very

306   The numerous analogies between two texts so far apart in time enable us to take a psychological view of the transformations they describe. The sequence of colours coincides by and large with the sequence of the planets. Grey and black correspond to Saturn [585] and the evil world; they symbolize the beginning in darkness, in the melancholy, fear, wickedness, and wretchedness of ordinary human life. It is Maier from whom the saying comes about the "noble substance which moves from lord to lord, in the beginning whereof is wretchedness with vinegar." [586] By "lord" he means the archon and ruler of the planetary house. He adds: "And so it will fare with me." The darkness and blackness can be interpreted psychologically as man's confusion and lostness; that state which nowadays results in an anamnesis, a thorough examination of all those contents which are the cause of the problematical situation, or at any rate its expression. This examination, as we know, includes the irrational contents that originate in the unconscious and express themselves in fantasies and dreams. The analysis and interpretation of dreams confront the conscious standpoint with the statements of the unconscious, thus widening its narrow horizon. This loosening up of cramped and rigid attitudes corresponds to the solution and separation of the elements by the *aqua permanens,* which was already present in the "body" and is lured out by the art. The water is a soul or spirit, that is, a psychic "substance," which now in its turn is applied to the initial material. This corresponds to using the dream's meaning to clarify existing problems. "Solutio" is defined in this sense by Dorn.[587]

307   The situation is now gradually illuminated as is a dark night by the rising moon. The illumination comes to a certain extent from the unconscious, since it is mainly dreams that put us on the track of enlightenment. This dawning light corresponds to the *albedo,* the moonlight which in the opinion of some alchemists heralds the rising sun. The growing redness (*rubedo*) which now follows denotes an increase of warmth and light

readily bring discordant minds into agreement, and will bind together the two serpents, that is, mutual hatreds, into one by the rod of his doctrine." * Cited in Picinellus, *Mundus symbolicus,* I, p. 152.

585 "In the first place Saturn reigns in the *nigredo*." * *Symb. aur. mensae,* p. 156.

586 Ibid., p. 568.

587 "Spec. phil.," *Theatr. chem.,* I, p. 303: "As bodies are dissolved by solution, so the doubts of the philosophers are resolved by knowledge." *

coming from the sun, consciousness. This corresponds to the increasing participation of consciousness, which now begins to react emotionally to the contents produced by the unconscious. At first the process of integration is a "fiery" conflict, but gradually it leads over to the "melting" or synthesis of the opposites. The alchemists termed this the rubedo, in which the marriage of the red man and the white woman, Sol and Luna, is consummated. Although the opposites flee from one another they nevertheless strive for balance, since a state of conflict is too inimical to life to be endured indefinitely. They do this by wearing each other out: the one eats the other, like the two dragons or the other ravenous beasts of alchemical symbolism.

308   Astrologically, as we have said, this process corresponds to an ascent through the planets from the dark, cold, distant Saturn to the sun. To the alchemists the connection between individual temperament and the positions of the planets was self-evident, for these elementary astrological considerations were the common property of any educated person in the Middle Ages as well as in antiquity. The ascent through the planetary spheres therefore meant something like a shedding of the characterological qualities indicated by the horoscope, a retrogressive liberation from the character imprinted by the archons. The conscious or unconscious model for such an ascent was the Gnostic redeemer, who either deceives the archons by guile or breaks their power by force. A similar motif is the release from the "bill of debt to fate." The men of late antiquity in particular felt their psychic situation to be fatally dependent on the compulsion of the stars, Heimarmene, a feeling which may be compared with that inspired by the modern theory of heredity, or rather by the pessimistic use of it. A similar demoralization sets in in many neuroses when the patient takes the psychic factors producing the symptoms as though they were unalterable facts which it is useless to resist. The journey through the planetary houses, like the crossing of the great halls in the Egyptian underworld, therefore signifies the overcoming of a psychic obstacle, or of an autonomous complex, suitably represented by a planetary god or demon. Anyone who has passed through all the spheres is free from compulsion; he has won the crown of victory and become like a god.

309   In our psychological language today we express ourselves

more modestly: the journey through the planetary houses boils down to becoming conscious of the good and the bad qualities in our character, and the apotheosis means no more than maximum consciousness, which amounts to maximal freedom of the will. This goal cannot be better represented than by the alchemical symbol of the μεσουράνισμα ἡλίου (position of the sun at noon) in Zosimos.[588] But at the zenith the descent begins. The mystic traveller goes back to the Nile mouth from which he started. He repeats, as it were, the descent of the soul which had led in the first place to the imprinting of the "chirographum." He retraces his steps through the planetary houses until he comes back to the dark Saturn. This means that the soul, which was imprinted with a horoscopic character at the time of its descent into birth, conscious now of its godlikeness, beards the archons in their lairs and carries the light undisguised down into the darkness of the world.

310   Here again psychology makes no special claims. What before was a burden unwillingly borne and blamed upon the entire family, is seen by the greatest possible insight (which can be very modest!) to be no more than the possession of one's own personality, and one realizes—as though this were not self-evident!—that one cannot live from anything except what one is.

311   On returning to the house of Saturn our pilgrim finds the long-sought Mercurius.[589] Maier passes remarkably quickly over this highly significant encounter and mentions merely their "numerous conversations" without, however, disclosing their content. This is the more surprising in that Mercurius either personifies the great teacher or else has the character of the arcane substance, both of which would be a fruitful source for further revelations. For Mercurius is the light-bringing Nous, who knows the secret of transformation and of immortality.

312   Let us assume that Maier's sudden silence is no mere accident but was intentional or even a necessity. This assumption is not entirely without justification since Maier was one of the founders of the international Rosicrucian Society,[590] and would therefore have no doubt been in a position to expatiate at length

---

[588] Berthelot, *Alch. grecs*, III, v bis (text vol., p. 118).

[589] More precisely, before he comes to the house of Saturn, "in one of the entrances." *Symb. aur. mensae*, p. 603.

[590] Ibid., p. 477. Cf. Waite, *The Real History of the Rosicrucians*, pp. 268ff.

upon the Hermetic arcana. What we know of the so-called Rosicrucian secrets does nothing to explain why they were hushed up. This, incidentally, is true of most "mysteries" of this kind. It is very significant that the "mysteries" of the early Church turned soon enough into "sacraments." The word "mystery" became a misnomer, since everything lay open in the rite. Andreas Rosencreutz used as a motto for his *Chymical Wedding:* "Mysteries profaned and made public fade and lose their grace. Therefore, cast not pearls before swine, nor spread roses for the ass." This attitude might have been a motive for silence. People had so often got to know of things that were kept secret in the mysteries under the most fearsome oaths and had wondered why on earth they should ever have been the object of secrecy. Self-importance or the prestige of the priesthood or of the initiates seemed the obvious deduction. And there can be no doubt that the mysteries often were abused in this way. But the real reason was the imperative need to participate in *a* or perhaps *the* secret without which life loses its supreme meaning. The secret is not really worth keeping, but the fact that it is still obstinately kept reveals an equally persistent psychic motive for keeping secrets, and that is the real secret, the real mystery. It is indeed remarkable and "mysterious" that this gesture of keeping something secret should be made at all. Why does man need to keep a secret, and for what purpose does he invent an artificial one which he even decks out as an ineffably holy rite? The thing hidden is always more or less irrelevant, for in itself it is no more than an image or sign pointing to a content that cannot be defined more closely. This content is certainly not a matter for indifference since it indicates the living presence of a numinous archetype. The essential thing is the hiding, an expressive gesture which symbolizes something unconscious and "not to be named" lying behind it; something, therefore, that is either not yet conscious or cannot or will not become conscious. It points, in a word, to the presence of an unconscious content, which exacts from consciousness a tribute of constant regard and attention. With the application of interest the continual perception and assimilation of the effects of the "secret" become possible. This is beneficial to the conduct of life, because the contents of the unconscious can then exert their compensatory effect and, if taken note of and recognized, bring about a balance that promotes health. On a primitive level, therefore, the chief effect of the mysteries is to promote health, growth, and fertility. If there were nothing good in the rite it would presumably never have come into existence or would long since have perished. The tremendous psychic effect of the Eleusinian mysteries, for instance, is beyond question. Psychotherapeutic experience has made the meaning of secrets once more a topical question, not only from the religious or philosophical point of view but also in respect of the demands of conscience with which individuation confronts a man.

313 Maier's silence is eloquent, as we soon find when we try to see the psychological equivalent of the descent and of the discovery of Mercurius. The maximal degree of consciousness confronts the ego with its shadow, and individual psychic life with a collective psyche. These psychological terms sound light enough but they weigh heavy, for they denote an almost unendurable conflict, a psychic strait whose terrors only he knows who has passed through it. What one then discovers about oneself and about man and the world is of such a nature that one would rather not speak of it; and besides, it is so difficult to put into words that one's courage fails at the bare attempt. So it need not be at all a frivolous evasion if Maier merely hints at his conversations with Mercurius. In the encounter with life and the world there are experiences that are capable of moving us to long and thorough reflection, from which, in time, insights and convictions grow up—a process depicted by the alchemists as the philosophical tree. The unfolding of these experiences is regulated, as it were, by two archetypes: the anima, who expresses *life,* and the "Wise Old Man," who personifies *meaning.*[591] Our author was led in the first place by the anima-sibyl to undertake the journey through the planetary houses as the precondition of all that was to follow. It is therefore only logical that, towards the end of the descent, he should meet Thrice-Greatest Hermes, the fount of all wisdom. This aptly describes the character of that spirit or thinking which you do not, like an intellectual operation, perform yourself, as the "little god of this world," but which happens to you as though it came from another, and greater, perhaps the great spirit of the world, not inappositely named Trismegistus. The long reflection, the "im-

591 For details see "Archetypes of the Collective Unconscious," pars. 66, 79.

mensa meditatio" of the alchemists is defined as an "internal colloquy with another, who is invisible." [592]

314   Possibly Maier would have revealed to us something more if Mercurius had not been in such a hurry to take upon himself "the role of arbiter between the owl and the birds who were fighting it." [593] This is an allusion to a work of Maier's entitled *Jocus severus* (Frankfurt a. M., 1617), where he defends the wisdom of alchemy against its detractors, a theme that also plays an important part in his *Symbola aureae mensae* in the form of argument and counterargument. One is therefore justified in assuming that Maier got into increasing conflict with himself and his environment the more he buried himself in the secret speculations of Hermetic philosophy. Indeed nothing else could have been expected, for the world of Hermetic images gravitates round the unconscious, and the unconscious compensation is always aimed at the conscious positions which are the most strongly defended because they are the most questionable, though its apparently hostile aspect merely reflects the surly face which the ego turns towards it. In reality the unconscious compensation is not intended as a hostile act but as a necessary and helpful attempt to restore the balance. For Maier it meant an inner and outer conflict which was not abolished, but only embittered, by the firmness of his convictions. For every one-sided conviction is accompanied by the voice of doubt, and certainties that are mere beliefs turn into uncertainties which may correspond better with the truth. The truth of the "sic et non" (yes and no), almost, but not quite, recognized by Abelard, is a difficult thing for the intellect to bear; so it is no wonder that Maier got stuck in the conflict and had to postpone his discovery of the phoenix until doomsday. Fortunately he was honest enough not to assert that he had ever made the lapis or the philosophical gold, and for this reason he never spread a veil of deception over his work. Thanks to his scrupulousness his late successors are at least able to guess how far he had progressed in the art, and where his labours came to a standstill. He never succeeded, as we can now see, in reaching the point where conflict and argument become logically superfluous, where "yes and no" are two aspects of the same thing. "Thou wilt never make the One which thou

[592] Ruland, *Lexicon*, p. 226.
[593] *Symb. aur. mensae*, pp. 603f.

seekest," says the master, "except first there be made one thing of thyself." [594]

g. *The Regeneration in Sea-water*

315   After these long digressions on the interrelated symbols that branch out from the sea and its various aspects, we will resume our discussion of salt and salt-water.

316   The *aqua pontica* (or *aqua permanens*) behaves very much like the baptismal water of the Church. Its chief function is ablution, the cleansing of the sinner, and in alchemy this is the "lato," the impure body; [595] hence the oft-repeated saying attributed to Elbo Interfector: [596] "Whiten the lato [597] and rend the books, lest your hearts be rent asunder." [598] In the *Rosarium* the ablution [599] of the lato occurs in variant form: it is cleansed not by water but by "Azoth and fire," [600] that is, by a kind of baptism in fire, which is often used as a synonym for water.[601] The equivalent of this in the Catholic rite is the plunging of a burning candle into the font, in accordance with Matthew 3 : 11: "He

---

594 Dorn, "Spec. phil.," *Theatr. chem.*, I, p. 276.

595 "Rosinus ad Sarrat.," *Art. aurif.*, I, p. 280: "But the lato is the unclean body." *

596 For instance in Maier, *Symb. aur. mensae*, p. 215.

597 The whitened lato is identical with the "crystalline salt." (Khunrath, *Hyl. Chaos*, p. 197.) The lato, too, is an arcane substance, but it has a negative character. Mylius says: "The lato is an imperfect yellow body compounded of Sun and Moon: when you have whitened it and restored it to its pristine yellowness, you have the lato again . . . Then you have passed through the door and have the beginning of the art." * It is the *prima materia lapidis* in the state of *vilitas*, 'baseness,' from which the "pearl of great price" arises. (*Phil. ref.*, p. 199.) This passage seems to be taken from "Consil. coniug.," *Ars chemica*, p. 134. The lato is the "black earth" (ibid., p. 80, also p. 39). According to Du Cange, "lato" has something to do with *"electrum."* Cf. Lippmann, *Entstehung und Ausbreitung der Alchemie*, I, p. 481.

598 "Dealbate Latonem et libros rumpite, ne corda vestra corrumpantur." *Ros. phil.* cites this saying from Geber, but in corrupt form: "reponite" instead of "rumpite."

599 Ablutio was understood by the alchemists as distillatio. Cf. Mylius, *Phil. ref.*, p. 35.

600 Quotation from Hermes: "Azoth and fire cleanse the lato, and remove the blackness from it" * (*Art. aurif.*, II, p. 277).

601 Mylius has: "Fire and water cleanse the lato and wipe off its blackness." * *Phil. ref.*, p. 297.

shall baptize you with the Holy Ghost, and with fire." [602] The alchemists did not hesitate to call the transformative process a "baptism." Thus the "Consilium coniugii" says: "And if we are baptized in the fountain of gold and silver, and the spirit of our body ascends into heaven with the father and the son, and descends again, then our souls shall revive and my animal body will remain white, that is, [the body] of the moon." [603] The subject of this sentence is Sol and Luna. The *Aurora consurgens* I distinguishes three kinds of baptism, "in water, in blood, and in fire," [604] the Christian ideas being here transferred directly to the chemical procedure. The same is true of the idea that baptism is a submersion in death, following Colossians 2 : 12: "(Ye are) buried with him in baptism, wherein also ye are risen with him." In his Table of Symbols, Penotus [605] correlates the "moon, the spirits and ghosts of the dead [*Manes et Lemures*], and gods of the underworld" with the "mystery of baptism," and the corresponding stage in the opus is the *solutio,* which signifies the total dissolution of the imperfect body in the *aqua divina,* its submersion, mortification,[606] and burial. The putrefaction takes place in the grave, and the foul smell that accompanies it is the stench of the graves.[607] The motif of imprisonment in the underworld is found in Greek alchemy, in the treatise of Komarios: "Lock them [the substances] in Hades." [608] The rebirth from the floods (κλύδωνες) of Hades and from the grave recurs in Cyril of Jerusalem: "That saving flood

[602] The fire symbolism connected with baptism is expressed particularly clearly in the hymn of St. Romanus, "De theophania": "I behold him in the midst of the floods, him who once appeared as dew in the fire in the midst of the three youths [Daniel 3 : 24f.], now a fire shining in the Jordan." * Pitra, *Analecta sacra,* I, p. 21.
[603] P. 128.* Cf. supra, par. 291.
[604] Parable 4. Another passage has: "But when he baptizes, he infuses the soul." * Ibid. [605] *Theatr. chem.,* II, p. 123.
[606] The classic example of this is the dissolution of Gabricus in the body of Beya, into "atoms" (*partes indivisibiles*). *Ros. phil.,* in *Art. aurif.,* II, p. 246.
[607] Morienus, "De transmut. metallica," *Art. aurif.,* II, p. 33.
[608] * The text is in a poor state here. The passage is apparently attributed to Stephanos, and occurs not only in the treatise of Komarios (Berthelot, *Alch. grecs.* IV, xx, 13, lines 17 and 20) but also in Zosimos (III, ii). Whether Stephanos (7th cent.) would have expressed himself in such an old-fashioned way is uncertain. The passage does in fact belong in the treatise of Komarios, where it also occurs in different words at 10, lines 22ff. This runs: "The waves injure them [the substances] . . . in Hades and in the grave where they lie. But when the grave is opened, they will rise up from Hades like the newborn from the belly." *

236

is both your sepulchre and your mother," [609] and in St. Augustine: "The water leads him down, as if dying, into the grave; the Holy Spirit brings him up, as if rising again, into heaven." [610]

317   The treatise of Ostanes [611] says that when preparing the ὕδωρ θεῖον, the vessel with the ingredients should be immersed in sea-water, and then the divine water will be perfected. It is, so to speak, gestated in the womb of the sea-water. The text says: "This [divine] water makes the dead living and the living dead, it lights the darkness and darkens the light, concentrates [δράσσεται] the sea-water and quenches fire." As this miraculous water occurs even in the oldest texts, it must be of pagan rather than of Christian origin. The oldest Chinese treatise known to us (A.D. 142) likewise contains this idea of the divine water: it is the "flowing pearl" (quicksilver), and the divine ch'i, meaning 'air, spirit, ethereal essence'. The various essences are likened to "spring showers in abundance," [612] and this recalls the "blessed water" in the treatise of Komarios, which brings the spring.[613] The age-old use of water at sacrifices and the great role it played in Egypt, where Western alchemy originated, may well have foreshadowed the water symbolism of later times. Folk ideas and superstitions such as we find in the Magic Papyri may have made their contribution, too; the following words might just as well have been taken from an alchemical treatise: "I am the plant named Baïs, I am a spout of blood . . . , the outgrowth of the abyss.[614] . . . I am the sacred bird Phoenix.[615] . . . I am Helios. . . . I am Aphrodite. . . . I am Kronos, who has showed forth the light. . . . I am Osiris, named water, I am Isis, named dew, I am Esenephys, named spring." [616] The personified ὕδωρ θεῖον might well have spoken like that.

318   The effect of Christian baptism is the washing away of sin and the acceptance of the neophyte into the Church as the earthly kingdom of Christ, sanctification and rebirth through

609 *Catecheses mystagogicae*, II, 4 (Migne, *P.G.*, vol. 33, col. 1080).*
610 Pitra, *Analecta sacra*, V, p. 150.*   611 Berthelot, *Alch. grecs*, IV, ii, 2.
612 *Isis*, XVIII, pp. 238 and 251.   613 Berthelot, *Alch. grecs*, IV, xx, 8, 9, 12.
614 The ἐναβύσσαιον ὕδωρ (abyssal water) is mentioned in the treatise of Christianos, "The Making of the Mystical Water" (Berthelot, VI, v, 6, line 12).
615 Probably the earliest reference to the phoenix is in Zosimos (Berthelot, III, vi, 5), where a quotation from Ostanes speaks of an "eagle of brass, who descends into the pure spring and bathes there every day, thus renewing himself." *
616 Preisendanz, *Pap. Graec. Mag.*, II, p. 73, Pap. XII, lines 228–38.*

grace, and the bestowal of an "indelible character" on the baptized. The effect of the *aqua permanens* is equally miraculous. The "Gloria mundi" says: "The mystery of every thing is life, which is water; for water dissolves the body into spirit and summons a spirit from the dead." [617] Dissolution into spirit, the body's volatilization or sublimation, corresponds chemically to evaporation, or any rate to the expulsion of evaporable ingredients like quicksilver, sulphur, etc. Psychologically it corresponds to the conscious realization and integration of an unconscious content. Unconscious contents lurk somewhere in the body like so many demons of sickness, impossible to get hold of, especially when they give rise to physical symptoms the organic causes of which cannot be demonstrated. The "spirit" summoned from the dead is usually the spirit Mercurius, who, as the *anima mundi*, is inherent in all things in a latent state. It is clear from the passage immediately following that it is salt of which it is said: "And that is the thing which we seek: all our secrets are contained in it." Salt, however, "takes its origin from Mercurius," so salt is a synonym for the arcane substance. It also plays an important part in the Roman rite: after being blessed it is added to the consecrated water, and in the ceremony of baptism a few grains of the consecrated salt are placed in the neophyte's mouth with the words: "Receive the salt of wisdom: may it be a propitiation for thee unto eternal life."

319   As the alchemists strove to produce an incorruptible "glorified body," they would, if they were successful, attain that state in the *albedo,* where the body became spotless and no longer subject to decay. The white substance of the ash [618] was therefore described as the "diadem of the heart," and its synonym, the white foliated earth (*terra alba foliata*), as the "crown of victory." [619] The ash is identical with the "pure water" which is

---

[617] *Mus. herm.*, p. 262 (Waite, I, p. 211). This opinion is put into the mouth of "Socrates," and corresponds more or less to Sermo XVI of the *Turba*.

[618] Ash is the calcined and annealed substance, freed from all decomposition.

[619] Senior, *De chemia*, p. 41: "The white foliated earth is the crown of victory, which is ash extracted from ash, and their second body." * The connection with 1 Thess. 2 : 19, ". . . our hope, or joy, or crown of glory" (DV), is doubtful, likewise with Isaiah 28 : 5, ". . . the Lord of hosts shall be a crown of glory" (DV). On the other hand, Isaiah 61 : 3, ". . . to give them a crown for ashes," is of importance for the alchemical connection between ashes, diadem, and crown. Cf. Goodenough, "The Crown of Victory."

"cleansed from the darkness of the soul, and of the black matter, for the wickedness (*malitia*) of base earthiness has been separated from it." [620] This "terrestreitas mala" is the "terra damnata" (accursed earth) mentioned by other authors; it is what Goethe calls the "trace of earth painful to bear," the moral turpitude that cannot be washed off. In Senior the ash is synonymous with *vitrum* (glass), which, on account of its incorruptibility and transparency, seemed to resemble the glorified body. Glass in its turn was associated with salt, for salt was praised as "that virgin and pure earth," and the "finest crystalline glass" is composed mainly of *sal Sodae* (soda salts), with sand added as a binding agent. Thus the raw material of glass-making (technically known as the "batch") is "formed from two incorruptible substances." [621] Furthermore, glass is made in the fire, the "pure" element. In the sharp or burning taste of salt the alchemists detected the fire dwelling within it, whose preservative property it in fact shares. Alexander of Macedon is cited as saying: "Know that the salt is fire and dryness." [622] Or, "the salts are of fiery nature." [623] Salt has an affinity with sulphur, whose nature is essentially fiery.[624] Glauber maintains that "fire and salt are in their essential nature one thing" and are therefore "held in high esteem by all sensible Christians, but the ignorant know no more of these things than a cow, a pig, or a brute, which live without understanding." He also says the "Abyssinians" baptized with water and fire. Without fire and salt the heathen would not have been able to offer sacrifice, and the evangelist Mark had said that "every one shall be salted with fire, and every sacrifice shall be salted with salt." [625]

h. The Interpretation and Meaning of Salt

320   Salt as much as ash is a synonym for the *albedo* (or *dealbatio*), and is identical with "the white stone, the white sun, the full moon, the fruitful white earth, cleansed and calcined." [626]

620 Ibid., p. 40.   621 Vigenerus, "De igne et sale," *Theatr. chem.*, VI, pp. 44f.
622 *Mus. herm.*, p. 217 (Waite, I, p. 176).
623 Vigenerus, p. 57.
624 *Mus. herm.*, p. 217.
625 *De natura salium*, pp. 16f. Glauber alludes here to Mark 9 : 49.
626 Mylius, *Phil. ref.*, p. 20.*

The connecting link between ash and salt is potash, and the burning and corrosive property of lye (caustic solution) is well known.[627] Senior mentions that the *dealbatio* was known as "salsatura" (marination).[628]

321   Some light is thrown on the numerous overlapping significations of salt, and the obscurity begins to clear up, when we are informed, further, that one of its principal meanings is *soul*. As the white substance it is the "white woman," and the "salt of our magnesia"[629] is a "spark of the *anima mundi*."[630] For Glauber the salt is feminine and corresponds to Eve.[631] The "Gloria mundi" says: "The salt of the earth is the soul."[632] This pregnant sentence contains within it the whole ambiguity of alchemy. On the one hand the soul is the "aqua permanens, which dissolves and coagulates," the arcane substance which is at once the transformer and the transformed, the nature which conquers nature. On the other hand it is the human soul imprisoned in the body as the *anima mundi* is in matter, and this soul undergoes the same transformations by death and purification, and finally by glorification, as the lapis. It is the tincture which "coagulates" all substances, indeed it even "fixes" (*figit*) itself; it comes "from the centre of the earth and is the destroyed earth, nor is there anything on the earth like to the tincture."[633] The soul is therefore not an earthly but a transcendental thing, regardless of the fact that the alchemists expected it to appear in a retort. This contradiction presented no difficulties to the medieval mind. There was a good reason for this: the philos-

---

[627] Cf. the *Liber de aluminibus et salibus,* attributed to Rhasis or to Garlandus (*Buch der Alaune und Salze,* ed. Ruska, pp. 81ff.). This purely chemical treatise of Arabic origin gives some idea of what the early medieval alchemists knew of chemistry.   [628] *De chemia,* p. 42.

[629] For the alchemists magnesia was as a rule an arcane substance and not a specifically chemical one. Cf. *Aion,* pars. 241f., 244.

[630] Khunrath, *Hyl. Chaos,* p. 197.

[631] *De Signatura salium,* p. 12. For Eve as the feminine element contained in the man see "Psychology and Religion," par. 47, n. 22.

[632] *Mus. herm.,* p. 217 (Waite, I, p. 176): "Sal terrae est anima."

[633] P. 218. How very much the tincture is the "baptismal water" can be seen from the Greek (Berthelot, VI, xviii, 4, line 2): "Being bodies they become spirits, so that he will baptize in the tincture of the spirit." * There is a similar passage in Pelagios (Berthelot, IV, i, 9, lines 17ff.). We are reminded of the famous passage about the *krater* in Zosimos (Berthelot, III, li, line 8): "baptized in the *krater*," referring to the baptism of Theosebeia into the Poimandres community.

ophers were so fascinated by their own psychisms that, in their naïveté, they faithfully reproduced the inner psychic situation externally. Although the unconscious, personified by the anima, is in itself transcendental, it can appear in the sphere of consciousness, that is, in this world, in the form of an "influence" on conscious processes.

322　Just as the world-soul pervades all things, so does salt. It is ubiquitous and thus fulfils the main requirement of an arcane substance, that it can be found everywhere. No doubt the reader will be as conscious as I am of how uncommonly difficult it is to give an account of salt and its ubiquitous connections. It represents the feminine principle of Eros, which brings everything into relationship, in an almost perfect way. In this respect it is surpassed only by Mercurius, and the notion that salt comes from Mercurius is therefore quite understandable. For salt, as the soul or spark of the *anima mundi,* is in very truth the daughter of the spiritus vegetativus of creation. Salt is far more indefinite and more universal than sulphur, whose essence is fairly well defined by its fiery nature.

323　The relationship of salt to the *anima mundi,* which as we know is personified by the Primordial Man or Anthropos, brings us to the analogy with Christ. Glauber himself makes the equation Sal: Sol $= A : \Omega$,[634] so that salt becomes an analogue of God. According to Glauber, the sign for salt $\ominus$ was originally ⊡,[635] a double totality symbol; the circle representing non-differentiated wholeness, and the square discriminated wholeness.[636] As a matter of fact there is another sign for salt, ♃ in contradistinction to ♀ Venus, who certainly has less to do with understanding and wisdom than has salt. Salt, says Glauber, was the "first fiat" at the creation.[637] Christ is the salt of wisdom which is given at baptism.[638] These ideas are elaborated by Georg von Welling: Christ is the salt, the fiat is the Word that is begotten from eternity for our preservation. Christ is the "sweet, fixed salt of silent, gentle eternity." The body, when salted by Christ, becomes tinctured and therefore incorruptible.[639]

324　The Christ parallel runs through the late alchemical speculations that set in after Boehme, and it was made possible by the

---

634 *De signatura salium,* p. 15.　　635 Ibid., p. 23.　　636 Cf. supra, par. 261.
637 *De natura salium,* p. 44.　　638 Ibid., p. 51.
639 *Opus Mago-Cabbalisticum,* pp. 6 and 31.

sal : *sapientia* equation. Already in antiquity salt denoted wit, good sense, good taste, etc., as well as spirit. Cicero, for instance, remarks: "In wit [*sale*] and humour Caesar . . . surpassed them all." [640] But it was the Vulgate that had the most decisive influence on the formation of alchemical concepts. In the Old Testament, even the "salt of the covenant" [641] has a moral meaning. In the New Testament, the famous words "Ye are the salt of the earth" (Matthew 5 : 13) show that the disciples were regarded as personifications of higher insight and divine wisdom, just as, in their role of ἀπόστολοι (proclaimers of the message), they functioned as "angels" (ἄγγελοι, 'messengers'), so that God's kingdom on earth might approximate as closely as possible to the structure of the heavenly hierarchy. The other well-known passage is at Mark 9 : 50, ending with the words: "Have salt in yourselves, and have peace one with another." The earliest reference to salt in the New Testament (Colossians 4 : 6) likewise has a classical flavour: "Let your speech be alway with grace, and seasoned with salt, that ye may know how ye ought to answer every man."

325 Here salt undoubtedly means insight, understanding, wisdom. In both Matthew and Mark the salt is liable to lose its savour. Evidently this salt must keep its tang, just as the wise virgins kept their lamps trimmed. For this purpose a flexibility of mind is needed, and the last thing to guarantee this is rigid insistence on the necessity of faith. Everyone will admit that it is the task of the Church to safeguard her store of wisdom, the *aqua doctrinae,* in its original purity, and yet, in response to the changing spirit of the times, she must go on altering it and differentiating it just as the Fathers did. For the cultured Greco-Roman world early Christianity was among other things a message in philosophical disguise, as we can see quite plainly from Hippolytus. It was a competing philosophical doctrine that reached a certain peak of perfection in St. Thomas. Until well into the sixteenth century the degree of philosophical truth of Christian doctrine corresponded to that of scientific truth today.

326 The physicians and natural philosophers of the Middle Ages nevertheless found themselves faced with problems for which the Church had no answer. Confronted with sickness and death, the physicians did not hesitate to seek counsel with the Arabs

640 *De officiis* I, §133 (trans. by Miller), pp. 136f. *
641 For instance, Leviticus 2 : 13.

and so resuscitate that bit of the ancient world which the Church thought she had exterminated for ever, namely the Mandaean and Sabaean remnants of Hellenistic syncretism. From them they derived a *sal sapientiae* that seemed so unlike the doctrine of the Church that before long a process of mutual assimilation arose which put forth some very remarkable blossoms. The ecclesiastical allegories kept, so far as I can judge, to the classical usage of Sal. Only St. Hilary (d. 367) seems to have gone rather more deeply into the nature of salt when he remarks that "salt contains in itself the element of water and fire, and by this is one out of two." [642] Picinellus observes: "Two elements which stir up an implacable enmity between themselves are found in wondrous alliance in salt. For salt is wholly fire and wholly water." [643] For the rest he advises a sparing use of salt: "Let the word be sprinkled with salt, not deluged with it," [644] and another, earlier allegorist, the Jesuit Nicholas Caussin,[645] does not mention salt at all.

327   This is not altogether surprising, for how do wisdom and revelation square with one another? As certain books of the Old Testament canon show, there is, besides the wisdom of God which expresses itself in revelation, a human wisdom which cannot be had unless one works for it. Mark 9 : 50 therefore exhorts us to make sure that we always have enough salt in us, and he is certainly not referring to divine revelation, for this is something no man can produce on his own resources. But at least he can cultivate and increase his own human wisdom. That Mark should offer this warning, and that Paul should express himself in a very similar way, is in accord with the traditional Judeo-Hellenism of the Jewish communities at that time. An authoritarian Church, however, leaves very little room for the salt of human wisdom. Hence it is not surprising that the *sal sapientiae* plays an incomparably greater role outside the Church. Irenaeus, reporting the views of the Gnostics, says: "The spiritual, they say, [is] sent forth to this end, that, being united here below with the psychic, it may take form, and be instructed simultaneously by intercourse with it. And this they declare

642 *Commentarium in Matthaei Evangelium*, IV, 10 (Migne, *P.L.*, vol. 9, col. 954).*
643 *Mundus symbolicus*, p. 711.
644 "Aspergatur sermo sapientia, non obruatur."
645 *Polyhistor symbolicus*.

to be the salt and the light of the world." [646] The union of the spiritual, masculine principle with the feminine, psychic principle is far from being just a fantasy of the Gnostics: it has found an echo in the Assumption of the Virgin, in the union of Tifereth and Malchuth, and in Goethe's "the Eternal Feminine leads us upward and on." Hippolytus mentions this same view as that of the Sethians. He says:

But when this wave is raised from the water by the wind and made pregnant in its nature, and has received within itself the reproductive power of the feminine, it retains the light scattered from on high together with the fragrance of the spirit [πνεύματος],[647] and that is Nous given shape in various forms. This [light] is a perfect God, who is brought down from the unbegotten light on high and from the spirit into man's nature as into a temple, by the power of nature and the movement of the wind. It is engendered from the water and commingled and mixed with the bodies as if it were the salt of all created things, and a light of the darkness struggling to be freed from the bodies, and not able to find a way out. For some very small spark of the light is mingled with the fragrance from above. . . . [Here follows a corrupt and controversial passage which I pass over.] . . . Therefore every thought and care of the light from above is how and in what way the Nous may be delivered from the death of the sinful and dark body, from the father below [τοῦ κάτωθεν],[648] who is the wind which raised up the waves in tumult and terror, and begot Nous his own perfect son, who is yet not his own son in substance. For he was a ray of light from on high, from that perfect light over-powered in the dark and terrible, bitter polluted water, and a shining spirit carried away over the water . . .[649]

328   This strangely beautiful passage contains pretty well everything that the alchemists endeavoured to say about salt: it is the spirit, the turning of the body into light (*albedo*), the spark of the *anima mundi,* imprisoned in the dark depths of the sea and begotten there by the light from above and the "reproductive power of the feminine." It should be noted that the alchemists could have known nothing of Hippolytus, as his *Philosophu-*

[646] *Adv. haer.,* I, vi, 1 (cf. trans. Roberts / Rambaut, I, p. 25).
[647] Here *pneuma* has the meaning of a holy spirit and not of wind.
[648] "Death" and the "father below" are both preceded by the same ἀπό (from) and are therefore parallel if not identical, in so far as the begetter of life is also the begetter of death. This is an indication of the ineluctable polaristic nature of the *auctor rerum.*
[649] *Elenchos,* V, 19, 14ff. Cf. Legge, *Philosophumena,* I, pp. 163f.

mena, long believed lost, was rediscovered only in the middle of the nineteenth century in a monastery on Mount Athos. Anyone familiar with the spirit of alchemy and the views of the Gnostics in Hippolytus will be struck again and again by their inner affinity.

329   The clue to this passage from the *Elenchos,* and to other similar ones, is to be found in the phenomenology of the self.[650] Salt is not a very common dream-symbol, but it does appear in the cubic form of a crystal,[651] which in many patients' drawings represents the centre and hence the self; similarly, the quaternary structure of most mandalas reminds one of the sign for salt ⊡ mentioned earlier. Just as the numerous synonyms and attributes of the lapis stress now one and now another of its aspects, so do the symbols of the self. Apart from its preservative quality salt has mainly the metaphorical meaning of sapientia. With regard to this aspect the "Tractatus aureus" states: "It is said in the mystic language of our sages, He who works without salt will never raise dead bodies. . . . He who works without salt draws a bow without a string. For you must know that these sayings refer to a very different kind of salt from the common mineral. . . . Sometimes they call the medicine itself 'Salt.' " [652] These words are ambiguous: here salt means "wit" as well as wisdom. As to the importance of salt in the opus, Johannes Grasseus says of the arcane substance: "And this is the Lead of the Philosophers, which they also call the lead of the air. In it is found the shining white dove, named the salt of the metals, wherein is the whole magistery of the work. This [dove] is the pure, chaste, wise, and rich Queen of Sheba." [653] Here salt, arcane substance (the paradoxical "lead of the air"), the white dove (*spiritus sapientiae*), wisdom, and femininity appear in one figure. The saying from the "Gloria mundi" is quite clear: "No man can understand this Art who does not know the salt and its preparation." [654] For the "Aquarium sapientum" the *sal sapientiae* comes from the *aqua benedicta* or *aqua pontica*, which, itself an extract, is named "heart, soul, and spirit." At first the

---

650 See *Aion,* ch. 13.

651 Cubic salt crystals are mentioned in Welling, *Opus Mago-Cabbalisticum,* p. 41.

652 *Mus. herm.,* p. 20 (Waite, I, p. 22).

653 "Arca arcani," *Theatr. chem.,* VI, p. 314.

654 *Mus. herm.,* p. 216 (Waite, I, p. 176).

aqua is contained in the prima materia and is "of a blood-red colour; but after its preparation it becomes of a bright, clear, transparent white, and is called by the sages the Salt of Wisdom." [655] Khunrath boldly summarizes these statements about the salt when he says: "Our water cannot be made without the salt of wisdom, for it is the salt of wisdom itself, say the philosophers; a fire, and a salt fire, the true Living Universal Menstruum." "Without salt the work has no success." [656] Elsewhere he remarks: "Not without good reason has salt been adorned by the wise with the name of Wisdom." Salt is the lapis, a "mystery to be hidden." [657] Vigenerus says that the Redeemer chose his disciples "that they might be the salt of men and proclaim to them the pure and incorruptible doctrine of the gospel." He reports the "Cabalists" as saying that the "computatio" [658] of the Hebrew word for salt (*melach*) gives the number 78. This number could be divided by any divisor and still give a word that referred to the divine Name. We will not pursue the inferences he draws from this but will only note that for all those reasons salt was used "for the service of God in all offerings and sacrifices." [659] Glauber calls Christ the *sal sapientiae* and says that his favourite disciple John was "salted with the salt of wisdom." [660]

330 Apart from its lunar wetness and its terrestrial nature, the most outstanding properties of salt are bitterness and wisdom. As in the double quaternio of the elements and qualities, earth and water have coldness in common, so bitterness and wisdom would form a pair of opposites with a third thing between. (See diagram on facing page.) The factor common to both, however incommensurable the two ideas may seem, is, psychologically, the function of *feeling*. Tears, sorrow, and disappointment are bitter, but wisdom is the comforter in all psychic suffering. Indeed, bitterness and wisdom form a pair of alternatives: where there is bitterness wisdom is lacking, and where wisdom is there can be no bitterness. Salt, as the carrier of this fateful alternative,

---

655 *Mus. herm.*, p. 88 (Waite, I, p. 80).   656 *Hyl. Chaos*, pp. 229, 254.

657 *Amphitheatrum*, p. 197. The lapis, however, corresponds to the self.

658 By "computatio" is meant the "isopsephia," that is, the sum which results from the numerical values of the letters in a word, this word being then equated with another word having the same numerical value.

659 "De igne et sale," *Theatr. chem.*, VI, pp. 129f.

660 *De natura salium*, pp. 25 and 51. Christ as *sal sapientiae* is another symbol of the self.

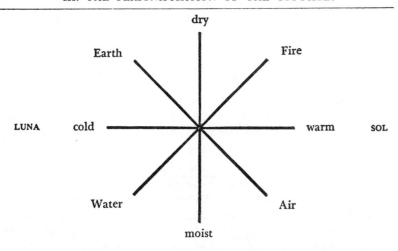

is co-ordinated with the nature of woman. The masculine, solar nature in the right half of the quaternio knows neither coldness, nor a shadow, nor heaviness, melancholy, etc., because, so long as all goes well, it identifies as closely as possible with consciousness, and that as a rule is the idea which one has of oneself. In this idea the shadow is usually missing: first because nobody likes to admit to any inferiority, and second because logic forbids something white to be called black. A good man has good qualities, and only the bad man has bad qualities. For reasons of prestige we pass over the shadow in complete silence. A famous example of masculine prejudice is Nietzsche's Superman, who scorns compassion and fights against the "Ugliest Man"—the ordinary man that everyone is. The shadow must not be seen, it must be denied, repressed, or twisted into something quite extraordinary. The sun is always shining and everything smiles back. There is no room for any prestige-diminishing weakness, so the *sol niger* is never seen. Only in solitary hours is its presence feared.

331   Things are different with Luna: every month she is darkened and extinguished; she cannot hide this from anybody, not even from herself. She knows that this same Luna is now bright and now dark—but who has ever heard of a dark sun? We call this quality of Luna "woman's closeness to nature," and the fiery brilliance and hot air that plays round the surface of things we like to call "the masculine mind."

332   Despite all attempts at denial and obfuscation there is an

247

unconscious factor, a black sun, which is responsible for the surprisingly common phenomenon of masculine split-mindedness, when the right hand mustn't know what the left is doing. This split in the masculine psyche and the regular darkening of the moon in woman toget er explain the remarkable fact that the woman is accused of all the darkness in a man, while he himself basks in the thought that he is a veritable fount of vitality and illumination for all the females in his environment. Actually, he would be better advised to shroud the brilliance of his mind in the profoundest doubt. It is not difficult for this type of mind (which besides other things is a great trickster like Mercurius) to admit a host of sins in the most convincing way, and even to combine it with a spurious feeling of ethical superiority without in the least approximating to a genuine insight. This can never be achieved without the participation of feeling; but the intellect admits feeling only when it is convenient. The novilunium of woman is a source of countless disappointments for man which easily turn to bitterness, though they could equally well be a source of wisdom if they were understood. Naturally this is possible only if he is prepared to acknowledge his black sun, that is, his shadow.

333   Confirmation of our interpretation of salt as Eros (i.e., as a feeling relationship) is found in the fact that the bitterness is the origin of the *colours* (par. 245). We have only to look at the drawings and paintings of patients who supplement their analysis by active imagination to see that colours are feeling-values. Mostly, to begin with, only a pencil or pen is used to make rapid sketches of dreams, sudden ideas, and fantasies. But from a certain moment on the patients begin to make use of colour, and this is generally the moment when merely intellectual interest gives way to emotional participation. Occasionally the same phenomenon can be observed in dreams, which at such moments are dreamt in colour, or a particularly vivid colour is insisted upon.

334   Disappointment, always a shock to the feelings, is not only the mother of bitterness but the strongest incentive to a differentiation of feeling. The failure of a pet plan, the disappointing behaviour of someone one loves, can supply the impulse either for a more or less brutal outburst of affect or for a modification and adjustment of feeling, and hence for its higher development. This culminates in wisdom if feeling is supplemented by

reflection and rational insight. Wisdom is never violent: where wisdom reigns there is no conflict between thinking and feeling.

335   This interpretation of salt and its qualities prompts us to ask, as in all cases where alchemical statements are involved, whether the alchemists themselves had such thoughts. We know from the literature that they were thoroughly aware of the moral meaning of the *amaritudo,* and by *sapientia* they did not mean anything essentially different from what we understand by this word. But how the wisdom comes from the bitterness, and how the bitterness can be the source of the colours, on these points they leave us in the dark. Nor have we any reason to believe that these connections were so self-evident to them that they regarded any explanation as superfluous. If that were so, someone would have been sure to blurt it out. It is much more probable that they simply said these things without any conscious act of cognition. Moreover, the sum of all these statements is seldom or never found consistently formulated in any one author; rather one author mentions one thing and another another, and it is only by viewing them all together, as we have tried to do here, that we get the whole picture.[661] The alchemists themselves suggest this method, and I must admit that it was their advice which first put me on the track of a psychological interpretation. The *Rosarium* says one should "read from page to page," and other sayings are "He should possess many books" and "One book opens another." Yet the complete lack, until the nineteenth century, of any psychological viewpoint (which even today meets with the grossest misunderstandings) makes it very unlikely that anything resembling a psychological interpretation penetrated into the consciousness of the alchemists. Their moral concepts moved entirely on the plane of synonym and analogy, in a word, of "correspondence." Most of their statements spring not from a conscious but from an unconscious act of thinking, as do dreams, sudden ideas, and fantasies, where again we only find out the meaning afterwards by careful comparison and analysis.

336   But the greatest of all riddles, of course, is the ever-recurring question of what the alchemists really meant by their substances. What, for instance, is the meaning of a "sal spirituale"? The

661 Olympiodorus (Berthelot, II, iv, 38) remarks: "Thus the key to the meaning of the circular art is the synopsis thereof." * And the *Turba* says: "The more I read the books, the more I am enlightened" * (ed. Ruska, Sermo XV, p. 125).

only possible answer seems to be this: chemical matter was so completely unknown to them that it instantly became a carrier for projections. Its darkness was so loaded with unconscious contents that a state of *participation mystique*,[662] or unconscious identity, arose between them and the chemical substance, which caused this substance to behave, at any rate in part, like an unconscious content. Of·this relationship the alchemists had a dim presentiment—enough, anyway, to enable them to make statements which can only be understood as psychological.

337   Khunrath says: "And the Light was made Salt, a body of salt, the salt of wisdom." [663] The same author remarks that the "point in the midst of the salt" corresponds to the "Tartarus of the greater world," which is hell.[664] This coincides with the conception of the fire hidden in the salt. Salt must have the paradoxical double nature of the arcane substance. Thus the "Gloria mundi" says that "in the salt are two salts," namely sulphur and the "radical moisture," the two most potent opposites imaginable, for which reason it was also called the Rebis.[665] Vigenerus asserts that salt consists of two substances, since all salts partake of sulphur and quicksilver.[666] These correspond to Khunrath's "king and queen," the two "waters, red and white." [667] During

---

662 I take the concept of *participation mystique*, in the sense defined above, from the works of Lévy-Bruhl. Recently this idea has been repudiated by ethnologists, partly for the reason that primitives know very well how to differentiate between things. There is no doubt about that; but it cannot be denied, either, that incommensurable things can have, for them, an equally incommensurable *tertium comparationis*. One has only to think of the ubiquitous application of "mana," the werewolf motif, etc. Furthermore, "unconscious identity" is a psychic phenomenon which the psychotherapist has to deal with every day. Certain ethnologists have also rejected Lévy-Bruhl's concept of the *état prélogique*, which is closely connected with that of *participation*. The term is not a very happy one, for in his own way the primitive thinks just as logically as we do. Lévy-Bruhl was aware of this, as I know from personal conversation with him. By "prelogical" he meant the primitive presuppositions that contradict only our rationalistic logic. These presuppositions are often exceedingly strange, and though they may not deserve to be called "prelogical" they certainly merit the term "irrational." Astonishingly enough Lévy-Bruhl, in his posthumously published diary, recanted both these concepts. This is the more remarkable in that they had a thoroughly sound psychological basis.

663 *Hyl. Chaos*, p. 74. Probably an allusion to John 1 : 9: "That was the true Light, which lighteth," etc.   664 Ibid., p. 194.

665 *Mus. herm.*, pp. 217f. (Waite, I, p. 177).   666 *Theatr. chem.*, VI, p. 127.

667 *Hyl. Chaos*, pp. 197f.

the work the salt "assumes the appearance of blood." [668] "It is certain," says Dorn, "that a salt, the natural balsam of the body, is begotten from human blood. It has within it both corruption and preservation against corruption, for in the natural order there is nothing that does not contain as much evil as good." [669] Dorn was a physician, and his remark is characteristic of the empirical standpoint of the alchemists.

338   The dark nature of salt accounts for its "blackness and foetid smell." [670] At the dissolution of living bodies it is the "last residue of corruption," but it is the "prime agent in generation." [671] Mylius expressly identifies salt with the uroboros-dragon.[672] We have already mentioned its identification with the sea of Typhon; hence one could easily identify it with the sea-monster Leviathan.[673] At all events there is an amusing relationship between salt and the Leviathan in Abraham Eleazar, who says with reference to Job 40 : 15: [674] "For Behemoth is a wild ox, whom the Most High has salted up with Leviathan and preserved for the world to come," [675] evidently as food for the inhabitants of paradise,[676] or whatever the 'world to come" may mean.

668 *Mus. herm.*, p. 216.
669 "Spec. phil.," *Theatr. chem.*, I, p. 307.
670 *Mus. herm.*, p. 216.
671 Steeb, *Coel. sephirot.*, pp. 26 and 29.
672 *Phil. ref.*, p. 195.
673 I cannot recall ever having come across this association in the texts.
674 AV; DV, 40 : 10.
675 *Uraltes Chymisches Werck*, II, p. 62. This story is told in abbreviated form in the Babylonian Talmud, "*Baba Bathra*," trans. by Slotki, II, pp. 296f. (74b): "All that the Holy One, blessed be He, created in this world He created male and female. Likewise, Leviathan the slant serpent and Leviathan the tortuous serpent He created male and female; and had they mated with one another they would have destroyed the whole world. What then did the Holy One, blessed be He, do? He castrated the male and killed the female, preserving it in salt for the righteous in the world to come; for it is written: And he will slay the dragon that is in the sea." He is also said to have done the same thing to Behemoth. By way of explanation I should like to add that the two prehistoric animals, Leviathan (water) and Behemoth (land), together with their females, form a quaternio of opposites. The *coniunctio oppositorum* on the animal level, i.e., in the unconscious state, is prevented by God as being dangerous, for it would keep consciousness on the animal level and hinder its further development. (Cf. *Aion*, pars. 181ff.) Regarding the connection between salt and the female element, it is significant that it was the female Leviathan who was salted.
676 According to an old tradition God, after the Fall, moved Paradise and placed it in the future.

339   Another direful aspect of salt is its relation to the malefic
Saturn, as is implied by Grasseus in that passage about the white
dove and the philosophical lead. Speaking of the identity of sea
and salt, Vigenerus points out that the Pythagoreans called the
sea the "tear of Kronos," because of its "bitter saltness." [677] On
account of its relation to Typhon salt is also endowed with a
murderous quality,[678] as we saw in the chapter on Sulphur,
where Sal inflicts on Sulphur an "incurable wound." This offers
a curious parallel to Kundry's wounding of Amfortas in *Parsifal*.
In the parable of Sulphur Sal plays the sinister new-moon role
of Luna.

340   As a natural product, salt "contains as much evil as good."
As the sea it is the παμμήτηρ, 'mother of all things'; as the tear of
Kronos it is bitterness and sadness; as the "sea-spume" it is the
scum of Typhon, and as the "clear water" it is Sapientia herself.

341   The "Gloria mundi" says that the aqua permanens is a "very
limpid water, so bitter as to be quite undrinkable." [679] In a
hymn-like invocation the text continues: "O water of bitter
taste, that preservest the elements! O nature of propinquity, that
dissolvest nature! O best of natures, which overcomest nature
herself! . . . Thou art crowned with light and art born . . .
and the quintessence ariseth from thee." [680] This water is like
none on earth, with the exception of that "fount in Judaea"
which is named the "Fount of the Saviour or of Blessedness."
"With great efforts and by the grace of God the philosophers
found that noble spring." But the spring is in a place so secret
that only a few know of its "gushing," and they know not the
way to Judaea where it might be found. Therefore the philosopher [681] cries out: "O water of harsh and bitter taste! For it is
hard and difficult for any man to find that spring." [682] This is an

677 Cf. Plutarch, "Isis and Osiris," 32, *Moralia* (trans. Babbitt, pp. 8off.): "The saying of the Pythagoreans, that the sea is a tear of Kronos."
678 Cf. The Gnostic view that Kronos is "a power of the colour of water, and all-
destructive." Hippolytus, *Elenchos*, V, 16, 2 (Legge, I, p. 154). For further associations of the "bright" water see "The Spirit Mercurius," par. 274.
679 *Mus. herm.*, p. 222 (Waite, I, p. 180).
680 Ibid., p. 213 (Waite, p. 173).*
681 Morienus, in whose treatise ("De transmutatione metallica") is found only the
expression "blessed water," then the idea of the "one fount" of the four qualities,
and finally, the important remark that no one attains the completion of the work
"save by the affliction of the soul." (*Art. aurif.*, II, pp. 18, 26, 34.)
682 *Mus. herm.*, p. 214.*

obvious allusion to the arcane nature and moral significance of the water, and it is also evident that it is not the water of grace or the water of the doctrine but that it springs from the *lumen naturae*. Otherwise the author would not have emphasized that Judaea was in a "secret place," for if the Church's teachings were meant no one would need to find them in a secret place, since they are accessible to everyone. Also, it would be quite incomprehensible why the philosopher should exclaim: "O water, held worthless by all! By reason of its worthlessness and tortuousness [683] no one can attain perfection in the art, or perceive its mighty virtue; for all four elements are, as it were, contained in it." There can be no doubt that this is the *aqua permanens* or *aqua pontica,* the primal water which contains the four elements.

342   The psychological equivalent of the chaotic water of the beginning [684] is the unconscious, which the old writers could grasp only in projected form, just as today most people cannot see the beam in their own eye but are all too well aware of the mote in their brother's. Political propaganda exploits this primitivity and conquers the naïve with their own defect. The only defence against this overwhelming danger is recognition of the shadow. The sight of its darkness is itself an illumination, a widening of consciousness through integration of the hitherto unconscious components of the personality. Freud's efforts to bring the shadow to consciousness are the logical and salutary answer to the almost universal unconsciousness and projection-proneness of the general public. It is as though Freud, with sure instinct, had sought to avert the danger of nation-wide psychic epidemics that threatened Europe. What he did not see was that the confrontation with the shadow is not just a harmless affair that can be settled by "reason." The shadow is the primitive who is still alive and active in civilized man, and our civilized reason means nothing to him. He needs to be ruled by a higher authority, such as is found in the great religions. Even when Reason triumphed at the beginning of the French Revolution it was

683 "Curvitatem," presumably an allusion to the winding course of water and the "rivuli" (streams) of the Mercurial serpent.
684 "Darkness there was: at first concealed in darkness this All was undiscriminated chaos." *Rig-veda*, X, 129, 2 (*Hymns of the Rig-veda,* trans. by Griffith, II, p. 575).

quickly turned into a goddess and enthroned in Notre-Dame.

343   The shadow exerts a dangerous fascination which can be countered only by another *fascinosum*. It cannot be got at by reason, even in the most rational person, but only by illumination, of a degree and kind that are equal to the darkness but are the exact opposite of "enlightenment." For what we call "rational" is everything that seems "fitting" to the man in the street, and the question then arises whether this "fitness" may not in the end prove to be "irrational" in the bad sense of the word. Sometimes, even with the best intentions this dilemma cannot be solved. This is the moment when the primitive trusts himself to a higher authority and to a decision beyond his comprehension. The civilized man in his closed-in environment functions in a fitting and appropriate manner, that is, rationally. But if, because of some apparently insoluble dilemma, he gets outside the confines of civilization, he becomes a primitive again; then he has irrational ideas and acts on hunches; then he no longer thinks but "it" thinks in him; then he needs "magical" practices in order to gain a feeling of security; then the latent autonomy of the unconscious becomes active and begins to manifest itself as it has always done in the past.

344   The good tidings announced by alchemy are that, as once a fountain sprang up in Judaea, so now there is a secret Judaea the way to which is not easily found, and a hidden spring whose waters seem so worthless [685] and so bitter that they are deemed of no use at all. We know from numerous hints [686] that man's inner life is the "secret place" where the *aqua solvens et coagulans*, the *medicina catholica* or panacea, the spark of the light of nature,[687] are to be found. Our text shows us how much the alchemists put their art on the level of divine revelation and regarded it as at least an essential complement to the work of redemption. True, only a few of them were the elect who formed the golden chain linking earth to heaven, but still they were the fathers of natural science today. They were the unwitting instigators of the schism between faith and knowledge, and

685 "Vilitas" was also something Christ was reproached with. Cf. John 1 : 46: "Can there any good thing come out of Nazareth?"
686 Cf. *Psychology and Alchemy*, par. 421.
687 Or as Morienus (*Art. aurif.*, II, p. 32) so graphically says: "Until it begins to shine like fishes' eyes."

it was they who made the world conscious that the revelation was neither complete nor final. "Since these things are so," says an ecclesiastic of the seventeenth century, "it will suffice, after the light of faith, for human ingenuity to recognize, as it were, the refracted rays of the Divine majesty in the world and in created things." [688] The "refracted rays" correspond to the "certain luminosity" which the alchemists said was inherent in the natural world.

345 Revelation conveys general truths which often do not illuminate the individual's actual situation in the slightest, nor was it traditional revelation that gave us the microscope and the machine. And since human life is not enacted exclusively, or even to a noticeable degree, on the plane of the higher verities, the source of knowledge unlocked by the old alchemists and physicians has done humanity a great and welcome service—so great that for many people the light of revelation has been extinguished altogether. Within the confines of civilization man's wilful rationality apparently suffices. Outside of this shines, or should shine, the light of faith. But where the darkness comprehendeth it not (this being the prerogative of darkness!) those labouring in the darkness must try to accomplish an opus that will cause the "fishes' eyes" to shine in the depths of the sea, or to catch the "refracted rays of the divine majesty" even though this produces a light which the darkness, as usual, does not comprehend. But when there is a light in the darkness which comprehends the darkness, darkness no longer prevails. The longing of the darkness for light is fulfilled only when the light can no longer be rationally explained by the darkness. For the darkness has its own peculiar intellect and its own logic, which should be taken very seriously. Only the "light which the darkness comprehendeth not" can illuminate the darkness. Everything that the darkness thinks, grasps, and comprehends by itself is dark; therefore it is illuminated only by what, to it, is unexpected, unwanted, and incomprehensible. The psychotherapeutic method of active imagination offers excellent examples of this; sometimes a numinous dream or some external event will have the same effect.

346 Alchemy announced a source of knowledge, parallel if not equivalent to revelation, which yields a "bitter" water by no

[688] Caussin, *Polyhistor symbolicus* (1618), p. 3.*

means acceptable to our human judgment. It is harsh and bitter or like vinegar,[689] for it is a bitter thing to accept the darkness and blackness of the *umbra solis* and to pass through this valley of the shadow. It is bitter indeed to discover behind one's lofty ideals narrow, fanatical convictions, all the more cherished for that, and behind one's heroic pretensions nothing but crude egotism, infantile greed, and complacency. This painful corrective is an unavoidable stage in every psychotherapeutic process. As the alchemists said, it begins with the *nigredo,* or generates it as the indispensable prerequisite for synthesis, for unless the opposites are constellated and brought to consciousness they can never be united. Freud halted the process at the reduction to the inferior half of the personality and tended to overlook the daemonic dangerousness of the dark side, which by no means consists only of relatively harmless infantilisms. Man is neither so reasonable nor so good that he can cope *eo ipso* with evil. The darkness can quite well engulf him, especially when he finds himself with those of like mind. Mass-mindedness increases unconsciousness and then the evil swells like an avalanche, as contemporary events have shown. Even so, society can also work for good; it is even necessary because of the moral weakness of most human beings, who, to maintain themselves at all, must have some external good to cling on to. The great religions are psychotherapeutic systems that give a foothold to all those who cannot stand by themselves, and they are in the overwhelming majority.

347 In spite of their undoubtedly "heretical methods" the alchemists showed by their positive attitude to the Church that they were cleverer than certain modern apostles of enlightenment. Also—very much in contrast to the rationalistic tendencies of today—they displayed, despite its "tortuousness," a remarkable understanding of the imagery upon which the Christian cosmos is built. This world of images, in its historical form, is irretrievably lost to modern man; its loss has spiritually impoverished the masses and compelled them to find pitiful substitutes, as

689 Maier (*Symb. aur. mensae,* p. 568): "There is in our chemistry a certain noble substance . . . in the beginning whereof is wretchedness with vinegar, but in its ending joy with gladness. And so I have supposed it will fare with me, that at first I shall taste, suffer, and experience much difficulty, bitterness, grief, and weariness, but in the end shall come to glimpse pleasanter and easier things." *

poisonous as they are worthless. No one can be held responsible for this development. It is due rather to the restless tempo of spiritual growth and change, whose motive forces go far beyond the horizon of the individual. He can only hope to keep pace with it and try to understand it so far that he is not blindly swallowed up by it. For that is the alarming thing about mass movements, even if they are good, that they demand and must demand blind faith. The Church can never explain the truth of her images because she acknowledges no point of view but her own. She moves solely within the framework of her images, and her arguments must always beg the question. The flock of harmless sheep was ever the symbolic prototype of the credulous crowd, though the Church is quick to recognize the wolves in sheep's clothing who lead the faith of the multitude astray in order to destroy them. The tragedy is that the blind trust which leads to perdition is practised just as much inside the Church and is praised as the highest virtue. Yet our Lord says: "Be ye therefore wise as serpents," [690] and the Bible itself stresses the cleverness and cunning of the serpent. But where are these necessary if not altogether praiseworthy qualities developed and given their due? The serpent has become a by-word for everything morally abhorrent, and yet anyone who is not as smart as a snake is liable to land himself in trouble through blind faith.

348   The alchemists knew about the snake and the "cold" half of nature,[691] and they said enough to make it clear to their successors that they endeavoured by their art to lead that serpentine Nous of the darkness, the *serpens mercurialis,* through the stages of transformation to the goal of perfection (*telesmus*).[692] The more or less symbolical or projected integration of the unconscious that went hand in hand with this evidently had so many favourable effects that the alchemists felt encouraged to express a tempered optimism.

---

[690] Matthew 10 : 16.

[691] Hippolytus reports the following saying of the Peratics: "The universal serpent is the wise word of Eve." * This was the mystery and the river of Paradise, and the sign that protected Cain so that no one should kill him, for the God of this world (ὁ θεὸς τοῦδε του κόσμου) had not accepted his offering. This God reminds us very much of the "prince of this world" in St. John. Among the Peratics it was naturally the demiurge, the "father below" (πατὴρ κάτωθεν). See *Elenchos*, V, 16, 8f. (Legge, I, p. 155f.).

[692] "This is the father of all perfection." * Ruska, *Tabula Smaragdina*, p. 2.

IV

REX AND REGINA

1. INTRODUCTION

349   We have already met the royal pair, and particularly the figure of the King, several times in the course of our inquiry, not to mention the material which was presented under this head in *Psychology and Alchemy*. Conforming to the prototype of Christ the King in the Christian world of ideas, the King plays a central role in alchemy and cannot, therefore, be dismissed as a mere metaphor. In the "Psychology of the Transference" I have discussed the deeper reasons for a more comprehensive treatment of this symbol. Because the king in general represents a superior personality exalted above the ordinary, he has become the carrier of a myth, that is to say, of the statements of the collective unconscious. The outward paraphernalia of kingship show this very clearly. The crown symbolizes his relation to the sun, sending forth its rays; his bejewelled mantle is the starry firmament; the orb is a replica of the world; the lofty throne exalts him above the crowd; the address "Majesty" approximates him to the gods. The further we go back in history the more evident does the king's divinity become. The divine right of kings survived until quite recent times, and the Roman Emperors even usurped the title of a god and demanded a personal cult. In the Near East the whole essence of kingship was based far more on theological than on political assumptions. There the psyche of the whole nation was the true and ultimate basis of kingship: it was self-evident that the king was the magical source of welfare and prosperity for the entire organic community of man, animal, and plant; from him flowed the life and prosperity of his subjects, the increase of the herds, and the fertility of the land. This signification of kingship was not invented *a posteriori;* it is a psychic *a priori* which reaches far back into prehistory and comes very close to being a natural revelation of the psychic structure. The fact that we explain this phenomenon on

rational grounds of expediency means something only for us; it means nothing for primitive psychology, which to a far higher degree than our objectively oriented views is based on purely psychic and unconscious assumptions.

350   The theology of kingship best known to us, and probably the most richly developed, is that of ancient Egypt, and it is these conceptions which, handed down by the Greeks, have permeated the spiritual history of the West. Pharaoh was an incarnation of God [1] and a son of God.[2] In him dwelt the divine life-force and procreative power, the *ka:* God reproduced himself in a human mother of God and was born from her as a God-man.[3] As such he guaranteed the growth and prosperity of the land and the people,[4] also taking it upon himself to be killed when his time was fulfilled, that is to say when his procreative power was exhausted.[5]

[1] A Fiji Islander told Hocart: "Only the chief was believed in: he was by way of being a human god" (*Kings and Councillors*, p. 61). "We must always bear in mind that the king is the god or gods" (p. 104).

[2] Pharaoh is the son of the Creator-god. "But at certain festivities the 'son' unites with the divine 'father' in the mystic fashion of the rite" (Jacobsohn, *Die dogmatische Stellung des Königs in der Theologie der alten Aegypter*, p. 46).

[3] Amon, the Father-god, unites himself, for instance, with Thutmosis I, and then, as the father, begets the son with the Queen (Jacobsohn, p. 17). Or again, the King lives on after his death as "Horus, the son of Hathor" (p. 20). A pyramid text says of Pharaoh: "Merenre is the Great, the son of the Great; Nut gave him birth" (p. 26). The *ka-mutef* makes the Queen the mother of the god (p. 62). Similar ideas are suggested by the names of the Canaanite kings Adoni-bezek and Adoni-zedek, which indicate an identification with the divine son of Ishtar, Adonis. Frazer (*The Golden Bough*, Pt. IV, p. 17), from whom I take this observation, comments: "Adoni-zedek means 'Lord of righteousness' and is therefore equivalent to Melchizedek, that is 'king of righteousness,' the title of that mysterious king of Salem and priest of God Most High."

[4] Among the Fiji Islanders the king is called "the Prosperity of the Land." "When the great chief, entitled the 'Lord of the Reef' is installed, they pray: . . . 'Let the fields resound, the land resound . . . let the fish come to land; let the fruit trees bear; let the land prosper' " (Hocart, p. 61).

[5] Frazer, *The Golden Bough*, Pt. III, p. 14ff. His death or sacrifice is followed by dismemberment. Classic examples are Osiris and Dionysus. Cf. Firmicus Maternus, *Liber de errore profanarum religionum* (Corp. Scrip. Eccl. Lat., II, p. 76): ". . . slew Osiris and tore him limb from limb, and cast forth the palpitating members of the wretched corpse along all the banks of the river Nile."* The same author says (7,7) concerning Dionysus: "For the stories of the Greeks claim to relate Liber to the Sun . . . Who has seen the infant sun? who has beguiled it, who has slain it? who has torn it to pieces, who has cut it up, who has feasted on its mem-

351   Father and son were consubstantial,[6] and after his death Pharaoh became the father-god again,[7] because his *ka* was consubstantial with the father.[8] The *ka* consisted, as it were, of Pharaoh's ancestral souls, fourteen of which were regularly worshipped by him,[9] corresponding to the fourteen *ka*s of the creator-god.[10] Just as Pharaoh corresponded on the human plane to the divine son, so his *ka* corresponded to the divine Procreator, the *ka-mutef*,[11] the "bull of his mother," and his mother corresponded to the mother of the gods (e.g., Isis).

352   This gives rise to a peculiar double trinity, consisting on the one hand of a divine series, father-god, divine son, the *ka-mutef*, and on the other hand a human series, father-god, human divine son (Pharaoh), and Pharaoh's *ka*. In the first series the father changes into the son and the son into the father through the

---

bers? . . . But this error also they seek to cover by a rational explanation, that of the undivided and divided mind, and thus too they think they can provide a reason for their worship." * In this connection we might also mention the bull-god of the eleventh nome of Lower Egypt: he was called "The Divided One," and in later times was associated with Osiris. For this reason the eleventh nome was tabooed. (Kees, *Der Götterglaube im alten Aegypten*, pp. 12 and 258).

[6] Cf. Jacobsohn, pp. 17 and 46.

[7] The dead king, resuscitated, is addressed as Amun, who drinks the milk of Isis (ibid., p. 41).

[8] The god, the king, and his *ka* form, as it were, a trinity composed of father, son, and procreative force (ibid., p. 58).

[9] To correspond with the 14 *ka*s of Ra, statues of 14 of the king's ancestors were carried at the processions. They were the previous royal incarnations of the father-god, who reproduced himself once more in the king (Jacobsohn, pp. 28, 32, 62, 67). Baynes says in this connection: "The safeguarding power of the continuity of tribal authority and tradition from earliest times is concentrated by means of mass-projection upon the person of the king. The distant heroic ancestors, the mighty figures of the mythic past are alive and present in the person of the king. He is the master symbol just because he is living history." ("On the Psychological Origins of Divine Kingship," p. 91.)

[10] It should be noted that Typhon tore the slain Osiris into 14 parts. Plutarch says: "The dismemberment of Osiris into 14 parts refers allegorically to the days of the waning of that satellite from the time of the full moon to the new moon." ("Isis and Osiris," 18, *Moralia*, trans. by Babbitt, V. pp. 44f.) Jacobsohn calls attention to the genealogical table of Jesus in Matthew 1 : 1ff. Verse 17 runs: "So all the generations from Abraham to David are fourteen generations; and from the carrying away into Babylon unto Christ are fourteen generations." This construction is somewhat arbitrary out of consideration for the number 14. Of the 14 ancestors of Pharaoh, Jacobsohn says (p. 67): "The conscious intention to bring out the number 14 is clearly discernible each time."   [11] Jacobsohn, p. 38.

procreative power of the *ka-mutef*. All three figures are consubstantial. The second, divine-human series, which is likewise bound into a unity by consubstantiality, represents the manifestation of God in the earthly sphere.[12] The divine mother is not included in either triunity; she stands outside it, a figure now wholly divine, now wholly human. We should mention in this connection a late Egyptian trinity amulet discussed by Spiegelberg: Horus and Hathor sit facing one another, and between them and over them hovers a winged serpent. The three deities all hold the *ankh* (symbol of life). The inscription says: "Baït is one, Hathor one, Akori one, one is their power. Greetings, Father of the World, greetings, three-formed God." [13] Baït is Horus. The amulet, which is three-cornered, may date from the first or second century A.D. Spiegelberg writes: "For my feeling this epigram, despite its Greek form, breathes an Egyptian spirit of Hellenistic nature and contains nothing Christian. But it is born of a spirit that made its contribution to the development of the dogma of the Trinity in Christianity." [14] The illustrations of the coniunctio in the *Rosarium,* showing King, Queen, and the dove of the Holy Ghost, correspond to the figures on the amulet exactly.[15]

2. GOLD AND SPIRIT

353   The striking analogy between certain alchemical ideas and Christian dogma is not accidental but in accordance with tradition. A good part of the symbolism of the king derives from this

---

[12] Jacobsohn stresses the homoousia of father, son, the king's *ka,* and the *ka-mutef* (pp. 38, 45f., 58, 62). In elucidating the *ka-mutef* as prototype of the ἅγιον πνεῦμα he cites (p. 65) the answer to the fifty-third question in the Heidelberg Catechism: "[I believe] that he [the Holy Ghost] is at the same time eternal God with the Father and the Son. Likewise, that he is also vouchsafed to me" (as personal *ka*). Jacobsohn also refers to the anecdote about Christ in *Pistis Sophia,* where the Holy Ghost appears as Christ's double (that is, as a proper *ka*). He enters the house of Mary, who at first mistakes him for Jesus. But he asks: "Where is Jesus my brother, that I may go to meet him?" Mary took him for a phantom and bound him to the foot of the bed. When Jesus came in, he recognized and embraced him, and they became one. (*Pistis Sophia,* ed. Schmidt, ch. 61, pp. 20ff. Cf. *Aion,* par. 131.)

[13] *

[14] Spiegelberg, "Der Gott Baït in dem Trinitätsamulett des Britischen Museums," pp. 225ff.

[15] For the complete series, see my "Psychology of the Transference."

source. Just as Christian dogma derives in part from Egypto-Hellenistic folklore, as well as from the Judaeo-Hellenistic philosophy of writers like Philo, so, too, does alchemy. Its origin is certainly not purely Christian, but is largely pagan or Gnostic. Its oldest treatises come from that sphere, among them the treatise of Komarios (1st cent.?) and the writings of Pseudo-Democritus (1st to 2nd cent.) and Zosimos (3rd cent.). The title of one of the latter's treatises is "The True Book of Sophe [16] the Egyptian and Divine Lord of the Hebrews, [and] of the Powers of Sabaoth." [17] Berthelot thinks that Zosimos really was the author, and this is quite possible. The treatise speaks of a knowledge or wisdom that comes from the Aeons:

Ungoverned (ἀβασίλευτος) and autonomous is its origin; it is non-material (αὖλος) and it seeks none of the material and wholly corruptible [18] bodies. For it acts without being acted upon (ἀπαθῶς). But, on their asking for a gift, the symbol of the chymic art comes forth from creation for those who rescue and purify the divine soul chained in the elements, that is, the divine Pneuma mingled with the flesh. For as the sun is the blossom of fire, and the heavenly sun is the right eye of the world, so also the copper, when purification makes it to blossom, is an earthly sun, a king upon earth, like the sun in heaven.[19]

354　　It is clear from this and from the text that follows that the "symbol of the chymic art" (τὸ σύμβολον τῆς χημείας), the king, is none other than gold, the king of metals.[20] But it is equally clear that the gold comes into being only through the liberation of the divine soul or pneuma from the chains of the "flesh." No doubt it would have suited our rational expectations better if the text had said not "flesh" but "ore" or "earth." Although the elements are mentioned as the prison of the divine psyche, the whole of nature is meant, Physis in general; not just ore and earth but

16 According to Berthelot, "Sophe" is a variant of "Cheops-Souphis." He cites a passage from the résumé of Africanus (3rd cent.) in Eusebius: "King Souphis wrote a book, which I purchased in Egypt as a very valuable thing" (Origines de l'alchimie, p. 58).

17 Berthelot, Alch. grecs, III, xlii.* So in Codex Parisiensis 2327, fol. 251 (Berthelot, Origines de l'alchimie, p. 58).

18 The text has παναφθόρων, but the sense requires παμφθόρων. Berthelot accordingly translates as 'corruptible'.　　19 Berthelot, Alch. grecs, III, xlii, 1.

20 Naturally this is still true of alchemy in later times. Thus Khunrath (Von hylealischen Chaos, p. 338) defines the King as gold refined from silver.

water, air, and fire, and besides these the "flesh," an expression
that already in the third century meant the "world" in a moral
sense as opposed to the spirit, and not simply the human body.
Consequently, there can be no doubt that the *chrysopoeia* (gold-
making) was thought of as a psychic operation running parallel
to the physical process and, as it were, independent of it. The
moral and spiritual transformation was not only independent of
the physical procedure but actually seemed to be its *causa
efficiens*. This explains the high-flown language, which would be
somewhat out of place in a merely chemical recipe. The psyche
previously imprisoned in the elements and the divine spirit
hidden in the flesh overcome their physical imperfection and
clothe themselves in the noblest of all bodies, the royal gold.
Thus the "philosophic" gold is an embodiment of psyche and
pneuma, both of which signify "life-spirit." It is in fact an
"aurum non vulgi," a living gold, so to speak, which corresponds
in every respect to the lapis. It, too, is a living being with a body,
soul, and spirit, and it is easily personified as a divine being or a
superior person like a king, who in olden times was considered
to be God incarnate.[21] In this connection Zosimos availed
himself of a primordial image in the form of the divine Anthropos, who at that time had attained a crucial significance in philosophy and religion, not only in Christianity but also in
Mithraism. The Bible as well as the Mithraic monuments and
the Gnostic writings bear witness to this. Zosimos has, moreover,
left us a long testimony on this theme.[22] The thoughts of this

[21] Rex as synonym for the lapis: "The Philosophers' stone . . . is the Chemical
King" ("Aquarium sapientum," *Mus. herm.*, p. 119; Waite, I, p. 103). In Lambspringk's Symbols he is the perfected arcane substance:

> "I have overcome and vanquished my foes,
> I have trodden the venomous Dragon under foot,
> I am a great and glorious King in the earth . . .
> Therefore Hermes has called me the Lord of the Forests." *

(*Mus. herm.*, p. 358; Waite, I, p. 292.) "The Philosophers' stone is the king descending from Heaven." ("Consil. coniug.," *Ars chemica*, p. 61.) In Hoghelande's "De
alchemiae difficultatibus" (*Theatr. chem.*, I, p. 162) there is a strange description
of the stone as a "tall and helmeted man" (homo galeatus et altus); it is also a
"king crowned with a red diadem." In Mylius (*Phil. ref.*, p. 17) it is the "princely
stone" (*princeps lapis*).

[22] For a literal translation of the text see *Psychology and Alchemy*, par. 456.

writer, directly or indirectly, were of decisive importance for the whole philosophical and Gnostic trend of alchemy in the centuries that followed. As I have dealt with this subject in considerable detail in *Psychology and Alchemy* I need not go into it here. I mention it only because the above passage from Zosimos is, to my knowledge, the earliest reference to the king in alchemy. As an Egyptian, Zosimos would have been familiar with the mystique of kingship, which at that time was enjoying a new efflorescence under the Caesars, and so it was easy for him to carry over the identity of the divine pneuma with the king into alchemical practice, itself both physical and pneumatic, after the older writings of Pseudo-Democritus had paved the way with their views on Θεῖα φύσις (divine nature).[23]

355 The definition of the king as pneuma carried considerably more weight than his interpretation as gold. Ruland's *Lexicon* defines Rex as follows: "Rex—King, Soul, Spiritual Water which gives Moisture to the Female and is restored to the Fountain whence it was derived. The Spirit is Water." [24] Here Rex is still the divine soul, the moist Osiris,[25] a life-giving, fertilizing pneuma and not primarily the physical gold. The mystique of the king comes out even more clearly in Khunrath: "When at last," he says, "the ash-colour, the whitening, and the yellowing are over, you will see the Philosophical Stone, our King and Lord of Lords, come forth from the couch and throne of his glassy sepulchre [26] onto the stage of this world, in his glorified body, regenerated and more than perfect, shining like a carbuncle, and crying out, Behold, I make all things new." [27] In his story of how the lapis is made, Khunrath describes the mystic birth of the king. Ruach Elohim (the spirit of God) penetrated

---

[23] Cf. the saying of Democritus, quoted in many variants: "Nature rejoices in nature, nature subdues nature, nature rules over nature." The truth of this dictum receives remarkable confirmation in the psychology of the individuation process.

[24] P. 276.

[25] Cf. the curious passage in Distinctio XIV of the "Allegoriae sapientum" (*Theatr. chem.*, V, p. 86): "For some say, the moistures are to be honoured, for they are high-minded kings that suffer not insult: be careful therefore with them and seek their good will, and they will give to thee with their eyes, that thou mayest have of them whatsoever thou willest." *

[26] A paraphrase for the retort as the place of rebirth.

[27] *Amphitheatrum*, p. 202.*

to the lowest parts and to the centre (*meditullium*) of the virginal *massa confusa*, and scattered the sparks and rays of his fruitfulness. "Thus the form impressed itself [*forma informavit*], and the purest soul quickened and impregnated the tohu-bohu, which was without form and void." This was a "mysterium typicum" (a "symbolical" mystery), the procreation of the "Preserver and Saviour of the Macrocosm and the Microcosm. The Word is become flesh . . . and God has revealed himself in the flesh, the spirit of God has appeared in the body. This, the son of the Macrocosm . . . that, the son of God, the God-man . . . the one in the womb of the Macrocosm, the other in the womb of the Microcosm," and both times the womb was virginal. "In the Book or Mirror of Nature, the Stone of the Wise, the Preserver of the Macrocosm, is the symbol of Christ Jesus Crucified, Saviour of the whole race of men, that is, of the Microcosm." [28] The "son of the Macrocosm" begotten by the divine pneuma (the Egyptian *ka-mutef*) is "of like kind and consubstantial with the Begetter." His soul is a spark of the world-soul. "Our stone is three and one, which is to say triune, namely earthly, heavenly, and divine." This reminds us of the Egyptian sequence: Pharaoh, *ka*, God. The triune stone consists of "three different and distinct substances: Sal-Mercurius-Sulphur." [29]

3. THE TRANSFORMATION OF THE KING

356 As the Egyptian mystique of kingship shows, the king, like every archetype, is not just a static image; he signifies a dynamic process whereby the human carrier of the mystery is included in the mysterious drama of God's incarnation. This happened at the birth of Pharaoh, at his coronation,[30] at the Heb-Sed festival, during his reign, and at his death. The texts and illustrations of the "birth-chamber" in the temple depict the divine procreation and birth of Pharaoh in the form of the mystic marriage of the Queen Mother and the Father-God. The Heb-Sed festival served to associate his *ka* with the cultivation of the soil and, presum-

[28] Ibid., p. 197.*
[29] Ibid., pp. 198f.
[30] Colin Campbell, *The Miraculous Birth of King Amon-Hotep III*, p. 82: "The Coronation, which bestowed on the divine being, the king, the two crowns of Egypt, advanced him a step further than birth in the divine scale of life."

ably, to preserve or strengthen his powers.[31] The identity of his *ka* with the Father-God was finally confirmed at his death and sealed for all time. The transformation of the king from an imperfect state into a perfect, whole, and incorruptible essence is portrayed in a similar manner in alchemy. It describes either his procreation and birth, in the form of a hierosgamos, or else his imperfect initial state and his subsequent rebirth in perfect form. In what follows I shall give a few examples of this transformation.

357   Among the older medieval treatises there is the so-called "Allegoria Merlini." [32] So far as the name Merlinus is concerned, I must leave it an open question whether it refers to the magician Merlin [33] or is a corruption of Merculinus.[34] The allegory tells us of a certain king who made ready for battle. As he

31 Ibid., pp. 83ff.: "The anniversary of the Coronation seems to have been held as a Sed festival, when the king was regarded as Osiris on earth." "The king is not 'dancing' or striding in the presence of his Osiris-self, as if worshipping him . . . no, the striding is a movement in the ceremony, preparatory to his taking possession of the throne, which marks his complete Osirification—the last act of the Sed festival" (p. 94). Breasted (*Development of Religion and Thought in Ancient Egypt*, p. 39) says of the Sed festival: "One of the ceremonies of this feast symbolized the resurrection of Osiris, and it was possibly to associate the Pharaoh with this auspicious event that he assumed the role of Osiris." On the significance of the Sed festival Frazer (*The Golden Bough*, Pt. IV, ii, p. 153) says: "The intention of the festival seems to have been to procure for the king a new lease of life, a renovation of his divine energies, a rejuvenescence." One of the inscriptions at Abydos runs: "Thou dost begin to renew thyself, to thee it is granted to blossom forth again like the young moon-god, thou dost grow young again . . . Thou art reborn in the renewal of the Sed festival" (Moret, *Du caractère religieux de la royauté pharaonique*, pp. 255f.). The Sed festival was held every 30 years, probably in connection with the quarters of the 120-year Sirius (= Isis) period. This festival, it should be noted, was also connected with a ceremony for making the fields fruitful: the king circumambulated a marked-off field four times, accompanied by the Apis bull. (Kees, *Der Götterglaube im alten Ägypten*, pp. 296f.) Similar ceremonies are still performed today. Amenophis IV caused the Aton, the symbol of his religious reformation, to be introduced at his Sed festival (Kees, p. 372).

32 Printed in *Art. aurif.*, I, pp. 392ff.

33 The name "Artus" which occasionally occurs, and which one might connect with the king of the same name in the Grail legend, is a corruption of "Horus." It is possible that the source for the "Allegoria Merlini" is the "Prophetia Merlini," which was well known in the Middle Ages. Cf. Geoffrey of Monmouth, *Histories of the Kings of Britain* (Book 7, pp. 170ff.).

34 The verses of a certain Merculinus are preserved in *Ros. phil.*, *Art. aurif.* (1610 edn.), II, pp. 242f.

was about to mount his horse he wished for a drink of water. A servant asked him what water he would like, and the king answered: "I demand the water which is closest to my heart, and which likes me above all things." When the servant brought it the king drank so much that "all his limbs were filled and all his veins inflated, and he himself became discoloured." His soldiers urged him to mount his horse, but he said he could not: "I am heavy and my head hurts me, and it seems to me as though all my limbs were falling apart." He demanded to be placed in a heated chamber where he could sweat the water out. But when, after a while, they opened the chamber he lay there as if dead. They summoned the Egyptian and the Alexandrian physicians, who at once accused one another of incompetence. Finally the Alexandrian physicians gave way to the Egyptian physicians, who tore the king into little pieces, ground them to powder, mixed them with their "moistening" medicines, and put the king back in his heated chamber as before. After some time they fetched him out again half-dead. When those present saw this, they broke out into lamentation, crying: "Alas, the king is dead." The physicians said soothingly that he was only sleeping. They then washed him with sweet water until the juice of the medicines departed from him, and mixed him with new substances. Then they put him back in the chamber as before. When they took him out this time he was really dead. But the physicians said: "We have killed him that he may become better and stronger in this world after his resurrection on the day of judgment." The king's relatives, however, considered them mountebanks, took their medicines away from them, and drove them out of the kingdom. They now wanted to bury the corpse, but the Alexandrian physicians, who had heard of these happenings, counselled them against it and said they would revive the king. Though the relatives were very mistrustful they let them have a try. The Alexandrian physicians took the body, ground it to powder a second time, washed it well until nothing of the previous medicines remained, and dried it. Then they took one part of sal ammoniac and two parts of Alexandrian nitre, mixed them with the pulverized corpse, made it into a paste with a little linseed oil, and placed it in a crucible-shaped chamber with holes bored in the bottom; beneath it they placed a clean crucible and let the corpse stand so for an hour. Then they heaped

267

fire upon it and melted it, so that the liquid ran into the vessel below. Whereupon the king rose up from death and cried in a loud voice: "Where are my enemies? I shall kill them all if they do not submit to me!" All the kings and princes of other countries honoured and feared him. "And when they wished to see something of his wonders, they put an ounce of well-purified mercury in a crucible, and scattered over it as much as a millet-seed of finger-nails or hair or of their blood, blew up a light charcoal fire, let the mercury cool down with these, and found the stone, as I do know."

358 This parable contains the primitive motif of the murder or sacrifice of the king for the purpose of renewing his kingly power and increasing the fertility of the land. Originally it took the form of killing the old and impotent king. In this tale the king was afflicted with a "dropsy" both real and metaphorical: he suffered from a general plethora and a total oedema because he drank too much of the special "water." One would be inclined to think that the "water closest to his heart which liked him above all things" was *eau de vie* and that he suffered from cirrhosis of the liver, were it not that the extraction of the moist psyche from the elements was a preoccupation of alchemy long before the distillation of alcohol.[35] The idea was to extract the pneuma or psyche or "virtue" from matter (e.g., from gold) in the form of a volatile or liquid substance, and thereby to mortify the "body." This *aqua permanens*[36] was then used to revive or reanimate the "dead" body and, paradoxically, to extract the soul again.[37] The old body had to die; it was either sacrificed or simply killed, just as the old king had either to die or to offer sacrifice to the gods (much as Pharaoh offered libations to his own statue). Something of this kind was celebrated at the Sed festival. Moret thinks the Sed ceremony was a kind of humanized regicide.[38]

359 Water has always played a role at sacrifices as the "animat-

---

35 The distillation of alcohol from wine was probably discovered at the beginning of the 12th cent. (Lippmann, *Entstehung und Ausbreitung der Alchemie*, II, p. 38.)

36 Its equivalent, the ὕδωρ θεῖον, can be translated either as 'divine water' or as 'sulphur water,' since θεῖον means both.

37 For instance in "Allegoriae sapientum" (*Theatr. chem.*, V, p. 67): "And know that it is the water which draweth forth what is hidden." *

38 Jacobsohn, *Die dogmatische Stellung des Königs in der Theologie der alten Ägypter*, p. 11.

ing" principle. A text from Edfu says: "I bring thee the vessels with the limbs of the gods [i.e., the Nile], that thou mayest drink of them; I refresh my heart that thou mayest rejoice." The water of the Nile was the real "consolamentum" of Egypt. In the Egyptian fairytale, Anubis found that the heart of his dead brother Bata, which Bata had placed on a cedar-flower, had turned into a cedar-cone. He put it in a vessel of cold water, and the heart soaked it up and Bata began to live again.[39] Here the water is life-giving. But of the *aqua permanens* it was said: "It kills and vivifies."

360   The king has numerous connections with water. In the parable of Sulphur cited earlier, the king drowns in it with Diana.[40] The hierosgamos was often celebrated in water. The motif of drowning also takes the form of an inward drowning, namely dropsy. Mater Alchimia is dropsical in the lower limbs.[41] Or the king is dropsical and conceals himself in the "belly of the horse" in order to sweat out the water.[42] The water appears also as a bath, as in the "Dicta Alani," where the "old man" sits in the bath.[43] Here I would recall the king's bath in Bernardus Trevisanus, which I have discussed earlier.[44] Water is used for baptism, immersion, and cleansing. The cleansing of Naaman (II Kings 5 : 10ff.) is often cited as an allegory of this.[45]

361   In our parable the wonderful water already has that decomposing and dissolving property which anticipates the king's dismemberment.[46] The dissolution of the initial material plays a

39 [Cf. Neumann, *The Origins and History of Consciousness*, pp. 69ff.]

40 The king who is imprisoned in the sea also belongs to this context. (Cf. Maier, *Symbolae aureae mensae*, p. 380.) See text in "Paracelsus as a Spiritual Phenomenon," pars. 181ff.

41 *Aurora consurgens* II, in *Art. aurif.*, I, p. 196: "Beware of dropsy and the flood of Noah." * (Cf. Ripley, *Opera omnia*, p. 69.)

42 Maier, p. 261: "The horse's belly is a great secret: our dropsical patient concealeth himself therein, that he may be restored to health and may free himself of all water [in turning] towards the sun." *

43 "So doth the old man sit in the bath, whom keep in a carefully sealed and closed vessel, until the visible Mercurius be invisible and hidden" (*Theatr. chem.*, III, p. 820).*

44 Cf. supra, pars. 74f.

45 Cf. *Aurora Consurgens*, pp. 97f.: "And to Naaman was it said: Go and wash seven times in the Jordan and thou shalt be clean. For there is one baptism for the remission of sins." *

46 "O blessed form of sea-water, which dissolvest the elements" (Tractatus aureus," *Ars chemica*, p. 20).*

great role in alchemy as an integral part of the process. Here I will mention only the unique interpretation of the *solutio* given by Dorn. In his "Speculativa philosophia" he discusses the seven stages of the work. The first stage begins with the "study of the philosophers," which is the way to the investigation of truth.

But the truth is that from which nothing can be missing, to which nothing can be added, nay more, to which nothing can be opposed. . . . The truth therefore is a great strength and an impregnable fortress . . . , an unconquerable pledge to them that possess it. In this citadel is contained the true and undoubted stone and treasure of the philosophers, which is not eaten into by moths, nor dug out by thieves, but remaineth for ever when all things else are dissolved, and is appointed for the ruin of many, but for the salvation of others. This is a thing most worthless to the vulgar, spurned above all things and hated exceedingly, yet it is not hateful but lovable, and to philosophers precious above gems.[47]

362   In his "Recapitulation of the First Stage" Dorn says:

It is the study of the Chemists to liberate that unsensual truth [48] from its fetters in things of sense, for through it the heavenly powers are pursued with subtle understanding. . . .[49] Knowledge is the sure and undoubted resolution [*resolutio*] by experiment of all opinions concerning the truth. . . . Experiment is manifest demonstration of the truth, and resolution the putting away of doubt. We cannot be resolved of any doubt save by experiment, and there is no better way to make it than on ourselves. Let us therefore verify what we have said above concerning the truth, beginning with ourselves. We have said above that piety consists in knowledge of ourselves,[50] and hence it is that we make philosophical knowledge begin from this also. But no man can know himself unless he know *what* and not

47 *Theatr. chem.*, I, p. 266.
48 In Dorn "veritas" is synonymous with "sapientia," as is shown by the passage that follows in the original text. There Truth says, "Come unto me, all ye who seek," which is a slight rephrasing of Ecclesiasticus 24 : 19: "Come unto me, all ye who desire me."
49 "Spec. phil.," p. 271.
50 Dorn stresses the great importance of self-knowledge for the performance of the *opus alchymicum* in other places as well. For instance, on p. 307 he says: "Therefore man, heaven and earth are one thing, likewise air and water. If man knows how to transmute things in the greater world . . . how much more so in the microcosm, that is, in himself, if he know that the greatest treasure of a man exists within the man, and not outside him." *

who he is,[51] on whom he depends and whose he is (for by the law of truth no one belongs to himself), and to what end he was made. With this knowledge piety begins, which is concerned with two things, namely, with the Creator and the creature that is made like unto him. For it is impossible for the creature to know himself of himself, unless he first know his Creator. . . .[52] No one can better know the Creator, than the workman is known by his work.[53]

363   Later Dorn says:

The chemical putrefaction is compared to the study of the philosophers, because as the philosophers are disposed to knowledge by study, so natural things are disposed by putrefaction to solution [*ad solutionem*]. To this is compared philosophical knowledge, for as by solution bodies are dissolved [*solvuntur*], so by knowledge are the doubts of the philosophers resolved [*resolvuntur*].[54]

He says in his "Physica Trithemii":

The first step in the ascent to higher things is the study of faith, for by this is the heart of man disposed to solution in water [*ad solutionem in aquam*].[55]

Finally, in his "Philosophia chemica," Dorn asserts:

Dissolution is knowledge, or the spagyric [56] union of the male with the female, the latter receiving from him all that ought to be received. This is the beginning of the special generation whereby the effect of our spagyric marriage is sensually apprehended, namely, the union of the twofold seed to form the embryo.[57]

364   It is evident from these statements that Dorn understood the alchemical *solutio* primarily as a spiritual and moral phenomenon and only secondarily as a physical one. The first part of the work is a psychic "solution" of doubts and conflicts, achieved by self-knowledge, and this is not possible without knowledge of God. The spiritual and moral *solutio* is conceived as a "spagyric marriage," an inner, psychic union which by analogy and magic correspondence unites the hostile ele-

[51] "Quid, non quis ipse sit" is an excellent formulation of the personalistic question Who? and of the impersonal and objective What? Quis refers to the ego, quid to the self. Cf. *Aion,* par. 252.   [52] "Spec. phil.," p. 272.   [53] P. 273.*
[54] P. 303.
[55] *Theatr. chem.,* I, p. 449.
[56] That is, alchemical or occult.
[57] *Theatr. chem.,* I, p. 475.

ments into *one* stone. By inquiring into the "quid," and by spiritual understanding, the selfish hardness of the heart—caused by original sin—is dissolved: the heart turns to water. The ascent to the higher stages can then begin. Egocentricity is a necessary attribute of consciousness and is also its specific sin.[58] But consciousness is confronted by the objective fact of the unconscious, often enough an avenging deluge. Water in all its forms—sea, lake, river, spring—is one of the commonest typifications of the unconscious, as is also the lunar femininity that is closely associated with water. The dissolution of the heart in water would therefore correspond to the union of the male with the female, and this in turn to the union of conscious and unconscious, which is precisely the meaning of the "spagyric marriage." [59] Similarly, the citadel or fortress is a feminine symbol, containing within it the treasure of the "truth," also personified as Wisdom.[60] This wisdom corresponds to salt, which is co-ordinated with the moon. The spagyric union produces an embryo whose equivalents are the homunculus and the lapis. The lapis, of course, is a symbol of the self.[61]

365   If after this glimpse into the psychology of the *solutio* we turn back to the "Allegoria Merlini," several things will become clear: the king personifies a hypertrophy of the ego which calls for compensation. He is about to commit an act of violence—a sure sign of his morally defective state. His thirst is due to his boundless concupiscence and egotism. But when he drinks he is overwhelmed by the water, i.e., by the unconscious, and medical help becomes necessary. The two groups of doctors further assist his dissolution by dismemberment and pulverization.[62] The

58 It is also regarded as the supreme sin. Cf. Wegmann, *Das Rätsel der Sünde*, ch. 3.
59 The water signifies the *sponsa* (bride) and *dilecta* (beloved) as well as Sapientia. Cf. Ecclesiasticus 24 : 5, where Wisdom "walked in the bottom of the deep, in the waves of the sea," and, as the love-goddess Ishtar, praises herself as a cedar, cypress, palm-tree, rose-plant, vine, etc. (13ff.).
60 "Spec. phil.," *Theatr. chem.*, I, p. 266, where Sapientia holds a long discourse.
61 Cf. *Psychology and Alchemy*, Part III, ch. 5, and *Aion*, pars. 121ff.
62 The method of the physicians was an imitation of Typhon's dismemberment of Osiris. Indeed, the king had already begun to drink his fill of Typhon's sea, in order to dissolve himself in it. The second version of the Visio Arislei in *Ros. phil.* likewise contains a dismemberment into "indivisible particles," but there it refers not to the king but to his son. His dismemberment takes place in the body of Beya, and thus represents a process of histolysis in the chrysalis state.

original of this may be the dismemberment of Osiris and Dionysus.[63] The king is subjected to various forms of dissolution: dismemberment, trituration, dissolution in water.[64] His transfer to the heated chamber is the prototype of the "laconicum" (sweat-bath) of the king, often shown in later illustrations; it is a therapeutic method which we meet again in the American Indian "sweat-lodge." The chamber also signifies the grave. The difference between the Egyptian and the Alexandrian physicians seems to be that the former moistened the corpse but the latter dried it (or embalmed or pickled it). The technical error of the Egyptians, therefore, was that they did not separate the conscious from the unconscious sufficiently, whereas the Alexandrians avoided this mistake.[65] At any rate they succeeded in reviving the king and evidently brought about his rejuvenation.

366   If we examine this medical controversy from the standpoint of alchemical hermeneutics many of the allusions can be understood in a deeper sense. For instance the Alexandrians, though making just as thorough use of the Typhonian technique of dismemberment, avoided the (Typhonian) sea-water and dried the pulverized corpse, using instead the other constituent of the *aqua pontica,* namely salt in the form of *sal ammoniac* (mineral salt

---

[63] Further material in "Transformation Symbolism in the Mass," pars. 353, 400.

[64] Variants of the latter are: the king immersed or drowning in the sea, the "sterile king of the sea," Mater Alchimia's dropsy, etc. The motif of the drowned king goes back to Osiris. In the lament of Isis for her son in the daily ritual, she says: "I have crossed the seas to the bounds of the earth, seeking the place where my Lord was; I have traversed Nadit in the night; I have sought . . . him who is in the water . . . in that night of the great affliction. I have found the drowned one of the earth of aforetime . . ." (Moret, *Mystères égyptiens*, p. 24).

[65] Concerning this separation see the Poimandres vision in the *Corpus hermeticum*, lib. I, 4: ". . . And I beheld a boundless vision: all was changed into a mild and joyous light, and I marvelled when I saw it. And in a little while, Darkness settled upon it, fearful and gloomy . . . And I saw the darkness changing into a watery substance, which was in great turmoil, and belched forth smoke as from a fire. And I heard it making an indescribable sound of lamentation; for there came forth from it an inarticulate cry, as it were a cry for light. But from the light there arose above the watery substance a Word, that one might hear it; a voice and pure fire and a spiritual Word (πνευματικὸν λόγον)." (Cf. Scott, *Hermetica*, I, pp. 114ff. and Mead, *Thrice-Greatest Hermes*, II, pp. 4f.) The separation of the four elements from the dark chaos then follows. (The text is corrupt, so I have translated it literally.) Concerning the "cry," cf. the drowning king's cry for help in Maier, *Symb. aur. mensae*, p. 380.

or rock-salt, also called *sal de Arabia*) and *sal nitri* (saltpetre).[66] Primarily the preservative quality of both salts is meant, but secondarily, in the mind of the adepts, "marination" meant the "in-forming" penetration of *sapientia* (Dorn's "veritas") into the ignoble mass, whereby the corruptible form was changed into an incorruptible and immutable one.

367   Certainly there is little trace of this in our somewhat crude parable. Also, the transformation of the king seems to betoken only the primitive renewal of his life-force, for the king's first remark after his resuscitation shows that his bellicosity is undiminished. In the later texts, however, the end-product is never just a strengthening, rejuvenation or renewal of the initial state but a transformation into a higher nature. So we are probably not wrong in attributing a fairly considerable age to this parable. One ground for this assumption is the conflict between the Alexandrian and Egyptian physicians, which may hark back to pre-Islamic times when the old-fashioned, magical remedies of the Egyptians still led to skirmishes with the progressive, more scientific medicine of the Greeks. Evidence for this is the "technical" blunder of the Egyptian method—contamination of conscious and unconscious—which the more highly differentiated consciousness of the Greeks was able to avoid.

4. THE REGENERATION OF THE KING
(*Ripley's "Cantilena"*)

368   It should not be overlooked that no reason was given why the king was in need of renewal. On a primitive level the need for renewal was self-evident, since the magic power of the king decreased with age. This is not so in later parables, where the original imperfection of the king itself becomes a problem.

369   Thus the author of the following parable, Sir George Ripley (1415–90), Canon of Bridlington, was already revolving in his mind the problem of the "sick king." I must leave to one side the question of how far this idea was influenced by the Grail Legend. It is conceivable that Ripley, as an Englishman, would have been acquainted with this tradition. Apart from the rather doubtful evidence of the "lapis exilis" ("lapsit exillis" in Wolf-

66 Ruland, *Lexicon*, pp. 281, 283.

ram von Eschenbach), I have not been able to find any more likely traces of the Grail cycle in alchemical symbolism, unless one thinks of the mystic vessel of transformation, the *tertium comparationis* for which would be the chalice in the Mass.

370   The first five verses of the *Cantilena* [67] are as follows:

> Behold! And in this *Cantilena* see
> The hidden Secrets of Philosophy:
> What Joy arises from the Merry Veines
> Of Minds elated by such dulcid Straines!
>
> Through Roman Countreys as I once did passe,
> Where Mercuries Nuptiall celebrated was,
> And feeding Stoutly (on the Bride-Groomes score)
> I learn'd these Novelties unknown before.
>
> There was a certaine Barren King by birth,
> Composèd of the Purest, Noblest Earth,
> By nature Sanguine and Devoute, yet hee
> Sadly bewailèd his Authoritie.
>
> Wherefore am I a King, and Head of all
> Those Men and Things that be Corporeall?
> I have no Issue, yet I'le not deny
> 'Tis Mee both Heaven and Earth are Rulèd by.
>
> Yet there is either a Cause Naturall
> Or some Defect in the Originall,

[67] *Opera omnia chemica* (Cassel, 1649), pp. 421ff. [Like all Ripley's works, the *Cantilena* did not appear in print until the middle of the 17th cent., long after his death. It was written in Latin and consists of 38 four-line stanzas (rhymed *aaaa*). Latin texts, which vary somewhat, appear in MSS. Ashmole 1394, pp. 67, 75; 1445, VIII, 2; 1479, 223, and English translations in MS. Ashmole 1445, VIII, pp. 2–12, 41–44, all dating from the 16th cent. and now at the Bodleian. The former of these translations (rhymed *aabb*), by an unknown hand, and entitled "George Ripley's Song," has been used here as a basis for the verses which follow. It was first published by F. Sherwood Taylor in *Ambix* (II, nos. 3 and 4, Dec. 1946). With the assistance of Mr. A. S. B. Glover, I have attempted to bring certain phrases in the *Ambix* version somewhat closer to the original Latin and hence to the prose translation made by Professor Jung in the Swiss edition of the *Mysterium*, and some of the verses have been recast. The Latin text given in the footnotes follows that of the Cassel edition throughout.—TRANS.]

Though I was borne without Corruption
And nourished 'neath the Pinions of the Sunne.[68]

371   The cleric's language betrays him: "original defect" is a
paraphrase of "original sin," and the "pinions of the sun" are
the "wings of the sun of justice" (Malachi 4 : 2: "The sun of
justice shall arise with healing in his wings"). Possibly there is
a connection here between the *Cantilena* and the remark of
Senior that the male without wings is under the winged female.[69]
The *Cantilena* condenses the winged female on the one hand
with the winged sun-disk of Malachi and on the other with the
idea of the nourishing mother—a kind of dreamlike contamination.

372   *Verses 6 and 7*

Each Vegetative which from the Earth proceeds
Arises up with its own proper Seeds;

68 "En philosophantium in hac cantilena
    Summa arcana concino voce cum amoena,
    Quae mentalis jubili pullulat a vena,
    Et mens audientium fit dulcore plena.

"In extremis partibus nuptiis Mercurii
    Accidit post studium semel quod interfui,
    Ubi vescens epulis tam grandis convivii
    Ignorata primitus haec novella didici.

"Quidam erat sterilis Rex in genitura,
    Cujus forma nobilis et decora pura
    Extitit, sanguineus erat hic natura,
    Attamen conqueritur sua contra jura.

"Rex caput corporum quare sum ego,
    Sterilis, inutilis sine prole dego,
    Cuncta tamen interim mundana ego rego,
    Et terrae nascentia quaeque, quod non nego.

"Causa tamen extitit quaedam naturalis
    Vel defectus aliquis est originalis;
    Quamvis sine maculis alvi naturalis
    Eram sub solaribus enutritus alis."

69 *De chemia*, p. 38: "It is the male which without wings is under the female, but
the female has wings. Wherefore they said: Cast the female upon the male, and
the male shall ascend upon the female." *

And Animalls, at Seasons, speciously
Abound with Fruit and strangly Multiply.

Alas, my Nature is Restricted so
No Tincture from my Body yet can flow.
It therefore is Infoecund: neither can
It ought availe, in Generating Man.[70]

Here again the ecclesiastical language is noticeable: the tincture is identical with the *aqua permanens,* the wonderful water of transformation which corresponds to the Church's "water of grace." The water that should flow from the body may be analogous to the "rivers from the belly of Christ," an idea that plays a great role not only in ecclesiastical metaphor but also in alchemy.[71] With regard to the ecclesiastical language I would call attention to Hugo Rahner's most instructive essay, "Flumina de ventre Christi." Origen speaks of "the river our saviour" (*salvator noster fluvius*).[72] The analogy of the pierced Redeemer with the rock from which Moses struck water was used in alchemy to denote the extraction of the *aqua permanens* or of the soul from the lapis; or again, the king was pierced by Mercurius.[73] For Origen water meant the "water of doctrine" and the "fount of science." It was also a "fountain of water springing up in the believer." St. Ambrose speaks of the "fountains of wis-

---

[70] "Ex terrae visceribus quoque vegetantur
Suis in seminibus, et qua animantur
Congruis temporibus fructu cumulantur,
Speciebus propriis et multiplicantur.

"Mea sed restringitur fortiter natura
Quod de meo corpore non fluit tinctura,
Infoecunda igitur mea est natura
Nec ad actum germinis multum valitura."

[71] Khunrath (*Hyl. chaos,* p. 268): "From the belly of Saturn's salt flow living waters leaping up to blessed life." (Cf. John 7 : 38: ". . . out of his belly shall flow rivers of living water.") Saturn's salt is the sapientia Saturni, the white dove hidden in the lead.

[72] *In Numeros homiliae,* 17, 4 (Migne, *P.G.,* vol. 12, col. 707).

[73] See fig. 150 in *Psychology and Alchemy.* Origen, *In Exodum homiliae,* 11, 2 (Migne, *P.G.,* vol. 12, col. 376) says of Christ: "Unless this rock had been smitten, it had not given water." *

dom and knowledge." [74] According to him paradise, with its fourfold river of the Logos, is the ground of the soul; [75] he also calls this river the innermost soul, since it is the "principle," the κοιλία (*venter*), and the νοῦς.[76] These few examples from the many collected by Rahner may suffice to put the significance of the *aqua permanens*, the arcane substance par excellence, in the right perspective. For the alchemists it was wisdom and knowledge, truth and spirit, and its source was in the inner man, though its symbol was common water or sea-water. What they evidently had in mind was a ubiquitous and all-pervading essence, an *anima mundi* and the "greatest treasure," the innermost and most secret numinosum of man. There is probably no more suitable psychological concept for this than the collective unconscious, whose nucleus and ordering "principle" is the self (the "monad" of the alchemists and Gnostics).

373 *Verses 8 and 9*

> My Bodies Masse is of a Lasting-Stuffe,
> Exceeding delicate, yet hard enough;
> And when the Fire Assays to try my Sprite,
> I am not found to Weigh a Graine too light.

> My Mother in a Sphaere gave birth to mee,
> That I might contemplate Rotunditie;
> And be more Pure of kind than other things,
> By Right of Dignity the Peer of Kings.[77]

74 *Commentarius in Cantica Canticorum*, 1 (Migne, *P.L.*, vol. 15, col. 1860). Dorn ("Spec. phil.," *Theatr. chem.*, I, p. 267) says: "Sweet is the ringing voice and grateful to the ears of them that philosophize! O inexhaustible fountain of riches to them that thirst after truth and justice! O solace to the want of them that are desolate! What more do ye seek, ye anguished mortals? Why, poor wretches, do you trouble your spirits with infinite cares? What madness is it, pray, that blinds you? seeing that all that you seek outside yourselves and not within yourselves is within you and not without you." *

75 Ambrose, *Explanatio Psalmorum XII* (ed. Petschenig, p. 337). In *Epistolae*, XLV, 3 (Migne, *P.L.*, vol. 16, col. 1142) he says: "That real paradise is not an earthly and visible one, it is not in any place, but in ourself, and it is quickened and vivified by the powers of the soul and the inpouring of the spirit." *

76 Rahner, "Flumina de ventre Christi," p. 289.

77 "Massa mei corporis semper est mansura
Valde delectabilis atque satis dura,
Hancque, cum examinat ignis creatura,
Nulla mei ponderis abest caritura.

The "house of the sphere" is the *vas rotundum,* whose roundness represents the cosmos and, at the same time, the world-soul,
which in Plato surrounds the physical universe from outside.
The secret content of the Hermetic vessel is the original chaos
from which the world was created. As the filius Macrocosmi and
the first man the king is destined for "rotundity," i.e., wholeness,
but is prevented from achieving it by his original defect.

374   *Verse 10*

> Yet to my Griefe I know, unlesse I feed
> On the Specifics I so sorely need
> I cannot Generate: to my Amaze
> The End draws near for me, Ancient of Daies.[78]

This verse confirms the decrepit condition of the king, who
apart from his original defect, or because of it, is also suffering
from senile debility. It was a bold stroke for a canon to identify
the king with the "Ancient of Days" from Daniel 7 : 9: "I beheld till the thrones were cast down, and the Ancient of Days
did sit, whose garments were white as snow, and the hair of his
head like pure wool: his throne was like the fiery flame, and his
wheels as burning fire." There can be no doubt that Ripley the
alchemist was here speculating over the head of Ripley the
cleric to hit upon an idea that in the Middle Ages must have
seemed like blasphemy: the identification of the transformative
substance with God. To our way of thinking this kind of allegory or symbolization is the height of absurdity and unintelligibility. It was even hard for the Middle Ages to swallow.[79]
But where it met with acceptance, as in philosophical alchemy,
it does much to explain the hymnlike or at any rate highly emotional language of some of the treatises. We have here, in fact,

---

> "Meque mater genuit sphaericae figurae
> Domi, quod rotunditas esset mihi curae.
> Foremque prae ceteris speciei purae,
> Et assistens regibus dignitatis jura."

[78] "Modo tamen anxia illud scio verum
Nisi fruar protinus ope specierum,
Generare nequeo, quia tempus serum
Est et ego stupeo antiquus dierum."

[79] Cf. the printer's apology in the Introduction to *Aurora consurgens* II (*Art.
aurif.,* I, p. 183), cited in *Psychology and Alchemy,* par. 464.

a new religious declaration: God is not only in the unspotted body of Christ and continually present in the consecrated Host but—and this is the novel and significant thing—he is also hidden in the "cheap," "despised," common-or-garden substance, even in the "uncleanness of this world, in filth." [80] He is to be found only through the art, indeed he is its true object and is capable of progressive transformation—"Deo adjuvante." This strange theologem did not, of course, mean that for the alchemists God was nothing but a substance that could be obtained by chemical transformation—far from it. Such an aberration was reserved rather for those moderns who put matter or energy in the place of God. The alchemists, so far as they were still pagans, had a more mystical conception of God dating from late antiquity, which, as in the case of Zosimos, could be described as Gnostic; or if they were Christians, their Christianity had a noticeable admixture of heathenish magical ideas about demons and divine powers and an *anima mundi* inherent or imprisoned in physical nature. The *anima mundi* was conceived as that part of God which formed the quintessence and real substance of Physis, and which was to God—to use an apt expression of Isidore [81]—as the "accrescent soul" ($\pi\rho o\sigma\phi\upsilon\grave{\eta}s$ $\psi\upsilon\chi\acute{\eta}$, 'grown-on') was to the divine soul of man. This accrescent soul was a second soul that grew through the mineral, vegetable, and animal kingdoms up to man, pervading the whole of nature, and to it the natural forms were attached like appendages ($\pi\rho o\sigma\alpha\rho\tau\acute{\eta}\mu\alpha\tau\alpha$). This strange idea of Isidore's is so much in keeping with the phenomenology of the collective unconscious that one is justified in calling it a projection of this empirically demonstrable fact in the form of a metaphysical hypostasis.

375   It will not have escaped the reader how primitive the idea of God's ageing and need of renewal is. It does in fact derive from ancient Egypt, though one is at a loss to imagine from what sources, other than the Bible, a Canon of Bridlington in the fifteenth century could have borrowed such a theology. His writings at any rate allow no conjectures in this respect. There is something of a clue, however, in the alchemical tradition itself, in the idea of a corrupt arcane substance whose corruption is due to original sin. A similar idea appears in the Grail tradition

[80] "In immunditia huius mundi, in stercore."
[81] Son of Basilides the Gnostic.

of the sick king, which has close connections with the transformation mystery of the Mass. The king is the forbear of Parsifal, whom one could describe as a redeemer figure, just as in alchemy the old king has a redeemer son or becomes a redeemer himself (the lapis is the same at the beginning and at the end). Further, we must consider certain medieval speculations concerning God's need of improvement and the transformation of the wrathful God of the Old Testament into the God of Love in the New: for, like the unicorn, he was softened by love in the lap of a virgin. Ideas of this kind are found as early as Bonaventure, the Franciscan saint, who died in 1274.[82] We should also remember that, in the figurative language of the Church, God the Father was represented as an old man and his birth as a rejuvenation in the Son. In a hymn to the Church as an analogy of the Mother of God Paulinus of Nola says:

> Sister and wife at once; for without the use of the body
> Mentally she unites, for the Spouse is God, not a man.
> Out of this mother is born the Ancient as well as the infant . . .[83]

376 Although the candidate for baptism ("reborn into a new infancy") is meant here, the point of the analogy is that God the Father, a bearded old man, is worshipped in God the Son as a newborn child.

377 The contrast between *senex* and *puer* touches at more than one point on the archetype of God's renewal in Egyptian theology, especially when the underlying homoousia comes out as clearly as in the verses of Ephraem Syrus: "The Ancient of Days, in his sublimity, dwelt as a babe in the womb." [84] "Thy Babe, O Virgin, is an old man; he is the Ancient of Days and precedes all time." [85]

378 Nowhere in this material, however, do we find the very specific motif of God's senescence, and the source Ripley could have used remains obscure. Even so, there is always the possibility of an autochthonous revival of the mythologem from the collective unconscious. Nelken has published a case of this kind. His patient was a primary-school teacher who suffered from paranoia. He developed a theory about a Father-God with immense pro-

[82] Further material in *Psychology and Alchemy*, pars. 522f. and n. 22.
[83] Poema 25, Migne, *P.L.* vol. 61, col. 637. Further material in Curtius, *European Literature and the Latin Middle Ages*, pp. 103ff.
[84] Ephraem Syrus, *Hymni et sermones*, II, col. 620.*   [85] Ibid., I, col. 136.*

creative powers. Originally he had 550 *membra virilia,* but in the course of time they were reduced to three. He also possessed two scrota with three testicles each. His colossal sperm production weakened him in the end, and finally he shrank to a five-ton lump and was found chained up in a ravine. This psychologem contains the motif of ageing and loss of procreative power. The patient was the rejuvenated Father-God or his avatar.[86] The embellishment of the archetypal theme is in this case completely original, so that we can safely take it as an autochthonous product.

379   In Ripley's case there is the more immediate possibility that he modified for his own purpose the conception of the Ancient of Days and his youthful son the Logos, who in the visions of Valentinus the Gnostic and of Meister Eckhart was a small boy. These concepts are closely related to those of Dionysus, youngest of the gods, and of the Horus-child, Harpocrates, Aion, etc. All naturally imply the renewal of the ageing god. The step from the world of Christian ideas back into paganism is not a long one,[87] and the naturalistic conclusion that the father dwindles when the son appears, or that he is rejuvenated in the son, is implicit in all these age-old conceptions, whose effect is all the stronger the more they are consciously denied. Such a combination of ideas is almost to be expected in a cleric like Ripley, even though, like all alchemists, he may not have been conscious of their full import.

380   *Verses 11–12*

Utterly perish'd is the Flower of Youth,
Through all my Veines there courses naught but Death.
Marvelling I heard Christ's voice,[88] that from above
I'le be Reborne, I know not by what Love.

---

[86] Nelken, "Analytische Beobachtungen über Phantasien eines Schizophrenen," pp. 538ff.   [87] Rahner, "Die Gottesgeburt," pp. 341ff.

[88] [The Swiss edition (II, p. 26, n. 85) has here "I heard that I should be reborn through Christ's Tree." This is based on the reading "Christi sed arbore" in line 2 of verse 11, which proves to be an error in transcription. The Cassel edition of the *Cantilena* (1649, and there appears to be no other) shows (p. 422) "Christi sed ab ore" (by Christ's mouth), in this agreeing with the 16th cent. Latin and English MSS. at the Bodleian. Since pars. 36–39 of the Swiss text are mainly concerned with the "arbor philosophica" mentioned elsewhere in Ripley's writings, they are here omitted with the author's consent.—TRANS.]

> Else I God's Kingdom cannot enter in:
> And therefore, that I may be Borne agen,
> I'le Humbled be into my Mother's Breast,
> Dissolve to my First Matter, and there rest.[89]

381   In order to enter into God's Kingdom the king must transform himself into the prima materia in the body of his mother,
and return to the dark initial state which the alchemists called
the "chaos." In this *massa confusa* the elements are in conflict
and repel one another; all connections are dissolved. Dissolution
is the prerequisite for redemption. The celebrant of the mysteries had to suffer a figurative death in order to attain transformation. Thus, in the Arisleus vision, Gabricus is dissolved into
atoms in the body of his sister-wife. We have seen from the analogy with the Ancient of Days what the alchemist's goal was: both
artifex and substance were to attain a perfect state, comparable
to the Kingdom of God. I will not discuss, for the moment, the
justification for this seemingly presumptuous comparison, but
would remind the reader that in the opinion of the alchemists
themselves the transformation was a miracle that could take
place only with God's help.

382   *Verse 13*

> Hereto the Mother Animates the King,
> Hasts his Conception, and does forthwith bring
> Him closely hidden underneath her Traine,
> Till, from herselfe, she'd made him Flesh againe.[90]

383   Here the "chymical wedding" takes the form of the ancient
rite of adoption, when the child to be adopted was hidden under
the skirts of the adoptive mother and then drawn forth again.[91]

89 "Me praedatum penitus iuventutis flore
　　Mors invasit funditus Christi sed ab ore
　　Me audivi coelitus grandi cum stupore
　　Renascendum denuo nescio quo amore.

　　"Regnum Dei aliter nequeo intrare
　　Hinc ut nascar denuo me humiliare
　　Volo matres sinibus meque adaptare
　　In primam materiam et me disgregare."

90 "Ad hoc mater propria regem animavit
　　Eiusque conceptui sese acceleravit,
　　Quem statim sub chlamyde sua occultavit
　　Donec eum iterum ex se incarnavit."

91 Cf. Diodorus, *Bibliotheke Historike*, 4, 39 (trans. by Oldfather, II, pp. 468f.)

In this way Ripley circumvented the scandal of the customary incest.

384   The adoption was represented in ancient times either by a figurative act of birth or by the suckling of the adoptive child. In this manner Heracles was "adopted" by Hera. In a hymn to Nebo [92] the god says to Asurbanipal:

> Small wert thou, Asurbanipal, when I left thee with the divine
>   Queen of Nineveh,
> Feeble wert thou, Asurbanipal, when thou didst sit in the lap of the
>   divine Queen of Nineveh,
> Of the four udders that were placed in thy mouth thou didst suck
>   from two,
> And in two thou didst bury thy face . . .[93]

385   Concealment under the skirt is a widely disseminated rite, and until quite recently was still practised by the Bosnian Turks. The motif of the "tutelary Madonna" in a mantle has a similar meaning, namely, the adoption of the believer.

386   Ripley's adoption scene may derive from the "lion-hunt" of Marchos,[94] where mention is made of a fire which "comes out over the coals, even as the pious mother steps over the body of her son." And again: "He likened the subtlety of the fire's heat to the stepping of the pious mother over the body of her son." [95] These sentences form part of a dialogue between King Marchos and his mother. In contrast to the *Cantilena,* however, it is not the king who is to be transformed but the lion (see pars. 409f.).

387   *Verses 14–17*

> 'Twas wonderfull to see with what a Grace
> This Naturall Union made at one Imbrace
> Did looke; and by a Bond both Sexes knitt,
> Like to a Hille and Aire surrounding it.
>
> The Mother unto her Chast Chamber [96] goes,
> Where in a Bed of Honour she bestowes
> Her weary'd selfe, 'twixt Sheets as white as Snow
> And there makes Signes of her approaching Woe.

[92] Nebo corresponds to the planet Mercury.
[93] Roscher, *Lexikon,* III, 1, col. 62, s.v. Nebo.   [94] Senior, *De chemia,* p. 63.
[95] Ibid., p. 63.*
[96] The "thalamus" refers to the mystic marriage. See infra, the "green lion."

Ranke Poison issuing from the Dying Man
Made her pure Orient face look foule and wan:
Hence she commands all Strangers to be gone,
Seals upp her Chamber doore, and lyes Alone.

Meanwhile she of the Peacocks Flesh did Eate
And Dranke the Greene-Lyons Blood with that fine Meate,
Which Mercurie, bearing the Dart of Passion,
Brought in a Golden Cupp of Babilon.[97]

388   The pregnancy diet described here is the equivalent of the
"cibatio," the "feeding" of the transformative substance. The
underlying idea is that the material to be transformed had to be
impregnated and saturated, either by imbibing the tincture, the
aqua propria (its "own water," the soul), or by eating its "feathers" or "wings" (volatile spirit), or its own tail (uroboros), or the
fruit of the philosophical tree. Here it is "peacock's flesh." The
peacock is an allusion to the *cauda pavonis* (peacock's tail). Immediately before the *albedo* or *rubedo* [98] "all colours" appear,
as if the peacock were spreading his shimmering fan. The basis
for this phenomenon may be the iridescent skin that often forms
on the surface of molten metal (e.g., lead).[99] The "omnes colores"

[97] "Mirum erat ilico cernere connexum
      Factum naturaliter primum ad complexum,
      Foedere complacito ad utrumque sexum
      Penitus post aeris montana transvexum.

"Mater tunc ingreditur thalamum pudoris
      Et sese in lectulo collocat honoris,
      Inter linteamina plenaque candoris
      Signa statim edidit futuri languoris.

"Moribundi corporis virus emanabat,
      Quod maternam faciem candidam foedabat,
      Hinc a se extraneos cunctos exserebat
      Ostiumque camerae firme sigillabat.

"Vescebatur interim carnibus pavonis
      Et bibebat sanguinem viridis leonis
      Sibi quem Mercurio telo passionis
      Ministrabat aureo scypho Babylonis."

[98] The sequence of alchemical operations is arbitrary in its details and varies from
author to author.
[99] Hoghelande seems to suggest something of the sort when he says that "colours
appear on the surface of the mercury" (*Theatr. chem.*, I, p. 150).

are frequently mentioned in the texts as indicating something like totality. They all unite in the *albedo,* which for many alchemists was the climax of the work. The first part was completed when the various components separated out from the chaos of the *massa confusa* were brought back to unity in the *albedo* and "all become one." Morally this means that the original state of psychic disunity, the inner chaos of conflicting part-souls which Origen likens to herds of animals,[100] becomes the "vir unus," the unified man. Eating the peacock's flesh is therefore equivalent to integrating the many colours (or, psychologically, the contradictory feeling-values) into a single colour, white. Norton's "Ordinall of Alchimy" says:

> For everie Colour whiche maie be thought,
> Shall heere appeare before that White be wrought.[101]

389   The lapis contains or produces all colours.[102] Hoghelande says that the "Hermaphroditic monster" contains all colours.[103] Poetic comparisons are also used, such as Iris, the rainbow,[104] or the iris of the eye.[105] The eye and its colours are mentioned by Hippolytus. He calls attention to the Naassene analogy between the four rivers of paradise and the senses. The river Pison, which waters Havilah, the land of gold, corresponds to the eye: "This, they say, is the eye, which by its bearing and its colours bears witness to what is said." [106] Abu'l-Qasim speaks of the tree with multicoloured blossoms.[107] Mylius says: "Our stone is the star-strewn Sol, from whom every colour proceeds by transformation, as flowers come forth in the spring." [108] The "Tractatus Aristotelis" gives a more elaborate description: "Everything that is

---

100 Cf. supra, par. 6, n. 26.   101 *Theatrum Chemicum Britannicum,* p. 54.
102 "This thing . . . maketh the colours to appear sporadically" * (*Turba,* Sermo XIII, lines 9ff.). "This, therefore, is the stone which we have called by all manner of names, which receiveth and drinketh the work, and out of which every colour appeareth" * (ibid., lines 24f.). Similarly Mylius (*Phil. ref.,* p. 119): "All the colours of the world shall be manifested." *   103 *Theatr. chem.,* I, p. 179.
104 "An earthly manifestation of the quintessence you may behold in the colours of the rainbow, when the rays of the sun shine through the rain." * "Gloria mundi," *Mus. herm.,* p. 251 (Waite, I. p. 202).
105 ". . . the pupil of the eye and Iris (rainbow) in the sky." (Olympiodorus, in Berthelot, *Alch. grecs,* II, iv, 38.)*
106 *Elenchos,* V. 9 (cf. Legge trans., I, p. 143).
107 Abu'l Qāsim Muhammad, *Kitāb al-'ilm al-muktasab* (ed. Holmyard), p. 23.
108 *Phil. ref.,* p. 121.

contained beneath the circle of the moon . . . is made into one at the quadrangular ending,[109] as if it were a meadow decked with colours and sweet-smelling flowers of divers kinds, which were conceived in the earth by the dew of heaven." [110]

390   The stages of the work are marked by seven colours which are associated with the planets.[111] This accounts for the relation of the colours to astrology, and also to psychology, since the planets correspond to individual character components. The *Aurora Consurgens* relates the colours to the soul.[112] Lagneus associates the four principal colours with the four temperaments.[113] The psychological significance of the colours comes out quite clearly in Dorn: "Truly the form which is the intellect of man is the beginning, middle, and end of the preparations, and this form is indicated by the yellow colour, which shows that man is the greater and principal form in the spagyric work, and one mightier than heaven." [114] Since the gold colour signifies intellect, the principal "informator" (formative agent) in the alchemical process, we may assume that the other three colours also denote psychological functions, just as the seven colours denote the seven astrological components of character. Consequently the synthesis of the four or seven colours would mean nothing less than the integration of the personality, the union of the four basic functions, which are customarily represented by the colour quaternio blue-red-yellow-green.[115]

391   The *cauda pavonis* was a favourite theme for artistic representation in the old prints and manuscripts. It was not the tail alone that was depicted, but the whole bird. Since the peacock stands for "all colours" (i.e., the integration of all qualities), an illustration in Khunrath's *Amphitheatrum sapientiae* logically shows it standing on the two heads of the Rebis, whose unity it

---

109 "In fine quadrangulari," i.e., at the synthesis of the four elements.
110 *Theatr. chem.*, V, p. 881.
111 Cf. Berthelot, *Alch. grecs,* Introduction, p. 76. Also infra, par. 577.
112 P. 95: "He who shall raise up his soul shall see its colours." *
113 *Citrinitas* $=$ the choleric temperament, *rubedo* $=$ the sanguine, *albedo* $=$ the phlegmatic, *nigredo* $=$ the melancholic. ("Harmonia chemica," *Theatr. chem.,* IV, p. 873.)
114 "Phil. chem.," *Theatr. chem.,* I, p. 485.
115 Cf. *Psychology and Alchemy,* pars. 212, 262, and "A Study in the Process of Individuation," pars. 564ff. (Picture 5).

obviously represents. The inscription calls it the "bird of Hermes" and the "blessed greenness," both of which symbolize the Holy Ghost or the Ruach Elohim, which plays a great role in Khunrath.[116] The *cauda pavonis* is also called the "soul of the world, nature, the quintessence, which causes all things to bring forth." [117] Here the peacock occupies the highest place as a symbol of the Holy Ghost, in whom the male-female polarity of the hermaphrodite and the Rebis is integrated.

392   Elsewhere Khunrath says that at the hour of conjunction the blackness and the raven's head and all the colours in the world will appear, "even Iris, the messenger of God, and the peacock's tail." He adds: "Mark the secrets of the rainbow in the Old and New Testament." [118] This is a reference to the sign of God's covenant with Noah after the flood (Gen. 10 : 12f.) and to the "one in the midst of the four and twenty elders," who "was to look upon like a jasper and a sardine-stone, and there was a rainbow round about the throne, in sight like unto an emerald" (Rev. 4 : 3f.),[119] and to the vision of the angel with a rainbow on his head (Rev. 10 : 1).[120] Iris as the "messenger of God" is of special importance for an understanding of the opus, since the integration of all colours points, as it were, to a coming of God, or even to his presence.

393   The colour green, stressed by Khunrath, is associated with Venus. The "Introitus apertus" says: "But in the gentle heat the mixture will liquefy and begin to swell up, and at God's command will be endowed with spirit, which will soar upward carrying the stone with it, and will produce new colours, first of all the green of Venus, which will endure for a long time." [121] Towards the end of this procedure, which was known as the regi-

116 Cf. the naïve prayer of the author in *Amphitheatrum sapientiae*, p. 221: "I beseech thee with all my heart, that thou wilt send me from thy holy heavens Ruach-Hokhmah-El, the Spirit of thy Wisdom, that it may ever be beside me as a familiar, may skilfully govern me, wisely admonish me and teach me; may be with me and pray with me and work with me; may give me right will and knowledge and experience and ability in physical and physico-medical matters." * The learned Dr. Khunrath would no doubt have been delighted to have the Holy Ghost as a laboratory assistant.
117 Cf. Fig. IV in the Appendix to *Amphitheatrum*.
118 Ibid., p. 202.
119 The emphasis is thus on the green colour.
120 ". . . and a rainbow was upon his head, and his face was as the sun."
121 *Mus. herm.*, p. 693 (Waite, II, p. 194).

men of Venus, the colour changes into a livid purple, whereupon the philosophical tree will blossom. Then follows the
regimen of Mars, "which displays the ephemeral colours of the
rainbow and the peacock at their most glorious." In "these days"
the "hyacinthine colour" [122] appears, i.e., blue.

394   The livid purple that appears towards the end of the regimen of Venus has something deathly about it. This is in accord
with the ecclesiastical view of purple, which expresses the "mystery of the Lord's passion." [123] Hence the regimen of Venus
leads by implication to passion and death, a point I would emphasize in view of the reference to the "dart of passion" in the
Cantilena. A passage from the "Aquarium sapientum" shows
that colours are a means of expressing moral qualities and situations: "While the digestion [124] and coction of the dead spiritual
body goes forward in man, there may be seen, as in the earthly
opus, many variegated colours and signs, i.e., all manner of sufferings, afflictions, and tribulations, the chiefest of which . . .
are the ceaseless assaults of the world, the flesh, and the devil." [125]

395   These statements concerning the regimen of Venus are confirmed in Penotus's Table of Symbols, where the peacock is correlated with the "mysterium coniugii" and with Venus, as is also
the green lizard. Green is the colour of the Holy Ghost, of life,
procreation and resurrection. I mention this because Penotus

122 Ibid., p. 694. It is worth pointing out that a remarkable change occurs during
the regimen Martis: whereas in the regimen Veneris the stone, the material to be
transformed, is "put into another vessel," in the regimen Martis we are told that
"The mother, being now sealed in her infant's belly, swells and is purified, and
because of the great . . . purity of the compound, no putridity can have place
in this regimen . . . Know that our Virgin Earth here undergoes the last degree of
cultivation, and prepares to receive and mature the fruit of the sun." * It is interesting that in this regimen the maternal substance is enclosed in the belly of its
own child. These are transformations that could be expressed only in terms of the
operation of *yin* and *yang*. Cf. the *I Ching* (Book of Changes).
123 Cf. Cassiodorus, *Expositio in Cantica Canticorum* (Migne, *P.L.*, vol. 70, cols.
1071, 1073, 1096).
124 Ruland, *Lexicon*, p. 126, s.v. Digestio: "A change of any substance into another
by a process of natural coction."
125 *Mus. herm.*, p. 131 (Waite, I, p. 111). The text continues: "All which things are
of good omen: namely that a man so troubled shall nonetheless in due time reach
the blessed and greatly desired conclusion, as also the Holy Scripture itself wit-
nesseth, wherein it is written (II Tim. 3 : 12), that all those who desire to live
godly in Christ Jesus shall suffer persecution, and that it is through many tribulations and straits that we must enter the kingdom of Heaven." *

correlates the *coniugium* with the "dii mortui" (dead gods), presumably because they need resurrecting. The peacock is an ancient Christian symbol of resurrection, like the phoenix. According to a late alchemical text,[126] the bronze tablets in the labyrinth at Meroë showed Osiris, after his regeneration by Isis, mounting a chariot drawn by peacocks, in which he drives along triumphing in his resurrection, like the sun.

396   In Dorn the "dead spiritual body" is the "bird without wings." It "changes into the raven's head and finally into the peacock's tail, after which it attains to the whitest plumage of the swan and, last of all, to the highest redness, the sign of its fiery nature." [127] This plainly alludes to the phoenix, which, like the peacock, plays a considerable role in alchemy as a symbol of renewal and resurrection,[128] and more especially as a synonym for the lapis.

397   The *cauda pavonis* announces the end of the work, just as Iris, its synonym, is the messenger of God. The exquisite display of colours in the peacock's fan heralds the imminent synthesis of all qualities and elements, which are united in the "rotundity" of the philosophical stone. For seventeen hundred years, as I have shown in *Psychology and Alchemy,* the lapis was brought into more or less clear connection with the ancient idea of the Anthropos. In later centuries this relationship extended to Christ, who from time immemorial was this same Anthropos or Son of Man, appearing in the gospel of St. John as the cosmogonic Logos that existed before the world was: "In the beginning was the Word, and the Word was with God, and the Word was God . . . All things were made by him, and without

126 Latin MS, 18th cent., "Figurarum Aegyptiorum secretorum," fol. 5 (author's possession).

127 "Congeries Paracelsicae," *Theatr. chem.,* I, p. 599.

128 Honorius of Autun, *Speculum de mysteriis ecclesiae* (Migne, *P.L.,* vol. 172, col. 936) says of the phoenix: "The phoenix is said to be red, and is Christ, of whom it is written: Who is this that cometh from Edom, with dyed garments from Bosra?" * (Cf. Isaiah 63 : 2: "Wherefore art thou red in thine apparel, and thy garments like him that treadeth in the winefat?" * Also verse 3: ". . . and their blood shall be sprinkled upon my garments.") Honorius continues: "Edom, which means red, is the name given to Esau, from the red pottage with which he was fed by Jacob his brother." * After relating the myth of the phoenix Honorius adds: "On the third day the bird is restored, because on the third day Christ was raised again by the Father." *

him was not any thing made that was made." According to the teachings of the Basilidians, the "God who is not" cast down a certain seed which, like a grain of mustard-seed, contained the whole plant, or, "like a peacock's egg, had in itself a varied multitude of colours." [129] In this seed was a "threefold sonship, consubstantial with the God who is not." In alchemy, the end of the work announced by the *cauda pavonis* was the birth of the *filius regius*. The display of colours in the Basilidian doctrine therefore occurred at the right place. Again one must ask: tradition—or spontaneous generation?

398   The peacock is an attribute of Juno, and one of the cognomens of Iris is Junonia. Just as the Queen Mother or the mother of the gods grants renewal, so the peacock annually renews his plumage, and therefore has a relation to all the changes in nature. De Gubernatis says:

The serene and starry sky and the shining sun are peacocks. The deep-blue firmament shining with a thousand brilliant eyes, and the sun rich with the colours of the rainbow, present the appearance of a peacock in all the splendour of its eye-bespangled feathers. When the sky or the thousand-rayed sun (*sahasrânsu*) is hidden by clouds, or veiled by autumnal mists, it again resembles the peacock, which, in the dark part of the year, like a great number of vividly coloured birds, sheds its beautiful plumage, and becomes drab and unadorned; the crow which had put on the peacock's feathers then caws with the other crows in funereal concert. In winter the peacock-crow has nothing left to it except its shrill disagreeable cry, which is not dissimilar to that of the crow. It is commonly said of the peacock that it has an angel's feathers, a devil's voice, and a thief's walk.[130]

This would explain Dorn's connecting the peacock with the raven's head (*caput corvi*).

399   Certain subsidiary meanings of the peacock in medieval literature are worth mentioning. Picinellus says that the peacock, contrasted with the sun, signifies the "righteous man, who, although adorned with the colours of a thousand virtues, yet has a share in the greater glory of the divine presence"; it also signifies the man who, "spotted by repeated sins, rises again to in-

---

[129] *Elenchos*, X, 14, 1 (Legge, II, p. 159).*
[130] *Zoological Mythology*, II, p. 323 (mod.).

tegrity of spirit." The peacock expresses the "inner beauty and perfection of the soul." [131] Merula mentions that the peacock will empty and destroy a vessel containing poison,[132] yet another peculiarity which may account for the peacock's position in alchemy, since it brings about and betokens the transformation of the poisonous dragon into the healing medicine. Merula also asserts that the peahen does not introduce her young to their father until they are fully grown, from which Picinellus drew an analogy with the Blessed Virgin, who likewise presents her charges to God only in the perfect state. Here again the motif of renewal through the mother is struck.[133]

400   If, therefore, the Queen Mother eats peacock flesh during her pregnancy, she is assimilating an aspect of herself, namely, her capacity to grant rebirth, whose emblem the peacock is. According to Augustine, peacock flesh has the peculiarity of not turning rotten.[134] It is, as the alchemists would say, a "cibus immortalis," like the fruits of the philosophical tree with which Arisleus and his companions were fed in the house of rebirth at the bottom of the sea. Peacock flesh was just the right food for the mother in her attempt to rejuvenate the old king and to give him immortality.

401   While peacock flesh [135] was the queen's diet, her drink was the

131 In order to hatch its eggs, the peacock seeks a lonely and hidden spot. Picinellus adds: "And assuredly solitude, the only recipe for preserving a spiritual disposition, offers the fullest occasion for inner felicity." *

132 I take this statement from Picinellus, as I was unable to ascertain which Merula is meant.

133 *Mundus Symbolicus*, I, p. 316.

134 *City of God*, XXI, 4 (trans. by Healey, II, p. 322): "Who was it but God that made the flesh of a dead peacock to remain always sweet, and without any putrefaction?" In the *Cyranides* the peacock is accounted "a most sacred bird." Its eggs are useful in preparing the gold colour. "When the peacock is dead, its flesh does not fade nor emit a foetid smell, but remains as if preserved with aromatic substances." * Its brain can be used to prepare a love-potion. Its blood, when drunk, expels demons, and its dung cures epilepsy. (Delatte, *Textes latins et vieux français relatifs aux Cyranides*, p. 171.)

135 In China (cf. the treatise of Wei Po-yang, in *Isis*, XVIII, p. 258) the nearest analogy is the "fluttering Chu-Niao," the scarlet bird; it has five colours, symbolizing totality, corresponding to the five elements and the five directions. "It is put into the cauldron of hot fluid to the detriment of its feathers." In Western alchemy the cock is plucked, or its wings are clipped, or it eats its own feathers.

blood of the green lion. Blood [136] is one of the best-known synonyms for the *aqua permanens,* and its use in alchemy is often based on the blood symbolism and allegories of the Church.[137] In the *Cantilena* the *imbibitio* (saturation) [138] of the "dead" [139] arcane substance is performed not on the king, as in the "Allegoria Merlini," but on the queen. The displacement and overlapping of images are as great in alchemy as in mythology and folklore. As these archetypal images are produced directly by the unconscious, it is not surprising that they exhibit its contamination of content [140] to a very high degree. This is what makes it so

[136] Ripley himself takes blood as synonymous with spirit: "The spirit or blood of the green lion" (*Opera omnia,* p. 139). In Rosencreutz's *Chymical Wedding* (p. 74) the lion holds a tablet with the inscription: "Hermes the Prince. After so many wounds inflicted on humankind, here by God's counsel and the help of the Art flow I, a healing medicine. Let him drink me who can: let him wash who will: let him trouble me who dare: drink, brethren. and live." *

[137] Cf. the parallel of the opus with the Mass in *Psychology and Alchemy,* pars. 480ff., and "Transformation Symbolism in the Mass," pars. 339ff.

[138] Cf. Mylius, *Phil. ref.,* p. 303, where he says that Mercurius is the green lion and "is the whole elixir of the *albedo* and the *rubedo,* and the *aqua permanens* and the water of life and death, and the virgin's milk, the herb of ablution [an allusion to the Saponaria, Berissa, and moly], and the fountain of the soul: of which who shall drink does not die, and it takes on colour and is their medicine and causes them to acquire colours, and it is this which mortifies and desiccates and moistens, makes warm and cool, and does contrary things," etc.* In short, Mercurius is the master-workman and the artifex. Therefore Mylius proceeds with the winged word: "And he is the dragon who marries himself and impregnates himself, and brings to birth in due time, and slays all living things with his poison." * (Usually he is said to "slay himself," too, and to "bring himself to life.") The uroboros has the wonderful quality of "aseity" (existence by self-origination) in common with the Godhead, for which reason it cannot be distinguished from him. This *aqua permanens,* unlike the ambiguous ὕδωρ θεῖον, is explicitly "divine." We can therefore understand the solemn exhortation in Dorn ("Spec. phil.," *Theatr. chem.,* I, p. 299): "Draw nigh, O Body, to this fountain, that with thy Mind thou mayest drink to satiety and hereafter thirst no more after vanities. O wondrous efficacy of this fount, which makest one of two, and peace between enemies! The fount of love can make *mind* out of spirit and soul, but this maketh *one man* of mind and body. We thank thee, O Father, that thou hast deigned to make thy sons partakers of thy inexhaustible fount of virtues. Amen." *

[139] The extraction of the soul from the prima materia is equivalent to the *mortificatio.* Then, in the *impraegnatio, informatio, impressio, imbibitio, cibatio,* etc., the soul returns to the dead body, and this is followed by its resuscitation or rebirth in a state of incorruptibility.

[140] The best instances of this interconnection of everything with everything else can be found in dreams, which are very much nearer to the unconscious even than myths.

difficult for us to understand alchemy. Here the dominant factor is not logic but the play of archetypal motifs, and although this is "illogical" in the formal sense, it nevertheless obeys natural laws which we are far from having explained. In this respect the Chinese are much in advance of us, as a thorough study of the *I Ching* will show. Called by short-sighted Westerners a "collection of ancient magic spells," an opinion echoed by the modernized Chinese themselves, the *I Ching* is a formidable psychological system that endeavours to organize the play of archetypes, the "wondrous operations of nature," into a certain pattern, so that a "reading" becomes possible. It was ever a sign of stupidity to depreciate something one does not understand.

402   Displacement and overlapping of images would be quite impossible if there did not exist between them an essential similarity of substance, a homoousia. Father, mother, and son are of the same substance, and what is said of one is largely true of the other. This accounts for the variants of incest—between mother and son, brother and sister, father and daughter, etc. The uroboros is one even though in the twilight of the unconscious its head and tail appear as separate figures and are regarded as such. The alchemists, however, were sufficiently aware of the homoousia of their basic substances not only to call the two protagonists of the coniunctio drama the *one* Mercurius, but to assert that the prima materia and the vessel were identical. Just as the *aqua permanens,* the moist soul-substance, comes from the body it is intended to dissolve, so the mother who dissolves her son in herself is none other than the feminine aspect of the father-son. This view current among the alchemists cannot be based on anything except the essential similarity of the substances, which were not chemical but psychic; and, as such, appurtenances not of consciousness, where they would be differentiated concepts, but of the unconscious, in whose increasing obscurity they merge together in larger and larger contaminations.

403   If, then, we are told that the queen drank blood, this image corresponds in every respect to the king drinking water,[141] to

141 The "Liber Platonis quartorum," which dates from the 10th cent., cites blood as a solvent (*Theatr. chem.,* V, p. 157), and says also that a particularly strong solvent is lion's dung (p. 159).

the king's bath in the trough of the oak, to the king drowning in the sea, to the act of baptism, to the passage through the Red Sea, and to the suckling of the child by the mother of the gods. The water and the containing vessel always signify the mother, the feminine principle best characterized by *yin,* just as in Chinese alchemy the king is characterized by *yang.*[142]

404   In alchemy the lion, the "royal" beast, is a synonym for Mercurius,[143] or, to be more accurate, for a stage in his transformation. He is the warm-blooded form of the devouring, predatory monster who first appears as the dragon. Usually the lion-form succeeds the dragon's death and eventual dismemberment. This in turn is followed by the eagle. The transformations described in Rosencreutz's *Chymical Wedding* give one a good idea of the transformations and symbols of Mercurius. Like him, the lion appears in dual form as lion and lioness,[144] or he is said to be Mercurius duplex.[145] The two lions are sometimes identified with the red and white sulphur.[146] The illustrations show a furious battle between the wingless lion (red sulphur) and the winged lioness (white sulphur). The two lions are prefigurations of the royal pair, hence they wear crowns. Evidently at this stage there is still a good deal of bickering between them, and this is precisely what the fiery lion is intended to express--the passionate emotionality that precedes the recognition of unconscious contents.[147] The quarrelling couple also represent the urobo-

142 Cf. the treatise of Wei Po-yang (pp. 231ff.), where *yin* and *yang* are the "charioteers" who lead from the inside to the outside. The sun is *yang,* the moon *yin* (p. 233). Our western image of the uroboros is expressed in the words: "*Yin* and *yang* drink and devour one another" (p. 244); "*Yang* donates and *yin* receives" (p. 245), and, in another form: "The Dragon breathes into the Tiger and the Tiger receives the spirit from the Dragon. They mutually inspire and benefit" (p. 252). As in western alchemy Mercurius duplex is designated "orientalis" and "occidentalis," so in China the dragon (*yang*) reigns over the East and the Tiger (*yin*) over the West. "The way is long and obscurely mystical, at the end of which the Ch'ien *(yang)* and the K'un (*yin*) come together" (p. 260).

143 Cf. n. 138.

144 See the illustration in Lambspringk's Symbols, *Mus. herm.,* p. 349 (Waite, I, p. 283).

145 That is to say, the "flying lion" is equated with Mercurius, who, in turn, consists of the winged and wingless dragon. Cf. Flamel, "Summarium philosophicum," *Mus. herm.,* p. 173 (Waite, I, p. 142).

146 Mylius, *Phil. ref.,* p. 190.

147 Emotional outbursts usually occur in cases of insufficient adaptation due to unconsciousness.

ros.[148] The lion thus signifies the arcane substance, described as *terra*,[149] the body or unclean body.[150] Further synonyms are the "desert place," [151] "poison, because it [this earth] is deadly," "tree, because it bears fruit," or "hidden matter [hyle], because it is the foundation of all nature and the substance [*subiectum*] of all elements." [152] In apparent contradiction to this Maier cites from Ripley's "Tractatus duodecim portarum" the remark that the green lion is a "means of conjoining the tinctures between sun and moon." [153] It is, however, psychologically correct to say that emotion unites as much as it divides. Basilius Valentinus takes the lion as the arcane substance, calling it the trinity composed of Mercurius, Sal, and Sulphur, and the equivalent of draco, aquila, rex, spiritus, and corpus.[154] The "Gloria Mundi" calls the green lion the mineral stone that "consumes a great quantity of its own spirit," [155] meaning self-impregnation by one's own soul (imbibitio, cibatio, nutritio, penetratio, etc.).[156]

405   Besides the green lion there was also, in the later Middle Ages, a red lion.[157] Both were Mercurius.[158] The fact that Ar-

[148] Maier, quoting Lully, says: "Some have called this earth the green lion mighty in battle; others the serpent that devours, stiffens, and mortifies his own tail" * (*Symb. aur. mensae*, p. 427).

[149] See n. 148.

[150] "But no unclean body enters, with one exception, which is commonly called by the philosophers the green Lion." * (Maier, p. 464, and Ripley, *Opera omnia*, p. 139.)

[151] Maier (p. 427) adds: "because the earth is depopulated of its spirits." *

[152] Ibid.

[153] "Medium coniungendi tincturas inter solem et lunam." (Maier, p. 464, Ripley, *Opera omnia*, p. 139.)

[154] *Chymische Schrifften*, pp. 248f.

[155] *Mus. herm.*, p. 219 (Waite, I, p. 178).*

[156] Further evidence for the lion as the arcane substance can be found in "Consil. coniugii" (*Ars chemica*, p. 64), where the lion signifies the "aes Hermetis" (bronze of Hermes). Another synonym for the lion is "vitrum" (glass), which on account of its transparency was also a symbol for the soul. (Cf. Caesarius of Heisterbach, *Dialogue on Miracles*, I.32 and IV.39 (trans. by Scott and Bland, I, pp. 42 and 237.) So, too, in Morienus, who counts the lion among the three substances that have to be kept secret. ("De transmut. metallica," *Art. aurif.*, II, pp. 51f.) *Ros. phil.* (*Art. aurif.*, II, p. 229) says: "In our green Lion is the true material . . . and it is called Adrop, Azoth, or the green Duenech." *

[157] The red lion is probably a later equivalent of sulphur rubeum (from the time of Paracelsus, it would seem). Mylius (*Phil. ref.*, p. 209, and Schema 23, p. 190) equates the two lions with red and white sulphur.

[158] Khunrath, *Hyl. Chaos*, p. 325.

tefius mentions a magic use of the lion (and of the snake) throws considerable light on our symbol: he is "good" for battle,[159] and here we may recall the fighting lions and the fact that the king in the "Allegoria Merlini" began drinking the water just when he was venturing forth to war. We shall probably not be wrong if we assume that the "king of beasts," known even in Hellenistic times as a transformation stage of Helios,[160] represents the old king, the Antiquus dierum of the *Cantilena*, at a certain stage of renewal, and that perhaps in this way he acquired the singular title of "Leo antiquus." [161] At the same time he represents the king in his theriomorphic form, that is, as he appears in his unconscious state. The animal form emphasizes that the king is overpowered or overlaid by his animal side and consequently expresses himself only in animal reactions, which are nothing but emotions. Emotionality in the sense of uncontrollable affects is essentially bestial, for which reason people in this state can be approached only with the circumspection proper to the jungle,[162] or else with the methods of the animal-trainer.

406   According to the statements of the alchemists the king changes into his animal attribute, that is to say he returns to his animal nature, the psychic source of renewal. Wieland made use of this psychologem in his fairytale "Der Stein der Weisen," [163] in which the dissipated King Mark is changed into an ass, though of course the conscious model for this was the transformation of Lucius into a golden ass in Apuleius.[164]

407   Hoghelande ranks the lion with the dog.[165] The lion has indeed something of the nature of the rabid dog we met with earlier, and this brings him into proximity with sulphur, the fiery

159 "Clavis maioris sapientiae" (*Theatr. chem.*, IV, p. 238). The treatise is probably of Harranite origin.

160 Paris Magic Papyrus, line 1665 (Preisendanz, *Pap. Graec. Magic.*, I, p. 126.) The lion is emblematic of the 6th hour.

161 Ventura, *Theatr. chem.*, II, p. 289.

162 Contact with wild nature, whether it be man, animal, jungle or swollen river, requires tact, foresight, and politeness. Rhinoceroses and buffaloes do not like being surprised.

163 Wieland, *Dschinistan, oder auserlesene Feen- und Geistermärchen.*

164 As in Apuleius the ass regains his human shape by eating roses, so he does here by eating a lily. In the Paris Magic Papyrus the ass is the solar emblem of the 5th hour.

165 Also with the griffin, camel, horse, and calf. (*Theatr. chem.*, I, p. 163.)

dynamism of Sol. In the same way the lion is the "potency" of King Sol.[166]

408   The aggressive strength of the lion has, like sulphur, an evil aspect. In Honorius of Autun the lion is an allegory of Antichrist and the devil,[167] in accordance with I Peter 5 : 8: ". . . your adversary the devil, as a roaring lion, walketh about, seeking whom he may devour." But in so far as the lion and lioness are forerunners of the (incestuous) coniunctio, they come into the category of those theriomorphic pairs who spend their time fighting and copulating, e.g., cock and hen, the two serpents of the caduceus, the two dragons, etc. The lion has among other things an unmistakable erotic aspect. Thus the "Introitus apertus" says: "Learn what the doves of Diana are,[168] who conquer the lion with caresses; the green lion, I say, who in truth is the Babylonish dragon, who kills all with his venom. Learn, lastly, what the caduceus of Mercury is, wherewith he works miracles, and what are those nymphs whom he holds enchanted, if thou wouldst fulfil thy wish" (i.e., the completion of the work).[169] The reference to the "Babylonish" dragon is not altogether accidental, since in ecclesiastical language "Babylon" is thoroughly ambiguous.[170] Nicholas Flamel likewise alludes to Babylon when he says that the stink and poisonous breath of burning mercury are nothing other than the "dragon's head which goes forth with great haste from Babylon, which is surrounded by two or three milestones." [171]

409   In the "lion hunt" of Marchos [172] the lion, as we have seen, takes the place of the king. Marchos prepares a trap and the lion, attracted by the sweet smell of a stone that is obviously an

---

[166] Dorn, "Spec. phil.," *Theatr. chem.*, I, p. 301.

[167] *Sermo in Dominica in Palmis* (Migne, *P.L.*, vol. 172, col. 916): "The devil is also called Dragon and lion."

[168] Eleazar (Abraham the Jew) mentions that the doves of Diana rouse the sleeping lion. Cf. *Uraltes Chymisches Werck*, Part I, p. 86.

[169] *Mus. herm.*, p. 654. "Si voto tuo cupis potiri" might mean rather more than this, since "votum" also means "vow."

[170] Revelation 17 : 5: "Mystery, Babylon the great, the mother of harlots and abominations of the earth."

[171] Presumably two or three miles from the city. "Summarium philosophicum," *Mus. herm.*, p. 173 (Waite, I, p. 142).

[172] Mentioned in the Arabic texts as Marqūš, king of Egypt. Cf. Ruska, *Tabula Smaragdina*, p. 57.

eye-charm,[173] falls into it and is swallowed by the magic stone. "And this stone, which the lion loves, is a woman." [174] The trap was covered by a "glass roof," and the interior, called by Senior the "cucurbita," is here called the "thalamus" (bridal chamber). The lion therefore falls like a bridegroom into the bridal chamber, where the magic stone that is "good for the eyes" and is a woman, lies on a bed of coals. This stone swallows (*transglutit*) the lion "so that nothing more of him was to be seen." This is a parallel of the Arisleus vision, where Beya causes Gabricus to disappear into her body.

410   In the "lion hunt" the incest, though veiled, is clear enough. The love-affair is projected on the lion, the animal nature or "accrescent soul" of the king; in other words it is enacted in his unconscious or in a dream. Because of his ambiguous character the lion is well suited to take over the role of this indecorous lover. As the king is represented by his animal and his mother by the magic stone, the royal incest can take place as though it were happening somewhere "outside," in quite another sphere than the personal world of the king and his mother. Indeed the marriage not only seems to be "unnatural" but is actually intended to be so. The tabooed incest is imposed as a task and, as the wealth of allegories shows, it is always in some symbolical form and never concrete. One has the impression that this "sacral" act, of whose incestuous nature the alchemists were by no means unconscious, was not so much banished by them into the *cucurbita* or glass-house but was taking place in it all the time. Whoever wished to commit this act in its true sense would therefore have to get outside himself as if into an external glass-house, a round *cucurbita* which represented the microcosmic space of the psyche. A little reason would teach us that we do not need to get "outside ourselves" but merely a little deeper *into* ourselves to experience the reality of incest and much else besides, since in each of us slumbers the "beastlike" primitive who may be roused by the doves of Diana (n. 168). This would account for the widespread suspicion that nothing good can come out of the psyche. Undoubtedly the hierosgamos of the substances is a projection of unconscious contents. These con-

173 "The stone which he who knows, places on his eyes." *
174 "Et hic lapis, quem diligit Leo, est foemina."

tents, it is usually concluded, therefore belong to the psyche and, like the psyche itself, are "inside" man, Q.E.D. As against this the fact remains that only a very few people are or ever were conscious of having any incestuous fantasies worth mentioning. If such fantasies are present at all they are *not yet* conscious, like the collective unconscious in general. An analysis of dreams and other products of the unconscious is needed to make these fantasies visible. To that end considerable resistances have to be overcome, as though one were entering a strange territory, a region of the psyche to which one feels no longer related, let alone identical with it; and whoever has strayed into that territory, either out of negligence or by mistake, feels outside himself and a stranger in his own house. I think one should take cognizance of these facts and not attribute to our personal psyche everything that appears as a psychic content. After all, we would not do this with a bird that happened to fly through our field of vision. It may well be a prejudice to restrict the psyche to being "inside the body." In so far as the psyche has a non-spatial aspect, there may be a psychic "outside-the-body," a region so utterly different from "my" psychic space that one has to get outside oneself or make use of some auxiliary technique in order to get there. If this view is at all correct, the alchemical consummation of the royal marriage in the *cucurbita* could be understood as a synthetic process in the psyche "outside" the ego.[175]

411　As I have said, the fact that one can get into this territory somehow or other does not mean that it belongs to me personally. The ego is Here and Now, but the "outside-of-the-ego" is an alien There, both earlier and later, before and after.[176] So it is not surprising that the primitive mind senses the psyche outside the ego as an alien country, inhabited by the spirits of the dead. On a rather higher level it takes on the character of a shadowy semi-reality, and on the level of the ancient cultures the shadows of that land beyond have turned into ideas. In Gnostic-Christian circles these were developed into a dogmatic, hierarchically arranged cosmogonic and chiliastic system which

175 Cf. my "Synchronicity: An Acausal Connecting Principle," pars. 949ff.
176 Considering, that is to say, that time is psychically relative, as the ESP experiments have shown. Cf. the writings of J. B. Rhine.

appears to us moderns as an involuntary, symbolic statement of the psyche concerning the structure of the psychic non-ego.[177]

412   This region, if still seen as a spectral "land beyond," appears to be a whole world in itself, a macrocosm. If, on the other hand, it is felt as "psychic" and "inside," it seems like a microcosm of the smallest proportions, on a par with the race of dwarfs in the casket, described in Goethe's poem "The New Melusine," or like the interior of the *cucurbita* in which the alchemists beheld the creation of the world, the marriage of the royal pair, and the homunculus.[178] Just as in alchemical philosophy the Anthroparion or homunculus corresponds, as the lapis, to the Anthropos, so the chymical weddings have their dogmatic parallels in the marriage of the Lamb, the union of sponsus and sponsa, and the hierosgamos of the mother of the gods and the son.

413   This apparent digression from our theme seemed to me necessary in order to give the reader some insight into the intricate and delicate nature of the lion-symbol, whose further implications we must now proceed to discuss.

414   The blood of the green lion drunk by the queen is handed to her in a "golden cup of Babylon." This refers to the "great whore" in Rev. 17 : 1ff., "that sitteth upon many waters, with whom the kings of the earth have committed fornication, and the inhabitants of the earth have been made drunk with the wine of her fornication . . . having a golden cup in her hand full of abominations and filthiness of her fornication . . ."

---

[177] I am aware of the problematical nature of this conception. But those who know the material will admit that it is no easy task to express this subtle but very important difference in conceptual terms. In actual practice the difference is immediately apparent, since, compared with personal contents, the products of the non-ego often have the quite specific character of "revelation," and are therefore felt as being inspired by an alien presence, or as perceptions of an object independent of the ego. Archetypal experiences often have a numinous effect and for that reason are of the greatest importance in psychotherapy.

[178] As this discussion started with the concept of Leo, I would like to draw the reader's attention to Bruno Goetz's novel *Das Reich ohne Raum* (1919). Goetz gives an excellent description of that feverish atmosphere, which ends with the sorcerer shrinking down a pair of lovers and putting them in a glass phial. This erotic fever seems to be connected with Leo, for a passage in the "Lion Hunt" runs: "His mother said to him: O Marchos, must this fire be lighter than the heat of fever? Marchos said to her: O mother, let it be in the state of fever. I return and enkindle that fire" *—the fire in the pit that serves Leo as a bridal bed. (Cf. Senior, *De chemia*, p. 63.)

415   The whore (*meretrix*) is a well-known figure in alchemy. She characterizes the arcane substance in its initial, "chaotic," maternal state. The "Introitus apertus" says that the chaos is like a mother of the metals. It is also called "our Luna" before the royal diadem is extracted from the "menstruum of our whore," [179] i.e., before the king is reborn from the moon-mother. The "Tractatus aureus de lapide" says of the arcane substance: "That noble whore Venus [180] is clothed and enveloped in abounding colour." This colour "has a reddish appearance." [181] The nobility of this Venus derives from the fact that she is also the queen, the "chaste bride" of the king.[182] In his "Practica de lapide" Basilius Valentinus says: "This tincture is the rose [183] of our Masters, of Tyrian hue, called also the red blood of the dragon, described by many, and the purple cloak [184] . . . with which the queen is covered." [185] A variant says: "That precious substance is the Venus of the ancients, the hermaphrodite, who has two sexes." [186] Maier writes: "In our chemistry there is Venus and Cupid. For Psyche is the female, Cupid the male, who is held to be the dragon." [187] The "opus ad rubeum" (reddening) takes place in the second house of Venus (Libra).[188] Accord-

---

179 *Mus. herm.*, pp. 653f. (Waite, II, p. 166).

180 In Abu'l Qasim (Holmyard, pp. 419f.) Venus is nicknamed "the noble, the impure, the green lion, the father of colours, the peacock of the Pleiades, the phoenix."

181 *Mus. herm.*, pp. 30f. (Waite, I, pp. 31f.). Quotation from Basilius Valentinus.

182 The contradiction between *meretrix* and *sponsa* is of very ancient origin: Ishtar, the "beloved" of the Song of Songs, is on the one hand the harlot of the gods (the "hierodule of heaven," Belti, the Black One), but on the other hand she is the mother and virgin. (Wittekindt, *Das Hohe Lied*, pp. 11f., 17, 24.) Unperturbed by the identity of the arcane substance with Venus, which he himself asserts, Khunrath (*Hyl. Chaos*, p. 62) calls the mother of the lapis a virgin and a "generatio casta" (chaste generation). Or again, he speaks of the "virgin womb of Chaos" (p. 75), inspired less by Christian tradition than by the insistence of the archetype, which had already prompted the same statements about Ishtar. Mother, daughter, sister, bride, matron, and whore are always combined in the anima archetype.

183 Concerning the rose, see infra, pars. 419f.

184 The richness of Venus's colours is also praised by Basilius Valentinus in his treatise on the seven planets (*Chymische Schrifften*, p. 167). Cf. supra, par. 140, n. 124.   185 *Mus. herm.*, p. 399 (Waite, I, p. 330).

186 D'Espagnet, *Bibliotheca Chemica*, II, p. 653.

187 *Symb. aur. mensae*, p. 178.

188 D'Espagnet, *Arcanum Hermeticae philosophiae opus* (1653), p. 82.

ingly the *Turba* remarks that Venus "precedes the sun." [189]
Flamel takes Venus as an important component of the arcane
substance; in an apostrophe to the Magnesia he says: "Thou
bearest within thee the many-formed image of Venus, the cup-
bearer and fire-spitting servant," [190] the latter referring to the
sulphurous aspect of Mercurius. Mercurius also plays the role
of cup-bearer in the *Cantilena*. In Flamel the lapis is born of the
conjunction of "Venus pugnax" (fighting Venus) [191] and Mercurius—evidently a reference to the quarrelling that precedes
their union (cf. the fighting lions). In Valentinus's poem on the
prima materia lapidis Venus is identified with the fountain, the
mother and bride of the king, in which her "fixed" father is
drowned:

> A stone there is, and yet no stone,
> In it doth Nature work alone.
> From it there welleth forth a fount
> In which her Sire, the Fixed, is drown'd:
> His body and life absorbed therein
> Until the soul's restored agen.[192]

416   In other texts Venus represents the queen at the wedding,
as in the "Introitus apertus": "See to it that you prepare the
couch of Venus carefully, then lay her on the marriage bed,"
etc.[193] In general, Venus appears as the feminine aspect of the
king, or as we should say, his anima. Thus Valentinus says of
Adam and Venus in the bath:

> So saith the Wise Man: Nought they be
> Except the Double Mercurie!

The King in the bath and the *connubium* with Venus [194] or with

189 "Venus, however, precedes the Sun, since she is eastern." * Sermo 67 (ed. Ruska),
p. 166.
190 *Theatr. chem.*, I, p. 883. The magnesia is also called "aphroselinum Orientis,"
the moonstone of the East (ibid., p. 885).
191 Her classical cognomen is "armata." According to Pernety (*Dict. mytho-hermétique*, p. 518) Venus is bound to Mars by a fire which is of the same nature as
the sun. Cf. the bull-slaying Venus with the sword in Lajard, *Recherches sur le
culte de Vénus*, Pl. IXff.
192 *Chymische Schrifften*, pp. 73f. Cf. infra, par. 547.
193 The text continues: "And in the fire you will see an emblem of the great
Work: black, the peacock's tail, white, yellow, and red." * *Mus. herm.*, p. 683
(Waite, II, p. 186).
194 Obscenely described in Figulus, *Rosarium novum Olympicum*, I, p. 73.

the mother are the same thing: the "man encompassed by the woman." Sometimes he and sometimes she is hermaphroditic,[195] because at bottom they are nothing other than Mercurius duplex. Venus or the whore corresponds to the erotic aspect of the lion, who in turn is an attribute of the king. As in the Apocalypse the seven-headed dragon is the riding-animal of the Great Whore, so in Valentinus the lion is the mount of Mercurius duplex (portrayed in his feminine aspect).[196] Khunrath equates Venus with the green lion.[197] Since Sulphur is to Sol as Leo is to Rex, we can see why Khunrath regards Venus as the *anima vegetativa* of sulphur.[198] The most subtle substance must, when mixed with Sol, be preserved in a bottle whose stopper is marked with the sign of the cross,[199] just as an evil spirit is banished by a crucifix.[200] The relation of the stone to Venus occurs as early as the Greek texts, which speak of the "Cytherean stone" and the "pearl of Cythera." [201] In the Arabic "Book of Krates" [202] Venus is endowed with tincturing power; she is therefore called "scribe." Since she holds the vessel from which quicksilver continually flows, the word "écrivain" very probably refers to Thoth-Mercurius. In the vision of Krates Venus appears surrounded by a number of Indians who shoot arrows at him. This image occurs again in Senior's vision of Hermes Trismegistus, at whom nine eagles shot their arrows. Mercurius is the archer who, chemically, dissolves the gold, and, morally, pierces the soul with the dart of passion. As Kyllenios he is identical with Cupid, who likewise shoots arrows in Rosencreutz's *Chymical Wedding*.[203]

417   The corrupt nature of Venus is stressed in "Rosinus ad Sarratantam":

195 The androgynous Venus is a very ancient prototype. Cf. Lajard, "Mémoire sur une représentation figurée de la Vénus orientale androgyne," likewise his *Recherches sur le culte de Vénus*, Pl. I, no. 1.   196 *Chymische Schrifften*, p. 62.
197 *Hyl. Chaos*, p. 91.
198 Ibid., p. 233. Other synonyms are *Sal Veneris, Vitriolum Veneris, Sal Saturni, leo rubeus et viridis, sulphur vitrioli*. They are all the *scintilla animae mundi*, the active principle that manifests itself in powerful instincts. Cf. Khunrath, *Hyl. Chaos*, p. 264.
199 Mylius, *Phil. ref.*, p. 17.
200 See Grimm's fairytale of the "Spirit in the Bottle," cited in my "The Spirit Mercurius," par. 239.
201 Berthelot, *Alch. grecs*, V, vii, 18 and 19.
202 Berthelot, *Chimie au moyen âge*, III, pp. 61ff.
203 "The Spirit Mercurius," par. 278.

And mark that Nature in the beginning of her origin intends to make the Sun or the Moon, but cannot, because of Venus, [who is] a corrupt [and] mixed quicksilver, or because of the foetid earth. Wherefore, as a child in its mother's womb accidentally contracts a weakness and a corruption by reason of the place, although the sperm was clean, [and] the child is nevertheless leprous and unclean because of the corrupt womb, so it is with all imperfect metals, which are corrupted by Venus and the foetid earth.[204]

418   Lastly, I would mention the king's daughter in the play in the *Chymical Wedding,* who was chosen as the bride but because of her coquetry was made captive by the King of the Moors. She agrees to be his concubine, and thus proves herself a regular *meretrix*. Rosencreutz's visit to the sleeping Venus shows that this two-faced goddess is somehow secretly connected with the opus.[205]

419   Evidently on account of its close connection with Venus the green lion has, surprisingly enough, rose-coloured blood, as mentioned by Dorn [206] and by his contemporary, Khunrath.[207] The latter ascribes rose-coloured blood to the *filius macrocosmi* as well.[208] This peculiarity of the green lion's blood establishes its connection not only with the filius, a well-known Christ parallel, but above all with the rose, whose symbolism produced not only the popular title "Rosarium" (rose-garden) but also the "Rosencreuz" (Rosie Cross). The white and the red rose [209] are syno-

---

204 *Art. aurif.,* I, p. 318.*

205 This is also suggested by the mysterious passage in Dorn: "Seek your lion in the East and the eagle to the South in taking up this work of ours . . . you should direct your way to the south; so shall you obtain your desire in Cyprus, of which nothing more may be said." * ("Congeries Paracelsicae," *Theatr. chem.,* I, p. 610.) For the alchemists Cyprus is definitely associated with Venus. In this connection I would also refer to Dorn's commentary on the *Vita longa* of Paracelsus, discussed in my "Paracelsus as a Spiritual Phenomenon." It is concerned with the "characteristics of Venus" in Paracelsus, which Dorn interprets as the "shield and buckler of love" (ibid., par. 234).

206 The idea of the rose-coloured blood seems to go back to Paracelsus: "Therefore I say to you (saith Paracelsus) . . ." (Dorn, *Theatr. chem.,* I, p. 609).

207 *Hyl. Chaos,* pp. 93 and 196.

208 On p. 276 he speaks of the "rose-coloured blood and aethereal water that flowed from the side of the Son of the Great World."

209 Figulus (*Rosarium novum Olympicum,* Part 2, p. 15) says: "I will not forbear to admonish thee not to reveal to anyone, however dear, the treasure of our secrets, lest the stinking goats browse upon the red and white roses of our rose-garden."

nyms for the *albedo* [210] and *rubedo*. The tincture is "of a rosy colour" and corresponds to the blood of Christ, who is "compared and united" with the stone.[211] He is the "heavenly foundation-stone and corner-stone." [212] The rose-garden is a "garden enclosed" and, like the rose, a soubriquet of Mary, the parallel of the "locked" prima materia.[213]

420 The relation of the love-goddess to red dates back to ancient times.[214] Scarlet [215] is the colour of the Great Whore of Babylon and her beast. Red is the colour of sin.[216] The rose is also an attribute of Dionysus. Red and rose-red are the colour of blood, a synonym for the *aqua permanens* and the soul, which are extracted from the prima materia and bring "dead" bodies to life.[217] The prima materia is called "meretrix" and is equated with "Great Babylon," just as are the dragon and the lion with the dragon of "Babel." The stone, the *filius regius,* is the son of this whore. In ecclesiastical tradition the son of the whore is Antichrist, begotten by the devil, as we read in the "Elucidarium" of Honorius of Autun.[218]

421 Certain of the ecclesiastical symbols prove to be acutely dualistic, and this is also true of the rose. Above all it is an allegory of Mary and of various virtues. Its perfume is the odour of sanctity, as in the case of St. Elizabeth and St. Teresa. At the same time it symbolizes human beauty (*venustas*), indeed the lust of the world (*voluptas mundi*).[219]

210 "The white rose is completed in summer-time in the East" * (Mylius, *Phil. ref.,* p. 124).   211 See infra, par. 485.

212 "Aquarium sapientum," *Mus. herm.,* p. 118 (Waite, I, p. 103).

213 "Gloria Mundi," *Mus. herm.,* p. 218 (Waite, I, p. 178): ". . . how the garden is to be opened, and the noble roses are to be seen in their field." *

214 Cf. "rosy Paphian," "rose-hued Aphrodite," "rose-hued Cyprian," etc. (Bruchmann, *Epitheta Deorum quae apud poetas Graecos leguntur,* s.v. Aphrodite, pp. 65, 68).

215 κόκκινος, *coccineus.* Cf. Rev. 17 : 4f.

216 Isaiah 1 : 18: ". . . though your sins be as scarlet, they shall be as white as snow; though they be red like crimson, they shall be as wool."

217 In keeping with these associations, the adulterous queen in Wieland's alchemical fairytale was changed into a pink goat.

218 "Antichrist shall be born in great Babylon of a whore of the tribe of Dan. He will be filled with the devil in his mother's womb and brought up by witches in Corozain" * (Migne, *P.L.,* vol. 172, col. 1163).

219 "Like to the rose that blooms in the midst of the thorns that enclose it,
     So are the pleasures of love never unshared with its gall." *

(Georgius Camerarius, cited in Picinellus, *Mundus Symbolicus,* I, pp. 665f.)

422   Like the rose, the figure of the mother-beloved shines in all the hues of heavenly and earthly love. She is the chaste bride and whore who symbolizes the prima materia, which "nature left imperfected." It is clear from the material we have cited that this refers to the anima. She is that piece of chaos which is everywhere and yet hidden, she is that vessel of contradictions and many colours—a totality in the form of a *massa confusa,* yet a substance endowed with every quality in which the splendour of the hidden deity can be revealed.

423   The food of the Queen Mother—peacock's flesh and lion's blood—consists of the goddess's own attributes, that is to say she eats and drinks herself. The "Consilium coniugii" formulates this as follows: "And so at length it sinks down into one content through saturation with the one ferment, water, for water is the ferment of water." [220] It is always the same idea, which is best expressed by the uroboros. Unexpectedly but not surprisingly we come across a similar formulation in ecclesiastical literature, in the remark of St. John Chrysostom that Christ was the first to eat his own flesh and drink his own blood (at the institution of the Last Supper).[221] Tertullian says: "In the same way the Lord applied to himself two Greek letters, the first and the last, as figures of the beginning and end which are united in himself. For just as Alpha continues on until it reaches Omega, and Omega completes the cycle back again to Alpha, so he meant to show that in him is found the course of all things from the beginning to the end and from the end back to the beginning, so that every divine dispensation should end in him through whom it began." [222] This thought corresponds exactly to what the alchemists sought to express by the uroboros, the ἓν τὸ πᾶν. The uroboros is a very ancient pagan symbol, and we have no reason to suppose that the idea of a self-generating and self-devouring being was borrowed from Christianity, e.g., from Tertullian, although the analogy with Christ, who as the one God begets himself and voluntarily offers himself for sacrifice, and then in the rite of the Eucharist, through the words of the consecration, performs his own immolation, is very striking. The concept of the uroboros must be much older, and may ultimately go back to

---

220 "Consil. coniugii," *Ars chemica,* p. 220.*
221 *In Matth. Homiliae,* 72 (73) (Migne, *P.G.,* vol. 57–58, col. 739).*
222 *Treatises on Marriage and Remarriage,* trans. by Le Saint, pp. 78f.*

ancient Egyptian theology, to the doctrine of the homoousia of the Father-God with the divine son, Pharaoh.

424   In the *Cantilena,* the mythologem of the uroboros is unexpectedly, and most unusually, translated into feminine form: it is not the father and son who merge into one another, but the mother who merges with her own substance, "eating her own tail" or "impregnating herself," as the king in the "Allegoria Merlini" drank his "own" water.[223] The queen is in a condition of psychic pregnancy: the anima has become activated and sends her contents into consciousness. These correspond to the peacock's flesh and the lion's blood. If the products of the anima (dreams, fantasies, visions, symptoms, chance ideas, etc.) are assimilated, digested, and integrated, this has a beneficial effect on the growth and development ("nourishment") of the psyche. At the same time the *cibatio* and *imbibitio* of the anima-mother indicate the integration and completion of the entire personality. The anima becomes creative when the old king renews himself in her. Psychologically the king stands first of all for Sol, whom we have interpreted as consciousness. But over and above that he represents a dominant of consciousness, such as a generally accepted principle or a collective conviction or a traditional view. These systems and ruling ideas "age" and thereby forcibly bring about a "metamorphosis of the gods" as described in Spitteler's *Olympian Spring.* It seldom occurs as a definite collective phenomenon. Mostly it is a change in the individual which may, under certain conditions, affect society "when the time is fulfilled." In the individual it only means that the ruling idea is in need of renewal and alteration if it is to deal adequately with the changed outer or inner conditions.

425   The fact that the king played a large role in medieval alchemy for several hundred years proves that, from about the thirteenth century onwards, the traces of the king's renewal surviving from Egyptian and Hellenistic times began to gain in importance because they had acquired a new meaning. For as the West started to investigate nature, till then completely unknown, the doctrine of the *lumen naturae* began to germinate too. Ecclesiastical doctrine and scholastic philosophy had both

---

[223] This pun is permissible, since one of the synonyms for the *aqua permanens* is "urina puerorum."

proved incapable of shedding any light on the nature of the physical world. The conjecture thereupon arose that just as the mind revealed its nature in the light of divine revelation, so nature herself must possess a "certain luminosity" which could become a source of enlightenment. It is therefore understandable that for those individuals whose particular interest lay in the investigation of natural things the dogmatic view of the world should lose its force as the *lumen naturae* gained in attraction, even though the dogma itself was not directly doubted. The more serious alchemists, if we are to believe their statements, were religious people who had no thought of criticizing revealed truth. There is in the literature of alchemy, so far as I can judge, no attack on dogma. The only thing of this kind is a depreciation of the Aristotelian philosophy sponsored by the Church in favour of Hermetic Neoplatonism.[224] Not only were the old Masters not critical of ecclesiastical doctrine, they were, on the contrary, convinced that their discoveries, real or imaginary, would enrich the doctrine of the correspondence of heavenly and earthly things, since they endeavoured to prove that the "mystery of faith" was reflected in the world of nature.[225] They could not guess that their passion for investigating nature would detract as much as it did from revealed truth, and that their scientific interests could be aroused only as the fascination of dogma began to pall. And so, as in dreams, there grew up in their unconscious the compensating image of the king's renewal.

426   These considerations make it the more comprehensible that it was a cleric who wrote the *Cantilena*. It is indeed something of a descent to the underworld when he makes Mercurius, "bearing the dart of passion," the emblem of Cupid,[226] hand the queen the blood-potion in a "golden cup of Babylon." This, as

---

224 Dorn ("Spec. Phil., "*Theatr. chem.*, I, p. 271) writes: "Whoever wishes to learn the alchemical art, let him learn not the philosophy of Aristotle, but that which teaches the truth . . . for his teaching consists entirely in amphibology, which is the best of all cloaks for lies. When he censured Plato and others for the sake of gaining renown, he could find no more commodious instrument than that which he used for his censure, namely amphibology, attacking his writings on the one hand, defending them by subterfuge on the other, and the reverse; and this kind of sophistry is to be found in all his writings." *

225 For the alchemists the world was an image and symbol of God.

226 Mercurius is also an "archer."

we have seen, is the golden cup "full of the abomination and filthiness of fornication," and it is quite obvious that she is being ruthlessly regaled with her own psychic substances. These are animal substances she has to integrate, the "accrescent soul"— peacock and lion with their positive and negative qualities; and the draught is given to her in the cup of fornication, which emphasizes still more the erotic nature of the lion, his lust and greed. Such an integration amounts to a widening of consciousness through profound insight.

427   But why should such an unpalatable diet be prescribed for the queen? Obviously because the old king lacked something, on which account he grew senile: the dark, chthonic aspect of nature. And not only this but the sense that all creation was in the image of God, the antique feeling for nature, which in the Middle Ages was considered a false track and an aberration. Dark and unfathomable as the earth is, its theriomorphic symbols do not have only a reductive meaning, but one that is prospective and spiritual. They are paradoxical, pointing upwards and downwards at the same time. If contents like these are integrated in the queen, it means that her consciousness is widened in both directions. This diet will naturally benefit the regeneration of the king by supplying what was lacking before. Contrary to appearances, this is not *only* the darkness of the animal sphere, but rather a spiritual nature or a natural spirit which even has its analogies with the mystery of faith, as the alchemists were never tired of emphasizing.

428   During her pregnancy, therefore, the queen undergoes something akin to a psychotherapeutic treatment, whereby her consciousness is enriched by a knowledge of the collective unconscious and, we may assume, by her inner participation in the conflict between her spiritual and chthonic nature. Often the law governing the progressive widening of consciousness makes the evaluation of the heights and depths into a moral task transcending the limits of convention. Failure to know what one is doing acts like guilt and must be paid for as dearly. The conflict may even turn out to be an advantage since, without it, there could be no reconciliation and no birth of a supraordinate third thing. The king could then be neither renewed nor reborn. The conflict is manifested in the long sickness of the queen.

429 *Verse 18*

> Thus great with Child, nine months she languishèd
> And Bath'd her with the Teares which she had shed
> For his sweete sake, who from her should be Pluckt
> Full-gorg'd with Milke which now the Greene-Lyon suckt.[227]

The uroboric relationship between queen and lion is quite evident here: she drinks his blood while he sucks her milk. This singular notion is explained by what we would consider an offensive identification of the queen with the mother of God, who, personifying humanity, takes God into her lap and suckles him at her breast. The lion, as an allegory of Christ, returns the gift by giving humanity his blood. This interpretation is confirmed in the later verses. Angelus Silesius makes use of a similar image in his epigram on the "humanized" God:

> God drank the Virgin's milk, left us his wine;
> How human things have humanized divine! [228]

430 *Verse 19*

> Her Skin in divers Colours did appeare,
> Now Black, then Greene, annon 'twas Red and Cleare.
> Oft-times she would sit upright in her Bed,
> And then again repose her Troubled Head.[229]

This display of colours is an indication of the queen's Venus and peacock nature (*cauda pavonis*). Psychologically it means that during the assimilation of the unconscious the personality passes through many transformations, which show it in different lights and are followed by ever-changing moods. These changes presage the coming birth.

[227] "Impraegnata igitur graviter languebat
   Certe novem mensibus in quibus madebat
   Fusis ante lachrymis quam parturiebat
   Lacte manans, viridis Leo quod sugebat."

[228] *Cherubinischer Wandersmann*, III, 11.

[229] "Eius tunc multicolor cutis apparebat
   Nunc nigra, nunc viridis, nunc rubea fiebat,
   Sese quod multoties sursum erigebat
   Et deorsum postea sese reponebat."

431 *Verse 20*

Thrice Fifty Nights she lay in grievous Plight,
As many Daies in Mourning sate upright.
The King Revivèd was in Thirty more,
His Birth was Fragrant as the Prim-Rose Flower.[230]

432   There are, in alchemy, two main kinds of smell, the "stench of graves" and the perfume of flowers, the latter being a symbol of resurgent life. In ecclesiastical allegory and in the lives of the saints a sweet smell is one of the manifestations of the Holy Ghost, as also in Gnosticism. In alchemy the Holy Ghost and Sapientia are more or less identical; hence the smell of flowers attests that the rebirth of the king is a gift of the Holy Ghost or of Sapientia, thanks to whom the regeneration process could take place.

433 *Verses 21–24*

Her Wombe which well proportion'd was at first
Is now Enlarg'd a Thousand fold at least,
That it bear Witnesse to his Genesis:
The End by Fires the best Approved is.

Her Chamber without Corners smoothly stands,
With Walls erected like her outstretched hands;
Or else the Fruit of her ripe Womb should spoil,
And a sicke Son reward her labouring Toil.

A burning Stove was plac'd beneath her Bed,
And on the same another Flourishèd:
Trimm'd up with Art, and very Temperate,
Lest her fine Limbes should freeze for lack of Heate.

Her Chamber doore was Lock'd and Bolted fast,
Admitting none to Vex her, first or last;

230 "Centum et quinquaginta noctibus languebat
    Et diebus totidem moerens residebat,
    In triginta postmodum rex reviviscebat,
    Cuius ortus vernulo flore redolebat."

The Furnace-mouth was likewise Fasten'd so
That thence no Vaporous Matter forth could go.[231]

This is the image of the homunculus in the Hermetic vessel!

434   *Verse 25*

And when the Child's Limbs there had putrefy'd,
The Foulness of the Flesh was laid aside,
Making her [232] fair as Luna, when anon
She coils towards [233] the Splendour of the Sun.[234]

This is an attempt to describe the transformation in the sealed chamber. It is not clear whether the mother has already given birth to the child, and whether "there" (*ibi*) refers to the chamber or to the gravid uterus. The latter seems to me more probable in view of the next verse. Altogether verse 25 is obscure and clumsy in the extreme. The only thing to emerge with any clar-

[231] "Ejus magnitudine primo coaequatus
         Venter in millecuplum crevit ampliatus,
         Ut super principio suo sit testatus
         Finis perfectissime ignibus probatus.

"Erat sine scopulis thalamus et planus,
Et cum parietibus erectus ut manus
Prolongatus aliter sequeretur vanus
Fructus neque filius nasceretur sanus."

"Stufa subtus lectulum erat collocata,
Una atque alia artificiata
Erat super lectulum valde temperata
Membrana frigescerent ejus delicata.

"Eratque cubiculi ostium firmatum,
Nulli praebens aditum suum vel gravatum,
Et camini etiam os redintegratum
Ab inde ne faceret vapor evolatum."

[232] [*Illam* could also refer to *tetredo*, 'foulness.'—TRANS.]

[233] *Spirificare* = *spiram facere*, 'to make a coil, wind like a snake.' *Spiritum facere* does not seem to me credible. *Sine coeli polis* (without the poles of heaven) is probably put in to fill up the line, and means no more than that this process does not take place in heaven but in the *cucurbita*.

[234] "Postquam computruerunt ibi membra prolis
          Carneae tetredinem deponebat molis,
          Illam Lunae similans sine coeli polis
          Postquam spirificans in splendorem Solis."

ity is the death and decomposition of the foetus in the uterus or in the chamber, and then the sudden appearance of Luna in the place of the mother after the "foulness of the flesh" had fallen away. Anyhow there is a tangle of thoughts here such as is frequently found in the texts. We must suppose that the poet meant something sensible with his apparent jumble of words, and that only his limited capacity for poetic expression prevented him from making himself intelligible. He was in fact trying to express a very difficult thought, namely the nature of the critical transformation. Chemically speaking, the "mother" overflowing with milk and tears is the solution, the "mother liquid" or matrix. She is the "water" in which the old king, as in the Arisleus vision, is dissolved into atoms. Here he is described as a *foetus in utero*. The dissolution signifies his death, and the uterus or *cucurbita* becomes his grave, that is, he disappears in the solution. At this moment something in the nature of a miracle occurs: the material solution loses its earthy heaviness, and solvent and solute together pass into a higher state immediately following the *cauda pavonis*, namely the *albedo*. This denotes the first stage of completion and is identified with Luna. Luna in herself is spirit, and she at once joins her husband Sol, thus initiating the second and usually final stage, the *rubedo*. With that the work is completed, and the lapis, a living being endowed with soul and spirit and an incorruptible body, has taken shape.

435   We know that what hovered before the mind of the alchemist during this transformation was the almost daily miracle of transubstantiation at the Mass. This would very definitely have been the case with Canon Ripley. We have already seen from a number of examples how much religious conceptions were mixed up with his alchemical interests. The queen in the *Cantilena* is neither a wife nor mother in the first place but a "tutelary madonna" who adopts the king as her son—an indication that she stands in the same relationship to the king as Mater Ecclesia to the believer. He dies and is buried as if in the Church or in consecrated ground, where he awaits resurrection in a glorified body.

436   The elevation of the "matrix," the chemical solution, from the state of materiality to Luna is the classic allegory of the Church, as Ripley doubtless knew. The goddess who suddenly

314

intervenes in the opus is depicted in the *Mutus liber,* where she appears equally suddenly during the procedure, as a naked female figure crowned with the sign of the moon and bearing a child in her arms. The miracle is there described as an intervention of the gods,[235] who, like god-parents, take the place of the earthly parents and arrange for the spiritual procreation of the *foetus spagyricus.* It is inevitable that Luna should stand for the Virgin and/or the Church in the *Cantilena* because the *senex-puer* is described by Ripley himself as the "Ancient of Days." Since the mother at this moment has brought about the histolysis of the old king, so that only a single homogeneous solution remains, we must assume that Luna, appearing in the place of the mother, has become identical with the solution and now carries the king in her body as her adopted son. This gives the king immortality in a divine and incorruptible body. In the *Mutus liber* there then follows an adoption by Sol and after that a *coniunctio Solis et Lunae,* and the adoptive child, now consubstantial with Sol and Luna, is included in the ceremony.

437   Something of this sort seems to occur in the *Cantilena:* Luna and her adoptive son are at first identical in one and the same solution. When Luna takes over this condition she is presumably in her *novilunium* and hastens to her union with Sol. The new moon is associated with uncanniness and snakiness, as we saw earlier.[236] I therefore interpret "spirificans in splendorem Solis" as "winding like a snake into the radiance of the sun." Woman is morally suspect in alchemy and seems closely akin to the serpent of paradise, and for this and other reasons Canon Ripley might easily think of the new moon's approach to the sun as a "spiram facere." [237] It should not be forgotten that a learned alchemist of the fifteenth century would have a knowledge of symbols at least as great as our own in the present exposition (if you discount the psychology), and in some cases perhaps greater. (There are still numerous unpublished MSS. in existence to which I have had no access.)

235 *Mutus liber.* Luna is shown in Pl. 5, and Sol or Phoebus Apollo in Pl. 6.
236 Supra, pars. 19ff., 172f.
237 As I have shown earlier, the alchemists thought the conjunction of the new moon was something sinister. Cf. particularly the "viperinus conatus" of the mother (supra, par. 14), a parallel of the early death of the mythological sun-god.

Verses 26–27

> Her time being come, the Child Conceiv'd before
> Issues re-borne out of her Wombe once more;
> And thereupon resumes a Kingly State,
> Possessing fully Heaven's Propitious Fate.
>
> The Mother's Bed which erstwhile was a Square
> Is shortly after made Orbicular;
> And everywhere the Cover, likewise Round
> With Luna's Lustre brightly did abound.[238]

439   The second strophe confirms that the entire solution has changed into Luna, and not only is *it* transformed, but the vessel containing the matrix. The "bed," which before was a square, now becomes round like the full moon. The "cooperculum" (cover) points more to a vessel than a bed, and this cover shines like the moon. As the cover is obviously the top part of the vessel it indicates the place where the moon rises, that is, where the content of the vessel is sublimated. The squaring of the circle, a favourite synonym for the magistery, has been accomplished. Anything angular is imperfect and has to be superseded by the perfect, here represented by the circle.[239] The mother is both content (mother liquid) and container, the two being often identified; for instance, the vessel is equated with the *aqua permanens*.[240] The production of the round and perfect means that the son issuing from the mother has attained perfection, i.e., the king has attained eternal youth and his body has become incorruptible. As the square represents the quaternio of mutually hostile elements, the circle indicates their reduction to unity. The One born of the Four is the Quinta Essentia. I need

---

[238] "Sic cum tempus aderat mater suum natum
    Prius quem conceperat, edidit renatum.
    Qui post partum regium repetebat statum,
    Possidens omnimodum foetum coeli gratum.

    "Lectus matris extitit qui quadrangularis
    Post notata tempora fit orbicularis,
    Cuius cooperculum formae circularis
    Undequaque candeat fulgor ut Lunaris."

[239] Cf. *Psychology and Alchemy*, par. 116.
[240] Ibid., par. 338.

not go into the psychology of this process here as I have done so already in *Psychology and Alchemy*.

440 *Verse 28*

> Thus from a Square, the Bed a Globe is made,
> And Purest Whiteness from the Blackest Shade;
> While from the Bed the Ruddy Son doth spring
> To grasp the Joyful Sceptre of a King.[241]

441 Vessel and content and the mother herself, who contains the father, have become the son, who has risen up from "blackest shade" to the pure whiteness of Luna and attained his redness (*rubedo*) through the *solificatio*. In him all opposites are fused together.

442 *Verse 29*

> Hence God unlock'd the Gates of Paradise,
> Rais'd him like Luna to th'Imperiall Place,
> Sublim'd him to the Heavens, and that being done,
> Crown'd him in Glory, aequall with the Sun.[242]

443 Here Ripley describes the renewal of the king and the birth of the son as the manifestation of a new redeemer—which sounds very queer indeed in the mouth of a medieval ecclesiastic. The sublimation of Luna ("uti Luna") to the "imperial place" is an unmistakable paraphrase on the one hand of the Assumption of the Virgin and on the other of the marriage of the bride, the Church. The unlocking of paradise means nothing less than the advent of God's Kingdom on earth. The attributes of sun and moon make the *filius regius* into the rearisen Primordial Man, who is the cosmos. It would be wrong to minimize the importance of this jubilee or to declare it is nonsense. One cannot dismiss all the alchemists as insane. It seems to me more advisable to examine the motives that led a cleric, of all people, to postu-

241 "Lecti sic quadrangulus factus est rotundus
Et de nigro maximo albus atque mundus
De quo statim prodiit natus rubicundus
Qui resumpsit regium sceptrum laetabundus."

242 "Hinc Deus paradysi portas reseravit,
Uti Luna candida illum decoravit,
Quam post ad imperii loca sublimavit
Soleque ignivomo digne coronavit."

late a divine revelation outside his credo. If the lapis were nothing but gold the alchemists would have been wealthy folk; if it were the panacea they would have had a remedy for all sickness; if it were the elixir they could have lived a thousand years or more. But all this would not oblige them to make religious statements about it. If nevertheless it is praised as the second coming of the Messiah one must assume that the alchemists really did mean something of the kind. Although they regarded the art as a charisma, a gift of the Holy Ghost or of the *Sapientia Dei*,[243] it was still man's work, and, even though a divine miracle was the decisive factor, the mysterious filius was still concocted artificially in a retort.

444   In the face of all this one is driven to the conjecture that medieval alchemy, which evolved out of the Arabic tradition sometime in the thirteenth century, and whose most eloquent witness is the *Aurora consurgens,* was in the last resort a continuation of the doctrine of the Holy Ghost, which never came to very much in the Church.[244] The Paraclete descends upon the single individual, who is thereby drawn into the Trinitarian process.[245] And if the spirit of procreation and life indwells in man, then God can be born in him—a thought that has not perished since the time of Meister Eckhart.[246] The verses of Angelus Silesius are in this respect quite unequivocal:

243 Angelus Silesius (*Cherub. Wandersmann,* III, 195) says of Sapientia:
    "As once a Virgin fashioned the whole earth,
      So by a Virgin it shall have rebirth."

244 That the Church has not done everything it might have been expected to do in regard to the doctrine of the Holy Ghost was a remark made to me spontaneously by Dr. Temple, the late Archbishop of Canterbury. For the psychological aspect of the doctrine of the Holy Ghost see "Dogma of the Trinity," pars. 234ff.

245 This conclusion is quite obvious in Angelus Silesius.

246 Cf. the magnificent sermon on the text "When all things were in the midst of silence" (Wisdom of Solomon 18 : 14) in Meister Eckhart (trans. by Evans, I, p. 3): "Here in time we make holiday because the eternal birth which God the Father bore and bears unceasingly in eternity is now born in time, in human nature. St. Augustine says this birth is always happening. But if it happen not in me what does it profit me? What matters is that it shall happen in me. We intend therefore to speak of this birth as happening in us, as being consummated in the virtuous soul; for it is in the perfect soul that God speaks his Word . . . There is a saying of the wise man: 'When all things were in the midst of silence, then leapt there down into me from on high, from the royal throne, a secret Word.' "

If by God's Holy Ghost thou art beguiled,
There will be born in thee the Eternal Child.

If it's like Mary, virginal and pure,
Then God will impregnate your soul for sure.

God make me pregnant, and his Spirit shadow me,
That God may rise up in my soul and shatter me.

What good does Gabriel's 'Ave, Mary' do
Unless he give me that same greeting too? [247]

445   Here Angelus expresses as a religious and psychological experience what the alchemists experienced in and through matter, and what Ripley is describing in his tortuous allegory. The nature of this experience is sufficient to explain the rapt language of certain verses in the *Cantilena*. He was speaking of something greater than the effects of grace in the sacraments: God himself, through the Holy Ghost, enters the work of man, in the form of inspiration as well as by direct intervention in the miraculous transformation. In view of the fact that such a miracle never did occur in the retort, despite repeated assertions that someone had actually succeeded in making gold, and that neither a panacea nor an elixir has demonstrably prolonged a human life beyond its due, and that no homunculus has ever flown out of the furnace—in view of this totally negative result we must ask on what the enthusiasm and infatuation of the adepts could possibly have been based.

446   In order to answer this difficult question one must bear in mind that the alchemists, guided by their keenness for research, were in fact on a hopeful path since the fruit that alchemy bore after centuries of endeavour was chemistry and its staggering discoveries. The emotional dynamism of alchemy is largely explained by a premonition of these then-unheard-of possibilities. However barren of useful or even enlightening results its labours were, these efforts, notwithstanding their chronic failure, seem to have had a psychic effect of a positive nature, something akin to satisfaction or even a perceptible increase in wisdom. Otherwise it would be impossible to explain why the alchemists did not turn away in disgust from their almost invariably futile

247 *Cherub. Wandersmann*, II, 101–104.

projects. Not that such disillusionments never came to them; indeed the futility of alchemy brought it into increasing disrepute. There remain, nevertheless, a number of witnesses who make it quite clear that their hopeless fumbling, inept as it was from the chemical standpoint, presents a very different appearance when seen from a psychological angle. As I have shown in *Psychology and Alchemy,* there occurred during the chemical procedure psychic projections which brought unconscious contents to light, often in the form of vivid visions. The medical psychologist knows today that such projections may be of the greatest therapeutic value. It was not for nothing that the old Masters identified their *nigredo* with melancholia and extolled the opus as the sovereign remedy for all "afflictions of the soul"; for they had discovered, as was only to be expected, that though their purses shrank their soul gained in stature—provided of course that they survived certain by no means inconsiderable psychic dangers. The projections of the alchemists were nothing other than unconscious contents appearing in matter, the same contents that modern psychotherapy makes conscious by the method of active imagination before they unconsciously change into projections. Making them conscious and giving form to what is unformed has a specific effect in cases where the conscious attitude offers an overcrowded unconscious no possible means of expressing itself. In these circumstances the unconscious has, as it were, no alternative but to generate projections and neurotic symptoms. The conscious milieu of the Middle Ages provided no adequate outlet for these things. The immense world of natural science lay folded in the bud, as also did that questing religious spirit which we meet in many of the alchemical treatises and which, we may well conjecture, was closely akin to the empiricism of scientific research.

447   Perhaps the most eloquent witness to this spirit was Meister Eckhart, with his idea of the birth of the son in human individuals and the resultant affiliation of man to God.[248] Part of this

248 The critical passages are: "And thus God the Father gives birth to his Son, in the very oneness of the divine nature. Mark, thus it is and in no other way that God the Father gives birth to his Son, in the ground and essence of the soul, and thus he unites himself with her." "St. John says: 'The light shineth in the darkness; it came unto its own and as many as received it became in authority sons of God; to them was given power to become God's sons.'" (Trans. by Evans, **I**, pp. 5 and 9.)

spirit was realized in Protestantism, another part was intuited by the mystics who succeeded Boehme, in particular by Angelus Silesius, who quite literally "perished in the work." He advanced even beyond Protestantism to an attitude of mind that would have needed the support of Indian or Chinese philosophy and would therefore not have been possible until the end of the nineteenth century at the earliest. In his own age Angelus could only wither away unrecognized, and this was the tragedy that befell him. A third part took shape in the empirical sciences that developed independently of all authority, and a fourth appropriated to itself the religious philosophies of the East and transplanted them with varying degrees of skill and taste in the West.

448   No thinking person will wish to claim that the present state of affairs represents a durable end-state. On the contrary, everyone is convinced that the tempo of change and transition has speeded up immeasurably. Everything has become fragmented and dissolved, and it is impossible to see how a "higher" synthesis could take place in any of the spiritual organizations that still survive without their having to be modified to an almost intolerable degree. One of the greatest obstacles to such a synthesis is sectarianism, which is always right and displays no tolerance, picking and fomenting quarrels for the holiest of reasons in order to set itself up in the place of religion and brand anyone who thinks differently as a lost sheep, if nothing worse. But have any human beings the right to totalitarian claims? This claim, certainly, is so morally dangerous that we would do better to leave its fulfilment to Almighty God rather than presume to be little gods ourselves at the expense of our fellow-men.

449   *Verse 30*

Four Elements, Brave Armes, and Polish'd well
God gave him, in the midst whereof did dwell
The Crownèd Maid, ordainèd for to be
In the Fifth Circle of the Mysterie.[249]

249 "Elementis quatuor Deus insignita
Arma tibi contulit decenter polita,
Quorum erat medio virgo redimita
Quae in quinto circulo fuit stabilita."

450   To the regenerated king, now endowed with the qualities of the cosmic Anthropos, God gives the four elements as the weapons with which he shall conquer the world. It is a figure that reminds us of the Manichaean "First Man," who, armed with the five elements, came down to fight against the darkness.[250] The elements are evidently conceived as circles, for the Quinta Essentia, the "Maid," appears in the fifth. The circular representation of the elements was well known in medieval alchemy.[251] The Maid is "crowned" (*redimita*), and in her we recognize the crowned Virgin, the Queen of Heaven, who recalls the old pictures of the *anima media natura* or *anima mundi*. She is the divine life indwelling in the world, or the pneuma that moved over the waters, implanted its seed in them, and so was held captive in the body of Creation. The *anima mundi* is the feminine half of Mercurius.[252]

451   In the *Cantilena* the Maid is the rejuvenated Queen Mother who now appears as the bride. Her redemption is achieved through the long sufferings of the mother, i.e., through the pains of the opus, which are compared to the Passion.[253]

452   The establishment of the Maid in the fifth circle is an indication that the quintessence, portraying the disharmonious elements as a unity, is equivalent to aether, the finest and most subtle substance. She therefore participates in the world of the spirit and at the same time represents the material, sublunary world. Her position corresponds on the one hand to that of Luna and on the other to that of the Blessed Virgin.

453   *Verses 31–35*

> With all delicious Unguent flowèd she
> When Purg'd from Bloody Menstruosity:
> On every side her Count'nance Brightly shone,
> She being Adorn'd with every Precious Stone.

250 Hegemonius, *Acta Archelai* (ed. Beeson), p. 10: "When the good father knew that darkness had come upon his earth, he brought forth from himself the virtue [or strength] which is called the mother of life, wherewith he surrounded the first man. These are the five elements, wind, light, water, fire, and matter; and clothed therewith, as preparation for war, he came down to fight against the darkness." *

251 See *Psychology and Alchemy*, figs. 64, 82, 114.   252 Ibid., pars. 499, 505f., fig. 208.

253 "In our vessel the Passion is enacted," says Mylius (*Phil. ref.*, p. 33). The motif of torture can be found in the visions of Zosimos. Cf. "Transformation Symbolism in the Mass," pars. 344ff., 410f. and "The Philosophical Tree," chs. 17 and 18.

A Lyon Greene did in her Lapp reside
(The which an Eagle [254] fed), and from his side
The Blood gush'd out: The Virgin drunck it upp,
While Mercuries Hand did th'Office of a Cupp.

The wondrous Milk she hasten'd from her Breast,
Bestow'd it frankly on the Hungry Beast,
And with a Sponge his Furry Face she dry'd
Which her own Milk had often Madefy'd.

Upon her Head a Diadem she did weare,
With fiery Feet sh'Advanced into the Aire;
And glittering Bravely in her Golden Robes
She took her Place amidst the Starry Globes.

The Dark Clouds being Dispers'd, so sate she there,
And woven to a Network in her Haire
Were Planets, Times, and Signes, the while the King
With his Glad Eyes was her Beleagering.[255]

[254] The eagle represents the next-higher stage of transformation after Leo. The lion is a quadruped and still earthbound, whereas the eagle symbolizes spirit.

[255] "Et unguento affluit haec delicioso
    Expurgata sanguine prius menstruoso
    Radiabat undique vultu luminoso
    Adornata lapide omni pretioso.

"Ast in eius gremio viridis iacebat
    Leo, cui aquila prandium ferebat;
    De leonis latere cruor effluebat,
    De manu Mercurii, quem Virgo bibebat.

"Lac, quod mirum extitit, illa propinabat
    Suis de uberibus, quod leoni dabat.
    Eius quoque faciem spongia mundabat,
    Quam in lacte proprio saepe madidabat.

"Illa diademate fuit coronata
    Igneoque pedibus aere ablata
    Et in suis vestibus splendide stellata,
    Empyreo medio coeli collocata.

"Signis, temporibus et ceteris planetis,
    Circumfusa, nebulis tenebrosis spretis,
    Quae, contexis crinibus in figuram retis,
    Sedit, quam luminibus Rex respexit laetis."

454   Here the apotheosis of the Queen is described in a way that
instantly reminds us of its prototype, the coronation of the Virgin Mary. The picture is complicated by the images of the Pietà
on the one hand and the mother, giving the child her breast, on
the other. As is normally the case only in dreams, several images
of the Mother of God have contaminated one another, as have
also the allegories of Christ as child and lion, the latter representing the body of the Crucified with the blood flowing from
his side. As in dreams, the symbolism with its grotesque con-
densations and overlappings of contradictory contents shows no
regard for our aesthetic and religious feelings; it is as though
trinkets made of different metals were being melted in a crucible
and their contours flowed into one another. The images have
lost their pristine force, their clarity and meaning. In dreams it
often happens—to our horror—that our most cherished convictions and values are subjected to just this iconoclastic mutilation. It also happens in the psychoses, when the patients sometimes come out with the most appalling blasphemies and hideous distortions of religious ideas. We find the same thing in
"belles" lettres—I need only mention Joyce's *Ulysses,* a book
which E. R. Curtius has not unjustly described as a work of Antichrist.[256] But such products spring more from the spirit of the
age than from the perverse inventive gifts of the author. In our
time we must expect "prophets" like James Joyce. A similar
spirit prevailed at the time of the Renaissance, one of its most
striking manifestations being the *Hexastichon* of Sebastian
Brant.[257] The illustrations in this little book are freakish beyond
belief. The main figure in each is an evangelical symbol, for instance the eagle of St. John, and round it and on it are allegories
and emblems of the principal events, miracles, parables, etc., in
the gospel in question. These creations may be compared with
the fantasies of George Ripley, for neither author had any
inkling of the dubious nature of what he was doing. Yet in spite
of their dreamlike quality these products seem to have been constructed with deliberate intent. Brant even numbered the main
components of his pictures according to the chapters of the Gospel, and again in Ripley's paraphrase of the sacred legend each

256 [Cf. Curtius, *James Joyce und sein Ulysses.*]
257 *Hexastichon Sebastiani Brant in memorabiles evangelistarum figuras* (1502).
See our Pls. 1 and 2.

item can easily be enucleated from its context. Brant thought of his pictures as mnemotechnical exercises that would help the reader to recall the contents of the gospels, whereas in fact their diabolical freakishness stamps itself on the mind far more than the recollection, say, that John 2 coincides with the marriage at Cana. The image of the Virgin with the wounded lion in her lap has the same kind of unholy fascination, precisely because it deviates so strangely from the official image to which we are accustomed.

455   I have compared the tendency to fantastic distortion to a melting down of images, but this gives the impression that it is an essentially destructive process. In reality—and this is especially so in alchemy—it is a process of assimilation between revealed truth and knowledge of nature. I will not attempt to investigate what the unconscious motives were that animated Sebastian Brant, and I need say nothing more about James Joyce here, as I have discussed this question in my essay "Ulysses: A Monologue." These melting processes all express a relativization of the dominants of consciousness prevailing in a given age. For those who identify with the dominants or are absolutely dependent on them the melting process appears as a hostile, destructive attack which should be resisted with all one's powers. Others, for whom the dominants no longer mean what they purport to be, see the melting as a longed-for regeneration and enrichment of a system of ideas that has lost its vitality and freshness and is already obsolete. The melting process is therefore either something very bad or something highly desirable, according to the standpoint of the observer.[258]

[258] One of my critics includes me among the "smelters," on the ground that I take an interest in the psychology of comparative religion. This description is justified in so far as I have called all religious ideas *psychic* (though their possible transcendental meaning is something I am not competent to judge). That is to say, I maintain that there is a relationship between Christian doctrine and psychology—a relationship which in my view need not necessarily turn out to the disadvantage of the former. My critic betrays a singular lack of confidence in the assimilating power of his doctrine when he deprecates with horror this incipient process of fusion. The Church was able to assimilate Aristotle despite his essentially alien way of thinking, and what has she not taken over from pagan philosophy, pagan cults, and—last but not least—from Gnosticism, without poisoning herself in the process! If Christian doctrine is able to assimilate the fateful impact of psychology, that is a sign of vitality, for life is assimilation. Anything that ceases to assimilate dies. The assimilation of Aristotle warded off the danger then threatening from

456   In the latter category we must distinguish two kinds of alchemists: those who believed that the revealed truth represented by the Church could derive nothing but gain if it were combined with a knowledge of the God in nature; and those for whom the projection of the Christian mystery of faith into the physical world invested nature with a mystical significance, whose mysterious light outshone the splendid incomprehensibilities of Church ceremonial. The first group hoped for a rebirth of dogma, the second for a new incarnation of it and its transformation into a natural revelation.

457   I lay particular stress on the phenomena of assimilation in alchemy because they are, in a sense, a prelude to the modern approximation between empirical psychology and Christian dogma—an approximation which Nietzsche clearly foresaw. Psychology, as a science, observes religious ideas from the standpoint of their psychic phenomenology without intruding on their theological content. It puts the dogmatic images into the category of psychic contents, because this constitutes its field of research. It is compelled to do so by the nature of the psyche itself; it does not, like alchemy, try to explain psychic processes in theological terms, but rather to illuminate the darkness of religious images by relating them to similar images in the psyche. The result is a kind of amalgamation of ideas of—so it would seem—the most varied provenience, and this sometimes leads to parallels and comparisons which to an uncritical mind unacquainted with the epistemological method may seem like a devaluation or a false interpretation. If this were to be construed as an objection to psychology one could easily say the same thing about the hermeneutics of the Church Fathers, which are often very risky indeed, or about the dubious nature of textual criticism. The psychologist has to investigate religious symbols because his empirical material, of which the theologian usually knows nothing, compels him to do so. Presumably no one would wish to hand over the chemistry of albuminous bodies to some other department of science on the ground that they are organic

the Arabs. Theological critics should remember these things before launching purely negative attacks on psychology. It is no more the intention of the psychologist than it was of the alchemist to disparage in any way the significance of religious symbols.

and that the investigation of life is a matter for the biologist. A rapprochement between empirical science and religious experience would in my opinion be fruitful for both. Harm can result only if one side or the other remains unconscious of the limitations of its claim to validity. Alchemy, certainly, cannot be defended against the charge of unconsciousness. It is and remains a puzzle whether Ripley ever reflected on his theological enormities and what he thought about them. From a scientific point of view, his mentality resembles that of a dream-state.

458   The coronation of the Virgin and the heavenly marriage bring us to the final strophes of the *Cantilena*.

459   *Verses 36–37*

> Thus He of all Triumphant Kings is Chiefe,
> Of Bodies sicke the only Grand Reliefe:
> Such a Reformist of Defects, that hee
> Is worshipp'd both by King and Commonalty.
>
> To Princes, Priests he yields an Ornament,
> The Sicke and Needy Sort he doth content:
> What man is there this Potion will not bless,
> As banishes all thought of Neediness? [259]

460   This is the apotheosis of the *filius regius,* as we find it in numerous treatises. Thus the "Tractatus aureus" [260] says: "The king comes forth from the fire and rejoices in the marriage. The son is become a warrior of the fire and surpasses the tinctures, for he himself is the treasure and himself is attired in the philosophic matter. Come hither, ye sons of wisdom, let us be glad and rejoice, for the dominion of death is over, and the son reigns; he is clothed with the red garment, and the purple is put on." The reborn king is the "wonder of the world," "an exceed-

[259] "Fit hic Regum omnium summus triumphator,
  Et aegrorum corporum grandis mediator,
  Omnium defectuum tantus reformator,
  Illi ut obediant Caesar et viator.

  "Praelatis et regibus praebens decoramen,
  Aegris et invalidis fit in consolamen.
  Quis est quem non afficit huius medicamen,
  Quo omnis penuriae pellitur gravamen."

[260] *Ars chemica,* ch. III, p. 22.

ing pure spirit"; [261] he is, the "Aquarium sapientum" assures us, "the most elect, the most subtile, the purest, and noblest of all the heavenly spirits, to whom all the rest yield obedience as to their King, who bestows on men all health and prosperity, heals all sickness, gives to the God-fearing temporal honour and long life, but to the wicked who abused him, eternal punishment. . . . In sum, they have designated him the chief of all things under heaven, and the marvellous end and epilogue of all philosophic works. Hence some devout philosophers of old have affirmed that he was divinely revealed to Adam, the first man, and thereafter was awaited with peculiar longing by all the holy Patriarchs." [262] "The Almighty," remarks the "Introitus," "has made him known by a most notable sign, whose birth [263] is declared throughout the East on the horizon of his hemisphere. The wise Magi saw it at the beginning of the era, and were astonished, and straightway they knew that the most serene King was born in the world. Do you, when you see his star, follow it to the cradle, and there you shall behold the fair infant. Cast aside your defilements, honour the royal child, open your treasure, offer a gift of gold; and after death he will give you flesh and blood, the supreme Medicine in the three monarchies of the earth." [264] The clothing of the elixir with the "kingly garment" is also found in the *Turba*.[265] The "Consilium coniugii" describes the king as "descending from heaven." [266] Mylius says of King Sol that "Phoebus with shining hair of gold sits in the midst, like a king and emperor of the world, grasping the sceptre and the helm." In him are "all the powers of heaven." [267] In another place he cites the following quotation: "And at last the

---

261 "Introitus apertus," *Mus. herm.*, p. 654 (Waite, II, p. 167).

262 *Mus. herm.*, p. 96 (Waite, I, p. 86).

263 Cf. "Rosinus ad Sarrat.," *Art. aurif.*, I, p. 281: "Then he touches the ferment with the prepared imperfect body, as it is said, until they become one in body, figure, and appearance, and then it is called the Birth. For then is born our stone, which is called king by the Philosophers, as it is said in the *Turba*: Honour our king coming out of the fire, crowned with a diadem." *

264 *Mus. herm.*, pp. 654f. (Waite, II, p. 167).*

265 "And ye shall see the *iksir* [elixir] clothed with the garment of the kingdom." * *Turba* (ed. Ruska), p. 147.

266 "The stone of the Philosophers is the king descending from heaven, and his hills are of silver, and his rivers of gold, and his earth precious stones and gems" * (*Ars chemica*, p. 61).

267 *Phil. ref.*, p. 10.

king will go forth crowned with his diadem, radiant as the sun, bright as the carbuncle." [268] Khunrath speaks of the "wondrous natural triune Son of the Great World," whom the sages name "their Son and crowned King, artificially hatched from the egg of the world." [269] Elsewhere he says of the *filius Mundi Maioris:*

The Son of the great World [Macrocosm] who is Theocosmos, i.e., a divine power and world (but whom even today, unfortunately, many who teach nature in a pagan spirit and many builders of medical science reject in the high university schools), is the exemplar of the stone which is Theanthropos, i.e., God and man (whom, as Scripture tells us, the builders of the Church have also rejected); and from the same, in and from the Great World Book of Nature, [there issues] a continuous and everlasting doctrine for the wise and their children: indeed, it is a splendid living likeness of our Saviour Jesus Christ, in and from the Great World which by nature is very similar to him (as to miraculous conception, birth, inexpressible powers, virtues, and effects); so God our Lord, besides his Son's Biblical histories, has also created a specific image and natural representation for us in the Book of Nature.[270]

461   These few examples, together with those already quoted in *Psychology and Alchemy,* may give the reader some idea of the way in which the alchemists conceived the triumphant king.

462

Verse 38

Wherefore, O God, graunt us a Peece of This,[271]
That through the Encrease [272] of its own Species

---

268 Ibid., p. 284. Cited in *Ros. phil. (Art. aurif.,* II, p. 329) as a quotation from Lully. A similar quotation in *Ros. phil.* (p. 272) is attributed to Ortulanus and Arnaldus: "Because the soul is infused into the body and a crowned king is born." * On p. 378 *Ros. phil.* cites an "Aenigma Hermetis de tinctura rubea": "I am crowned and adorned with a diadem and clothed with kingly garments; for I cause joy to enter into bodies." * The "Tractatulus Avicennae" (*Art. aurif.,* I, p. 422) says: "Despise not the ash, for God will grant it liquefaction, and then finally by divine permission the king is crowned with a red diadem. It behoves thee therefore to attempt this magistery." *

269 *Hyl. Chaos,* pp. 236f.

270 Ibid., pp. 286f. Cf. the passage from *Amphitheatrum,* p. 197 (supra, par. 355, n. 28).

271 "Illius species" = a piece of the king, as it were, who is now suddenly a substance.

272 The "multiplicatio" often means a spontaneous renewal of the tincture, com-

> The Art may be Renew'd, and Mortal Men
> Enjoy for aye its Thrice-Sweet Fruits. AMEN.[273]

463   Here ends the *Cantilena,* one of the most perfect parables of
the renewal of the king. It does not, of course, compare with the
much more elaborate development of the myth in Christian
Rosencreutz. (His *Chymical Wedding* is so rich in content that
I could touch on it only lightly here.) The latter part of *Faust II*
likewise contains the same motif of the transformation of the
old man into a boy, together with all the necessary indicia of the
heavenly marriage. This theme, too, as in alchemy, runs through
the whole of *Faust* and repeats itself on three different levels
(Gretchen, Helen, Queen of Heaven), just as the king's renewal
takes a form that was destined to fail three times before Faust's
death (the Boy Charioteer, the Homunculus, and Euphorion).

5. THE DARK SIDE OF THE KING

464   Besides the *Cantilena,* there are various other descriptions [274]
of the king's renewal, enriched with numerous details, which I
will not discuss here so as not to overburden this chapter. The
material we have adduced may suffice to illustrate the essential
features of the transformation process. Nevertheless, the myth
of the king's renewal has so many ramifications that our exposition so far does not cover the entire range of the symbol. In this
section, therefore, I shall try to shed a little more light on the
critical phase of the *nigredo,* the phase of decay and death.

---

parable to the widow's cruse of oil. Mylius (*Phil. ref.,* p. 92) lays down the following
rule: "Project therefore on any body as much of it as you please, since its Tincture
shall be multiplied twofold. And if one part of it in the first place converts with
its bodies a hundred parts: in the second it converts a thousand, in the third ten
thousand, in the fourth a hundred thousand, in the fifth a million, into the true
sun-making and moon-making (substance)." *

273 "Nostrum Deus igitur nobis det optamen
       Illius in speciem per multiplicamen,
       Ut gustemus practicae per regeneramen
       Eius fructus, uberes et ter dulces. Amen."

274 Cf. the king's bath in Bernardus Trevisanus, supra, pars. 74f. For a detailed
parable see the "Tractatus aureus de lapide," in *Mus. herm.,* pp. 41ff. (Waite, I,
pp. 41ff.).

"Third Picture of John"

From the Hexastichon *of Sebastian Brant (1502), fol. a.vr*

"Second Picture of Luke"

From the Hexastichon *of Sebastian Brant (1502), fol. c.iiir*

"Jezoth le Juste"

From an 18th cent. ms., "Abraham le Juif," Bibliothèque Nationale,
Fr. 14765, Pl. 8

The Two Unipeds

From a Latin ms., "Figurarum aegyptiorum secretarum"
(author's collection), p. 20

4

The "Revelation of the Hidden"

From the author's "Figurarum aegyptiorum secretarum,"

p. 27

The Worldly and the Spiritual Power

From the author's "Figurarum aegyptiorum secretarum,"
p. 31

The Royal Pair

From the author's "Figurarum aegyptiorum secretarum,"
p. 33

The Eye-Motif in a Modern Painting
Author's collection

The Eye-Motif in a Modern Painting
Author's collection

The Nigredo
From the Theatrum chemicum, *Vol. IV (1613), p. 570*

465   The king's decline, as we saw, was due to imperfection or sickness. In the *Cantilena* his sickness was sterility. The figure of the sterile king may perhaps come from the "Arisleus Vision," [275] where the King of the Sea rules over an unfruitful country, although he himself is not sterile. Usually the king is connected in some way with the world of darkness. Thus, in the "Introitus," he is at first the "secret, infernal fire," [276] but as the reborn *puellus regius* (kingly boy) he is an allegory of Christ. In Michael Maier the king is dead and yet imprisoned alive in the depths of the sea, whence he calls for help.[277] The following story of the king is from Trismosin's *Splendor solis:*

The old Philosophers declared they saw a Fog rise, and pass over the whole face of the earth, they also saw the impetuosity of the Sea, and the streams over the face of the earth, and how these same became foul and stinking in the darkness. They further saw the king of the Earth sink, and heard him cry out with eager voice,[278] "Whoever saves me shall live and reign with me for ever in my brightness on my royal throne," and Night enveloped all things. The day after, they saw over the King an apparent Morning Star, and the light of Day clear up the darkness, and bright Sunlight pierce through the clouds, with manifold coloured rays of brilliant brightness, and a sweet perfume from the earth, and the Sun shining clear. Herewith was completed the Time when the King of the Earth was released and renewed, well apparelled, and quite handsome, surprising with his beauty the Sun and Moon. He was crowned with three costly crowns,

---

[275] *Art. aurif.,* I, pp. 146ff.

[276] *Mus. herm.,* p. 654 (Waite, II, p. 167).

[277] *Symb. aur. mensae,* p. 380: "And although that king of the philosophers seems dead, yet he lives, and cries out from the deep: He who shall deliver me from the waters and bring me back to dry land, him will I bless with riches everlasting. But although that cry is heard by many, yet are none near at hand to be moved with compassion for the king and to seek him. For who, say they, will plunge into the sea? Who will relieve another's danger at the cost of his own? For few there are who credit his lamentation and they think the voice they hear to be the loud cries and echoes of Scylla and Charybdis. So they stay idle at home, and have no care for the king's treasure nor for his safety." * Cf. *Psychology and Alchemy,* pars. 434ff.

[278] Possibly a reference to Psalm 69 : 2f.: "I sink in deep mire, where there is no standing; I am come into deep waters, where the floods overflow me. I am weary of crying, my throat is dried; mine eyes fail while I wait for my God." Verse 14f.: "Deliver me out of the mire, and let me not sink; let me be delivered from them that hate me, and out of the deep waters. Let not the waterflood overflow me, neither let the deep swallow me up, and let not the pit shut her mouth upon me."

the one of Iron, the other of Silver, and the third of pure Gold. They saw in his right hand a Sceptre with Seven Stars, all of which gave a golden Splendour [etc., etc.].[279]

466   The seven stars are a reference to Rev. 1 : 16: "And he had in his right hand seven stars." He who held them was "like unto the Son of man," in agreement with the *puellus regius* in the "Introitus." The king sinking in the sea is the arcane substance, which Maier calls the "antimony of the philosophers." [280] The arcane substance corresponds to the Christian dominant, which was originally alive and present in consciousness but then sank into the unconscious and must now be restored in renewed form. Antimony is associated with blackness: antimony trisulphide is a widely used Oriental hair-dye *(kohl)*. On the other hand antimony pentasulphide, "gold-sulphur" *(Sulphur auratum antimonii)* is orange-red.

467   The sunken king of alchemy went on living as the "metal king," the "regulus" of metallurgy. This is the name for the lumps of metal formed beneath the slag in melting and reducing ores. The term *Sulphur auratum antimonii,* like gold-sulphur, indicates the strong predominance of sulphur in combination with antimony. Sulphur, as we have seen, is the active substance of Sol and is foul-smelling: sulphur dioxide and sulphuretted hydrogen give one a good idea of the stink of hell. Sulphur is an attribute of Sol as Leo is of Rex. Leo, too, is ambiguous: on the one hand he is an allegory of the devil and on the other is connected with Venus. The antimony compounds known to the alchemists (Sb_2S_5, Sb_2S_3) therefore contained a substance which clearly exemplified the nature of Rex and Leo, hence they spoke of the "triumph of antimony." [281]

468   As I have shown in *Psychology and Alchemy*,[282] the sunken king forms a parallel to Parable VII of *Aurora Consurgens:* [282a]

279 *Splendor Solis: Alchemical Treatises of Solomon Trismosin,* pp. 29f. See also *Psychology and Alchemy,* fig. 166.

280 "The true antimony of the philosophers [lies] in the deep sea, that the son of the king may lurk submerged" * *(Symb. aur. mensae,* p. 380).

281 Ibid., p. 378, referring to *The Triumphal Chariot of Antimony* of Basilius Valentinus, which, it seems, was first published in German in 1604. The Latin edition appeared later, in 1646. See Schmieder, *Geschichte der Alchemie,* p. 205.

282 Pars. 434ff.   282a P. 133.

Be turned to me with all your heart and do not cast me aside because I am black and swarthy, because the sun hath changed my colour and the waters have covered my face and the land hath been polluted and defiled in my works; for there was darkness over it, because I stick fast in the mire of the deep and my substance is not disclosed. Wherefore out of the depths have I cried, and from the abyss of the earth with my voice to all you that pass by the way. Attend and see me, if any shall find one like unto me, I will give into his hand the morning star.

469   The "mire of the deep" refers to Psalm 68 : 3 (Vulgate): "Infixus sum in limo profundi et non est substantia" (AV 69 : 2: "I sink in deep mire, where there is no standing"). David's words are interpreted by Epiphanius [283] as follows: there is a material which consists of "miry reflections" and "muddy thoughts of sin." But of Psalm 130 : 1: "Out of the depths have I cried to thee, O Lord," he gives the following interpretation: "After the saints are so graced that the Holy Ghost dwells within them, he gives them, after having made his habitation in the saints, the gift to look into the deep things of God, that they may praise him from the depths, as also David declares: 'Out of the depths,' he says, 'have I cried to thee, O Lord.' " [284]

470   These contradictory interpretations of the "depths" (*profunda*) come much closer together in alchemy, often so close that they seem to be nothing more than two different aspects of the same thing. It is natural that in alchemy the depths should mean now one and now the other, to the despair of all lovers of consistency. But the eternal images are far from consistent in meaning. It is characteristic of the alchemists that they never lost sight of this polarity, thereby compensating the world of dogma, which, in order to avoid ambiguity, emphasizes the one pole to the exclusion of the other. The tendency to separate the opposites as much as possible and to strive for singleness of meaning is absolutely necessary for clarity of consciousness, since discrimination is of its essence. But when the separation is carried so far that the complementary opposite is lost sight of, and the blackness of the whiteness, the evil of the good, the depth of the heights, and so on, is no longer seen, the result is one-sidedness, which is then compensated from the unconscious without our

[283] *Panarium* (ed. Holl), Haer. 36, cap. 4 (II, pp. 47ff.).
[284] *Ancoratus* (ed. Holl), vol. I, p. 20.

help. The counterbalancing is even done against our will, which in consequence must become more and more fanatical until it brings about a catastrophic enantiodromia. Wisdom never forgets that all things have two sides, and it would also know how to avoid such calamities if ever it had any power. But power is never found in the seat of wisdom; it is always the focus of mass interests and is therefore inevitably associated with the illimitable folly of the mass man.

471   With increasing one-sidedness the power of the king decays, for originally it had consisted just in his ability to unite the polarity of all existence in a symbol. The more distinctly an idea emerges and the more consciousness gains in clarity, the more monarchic becomes its content, to which everything contradictory has to submit. This extreme state has to be reached, despite the fact that the climax always presages the end. Man's own nature, the unconscious, immediately tries to compensate, and this is distasteful to the extreme state, which always considers itself ideal and is moreover in a position to prove its excellence with the most cogent arguments. We cannot but admit that it is ideal, but for all that it is imperfect because it expresses only one half of life. Life wants not only the clear but also the muddy, not only the bright but also the dark; it wants all days to be followed by nights, and wisdom herself to celebrate her carnival, of which indeed there are not a few traces in alchemy. For these reasons, too, the king constantly needs the renewal that begins with a descent into his own darkness, an immersion in his own depths, and with a reminder that he is related by blood to his adversary.

472   According to the *Ancoratus* of Epiphanius, the phoenix emerges from his ashes first in the form of a worm:

When the bird is dead, indeed utterly consumed, and the flames are extinguished, there are left only the crude remnants of the flesh. From this there comes forth in one day an unseemly worm, which puts on wings and becomes as new; but on the third day it matures, and after growing to full stature with the aid of the medicines found in that place, it shows itself, and hastens upward once more to its own country, and there rests.[285]

So, too, the king rises from his "infernal fire" as a crowned dragon.[286] He is the Mercurial serpent, which is especially con-

285 Ibid., pp. 104f.   286 See *Psychology and Alchemy*, figs. 10–12, 46, 47.

nected with evil-smelling places ("it is found on the dung-hills").[287] The fact that the passage in the *Ancoratus* stresses the "one day" may perhaps throw some light on the apparently unique reference in Khunrath's *Amphitheatrum* to the "filius unius (SVI) diei" [288] as a designation for the "Hermaphrodite of nature," i.e., the arcane substance. He is there synonymous with "Saturn,[289] the ambisexual Philosophic Man of the philosophers, the lead of the sages, the Philosophic World-Egg . . . the greatest wonder of the world, the Lion, green and red . . . A lily among thorns." [290]

473   As we have seen, the *filius regius* is identical with Mercurius and at this particular stage also with the Mercurial serpent. This stage is indicated in Khunrath by Saturn, the dark, cold *maleficus;* by the world-egg, obviously signifying the initial state, and finally by the green and red lion, representing the animal soul of the king. All this is expressed by the dragon or serpent as the *summa summarum.* The dragon as the lowest and most inchoate

287 Cf. "The Spirit Mercurius," par. 269 and n. 41, and "Paracelsus as a Spiritual Phenomenon," par. 182, n. 61.

288 P. 195, "the son of one (HIS) day; wherein are warm, cold, moist and dry." The Mercurial Serpent "giving birth in a single day," however, is mentioned in "De lapide philosophorum" of Albertus Magnus (*Theatr. chem.*, IV, pp. 98f.). See infra, pars. 712 and 718. Cf. also *Das Buch der Alaune und Salze* (ed. Ruska), pp. 58f.

289 As regards the Saturn/lead equation, it should be noted that although astrologically Saturn is a malefic planet of whom only the worst is expected, he is also a purifier, because true purity is attained only through repentance and expiation of sin. Thus Meister Eckhart says in his sermon on the text, "For the powers of heaven shall be shaken" (Luke 21 : 26): "Further we must note how (God) has decked the natural heavens with seven planets, seven noble stars which are nearer to us than the rest. The first is Saturn, then comes Jupiter, then Mars, and then the Sun; after that comes Venus, and then Mercury, and then the Moon. Now when the soul becomes a spiritual heaven, our Lord will deck her with these same stars spiritually, as St. John saw in his Apocalypse when he espied the King of Kings seated upon the throne of the majesty of God, and having seven stars in his hand. Know that the first star, Saturn, is the purger . . . In the heaven of the soul Saturn becomes of angelic purity, bringing as reward the vision of God, as our Lord said, 'Blessed are the pure in heart for they shall see God.' " (Evans, I, p. 168.) It is in this sense that Saturn should be understood here. Cf. Vigenerus ("De igne et sale," *Theatr. chem.*, VI, p. 76): "Lead signifies the vexations and troubles wherewith God visits us and brings us back to repentance. For as lead burns up and removes all the imperfections of metals, for which reason Boethus the Arab called it the water of sulphur, so likewise tribulation in this life cleanses us from the many blemishes which we have incurred: wherefore St. Ambrose calls it the key of heaven." *   290 Song of Songs 2 : 2.

form of the king is, we are constantly told, at first a deadly poison but later the alexipharmic itself.

474   In the myth of the phoenix as reported by Pliny we again meet the worm: ". . . from its bones and marrow is born first a sort of maggot, and this grows into a chicken." [291] This version is repeated in Clement of Rome,[292] Artemidorus,[293] Cyril of Jerusalem,[294] St. Ambrose,[295] and Cardan.[296] In order to understand the phoenix myth it is important to know that in Christian hermeneutics the phoenix is made an allegory of Christ, which amounts to a reinterpretation of the myth.[297] The self-burning of the phoenix corresponds to Christ's self-sacrifice, the ashes to his buried body, and the miraculous renewal to his resurrection.[298] According to Horapollo (4th cent.), whose views were taken over by later writers,[299] the phoenix signifies the soul and its journey to the land of rebirth.[300] It stands for the "long-last-

---

[291] *Natural History*, X, ii (trans. by Rackham, III, p. 294).*

[292] *The Apostolic Constitutions*, V, 7 (trans. by Smith and others, p. 134).

[293] *Onirocriticon*, lib. IV, cap. 47.

[294] *Catecheses Mystagogicae*, XVIII, 8 (ed. Reischl and Rupp, II, pp. 307ff.).

[295] *De Excessu fratris*, lib. II, cap. 59 (ed. Faller, p. 281), and *Hexaemeron*, V, cap. 23 (Migne, *P.L.*, vol. 14, col. 238).   [296] *De subtilitate*, p. 602.

[297] The fact that the myth was assimilated into Christianity by interpretation is proof, first of all, of the myth's vitality; but it also proves the vitality of Christianity, which was able to interpret and assimilate so many myths. The importance of hermeneutics should not be under-estimated: it has a beneficial effect on the psyche by consciously linking the distant past, the ancestral heritage which is still alive in the unconscious, with the present, thus establishing the vitally important connection between a consciousness oriented to the present moment only and the historical psyche which extends over infinitely long periods of time. As the most conservative of all products of the human mind, religions are in themselves the bridges to the ever-living past, which they make alive and present for us. A religion that can no longer assimilate myths is forgetting its proper function. But its spiritual vitality depends on the continuity of myth, and this can be preserved only if each age translates the myth into its own language and makes it an essential content of its view of the world. The *Sapientia Dei* which reveals itself through the archetype always ensures that the wildest deviations shall return to the middle position. Thus the fascination of philosophical alchemy comes very largely from the fact that it was able to give new expression to nearly all the most important archetypes. Indeed, as we have seen already, it even tried to assimilate Christianity.

[298] Numerous examples of these parallels can be found in Picinellus, *Mundus Symbolicus*, I, pp. 322ff.

[299] Cf. the edition of his *Hieroglyphica* in Caussin, *De Symbolica Aegyptorum sapientia* (1618), p. 142.

[300] *The Hieroglyphics of Horapollo* (trans. by Boas), p. 75 (Book I, No. 34).

ing restitution of things" (ἀποκατάστασιν πολυχρόνιον); indeed, it is renewal itself.[301] The idea of apocatastasis or restitution (Acts 3 : 21) and re-establishment in Christ (Ephesians 1 : 10, DV) [302] may well have helped the assimilation of the phoenix allegory, quite apart from the main motif of renewal.

475   Khunrath's insertion of the word "SVI," in capital letters, after "unius" plainly indicates that he was referring to something divine. This can only be some analogy of God or Christ. Nowhere else in the alchemical texts is this "one" day mentioned, except for an occasional remark that by the special grace of God the opus could be completed in one day. Khunrath's "SVI" seems to refer rather to God, in the sense that the *filius regius* is born on "His" day, the day that belongs to God or is chosen by him. Since the phoenix is mainly an allegory of resurrection, this one day of birth and renewal must be one of the three days of Christ's burial and descent into hell. But there is nothing about this one day in Christian dogma, unless Khunrath, who had a speculative mind, was anticipating the arguments of certain Protestant dogmaticians who, following Luke 23 : 43,[303] propounded the theory that after his death Christ did not immediately descend into hell (as in Catholic dogma), but remained in paradise until Easter morning. And just as there was an earthquake at the moment when Christ's soul separated from his body in death, so there was another earthquake on Easter morning (Matthew 28 : 2). During this earthquake Christ's soul was reunited with his body,[304] and only then did he descend into hell to "preach to the spirits in prison" (I Peter 3 : 19). Meanwhile the angel at the tomb appeared in his place and spoke to the women. The descent into hell is supposed to be limited to this short space of time.[305]

476   On this view the "one day" would be Easter Day. In alchemy the uniting of the soul with the body is the miracle of the coniunctio, by which the lapis becomes a living body. The phoenix

301 Ibid., p. 96 (Book II, No. 57): "For when this bird is born, there is a renewal of things." *

302 Likewise Col. 1 : 20, and in a certain sense Rom. 8 : 19ff.

303 "Today shalt thou be with me in paradise."

304 According to the dogma, Christ descended with his body into limbo.

305 These speculations belong to the 17th cent., whereas Khunrath wrote in the 16th cent. See the article by M. Lauterburg on Christ's descent into hell in Herzog and Hauck, *Realenzyklopaedie für protestantische Theologie*, VIII, p. 204.

signifies precisely this moment.[306] The alchemical transformation was often compared to the rising of the sun. But apart from the fact that there is not the slightest ground for supposing that such speculations ever entered Khunrath's head, the Easter morning hypothesis does not seem very satisfactory. The special element of the *worm* is missing, which Epiphanius stresses in connection with the one day. It seems as though this element should not be overlooked in explaining the *filius unius diei.* The one day probably refers to Genesis 1 : 5: "And there was evening and there was morning, one day" (RSV).[307] This was after the separation of light from darkness (or the creation of light), and here it should be remembered that darkness precedes the light and is its mother.[308] The son of this one day is the Light, the Logos (John 1 : 5), who is the Johannine Christ.[309] So interpreted, the son of one day immediately becomes related to the "Hermaphrodite of nature," [310] the Philosophic Man, and to Saturn, the tempter and oppressor,[311] who, as Ialdabaoth and the highest archon, is correlated with the lion. All these figures are synonyms for Mercurius.

477   There is a didactic poem, *Sopra la composizione della pietra dei Philosophi,* by Fra Marcantonio Crasselame, which was published in a work significantly entitled *La Lumière sortant par soi-mesme des Ténèbres.*[312] As the title shows, this is not the light that was created by the Logos, but a spontaneous, self-

306 Cf. the aforementioned "Ortus," which is identical with the phoenix and shares its display of colours. In his excerpts from Epiphanius Caussin cites: "The bird phoenix is more beauteous than the peacock; for the peacock has wings of gold and silver, but the phoenix of jacinth and emerald, and adorned with the colours of precious stones: she has a crown upon her head" * (*Symb. Aegypt. sap.,* p. 142).   307 Vulgate: "Factumque est vespere et mane, dies unus."

308 Gen. 1 : 2: "And darkness was upon the face of the deep." Cf. Boehme ("Tabulae principiorum," I, 3, in *De signatura rerum,* Amsterdam edn., p. 271), who calls darkness the first of the three principles.

309 John 8 : 12: "I am the light of the world."

310 Among the Valentinians (Irenaeus, *Adversus haereses,* I, 5, 1) the demiurge and king of all things who was created by Achamoth was called the "Father-Mother"—an hermaphrodite. Similar traditions may have been known to the alchemists, though I have found no trace of any such connections.

311 The alchemical figures, especially the gods of metals, should always be thought of astrologically as well.

312 [The first edition was published at Venice (1666) with the title *Lux obnubilata suapte natura refulgens;* the French edition (1687), which contains the Italian poem at pp. 3ff., is cited below: poem in the text, Crasselame's commentary in the foot-

begotten light. The poem begins with the creation of the world and declares that the Word created chaos:

At the Omnipotent's first word, shadowy Chaos, formless mass, came from the void.

But who knows how all things were made? Only the "sons of the Art":

O emulous Sons of Divine Hermes, to whom the paternal Art makes Nature visible without any veil, you, you alone, know how the eternal Hand fashioned earth and Heaven out of shapeless Chaos. Your own great Work clearly shows you that God made Everything in the same manner as the Physical Elixir is produced.

478 The *opus alchymicum* recapitulates the secret of creation which began with the incubation of the waters. Mercurius, a living and universal spirit, descends into the earth and mingles with the impure sulphurs, thus becoming fixed:

If I be clearly understood, your unknown Mercury is nothing other than a living innate universal Spirit which, ever agitated in aerial vapour, descends from the Sun to fill the empty Centre of the Earth; whence it later issues forth from the impure Sulphurs and, from volatile, becomes fixed and, having taken form, imparts its form to the radical moisture.

479 But through his descent Mercurius is made captive and can be freed only by the art:

But where is this golden Mercury, this radical moisture, which, dissolved in sulphur and salt, becomes the animated seed of the metals? Ah, he is incarcerated and held so fast that even Nature cannot release him from the harsh prison, unless the Master Art open the way.

480 It is a spirit of light that descends from the sun,[313] a living

---

notes. Crasselame was the pseudonym of Otto Tachenius. Grateful acknowledgment is made to Professor Charles Singleton for the prose translation of the Italian verses.—EDITORS.]

313 "It establishes a twofold motion in Mercurius, one of descent and the other of ascent, and as the former serves to give form to the materials by means of the rays of the sun and of the other stars which by their nature are directed towards lower bodies, and by the action of its vital spirit to awaken the natural fire which is as it were asleep in them, so the movement of ascent serves naturally to purify the bodies." (P. 112) The first descent comes within the story of the Creation and is therefore left out of account by most of the alchemists. Accordingly, they begin their work with the ascent and complete it with the descent, whose purpose is to reunite the freed soul (the *aqua permanens*) with the dead (purified) body, thus bringing the *filius* to birth.

spirit that lives in all creatures as the spirit of wisdom,[314] and teaches man the art whereby the "soul enchained in the elements" may be freed. From Mercurius comes the illumination of the adept, and it is through his work that Mercurius is freed from his chains. This Mercurius duplex, who ascends and descends, is the uroboros, by definition an "increatum." [315] It is the snake that begets itself from itself.[316] Although the poem takes Mercurius chiefly as a spirit of light, the uroboros is a Ἑρμῆς καταχθόνιος (subterranean Hermes). Mercurius is a compound of opposites, and the alchemists were primarily concerned with his dark side, the serpent.

481   It is an age-old mythological idea that the hero, when the light of life is extinguished, goes on living as a snake and is worshipped as a snake.[317] Another widespread primitive idea is the snake-form of the spirits of the dead. This may well have given rise to the worm version of the phoenix myth.

482   In Amente, the Egyptian underworld, dwells the great seven-headed snake,[318] and in the Christian underworld is the most

314 "From it goes forth Splendour, from its light Life, from its movement Spirit" (p. 113).

315 Cf. "The Spirit Mercurius," par. 283, and *Psychology and Alchemy*, pars. 430ff. Crasselame was influenced by Paracelsus. He identifies his Mercurius with the "Illiastes"; cf. "Paracelsus as a Spiritual Phenomenon," pars. 160, 168, n. 62, 170ff. and n. 10.

316 The "Epistola ad Hermannum" (*Theatr. chem.*, V, p. 900) says of the lapis: "It ascends of itself, blackens, descends and whitens, grows and diminishes . . . is born, dies, rises again, and thereafter lives forever." *

317 Examples are Trophonios in his cave (Rohde, *Psyche*, trans. Hillis, p. 105, n. 12) and Erechtheus in the crypt of the Erechtheion (p. 98). The heroes themselves often have the form of snakes (p. 137), or else the snake is their symbol (p. 290, n. 105). The dead in general are frequently depicted as snakes (p. 170). Like the "hero" of alchemy, Mercurius, another ancient alchemical authority, the Agathodaimon, also has the form of a snake.

318 Cf. the snake-boat of Ra in the underworld (Budge, *The Egyptian Heaven and Hell*, I, pp. 66, 86). The snake-monster *par excellence* is the Apep-serpent (Budge, *The Gods of the Egyptians*, I, p. 269). Its equivalent in Babylonia is Tiamat (I, p. 277). The Book of the Apostle Bartholomew (Budge, *Coptic Apocrypha in the Dialect of Upper Egypt*, p. 180) says with reference to the resurrection of Christ: "Now Abbaton, who is Death, and Gaios, and Tryphon, and Ophiath, and Phthinon, and Sotomis, and Komphion, who are the six sons of Death, wriggled into the tomb of the Son of God on their faces, in the form of serpents." Budge comments (intro., p. lxiii): "In the Coptic Amente lived Death with his six sons, and in the form of a seven-headed serpent, or of seven serpents, they wriggled into the tomb of the Lord to find out when his body was going to Amente. The seven-

celebrated snake of all, the devil, "that old serpent." [319] Actually
it is a pair of brothers that inhabit hell, namely death and the
devil, the devil being characterized by the snake and death by
worms. In old German the concepts of worm, snake, and dragon
coalesce, as they do in Latin (*vermis, serpens, draco*). The underworld signifies hell [320] and the grave.[321] The worm or serpent is
all-devouring death. The dragon-slayer is therefore always a conqueror of death. In Germanic mythology, too, hell is associated
with worms. The *Edda* says:

> A hall did I see
> Far from the sun,
> On the shore of death,
> The door to the north.
> Dripping poison
> Drops from the roof;
> The chamber walls
> Are bodies of worms.[322]

Hell in Old English is called the "worm's hall" (*wyrmsele*)
and in Middle High German it is the "worm-garden." [323]

483   Like the heroes and spirits of the dead, the gods too (par-

---

headed serpent of the Gnostics is only a form of the serpent of Nau . . . and the
belief in this monster is as old at least as the 6th dynasty." The "seven Uraei of
Amente," mentioned in the Book of the Dead (ch. 83) are probably identical with
the "worms in Rastau, that live upon the bodies of men and feed upon their
blood" (Papyrus of Nektu-Amen). When Ra stabbed the Apep-serpent with his
lance, it threw up everything it had devoured (Budge, *Osiris and the Egyptian
Resurrection,* I, p. 65). This is a motif which recurs in the primitive whale-dragon
myths. Generally the hero's father and mother come up with him out of the monster's belly (cf. *Symbols of Transformation,* par. 538, n. 85), or everything that
death had swallowed (par. 310). It is clear that this motif is a prefiguration of the
apocatastasis on a primitive level.

[319] Rev. 20 : 2. Honorius of Autun, *Speculum de mysteriis ecclesiae* (Migne, *P.L.,*
vol. 172, col. 937): "The seven-headed dragon, the prince of darkness, drew down
from heaven with his tail a part of the stars, and covered them over with a cloud
of sins, and drew over them the shadow of death." *

[320] Isaiah 38 : 10: ". . . in the cutting off of my days I shall go to the gates of hell"
(AV/DV).

[321] Job 17 : 13f.: ". . . the grave is mine house: I have made my bed in the darkness. I have said to corruption, Thou art my father; to the worm, Thou art my
mother and my sister." Job 21 : 26: "They shall lie down alike in the dust, and
the worms shall cover them."

[322] Niedner, *Thule,* II, p. 39.

[323] Grimm, *Teutonic Mythology* (trans. by Stallybrass), IV, p. 1540.

ticularly the earth-gods), are associated with the snake, as are Hermes and Asklepios.[324] Indeed, the Greek god of healing, on being hatched from the egg, seems to have taken the form of a snake.[325] An inscription on the temple of Hathor at Dendereh reads: [326]

The sun, who has existed from the beginning, rises up like a falcon out of the midst of his lotus-bud. When the doors of his petals open in sapphire-coloured splendour, he has sundered the night from the day. Thou risest up like the sacred snake as a living spirit, creating the beginnings and shining in thy glorious form in the barge of the sunrise. The divine Lord whose image dwells in secret in the temple at Dendereh is made the creator of the world by his work. Coming as one, he multiplies himself a millionfold when the light goes forth from him in the form of a child.[327]

The comparison of the god to a snake reminds us of his chthonic form in the underworld, just as the rejuvenated phoenix (falcon) first takes the form of a worm.[328] As Christianity borrowed a good deal from the Egyptian religion it is not surprising that

---

[324] Cf. Nietzsche, *Thus Spake Zarathustra* (trans. by Common), p. 121: "When did ever a dragon die of a serpent's poison?" says Zarathustra to the snake that had bitten him. He is a hero of the race of dragons, for which reason he is also called the "stone of wisdom" (p. 205).

[325] Cf. Lucian's story of Alexander the mountebank, who produced an egg with Asklepios inside it. ("Pseudomantis," 12, in *Works*, I, pp. 144ff.)

[326] Brugsch, *Religion und Mythologie der alten Ägypter*, pp. 103f.

[327] It is astonishing to see how alchemy made analogous use of the same images: the opus is a repetition of the Creation, it brings light from the darkness (*nigredo*), the lapis is "one," it is produced in the form of *puer, infans, puellus,* and can be multiplied indefinitely.

[328] The worm stands for the most primitive and archaic form of life from which ultimately developed the direct opposite of the earth-bound creature—the bird. This pair of opposites—snake and bird—is classical. The eagle and serpent, the two animals of Zarathustra, symbolize the cycle of eternal return. "For thine animals know well, O Zarathustra, who thou art and must become: behold, thou art the teacher of the eternal return" (*Thus Spake Zarathustra*, p. 264). Cf. the "ring of return" (p. 273) and "alpha and omega" (p. 275). The shepherd into whose mouth the serpent crawled is also connected with the idea of eternal return (pp. 207f.). He forms with the snake the circle of the uroboros. "The circle did not evolve: it is the primary law" (Aphorism 29 in Horneffer, *Nietzsches Lehre von der Ewigen Wiederkunft*, p. 78). Cf. also the teaching of Saturninus that the angels first created a man who could only crawl like a worm. (Irenaeus, *Adv. haer.*, I, XXIV, 1.) As Hippolytus remarks (*Elenchos*, VII, 28, 3), because of the weakness of the angels who created him, man "grovelled like a worm."

the allegory of the snake found its way into the world of Christian ideas (John 3 : 14) and was readily seized on by the alchemists.[329] The dragon is an allegory of Christ as well as of the Antichrist.[330] A remarkable parallel occurs in the anonymous treatise, "De promissionibus" (5th cent.).[331] It concerns a version of the legend of St. Sylvester, according to which this saint imprisoned a dragon in the Tarpeian Rock and so rendered him harmless. The other version of this story is related by a "certain monk" who discovered that the alleged dragon, to whom offerings of virgins were made, was nothing but a mechanical device. St. Sylvester locked the dragon up with a chain, as in Rev. 20 : 1; but in the parallel story the artificial dragon "brandished a sword in its mouth," like the Son of Man in Rev. 1 : 16.[332]

6. THE KING AS ANTHROPOS

484   I have drawn attention earlier [333] to the passage in Hippolytus where the Gnostic interpretation of Psalm 24 : 7–10 is discussed. The rhetorical question of the psalm, "Who is this king of glory?" is answered in Hippolytus thus: "A worm and no man, the reproach of men and the outcast of the people.[334] He is the king of glory, mighty in battle." This passage, says Hippolytus, refers to Adam and his "ascension and rebirth, that he may be born spiritual, not fleshly." [335] The worm therefore signifies the second Adam, Christ. Epiphanius also mentions the worm as an allegory of Christ,[336] though without substantiating it further.

329 Cf. *Psychology and Alchemy*, fig. 217. There is also an indirect hint of this in the hanging up of the snake on a tree. Cf. the alchemical myth of Cadmus (supra, pars. 84ff.), and *Psychology and Alchemy*, fig. 150.

330 Honorius of Autun, *Spec. de myst. eccl.* (Migne, *P.L.*, vol. 172, col. 915).

331 Migne, *P.L.*, vol. 51, col. 833.

332 Cf. *Symbols of Transformation*, pars. 572ff.

333 Cf. supra, par. 146; also "Paracelsus as a Spiritual Phenomenon," par. 182.

334 This is another quotation, namely from Psalm 21 : 7 (DV). It is interesting that this psalm begins with the words: "My God, my God, why hast thou forsaken me?" an indication that the transformation of the King of Glory into the least of his creatures is felt as abandonment by God. The words are the same as Matthew 27 : 46: "Eli, Eli, lama sabachthani."

335 *Elenchos*, V, 8, 18 (Legge, I, p. 134).*

336 *Ancoratus*, 45 (ed. Holl, p. 55).

485   This train of thought is consciously or unconsciously continued in alchemy. The "Aquarium sapientum" says: [337]

And firstly it is here to be noted, that the Sages have called this decomposed product, on account of its blackness (Cant. 1), the raven's head. In the same way Christ (Isa. 53) had no form nor comeliness, was the vilest of all men, full of griefs and sicknesses, and so despised that men even hid their faces from him, and he was esteemed as nothing. Yea, in the 22nd Psalm [Vulgate] he complains of this, that he is a worm and no man, the laughing-stock and contempt of the people; indeed, it is not unfitly compared with Christ when the putrefied body of the Sun lies dead, inactive, like ashes, in the bottom of the phial, until, as a result of greater heat, its soul by degrees and little by little descends to it again, and once more infuses, moistens, and saturates the decaying and all but dead body, and preserves it from total destruction. So also did it happen to Christ himself, when at the Mount of Olives, and on the cross, he was roasted [338] by the fire of the divine wrath [339] (Matt. 26, 27), and complained that he was utterly deserted by his heavenly Father, yet none the less was always (as is wont to happen also to an earthly body through assiduous care and nourishing) comforted and strengthened (Matt. 4, Luke 22) and, so to speak, imbued, nourished, and supported with divine nectar; yea, when at last, in his most sacred passion, and at the hour of death, his strength and his very spirit were completely withdrawn from him, and he went down to the lowest and deepest parts below the earth (Acts 1, Eph. 1, I Peter 3), yet even there he was preserved, refreshed, and by the power of the eternal Godhead raised up again, quickened, and glorified (Rom. 14), when finally his spirit, with its body dead in the sepulchre, obtained a perfect and indissoluble union, through his most joyful resurrection and victorious ascension into heaven, as Lord and Christ (Matt. 28) and was exalted

337 *Mus. Herm.*, pp. 117f.

338 "Assatus." The word was used by the alchemists to denote the roasting of the ore.

339 "The fire of divine wrath" suggests Boehme's "divine wrath-fire." I do not know whether there is direct connection between them. In our treatise God's wrath, falling upon Christ, turns against God himself. Boehme discusses this question in "Aurora" (*Works*, I), VIII, 20ff., pp. 62ff., and *Quaestiones theosophicae* (Amsterdam edn., 1682, pp. 3, 11ff.), and says that on the one hand the wrath-fire comes from the "dryness," one of the seven "qualities" of Creation, and on the other hand it is connected with the first principle of "divine revelation," the darkness (Gen. 1 : 2), which "reaches into the fire" ("Tabula principiorum," I, pp. 2ff.). The fire is hidden in the centre of the light as well as in all creatures, and was kindled by Lucifer.

(Mark 16) to the right hand of his Father; with whom through the power and virtue of the Holy Spirit as true God and man he reigns and rules over all things in equal power and glory (Ps. 8), and by his most powerful word preserveth and upholdeth all things (Hebr. 1) and maketh all things one (Acts 17). And this wondrous Union and divine Exaltation angels and men, in heaven and on earth and under the earth (Philipp. 2, I Peter 1) can scarce comprehend, far less meditate upon, without fear and terror; and his virtue, power, and roseate Tincture [340] is able even now to change, and tint, and yet more, perfectly to cure and heal us sinful men in body and soul: of which things we shall have more to say below . . . Thus, then, we have briefly and simply considered the unique heavenly foundation and corner-stone Jesus Christ, that is to say, *how he is compared and united with the earthly philosophical stone of the Sages, whose material and preparation, as we have heard, is an outstanding type and lifelike image of the incarnation of Christ.*

486   The various fatalities which the old king has to suffer—immersion in the bath or in the sea, dissolution and decomposition, extinction of his light in the darkness, incineration in the fire, and renewal out of the chaos—are derived by the alchemists from the dissolution of the "matter" in acids, from the roasting of ores, the expulsion of sulphur or mercury, the reduction of metallic oxides, and so forth, as if these chemical procedures yielded a picture which, with a little straining of the imagination, could be compared with Christ's sufferings and his final triumph. The fact that they projected the Passion as an unconscious premise into the chemical transformations was not at all clear to the alchemists.[341] Naturally, under these circumstances, they were able to prove with complete success that their alleged observations coincided with the Passion. Only, it was not a question of their making observations on matter, but of introspection. Since, however, genuine projections are never voluntarily made but always appear as preconscious factors, there must have been something in the unconscious of the alchemists which lent itself to projection (i.e., had a tendency to become conscious

---

340 The rose-coloured tincture brings Christ into connection with the lion. (Cf. supra, pars. 419f.

341 We have an amusing example of this tendency in Dom Pernety *(Les Fables égyptiennes et grecques)*, who demonstrates the alchemical nature of ancient mythology without seeing that this was the matrix from which the alchemical ideas arose.

because of its energy charge), and on the other hand found in the alchemical operations a "hook" that attracted it, so that it could express itself in some way. Projection is always an indirect process of becoming conscious—indirect because of the check exercised by the conscious mind, by the pressure of traditional or conventional ideas which take the place of real experience and prevent it from happening. One feels that one possesses a valid truth concerning the unknown, and this makes any real knowledge of it impossible. The unconscious factor must necessarily have been something that was incompatible with the conscious attitude. What it was in reality we learn from the statements of the alchemists: a myth that had much in common not only with many mythologems of pagan origin but above all with Christian dogma. If it were identical with the dogma and appeared in projection it would show that the alchemists had a thoroughly anti-Christian attitude (which was not the case). Lacking such an attitude a projection of this kind would be psychologically impossible. But if the unconscious complex represented a figure that deviated from the dogma in certain essential features, then its projection becomes possible, for it would then be in opposition to the dogma approved by consciousness and would have arisen by way of compensation.

487   In this and my other writings I have constantly stressed the peculiar nature of the alchemists' statements and need not recapitulate what I have said. I should only like to point out that the central idea of the *filius philosophorum* is based on a conception of the Anthropos in which the "Man" or the "Son of Man" does not coincide with the Christian, historical redeemer figure. The alchemical Anthropos comes closer to the Basilidian conception of him as reported by Hippolytus: "For he [the Redeemer] . . . is in their view the inner spiritual man in the psychic . . . which is the Sonship that left the soul here not to die but to remain according to its nature, just as the first Sonship left behind on high the Holy Ghost, who is conterminous with him, in the appropriate place, clothing himself in his own soul." [342]

488   The inner spiritual man bears a resemblance to Christ—that is the unconscious premise for the statements about the *filius*

[342] *Elenchos*, VII, 27, 4f. (Legge, II, p. 78).

regius.[343] This idea contradicts the dogmatic view and therefore has every reason to be repressed and projected. At the same time it is the logical consequence of a spiritual situation in which the historical figure had long since disappeared from consciousness, while his spiritual presence was stressed all the more strongly in the form of the inner Christ or God who is born in the soul of man. The outward fact of the dogmatic Christ was answered from within by that inner primordial image which had produced a Purusha or a Gayomart long before the Christian era and made the assimilation of the Christian revelation possible. The ultimate fate of every dogma is that it gradually becomes soulless. Life wants to create new forms, and therefore, when a dogma loses its vitality, it must perforce activate the archetype that has always helped man to express the mystery of the soul. Note that I do not go so far as to say that the archetype actually *produces* the divine figure. If the psychologist were to assert that, he would have to possess a sure knowledge of the motives that underlie all historical development and be in a position to demonstrate this knowledge. But there is no question of that. I maintain only that the psychic archetype makes it possible for the divine figure to take form and become accessible to understanding. But the supremely important motive power which is needed for this, and which sets the archetypal possibilities in motion at a given historical moment, cannot be explained in terms of the archetype itself. Only experience can establish which archetype has become operative, but one can never predict that it *must* enter into manifestation. Who, for instance, could logically have foretold that the Jewish prophet Jesus would give the decisive answer to the spiritual situation in the age of Hellenistic syncretism, or that the slumbering image of the Anthropos would waken to world dominion?

489   The limitations of human knowledge which leave so many incomprehensible and wonderful things unexplained do not, however, exempt us from the task of trying to understand the revelations of the spirit that are embodied in dogma, otherwise there is a danger that the treasures of supreme knowledge which lie hidden in it will evaporate into nothing and become a bloodless phantom, an easy prey for all shallow rationalists. It would be a great step forward, in my opinion, if at least it were recog-

[343] Cf. *Psychology and Alchemy,* par. 451.

nized how far the truth of dogma is rooted in the human psyche, which is not the work of human hands.

490   The inner spiritual man of the Gnostics is the Anthropos, the man created in the image of the Nous, the ἀληθινὸς ἄνθρωπος (true man).[344] He corresponds to the *chên-yên* (true man) of Chinese alchemy. The *chên-yên* is the product of the opus. On the one hand he is the adept who is transformed by the work,[345] on the other he is the homunculus or filius of Western alchemy, who also derives from the true man.[346] The treatise of Wei Po-yang says:

> The ear, the eye, and the mouth constitute the three precious things. They should be closed, to stop communication. The True Man living in a deep abyss, floats about the centre of the round vessel . . . The mind is relegated to the realm of Nonexistence so as to acquire an enduring state of thoughtlessness. When the mind is integral, it will not go astray. In its sleep, it will be in God's embrace, but during its waking hours it is anxious about the continuation or termination of its existence.[347]

This true man is Dorn's "vir unus" and at the same time the lapis Philosophorum.[348]

491   The "true man" expresses the Anthropos in the individual human being. Compared with the revelation of the Son of Man in Christ this seems like a retrograde step, for the historical uniqueness of the Incarnation was *the* great advance which gathered the scattered sheep about one shepherd. The "Man" in the individual would mean, it is feared, a scattering of the flock. This would indeed be a retrograde step, but it cannot be blamed on the "true man"; its cause is rather all those bad human qualities which have always threatened and hindered the work of civilization. (Often, indeed, the sheep and the shepherd are just about equally inept.) The "true man" has nothing to do with this. Above all he will destroy no valuable cultural form since he himself is the highest form of culture. Neither in the East nor in the West does he play the game of shepherd and

---

344 Cf. Leisegang, *Der heilige Geist,* pp. 78f.

345 Wei Po-yang, "An Ancient Chinese Treatise on Alchemy," p. 241.

346 Cf. the Anthropos doctrine in Zosimos. (*Psychology and Alchemy,* par. 456.)

347 P. 251.

348 It is highly remarkable that there should be an Anthropos doctrine in China, where the basic philosophical assumptions are so very different.

sheep, because he has enough to do to be a shepherd to himself.

492   If the adept experiences his own self, the "true man," in his work, then, as the passage from the "Aquarium sapientum" shows, he encounters the analogy of the true man—Christ—in new and direct form, and he recognizes in the transformation in which he himself is involved a similarity to the Passion. It is not an "imitation of Christ" but its exact opposite: an assimilation of the Christ-image to his own self, which is the "true man." [349] It is no longer an effort, an intentional straining after imitation, but rather an involuntary experience of the reality represented by the sacred legend. This reality comes upon him in his work, just as the stigmata come to the saints without being consciously sought. They appear spontaneously. The Passion *happens to* the adept, not in its classic form—otherwise he would be consciously performing spiritual exercises—but in the form expressed by the alchemical myth. It is the arcane substance that suffers those physical and moral tortures; it is the king who dies or is killed, is dead and buried and on the third day rises again. And it is not the adept who suffers all this, rather *it* suffers in him, *it* is tortured, *it* passes through death and rises again. All this happens not to the alchemist himself but to the "true man," who he feels is near him and in him and at the same time in the retort. The passion that vibrates in our text and in the *Aurora* is genuine, but would be totally incomprehensible if the lapis were nothing but a chemical substance. Nor does it originate in contemplation of Christ's Passion; it is the real experience of a man who has got involved in the compensatory contents of the unconscious by investigating the unknown, seriously and to the point of self-sacrifice. He could not but see the likeness of his projected contents to the dogmatic images, and he might have been tempted to assume that his ideas were nothing else than the familiar religious conceptions, which he was using in order to explain the chemical procedure. But the texts show clearly that, on the contrary, a real experience of the opus had an increasing tendency to assimilate the dogma or to amplify itself with it. That is why the text says that Christ was "compared and united" with the stone. The alchemical Anthropos showed itself to be independent of any dogma.[350]

349 Who, *nota bene,* is not to be confused with the ego.
350 A reverse process set in during the 17th cent., exemplified most clearly in

493   The alchemist experienced the Anthropos in a form that was imbued with new vitality, freshness and immediacy, and this is reflected in the enthusiastic tone of the texts. It is therefore understandable that every single detail of the primordial drama would be realized in quite a new sense. The *nigredo* not only brought decay, suffering, death, and the torments of hell visibly before the eyes of the alchemist, it also cast the shadow of its melancholy over his own solitary soul.[351] In the blackness of a despair which was not his own, and of which he was merely the witness, he experienced how *it* turned into the worm and the poisonous dragon.[352] From inner necessity the dragon destroyed itself (*natura naturam vincit*) and changed into the lion,[353] and the adept, drawn involuntarily into the drama, then felt the need to cut off its paws [354] (unless there were two lions who devoured one another). The dragon ate its own wings as the eagle did its feathers.[355] These grotesque images reflect the conflict of opposites into which the researcher's curiosity had led him. His work began with a *katabasis*, a journey to the underworld as

Boehme. (The "Aquarium sapientum" represents the critical point between the two.) After that, the dogmatic figure of Christ began to predominate and enriched itself with alchemical ideas.

351 As Morienus (*Art. aurif.*, II, p. 18) says: "For the entry into rest is exceeding narrow, and no man can enter therein save by affliction of the soul." *

352 "There is in our chemistry a certain noble substance, which moves from lord to lord" * (Maier, *Symb. aur. mensae*, p. 568). "Verus Mercurii spiritus" and "sulphuris anima" are parallels to dragon and eagle, king and lion, spirit and body (*Mus. herm.*, p. 11). The "senex-draco" must be reborn as the king (*Verus Hermes*, p. 16). King and Queen are represented with a dragon's tail (Eleazar, *Uraltes Chymisches Werck*, pp. 82ff.). There, on p. 38, it is said that a black worm and dragon come from the king and queen in the *nigredo*. The worm Phyton sucks the king's blood (p. 47).

353 Since the alchemical symbols are saturated with astrology, it is important to know that the chief star in Leo is called Regulus ("little king") and that the Chaldaeans regarded it as the lion's heart (Bouché-Leclercq, *L'Astrologie grecque*, pp. 438f.). Regulus is a favourable sign at the birth of kings. "Cor" (heart) is one of the names of the arcane substance. It signifies "fire, or any great heat" (Ruland, *Lexicon*, p. 114).

354 Cf. *Psychology and Alchemy*, fig. 4, top left. Also the inscription in *Pandora* (ed. Reusner), p. 227: "Kill the lion in his blood." The symbol derives from Senior (*De chemia*, p. 64).

355 See the eagle with the head of a king consuming his feathers in the Ripley Scrowle: *Psychology and Alchemy*, fig. 228.

Dante also experienced it,[356] with the difference that the adept's soul was not only impressed by it but radically altered. *Faust I* is an example of this: the transformation of an earnest scholar, through his pact with the devil, into a worldly cavalier and crooked careerist. In the case of the fanciful Christian Rosencreutz the descent to Venus led only to his being slightly wounded in the hand by Cupid's arrow. The texts, however, hint at more serious dangers. Olympiodorus says: [357] "Without great pains this work is not perfected; there will be struggles, violence, and war. And all the while the demon Ophiuchos [358] instils negligence (ὀλιγωρίαν), impeding our intentions; everywhere he creeps about, both within and without, causing oversights, anxiety, and unexpected accidents, or else keeping us from the work by harassments (λύπαις) and injuries." The philosopher Petasios (Petesis), quoted by Olympiodorus, expresses himself even more strongly: "So bedevilled (δαιμονοπληξίας) and shameless (ἀναιδείας) is the lead [359] that all who wish to investigate it fall into madness through ignorance." That this is not just empty talk is shown by other texts, which often emphasize how much the psyche of the laborant was involved in the work. Thus Dorn, commenting on the quotation from Hermes, "All obscurity shall yield before thee," says:

For he saith, All obscurity shall yield before thee; he saith not, before the metals. By obscurity is to be understood naught else but the darkness of diseases and sickness of body and mind . . . The

356 So far I have found no reference to Dante in any of the texts.

357 Berthelot, *Alch. grecs*, II, iv, 28.

358 It is difficult to explain why the constellation Ophiuchos (Anguitenens, Serpentarius, the Serpent-Holder) is called a demon. Astronomically speaking he stands on Scorpio and is therefore connected astrologically with poison and physicians. And indeed, in the ancient world he signified Asklepios (Roscher, *Lexikon*, VI, cols. 921f.). Hippolytus (*Elenchos*, IV, 47, 5ff.) states that whereas the constellation Engonasi (The Kneeler) represents Adam and his labours, and hence the first creation, Ophiuchos represents the second creation or rebirth through Christ, since he prevents the Serpent from reaching the Crown (στέφανος, corona borealis, the Wreath of Ariadne, the beloved of Dionysus). (Cf. Bouché-Leclercq, p. 609, n. 1.) This interpretation does not fit in badly with the "saviour" Asklepios. But since, according to the ancients, snake-charmers are born under this constellation, a nefarious connotation may have crept in (also, perhaps, through the "poisonous" Scorpio).

359 Μόλυβδος, another name for the arcane substance.

author's intention is, in sum, to teach them that are adepts in spagyric medicine how with a very small dose, such as is suggested by a grain of mustard seed,[360] however it be taken, to cure all diseases indifferently, by reason of the simplicity of union[361] effective in the medicine, so that no variety of the multitude of maladies may resist it. But manifold as are the obscurities of the weaknesses of the mind, as insanity [*vesania*], mania, frenzy [*furia*], stupidity [*stoliditas*], and others like, by which the spirit [*animus*] is darkened and impaired, yet by this single spagyric medicine they are perfectly cured. And it not only restores health to the spirit [*animo*], but also sharpens the ingenuity and mind of men, that all things may be miraculously easy[362] for them in understanding [*intellectu*] and perception [*perceptu*], and nothing be hid from them which is in the upper or lower world.[363]

The sentence from the "Tabula smaragdina," "He will conquer every subtle thing," Dorn interprets as follows: the subtle thing is Mercurius, or the "spiritual obscurities that occupy the mind"; in other words it is spirit. Hence the darkness is a demon that possesses the spirit (as in Olympiodorus) and can be cast out by the work ("it expels every subtle thing").[364] Sickness is an imprinting of evil (*impressio mali*) and is healed through the "repression of evil by the action of the true and universal centre upon the body." This centre is the unarius or the One, in which the unitary man (*unicus homo*) is rooted. If, therefore, he is to recover from his bodily and spiritual sicknesses, "let him study to know and to understand exactly the centre, and apply himself wholly thereto, and the centre will be freed from all imperfec-

360 An allusion to Matthew 13 : 31: "The kingdom of heaven is like to a grain of mustard seed."

361 "Unionis simplicitas" refers probably to the doctrine of the "res simplex," signifying the Platonic "Idea." "The simple is that which Plato calls the intelligible, not the sensible." "The simple is the unexpected part," it is "indivisible" and "of one essence." The soul is "simplex." "The work is not brought to perfection unless it ends in the simple." "The conversion of the elements to the simple." "Man is the most worthy of living things and nearest to the simple, and this because of his intelligence." Quotations from "Liber Platonis quartorum," *Theatr. chem.*, V, pp. 120, 122, 130, 139, 179, 189.*

362 Cf. "Spec. phil.," *Theatr. chem.*, I, p. 298: "They found the virtue [power] of it [truth] to be such, that it performed miracles." * (Cf. also "Phil. chemica," *Theatr. chem.*, I, pp. 497 and 507.)

363 "Physica Trismegisti," *Theatr. chem.*, I, p. 433.

364 Ibid., p. 434.

tions and diseases,[365] that it may be restored to its state of original monarchy." [366]

494 These passages from Dorn refer less to the dangers of the work than to the healing through the outcome of the work. But the means of healing come from Mercurius, that spirit [367] of whom the philosophers said: "Take the old black spirit, and destroy therewith the bodies until they are changed." [367a] The destruction of the bodies is depicted as a battle, as in Sermo 42 of the *Turba:* "Excite war between the copper and the quicksilver, since they strive to perish and first become corrupt." "Excite the battle between them and destroy the body of the copper, till it becomes powder." [368] This battle is the *separatio, divisio, putrefactio, mortificatio,* and *solutio,* which all represent the original chaotic state of conflict between the four hostile elements. Dorn describes this vicious, warlike quaternity allegorically as the four-horned serpent, which the devil, after his fall from heaven, sought to "infix" in the mind of man.[369] Dorn puts the motif of war on a moral plane [370] and thereby approximates it to the modern concept of psychic dissociation, which, as we know, lies at the root of the psychogenic psychoses and neuroses. In the "furnace of the cross" and in the fire, says the "Aquarium sapientum," "man, like the earthly gold, attains to the true black Raven's Head; that is, he is utterly disfigured and is held in derision by the world,[371] and this not only for forty days and nights,

365 The centre, therefore, cannot be simply God (the "One"), since only in man can it be attacked by disease.
366 "De tenebris contra naturam," *Theatr. chem.,* I, pp. 530f.*
367 Cf. "The Spirit Mercurius."
367a *Turba,* Sermo XLVII, p. 152.* (Another reading for "veterum" is "et unientem.")
368 * Ibid., p. 149.
369 "The devil seeking to erect them [the horns] into heaven, and being cast down therefrom, attempted thereafter to infix them in the mind of men, namely, ambition, brutality, calumny, and dissension." * ("De tenebris contra naturam," *Theatr. chem.,* I, p. 531.)
370 Likewise the "Aquarium sapientum," *Mus. herm.,* p. 129 (Waite, I, p. 110) says: "Man is placed by God in the furnace of tribulation, and like the Hermetic compound he is troubled at length with all kinds of straits, divers calamities and anxieties, until he die to the old Adam and the flesh, and rise again as in truth a new man." *
371 Here the author refers to Wisdom of Solomon, ch. 5, obviously meaning verses 3 and 4: ". . . These are they whom we had some little time in derision and for a parable of reproach. We fools esteemed their life madness and their end without

or years,[372] but often for the whole duration of his life; so much so that he experiences more heartache in his life than comfort and joy, and more sadness than pleasure . . . Through this spiritual death his soul is entirely freed." [373] Evidently the *nigredo* brought about a deformation and a psychic suffering which the author compared to the plight of the unfortunate Job. Job's unmerited misfortune, visited on him by God, is the suffering of God's servant and a prefiguration of Christ's Passion. One can see from this how the figure of the Son of Man gradually lodged itself in the ordinary man who had taken the "work" upon his own shoulders.

495   In the second century of our era Wei Po-yang, quite uninfluenced by Western alchemy and unhampered by the preconceptions of our Christian psychology, gave a drastic account of the sufferings caused by a technical blunder during the opus:

> Disaster will come to the black mass: gases from food consumed will make noises inside the intestines and stomach. The right essence will be exhaled and the evil one inhaled. Days and nights will be passed without sleep, moon after moon. The body will then be tired out, giving rise to an appearance of insanity. The hundred pulses will stir and boil so violently as to drive away peace of mind and body . . . Ghostly things will make their appearance, at which he will marvel even in his sleep. He is then led to rejoice, thinking that he is assured of longevity. But all of a sudden he is seized by an untimely death.[374]

So we can understand why Khunrath writes:

> But chiefly pray to God . . . for the good gift of discretion, the good spirit of discriminating good from evil, who may lead thee into true knowledge and understanding of the Light of Nature, into her Great Book. So wilt thou extricate thyself from the labyrinth of very very

---

honour" (DV). He also mentions Job 30, where verse 10 would be relevant: "They abhor me and flee far from me, and are not afraid to spit in my face."

[372] Genesis 8 : 6: Noah sent forth the raven after 40 days. Gen. 7 : 7: rising of the flood. Gen. 7 : 4: "I will rain upon the earth forty days and forty nights." Luke 4 : 1f: "Jesus . . . was led by the Spirit into the wilderness, being forty days tempted of the devil." Exodus 34 : 28: Moses was with the Lord forty days and forty nights. Deut. 8 : 2: The children of Israel wandered forty years in the wilderness.

[373] *Mus. herm.,* p. 130 (Waite, I, p. 111).*

[374] "An Ancient Chinese Treatise on Alchemy," p. 238. Cf. the motif of torture in "Transformation Symbolism in the Mass," pars. 345ff., 410f.

many deceitful Papers, and even books of Parchment, and arrive right well at the ground of truth.[375]

496   The depressions of the adept are also described in the "Tractatus aureus":

My son, this is the hidden stone of many colours, which is born in one colour; know this and conceal it. By this, the Almighty favouring, the greatest diseases are escaped, and every sorrow,[376] distress, evil, and hurtful thing is made to depart. It leads from darkness to light, from this desert wilderness to a secure habitation, and from poverty and straits into freedom.[377]

497   These testimonies suffice to show that the adept was not only included in his work but also knew it.

7. THE RELATION OF THE KING-SYMBOL TO CONSCIOUSNESS

498   The apotheosis of the king, the renewed rising of the sun, means, on our hypothesis, that a new dominant of consciousness has been produced and that the psychic potential is reversed. Consciousness is no longer under the dominion of the unconscious, in which state the dominant is hidden in the darkness, but has now glimpsed and recognized a supreme goal. The apotheosis of the king depicts this change, and the resultant feeling of renewal is expressed nowhere more plainly than in some of our loveliest chorals. Ripley's *Cantilena* includes mother Luna, the maternal aspect of night, in this transfiguration, which reminds us of the apotheosis at the end of *Faust II*. It is as though the moon had risen in the night with as much splendour as the sun. And just as the Queen "flows with all delicious unguent" so, in the Acts of Thomas,[378] a sweet smell pours from the heavenly goddess. She is not only the mother but the "Kore, daughter of the light." She is the Gnostic Sophia,[379] who corresponds to the alchemical mother. If our interpretation of King

---

[375] *Hyl. Chaos,* pp. 186f.
[376] Instead of "tristitia" the usual synonym for the nigredo is "melancholia," as in "Consil. coniugii" (*Ars chemica,* pp. 125f.): "Melancholia id est nigredo."
[377] *Ars chemica,* p. 14.
[378] Cf. James, *The Apocryphal New Testament,* p. 367.
[379] Bousset, *Hauptprobleme der Gnosis,* pp. 58ff.

Sol is correct,[380] then the apotheosis must also have made mother Luna visible, that is to say made the unconscious conscious. What at first sight seems a contradiction in terms resolves itself, on closer examination, as the coming into consciousness of an essential content of the unconscious. It is primarily the feminine element in man, the anima,[381] that becomes visible; secondly the moonlight, which enables us to see in the dark, and represents an illumination of the unconscious, or its permeability to light; and thirdly, the moon stands for the rotundum, about which I have written in *Psychology and Alchemy*.[382] In the sublunary world her roundness (*plenilunium, circulus lunaris*)[383] corresponds, as the mirror-image of the sun, to the Anthropos, the psychological self, or psychic totality.

499   The moon is the connecting-link between the concept of the Virgin Mother and that of the child, who is round, whole, and perfect. The new birth from the moon can therefore be expressed as much by the Christian's joy at Eastertide as by the mystic dawn, the *aurora consurgens;* for the risen king is the "soul, which is infused into the dead stone."[384] The idea of roundness is also found in the crown, symbol of kingship. "Corona regis" is cited as synonymous with ashes, body, sea, salt, mother and Blessed Virgin,[385] and is thus identified with the feminine element.

500   This peculiar relationship between rotundity and the mother is explained by the fact that the mother, the unconscious, is the place where the symbol of wholeness appears. The fact that the rotundum is, as it were, contained in the anima and is prefigured by her lends her that extraordinary fascination which char-

---

[380] The coincidence of the apotheosis of the king with the birth of Christ is indicated in D'Espagnet, *Arcanum Hermeticae philosophiae opus*, p. 82: "But lastly, [the opus] comes to an end in the other royal throne of Jove, from which our most mighty king shall receive a crown adorned with most precious rubies. 'Thus in its own footsteps does the year revolve upon itself.' " *

[381] The anima mediates between consciousness and the collective unconscious, just as the persona does between the ego and the environment. Cf. *Two Essays on Analytical Psychology*, pars. 305ff., 339, 507.

[382] Pars. 107f. and n. 38, 116. Cf. "Transformation Symbolism in the Mass," pars. 366ff.

[383] Cf. Albertus Magnus, "Super arborem Aristotelis" (*Theatr. chem.*, II, p. 527): "The stork sat there, as if calling itself the circle of the moon." * The stork, like the swan and goose, has a maternal significance.

[384] "Exercit. in Turbam," *Art. aurif.*, I, p. 181.*   [385] Ibid., p. 180.

acterizes the "Eternal Feminine" in the good as well as the bad sense. At a certain level, therefore, woman appears as the true carrier of the longed-for wholeness and redemption.

501   The starting-point of our explanation is that the king is essentially synonymous with the sun and that the sun represents the daylight of the psyche, consciousness, which as the faithful companion of the sun's journey rises daily from the ocean of sleep and dream, and sinks into it again at evening. Just as in the round-dance of the planets, and in the star-strewn spaces of the sky, the sun journeys along as a solitary figure, like any other one of the planetary archons, so consciousness, which refers everything to its own ego as the centre of the universe, is only one among the archetypes of the unconscious, comparable to the King Helios of post-classical syncretism, whom we meet in Julian the Apostate, for instance. This is what the complex of consciousness would look like if it could be viewed from one of the other planets, as we view the sun from the earth. The subjective ego-personality, i.e., consciousness and its contents, is indeed seen in its various aspects by an unconscious observer, or rather by an observer placed in the "outer space" of the unconscious. That this is so is proved by dreams, in which the conscious personality, the ego of the dreamer, is seen from a standpoint that is "toto coelo" different from that of the conscious mind. Such a phenomenon could not occur at all unless there were in the unconscious other standpoints opposing or competing with ego-consciousness. These relationships are aptly expressed by the planet simile. The king represents ego-consciousness, the subject of all subjects, as an object. His fate in mythology portrays the rising and setting of this most glorious and most divine of all the phenomena of creation, without which the world would not exist as an object. For everything that is only is because it is directly or indirectly known, and moreover this "known-ness" is sometimes represented in a way which the subject himself does not know, just as if he were being observed from another planet, now with benevolent and now with sardonic gaze.

502   This far from simple situation derives partly from the fact that the ego has the paradoxical quality of being both the subject and the object of its own knowledge, and partly from the fact that the psyche is not a unity but a "constellation" consisting of other luminaries besides the sun. The ego-complex is not

357

the only complex in the psyche.[386] The possibility that unconscious complexes possess a certain luminosity, a kind of consciousness, cannot be dismissed out of hand, for they can easily give rise to something in the nature of secondary personalities, as psychopathological experience shows. But if this is possible, then an observation of the ego-complex from another standpoint somewhere in the same psyche is equally possible. As I have said, the critical portrayal of the ego-complex in dreams and in abnormal psychic states seems to be due to this.

503 The conscious mind often knows little or nothing about its own transformation, and does not want to know anything. The more autocratic it is and the more convinced of the eternal validity of its truths, the more it identifies with them. Thus the kingship of Sol, which is a natural phenomenon, passes to the human king who personifies the prevailing dominant idea and must therefore share its fate. In the phenomenal world the Heraclitan law of everlasting change, πάντα ῥεῖ, prevails; and it seems that all the true things must change and that only that which changes remains true.

504 Pitilessly it is seen from another planet that the king is growing old, even before he sees it himself: ruling ideas, the "dominants," change, and the change, undetected by consciousness, is mirrored only in dreams. King Sol, as the archetype of consciousness, voyages through the world of the unconscious, one of its multitudinous figures which may one day be capable of consciousness too. These lesser lights are, on the old view, identical with the planetary correspondences in the psyche which were postulated by astrology. When, therefore, an alchemist conjured up the spirit of Saturn as his familiar, this was an attempt to bring to consciousness a standpoint outside the ego, involving a relativization of the ego and its contents. The intervention of the planetary spirit was besought as an aid. When the king grows old and needs renewing, a kind of planetary bath is instituted—a bath into which all the planets pour their "influences."[387] This expresses the idea that the dominant, grown feeble with age,

---

[386] The primitive assertion that the individual has a plurality of souls is in agreement with our findings. Cf. Tylor, *Primitive Culture*, I, pp. 391ff.; Schultze, *Psychologie der Naturvölker*, p. 268; Crawley, *The Idea of the Soul*, pp. 235ff.; and Frazer, *Taboo and the Perils of the Soul*, pp. 27 and 80, and *Balder the Beautiful*, II, pp. 221ff.   [387] Cf. *Psychology and Alchemy*, figs. 27, 57, 257.

needs the support and influence of those subsidiary lights to fortify and renew it. It is, as it were, dissolved in the substance of the other planetary archetypes and then put together again. Through this process of melting and recasting there is formed a new amalgam of a more comprehensive nature, which has taken into itself the influences of the other planets or metals.[388]

505   In this alchemical picture we can easily recognize the projection of the transformation process: the aging of a psychic dominant is apparent from the fact that it expresses the psychic totality in ever-diminishing degree. One can also say that the psyche no longer feels wholly contained in the dominant, whereupon the dominant loses its fascination and no longer grips the psyche so completely as before. On the other hand its content and meaning are no longer properly understood, or what is understood fails to touch the heart. A "sentiment d'incomplétude" of this kind produces a compensatory reaction which attracts other regions of the psyche and their contents, so as to fill up the gap. As a rule this is an unconscious process that always sets in when the attitude and orientation of the conscious mind have proved inadequate. I stress this point because the conscious mind is a bad judge of its own situation and often persists in the illusion that its attitude is just the right one and is only prevented from working because of some external annoyance. If the dreams were observed it would soon become clear why the conscious assumptions have become unworkable. And if, finally, neurotic symptoms appear, then the attitude of consciousness, its ruling idea, is contradicted, and in the unconscious there is a stirring up of those archetypes that were the most suppressed by the conscious attitude. The therapist then has no other course than to confront the ego with its adversary and thus initiate the melting and recasting process. The confrontation is expressed, in the alchemical myth of the king, as the collision of the masculine, spiritual father-world ruled over by King Sol with the feminine, chthonic mother-world symbolized by the *aqua permanens* or by the chaos.

506   The illegitimate aspect of this relationship appears as incest, veiled, in the *Cantilena,* by adoption—which nevertheless results in the pregnancy of the mother. As I have explained elsewhere,

[388] Ibid., fig. 149.

359

incest expresses the union of elements that are akin or of the same nature; that is to say the adversary of Sol is his own feminine chthonic aspect which he has forgotten. Sol's reflected light is the feminine Luna, who dissolves the king in her moistness. It is as though Sol had to descend into the watery deep of the sublunary world in order to unite the "powers of Above and Below" (as in Faust's journey to the Mothers). The unworkable conscious dominant disappears in menacing fashion among the contents rising up from the unconscious, thus bringing about a darkening of the light. The warring elements of primeval chaos are unleashed, as though they had never been subjugated. The battle is fought out between the dominant and the contents of the unconscious so violently that reason would like to clamp down on unreason. But these attempts fail, and go on failing until the ego acknowledges its impotence and lets the furious battle of psychic powers go its own way. If the ego does not interfere with its irritating rationality, the opposites, just *because* they are in conflict, will gradually draw together, and what looked like death and destruction will settle down into a latent state of concord, suitably expressed by the symbol of pregnancy.[389] In consequence the king, the previous dominant of consciousness, is transformed into a real and workable whole, whereas before he had only pretended to wholeness.

507   The *Cantilena* shows us what that dominant was which is subjected to transformation not only in Ripley but in many other alchemists: it was the Christian view of the world in the Middle Ages. This problem is of such dimensions that one cannot expect a medieval man to have been even remotely conscious of it. It was bound to work itself out in projection, unconsciously. For this reason, too, it can hardly be grasped even today —which is why the psychological interpretation of the One, the *filius regius,* meets with the greatest difficulties. From the hymn-like manner in which the alchemists praised their "son" it is quite evident that they meant by this symbol either Christ himself or something that corresponded to him. Naturally they were not concerned with the historical personality of Jesus, which at

[389] The phase of the conflict of opposites is usually represented by fighting animals, such as the lion, dragon, wolf, and dog. Cf. Lambspringk's Symbols in the *Musaeum hermeticum.*

that time was completely covered up by the dogmatic figure of the second Person of the Trinity. The latter symbol had slowly crystallized out in the course of the centuries, though it was clearly prefigured in the Logos of St. John. Nor was the conception of God as *senex* and *puer* peculiar to the alchemists, for many clerics who were not alchemists took it as a transformation of the wrathful and vindictive Yahweh of the Old Testament into the God of Love of the New. Thus the archetype of the king's renewal manifested itself not only among the "philosophers" but also in ecclesiastical circles.[390]

508   There can be a psychological explanation of the *filius regius* only when this image has sloughed off its projected form and become a purely psychic experience. The Christ-lapis parallel shows clearly enough that the *filius regius* was more a psychic event than a physical one, since as a physical event it can demonstrably never occur and as a religious experience it is beyond question. There are many passages in the texts that can be interpreted—strange as this may sound—as an experience of Christ in matter. Others, again, lay so much emphasis on the lapis that one cannot but see in it a renewal and completion of the dogmatic image. An unequivocal substitution of the *filius regius* for Christ does not, to my knowledge, occur in the literature, for which reason one must call alchemy Christian even though heretical. The Christ-lapis remains an ambiguous figure.

509   This is of considerable importance as regards a psychological interpretation of the *filius regius*. In any such view the place of matter, with its magical fascination, is taken by the unconscious, which was projected into it. For our modern consciousness the dogmatic image of Christ changed, under the influence of evangelical Protestantism, into the personal Jesus, who in liberal rationalism, which abhorred all "mysticism," gradually faded into a mere ethical prototype. The disappearance of the feminine element, namely the cult of the Mother of God, in Protestantism was all that was needed for the spirituality of the dogmatic image to detach itself from the earthly man and gradually sink into the unconscious. When such great and significant images fall into oblivion they do not disappear from the human sphere, nor do they lose their psychic power. Anyone in the Mid-

390 Cf. *Psychology and Alchemy*, pars. 520ff.

dle Ages who was familiar with the mysticism of alchemy remained in contact with the living dogma, even if he was a Protestant. This is probably the reason why alchemy reached its heyday at the end of the sixteenth and in the seventeenth century: for the Protestant it was the only way of still being Catholic. In the opus alchymicum he still had a completely valid transformation rite and a concrete mystery. But alchemy did not flourish only in Protestant countries; in Catholic France it was still widely practised during the eighteenth century, as numerous manuscripts and published works testify, such as those of Dom Pernety (1716–1800?), Lenglet du Fresnoy (1674–1752?), and the great compilation of Manget, published 1702. This is not surprising, as in France at that time the modern anti-Christian "schism" was brewing which was to culminate in the Revolution—that relatively harmless prelude to the horrors of today. The decline of alchemy during the Enlightenment meant for many Europeans a descent of all dogmatic images—which till then had been directly present in the ostensible secrets of chemical matter—to the underworld.

510   Just as the decay of the conscious dominant is followed by an irruption of chaos in the individual,[391] so also in the case of the masses (Peasant Wars, Anabaptists, French Revolution, etc.), and the furious conflict of elements in the individual psyche is reflected in the unleashing of primeval blood-thirstiness and lust for murder on a collective scale. This is the sickness so vividly described in the *Cantilena*. The loss of the eternal images is in truth no light matter for the man of discernment. But since there are infinitely many more men of no discernment, nobody, apparently, notices that the truth expressed by the dogma has vanished in a cloud of fog, and nobody seems to miss anything. The discerning person knows and feels that his psyche is disquieted by the loss of something that was the life-blood of his ancestors. The undiscerning (ἄνοοι) miss nothing, and only discover afterwards in the papers (much too late) the alarming symptoms that have now become "real" in the outside world because they were not perceived before inside, in oneself, just as the presence of the eternal images was not noticed. If they had been, a threnody for the lost god would have arisen, as once before in antiquity at

391 Ibid., pars. 38, 56ff.

the death of Great Pan.[392] Instead, all well-meaning people assure us that one has only to believe he is still there—which merely adds stupidity to unconsciousness. Once the symptoms are really outside in some form of sociopolitical insanity, it is impossible to convince anybody that the conflict is in the psyche of every individual, since he is now quite sure where his enemy is. Then, the conflict which remains an intrapsychic phenomenon in the mind of the discerning person, takes place on the plane of projection in the form of political tension and murderous violence. To produce such consequences the individual must have been thoroughly indoctrinated with the insignificance and worthlessness of his psyche and of psychology in general. One must preach at him from all the pulpits of authority that salvation always comes from outside and that the meaning of his existence lies in the "community." He can then be led docilely to the place where of his own natural accord he would rather go anyway: to the land of childhood, where one makes claims exclusively on others, and where, if wrong is done, it is always somebody else who has done it. When he no longer knows by what his soul is sustained, the potential of the unconscious is increased and takes the lead. Desirousness overpowers him, and illusory goals set up in the place of the eternal images excite his greed. The beast of prey seizes hold of him and soon makes him forget that he is a human being. His animal affects hamper any reflection that might stand in the way of his infantile wish-fulfilments, filling him instead with a feeling of a new-won right to existence and intoxicating him with the lust for booty and blood.

511   Only the living presence of the eternal images can lend the human psyche a dignity which makes it morally possible for a man to stand by his own soul, and be convinced that it is worth his while to persevere with it. Only then will he realize that the conflict is *in him,* that the discord and tribulation are his riches, which should not be squandered by attacking others; and that, if

392 In late antiquity Pan was no longer a grotesque pastoral deity but had taken on a philosophical significance. The Naassenes regarded him as one of the forms of the "many-formed Attis" (*Elenchos,* V, 9, 9) and as synonymous with Osiris, Sophia, Adam, Korybas, Papa, Bakcheus, etc. The story of the dirge is in Plutarch, "The Obsolescence of Oracles," 17 (*Moralia,* V, pp. 401ff.). (Cf. "Psychology and Religion," par. 145). Its modern equivalent is Zarathustra's cry "God is dead!" (*Thus Spake Zarathustra,* p. 67).

fate should exact a debt from him in the form of guilt, it is a debt to himself. Then he will recognize the worth of his psyche, for nobody can owe a debt to a mere nothing. But when he loses his own values he becomes a hungry robber, the wolf, lion, and other ravening beasts which for the alchemists symbolized the appetites that break loose when the black waters of chaos—i.e., the unconsciousness of projection—have swallowed up the king.[393]

512   It is a subtle feature of the *Cantilena* that the pregnancy cravings of the mother are stilled with peacock's flesh and lion's blood, i.e., with her own flesh and blood.[394] If the projected conflict is to be healed, it must return into the psyche of the individual, where it had its unconscious beginnings. He must celebrate a Last Supper with himself, and eat his own flesh and drink his own blood; which means that he must recognize and accept the other in himself. But if he persists in his one-sidedness, the two lions will tear each other to pieces. Is this perhaps the meaning of Christ's teaching, that each must bear his own cross? For if you have to endure yourself, how will you be able to rend others also?

513   Such reflections are justified by the alchemical symbolism, as one can easily see if one examines the so-called allegories a little more closely and does not dismiss them at the start as worthless rubbish. The miraculous feeding with one's own substance—so strangely reflecting its prototype, Christ—means nothing less than the integration of those parts of the personality

---

[393] "In the midst of the Chaos a small globe is happily indicated, and this is the supreme point of junction of all that is useful for this quest. This small place, more efficient than all the entirety, this part which comprises its whole, this accessory more abundant than its principal, on opening the store of its treasures, causes the two substances to appear which are but a single one. . . . Of these two is composed the unique perfect, the simple abundant, the composite without parts, the only indivisible hatchet of the sages, from which emerges the scroll of destiny, extending evenly beyond the Chaos, after which it advances in ordered fashion to its rightful end." ("Recueil stéganographique," *Le Songe de Poliphile*, II, f.) In these words Béroalde de Verville describes the germ of unity in the unconscious.
[394] Because of his fiery nature, the lion is the "affective animal" *par excellence*. The drinking of the blood, the essence of the lion, is therefore like assimilating one's own affects. Through the wound the lion is "tapped," so to speak: the affect is pierced by the well-aimed thrust of the weapon (insight), which sees through the motive for the affect. In alchemy, the wounding or mutilation of the lion signifies the subjugation of concupiscence.

which are still outside ego-consciousness. Lion and peacock, emblems of concupiscence and pride, signify the overweening pretensions of the human shadow, which we so gladly project on our fellow man in order to visit our own sins upon him with apparent justification. In the age-old image of the uroboros lies the thought of devouring oneself and turning oneself into a circulatory process, for it was clear to the more astute alchemists that the prima materia of the art was man himself.[395] The uroboros is a dramatic symbol for the integration and assimilation of the opposite, i.e., of the shadow. This "feed-back" process is at the same time a symbol of immortality, since it is said of the uroboros that he slays himself and brings himself to life, fertilizes himself and gives birth to himself. He symbolizes the One, who proceeds from the clash of opposites, and he therefore constitutes the secret of the prima materia which, as a projection, unquestionably stems from man's unconscious. Accordingly, there must be some psychic datum in it which gives rise to such assertions, and these assertions must somehow characterize that datum even if they are not to be taken literally. What the ultimate reason is for these assertions or manifestations must remain a mystery, but a mystery whose inner kinship with the mystery of faith was sensed by the adepts, so that for them the two were identical.

8. THE RELIGIOUS PROBLEM OF THE KING'S RENEWAL

514   Medical psychology has recognized today that it is a therapeutic necessity, indeed, the first requisite of any thorough psychological method, for consciousness to confront its shadow.[396] In the end this must lead to some kind of union, even though the union consists at first in an open conflict, and often remains so for a long time. It is a struggle that cannot be abolished by rational means.[397] When it is wilfully repressed it continues in

[395] Thus Morienus (7th–8th cent.) states: "This thing is extracted from thee, for thou art its ore; in thee they find it, and, to speak more plainly, from thee they take it; and when thou hast experienced this, the love and desire for it will be increased in thee. And thou shalt know that this thing subsists truly and beyond all doubt" * (*Art. aurif.*, II, p. 37).

[396] In Freud this is done by making conscious the repressed contents; in Adler, by gaining insight into the fictitious "life-style."

[397] This sentence needs qualifying as it does not apply to all conflict situations. Anything that can be decided by reason without injurious effects can safely be left

the unconscious and merely expresses itself indirectly and all the more dangerously, so no advantage is gained. The struggle goes on until the opponents run out of breath. What the outcome will be can never be seen in advance. The only certain thing is that both parties will be changed; but what the product of the union will be it is impossible to imagine. The empirical material shows that it usually takes the form of a subjective experience which, according to the unanimous testimony of history, is always of a religious order. If, therefore, the conflict is consciously endured and the analyst follows its course without prejudice, he will unfailingly observe compensations from the unconscious which aim at producing a unity. He will come across numerous symbols similar to those found in alchemy—often, indeed, the very same. He will also discover that not a few of these spontaneous formations have a numinous quality in harmony with the mysticism of the historical testimonies. It may happen, besides, that a patient, who till then had shut his eyes to religious questions, will develop an unexpected interest in these matters. He may, for instance, find himself getting converted from modern paganism to Christianity or from one creed to another, or even getting involved in fundamental theological questions which are incomprehensible to a layman. It is unnecessary for me to point out here that not every analysis leads to a conscious realization of the conflict, just as not every surgical operation is as drastic as a resection of the stomach. There is a minor surgery, too, and in the same way there is a minor psychotherapy whose operations are harmless and require no such elucidation as I am concerned with here. The patients I have in mind are a small minority with certain spiritual demands to be satisfied, and only these patients undergo a development which presents the doctor with the kind of problem we are about to discuss.

515 Experience shows that the union of antagonistic elements is an irrational occurrence which can fairly be described as "mystical," provided that one means by this an occurrence that cannot be reduced to anything else or regarded as in some way unauthentic. The decisive criterion here is not rationalistic opinions or regard for accepted theories, but simply and solely the value

to reason. I am thinking, rather, of those conflicts which reason can no longer master without danger to the psyche.

for the patient of the solution he has found and experienced. In this respect the doctor, whose primary concern is the preservation of life, is in an advantageous position, since he is by training an empiricist and has always had to employ medicines whose healing power he knew even though he did not understand how it worked. Equally, he finds all too often that the scientifically explained and attested healing power of his medicines does not work in practice.

516   If, now, the alchemists meant by their old king that he was God himself, this also applies to his son. They themselves must have shrunk from thinking out the logical consequences of their symbolism, otherwise they would have had to assert that God grows old and must be renewed through the art. Such a thought would have been possible at most in the Alexandrian epoch, when gods sprang up like mushrooms. But for medieval man it was barely conceivable.[398] He was far more likely to consider that the art would change something in himself, for which reason he regarded its product as a kind of φάρμακον. Had he had any idea of "psychology," he would almost certainly have called his healing medicament "psychic" and would have regarded the king's renewal as a transformation of the conscious dominant— which naturally has nothing to do with a magical intervention in the sphere of the gods.

517   Man's ideas and definitions of God have followed one another kaleidoscopically in the course of the millennia, and the evangelist Mark would have been very much astonished if he could have taken a look at Harnack's *History of Dogma*. And yet it is not a matter of indifference which definitions of his conscious dominant man considers to be binding, or what sort of views he happens to have in this regard. For on this depends whether consciousness will be king or not. If the unconscious rules to the exclusion of all else, everything is liable to end in destruction, as the present state of things gives us reason to fear. If the dominant is too weak, life is wasted in fruitless conflict because Sol and Luna will not unite. But if the son is the dominant, then Sol is his right eye and Luna his left. The dominant must contain them both, the standpoint of ego-consciousness and

398 There were, nevertheless, some who would have liked to have the Holy Ghost as a familiar during their work. (See supra, n. 116.)

the standpoint of the archetypes in the unconscious. The binding force that inevitably attaches to a dominant should not mean a prison for one and a *carte-blanche* for the other, but duty and justice for both.

518   What the nature is of that unity which in some incomprehensible way embraces the antagonistic elements eludes our human judgment, for the simple reason that nobody can say what a being is like that unites the full range of consciousness with that of the unconscious. Man knows no more than his consciousness, and he knows himself only so far as this extends. Beyond that lies an unconscious sphere with no assignable limits, and it too belongs to the phenomenon Man. We might therefore say that perhaps the One is like a man, that is, determined and determinable and yet undetermined and indeterminable. Always one ends up with paradoxes when knowledge reaches its limits. The ego knows it is part of this being, but only a part. The symbolic phenomenology of the unconscious makes it clear that although consciousness is accorded the status of spiritual kingship with all its attendant dangers, we cannot say what kind of king it will be. This depends on two factors: on the decision of the ego and the assent of the unconscious. Any dominant that does not have the approval of the one or the other proves to be unstable in the long run. We know how often in the course of history consciousness has subjected its highest and most central ideas to drastic revision and correction, but we know little or nothing about the archetypal processes of change which, we may suppose, have taken place in the unconscious over the millennia, even though such speculations have no firm foundation. Nevertheless the possibility remains that the unconscious may reveal itself in an unexpected way at any time.*

519   The alchemical figure of the king has provoked this long discussion because it contains the whole of the hero myth including the king's—and God's—renewal, and on the other hand because, as we conjecture, it symbolizes the dominant that rules consciousness. "King Sol" is not a pleonasm; it denotes a consciousness which is not only conscious as such but is conscious in a quite special way. It is controlled and directed by a dominant that, in the last resort, is the arbiter of values. The sun is the common light of nature, but the king, the dominant, introduces

* [For par. 518a, inadvertently omitted at this point in the first edition, see supra, p. vii.]

the human element and brings man nearer to the sun, or the sun nearer to man.[399]

520   Consciousness is renewed through its descent into the unconscious, whereby the two are joined. The renewed consciousness does not *contain* the unconscious but forms with it a totality symbolized by the son. But since father and son are of one being, and in alchemical language King Sol, representing the renewed consciousness, *is* the son, consciousness would be absolutely identical with the King as dominant. For the alchemists this difficulty did not exist, because the King was projected into a postulated substance and hence behaved merely as an object to the consciousness of the artifex. But if the projection is withdrawn by psychological criticism, we encounter the aforesaid difficulty that the renewed consciousness apparently coincides with the renewed king, or son. I have discussed the psychological aspect of this problem in the second of the *Two Essays on Analytical Psychology,* in the chapter on the "mana personality." The difficulty cannot be resolved by purely logical argument but only by careful observation and analysis of the psychic state itself. Rather than launch out into a detailed discussion of case-histories I would prefer to recall the well-known words of Paul, "I live, yet not I, but Christ liveth in me" (Gal. 2 : 20), which aptly describe the peculiar nature of this state. From this we can see that that other, earlier state, when the king aged and disappeared, is marked by a consciousness in which a critical ego knowingly took the place of the sick king, looking back to an earlier "mythical" time when this ego still felt absolutely dependent on a higher and mightier non-ego. The subsequent disappearance of the feeling of dependence and the simultaneous strengthening of criticism are felt as progress, enlightenment, liberation, indeed as redemption, although a one-sided and limited being has usurped the throne of a king. A personal ego seizes the reins of power to its own destruction; for mere egohood, despite possessing an *anima rationalis,* is not even sufficient for the guidance of personal life, let alone for the guidance of men. For this purpose it always needs a "mythical" dominant, yet

399 Cf. the *solificatio* in the Isis mysteries: "And a garland of flowers was upon my head, with white palm-leaves sprouting out on every side like rays; thus I was adorned like unto the sun, and made in the fashion of an image" (*The Golden Ass,* trans. by Adlington, pp. 582f.).

such a thing cannot simply be invented and then believed in. Contemplating our own times we must say that though the need for an effective dominant was realized to a large extent, what was offered was nothing more than an arbitrary invention of the moment. The fact that it was also believed in goes to prove the gullibility and cluelessness of the public and at the same time the profoundly felt need for a spiritual authority transcending egohood. An authority of this kind is never the product of rational reflection or an invention of the moment, which always remains caught in the narrow circle of ego-bound consciousness; it springs from traditions whose roots go far deeper both historically and psychologically. Thus a real and essentially religious renewal can be based, for us, only on Christianity. The extremely radical reformation of Hinduism by the Buddha assimilated the traditional spirituality of India in its entirety and did not thrust a rootless novelty upon the world. It neither denied nor ignored the Hindu pantheon swarming with millions of gods, but boldly introduced Man, who before that had not been represented at all. Nor did Christ, regarded simply as a Jewish reformer, destroy the law, but made it, rather, into a matter of conviction. He likewise, as the regenerator of his age, set against the Greco-Roman pantheon and the speculations of the philosophers the figure of Man, not intending it as a contradiction but as the fulfilment of a mythologem that existed long before him—the conception of the Anthropos with its complex Egyptian, Persian, and Hellenistic background.

521   Any renewal not deeply rooted in the best spiritual tradition is ephemeral; but the dominant that grows from historical roots act like a living being within the ego-bound man. He does not possess it, it possesses him; therefore the alchemists said that the artifex is not the master but rather the minister of the stone —clearly showing that the stone is indeed a king towards whom the artifex behaves as a subject.

522   Although the renewed king corresponds to a renewed consciousness, this consciousness is as different from its former state as the *filius regius* differs from the enfeebled old king. Just as the old king must forgo his power and make way for the little upstart ego, so the ego, when the renewed king returns, must step into the background. It still remains the *sine qua non* of con-

sciousness,[400] but it no longer imagines that it can settle everything and do everything by the force of its will. It no longer asserts that where there's a will there's a way. When lucky ideas come to it, it does not take the credit for them, but begins to realize how dangerously close it had been to an inflation. The scope of its willing and doing becomes commensurate with reality again after an Ash Wednesday has descended upon its presumptuousness.[401]

523   We can compare the logical sequence of psychological changes with the alchemical symbolism as follows:

Ego-bound state with feeble dominant	Sick king, enfeebled by age, about to die
Ascent of the unconscious and/or descent of the ego into the unconscious	Disappearance of the king in his mother's body, or his dissolution in water
Conflict and synthesis of conscious and unconscious	Pregnancy, sick-bed, symptoms, display of colours
Formation of a new dominant; circular symbols (e.g., mandala) of the self	King's son, hermaphrodite, rotundum [402]

524   Though the comparison holds good on average, the symbolism of the *Cantilena* differs from the above schema in that the apotheosis of the *filius regius* takes place simultaneously with that of Queen Luna, thus paralleling the marriage in the Apocalypse. The Christian prototype gained the upper hand in Ripley, whereas usually the coniunctio precedes the production of the lapis and the latter is understood as the child of Sol and Luna. To that extent the lapis exactly corresponds to the psychological idea of the self, the product of conscious and unconscious. In Christian symbolism, on the other hand, there is a marriage of the Lamb (the Apocalyptic Christ) with the bride (Luna-Ecclesia). Because the lapis is itself androgynous, a synthesis of

400 Consciousness consists in the relation of a psychic content to the ego. Anything not associated with the ego remains unconscious.

401 This ever-repeated psychological situation is archetypal and expresses itself, for instance, in the relation of the Gnostic demiurge to the highest God.

402 The conjunction symbolism appears in two places: first, at the descent into the darkness, when the marriage has a nefarious character (incest, murder, death); second, before the ascent, when the union has a more "heavenly" character.

male and female, there is no need for another coniunctio. The symbolical androgyny of Christ does not, curiously enough, eliminate the marriage of the Lamb—the two things exist side by side.

525   We have here a discrepancy between the alchemical and psychological symbolism and the Christian. It is indeed difficult to imagine what kind of coniunctio beyond the union of conscious (male) and unconscious (female) in the regenerated dominant could be meant, unless we assume, with the dogmatic tradition, that the regenerated dominant also brings the *corpus mysticum* of mankind (Ecclesia as Luna) into glorious reality. Among the alchemists, who were mostly solitaries by choice, the motif of the Apocalyptic marriage, characterized as the marriage of the Lamb (Rev. 19 : 7ff.), is missing, the accent here lying on the sacrificial appellation "lamb." According to the oldest and most primitive tradition the king, despite his dignity and power, was a victim offered up for the prosperity of his country and his people, and in his godlike form he was even eaten. As we know, this archetype underwent an extremely complicated development in Christianity. From the standpoint of Christian symbolism the alchemists' conception of the goal lacked, firstly, the motif of the heavenly marriage and, secondly, the almost more important motif of sacrifice and the totem meal. (The mourned gods of Asia Minor—Tammuz, Adonis, etc. —were, in all probability, originally sacrifices for the fruitfulness of the year.) The lapis was decidedly an ideal for hermits, a goal for isolated individuals. Besides that, it was a food (*cibus immortalis*), could be multiplied indefinitely, was a living being with body, soul, and spirit, an androgyne with incorruptible body, etc. Though likened to King Sol and even named such, it was not a sponsus, not a victim, and belonged to no community; it was like the "treasure hid in a field, the which when a man hath found, he hideth" (Matt. 13 : 44), or like "one pearl of great price," for which a man "went and sold all that he had, and bought it" (Matt. 13 : 46). It was the well-guarded, precious secret of the individual.[403] And though the old Masters empha-

---

[403] Cf. Oxyrhynchos Fragment 5 (discovered 1897): "Jesus saith, Wherever there are (two), they are not without God, and wherever there is one alone, I say, I am with him. Raise the stone, and there thou shalt find me; cleave the wood, and there am I." (Grenfell and Hunt, *New Sayings of Jesus*, p. 38.) The text is fragmentary. See Preuschen, *Antilegomena*, p. 43.

sized that they would not hide their secret "jealously"[404] and would reveal it to all seekers, it was perfectly clear that the stone remained the preoccupation of the individual.

526   In this connection it should not be forgotten that in antiquity certain influences, evidently deriving from the Gnostic doctrine of the hermaphroditic Primordial Man,[405] penetrated into Christianity and there gave rise to the view that Adam had been created an androgyne.[406] And since Adam was the prototype of Christ, and Eve, sprung from his side, that of the Church, it is understandable that a picture of Christ should develop showing distinctly feminine features.[407] In religious art the Christ-image has retained this character to the present day.[408] Its veiled androgyny reflects the hermaphroditism of the lapis, which in this respect has more affinity with the views of the Gnostics.

527   In recent times the theme of androgyny has been subjected to quite special treatment in a book by a Catholic writer which merits our attention. This is *Die Gnosis des Christentums,* by Georg Koepgen, an important work that appeared in 1939 with the episcopal imprimatur in Salzburg, and since then has been placed on the Index. Of the Apollinian-Dionysian conflict in antiquity, Koepgen says it found its solution in Christianity because "in the person of Jesus the male is united with the female." "Only in him do we find this juxtaposition of male and female in unbroken unity." "If men and women can come together as equals in Christian worship, this has more than an accidental significance: it is the fulfilment of the androgyny that was made manifest in Christ" (p. 316). The change of sex in the believer is suggested in Rev. 14 : 4: "These are they that were not defiled with women; for they are virgins." Koepgen says of this passage: "Here the new androgynous form of existence becomes visible. Christianity is neither male nor female, it is male-female in the sense that the male paired with the female in

404 Particularly in the *Turba.*

405 Cf. the androgynous statue in the form of a cross, in Bardesanes.

406 As late as Boehme, Adam was described as a "male virgin." Cf. "Three Principles of the Divine Essence" (*Works,* I), X, 18, p. 68, and XVII, 82, p. 159. Such views had been attacked by Augustine.

407 Cf. the picture of his baptism in the Reichenau Codex Lat. Mon. 4453, reproduced in Goldschmidt, *German Illumination,* II, 27.

408 How different is the picture of the "Holy Shroud" in Turin! Cf. Vignon, *The Shroud of Christ.*

Jesus's soul. In Jesus the tension and polaristic strife of sex are resolved in an androgynous unity. And the Church, as his heir, has taken this over from him: she too is androgynous." As regards her constitution the Church is "hierarchically masculine, yet her soul is thoroughly feminine." "The virgin priest . . . fulfils in his soul the androgynous unity of male and female; he renders visible again the psychic dimension which Christ showed us for the first time when he revealed the 'manly virginity' of his soul." [409]

528   For Koepgen, therefore, not only Christ is androgynous but the Church as well, a remarkable conclusion the logic of which one cannot deny. The consequence of this is a special emphasis on bisexuality and then on the peculiar identity of the Church with Christ, which is based also on the doctrine of the *corpus mysticum*. This certainly forestalls the marriage of the Lamb at the end of time, for the androgyne "has everything it needs" [410] and is already a *complexio oppositorum*. Who is not reminded here of the fragment from the Gospel according to the Egyptians cited by Clement of Alexandria: "When ye have trampled on the garment of shame, and when the two become one and the male with the female is neither male nor female." [411]

529   Koepgen introduces his book with a dedication and a motto. The first is: "Renatis praedestinatione" (To those who are reborn out of predestination), and the second is from John 14 : 12: "He that believeth on me, the works that I do he shall do also, and greater works than these shall he do." The dedication echoes the motif of election, which the author shares with the alchemists. For Morienus had said of alchemy:

God vouchsafes this divine and pure science to his faithful and his servants, that is, to those on whom nature made it proper to confer it from the beginning of things. For this thing can be naught else but the gift of God most high, who commits and shows it as he will, and to whom he will of his faithful servants. For the Lord selects of his

[409] Koepgen notes: "Not even the reformers, who twisted the ideal of virginity in the interests of a bourgeois ethos, ventured to change anything in this respect. Even for them Christ was an androgynous unity of man and virgin. The only puzzling thing is that they acknowledged the virginity of Christ while disapproving the virginity of the priesthood." (p. 319).

[410] Senior, *De chemia*, p. 108. Cf. ἀπροσδεής ('in need of nothing') as an attribute of the Valentinian monad. (Hippolytus, *Elenchos*, VI, 29, 4.)

[411] *Stromata*, III, 13, 92,* cited in James, *The Apocryphal New Testament*, p. 11.

servants those whom he wills and chooses, to seek after this divine science which is concealed from man, and having sought it to keep it with them.[412]

Dorn says much the same: "For it sometimes comes about, after many years, many labours, much study . . . that some are chosen, when much knocking,[413] many prayers, and diligent enquiry have gone before." [414]

530   The quotation from John is taken from the fourteenth chapter, where Christ teaches that whoever sees him sees the Father. He is in the Father and the Father is in him. The disciples are in him and he in them, moreover they will be sent the Holy Ghost as Paraclete and will do works that are greater than his own. This fourteenth chapter broaches a question that was to have great repercussions for the future: the problem of the Holy Ghost who will remain when Christ has gone, and who intensifies the interpenetration of the divine and the human to such a degree that we can properly speak of a "Christification" of the disciples. Among the Christian mystics this identity was carried again and again to the point of stigmatization. Only the mystics bring creativity into religion. That is probably why they can feel the presence and the workings of the Holy Ghost, and why they are nearer to the experience of brotherhood in Christ.

531   Koepgen thinks along the same lines, as his dedication and motto show. It is easy to see what happens when the logical conclusion is drawn from the fourteenth chapter of John: the *opus Christi* is transferred to the individual. He then becomes the bearer of the mystery, and this development was unconsciously prefigured and anticipated in alchemy, which showed clear signs of becoming a religion of the Holy Ghost and of the Sapientia Dei. Koepgen's standpoint is that of creative mysticism, which has always been critical of the Church. Though this is not obviously so in Koepgen, his attitude betrays itself indirectly in the living content of his book, which consistently presses for a deepening and broadening of the dogmatic ideas. Because he re-

412 "De transmut. metallica," *Art. aurif.*, II, pp. 22f.* This seemingly pointless and selfish procedure becomes understandable if the alchemical opus is regarded as a divine mystery. In that case its mere presence in the world would be sufficient.

413 "For the first Chief of the spagyrics saith: Knock and it shall be opened unto you" * (Matthew 7 : 7). "Phys. Trismegisti," *Theatr. chem.*, I, p. 413.

414 Ibid.* Eleazar (*Uraltes Chymisches Werck*, II, p. 53) says: "For this stone belongeth only to the proven and elect of God."

mained fully conscious of his conclusions, he does not stray so very far outside the Church, whereas the alchemists, because of their unconsciousness and naïve lack of reflection, and unhampered by intellectual responsibility, went very much further in their symbolism. But the point of departure for both is the procreative, revelatory working of the Holy Ghost, who is a "wind that bloweth where it listeth," and who advances beyond his own workings to "greater works than these." The creative mystic was ever a cross for the Church, but it is to him that we owe what is best in humanity.[415]

9. REGINA

532   We have met the figure of the Queen so often in the course of our exposition that we need say only a few words about her here. We have seen that as Luna she is the archetypal companion of Sol. Together they form the classic alchemical syzygy, signifying on the one hand gold and silver, or something of the kind,[416] and on the other the heavenly pair described in *Aurora Consurgens:*

Therefore I will rise and go into the city, seeking in the streets and the broad ways a chaste virgin to espouse, comely in face, more

[415] I can only agree with Aldous Huxley when he writes in *Grey Eminence* (1943): "By the end of the seventeenth century, mysticism has lost its old significance in Christianity and is more than half dead. 'Well, what of it?' may be asked. 'Why shouldn't it die? What use is it when it's alive?'—The answer to these questions is that where there is no vision, the people perish; and that, if those who are the salt of the earth lose their savour, there is nothing to keep that earth disinfected, nothing to prevent it from falling into complete decay. The mystics are channels through which a little knowledge of reality filters down into our human universe of ignorance and illusion. A totally unmystical world would be a world totally blind and insane" (p. 98). "In a world inhabited by what the theologians call unregenerate or natural men, church and state can probably never become appreciably better than the best of the states and churches of which the past has left us a record. Society can never be greatly improved, until such time as most of its members choose to become theocentric saints. Meanwhile, the few theocentric saints who exist at any given moment are able in some slight measure to qualify and mitigate the poisons which society generates within itself by its political and economic activities. In the gospel phrase, theocentric saints are the salt which preserves the social world from breaking down into irremediable decay" (p. 296).

[416] Hoghelande (*Theatr. chem.*, I, p. 162): "So also the King and Queen are called the composite of the stone . . . Thus man and woman are called Male and Female, because of their union and action and passion. Rosinus [says]: The secret of the art of gold consists in the male and the female." *

comely in body, most comely in her garments, that she may roll back the stone from the door of my sepulchre and give me wings like a dove, and I will fly with her into heaven and then say: I live for ever, and will rest in her, for the Queen stood on my right hand in gilded clothing, surrounded with variety. . . . O Queen of the heights, arise, make haste, my love, my spouse, speak, beloved, to thy lover, who and of what kind and how great thou art. . . . My beloved, who is ruddy, hath spoken to me, he hath sought and besought: I am the flower of the field and the lily of the valleys, I am the mother of fair love and of fear and of knowledge and of holy hope. As the fruitful vine I have brought forth a pleasant odour, and my flowers are the fruit and honour and riches. I am the bed of my beloved, . . . wounding his heart with one of my eyes and with one hair of my neck. I am the sweet smell of ointments giving an odour above all aromatical spices, and like unto cinnamon and balsam and chosen myrrh.[417]

533   The prototype of this spiritual *Minne* is the relationship of King Solomon to the Queen of Sheba. Johannes Grasseus says of the white dove that is hidden in the lead: "This is the chaste, wise, and rich Queen of Sheba, veiled in white, who was willing to give herself to none but King Solomon. No human heart can sufficiently investigate all this." [418] Penotus says:

You have the virgin earth, give her a husband who is fitting for her! She is the Queen of Sheba, hence there is need of a king crowned with a diadem—where shall we find him? We see how the heavenly sun gives of his splendour to all other bodies, and the earthly or mineral sun will do likewise, when he is set in his own heaven, which is named the "Queen of Sheba," who came from the ends of the earth to behold the glory of Solomon. So, too, our Mercury has left his own lands and clothed himself with the fairest garment of white, and has given himself to Solomon, and not to any other who is a stranger [*extraneo*] and impure.[419]

534   Here Mercurius in feminine form is the queen, and she is the "heaven" wherein the sun shines. She is thus thought of as a medium surrounding the sun—"a man encompassed by a woman," as was said of Christ [420]—or as Shiva in the embrace of

417 Parable XII, pp. 135ff.   418 "Arca arcani," *Theatr. chem.*, VI, p. 314.
419 *Theatr. chem.*, II, p. 149.
420 St. Gregory, *In I Regum expos.* (Migne, *P.L.*, vol. 79, col. 23). Mylius (*Phil. ref.*, p. 8) says of God: "Whom the divine Plato declared to dwell in the substance of fire; meaning thereby the unspeakable splendour of God in himself and the love that surrounds him." *

Shakti. This medium has the nature of Mercurius, that paradoxical being, whose one definable meaning is the unconscious.[421] The queen appears in the texts as the maternal vessel of Sol and as the aureole of the king, i.e., as a crown.[422] In the "Tractatus aureus de Lapide" [423] the queen, at her apotheosis,[424] holds a discourse in which she says:

After death is life restored to me. To me, poor as I am, were entrusted the treasures of the wise and mighty. Therefore I, too, can make the poor rich, give grace to the humble, and restore health to the sick. But I am not yet equal to my most beloved brother, the mighty king, who has yet to be raised from the dead. But when he comes, he will verily show that my words are the truth.

535   In this "soror et sponsa" we can easily discern the analogy with the Church, which, as the *corpus mysticum*, is the vessel for the *anima Christi*. This vessel is called by Penotus the "Queen of Sheba," referring to the passage in Matthew 12 : 42 (also Luke 11 : 31): "For she [the queen of the south] came from the uttermost parts of the earth to hear the wisdom of Solomon." In this connection I would like to mention a passage in the "Speculum de Mysteriis" of Honorius of Autun, which likewise refers to the "queen of the south." He says: [425]

John abandoned his bride and, himself a virgin, followed the son of a virgin. And because for love of her he despised the bond of the flesh, Christ loved him before all the disciples. For while the Queen of the South gave her body and her blood to the disciples, John lay in the bosom of Jesus and drank from that fount of wisdom; which secret of the Word he afterward committed to the world; the Word, namely, which is hidden in the Father, because in the bosom of Jesus are hidden all the treasures of wisdom and knowledge.[426]

536   In the passage from the "Tractatus aureus" it is the Queen of the South who is entrusted with the treasures of the wise and

421 Cf. "The Spirit Mercurius," pars. 271, 284.

422 *Aurora Consurgens*, p. 141: "I am the crown wherewith my beloved is crowned."

423 *Mus, herm.*, p. 50 (Waite, I, p. 48).

424 "Adorned with a most excellent crown composed of pure diamonds" probably refers to the wreath of stars about her head.

425 Migne, *P.L.*, vol. 172, col. 834.

426 Colossians 2 : 3: ". . . so as to know the mystery of God the Father and of Christ Jesus, in whom are hidden all the treasures of wisdom and knowledge" (DV).

mighty, and in Honorius she gives her body and blood to the disciples. In both cases she seems to be identified with Jesus. We can see from this how close was the thought of Christ's androgyny, and how very much the queen and the king are one, in the sense that body and soul or spirit and soul are one.[427] As a matter of fact the queen corresponds to the soul (anima) and the king to spirit, the dominant of consciousness.[428] In view of this interpretation of the queen we can understand why the secret of the work was sometimes called the "Reginae Mysteria." [429]

537   The close connection between king and queen is due to the fact that occasionally they both suffer the same fate: she is dissolved with him in the bath (in another version she is the bath itself). Thus Eleazar says of the king's bath: "For in this fiery sea the king cannot endure; it robs the old Albaon [430] of all his strength and consumes his body and turns it to blood-red blood. Nor is the queen freed; she must perish in this fiery bath." [431]

538   Further, it is not surprising that king and queen form as it were a unity, since they are in effect its forerunners. The situation becomes worthy of note only because of the interpretation we have given it: that in the mythologem the king, as the dominant of consciousness, is almost identical with the archetypal figure that personifies the unconscious, namely the anima. The two figures are in some respects diametrically opposed to one another, as are conscious and unconscious; but, just as male and female are united in the human organism, so the psychic material remains the same whether in the conscious or in the unconscious state. Only, sometimes it is associated with the ego, sometimes not.

539   The anima in her negative aspect—that is, when she remains

427 The alchemists were in some doubt as to whether to call the body or the soul feminine. Psychologically, this consideration applies only to the soul as the representative of the body, for the body itself is experienced only indirectly through the soul. The masculine element is spirit.

428 This is true only of the male artifex. The situation is reversed in the case of a woman.

429 Thus Maier (Symb. aur. mensae, p. 336) says: "He who works through the talent of another and the hand of a hireling, will find that his works are estranged from the truth. And conversely, he who performs servile work for another, as a servant in the Art, will never be admitted to the mysteries of the Queen." * Cf. Psychology and Alchemy, par. 421.

430 The materia prima, raw material, black earth.

431 Uraltes Chymisches Werck, II, p. 72.

unconscious and hidden—exerts a possessive influence on the subject. The chief symptoms of this possession are blind moods and compulsive entanglements on one side, and on the other cold, unrelated absorption in principles and abstract ideas. The negative aspect of the anima indicates therefore a special form of psychological maladjustment. This is either compensated from the conscious side or else it compensates a consciousness already marked by a contrary (and equally incorrect) attitude. For the negative aspect of the conscious dominant is far from being a "God-given" idea; it is the most egoistic intention of all, which seeks to play an important role and, by wearing some kind of mask, to appear as something favourable (identification with the persona!). The anima corresponding to this attitude is an intriguer who continually aids and abets the ego in its role, while digging in the background the very pits into which the infatuated ego is destined to fall.

540　But a conscious attitude that renounces its ego-bound intentions—not in imagination only, but in truth—and submits to the suprapersonal decrees of fate, can claim to be serving a king. This more exalted attitude raises the status of the anima from that of a temptress to a psychopomp.[432] The transformation of the kingly substance from a lion into a king has its counterpart in the transformation of the feminine element from a serpent into a queen. The coronation, apotheosis, and marriage signalize the equal status of conscious and unconscious that becomes possible at the highest level—a *coincidentia oppositorum* with redeeming effects.

541　It would certainly be desirable if a psychological explanation and clarification could be given of what seems to be indicated by the mythologem of the marriage. But the psychologist does not feel responsible for the existence of what cannot be known; as the handmaid of truth he must be satisfied with establishing the existence of these phenomena, mysterious as they are. The union of conscious and unconscious symbolized by the royal marriage is a mythological idea which on a higher level assumes the character of a psychological concept. I must expressly emphasize that the psychological concept is definitely not

---

[432] "Come then, to higher spheres conduct him!
Divining *you*, he knows the way."

(*Faust II*, trans. by MacNeice, p. 303.)

derived from the mythologem, but solely from practical investigation of both the historical and the case material. What this empirical material looks like has been shown in the dream-series given in *Psychology and Alchemy*. It serves as a paradigm in place of hundreds of examples, and it may therefore be regarded as more than an individual curiosity.

542   The psychological union of opposites is an intuitive idea which covers the phenomenology of this process. It is not an "explanatory" hypothesis for something that, by definition, transcends our powers of conception. For, when we say that conscious and unconscious unite, we are saying in effect that this process is inconceivable. The unconscious is unconscious and therefore can neither be grasped nor conceived. The union of opposites is a transconscious process and, in principle, not amenable to scientific explanation. The marriage must remain the "mystery of the queen," the secret of the art, of which the *Rosarium* reports King Solomon as saying:

This is my daughter, for whose sake men say that the Queen of the South came out of the east, like the rising dawn, in order to hear, understand, and behold the wisdom of Solomon. Power, honour, strength, and dominion are given into her hand; she wears the royal crown of seven glittering stars, like a bride adorned for her husband, and on her robe is written in golden lettering, in Greek, Arabic, and Latin: "I am the only daughter of the wise, utterly unknown to the foolish." [433]

543   The Queen of Sheba, Wisdom, the royal art, and the "daughter of the philosophers" are all so interfused that the underlying psychologem clearly emerges: the art is queen of the alchemist's heart, she is at once his mother, his daughter, and his beloved, and in his art and its allegories the drama of his own soul, his individuation process, is played out.

[433] *Art. aurif.*, II, p. 294f. Cf. *Aurora Consurgens*, pp. 53f.

V

ADAM AND EVE

1. ADAM AS THE ARCANE SUBSTANCE

544   Like the King and Queen, our first parents are among those figures through whom the alchemists expressed the symbolism of opposites. Adam is mentioned far more frequently than Eve, and for this reason we shall have to concern ourselves first and principally with him. He will give us plenty to get on with, as he figures in a great variety of significations which enter the world of alchemical ideas from the most heterogeneous sources.

545   Ruland defines Adam as a synonym for the *aqua permanens,* in contradistinction to Eve, who signifies earth. Water is the prime arcane substance, and is therefore the agent of transformation as well as the substance to be transformed. As "water" is synonymous with Mercurius, we can understand the remark of John Dee that "that other Mercurius" who appears in the course of the work is the "Mercurius of the Philosophers, that most renowned Microcosm and Adam." [1] Adam is mentioned as the arcane substance in Rosinus. His correlates are lead and "Azoch," [2] both, like Adam,[3] of hermaphroditic nature. Similarly, Dorn says that the lapis was called "Adam, who bore his invisible Eve hidden in his body." [4] This archaic idea occasion-

---

1 "Monas hieroglyphica," *Theatr. chem.,* II, p. 222.*

2 Azoch = Azoth = "Mercurius duplex." Cf. Ruland, *Lexicon,* p. 66, s.v. Azoch.

3 "Take Adam and that which is made like to Adam: here hast thou named Adam and hast been silent concerning the name of the woman or Eve, not naming her, for thou knowest that men who are like unto thee in the world know that that which is made like unto thee is Eve" * ("Rosinus ad Euthiciam," *Art. aurif.,* I, p. 248).

4 "Congeries Paracelsicae chemicae," *Theatr. chem.,* I, p. 578: "Wherefore with the most powerful talent and understanding they asserted that their stone was a living thing, which they also called their Adam, who bore his invisible Eve hidden in his body from the moment when they were united by the power of the great Creator of all things. And for that reason the Mercury of the Philosophers may fittingly be called nothing else than their most secret compound Mercury, and not the

ally turns up in the products of the insane today.[5] The dual nature of Adam is suggested in the "Gloria mundi": "When Almighty God had created Adam and set him in paradise, he showed him two things in the future, saying, 'Behold, Adam, here are two things: one fixed and constant, the other fugitive.' "[6]

546 As the transformative substance, therefore, Adam is also the king [7] who is renewed in the bath. Basilius Valentinus says in his poem: "Adam sat in the bath which the old Dragon had prepared, and in which Venus found her companion." [8]

547 It was a bold stroke, even for a Baroque imagination, to bring together Adam and Venus. In the poem Venus is the "fountain that flows from the stone and submerges her father, absorbing his body and life into herself." She is thus a parallel figure to Beya, who dissolved Gabricus into atoms in her body. In the same section in which Ruland mentions Adam as a synonym for water he states that he was also called the "tall man." [9] Ruland was a Paracelsist, so this expression may well coincide with the "great man" of Paracelsus, the Adech,[10] whom Ruland defines as "our inner and invisible man." [11]

548 Accordingly the arcane substance would appear to be the "inner" man or Primordial Man, known as Adam Kadmon in the Cabala. In the poem of Valentinus, this inner man is swamped by the goddess of love—an unmistakable psychologem for a definite and typical psychic state, which is also symbolized very aptly by the Gnostic love-affair between Nous and Physis. In both cases the "higher spiritual man" is the more comprehen-

---

vulgar one. . . . There is in Mercury whatever the wise seek . . . the matter of the stone of the philosophers is naught else than . . . Adam the true hermaphrodite and microcosm." * "Nature first requires of the artifex that the philosophic Adam be drawn to the Mercurial substance" * (p. 589). ". . . the composition of the most holy Adamic stone is made from the Adamic Mercury of the sages" * (p. 590).

5 For instance, Adam as "God the Father" fused together with Eve. Cf. Nelken, p. 542.

6 Mus. herm., p. 228.*

7 "Adam was the Lord, King, and Ruler." * Ibid., p. 269.

8 "De prima materia," Mus. herm., p. 425.* Cf. supra, pars. 415f.

9 Cf. Hoghelande (Theatr. chem., I, p. 162): "A tall and helmeted man."

10 A Paracelsan neologism, presumably a compound of "Adam" and "Enoch." Cf. "Paracelsus as a Spiritual Phenomenon" par. 168.

11 Dorn (in his edition of Paracelsus' De vita longa, p. 178) calls him the "invisibilis homo maximus."

sive, supra-ordinate totality which we know as the self. The bath, submersion, baptism, and drowning are synonymous, and all are alchemical symbols for the unconscious state of the self, its embodiments, as it were—or, more precisely, for the unconscious process by which the self is "reborn" and enters into a state in which it can be experienced. This state is then described as the "filius regius." The "old dragon" who prepared the bath, a primeval creature dwelling in the caverns of the earth, is, psychologically, a personification of the instinctual psyche, generally symbolized by reptiles. It is as though the alchemists were trying to express the fact that the unconscious itself initiates the process of renewal.

549   Adam's bath is also mentioned in a Latin manuscript in my possession, where an unspecified being or creature addresses Adam thus: "Hear, Adam, I will speak with you. You must go with me into the bath; you know in what manner we are influenced the one by the other, and how you must pass through me. Thus I step up to you with my sharpened arrows, aiming them at your heart . . ." [12]

550   Here again Adam is the transformative substance, the "old Adam" who is to renew himself. The arrows recall the *telum passionis* of Mercurius and the shafts of Luna, which the alchemists, via the mysticism of Hugh of St. Victor [13] and others, referred to that well-known passage in the Song of Songs: "Thou hast wounded my heart," as we have seen earlier.[14] The speaker in the manuscript must be feminine, as immediately before there is a reference to the cohabitation of man and woman.

551   Both texts point to a hierosgamos which presupposes a kind of consanguineous relationship between *sponsus* and *sponsa*. The relationship between Adam and Eve is as close as it is difficult to define. According to an old tradition Adam was androgynous before the creation of Eve.[15] Eve therefore was more himself than if she had been his sister. Adam's highly unbiblical marriage is emphasized as a hierosgamos by the fact that God himself was present at the ceremony as best man *(paranymphus)*.[16] Traces of cabalistic tradition are frequently notice-

12 Ms. from 18th cent., "Figurarum aegyptiorum," fol. 17.

13 *De laude charitatis* (Migne, *P.L.*, vol. 176, col. 974).   14 See supra, pars. 24f.

15 Cf. Wünsche, "Schöpfung und Sündenfall," p. 10. Adam had two faces. God sawed him into two halves—Adam and Eve.

16 Ibid., p. 24.

able in the alchemical treatises from the sixteenth century on. Both our texts are fairly late and so fall well within this tradition.

552   We must now turn to the question of why it was that Adam should have been selected as a symbol for the prima materia or transformative substance. This was probably due, in the first place, to the fact that he was made out of clay, the "ubiquitous" *materia vilis* that was axiomatically regarded as the prima materia and for that very reason was so tantalizingly difficult to find, although it was "before all eyes." It was a piece of the original chaos, of the *massa confusa,* not yet differentiated but capable of differentiation; something, therefore, like shapeless, embryonic tissue. Everything could be made out of it.[17] For us the essential feature of the prima materia is that it was defined as the "massa confusa" and "chaos," referring to the original state of hostility between the elements, the disorder which the artifex gradually reduced to order by his operations. Corresponding to the four elements there were four stages of the process (*tetrameria*), marked by four colours, by means of which the originally chaotic arcane substance finally attained to unity, to the "One," the lapis, which at the same time was an homunculus.[18] In this way the Philosopher repeated God's work of creation described in Genesis 1. No wonder, therefore, that he called his prima materia "Adam" and asserted that it, like him, consisted or was made out of the four elements. "For out of the four elements were created our Father Adam and his children," says the *Turba.*[19] And Gabir ibn Hayyan (Jabir)[20] says in his "Book of Balances":

The Pentateuch says, regarding the creation of the first being, that his body was composed of four things, which thereafter were transmitted by heredity: the warm, the cold, the moist, and the dry. He was in fact composed of earth and water, a body and a soul. Dryness came to him from the earth, moisture from the water, heat from the spirit, and cold from the soul.[21]

[17] Further material in *Psychology and Alchemy,* pars. 425ff., 430f., 433.
[18] "The second Adam who is called the philosophic man." * (*Aurora consurgens, I,* Parable VI.)   [19] Sermo VIII (ed. Ruska), p. 115.*
[20] The Latin Geber, author of the classical "Summa perfectionis," was formerly thought to be identical with Jabir. For the present state of the Jabir controversy see Lippmann, *Entstehung und Ausbreitung der Alchemie,* II, p. 89.
[21] Berthelot, *Chimie au moyen âge,* III, pp. 148f.

The later literature often mentions Adam as a *compositio elementorum*.[22] Because he was composed out of the four cosmic principles he was called the Microcosm.[23] The "Tractatus Micreris" says: [24]

Even so is man called the lesser world [*mundus minor*], because in him is the figure of the heavens, of the earth, of the sun and moon, a visible figure upon earth and [at the same time] invisible, wherefore he is named the lesser world. Therefore the old Philosophers said of him, When the water fell upon the earth, Adam was created, who is the lesser world.[25]

Similar views of Adam are found elsewhere; thus the *Pirke de Rabbi Eliezer* says that God collected the dust from which Adam was made from the four corners of the earth.[26] Rabbi Meir (2nd cent.) states that Adam was made from dust from all over the world. In Mohammedan tradition Tabari, Masudi, and others say that when the earth refused to provide the material for Adam's creation the angel of death came along with three kinds of earth: black, white, and red.[27] The Syrian "Book of the Cave of Treasures" relates:

And they saw God take a grain of dust from the whole earth, and a drop of water from the whole sea, and a breath of wind from the upper air, and a little warmth from the nature of fire. And the angels saw how these four weak elements, the dry, the moist, the cold, and the warm, were laid in the hollow of his hand. And then God made Adam.[28]

The poet Jalal-ud-din Rumi says that the earth from which Adam was made had seven colours.[29] A collection of English

[22] For instance in Mylius, *Phil. ref.*, p. 168.

[23] Adam's body came from the earth of Babylonia, his head from the land of Israel, and his limbs from the remaining countries. (*Talmud*, ed. Epstein, "Sanhedrin," 38a; I, p. 241.)   [24] *Theatr. chem.*, V, p. 109.

[25] Here the text develops the comparison of Adam with the arcane substance.

[26] "He [God] began to collect the dust of the first man from the four corners of the world; red, black, white, and green. Red, this is the blood; black refers to the entrails; white refers to the bones and sinews; green refers to the body." * *Pirke de Rabbi Eliezer* (trans. by Friedlander), ch. 11, pp. 77f. (modified). According to other sources, green refers to the skin and the liver. Cf. *Jewish Encyclopaedia*, I, pp. 173ff., s.v. Adam, for further material.

[27] Ibid., p. 174.   [28] Bezold, *Die Schatzhöhle*, p. 3.

[29] Kohut, "Die talmudisch-midraschische Adamssage in ihrer Rückbeziehung auf die persische Yima- und Meshiasage."

riddles from the fifteenth century asks the following questions concerning Adam's creation:

Questions bitwene the Maister of Oxinford and his scoler: Whereof was Adam made? Of VIII thingis: the first of earthe, the second of fire, the IIId of wynde, the IIIIth of clowdys, the Vth of aire where thorough he speketh and thinketh, the VIth of dewe whereby hi sweteth, the VIIth of flowres wherof Adam hath his ien, the VIIIth is salte wherof Adam hath salt teres.[30]

553   This material clearly shows the tetradic and ogdoadic nature of Adam, and there is also that characteristic uncertainty as to three and seven: four elements, four colours, four qualities, four humours,[31] and three and seven colours.[32]

554   Dorn calls the ternarius (the number three) "peculiar to Adam" (*Adamo proprius*). And because the ternarius was the "offspring of the unarius" (the number one), the devil, whose nature is binary, could do nothing against him, but had to make his attack upon Eve,[33] "who was divided from her husband as a natural binarius from the unity of his ternarius."[34] Vigenerus, commenting on I Cor. 15 : 47,[35] writes:

For the elements are circular [in their arrangement], as Hermes makes clear, each being surrounded by two others with which it

---

[30] Grimm (*Teutonic Mythology*, II, p. 565) cites a Latin version from the Rituale Ecclesiae Dunelmensis (10th cent.) and other material besides. The above quotation is from Koehler, *Kleinere Schriften zur erzählenden Dichtung des Mittelalters*, II, p. 2. The "questions" go back to an Anglo-Saxon "Dialogue between Saturn and Solomon" (Thorpe, *Analecta Anglo-Saxonica*, pp. 95ff.).

[31] Isidore of Seville, *De natura rerum*, IX (ed. Becker, p. 21). Cited in *Jewish Encyclopaedia*, I, p. 174, s.v. Adam.

[32] Cf. the seven sons of Adam and the seven metals from the blood of Gayomart. There is the same uncertainty in the legend of the seven sleepers recounted in the 18th Sura of the Koran: in some versions there are seven, in others eight sleepers, or the eighth is a dog, or there are three men and a dog, and so on. (See "Concerning Rebirth," par. 242, n. 6.) Similarly, Adam sometimes has three colours, red, black, and white, and sometimes four, white, black, red, and green. (Cf. *Jewish Encyclopaedia*, I, p. 174.)

[33] Elsewhere he says of the devil: "For he knew that through the ternarius no entry could lie open to Adam, since the unarius protected the ternarius, and therefore he sought to enter the binarius of Eve" * ("Duellum animi cum corpore," *Theatr. chem.*, I, p. 542).

[34] "De tenebris contra naturam," *Theatr. chem.*, I, p. 527.*

[35] "The first man was of the earth, earthy; the second man is from heaven, heavenly" (DV).

387

agrees in one of those qualities peculiar to itself, as [for instance] earth is between fire and water, partaking in the dryness of fire and the coldness of water. And so with the rest. . . .[36] Man, therefore, who is an image of the great world, and is called the microcosm or little world (as the little world, made after the similitude of its arche- type, and compounded of the four elements, is called the great man), has also his heaven and his earth. For the soul and the understanding are his heaven; his body and senses his earth. Therefore, to know the heaven and earth of man, is the same as to have a full and complete knowledge of the whole world and of the things of nature.[37]

555   The circular arrangement of the elements in the world and in man is symbolized by the mandala and its quaternary struc- ture. Adam would then be a quaternarius, as he was composed of red, black, white, and green dust from the four corners of the earth, and his stature reached from one end of the world to the other.[38] According to one Targum, God took the dust not only from the four quarters but also from the sacred spot, the "centre of the world." [39] The four quarters reappear in the (Greek) let- ters of Adam's name: *anatole* (sunrise, East), *dysis* (sunset, West), *arktos* (Great Bear, North), *mesembria* (noon, South).[40] The "Book of the Cave of Treasures" states that Adam stood on the spot where the cross was later erected, and that this spot was the centre of the earth. Adam, too, was buried at the centre of the earth—on Golgotha. He died on a Friday, at the same hour as the Redeemer.[41] Eve bore two pairs of twins—Cain and Lebhûdhâ, Abel and Kelîmath—who later married each other (marriage quaternio). Adam's grave is the "cave of treasures." All his descendants must pay their respects to his body and "not depart from it." When the Flood was approaching, Noah took Adam's body with him into the ark. The ark flew over the flood on the wings of the wind from east to west and from north to south, thus describing a cross upon the waters.

[36] "De igne et sale," *Theatr. chem.*, VI, p. 3.*
[37] Ibid.*
[38] *Pirke de Rabbi Eliezer*, p. 79.
[39] *Jewish Encyclopaedia*, s.v. Adam.
[40] Mentioned in Zosimos, in Berthelot, *Alch. grecs*, III, xlix, 6. Cf. also *Sibylline Oracles* (ed. Geffcken), pp. 47ff.
[41] In the sixth hour, on a Friday, "Heva mounted the tree of transgression, and in the sixth hour the Messiah mounted the cross" (Bezold, *Die Schatzhöhle*, p. 62). Cf. Augustine's interpretation of the crucifixion as Christ's marriage with the "matrona." (Infra, par. 568.)

556   At the midpoint where Adam was buried, the "four corners come together; for when God created the earth his power ran along in front of it, and the earth ran after his power from four sides like winds and gentle breezes, and there his power stopped and came to rest. And there will be accomplished the redemption for Adam and all his children." Over the grave where the cross would stand there grew a tree, and there too was the altar of Melchizedek. When Shem laid the body on the ground,

> the four sides moved away from one another, the earth opened in the form of a cross, and Shem and Melchizedek laid the body inside. And as soon as they had done this, the four sides moved together again and covered the body of our Father Adam, and the doors of the earth were closed. And the same spot was named the Place of the Skull, because the head of all men was laid there, and Golgotha, because it was round . . . and Gabbatha, because all the nations were gathered in it.[42]

"There the power of God will appear, for the four corners of the world have there become one," say the Ethiopic *Clementines*.[43] God said to Adam: "I shall make thee God, but not now; only after the passing of a great number of years." [44] The apocryphal "Life of Adam and Eve" says that the east and north of paradise were given to Adam, but the west and south to Eve.[45] The *Pirke de Rabbi Eliezer* relates that Adam was buried in the double cave Machpelah, and that Eve, Abraham and Sara, Isaac and Rebecca, Jacob and Leah were buried there too. "Therefore the cave was named Kiriath Arba', the City of Four, because four husbands and wives were buried there." [46]

557   I do not want to pile up proofs of Adam's quaternary nature, but only to give it due emphasis. Psychologically the four are the four orienting functions of consciousness, two of them perceptive (irrational), and two discriminative (rational). We could say that all mythological figures who are marked by a quaternity have ultimately to do with the structure of consciousness. We

---

42 Bezold, pp. 27ff.

43 Ibid., p. 76.

44 "Testament of Adam," in Riessler, *Altjüdisches Schrifttum ausserhalb der Bibel*, p. 1087.

45 Charles, *Apocrypha and Pseudepigrapha of the Old Testament*, II, p. 142.

46 Ch. 20, pp. 148f. Dr. R. Schärf points out that the cave is not identical with the City of Four, since Kirjath Arba' is a name for Hebron, where the cave is.

can therefore understand why Isaac Luria attributed every psychic quality to Adam: he is the psyche *par excellence*.[47]

558   The material I have presented is so suggestive that no detailed commentary is needed. Adam stands not only for the psyche but for its totality; he is a symbol of the self, and hence a visualization of the "irrepresentable" Godhead. Even if all the texts here cited were not available to the alchemists, a knowledge of the Zosimos treatises or of certain Cabalistic traditions would have been sufficient to make quite clear to them what was meant when the arcane substance was called Adam. I need hardly point out how important these historical statements are from the psychological point of view: they give us valuable indications of the way in which the corresponding dream-symbols should be evaluated. We do not devalue statements that originally were intended to be metaphysical when we demonstrate their psychic nature; on the contrary, we confirm their factual character. But, by treating them as psychic phenomena, we remove them from the inaccessible realm of metaphysics, about which nothing verifiable can be said, and this disposes of the impossible question as to whether they are "true" or not. We take our stand simply and solely on the facts, recognizing that the archetypal structure of the unconscious will produce, over and over again and irrespective of tradition, those figures which reappear in the history of all epochs and all peoples, and will endow them with the same significance and numinosity that have been theirs from the beginning.

2. THE STATUE

559   An old tradition says that Adam was created "a lifeless statue." It is worthy of remark that the statue plays a mysterious

---

[47] "Therefore in Adam the first man . . . were contained all those ideas or species aforesaid, from the practical soul to the emanative simplicity." * [I am indebted to Prof. G. Scholem for the following interpretative translation of the last few words: ". . . from the *nefesh* (i.e., the lowest of the five parts of the soul) of the world of *'asiyah* (i.e., the lowest of the four worlds of the Cabalistic cosmos) to the *yehidah* (the highest soul) of the world of *'atsiluth* (the highest world of the Cabalistic cosmos)."—TRANS.] Knorr von Rosenroth, "De revolutionibus animarum," Part I, cap. I, sec. 10, *Kabbala denudata*, II, Part 3, p. 248.

role in ancient alchemy. One of the earliest Greek treatises, the Book of Komarios,[48] says:

After the body had been hidden in the darkness, [the spirit] found it full of light. And the soul united with the body, since the body had become divine through its relation to the soul, and it dwelt in the soul. For the body clothed itself in the light of divinity, and the darkness departed from it, and all were united in love, body, soul, and spirit, and all became one; in this the mystery is hidden. But the mystery was fulfilled in their coming together, and the house was sealed, and the statue [ἀνδρίας] was erected, filled with light and divinity.[49]

Here the statue evidently denotes the end-product of the process, the lapis Philosophorum or its equivalent.

560   The statue has a somewhat different significance in the treatise of Senior,[50] who speaks of the "water that is extracted from the hearts of statues." Senior is identical with the Arabian alchemist Ibn 'Umail al-Tamimi. He is reported to have opened tombs and sarcophagi in Egypt and to have removed the mummies.[51] Mummies were supposed to possess medicinal virtues, and for this reason bits of corpses had long been mentioned in European pharmacy under the name of "mumia." [52] It is possible that "mumia" was also used for alchemical purposes. It is mentioned in Khunrath as synonymous with the prima materia.[53] In Paracelsus, who may have been Khunrath's source for this, "Mumia balsamita" has something to do with the elixir, and is even called the physical life-principle itself.[54] Senior's statues may well have been Egyptian sarcophagi, which as we know were portrait-statues. In the same treatise there is a description of a statue (of Hermes Trismegistus) in an under-

48 Berthelot, Alch. grecs, IV, xx.

49 Ibid., IV, xx, 15.

50 De chemia, p. 64: "Then I gather together the head, hands and feet [of the lion] and warm with them the water extracted from the hearts of statues, from the white and yellow stones, which falls from heaven in time of rain." *

51 Stapleton, "Muhammad bin Umail."

52 Already in the Cyranides we find: "Also the laudanum of his [the goat's] beard, i.e., mumia or hyssop or sweat." * (Delatte, Textes latins et vieux français relatifs aux Cyranides, p. 129.)

53 Von hyl. Chaos, pp. 310f.: "The foundations of all that is created . . . are contained in . . . the radical moisture, the seed of the world, the Mumia, the materia prima." *

54 Cf. "Paracelsus as a Spiritual Phenomenon," pars. 170 and n. 5, 190.

ground chapel. Senior says: "I shall now make known to you what that wise man who made the statue has hidden in that house; in it he has described that whole science, as it were, in the figure, and taught his wisdom in the stone, and revealed it to the discerning." Michael Maier comments: "That is the statue from whose heart the water is extracted." He also mentions that a stone statue which pronounced oracles was dedicated to Hermes in Achaia Pharis.

561   In Raymond Lully (Ramon Llull) there is an "oil that is extracted from the heart of statues," and moreover "by the washing of water and the drying of fire." [55] This is an extremely paradoxical operation in which the oil evidently serves as a mediating and uniting agent.

562   There is an allusion to the statues in Thomas Norton's "Ordinall of Alkimy":

> But holy *Alkimy* of right is to be loved,
> Which treateth of a precious Medicine,
> Such as trewly maketh *Gold* and *Silver* fine:
> Whereof example for Testimonie
> Is in a Citty of *Catilony*.
> Which *Raymund Lully, Knight,* men [do] suppose,
> Made in seaven Images the trewth to disclose;
> Three were good *Silver,* in shape like Ladies bright,
> Everie each of Foure were *Gold* and like a Knight:
> In borders of their Clothing Letters did appeare,
> Signifying in Sentence as it sheweth here.[56]

563   The "seven" refer to the gods of the planets, or the seven metals.[57] The correlation of the "three" (Venus, moon, earth) with silver (Luna) and of the "four" with gold (Sol) is remarkable in that three is usually considered a masculine and four a feminine number.[58] As Lully was undoubtedly acquainted with

---

[55] *Codicillus*, 1651, p. 88.* Cf. Maier, *Symbola*, p. 19. Concerning the oil Lully says: "This oil is the tincture, gold and the soul, and the unguent of the philosophers" * (*Codicillus*, p. 96). A follower of Lully, Christopher of Paris, says: "That oil or divine water . . . is called the Mediator" * ("Elucidarius," *Theatr. chem.*, VI, p. 214). It is therefore not surprising that Pernety (*Dict. mytho-hermétique*, p. 472) quotes the first *Codicillus* passage thus: "You extract this *God* [deum for oleum] from the hearts of statues by a moist bath of water and by a dry bath of fire."
[56] *Theatr. chem. Brit.*, pp. 20f.
[57] Of these Norton discusses iron, copper, and lead.
[58] Cf. "The Phenomenology of the Spirit in Fairytales," pars. 425, 437ff.

Senior this legend seems like a concretization of Senior's saying.[59]

564   The idea of a precious substance hidden in the "statue" is an old tradition and is particularly true of the statues of Hermes or Mercurius. Pseudo-Dionysius [60] says that the pagans made statues (ἀνδριάντας) of Mercurius and hid in them a simulacrum of the god. In this way they worshipped not the unseemly herm but the image hidden inside.[61] Plato is referring to these statues when he makes Alcibiades say that Socrates "bears a strong resemblance to those figures of Silenus in statuaries' shops, represented holding pipes or flutes; they are hollow inside, and when they are taken apart you see that they contain little figures [ἀγάλματα] of gods." [62]

565   It must have appealed very much to the imagination of the alchemists that there were statues of Mercurius with the real god hidden inside. Mercurius was their favourite name for that being who changed himself, during the work, from the prima materia into the perfected lapis Philosophorum. The figure of Adam readily lent itself as a biblical synonym for the alchemical Mercurius, first because he too was androgynous, and second because of his dual aspect as the first and second Adam. The second Adam is Christ, whose mystical androgyny is established in ecclesiastical tradition.[63] I shall come back to this aspect of Adam later.

566   According to the tradition of the Mandaeans, Adam was created by the seven in the form of a "lifeless bodily statue" which could not stand erect. This characteristic expression

---

59 I have had access to only a few of the dozens of Lully treatises that exist, so I have not attempted to trace the origin of the story.

60 Dionysius is cited in the alchemical literature. See *Theatr. chem.*, VI, p. 91.

61 "They made in them [the statues] both doors and hollows, in which they placed images of the gods they worshipped. And so statues of Mercury after this kind appeared of little worth, but contained within them ornaments of gods" * (Pachymeres' paraphrase of Dionysius the Areopagite, *De caelesti hierarchia,* in Migne, *P.G.,* vol. 3, col. 162).

62 *Symposium,* 215a; trans. by Hamilton, p. 100. In his commentary on this passage R. G. Bury *(The Symposium of Plato,* p. 143) says: "The interiors [of the statuettes] were hollow and served as caskets to hold little figures of gods wrought in gold or other precious metals."

63 One has only to read the meditations of St. Teresa of Avila or of St. John of the Cross on Song of Songs 1 : 1: "Let him kiss me with the kiss of his mouth, for thy breasts *(ubera)* are better than wine" (DV). Usually (as in AV and RSV) the passage is falsified: "love" for "breasts."

"bodily statue" frequently recurs in their literature and recalls the Chaldaean myth handed down by the Naassenes, that man's body was created by the demons and was called a statue (ἀνδριάς).[64] Ptahil, the world-creator, tried to "throw the soul into the statue," but Manda d'Hayye, the redeemer, "took the soul in his arms" and completed the work without Ptahil.[65] In this connection we may note that there is a description of the statue of Adam in Cabalistic literature.[66]

567   As Adam has always been associated with the idea of the second Adam in the minds of Christian writers,[67] it is readily understandable that this idea should reappear among the alchemists. Thus Mylius says:

> There now remains the second part of the philosophical practice, by far the more difficult, by much the more sublime. In this we read that all the sinews of talent, all the mental efforts of many philosophers have wearied themselves. For it is more difficult to make a man live again, than to slay him. Here is God's work besought: for it is a great mystery to create souls, and to mould the lifeless body into a living statue.[68]

This living statue refers to the end-result of the work; and the work, as we have seen, was on the one hand a repetition of the creation of the world, and on the other a process of redemption, for which reason the lapis was paraphrased as the risen Christ.

[64] The corresponding passage in Hippolytus, *Elenchos*, V, 7, 6, runs: "But the Assyrians say that the fish-eating Oannes [the first man] was born among them, and the Chaldaeans say the same thing about Adam; and they assert that he was the man whom the earth brought forth alone, and that he lay unbreathing and unmoved as a statue [ἀνδριάντα], an image of him on high who is praised as the man Adamas, begotten of many powers" (Legge trans., I, p. 122, modified).

[65] Bousset, *Hauptprobleme der Gnosis*, pp. 34f. This story from the Genza (holy book of the Mandaeans) may throw light on the passage in Senior, where he says that the male reptile "will cast his semen upon the marble in a statue" * (*De chemia*, p. 78).

[66] Kohen, *Emek ha-Melech*. [This reference is untraceable.—EDITORS.]

[67] Cf. the pregnant sentences in Ephraem Syrus ("De poenitentia," *Opera omnia*, p. 572): "Two Adams are created: the one, our father, unto death, because he was created mortal, and sinned; the second, our father, unto resurrection, since when he was immortal he by death overcame death and sin. The first Adam, here, is father; the second, there, is also father of the first Adam." *

[68] *Phil. ref.*, p. 19.* It is by no means certain that Mylius, who seldom or never gives his sources, is the originator of this thought. He might just as easily have copied it from somewhere, though I cannot trace the source.

The texts sometimes strike a chiliastic note with their references to a golden age when men will live forever without poverty and sickness.[69] Now it is remarkable that the statue is mentioned in connection with the eschatological ideas of the Manichaeans as reported by Hegemonius: the world will be consumed with fire and the souls of sinners chained for all eternity, and "then shall these things be, when the statue shall come." [70] I would not venture to say whether the Manichaeans influenced the alchemists or not, but it is worth noting that in both cases the statue is connected with the end-state. The tradition reported by Hegemonius has been confirmed by the recently discovered original work of Mani, the *Kephalaia*.[71] This says:

At that time [the Father of Greatness] made the messenger and Jesus the radiant and the Virgin of Light and the Pillar of Glory and the gods. . . .[72] The fourth time, when they shall weep, is the time when the statue [ἀνδριάς] shall raise itself on the last day. . . .[73] At that same hour, when the last statue shall rise, they shall weep. . . .[74] The first rock is the pillar [στῦλος] of glory, the perfect man, who has been summoned by the glorious messenger. . . . He bore the whole world and became the first of all bearers. . . .[75] The intellectual element [νοερόν] [gathered itself] into the pillar of glory, and the pillar of glory into the first man. . . .[76] The garments, which are named the Great Garments, are the five intellectual elements, which have [made perfect] the body of the pillar of glory, the perfect man.[77]

It is clear from these extracts that the statue or pillar is either the perfect Primordial Man (τέλειος ἄνθρωπος) or at least his body, both at the beginning of creation and at the end of time.

568   The statue has yet another meaning in alchemy which is worth mentioning. In his treatise "De Igne et Sale" Vigenerus calls the sun the "eye and heart of the sensible world and the image of the invisible God," adding that St. Dionysius called it the "clear and manifest statue of God." [78] This statement probably refers to Dionysius's *De divinis nominibus* (ch. IV): "The

69 "Paracelsus as a Spiritual Phenomenon" par. 214.
70 *Acta Archelai*, XIII, p. 21.*
71 Schmidt, *Manichäische Handschriften der Staatlichen Museen, Berlin*, I.
72 Ch. XXIV, p. 72, vv. 33f.   73 Ch. LIX, p. 149, v. 29f.   74 P. 150, v. 8.
75 Ch. LXII, p. 155, v. 10ff.
76 Ch. LXXII, p. 176, v. 3ff.
77 P. 177, v. 2ff.
78 *Theatr. chem.*, VI, p. 91.*

sun is the visible image of divine goodness." [79] Vigenerus translated εἰκών not by "imago" but by "statua," which does not agree with the Latin text of the collected edition brought out by Marsilio Ficino in 1502–3, to which he may have had access. It is not easy to see why he rendered εἰκών by "statua," unless perhaps he wished to avoid repeating the word "imago" from the end of the preceding sentence. But it may also be that the word "cor" recalled to his mind Senior's phrase "from the hearts of statues," as might easily happen with so learned an alchemist. There is, however, another source to be considered: it is evident from this same treatise that Vigenerus was acquainted with the *Zohar*. There the Haye Sarah on Genesis 28 : 22 says that Malchuth is called the "statue" when she is united with Tifereth.[80] Genesis 28 : 22 runs: "And this stone, which I have set for a pillar, shall be God's house." [81] The stone is evidently a reminder that here the upper (Tifereth) has united with the lower (Malchuth): Tifereth the son [82] has come together with the "Matrona" [83] in the hierosgamos. If our conjecture is correct, the statue could therefore be the Cabalistic equivalent of the lapis Philosophorum, which is likewise a union of male and female. In the same section of Vigenerus's treatise the sun does in fact appear as the bridegroom.[84] As Augustine is quoted a few lines later, it is possible that Vigenerus was thinking of that passage where Augustine says:

Like a bridegroom Christ went forth from his chamber, he went out with a presage of his nuptials into the field of the world. He ran like a giant exulting on his way, and came to the marriage bed of the cross, and there, in mounting it, he consummated his marriage. And

[79] *Divine Names* (trans. by Rolt), p. 93.* An older authority than Dionysius is Theophilus of Antioch (2nd cent.), who says: "The sun is a type of God, and the moon of man" (*Three Books to Autolycus*, II, 15; trans. by Pratten and others, p. 82).*

[80] *Kabbala denudata*, I, Part 1, p. 546.

[81] This was the stone of Bethel, which Jacob set up after his dream of the ladder.

[82] "It is the brightest, which belongs to Tifereth." * *Kabbala denudata*, p. 202.

[83] Malchuth = *sponsa* (pp. 366, 477). The "ecclesia Israel" is also called Malchuth (p. 480). Besides this, Tifereth and Malchuth are brother and sister (p. 120). "Malchuth is also called by the name of mother, since she is the mother of all things that exist under her, even to the bound of the whole Abyss" * (p. 120).

[84] "His [the sun's] beauty is compared with that of a bridegroom coming forth from his bridechamber. And he is as a bridegroom issuing from his couch" * (*Theatr. chem.*, VI, p. 92).

396

when he perceived the sighs of the creature, by a loving exchange he gave himself up to the torment in place of his bride. He yielded up also the carbuncle, as the jewel of his blood, and he joined the woman to himself for ever. "I have espoused you to one husband," says the apostle, "that I may present you as a chaste virgin to Christ" [2 Cor. 11 : 2].[85]

569   Since Adam signifies not only the beginning of the work, the prima materia, but also the end, the lapis, and the lapis is the product of the royal marriage, it is possible that Vigenerus's "statua Dei," replacing the more usual "imago Dei," has some connection with the Cabalistic interpretation of the stone of Bethel, which in turn marked the union of Tifereth and Malchuth. The statue stands for the inert materiality of Adam, who still needs an animating soul; it is thus a symbol for one of the main preoccupations of alchemy.

3. ADAM AS THE FIRST ADEPT

570   Not always in alchemy is Adam created out of the four elements. The "Introitus apertus," for instance, says that the soul of the gold is united with Mercurius in lead, "that they may bring forth Adam and his wife Eve." [86] Here Adam and Eve take the place of King and Queen. But in general Adam, being composed of the four elements, either *is* the prima materia and the arcane substance itself,[87] or he brought it with him from paradise, at the beginning of the world, as the first adept. Maier mentions that Adam brought antimony (then regarded as an arcane substance) [88] from paradise.[89] The long line of "Philos-

85 *Sermo suppositus*, 120, 8 (Migne, *P.L.*, vol. 39, cols. 1984f.).*
86 *Mus. herm.*, p. 688 (Waite, II, p. 189).
87 As the "chaos," the materia prima likewise consists of four elements (*Theatr. chem.*, VI, p. 228) which are in conflict. The task of the opus is to reconcile them so that they give rise to the One, the filius philosophorum. The Gnostics of Hippolytus thought in the same way; they spoke of the ascent and rebirth of Adam "that he may be born spiritual, not fleshly" (*Elenchos*, V, 8, 18). He is called "mighty in war," but the war is in his own body, which "is made from warring elements" (V, 8, 19; Legge, I, p. 134).
88 "More medicinal virtue lies hid in antimony than in any other simple, and therefore more of the tinging virtue of the tincture." * (*Symbola*, p. 379.)
89 Similarly Mylius says: "And therefore it is said that the stone is in every man. And Adam brought it forth with him from Paradise, from which material our stone or Elixir is produced in every man." * (*Phil. ref.*, p. 30.)

ophers" begins with him. The "Aquarium sapientum" asserts that the secret of the stone was revealed to Adam from above and was subsequently "sought after with singular longing by all the Holy Patriarchs." [90] The "Gloria mundi" says: "The Lord endowed Adam with great wisdom, and such marvellous insight that he immediately, without the help of any teacher—simply by virtue of his original righteousness—had a perfect knowledge of the seven liberal arts, and of all animals, plants, stones, metals, and minerals. Nay, what is more, he had a perfect understanding of the Holy Trinity, and of the coming of Christ in the flesh." [91] This curious opinion is traditional and comes mainly from Rabbinic sources.[92] Aquinas, too, thought that Adam, because of his perfection, must have had a knowledge of all natural things.[93] In Arabian tradition Shîth (Seth) learnt medicine from him.[94] Adam also built the Ka'ba, for which purpose the angel Gabriel gave him the ground-plan and a precious stone. Later the stone turned black because of the sins of men.[95]

571   The Jewish sources are even more explicit. Adam understood all the arts,[96] he invented writing, and from the angels he learnt husbandry and all the professions including the art of the smith.[97] A treatise from the eleventh century lists thirty kinds of fruit which he brought with him from paradise.[98] Maimonides states that Adam wrote a book on trees and plants.[99] Rabbi Eliezer credits Adam with the invention of the leap-year.[100] According to him, the tables on which God later inscribed the law came from Adam.[101] From Eliezer, probably, derives the statement of Bernardus Trevisanus that Hermes Trismegistus found seven stone tables in the vale of Hebron, left over from ante-

---

[90] *Mus. herm.*, p. 97.   [91] *Mus. herm.*, p. 268 (Waite, I, p. 216).

[92] In the Naassene view the Chaldaeans equated Oannes with Adam. Cf. n. 64, supra.

[93] *Summa theol.*, I, q. 94, ad 3 (I, pp. 480ff.).

[94] Chwolsohn, *Die Ssabier*, II, p. 601.

[95] Wünsche, "Salomos Thron und Hippodrom," p. 50.

[96] Kohut, "Die talmudisch-midraschische Adamssage," p. 80.

[97] *Jewish Encyclopaedia,* s.v. Adam.

[98] "Alfabet des Ben-Sira." Cf. Scheftelowitz, *Die altpersische Religion und das Judentum,* p. 218.

[99] Chwolsohn, *Die Ssabier*, I, p. 709.

[100] "Adam handed on the tradition to Enoch, who was initiated into the principle of intercalation" * (*Pirke de Rabbi Eliezer,* 8, trans. by Friedlander, p. 52).

[101] "Adam said: these are the tables, on which the Holy One, blessed be He, will write with his own finger." * (Cf. *Pirke de Rabbi Eliezer,* 20, p. 148.)

diluvian times. On them was a description of the seven liberal arts. Adam had put these tables there after his expulsion from paradise.[102] According to Dorn, Adam was the first "practitioner and inventor of the arts." He had a knowledge of all things "before and after the Fall," and he also prophesied the renewal and chastening of the world by the flood.[103] His descendants set up two stone tables on which they recorded all the "natural arts" in hieroglyphic script. Noah found one of these tables at the foot of Mount Ararat, bearing a record of astronomy.[104]

572   This legend probably goes back to Jewish tradition, to stories like the one mentioned in the *Zohar*:

When Adam was in paradise, God sent the holy angel Raziel,[105] the keeper of the higher secrets, to him with a book, in which the higher holy wisdom was set forth. In this book two and seventy kinds of wisdom were described in six hundred and seventy sections. By means of this book there were given to him fifteen hundred keys to wisdom, which were known to none of the higher holy men, and all remained secret until this book came to Adam. . . . Henceforth he kept this book hid and secret, daily using this treasure of the Lord, which discovered to him the higher secrets of which even the foremost angels knew nothing, until he was driven out of paradise. But when he sinned and transgressed the command of the Lord, this book fled from him. . . . He bequeathed it to his son Seth. And from Seth it came to Enoch, and from him . . . to Abraham.[106]

573   In the *Clementine Homilies* (2nd cent.) Adam is the first of a series of eight incarnations of the "true prophet." The last is Jesus.[107] This idea of a pre-existent seer may spring from Jewish or Judaeo-Christian tradition, but in China it is vividly realized

---

102 *Theatr. chem.*, I, pp. 774f.

103 "The world is to be renewed, or rather, chastened and little short of destroyed, by water" * ("Congeries Paracelsicae," *Theatr. chem.*, I, p. 617).

104 *Theatr. chem.*, I, pp. 617f.

105 From Aramaic *ras* = 'secret'.

106 Peter Beer, *Geschichte, Lehre und Meinungen aller bestandenen und noch bestehenden religiösen Sekten der Juden und der Geheimlehre oder Cabbalah*, II, pp. 11f. The mystical book Sefer Raziel is one of the oldest texts of the Cabala (1st edn., Amsterdam, 1701). It is identified with "Sifre de-Adam Kadmaa," cited in the *Zohar*. (Cf. *Jewish Encyclopaedia*, s.v. Adam.) According to another version the book was made of precious stones and contained the names of the seven charms which God gave to Adam. (Grunwald, "Neue Spuk- und Zauberliteratur," pp. 167f.)

107 The series consists of Adam, Enoch, Noah, Abraham, Isaac, Jacob, Moses, Christ. *Clementine Homilies* (trans. by Smith and others), pp. 283 and 259.

in the figure of P'an Ku.[108] He is represented as a dwarf clad in a bear-skin or in leaves; on his head he has two horns.[109] He proceeded from *yang* and *yin*, fashioned the chaos, and created heaven and earth. He was helped by four symbolic animals—the unicorn, the phoenix, the tortoise, and the dragon.[110] He is also represented with the sun in one hand and the moon in the other. In another version he has a dragon's head and a snake's body. He changed himself into the earth with all its creatures and thus proved to be a real *homo maximus* and Anthropos. P'an Ku is of Taoist origin and nothing seems to be known of him before the fourth century A.D.[111] He reincarnated himself in Yüan-shih T'ien-tsun, the First Cause and the highest in heaven.[112] As the fount of truth he announces the secret teaching, which promises immortality, to every new age. After completing the work of creation he gave up his bodily form and found himself aimlessly floating in empty space. He therefore desired rebirth in visible form. At length he found a holy virgin, forty years old, who lived alone on a mountain, where she nourished herself on air and clouds. She was hermaphroditic, the embodiment of both *yang* and *yin*. Every day she collected the quintessence of sun and moon. P'an Ku was attracted by her virgin purity, and once, when she breathed in, he entered into her in the form of a ray of light, so that she became pregnant. The pregnancy lasted for twelve years, and the birth took place from the spinal column. From then on she was called T'ai-yüan Sheng-mu, "the Holy Mother of the First Cause." [113] The relatively late date of the legend leaves the possibility of Christian influence open. All the same, its analogy with Christian and Persian ideas does not prove its dependence on these sources.

574   The series of eight incarnations of the "true prophet" is distinguished by the special position of the eighth, namely Christ.

108 *P'an* means 'egg-shell,' *Ku* 'firm, to make firm; 'undeveloped and unenlightened, i.e., the embryo' (Hastings, *Encyclopaedia of Religion and Ethics*, IV, 141a).
109 Moses, too, is represented with horns.
110 Cf. the Christian relation of the Anthropos to the tetramorph (angel, eagle, lion, ox). See *Psychology and Alchemy*, fig. 53.
111 He is supposed to have been invented, so to speak, by the Taoist philosopher Ko Hung, 4th cent.
112 He is an "increatum" made of uncreated, incorruptible air.
113 For these statements see Werner, *Myths and Legends of China*, pp. 76ff. Krieg (*Chinesische Mythen und Legenden*, pp. 7ff.) gives a very fine recension of the P'an-Ku legend, in which he brings together a number of Taoist-alchemical motifs.

The eighth prophet is not merely the last in the series; he corresponds to the first and is at the same time the fulfilment of the seven, and signifies the entry into a new order. I have shown in *Psychology and Alchemy* (pars. 200ff.), with the help of a modern dream, that whereas the seven form an uninterrupted series, the step to the eighth involves hesitation or uncertainty and is a repetition of the same phenomenon that occurs with three and four (the Axiom of Maria). It is very remarkable that we meet it again in the Taoist series of "eight immortals" (*hsien-yên*): the seven are great sages or saints who dwell in heaven or on the earth, but the eighth is a *girl* who sweeps up the fallen flowers at the southern gate of heaven.[114] The parallel to this is Grimm's tale of the seven ravens: there the seven brothers have one sister.[115] One is reminded in this connection of Sophia, of whom Irenaeus says: "This mother they also call the Ogdoad, Sophia, Terra, Jerusalem, Holy Spirit, and, with a masculine reference, Lord."[116] She is "below and outside the Pleroma." The same thought occurs in connection with the seven planets in Celsus's description of the "diagram of the Ophites," attacked by Origen.[117] This diagram is what I would call a mandala—an ordering pattern or pattern of order which is either consciously devised or appears spontaneously as a product of unconscious processes.[118] The description Origen gives of the diagram is unfortunately not particularly clear, but at least we can make out that it consisted of ten circles, presumably concentric, since he speaks of a circumference and a centre.[119] The outermost circle was labelled "Leviathan" and the innermost "Behemoth," the two apparently coinciding, for "Leviathan" was the name for the centre as well as the circumference.[120] At the same time, "the

114 Wilhelm, *The Chinese Fairy Book* (trans. by Martens), pp. 76ff.

115 *Grimm's Fairy Tales* (trans. by Hunt and Stern), p. 137.

116 *Adv. haer.*, I, v. 3. (trans. by Roberts and Rambaut, I, p. 22).

117 *Contra Celsum* VI, 24 (trans. by Chadwick, p. 337).

118 Cf. "A Study in the Process of Individuation" and "Concerning Mandala Symbolism."

119 "It contained a drawing of ten circles, which were separated from one another and held together by a single circle, which was said to be the soul of the universe and was called Leviathan." * (*Contra Celsum*, VI, 25, p. 340.)

120 The passage runs: "We also found that Behemoth is mentioned in it as if it were some being fixed below the lowest circle. The inventor of this horrible diagram depicted Leviathan upon the circumference of the circle and at its centre, putting in the name twice." * (Ibid.)

impious diagram said that the Leviathan . . . is the soul that has permeated the universe." [121]

575   Origen had got hold of a diagram like the one used by Celsus and discovered in it the names of the seven angels Celsus alludes to. The prince of these angels was called the "accursed God," and they themselves were called sometimes gods of light and sometimes "archons." The "accursed God" refers to the Judaeo-Christian world-creator, as Origen duly notes. Yahweh appears here obviously as the prince and father of the seven archons.[122] The first of them had a "lion's form" and was named Michael; the second was a bull and was named Suriel, the bull-formed; the third, Raphael, had the form of a snake; the fourth, named Gabriel, the form of an eagle; the fifth, Thauthabaoth, the form of a bear; the sixth, Erataoth, the form of a dog; and the seventh had the form of an ass and was called Onoël or Taphabaoth or Tharthataoth.[123]

576   It is to be presumed that these names were distributed among the eight inner circles. The seven archons correspond to the seven planets and represent so many spheres with doors which the celebrant has to pass through on his ascent. Here, says Origen, is the origin of the Ogdoad, which, clearly, must consist of the seven and their father Yahweh. At this point Origen mentions, as the "first and seventh," Ialdabaoth, of whom we have not heard before. This supreme archon, as we know from other sources too, is lion-headed or lion-like.[124] He would therefore correspond to Michael in the Ophitic diagram, the first in the list of archons. "Ialdabaoth" means "child of chaos"; thus he is the first-born of a new order that supersedes the original state of chaos. As the first son, he is the last of the series,[125] a feature he shares with Adam and also with Leviathan, who, as we have seen, is both circumference and centre. These analogies suggest that the diagram showed a series of concentric circles.[126]

121 Ibid.*   122 Ibid., VI, 27, pp. 342f.

123 Ibid., VI, 30, p. 346.

124 ". . . and they say that the star Saturn is in sympathy with the lion-like Archon" (VI, 31, p. 347).* Cf. Bousset, *Hauptprobleme der Gnosis*, pp. 351ff.

125 In the prayer to Ialdabaoth the celebrant addresses him thus: "And thou, Ialdabaoth, first and seventh . . . a perfect work for Son and Father." * (Origen, VI, 31, p. 347.)

126 Leisegang (*Die Gnosis*, p. 169) gives a different reconstruction but does not take account of the seven spheres of the archons.

The old world-picture, with the earth as the centre of the universe, consisted of various "heavens"—spherical layers or spheres —arranged concentrically round the centre and named after the planets. The outermost planetary sphere or archon was Saturn. Outside this would be the sphere of the fixed stars (corresponding to Leviathan as the tenth circle in the diagram), unless we postulated some place for the demiurge or for the father or mother of the archons. It is evident from the text that an Ogdoad is meant,[127] as in the system of Ptolemy reported by Irenaeus.[128] There the eighth sphere was called Achamoth (Sophia, Sapientia),[129] and was of feminine nature, just as in Damascius the hebdomad was attributed to Kronos and the ogdoad to Rhea.[130] In our text the virgin Prunicus is connected with the mandala of seven circles: [131] "They have further added on top of one another sayings of the prophets, circles included in circles . . . and a power flowing from a certain Prunicus, a virgin, a living soul." [132]

577   The "circles included in circles" point decisively to a concentric arrangement, as we find it, significantly enough, in Herodotus's description [133] of the seven circular walls of Ecbatana.[134] The ramparts of these walls were all painted in different colours; of the two innermost and highest walls one was silvered and the other gilded. The walls obviously represented the concentric circles of the planets, each characterized by a special colour.

578   In the introduction to his diagram Celsus reports on the idea, found among the Persians and in the Mithraic mysteries, of a

127 VI, 31, p. 347.
128 *Adv. haer.* I, ivff. (trans. by Roberts and Rambaut, I, pp. 16ff.)
129 The demiurge is the hebdomad, but Achamoth is the ogdoad. (Leisegang, p. 317.)
130 Damascius, *De Principiis* (ed. Ruelle), § 266 (II, pp. 132f.)*
131 *Contra Celsum*, p. 350.* The Gnostics, Origen remarks, likened this Prunicus to the "woman with the bloody flux," who was thus afflicted for twelve years. T'ai-yüan, "the Holy Mother of the First Cause," had a pregnancy lasting for twelve years. (See supra, par. 573.)
132 Irenaeus (*Adv. haer.* I, iv, 2) says that, according to the Valentinians, "the whole soul of the world and of the creator of the world" proceeded from Sophia's longing for the life-giver (Christ). (Cf. *Writings*, I, p. 17.)
133 *The Histories*, I, 98 (trans. by de Selincourt, pp. 54f).
134 Concerning the mandala as the plan of a primitive settlement see my "Psychology of the Transference," pars. 433ff.

stairway with seven doors and an eighth door at the top. The first door was Saturn and was correlated with lead, and so on. The seventh door was gold and signified the sun. The colours are also mentioned.[135] The stairway represents the "passage of the soul" (*animae transitus*). The eighth door corresponds to the sphere of the fixed stars.

579   The archetype of the seven appears again in the division of the week and the naming of its days, and in the musical octave, where the last note is always the beginning of a new cycle. This may be a cogent reason why the eighth is feminine: it is the *mother* of a new series. In Clement's line of prophets the eighth is Christ. As the first and second Adam he rounds off the series of seven, just as, according to Gregory the Great, he, "coming in the flesh, joined the Pleiades, for he had within himself, at once and for ever, the works of the sevenfold Holy Spirit." [136] These references should suffice to show the special nature of the eighth and its tendency to be feminine in Christian gnosis.

580   Adam's dual nature reappears in Christ: he is male-female. Boehme expresses this by saying that Christ was a "virgin in mind." [137] She is "an image of the holy number Three," [138] "eternally uncreated and ungenerated." [139] Where the "Word" is, there is the virgin, for the "Word" is in her.[140] She is the "woman's seed," [141] which shall bruise the head of the serpent (Gen. 3 : 15).[142] He who shall tread on its head is Christ, who thus appears identical with the seed of the woman or with the virgin. In Boehme the virgin has the character of an anima, for "she is given to be a companion to thee in thy soul," [143] and at the same time, as divine power and wisdom, she is in heaven and in paradise.[144] God took her to him to be his "spouse." [145] She

135 "For these two metals recall the colours of the sun and moon." * (Cf. *Contra Celsum*, p. 334.)

136 *Moralia in Job*, cap. 38, bk. 29, chap. 31 (Migne, *P.L.*, vol. 76, col. 519).*

137 *Three Principles of the Divine Essence* (*Works*, I), XVIII, 20, p. 170.

138 *A High and Deep Search concerning the Threefold Life of Man* (*Works*, II), V, 41, p. 47.

139 Ibid., XI, 12, p. 110. Cf. the increatum of Paracelsus and the alchemists (*Psychology and Alchemy*, pars. 430f.).   140 *A High and Deep Search*, VI, 77–8, p. 67.

141 *Zweyte Apologie wieder Balthasar Tilken* (Amsterdam edn., 1682), II, 227, p. 306.   142 *Mysterium Magnum* (*Works*, III), IX, 11, p. 36; XXIII, 38, p. 104.

143 *Three Principles* (*Works*, I), XVII, 78, p. 159.

144 Ibid., XIII, 9, p. 94.

145 *Menschwerdung Christi*, Part I, ch. 11, 10.

expresses all the profundity and infinity of the Godhead,[146] thus corresponding to the Indian Shakti.[147] The androgynous unity of Shiva and Shakti is depicted in Tantric iconography as permanent cohabitation.[148]

581 Boehme's ideas had a strong influence on Franz von Baader, who asserted that God gave Adam a helpmeet (*adjutor*) through whom Adam "was to have brought forth without an external woman," as Mary did without a man. But Adam "fell for" [149] the bestial act of copulation and was in danger of himself sinking to the level of a beast. God, recognizing this possibility, thereupon created Eve as a "salutary counter-institution [*rettende Gegenanstalt*], to prevent an otherwise unavoidable and deeper descent of man . . . into animal nature." [150] When Adam threatened to sink into it nevertheless, his divine androgyny departed from him, but was preserved in Eve as the "woman's seed," with the help of which man would free himself from the "seed of the serpent." For "he who was born in the Virgin Mary is the same who had to depart from Adam on account of his fall." [151]

582 The presence of a divine pair or androgyne in the human soul is touched upon by Origen: "They say that as the sun and moon stand as the two great lights in the firmament of heaven, so in us Christ and the Church." [152] And thus, too, Adam and Eve are in each of us, as Gregory the Great says; Adam standing for the spirit, Eve for the flesh.[153]

583 Origen, like Clement of Rome, credits Adam with the gift of prophecy, "for he prophesied a great mystery in Christ and the Church, saying, 'Therefore shall a man leave his father and mother, and shall cleave unto his wife, and they shall be one flesh.' " [154] (Gen. 2 : 24; cf. Matt. 19 : 5 and Mark 10 : 7.)

146 *A High and Deep Search* (*Works*, II), V, 56, p. 48.

147 Avalon, *The Serpent Power.*

148 For this motif see *Symbols of Transformation*, pars. 306, 349, 620.

149 Lit., "vergaffte sich." This expression derives from Paracelsus. See *Liber Azoth* (ed. Sudhoff, vol. XIV) p. 574.   150 von Baader, *Werke*, VII, p. 229.

151 Ibid., p. 231.

152 *In Genesim Hom.*, I, 7 (Migne, *P.G.*, vol. 12, col. 151).

153 "Every man has in himself both Adam and Eve. For as in that first transgression of man, the serpent suggested, Eve delighted, and Adam consented, so we see every day that when the devil suggests, the flesh delights, and the spirit consents." *
In Septem Psalmos poenitentiales, V, § 8 (Migne, *P.L.*, vol. 79, col. 608).

154 *In Cant. hom.* II (Migne, *P.G.*, vol. 13, cols. 47ff.).

584   I shall end this account of the excellent equipment of the first man with an Arabian legend, which is not without a deeper meaning. When Adam left Paradise, God sent the angel Gabriel to him with an offer of three gifts of which he should choose one: modesty, intelligence, and religion. Without hesitation Adam chose intelligence. Thereupon Gabriel commanded modesty and religion to return at once to heaven. But they refused, invoking God's own command never to part from intelligence, wherever it might be found. For the Prophet had said: "Never submit to one who has no trace of intelligence." [155]

4. THE POLARITY OF ADAM

585   There has always existed a widely felt need to think of the first man as having a "light" nature; hence the frequent comparison with the sun. The alchemists did not insist on this aspect, so I need say only a few words about it here. Usually, however, in the non-alchemical literature Adam is a "light" figure whose splendour even outshines that of the sun. He lost his radiance owing to the Fall.[156] Here we have a hint of his dual nature: on the one hand shining and perfect, on the other dark and earthy. Haggadic interpretation derives his name from *adamah*, earth.[157]

586   His dual nature is confirmed by Origen: one Adam was made out of earth, the other "after the image and likeness of God. He is our inner man, invisible, incorporeal, unspotted, and immortal." [158] Similar views are expressed by Philo.[159] It is worth noting that in Colossians 1 : 15 Christ is this "image of the invisible God, the firstborn of every creature."

[155] "Le Livre des Balances," in Berthelot, *Chimie au moyen âge*, III, p. 140.

[156] Irenaeus, *Adv. haer.*, I, 30, 9; Bousset, *Hauptprobleme der Gnosis*, p. 198; Bezold, *Die Schatzhöhle*, p. 3; Kohut, "Adamssage," pp. 72 and 87; *Jewish Encyclopaedia*, s.v. Adam; Wünsche, "Schöpfung und Sündenfall des ersten Menschenpaares," p. 11.

[157] Gruenbaum, *Jüdisch-deutsche Chrestomathie*, p. 180. *Adamah* is also related to Hebrew *dam*, 'blood.' "Adam" would therefore mean "made of red earth."

[158] *In Genesim Hom.*, I, 13.*

[159] Philo distinguishes between the mortal Adam made of earth and the Adam created after the image of God and says of the latter: "He that was created after the [divine] image was an idea, or genus, or imprint, or object of thought, incorporeal, neither male nor female, by nature incorruptible" * ("On the Account of the World's Creation given by Moses," §134, *Works*, I, pp. 106f., mod.).

587   Adam's dual nature is reflected in his hermaphroditism. Thus Dorn says that the "fiery and perfect Mercurius" is the "true hermaphroditic Adam." [160] This idea occurs among the Naassenes. "These men," says Hippolytus, "worship as the beginning of all things, according to their own statement, a Man and a Son of Man. But this Man is masculo-feminine [ἀρσενόθηλυς] and is called by them Adamas; and hymns to him are many and various." He quotes as an example: "From thee the father, through thee the mother, the two immortal names, parents of the Aeons, O citizen of heaven, O Man of the Great Name!" [161] Adam is masculo-feminine also in Jewish tradition. In *Midrash Rabbah* VIII, 1 [162] he is an androgyne, or a man and woman grown into one body with two faces. God sawed the body in two and made each half a back.[163] Through his androgyny Adam has affinities with Plato's sphere-shaped Original Being as well as with the Persian Gayomart. This idea has left a few traces in alchemy. For instance, Glauber attributes the sign of the circle to Adam and the square to Eve.[164] The circle is usually the sign for gold and sun. It is found in the latter sense in the "Book of the Cave of Treasures": "Then God made Adam. . . . And when the angels saw his glorious appearance, they were moved by the beauty of the sight; for they saw the form of his countenance, while it was enkindled, in shining splendour like to the ball of the sun, and the light of his eyes like to the sun, and the form of his body like to the light of a crystal." [165] An Arabic Hermes-text on the creation of Adam relates that, when the virgin (Eve) came to power, the angel Harus (Horus) arose from

160 "Congeries Paracelsicae," *Theatr. chem.*, I, p. 578.

161 *Elenchos*, V, 6, 4f (Legge, I, p. 120).

162 Ed. Freedman and Simon, II, p. 54. Cf. also Scheftelowitz, *Die altpersische Religion und das Judentum*, p. 217, and Bousset, *Hauptprobleme der Gnosis*, p. 198.

163 Adam's back is of significance. An Islamic legend says: "Then God also made a covenant with the descendants of Adam: for he touched his back, and lo, all men who will be born until the end of the world crept forth from his back, in stature no greater than ants, and ranged themselves to his right hand and to his left." (Weil, *Biblische Legende der Muselmänner*, p. 34.) Then God sent these little souls back into Adam's backbone, where they died and were changed into a single spirit. (Ghazali, *Die kostbare Perle im Wissen des Jenseits*, ed. Brugsch, p. 7.) Citations from Aptowitzer, "Arabisch-jüdische Schöpfungstheorien," p. 216.

164 *De Signatura salium, metallorum et planetarum*, p. 12.

165 Bezold, *Die Schatzhöhle*, p. 3.

the unanimous will of the planets. This Harus took sixty spirits from the planets, eighty-three from the zodiac, ninety from the highest heaven, one hundred and twenty-seven from the earth, three hundred and sixty spirits in all, mixed them together and created out of them Adamanus, the first man, "after the form of the highest heaven." [166] The number 360 and the "form of heaven" both indicate his circular shape.

588 Aside, however, from his androgyny there is a fundamental polarity in Adam which is based on the contradiction between his physical and spiritual nature. This was felt very early, and is expressed in the view of Rabbi Jeremiah ben Eleazar that Adam must have had two faces, in accordance with his interpretation of Psalm 139 : 5: "Thou hast beset me behind and before"; [167] and in the Islamic view that Adam's soul was created thousands of years before his body and then refused to enter the figure made of clay, so that God had to put it in by force.[168]

589 According to a Rabbinic view Adam even had a tail.[169] His condition at first was altogether most inauspicious. As he lay, still inanimate, on the ground, he was of a greenish hue, with thousands of impure spirits fluttering round who all wanted to get into him. But God shooed them away till only one remained, Lilith, the "mistress of spirits," who succeeded in so attaching herself to Adam's body that she became pregnant by him. Only when Eve appeared did she fly away again.[170] The daemonic Lilith seems to be a certain aspect of Adam, for the legend says that she was created with him from the same earth.[171] It throws a bad light on Adam's nature when we are told that countless demons and spooks arose from his nocturnal emissions (*ex nocturno seminis fluxu*). This happened during the one hundred and thirty years which he had to spend apart from Eve, banished from the heavenly court "under the anathema of excommunication." [172] In Gnosticism the original man Adamas, who is noth-

166 Reitzenstein and Schaeder, *Studien zum antiken Synkretismus aus Iran und Griechenland*, p. 114.
167 *Jewish Encyclopaedia*, s.v. Adam.
168 Ibid.
169 Ibid.
170 *Zohar* I, 34 (trans. by Sperling and Simon, I, p. 129), and III, 19 (IV, p. 359).
171 According to Ben Sira. Cf. van Dale, *Dissertationes de origine ac progressu Idololatriae et Superstitionum,* p. 112.
172 Ibid., pp. 111.

ing but a paraphrase of Adam,[173] was equated with the ithyphallic Hermes and with Korybas, the pederastic seducer of Dionysus,[174] as well as with the ithyphallic Cabiri.[175] In the *Pistis Sophia* we meet a Sabaoth Adamas, the ruler (τύραννος) of the Aeons, who fights against the light of Pistis Sophia [176] and is thus wholly on the side of evil. According to the teachings of the Bogomils, Adam was created by Satanaël, God's first son and the fallen angel, out of mud. But Satanaël was unable to bring him to life, so God did it for him.[177] Adam's inner connection with Satan is likewise suggested in Rabbinic tradition, where Adam will one day sit on Satan's throne.[178]

590   As the first man, Adam is the *homo maximus*, the Anthropos, from whom the macrocosm arose, or who *is* the macrocosm. He is not only the prima materia but a universal soul which is also the soul of all men.[179] According to the Mandaeans he is the

[173] According to the teaching of the Barbeliots (Irenaeus, *Adv. haer.* I, 29, 2f.; *Writings*, I, p. 102), the Autogenes, who was sent forth by Ennoia and the Logos, created "the perfect and true man, who is called Adamas."

[174] Cf. *Scholia in Lucianum*, "De dea Syria," 28 (ed. Rabe, p. 187), and Roscher, *Lexikon*, s.v. κόρυβος, col. 1392 b.

[175] Hippolytus, *Elenchos*, V, 8, 9ff. (Legge trans., I, pp. 133ff.).

[176] *Pistis Sophia* (trans. by Mead), pp. 19 and 30. For Adam as "head of the Aeon" see Lidzbarski, *Das Johannesbuch der Mandäer*, p. 93, line 4.

[177] Euthymios Zigabenos, *Panoplia Dogmatica* (Migne, *P.G.*, vol. 130).

[178] Wünsche, *Die Sagen vom Lebensbaum und Lebenswasser*, p. 23.

[179] For a comprehensive survey of the Adam material see Murmelstein, "Adam, ein Beitrag zur Messiaslehre." Concerning the universal soul see ibid., XXXV, p. 269, and XXXVI, p. 52; also Aptowitzer, "Arabisch-jüdische Schöpfungstheorien," p. 214: "While Adam lay there a lifeless body, God showed him all the righteous who would one day issue from him. These have their origin in the separate parts of Adam's body: one from his head, the other from his hair, and others from his forehead, eyes, nose, mouth, ear and jawbone. Proof of this can be found in Job 38 : 4, where [as interpreted by the midrash] God says to Job: 'Tell me how thou art made, from what part of Adam's body thou comest; if thou canst tell me this, then mayest thou contend with me.'" "The first Adam was as great as the world from one end to the other, therefore the angels would have cried 'Holy!' before him, but God made him small by taking away pieces of his limbs, which then lay round about Adam. Adam said to God: 'Wherefore dost thou rob me?' God answered him: 'I will recompense thine injuries many times, for it hath been said, The son of David shall not come until all the souls in thy body are become earth. Take these pieces and carry them into all regions of the earth; wherever thou dost cast them, they will be turned to dust, and there shall the earth be inhabited by thy descendants. The places which thou shalt appoint for Israel shall belong to Israel, and the places which thou shalt appoint for the other peoples

"mystery of the worlds." [180] The conception of the Anthropos first penetrated into alchemy through Zosimos, for whom Adam was a dual figure—the fleshly man and the "man of light." [181] I have discussed the significance of the Anthropos idea at such length in *Psychology and Alchemy* that no further documentation is needed here. I shall therefore confine myself to material that is of historical interest in following the thought-processes of the alchemists.

591   Already in Zosimos [182] three sources can be distinguished: Jewish, Christian, and pagan. In later alchemy the pagan-syncretistic element naturally fades into the background to leave room for the predominance of the Christian element. In the sixteenth century, the Jewish element becomes noticeable again, under the influence of the Cabala, which had been made accessible to a wider public by Johann Reuchlin [183] and Pico della Mirandola.[184] Somewhat later the humanists then made their contribution from the Hebrew and Aramaic sources, and especially from the *Zohar*. In the eighteenth century an allegedly Jewish treatise appeared, Abraham Eleazar's *Uraltes Chymisches Werck*,[185] making copious use of Hebraic terminology and claiming to be the mysterious "Rindenbuch" of Abraham the Jew, which, it was said, had revealed the art of gold-making to Nicholas Flamel (1330–1417).[186] In this treatise there is the following passage:

For Noah must wash me in the deepest sea, with pain and toil, that my blackness may depart; I must lie here in the deserts among many serpents, and there is none to pity me; I must be fixed to this black cross, and must be cleansed therefrom with wretchedness and vine-

shall belong to the other peoples." In this Haggadah (discourse), therefore, it is said that all the generations of men were contained in Adam; in his soul, all souls, and in his body, all bodies.

180 Lidzbarski, *Das Johannesbuch der Mandäer*, p. 168, line 7.

181 Cf. the Zosimos text in *Psychology and Alchemy*, par. 456.

182 Berthelot, *Alch. grecs*, III, xlix, 4–12.

183 Reuchlin, *De verbo mirifico*, and *De arte cabbalistica*.

184 "Apologia tredecim Quaestionum," *Opera* (Venice, 1557).

185 *Uraltes Chymisches Werck*, 2nd edn., 1760. Published in Leipzig by Julius Gervasius von Schwartzburg.

186 See preface to the book. The MS is said to have been in the possession of Cardinal Richelieu. The story goes that Flamel bought the treatise, which was written on sheets of bark, for two florins from an unknown person. It is a late forgery from the beginning of the 18th cent. The first edition appeared in 1735.

gar [187] and made white, that the inwards of my head may be like the sun or Marez,[188] and my heart may shine like a carbuncle, and the old Adam come forth again from me. O! Adam Kadmon, how beautiful art thou! And adorned with the rikmah [189] of the King of the World! Like Kedar [190] I am black henceforth; ah! how long! O come, my Mesech,[191] and disrobe me, that mine inner beauty may be revealed. . . . O that the serpent roused up Eve! To which I must testify with my black colour that clings to me, and that is become mine by the curse of this persuasion, and therefore am I unworthy of all my brothers. O Sulamith afflicted within and without, the watchmen of the great city will find thee and wound thee, strip thee of thy garments and smite thee, and take away thy veil. . . . Yet shall I be blest again when I am delivered from the poison brought upon me by the curse, and mine inmost seed and first birth comes forth. For its father is the sun, and its mother the moon. Yea, I know else of no other bridegroom who should love me, because I am so black. Ah! do thou tear down the heavens and melt my mountains! For thou didst crumble the mighty kingdoms of Canaan like dust, and crush them with the brazen serpent of Joshua and offer them up to Algir $\triangle$ [fire], that she who is encompassed by many mountains may be freed.[192]

592   It is evident that the speaker is the feminine personification of the prima materia in the *nigredo* state. Psychologically this dark figure is the unconscious anima. In this condition she corresponds to the *nefesh* of the Cabalists.[193] She is "desire"; for as Knorr von Rosenroth trenchantly remarks: "The mother is nothing but the inclination of the father for the lower." [193a] The

---

187 This phrase occurs also in Maier, *Symbola*, p. 568: "There is in our chemistry a certain noble substance which moves from lord to lord, in the beginning whereof is wretchedness with vinegar, but in the end joy with gladness." *

188 Eleazar states that Marez, $\triangledown$, signifies earth, Hebrew *erets*.

189 Hebrew *riqma*, 'many-coloured garment.'

190 The men of Kedar lived in black tents.

191 Mixed drink, spiced wine.

192 *Uraltes Chymisches Werck*, II, pp. 51f.

193 "The psyche, which by them is called *nefesh*, is the vital spirit, not in so far as it is wholly corporeal, but as that which is inborn and primitive and seminal, which later writers call the Archeus. This corresponds to the vegetative or plastic soul of the Philosophers, and the affective or concupiscible soul of the Platonists." * (Knorr's note to § 7 of the "Tractatus de revolutionibus animarum," *Kabbala denudata*, II, Part 3, p. 247.) *Nefesh* is a kind of blood-soul, hence the prohibition against shedding blood (Leviticus 17 : 14).   193a *

blackness comes from Eve's sin. Sulamith (the Shulamite) [194] and Eve (Havva, earth) are contaminated into a single figure, who contains in herself the first Adam, like the mother her child, and at the same time awaits the second Adam, i.e., Adam before the Fall, the perfect Original Man, as her lover and bridegroom. She hopes to be freed by him from her blackness. Here again we encounter the mysticism of the Song of Songs as in the *Aurora consurgens* I. Jewish gnosis (Cabala) combines with Christian mysticism: sponsus and sponsa are called on the one hand Tifereth and Malchuth and on the other Christ and the Church.[195] The mysticism of the Song of Songs [196] appeared in Jewish-Gnostic circles during the third and fourth centuries, as is proved by the fragments of a treatise called *Shiur Koma* ("The Measure of the Body"). It concerns a "mysticism only superficially Judaicized by references to the description of the Beloved in the Song of Songs." [197] The figure of Tifereth belongs to the Sefiroth system, which is conceived to be a tree. Tifereth occupies the middle position. Adam Kadmon is either the whole tree or is thought of as the mediator between the supreme authority, En Soph, and the Sefiroth.[198] The black Shulamite in our text

[194] [The Hebrew word used in Song of Songs 6 : 13 is "Shulamith" or "Shulammit," translated in most versions of the Bible as "the Shulamite" (the girl from Shulem or ancient Shunem). Cf. Sellin, *Introduction to Old Testament*, pp. 223ff. "Sulamith" or "Shulamith" is also used as a personal name by modern Jews.—TRANS.]

[195] "Adam is called by the Cabalists Adam Kadmon, to distinguish him from Adam the first man . . . because of all things that came forth from God he occupies the first place, as the first man among the species of men. Nothing can more fitly be signified thereby than the soul of the Messiah, of which Paul speaks in I Corinthians 15 : 45–49." * (Knorr's note to "Tract. de revolut. animarum," *Kabbala denudata*, II, Part 3, p. 244.)

[196] "The love of the 'King' for the 'Queen' is the love of God for 'Zion', or for that power which is also called 'Shalom,' peace or fulfilment; for 'Shulamith,' who is praised in the Song of Songs" (Müller, *Der Sohar und seine Lehre*, p. 46).

[197] Scholem, "Kabbala," in *Encyclopaedia Judaica*, IX, cols. 630ff.

[198] *Kabbala denudata*, I, p. 28, s.v. homo. Wünsche ("Kabbala," in Herzog and Hauck, *Realenzyklopädie*, IX, p. 676) says: "Concerning Adam Kadmon the Cabalistic writings are not altogether clear. Sometimes he is conceived as the Sephiroth in their entirety, sometimes as a first emanation existing before the Sephiroth and superior to them, through which God . . . was made manifest and . . . revealed himself to the whole of Creation as a kind of prototype (macrocosm). In the latter event it looks as though Adam Kadmon were a first revelation interposed between God and the world, a second God, so to speak, or the divine Logos." This view agrees with that of the *Kabbala denudata*, which was influenced by Isaac Luria.

corresponds to Malchuth as a widow, who awaits union with Tifereth and hence the restoration of the original wholeness. Accordingly, Adam Kadmon here takes the place of Tifereth. He is mentioned in Philo and in the midrashic tradition. From the latter source comes the distinction between the heavenly and earthly Adam in I Cor. 15 : 47: "The first man was of the earth, earthy; the second man is from heaven, heavenly" (DV), and verse 45: "The first man, Adam, became a living soul; the last Adam became a life-giving spirit" (DV). Thus the original hylic-psychic man is contrasted with the later pneumatic man.

593   The *Tractatus de Revolutionibus Animarum,* of Knorr von Rosenroth, Part I, ch. 1, § 10, contains a passage which is of importance for the psychological interpretation of Adam:

Ezekiel 34 : 31 says, "Ye are Adam." [199] This means, you are rightly called by the name of Adam. The meaning is: If the text were to be understood literally, it could rightly be objected that all the peoples of the world or the Gentiles are men after the same manner as the Israelites, that is, of upright stature. Wherefore it would have to be said: Ye are men. But in truth (the meaning is this: out of your souls was composed the microcosm of Adam). . . . [200] § 11. Ye are Adam. (He says, as it were, that all the souls of the Israelites were in truth nothing but the first-created Adam.) And you were his sparks and his limbs.[201]

Here Adam appears on the one hand as the body of the people of Israel [202] and on the other as its "general soul." This conception can be taken as a projection of the interior Adam: the *homo maximus* appears as a totality, as the "self" of the people.

Here Adam Kadmon is "a mediator between En Soph and the Sefiroth" (*Jewish Encyclopaedia,* III, p. 475, s.v. Cabala). Dr. S. Hurwitz refers me to the *Zohar* (III, 48a): "As soon as man was created everything was created, the upper and the lower worlds, for everything is contained in man." According to this view Adam Kadmon is the *homo maximus,* who is himself the world. Man and his heavenly prototype are "twins" (*Talmud,* "Sanhedrin," 46b, ed. Epstein, I, p. 306). Adam Kadmon is the "highest man" of the divine chariot (Merkabah), the "highest crown" (Kether), the anima generalis. Isaac Luria says he contains in himself the ten Sefiroth. They went forth from him in ten concentric circles, and these are his *nefesh,* souls. (Cf. supra, pars. 574ff., the diagram of the Ophites in Origen, *Contra Celsum.*)

199 Ezek. 34 : 31 apparently says nothing of the kind. What it does say, however, is: "And ye my flock, the flock of my pasture, are men" (AV). "Man" = "Adam." "Adam" here is a collective concept.

200 The parentheses are Knorr von Rosenroth's.

201 *Kabbala denudata,* II, Part 3, pp. 248f.*   202 Cf. ibid., ch. 3, sect. 1, pp. 255f.

As the inner man, however, he is the totality of the individual, the synthesis of all parts of the psyche, and therefore of the conscious and the unconscious. § 20 says: "And therefore our masters have said: The son of David shall not come until all the souls that were in the body (of the first-created) have fully gone out." [203] The "going out" of the souls from the Primordial Man can be understood as the projection of a psychic integration process: the saving wholeness of the inner man—i.e., the "Messiah"—cannot come about until all parts of the psyche have been made conscious. This may be sufficient to explain why it takes so long for the second Adam to appear.

594   The same treatise says: "From En Soph, from the most general One, was produced the universe, which is Adam Kadmon, who is One and Many, and of whom and in whom are all things." "The differences of genera are denoted by concentric circles" which proceed from him or are contained in him. He is thus something like a schema of the psychic structure, in which the "specific differences [those characterizing species] are denoted by a straight line" [204] (i.e., in a concentric system, by the radius). "Thus in Adam Kadmon are represented all the orders of things, both genera and species and individuals." [205]

595   Among the pagan sources we must distinguish an Egyptian one, concerned with the very ancient tradition of the God-man Osiris and the theology of kingship; a Persian one, derived from Gayomart; and an Indian one, derived from Purusha.[206] The

203 Ibid., p. 251.* Knorr's parentheses.
204 "Sed differentias specificas designari per rectilineum." The so-called "numerical differences" are concerned with the opposites. The text says: "The numerical differences refer to the balance-like arrangement in which there is a turning [in which two principles are related, i.e., "turned"] face to face, and two or more things of the same perfection or species are distinguished only as male and female. And these numerical differences [i.e., relationships] are also denoted by such expressions as "facing," "turning the back," etc." * Diss. VI, § 9, p. 118.
205 "Ab Aen-Soph, i.e., Uno generalissimo, productum esse Universum, qui est Adam Kadmon, qui est unum et multum, et ex quo et in quo omnia. . . . Differentias autem generum notari per circulos homocentricos, sicut Ens, substantiam; haec, corpus; hoc, vivens; istud, sensitivum; et haec, rationale continet. . . . Et hoc modo in Adam Kadmon repraesentantur omnium rerum ordines, tum genera, quam species et individua." (Ibid.) Cf. Scholem, *Major Trends in Jewish Mysticism*, p. 215.
206 For the Egyptian source see the account in Bousset, *Hauptprobleme der Gnosis*, and Reitzenstein and Schaeder, *Studien zum antiken Synkretismus*. For the Indian,

Christian source for alchemical ideas is the aforementioned Pauline doctrine of the first and second Adam.

5. THE "OLD ADAM"

596   After these preliminary remarks we can turn back to Eleazar's text, beginning with the significant passage in the middle where Adam appears. The reader is immediately struck by the expression "the old Adam," who is evidently equated with Adam Kadmon. Rather than "the old" Adam we would expect "the second" or "the original" Adam, chiefly because "the old Adam" means above all the old, sinful, unredeemed man, in accordance with Romans 6 : 6: "Knowing this, that our old man is crucified with him, that the body of sin might be destroyed, that henceforth we should not serve sin." That this passage must have been at the back of the author's mind is shown by the sentence: "I must be fixed to this black cross, and must be cleansed therefrom with wretchedness and vinegar."

597   The author purports to be a Jew, but was clumsy enough not only to perpetrate anachronisms but to reveal his own unquestionably Christian psychology. He had a good knowledge of the Bible and was familiar with "Biblical" language. The language of his book is the stylistically and grammatically fluid German of the eighteenth century. He has a liking for edifying rhetoric (could he have been a theologian?) One thing is clear, at any rate, and that is that the expression "the old Adam" on the lips of such a person can have only one meaning, namely, the "old man" whom we are to put off (Eph. 4 : 22) in accordance with the command in Colossians 3 : 9: "Put off the old man with his deeds." These passages must have been known to the author, and he could easily have avoided the resultant contradiction or ambiguity by putting, instead of "old," "original," or something of that kind.

598   I must beg the reader's indulgence for apparently splitting hairs and harping somewhat pedantically on this little defect in the style of a none too careful author. But it is more than a question of a mere slip of the pen: a text that is riddled with ambiguities, that sets up the most unexpected relationships (Adam and the Shulamite!) and blends together the most heterogeneous sit-

see Deussen, *Geschichte der Philosophie*, I, 1, p. 228, and for its relations with the belief in the Messiah, see Abegg, *Der Messiasglaube in Indien und Iran*.

uations, has unquestionable affinities with the structure of a dream and consequently necessitates a careful examination of its figures. A cliché like "the old Adam," which can have no other meaning, does not occur in a dream-text without a very good reason, even though the author might have excused it as a mere "slip." Even if—as seems to be the case here—he understood the "old" Adam as the "Ur-" or "original" Adam, he was compelled by some obscure intention to pick on "the old Adam," which in this context is thoroughly ambiguous. Had it occurred in a real dream it would be a technical blunder for the interpreter to overlook this ostensible slip. As we know, these *quid pro quos* invariably happen at the critical places, where two contrary tendencies cross.

599 Our suspicions have been aroused, and in what follows we shall pursue them on the assumption that "the old Adam" is not a mere accident but is one of those irritating ambiguities of which there is no lack in the alchemical texts. They are irritating because seldom if ever can it be ascertained with any certainty whether they arose from a conscious intention to deceive or from an unconscious conflict.

600 The "old" Adam, evidently, can "come forth again" from the Shulamite, the black mother, only because he had once got into her in some way. But that can only have been the old, sinful Adam, for the blackness of the Shulamite is an expression for sin, the original sin, as the text shows. Behind this idea lies the archetype of the Anthropos who had fallen under the power of Physis, but it seems doubtful whether our author had any conscious knowledge of this myth. Had he really been familiar with Cabalistic thought he would have known that Adam Kadmon, the spiritual First Man, was an "Idea" in the Platonic sense, which could never be confused with the sinful man. By his equation "old Adam" = Adam Kadmon the author has contaminated two opposites. The interpretation of this passage must therefore be: from the black Shulamite comes forth the antithesis "old Adam": Adam Kadmon. Her obvious connection with the earth as the mother of all living things makes it clear that her son was the sinful Adam, but not Adam Kadmon, who, as we have seen, is an emanation of En Soph. Nevertheless, by contaminating the two, the text makes both of them issue from

416

the Shulamite. The "old" Adam and the Primordial Man appear to be identical, and the author could excuse himself by saying that by "old" he meant the first or original Adam—a point which it is not easy to deny.

601   As high as the Primordial Man stands on the one side, so low on the other is the sinful, empirical man. The phenomenon of contamination, which we meet so frequently in the psychology of dreams and of primitives, is no mere accident but is based on a common denominator; at some point the opposites prove to be identical, and this implies the possibility of their contamination. One of the commonest instances of this is the identity of the god and his animal attribute. Such paradoxes derive from the non-human quality of the god's and the animal's psychology. The divine psyche is as far above the human as the animal psyche reaches down into subhuman depths.

602   The "old Adam" corresponds to the primitive man, the "shadow" of our present-day consciousness, and the primitive man has his roots in the animal man (the "tailed" Adam),[207] who has long since vanished from our consciousness. Even the primitive man has become a stranger to us, so that we have to rediscover his psychology. It was therefore something of a surprise when analytical psychology discovered in the products of the unconscious of modern man so much archaic material, and not only that but the sinister darkness of the animal world of instinct. Though "instincts" or "drives" can be formulated in physiological and biological terms they cannot be pinned down in that way, for they are also psychic entities which manifest themselves in a world of fantasy peculiarly their own. They are not just physiological or consistently biological phenomena, but are at the same time, even in their content, meaningful fantasy structures with a symbolic character. An instinct does not apprehend its object blindly and at random, but brings to it a certain psychic "viewpoint" or interpretation; for every instinct is linked *a priori* with a corresponding image of the situation, as can be proved indirectly in cases of the symbiosis of plant and animal. In man we have direct insight into that remarkable world

207 Cf. supra, par. 589. According to the Valentinians, man is covered in a "pelt-like garment" (δερμάτικον χιτῶνα). Irenaeus, *Adv. haer.*, I, 5, 5 (Migne, *P.G.*, vol. 7, cols. 501f.).

of "magical" ideas which cluster round the instincts and not only express their form and mode of manifestation but "trigger them off." [208] The world of instinct, simple as it seems to the rationalist, reveals itself on the primitive level as a complicated interplay of physiological facts, taboos, rites, class-systems, and tribal lore, which impose a restrictive form on the instinct from the beginning, preconsciously, and make it serve a higher purpose. Under natural conditions a spiritual limitation is set upon the unlimited drive of the instinct to fulfil itself, which differentiates it and makes it available for different applications. Rites on a primitive level are uninterpreted gestures; on a higher level they become mythologized.

603 The primary connection between image and instinct explains the interdependence of instinct and religion in the most general sense. These two spheres are in mutually compensatory relationship, and by "instinct" we must understand not merely "Eros" but everything that goes by the name of "instinct." [209] "Religion" on the primitive level means the psychic regulatory system that is coordinated with the dynamism of instinct. On a higher level this primary interdependence is sometimes lost, and then religion can easily become an antidote to instinct, whereupon the originally compensatory relationship degenerates into conflict, religion petrifies into formalism, and instinct is vitiated. A split of this kind is not due to a mere accident, nor is it a meaningless catastrophe. It lies rather in the nature of the evolutionary process itself, in the increasing extension and differentiation of consciousness. For just as there is no energy without the tension of opposites, so there can be no consciousness without the perception of differences. But any stronger emphasis of differences leads to polarity and finally to a conflict which maintains the necessary tension of opposites. This tension is needed on the one hand for increased energy production and on the other for the further differentiation of differences, both of which are indispensable requisites for the development of consciousness. But although this conflict is unquestionably useful it

208 Cf. "Instinct and the Unconscious," par. 277.
209 It makes no difference here that the definition and classification of the instincts are an extremely controversial matter. The word "instinct" still denotes something that is known and understood by everyone.

also has very evident disadvantages, which sometimes prove injurious. Then a counter-movement sets in, in the attempt to reconcile the conflicting parties. As this process has repeated itself countless times in the course of the many thousand years of conscious development, corresponding customs and rites have grown up for the purpose of bringing the opposites together. These reconciling procedures are rites performed by man, but their content is an act of help or reconciliation emanating from the divine sphere, whether in the present or in the past. Generally the rites are linked up with the original state of man and with events that took place in the age of the heroes or ancestors. This is as a rule a defective state, or a situation of distress, which is helped by divine intervention, and the intervention is repeated in the rite. To take a simple example: When the rice will not grow, a member of the rice-totem clan builds himself a hut in the rice-field and tells the rice how it originally grew from the rice-ancestor. The rice then remembers its origin and starts growing again. The ritual anamnesis of the ancestor has the same effect as his intervention.

604   The prime situation of distress consists either in a withdrawal of the favourable gods and the emergence of harmful ones, or in the alienation of the gods by man's negligence, folly, or sacrilege, or else (as in the Taoist view) in the separation [210] of heaven and earth for unfathomable reasons, so that they can now come together again only if the wise man re-establishes Tao in himself by ritual meditation. In this way he brings his own heaven and earth into harmony.[211]

---

210 Cf. supra, par. 18, the separation of Tifereth and Malchuth as the cause of evil.
211 As an example of "being in Tao" and its synchronistic accompaniments I will cite the story, told me by the late Richard Wilhelm, of the rain-maker of Kiaochau: "There was a great drought where Wilhelm lived; for months there had not been a drop of rain and the situation became catastrophic. The Catholics made processions, the Protestants made prayers, and the Chinese burned joss-sticks and shot off guns to frighten away the demons of the drought, but with no result. Finally the Chinese said, 'We will fetch the rain-maker.' And from another province a dried up old man appeared. The only thing he asked for was a quiet little house somewhere, and there he locked himself in for three days. On the fourth day the clouds gathered and there was a great snow-storm at the time of the year when no snow was expected, an unusual amount, and the town was so full of rumours about the wonderful rain-maker that Wilhelm went to ask the man

605   Just as the rice spoils in the defective state, so too man degenerates, whether from the malignity of the gods or from his own stupidity or sin, and comes into conflict with his original nature. He forgets his origination from the human ancestor, and a ritual anamnesis is therefore required. Thus the archetype of Man, the Anthropos, is constellated and forms the essential core of the great religions. In the idea of the *homo maximus* the Above and Below of creation are reunited.

6. THE TRANSFORMATION

606   The appearance of Adam Kadmon has characteristic consequences for the Shulamite: it brings about a *solificatio,* an illumination of the "inwards of the head." This is a veiled but, for the psychology of alchemy, typical allusion to the "transfiguration" (*glorificatio*) of the adept or of his inner man. For Adam is "interior homo noster," the Primordial Man in us.

607   Seen in the light of the above remarks, Eleazar's text assumes a by no means uninteresting aspect and, since its train of thought is characteristic of the basic ideas of alchemy, a meaning with many facets. It depicts a situation of distress corresponding to the alchemical *nigredo:* the blackness of guilt has covered the bridal earth as with black paint. The Shulamite comes into the same category as those black goddesses (Isis, Artemis, Parvati, Mary) whose names mean "earth." Eve, like Adam, ate of the tree of knowledge and thereby broke into the realm of divine privileges—"ye shall be as gods, knowing good and evil." In other words she inadvertently discovered the possibility of *moral* consciousness, which until then had been outside man's range. As a result, a polarity was torn open with momentous

how he did it. In true European fashion he said: 'They call you the rain-maker, will you tell me how you made the snow?' And the little Chinese said: 'I did not make the snow, I am not responsible.' 'But what have you done these three days?' 'Oh, I can explain that. I come from another country where things are in order. Here they are out of order, they are not as they should be by the ordinance of heaven. Therefore the whole country is not in Tao, and I also am not in the natural order of things because I am in a disordered country. So I had to wait three days until I was back in Tao and then naturally the rain came.'" From "Interpretation of Visions," Vol. 3 of seminars in English by C. G. Jung (new edn., privately multigraphed, 1939), p. 7.

consequences. There was a sundering of earth from heaven, the original paradise was shut down, the glory of the First Man was extinguished, Malchuth became a widow, the fiery *yang* went back aloft, and the damp *yin* enveloped humanity with darkness, degenerated through ever-increasing wantonness, and finally swelled into the black waters of the Deluge, which threatened to drown every living thing but on the other hand could be understood more hopefully as an ablution of the blackness. Noah, too, appears in a different light: he is no longer seen as someone runing away from the catastrophe but as Lord of the Waters, the minister of the ablution. This operation does not seem to be enough, however, for the Shulamite promptly gets herself into the opposite kind of pickle—into the dry desert, where, like the children of Israel, she is menaced by evil in the form of poisonous serpents.[212] This is an allusion to the tribulations of the Exodus, which in a sense was a repetition of the expulsion from paradise, since bidding farewell to the fleshpots of Egypt was quite as painful a prospect as the stony ground from which our first parents had to wrest a living in the sweat of their brows. But even with this last extremity the goal is not reached, for the Shulamite has still to be fixed to a black cross. The idea of the cross points beyond the simple antithesis to a double antithesis, i.e., to a quaternio. To the mind of the alchemist this meant primarily the intercrossing elements:

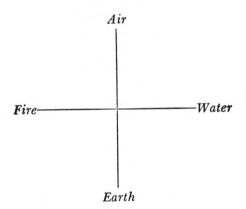

212 In this connection Eleazar makes use of the symbol (significant only for a Christian) of the snake set up on a pole, a prefiguration of Christ (John 3 : 14).

or the four qualities:

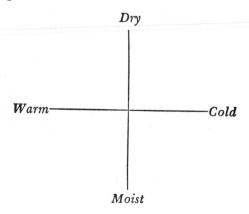

We know that this fastening to a cross denotes a painful state of suspension, or a tearing asunder in the four directions.[213] The alchemists therefore set themselves the task of reconciling the warring elements and reducing them to unity. In our text this state is abolished when the distressing blackness is washed off with "wretchedness and vinegar." This is an obvious allusion to the "hyssop and gall" which Christ was given to drink. In the oft-quoted text of Maier, "wretchedness and vinegar" stand for the melancholia of the *nigredo,* as contrasted with the "joy and gladness" of the redeemed state. The washing with wretchedness and vinegar finally brings about the whitening as well as a *solificatio* of the "inwards of the head," presumably the brain or even the soul. We can only interpret this as meaning that the Shulamite experienced a transformation similar to Parvati's, who, saddened by her blackness, was given a golden skin by the gods. Here we must emphasize that it is the lapis or hermaphrodite which, as the god who is quartered or torn asunder or crucified on the Four, represents and suffers the discord of the elements, and at the same time brings about the union of the Four and besides that is identical with the product of the union. The

213 I am informed that the American Indian punishment for a fallible medicineman was to have him pulled asunder by four horses, all going in opposite directions. (I cannot vouch for the truth of this statement, but the important thing is the idea as such.)

alchemists could not help identifying their Primordial Man with Christ, for whom our author substitutes Adam Kadmon.

608   Since sun and gold are equivalent concepts in alchemy, the *solificatio* means that the "inwards of the head"—whatever we are to understand by that—are transformed into light, or "Marez," the precious white earth. The Shulamite's heart, too, will shine "like a carbuncle." From the time of the Middle Ages the carbuncle was regarded as a synonym for the lapis.[214] Here the allegory is transparent: as the head is illuminated, so the heart burns in love.

609   The difference between Parvati and the Shulamite is, therefore, that whereas Parvati is transformed outwardly the Shulamite is transformed inwardly. Outwardly she remains as black as ever. Unlike the Shulamite of the Song of Songs, whose skin is "swarthy," our Shulamite declares that her blackness "clings" to her as if painted on, and that one has only to disrobe her to bring her "inner beauty" to light. By the sin of Eve she is plunged, as it were, in ink, in the "tincture," and blackened, just as in Islamic legend the precious stone that Allah gave Adam was blackened by his sin. If the poison of the curse is taken from her —which will obviously happen when the Beloved appears—then her "innermost seed," her "first birth," will come forth. According to the text this birth can refer only to the appearance of Adam Kadmon. He is the only one who loves her despite her blackness. But this blackness seems to be rather more than a veneer, for it will not come off; it is merely compensated by her inner illumination and by the beauty of the bridegroom. As the Shulamite symbolizes the earth in which Adam lay buried, she also has the significance of a maternal progenitrix. In this capacity the black Isis put together again the limbs of her dismembered brother-spouse, Osiris. Thus Adam Kadmon appears here in the classic form of the son-lover, who, in the hierosgamos of sun and moon, reproduces himself in the mother-beloved. Consequently the Shulamite takes over the ancient role of the hierodule of Ishtar. She is the sacred harlot (*meretrix*), which is one of the names the alchemist gave his arcane substance.

610   The Shulamite's reversion to type is not a stroke of genius

---

[214] Wolfram von Eschenbach calls the carbuncle a healing stone which lies under the horn of the unicorn. Cf. *Psychology and Alchemy*, par. 552.

on the part of our author, but merely the traditional alchemical view that "our infant," the son of the Philosophers, is the child of sun and moon. But in so far as he represents the hermaphroditic Primordial Man himself, the son is at the same time the father of his parents. Alchemy was so saturated with the idea of the mother-son incest that it automatically reduced the Shulamite of the Song of Songs to her historical prototype.[215]

611   We have paid due attention to the recalcitrant nature of the Shulamite's blackness. Now it is significant that the "old Adam" is mentioned at the very moment when the perfect, prelapsarian Adam, the shining Primordial Man, is obviously meant. Just as the black Shulamite misses the final apotheosis, the total *albedo,* so we lack the necessary confirmation that the first Adam is changed into the second, who at the same time is the father of the first. We cannot suppress the suspicion that, just as the blackness will not disappear, so the old Adam will not finally change. This may be the deeper reason why the expression "the old Adam" did not worry the author but, on the contrary, seemed just right. It is, unfortunately, far truer to say that a change for the better does *not* bring a total conversion of darkness into light and of evil into good, but, at most, is a compromise in which the better slightly exceeds the worse. The complication introduced by the "old" Adam, therefore, does not seem to be merely fortuitous, since it forms a factor in an archetypal quaternio composed as follows:

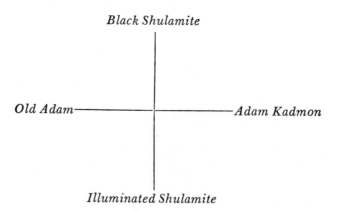

Black Shulamite

Old Adam ———————————— *Adam Kadmon*

Illuminated Shulamite

[215] The passage we have cited may be decisive in regard to the origin and date of

or

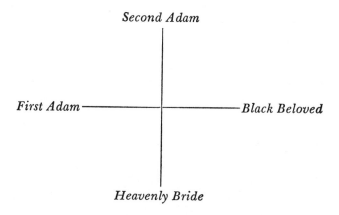

Second Adam

First Adam ——————————————— *Black Beloved*

Heavenly Bride

612   This structure corresponds to the marriage quaternio discussed in the "Psychology of the Transference," [216] which is based on certain psychic facts and has the following structure:

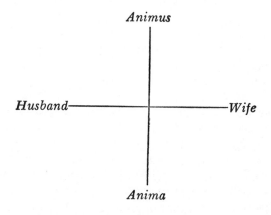

Animus

Husband ——————————— *Wife*

Anima

the treatise, both of which were contested by Robert Eisler, who, without having seen the book, doubted Scholem's view that it is a late forgery. (Eisler, "Zur Terminologie und Geschichte der jüdischen Alchemie," pp. 194 and 202.) See also Kopp (*Die Alchemie in älterer und neuerer Zeit*, II, pp. 314ff.), who established a first edition in 1735 and regards the publisher Gervasius von Schwartzenburg as the author.

216 Pars. 422ff.

or

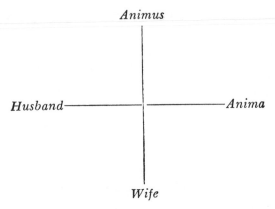

$$Husband \text{———————}|\text{———————} Anima$$

Animus

Wife

613   Although this quaternio plays a considerable role in alchemy, it is not a product of alchemical speculation but an
archetype which can be traced back to the primitive marriage-
class system (four-kin system). As a quaternity it represents a
whole judgment and formulates the psychic structure of man's
totality. This expresses on the one hand the structure of the individual, i.e., a male or female ego in conjunction with the contrasexual unconscious, and on the other hand the ego's relation
to the other sex, without which the psychological individual
remains incomplete. (By this I mean primarily a *psychic* relationship.) But in this schema the idea of *transformation,* so
characteristic of alchemy, is missing. As a scientific discipline,
empirical psychology is not in a position to establish whether
the conscious ego ranks "higher" or "lower" than the anima,
which, like the ego, has a positive and a negative aspect. Science
does not make value-judgments, and though psychology has a
concept of "value" it is nothing but a concept of "intensity": one
complex of ideas has a higher value when its power of assimilation proves stronger than that of another.[217] The alchemical idea
of transformation is rooted in a spiritual concept of value which
takes the "transformed" as being *more* valuable, better, higher,
more spiritual, etc., and the empirical psychologist has nothing
to set against this. But since evaluating and estimating are functions of feeling and nevertheless do play a role in psychology,
value must somehow be taken into account. This happens when

217 Cf. my "On Psychic Energy," pars. 18ff.

426

an assertion or value-judgment is accepted as an intrinsic part of the description of an object.

614 The moral as well as the energic value of the conscious and the unconscious personality is subject to the greatest individual variations. Generally the conscious side predominates, though it suffers from numerous limitations. The schema of the psychological structure, if it is to be compared with the alchemical schema, must therefore be modified by the addition of the idea of transformation. This operation is conceivable in principle, as the process of making the anima and animus conscious does in fact bring about a transformation of personality. Hence it is the psychotherapist who is principally concerned with this problem. The foremost of his therapeutic principles is that conscious realization is an important agent for transforming the personality. The favourable aspect of any such transformation is evaluated as "improvement"—primarily on the basis of the patient's own statements. The improvement refers in the first place to his psychic health, but there can also be a moral improvement. These statements become increasingly difficult or impossible to verify when the evaluation imperceptibly encroaches upon territory hedged about with philosophical or theoretical prejudices. The whole question of "improvement" is so delicate that it is far easier to settle it by arbitrary decision than by careful deliberation and comparison, which are an affront to all those "terrible simplifiers" who habitually cultivate this particular garden.

615 Although the fact of transformation and improvement cannot be doubted, it is nevertheless very difficult to find a suitable term for it which is not open to misunderstanding and can be fitted into our schema. Medieval man, like our own simplifiers, was naïve enough always to know what was "better." We are not so sure, and besides this we feel to some extent answerable to those who hold a different opinion. We cannot cherish the joyful belief that everybody else is in the wrong. For this reason we shall probably have to give up the idea of expressing in the terminology of our schema the kind of transformation which is bound up with conscious realization and the wholeness (individuation) it brings in its train.

616 For a naïve-minded person the imperfect, corrupt old Adam

427

is simply contrasted with the perfect "Primordial Man," and the dark Eve with an illuminated and altogether nobler being. The modern viewpoint is much more realistic, as it withdraws the archetypal schema, which referred originally to a mythological situation, back from projection, and peoples the stage not with mythical lay-figures but with real human beings and their psyches. The man, or the masculine ego-consciousness, is then contrasted with an animus, the masculine figure in a woman's unconscious, who compels her either to overvalue him or to protest against him. The corresponding figure that contrasts with the woman and her feminine ego-consciousness is the anima, the source of all the illusions, over- and under-valuations of which a man makes himself guilty in regard to a woman. There is nothing to indicate in this schema that the man is better than the animus or vice versa, or that the anima is a "higher" being than the woman. Nor does it indicate in which direction the line of development is moving. Only one thing is clear, that when, as a result of a long, technical and moral procedure the patient obtains a knowledge of this structure, based on experience, and accepts the responsibility entailed by this knowledge, there follows an integration or *completeness* of the individual, who in this way approaches *wholeness* but not *perfection,* which is the ideal of certain world philosophies. In the Middle Ages "philosophy" prevailed over fact to such an extent that the base metal lead was credited with the power to turn into gold under certain conditions, and the dark, "psychic" man with the capacity to turn himself into the higher "pneumatic" man. But just as lead, which theoretically could become gold, never did so in practice, so the sober-minded man of our own day looks round in vain for the possibility of final perfection. Therefore, on an objective view of the facts, which alone is worthy of the name of science, he sees himself obliged to lower his pretensions a little, and instead of striving after the ideal of perfection to content himself with the more accessible goal of approximate completeness. The progress thereby made possible does not lead to an exalted state of spiritualization, but rather to a wise self-limitation and modesty, thus balancing the disadvantages of the lesser good with the advantage of the lesser evil.

617   What prevents us from setting up a psychological schema

428

fully corresponding to the alchemical one is ultimately, therefore, the difference between the old and the modern view of the
world, between medieval romanticism and scientific objectivity.

618   The more critical view which I have outlined here on the
objective basis of scientific psychology is, however, implied in
the alchemical schema. For even as the old Adam comes forth
again and is present in the schema just as much as Adam Kadmon, so the blackness does not depart from the Shulamite, an
indication that the transformation process is not complete but is
still going on. That being so, the old Adam is not yet put off and
the Shulamite has not yet become white.

619   In the Cabalistic view Adam Kadmon is not merely the universal soul or, psychologically, the "self," but is himself the
process of transformation, its division into three or four parts
(trimeria or tetrameria). The alchemical formula for this is the
Axiom of Maria: "One becomes two, two becomes three, and
out of the Third comes the One as the Fourth." [218] The treatise
of Rabbi Abraham Cohen Irira (Hacohen Herrera) says: "Adam
Kadmon proceeded from the Simple and the One, and to that
extent he is Unity; but he also descended and fell into his own
nature, and to that extent he is Two. And again he will return to
the One, which he has in him, and to the Highest; and to that
extent he is Three and Four." [219] This speculation refers to the
"essential Name," the Tetragrammaton, which is the four letters
of God's name, "three different, and the fourth a repetition of
the second." [220] In the Hebrew word YHVH (written without
vowels), *he* is feminine and is assigned as a wife to *yod* [221] and to

---

[218] Berthelot, *Alch. grecs*, VI, v, 6.*

[219] *Kabbala denudata*, I, Part 3, "Porta coelorum," ch. 8, § 3, p. 116.*

[220] Ibid., § 4: "And this is the reason why the Essential Name has four letters,
three different, and the fourth a repetition of the second: for the first *he* is the
spouse of the *yod;* and the second, the spouse of the *vau*. The first emanated from
yod, directly, and the second from *vau,* in a converse and reflex way." *

[221] Another view of the *yod* can be found in the *Zohar*, III, 191 (Vol. V, p. 267):
"He then cited the verse, 'I am black, but comely.' This means that when she (the
Moon) is very lovesick for her Beloved, she shrinks to nothing until only a dot is
left of her, and she is hidden from all her hosts and camps. Then she says, 'I am
black,' like the letter Yod, in which there is no white space, and I have no room to
shelter you under my wings; therefore 'do not look at me,' for ye cannot see me
at all."

vau. As a result *yod* [222] and *vau* [223] are masculine, and the feminine *he,* though doubled, is identical and therefore a single unit. To that extent the essential Name is a triad. But since *he* is doubled, the Name is also a tetrad or quaternity [224]—a perplexity which coincides most strangely with the Axiom of Maria. On the other hand the Tetragrammaton consists of a double marriage and thus agrees in an equally remarkable manner with our Adam diagrams. The doubling of the feminine *he* is archetypal,[225] since the marriage quaternio presupposes both the difference and the identity of the feminine figures. This is true also of the two masculine figures, as we have seen, though here their difference usually predominates—not surprisingly, as these things are mostly products of the masculine imagination. Consequently the masculine figure coincides with man's consciousness, where differences are practically absolute. Though the feminine figure

[222] "Yod, because it is simple, is something single and primary, and like the number '1,' which, among numbers and as a point, is the first of all bodies. But the point by moving along its length produces a line, namely *vau.*" * (*Kabbala denudata,* Vol. 1, Part 3, Diss. VII, § 1, p. 142.) "The letter *yod,* because it is a point, is made the beginning and the middle and the end; indeed, it is also the beginning of the Decads and the end of the unities and therefore it returns to the One." * (Introductio in Librum Sohar, § 1, ch. XXXVII, § 1, *Kabbala denudata,* II, Part 1, p. 203.) With regard to the function of *yod,* Sect. VI, ch. I, p. 259 is significant: "When the Wisdom of the Blessed One saw that even in this splendour the worlds could not be manifested, since the Light was still too weak there, he again signalled to this letter *yod* that it should once more descend and break through the sphere of splendour and give forth its light, which was a little denser." * The point is the "inner point," which is the same as the "inner rose," the "community of Israel," the "Bride." Further attributes of the rose are: sister, companion, dove, perfect one, twin. ("Tres discursus initiales Libri Sohar," Comm. in Disc. I, § 12f., *Kabbala denudata,* II, Part 2, p. 151.) *Yod* is attached to the "summit of the crown" and descends upon Sapientia (Hokhmah): "It scattered light and an eminent influence on that Wisdom." * ("Theses Cabbalisticae," I, § 19, *Kabbala denudata,* I, Part 2, p. 151.) *Yod* is the "vas" or "vasculum" into which the "fount of the sea" pours, and from which the "fount gushing forth wisdom" issues. ("Pneumatica Kabbalistica," Diss. I, ch. I, § 7 and 10, *Kabbala denudata,* II, Part 3, pp. 189f.)

[223] "*Vau* denotes life, which is the emanation and movement of the essence that is manifested in it; and it is the medium of union and connection between the essence and the understanding." * (Herrera, "Porta coelorum," Diss. VII, ch. I, § 3, *Kabbala denudata,* I, Part 3, p. 141.)

[224] A whole series of quaternions are associated with the Tetragrammaton. Cf. "Porta coelorum," Diss. VII, ch. III, § 5, p. 145.

[225] "*He* denotes Being, which is composed of essence and existence." "The last *he* is the image of the intellect or mind." * (Ibid., ch. I, § 2 and 4, p. 141.)

is doubled it is so little differentiated that it appears identical. This double yet identical figure corresponds exactly to the anima, who, owing to her usually "unconscious" state, bears all the marks of non-differentiation.

620　If we apply these considerations to the alchemical schema, we shall be able to modify it in a way that was not possible with the psychological one. We thus arrive at a formula which reduces both to the same denominator:

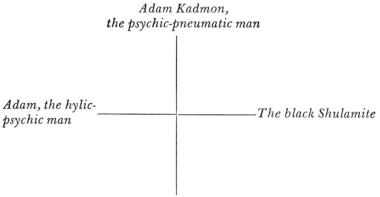

Adam Kadmon,
the psychic-pneumatic man

Adam, the hylic-
psychic man ————————————————*The black Shulamite*

The illuminated Shulamite

621　The critical point, namely the fact that the transformation is not complete, comes out in the text itself; the desired perfection is relegated to the future, "that she who is encompassed by many mountains shall be freed." For this a divine miracle is needed, the crushing and burning of Canaan, the tearing down of heaven, and the melting of mountains. One can see from these tours de force the magnitude of the difficulties that have to be overcome before perfection is reached.

622　The reference to the mountains which encompass the Shulamite has a strange parallel in Parvati, whose name means "mountain dweller" and who was deemed the daughter of Himavat (Himalaya).[226] Grieving over her blackness, for which her husband Shiva reproached her, she left him and withdrew to the

226 Song of Songs says of the Shulamite (4 : 8): "Come with me from Lebanon, my spouse, with me from Lebanon; come down from the top of Amana, from the top of Shenir and Hermon, from the lions' dens, from the mountains of the leopards" (AV, mod.). According to Wittekindt (*Das Hohe Lied*, p. 166) Lebanon, lion, and leopard refer to Ishtar.

solitude of the forest. And in her loneliness and seclusion the Shulamite exclaims:

What shall I say? I am alone among the hidden; nevertheless I rejoice in my heart, because I can live privily, and refresh myself in myself. But under my blackness I have hidden the fairest green.[227]

623   The state of imperfect transformation, merely hoped for and waited for, does not seem to be one of torment only, but of positive, if hidden, happiness. It is the state of someone who, in his wanderings among the mazes of his psychic transformation, comes upon a secret happiness which reconciles him to his apparent loneliness. In communing with himself he finds not deadly boredom and melancholy but an inner partner; more than that, a relationship that seems like the happiness of a secret love, or like a hidden springtime, when the green seed [228] sprouts from the barren earth, holding out the promise of future harvests. It is the alchemical *benedicta viriditas,* the blessed greenness, signifying on the one hand the "leprosy of the metals" (verdigris), but on the other the secret immanence of the divine spirit of life in all things. "O blessed greenness, which generatest all things!" cries the author of the *Rosarium.*[229] "Did not the spirit of the Lord," writes Mylius, "which is a fiery love, give to the waters when it was borne over them a certain fiery vigour, since nothing can be generated without heat? God breathed into created things . . . a certain germination or greenness, by which all things should multiply . . . They called all things green, for to be green means to grow . . . Therefore this virtue of generation and the preservation of things might be called the Soul of the World." [230]

624   Green signifies hope and the future, and herein lies the reason for the Shulamite's hidden joy, which otherwise would be difficult to justify. But in alchemy green also means perfection. Thus Arnaldus de Villanova says: "Therefore Aristotle says in his book, Our gold, not the common gold, because the green which is in this substance signifies its total perfection, since by our magistery that green is quickly turned into truest gold." [231]

227 Eleazar, *Uraltes Chymisches Werck,* II, p. 52.
228 "For by greenness virginity would appear to be prefigured" * (Mennens, "Aureum vellus," *Theatr. chem.,* V, p. 434).
229 *Art. aurif.,* II, p. 220.*   230 *Phil. ref.,* p. 11.*
231 "Speculum alchimiae," *Theatr. chem.,* IV, p. 605.*

Hence the Shulamite continues:

But I must be like a dove with wings, and I shall come and be free at vespertime, when the waters of impurity are abated, with a green olive leaf; then is my head of the fairest Asophol,[232] and my hair curly-gleaming as the ☽. And Job says (27 : 5),[233] that out of my ▽[234] shall come forth blood. For it is all as △,[235] shining red Adamah,[236] mingled with a glowing △. Though I am poisonous, black, and hateful without, yet when I am cleansed I shall be the food of heroes; as out of the lion which Samson slew there afterward came forth honey. Therefore says Job 28 : 7: *Semitam non cognovit ille avis, neque aspicit eam oculus vulturis.*[237] For this stone belongeth only to the proven and elect of God.[238]

625   It is the hope of the dark Shulamite that one day, at "vespertime," probably in the evening of life, she will become like Noah's dove, which, with the olive leaf in its beak, announced the end of the flood and appeared as the sign of God's reconciliation with the children of men.[239] The Song of Songs (2 : 14) says: "O my dove, that art in the clefts of the rock, in the secret places of the stairs, let me see thy countenance, let me hear thy voice . . ." In our text her head will be of gold, like the sun, and her hair like the moon. She thus declares herself to be a conjunction of the sun and moon. Indeed, a golden head and "bushy" hair are attributes of the Beloved.[240] She is, in fact, min-

---

[232] "Asophol" means gold.

[233] This must refer to Job 28 : 5: "As for the earth, out of it cometh bread, and under it is turned up as it were fire" (AV). (". . . but underneath it is turned up as by fire." RSV.)

[234] Earth.

[235] Fire.

[236] "Adamah" means red earth, synonymous with "laton."

[237] The Vulgate has: "Semitam ignoravit avis, nec intuitus est eam oculus vulturis" (DV: The bird hath not known the path, neither hath the eye of the vulture beheld it). Our text obviously does not follow the Vulgate, but seems to be based on Luther's version.

[238]   "Three things make the shining stone;
                 Save where God's own breath has blown
                 No man it possesses." *

Joh. de Tetzen, "Processus de lapide philosophorum," *Drey Chymische Bücher,* p. 64.

[239] Genesis 8 : 11.

[240] Song of Songs 5 : 11: "His head is as the most fine gold, his locks are bushy, and black as a raven."

433

gled with the Beloved, from which it is evident that the perfect state melts *sponsus* and *sponsa* into *one* figure, the sun-and-moon child.[241] The black Shulamite, well matched by her "bushy locks, black as a raven," becomes the moon, which in this way acquires its "curly-gleaming" hair.[242]

7. ROTUNDUM, HEAD, AND BRAIN

626   Although the above passage from the Song of Songs is chiefly responsible for the "golden head," it should be emphasized that this motif also occurs in alchemy without direct reference to the Song of Songs. "His head was of fine gold," says the "Splendor solis" of the dismembered man whose body was "white like salt." [243] In Greek alchemy the adepts were called "children of the golden head." [244] The "simple" (i.e., arcane) substance was called the "Golden Head, after the god-sent Daniel, God's mouthpiece." [245] According to legend, Pope Sylvester II (d. 1003), famed as the transmitter of Arabian science, possessed a golden head that imparted oracles.[246] This legend may perhaps date back to the Harranite ceremony of the oracular head.[247] The head has also the subsidiary meaning of the *corpus rotundum*,

241 Hebrew *shemesh* (sun) is masculine as well as feminine. The Book Bahir says: "And why is the gold called ZaHaB? Because in it are comprised three principles: the Male (Zakhar), and this is indicated by the letter *Zayin*, the soul, and that is indicated by He. And what is its function? *He* is the throne for Zayin . . . and *Beth* (guarantees) their continuance." (Scholem, *Das Buch Bahir*, p. 39, sect. 36.) For the sun-moon conjunction see the vision of the sun-woman (Rev. 11 : 19), discussed in "Answer to Job," pars. 710ff. [According to Sellin, *Introduction to Old Testament*, p. 224, it has been suggested that the Song of Songs may contain festal hymns on the relations of the sun (*Shelems*) and the moon (*Shelamith*).—TRANS.]

242 Cf. the motif of curly-headedness in the discussion of Aelia Laelia Crispis, supra, par. 37.

243 Salomon Trismosin, *Aureum Vellus*, Tractatus Tertius, p. 28.

244 Berthelot, *Alch. grecs*, III, x, 1.

245 Χρυσέα κεφαλὴ κατὰ τὸν θεσπέσιον Δανιὴλ τὸν θεηγόρον (Berthelot, *Alch. grecs*, IV, vi, 1). This refers to Daniel 2 : 31f., describing Nebuchadnezzar's dream of the great image with feet of clay.

246 Thorndike, *A History of Magic and Experimental Science*, I, p. 705. Sylvester II, formerly Gerbert of Rheims, was, it appears, interested in alchemy. Evidence for this is an alleged letter to Gerbert (early 12th cent.) on the squaring of the circle (Bodleian MS. Digby 83). Thorndike attributes the letter to Gerbert himself.

247 Cf. "Transformation Symbolism in the Mass," pars. 365f.

signifying the arcane substance.[248] This is particularly relevant to our text, as the "inwards" of the head turned to gold and/or white earth. The latter is the *terra alba foliata* (foliated white earth), which in this case would be the brain. This conjecture is corroborated by the fact that the "inwards of the head" is, as it were, a literal translation of ἐγκέφαλος μυελός (marrow in the head). Besides this the brain is a synonym for the arcane substance, as is clear from a Hermes quotation in the *Rosarium:* "Take his brain, powder it with very strong vinegar . . . until it turns dark." [249] The brain was of interest to the alchemists because it was the seat of the "spirit of the supracelestial waters," [250] the waters that are above the firmament (Genesis 1 : 7). In the "Visio Arislei" the brain of the King of the Sea is the birthplace of the brother-sister pair.[251] The "Liber quartorum" calls the brain the "abode of the divine part." [252] For the brain has a "proximity to the rational soul," which in turn pos-

---

248 Cf. *Psychology and Alchemy*, pars. 116, 220; also the "round thing" or "Moor's head" in Rosencreutz, *Chymical Wedding*, pp. 147–8; the golden ball heated by the sun (p. 113), *cibatio* (feeding) with the blood of the beheaded (p. 117), death's head and sphere (p. 120). The cranium is mentioned as the place of origin of the prima materia in Ventura (*Theatr. chem.*, II, p. 271), and in "Liber Platonis quartorum" (*Theatr. chem.*, V, p. 151): "The vessel necessary in this work must be round in shape, that the artifex may be the transformer of this firmament and of the brain-pan." * Albertus Magnus ("Super arborem Aristotelis," *Theatr. chem.*, II, p. 525) says: "His head lives forever and therefore his head is called the life of glory and the angels serve it. And God placed this image in the paradise of delights and in it he set his own image and likeness," * and on p. 526: ". . . until the black head of the Ethiopian bearing the likeness be well washed." * Among the Naassenes of Hippolytus the head of the primordial man Edem signified paradise, and the four rivers that issue from it signified the four senses. (*Elenchos*, V, 9, 15; Legge, I, p. 143.) The same author describes the "talking head" as a magic trick. (*Elenchos*, IV, 41; Legge, I, p. 102.) There is some connection between the text of Albertus Magnus and the report in Hippolytus, at any rate in meaning; perhaps the common source is I Corinthians 11 : 3: "But I would have you know that the head of every man is Christ, and the head of the woman is the man, and the head of Christ is God" (DV). Compare the Albertus text with verse 7: "A man indeed ought not to cover his head, because he is the image and glory of God." For the head as a trophy of revenge see "Peredur son of Efrawg" in the *Mabinogion* (trans. by Jones), pp. 183ff. As early as the Greek alchemists the "simple thing" (ἁπλοῦν), i.e., the prima materia, was called the "golden head." (Berthelot, *Alch. grecs*, IV, vi, 1.)

249 *Art. aurif.*, II, p. 264.*
250 Steeb, *Coelum Sephiroticum*, pp. 117f.*
251 *Art. aurif.*, I, p. 147.   252 *Theatr. chem.*, V, pp. 124, 127, 187.

sesses "simplicitas," a feature it shares with God.[253] Because the brain seemed secretly to participate in the alchemical process,[254] Wei Po-yang states that "when the brain is properly tended for the required length of time, one will certainly attain the miracle." [255] References to the brain are also found in Greek alchemy, an especially large role being played by the λίθος ἐγκέφαλος (brain-stone), which was equated with the λίθος οὐ λίθος (stone that is no stone).[256] The latter is one of the terms Zosimos uses for the brain; he also calls it "not given and given by God," and the "Mithraic secret." [257] The treatise on the "Stone of Philosophy" says that "alabaster is whitest brain stone." [258] In the Table of Symbols in Penotus the brain is correlated with the *moon,* the mystery of baptism, and the "infernal gods." [259] The new moon signifies the *albedo* and the white stone; [260] baptism has its parallel in the children of the King of the Sea, who were imprisoned in the glass-house at the bottom of the sea and transformed; [261] the infernal gods can be correlated with the brain as the seat of consciousness and intelligence, for consciousness leads an "ungodly" existence, having fallen away from the divine totality.[262]

---

253 Ibid., p. 124. P. 128: "We must convert the member (i.e., the brain or heart) at the beginning of the work into that from which it is generated, and then we convert it through the spirit into whatsoever we will." * "Member" means here a part of the body ("membrum cerebri," p. 127). What is meant is a transformation of the brain into the *res simplex,* to which it is in any case related, "for it is a triangle in shape and is nearer than all members of the body to the likeness of the simple." *

254 This seems to have made a particularly strong impression on Albertus Magnus, who believed he had proof that gold is formed in the head: "The greatest mineral virtue is in every man, and especially in the head between the teeth, so that in due time gold is found in tiny oblong grains . . . Wherefore it is said that the stone is in every man." * (Cited in Ripley, "Axiomata philosophica," *Theatr. chem.,* II, p. 134.) Can there have been gold-fillings in those days?

255 *Isis,* XVIII, p. 260.   256 Berthelot, *Alch. grecs,* I, iii, 1.

257 Ibid., III, ii, 1.   258 Ibid., III, xxix, 4.

259 "Characteres secretorum celandorum," *Theatr. chem.,* II, p. 123.

260 The alchemists connected the "white stone" with Rev. 2 : 17: ". . . and I will give him a white pebble (*calculum, ψῆφον*) and upon the pebble a new name written, which no one knows except him who receives it." (DV).

261 "Visio Arislei," *Art. aurif.,* I, p. 148.

262 Hence the devil is expressly called "Lucifer." Penotus therefore correlates the brain with the snake, to whom our first parents owed their first independent action. The Gnostic Naas and the *serpens mercurialis* of the alchemists play a similar role.

627   Zosimos is the connecting link between alchemy and Gnosticism, where we find similar ideas. There the brain (or cerebellum) "is in shape like the head of a dragon." [263] The wicked Korybas, having affinities on the one hand with Adam and on the other with the Kyllenic Hermes,[264] comes "from the head on high and from the uncharacterized brain," [265] and penetrates all things; "we know not how and in what fashion he comes." Here Hippolytus paraphrases John 5 : 37: "We have heard his voice, but we have not seen his shape," an allusion to a partially unconscious factor. To emphasize this aspect, Hippolytus goes on to say that Korybas dwells in the "image of clay" (ἐν τῷ πλάσματι τῷ χοϊκῷ), i.e., in man.[266] "This," he continues, "is the God who dwells in the flood, of whom the Psalter says that he calls aloud and cries out from many waters." [267] We can take this as the longing of the unconscious for consciousness. When one considers that this passage dates from an age (*ca.* 2nd cent.) that had not the remotest conception of psychology in the modern sense, one must admit that Hippolytus, with the scanty means at his disposal, has managed to give a fairly decent account of the psychological facts. The Adam of whom the Naassenes speak is a "rock."

This, they say, is Adamas, the chief corner-stone [λίθος ὁ ἀκρογωνιαῖος], who has become the head [κεφαλήν] of the corner. For in the head is the characterized [χαρακτηριστικόν] brain, the substance from which the whole family is named [χαρακτηρίζεται], the "Adam whom I place in the foundations of Zion." [268] Allegorically, they mean the image [πλάσμα] of Man. But he who is so placed is Adam [the inner man,

263 Hippolytus, *Elenchos*, IV, 51, 13 (Legge, I, p. 117).*
264 The parallels include Attis, Osiris, the serpent, and Christ.
265 ἀπό τοῦ ἀχαρακτηρίστου ἐγκεφάλου.
266 He adds: "But no one is aware of it," another reference to unconsciousness.
267 *Elenchos*, V, 8, 13ff. (Legge, I, p. 133). Cf. Psalm 29 : 3: "The voice of the Lord is upon the waters," and verse 10: "The Lord sitteth upon the flood." For an alchemical parallel in Maier see *Psychology and Alchemy*, pars. 434ff.
268 This stone in the foundations of Zion may refer to Zech. 4 : 9f.: "The hands of Zorobabel have laid the foundation of this house, and his hands shall finish it . . . And they shall rejoice and shall see the tin plummet in the hand of Zorobabel. These are the seven eyes of the Lord that run to and fro through the whole earth" (DV). One of the alchemists brought this passage into connection with the lapis philosophorum on the ground that the "eyes of the Lord" were on the foundation-stone. (Cf. supra, par. 45.)

the foundation of Zion] . . . who has fallen from Adam the arch-man [ἀρχανθρώπου] on high.[269]

628   These extracts are sufficient to show how original are the bases of alchemical ideas. If no continuity of tradition can be proven, we would be forced to assume that the same ideas can arise spontaneously, again and again, from an archetypal foundation.

8. ADAM AS TOTALITY

629   Now that we have seen the significance of the brain and the moon-earth as the arcane substance, we can take up our commentary on Eleazar's text.

630   An alchemical recipe says: "Sow the gold in foliated white earth." [270] Thus the gold (sun) and the white earth, or moon [271] are united. In Christianity, as in alchemy, earth and moon are

---

[269] *Elenchos*, V, 7, 35f. (Legge, I, p. 129). The passages in parentheses are uncertain.

[270] "Seminate aurum in terram albam foliatam." *Ros. phil., Art. aurif.,* II, p. 336 has: "Seminate ergo *animam* in terram albam foliatam." Concerning terra foliata see Emblema VI in Maier, *Scrutinium chymicum,* pp. 16ff. The symbol probably derives from Senior, *De chemia,* pp. 24f.: "Likewise they call this water the life-giving Cloud, the lower world, and by this they understand the foliate Water, which is the gold of the Philosophers, which Lord Hermes called the Egg with many names. The lower world is the body and burnt ashes, to which they reduce the venerable Soul. And the burnt ashes and the soul are the gold of the sages which they sow in their white earth, and [in] the earth scattered with stars, foliate, blessed, and thirsting, which he called the earth of leaves and the earth of silver and the earth of gold." * "[Wherefore] Hermes said: Sow the gold in white foliate earth. For white foliate earth is the crown of victory, which is ashes extracted from ashes" * (p. 41). The "Liber de magni lapidis compositione" (*Theatr. chem.,* III, p. 33) mentions the "star Diana" as a synonym for *terra.*

[271] In their use of the terms Luna and Terra the alchemists often make no distinction between the two. The following two sentences occur almost side by side in "Clangor buccinae" (*Art. aurif.,* I, p. 464): "Therefore *Luna* is the mother and the field in which the seed should be sown and planted," * and "for I [says Sol] am as seed sown in good *earth.*" * The generative pair are always Sol and Luna, but at least as often the earth is the mother. It seems that Luna represents the beloved and bride, while earth represents the maternal element. The "Introitus apertus," *Mus. herm.,* p. 694 (Waite, II, pp. 194f.) says: "Know that our virgin earth here undergoes the last degree of cultivation, that the fruit of the Sun may be sown and ripened." * The earth is the "mother of metals" and of all creatures. As *terra alba,* it is the "perfect white stone" (*Art. aurif.,* II, p. 490); but this phase of the

closely related, conjoined by the figure of the divine mother. The sun-moon conjunction takes place in the head, an indication of the psychic nature of this event.[272] As I said, the concept of the "psychic," as we understand it today, did not exist in the Middle Ages, and even the educated modern man finds it difficult to understand what is meant by "reality of the psyche." So it is not surprising that it was incomparably more difficult for medieval man to imagine something between "esse in re" and "esse in intellectu solo." [273] The way out lay in "metaphysics." [274] The alchemist was therefore compelled to formulate his quasi-chemical facts metaphysically too.[275] Thus the white earth corresponds to the earth that signified "mankind, is exalted above all the circles of the World, and placed in the intellectual heaven

---

albedo is called "full moon" and "fruitful white earth" (Mylius, *Phil. ref.*, p. 20). Just as Luna longs for her lover, so the earth draws down the moon's soul. (Ripley, *Opera omnia*, p. 78.) Luna says to Sol: "I shall receive a soul from thee by flattery" * (Senior, *De chemia*, p. 8). The "Tractatus Micreris" (*Theatr. chem.*, V, p. 109) says: "From water falling upon the earth Adam was created, who is also the lesser world." * Mylius (*Phil. ref.*, p. 185): "Earth is called the mother of the elements, for she bears the son in her womb." * "Gloria mundi" (*Mus. herm.*, p. 221; Waite, I, p. 179) endows the filius with the dual birth of the hero: "although at his first birth he is begotten by the Sun and the Moon, he embodies certain earthly elements." * "The father receives the son, that is, the earth retains the spirit." * (Mylius, *Phil. ref.*, p. 137.) This whole identification of earth and moon is attested in antiquity: "For the lowest part of all the world is the earth, but the lowest part of the aether is the moon; and they have called the moon the aethereal earth." * (Macrobius, *In somnium Scipionis*, I, 19, 10.) Pherecydes says the moon is the heavenly earth from which souls are born. In Firmicus Maternus (*Matheseos*, V, praef. 5) the moon is even "the mother of mortal bodies." For the connection between the moon and the earth's fertility see Rahner, "Mysterium Lunae," pp. 61ff.

272 Cf. "Psychology of the Transference," pars. 469ff.

273 Proof of this is the controversy about universals, which Abelard sought to resolve by means of his "conceptualism." Cf. *Psychological Types* pars. 68ff.

274 Theosophy and kindred systems are still based on this principle.

275 The presbyter Jodocus Greverus says in his "Secretum" (*Theatr. chem.*, III, pp. 785f.): "But do thou therefore, dear reader, receive the legitimate meaning of my words, and understand that philosophers are like to gardeners and husbandmen, who first choose their seeds, and when they are selected, sow them not in common earth, but in cultivated fields or prepared gardens." * "But the Sun and Moon of the philosophers being taken as good seed, the earth itself is to be cleared of all its refuse and weeds, and worked with diligent tending, and after it has been thus tilled the aforesaid seeds of Sun and Moon are to be set therein." *

of the most holy Trinity." [276] (Where, we may add, it is obviously added to the Trinity as the "Fourth," thereby making it a totality.) [277] This cheerful piece of heterodoxy remained unconscious and its consequences never appeared on the surface.

631   The conclusion which Eleazar draws requires elucidation. It is in itself remarkable that he should paraphrase, in connection with the perfect state, i.e., the *coniunctio Solis et Lunae,* just that passage in Job (supra, par. 624) and say: "Out of my earth shall come forth blood." This is feasible only if the coniunctio symbolizes the production of the hermaphroditic second Adam, namely Christ and the *corpus mysticum* of the Church. In the ecclesiastical rite the equivalent of the coniunctio is the mixing of substances, or the Communion in both kinds. The passage from Job must therefore be interpreted as though Christ were speaking: "From my earth, my body, will come forth blood." In the Greek Orthodox rite the loaf of bread stands for Christ's body. The priest pierces it with a small silver lance, to represent by analogy the wound in his side from which blood and grace flow, and perhaps also the slaying of the victim (*mactatio Christi*).

632   The alchemical earth, as we saw, is the arcane substance, here equated with the body of Christ and with *adamah,* the red earth of paradise. From *adamah* is traditionally derived the name Adam, so that here again the paradisal earth is connected with the corpus mysticum. (This specifically Christian idea comports ill with the alleged Jewish authorship.) Nevertheless, it is strange that, as Eleazar says, this earth is "mingled with fire."

---

276 "De arte chymica," *Art. aurif.,* I, p. 613.* This earth is in the truest sense paradise, the "garden of happiness and wisdom." "For it is the gift of God, having the mystery of the union of Persons in the Holy Trinity. O most wondrous knowledge, which is the theatre of all nature, and its anatomy, earthly astrology, proof of God's omnipotence, testimony to the resurrection of the dead, pattern of the remission of sins, infallible rehearsal of the judgment to come and mirror of eternal blessedness." * (Greverus, *Theatr. chem.,* III, p. 809.)

277 "Male and female created he them. From this we learn that every figure which does not comprise male and female elements is not a higher [heavenly] figure. . . . Observe this: God does not make his abode in any place where male and female are not joined together." (*Zohar,* I, p. 177, mod.) Cf. "When we have trampled on the garment of shame, and when the two become one and the male with the female is neither male nor female" (*Stromata,* III, 13, 92). According to the *Zohar* (IV, p. 338), a male and female principle are to be distinguished in God himself. Cf. Wünsche, "Kabbala," Herzog and Hauck, *Realenzyklopädie,* IX, p. 679, line 43.

This recalls the alchemical idea of the "ignis gehennalis," the "central fire" [278] by whose warmth all nature germinates and grows, because in it dwells the Mercurial serpent, the salamander whom the fire does not consume, and the dragon that feeds on the fire.[279] Though this fire is a portion of the fire of God's spirit (Boehme's "divine wrath-fire"), it is also Lucifer, the most beautiful of God's angels, who after his fall became the fire of hell itself. Eleazar says: "This old Father-Begetter [280] will one day be drawn from the primordial Chaos,[281] and he is the fire-spewing dragon." The dragon floating in the air is the universal "Phyton,[282] the beginning of all things." [283]

633 Another source for the fire mingled with earth might be the image of the Son of Man in Revelation 1 : 14f.:

His head and his hairs were white like wool, as white as snow, and his eyes were as a flame of fire, and his feet like unto fine brass,[284] as if they burned in a furnace, and his voice as the sound of many waters. And he had in his right hand seven stars, and out of his mouth went a sharp two-edged sword, and his countenance was as the sun shineth in his strength.

Here again the head is compared to the sun, combined with the whiteness of the full moon. But the feet stand in the fire and glow like molten metal. We find the lower fire in Job 28 : 5: "Terra igne subversa est" (DV: "the earth hath been overturned with fire"). But "out of it cometh bread"—an image of the union of supreme opposites! In the Apocalyptic image we would hardly recognize the Son of Man, who is the true incarnation of God's love. But actually this image comes nearer to the paradoxes of the alchemists than does the Christ of the gospels, whose inner polarity was reduced to vanishing-point after the "Get thee be-

278 "Wherefore in the centre of the earth there is a most vast and raging fire, gathered together from the rays of the sun. It is called the abyss or nether world, and there is no other sublunar fire; for the dregs or earthly remains of the aforesaid principles, i.e., of the sun's heat and of water, are fire and earth, set aside for the damned." * (Mennens, *Theatr. chem.*, V, p. 370.)

279 "For he it is that overcomes fire, and by fire is not overcome; but in it amicably rests, rejoicing therein." * (*The Works of Geber,* trans. by Russell, p. 135.)

280 Identified by Eleazar with Albaon = black lead.

281 This expression derives from Khunrath, *Hyl. Chaos.*

282 Cf. "The Spirit Mercurius" par. 263.

283 *Uraltes Chymisches Werck,* I, p. 63.

284 Χαλκολιβάνῳ, rendered by the Vulgate as *aurichalcum,* from ὀρείχαλκος, a copper alloy.

hind me, Satan" incident. In the Apocalypse it becomes visible again, and even more so in the symbolism of alchemy.[285]

634   Our conjecture that Eleazar had in mind the Apocalyptic figure of the Son of Man is confirmed to the extent that there is an illustration of the "fils de l'homme ☿" (= Mercurius) in a French manuscript (18th cent.),[286] bearing the name "Jezoth le Juste," who is assigned the significant number 4 × 4 in the form of sixteen points (Pl. 3).[287] This refers to the four cherubim in the vision of Ezekiel, each of which had four faces (Ezek. 1 : 10, 10 : 14). In unorthodox fashion he is dressed like a woman, as is often the case with the hermaphroditic Mercurius in alchemical illustrations of the seventeenth and eighteenth centuries. Models for this figure are the visions of St. John the Divine (Rev. 1 and 4) and of Daniel (7 : 9ff.). "Jezoth" (= Yesod) is the ninth and middle Sefira in the lowest triad of the Cabalistic tree, and was interpreted as the creative and procreative power in the universe. Alchemically he corresponds to the *spiritus vegetativus,* Mercurius.[288] Just as Mercurius has a phallic aspect in alchemy, being related to Hermes Kyllenios,[289] so in the *Zohar* has Yesod; indeed the "Zaddik" or "Just One," as Yesod is also called, is the organ of generation.[290] He is the

---

[285] Cf. the dual aspect of the Cabalistic Tifereth, who corresponds to the Son of Man: "To the right he is called the Sun of righteousness, Malachi 4 : 2, but to the left [he is called the Sun] from the heat of the fire of Geburah." * *(Kabbala denudata,* I, Part 1, p. 348.) Of the second day, which is assigned to Geburah, it is said: "On that day Gehenna was created" (ibid., p. 439).

[286] Bibliothèque Nationale, Fr. 14765, pl. 8.

[287] Cf. the 4 × 4 structure in *Aion,* par. 410.

[288] "In natural things Yesod contains in itself quicksilver, for this is the foundation of the whole art of transmutation" * *(Kabbala denudata,* I, p. 441).

[289] Cf. "The Spirit Mercurius," par. 278.

[290] "Yesod in human beings denotes the genital member of either sex" * *(Kab. den.,* I, p. 440). The divine name assigned to him is El-chai: "Wherefore Adonai burns with continual lust to fly to the measure of El-chai" * (p. 441). Yesod is also called "firm" and "true," because he leads the "influx" of Tifereth down into Malchuth: "It is this firm step between Him and Her, that the most subtle nature of the semen sent down from above shall not be moved" * (p. 560). His cognomina are, among others: "redeeming angel, fount of living waters, tree of knowledge of good and evil, Leviathan, Solomon, Messiah the son of Joseph." * The ninth Sephira (Yesod) is named "member of the covenant (or of circumcision)." *(Kabbala denudata,* I, Part 2, Apparatus in Librum Sohar, p. 10.) "The Zohar makes prominent use of phallic symbolism in connection with speculations concerning the Sefira Yesod" (Scholem, *Major Trends,* p. 228). The author adds: "There is of

"spout of the waters" (*effusorium aquarum*),[291] or the "tube" (*fistula*) and "waterpipe" (*canalis*),[292] and the "spring of bubbling water" (*scaturigo*).[293] Such comparisons mislead the modern mind into one-sided interpretations, for instance that Yesod is simply the penis, or, conversely, that the obviously sexual language has no basis in real sexuality. But in mysticism one must remember that no "symbolic" object has only one meaning; it is always several things at once. Sexuality does not exclude spirituality nor spirituality sexuality, for in God all opposites are abolished. One has only to think of the *unio mystica* of Simeon ben Yochai in *Zohar* III, which Scholem (see n. 290) barely mentions.

635   Yesod has many meanings, which in the manuscript are related to Mercurius. In alchemy Mercurius is the "ligament" of the soul, uniting spirit and body. His dual nature enables him to play the role of mediator; he is bodily and spiritual and is himself the union of these two principles. Correspondingly, in Yesod is accomplished the mystery of the "unitio" [294] of the upper, Tifereth, and the lower, Malchuth. He is also called the "covenant of peace." [295] Similar designations are "bread," "chief of the Faces" [296] (i.e., of the upper and lower), the "apex" which touches earth and heaven,[297] "propinquus" (the Near One), since he is nearer to the Glory (Shekinah), i.e., Malchuth, than

course ample room here for psychoanalytical interpretations." In so far as the Freudian school translates psychic contents into sexual terminology there is nothing left for it to do here, since the author of the *Zohar* has done it already. This school merely shows us all the things that a penis can be, but it never discovered what the phallus can symbolize. It was assumed that in such a case the censor had failed to do its work. As Scholem himself shows and emphasizes particularly, the sexuality of the *Zohar*, despite its crudity, should be understood as a symbol of the "foundation of the world."

291 "He is the spout for the waters from on high . . . and upon it are two olives, Nezach and Hod, the two testicles of the male" * (*Kabbala denudata*, I, Part 1, p. 330).

292 P. 544, "fons" p. 215.

293 P. 551.

294 Ibid., p. 165, s.v. Botri.

295 P. 210, 5: "But the covenant of peace or perfection is so called because this mode makes peace and perfection between Tifereth and Malchuth, so that it is said thereof in I Chron. 29 : 11, 'for this mode, which is called *Qol* [i.e., "All"], is in heaven and earth,' the Targum using this paraphrase, that it is united with heaven and earth." *

296 P. 500.   297 Pp. 674 and 661.

to Tifereth,[298] and the "Strong One of Israel." [299] Yesod unites the emanation of the right, masculine side (Nezach, life-force) with the left, feminine side (Hod, beauty).[300] He is called "firm, reliable, constant" [301] because he leads the emanation of Tifereth down into Malchuth.[302]

636   Mercurius is often symbolized as a tree, and Yesod as *frutex* (tree-trunk) and *virgultum* (thicket).[303] Mercurius is the *spiritus vegetativus,* spirit of life and growth, and Yesod is described as "vivus," living,[304] or "living for aeons." [305] Just as Mercurius is the prima materia and the basis of the whole process, so Yesod means "foundation." [306] "In natural things Yesod contains in himself quicksilver, for this is the basis of the whole art of transmutation"; [307] not, of course, ordinary quicksilver, but "that which not without mystery is called a star." From this star flow "the waters of the good God El, or quicksilver. . . . This quicksilver . . . is called the Spherical Water," or "the water of baptism." [308]

This water is called the daughter of Matred, that is . . . of a man who labours unweariedly at making gold. For this water flows not out of the earth, nor is it dug out of mines, but is brought forth and perfected with great labour and much diligence. His wife is called the Water of gold, or such kind of water as gives rise to gold. And if this workman is espoused with her, he will engender a daughter, who will be the Water of the king's bath.[309]

298 P. 677: "Near . . . and better than the brother from afar, who is Tifereth." *
299 P. 14: "For the Strong One of Israel is the name midway between Nezach and Hod." *
300 As *castella munita* (fortified strongholds) and *botri* (grapes), Nezach and Hod signify the testicles. (Pp. 156 and 165).
301 Yesod is also called, like Tifereth, amicus fidelis, the faithful friend: "In the Zohar, in speaking of that youth, it is said that the Just One (Yesod) shall be called the faithful friend, according to Song of Songs 7 : 10, 'I am my beloved's.' And hence Yesod is called Friend, for he unites two lovers and friends; for through him is effected the union of Tifereth and Malchuth" * (p. 247).
302 P. 560. The symbolism is sexual (cf. supra, n. 290). The attribute "strong," "mighty" applies to Tifereth as well as to Yesod.
303 P. 710.
304 P. 340.
305 P. 165.
306 P. 660: Proverbs 10 : 25: "But the righteous is an everlasting foundation."
307 P. 441.   308 Pp. 441f.*
309 P. 442.* This appears to come from the alchemical treatise "Ash Metsareph," on which Knorr elaborates in his "Apparatus."

On the basis of isopsephic [310] speculation the water of gold was identified with Yesod. The tablet with sixteen signs for gold or sun ⊙ at the feet of the *fils de l'homme* seems to point to this (Pl. 3). The *Kabbala denudata* reproduces a "Kamea" [311] containing not 2×8 but $8 \times 8 = 64$ numbers,[312] "which represent the sum of the name of the golden water." [313]

637 As the prima materia is also called lead and Saturn, we should mention that the Sabbath is co-ordinated with Yesod, as is the letter Teth,[314] which stands under the influence of Shabtai (Saturn). In the same way that Mercurius, as a volatile substance, is named the bird, goose, chick of Hermes, swan, eagle, vulture, and phoenix, Yesod (as well as Tifereth) is called "pullus avis" [315] also "penna, ala" (feather, wing).[316] Feathers and wings play a role in alchemy too: the eagle that devours its own feathers or wings,[317] and the feathers of the phoenix in Michael Maier.[318] The idea of the bird eating its own feathers is a variant of the uroboros, which in turn is connected with Leviathan. Leviathan and the "great dragon" are names for both Yesod and Tifereth.[319]

638 Yesod is as a part to the whole, and the whole is Tifereth,

310 See supra, par. 329, n. 658.

311 From Ital. *cameo*, L. *cammaeus*.

312 As a multiple of 4, 64 thus represents the highest totality. The 64 hexagrams of the *I Ching* should probably be understood in the same way. They represent the course of the "valley spirit," Tao, winding like a dragon or water. Cf. Rousselle, "Drache und Stute," p. 28; also Tscharner, *Das Vermächtnis des Laotse*, p. 11.

313 *Kabbala denudata*, I, Part 1, p. 443.

314 "In the Zohar this letter is called the fount of life" * (pp. 439 and 366).

315 P. 144: "Aprokh: the chick of any bird. Deut. 22 : 6; Ps. 84 : 4. In Raya Mehimna, R. Simeon ben Yochai says that by this name is to be understood the grade Tifereth, as is apparent from its six members (limbs), which are six wings, wherewith it flies up and down. But in Tikkunim at the beginning of the book of R. Bar, Bar Channa: this name is said to refer to the Just One under the mystery of light reflected from the depths to the height. His words are these: Aephrochim are flowers, which do not yet bear perfect fruit. They are the Sefiroth under the notion of a tree, which is turned from the depths upwards, and this with reference to Yesod." *

316 "Feather, wing . . . the genital member . . . this name is expounded of Yesod, who is surnamed the Just One" * (p. 22).

317 See *Psychology and Alchemy*, fig. 228.

318 "The phoenix . . . from the glittering feathers about whose neck . . . is made a medicine most useful for restoring to the desired state of health all affections contrary to human nature" * (*Symbola*, p. 599).

319 *Kabbala denudata*, I, Part 1, pp. 499 and 737.

445

who is named the sun.[320] The feet of the Apocalyptic Son of Man, glowing as if in the fire, may have a connection with Malchuth, since the feet are the organ that touches the earth. The earth, Malchuth, is Yesod's "footstool." [321] Malchuth is also the "furnace", "the place destined for the cooking and decoction of the influence sent down to her by her husband for the nourishment of the hosts." [322]

639   After this digression, let us turn back once more to Eleazar's text. The golden head with the silver moon-hair and the body made of red earth mingled with fire are the "inside" of a black, poisonous, ugly figure, which is how the Shulamite now appears. Obviously these negative qualities are to be understood in a moral sense, although chemically they signify the black lead of the initial state. But "inside" is the second Adam, a mystic Christ, as is made clear by the allegory of the lion which Samson slew, and which then became the habitation of a swarm of honey-bees: "Out of the eater came forth meat, and out of the strong came forth sweetness." [323] These words were interpreted as referring to the *corpus Christi*, the Host,[324] which Eleazar calls the "food of heroes." This strange expression and the still stranger conception of the "Christ" present in the Host are an allusion to the alchemical secret. That is why the author can say with Job 28 : 7 that the way is unknown, "neither hath the eye of the vulture beheld it." It is shrouded in mystery, for "the stone belongeth only to the proven and elect of God."

640   The lapis also figures in the Cabala: "Sometimes Adonai, the name of the last Sefira, and Malchuth herself, the Kingdom, are so called; for the latter is the foundation of the whole fabric of the world." [325] The stone is, indeed, of supreme importance, because it fulfils the function of Adam Kadmon as the "capital-stone, from which all the upper and lower hosts in the work of

320 Ibid., p. 348.

321 Pp. 157, 266, 439.

322 The text continues: "As is well known, the woman by her warmth cooks the seed for generation" * (p. 465).

323 Judges 14 : 14.

324 "This is to be understood of the Son of God, who after having long imitated the terrible lion in rebuking the world's sins, a little later, when he instituted the most holy sacrament of the Eucharist as his death drew nigh, turned himself into exceeding sweet honeycombs" * (Picinellus, *Mundus Symbolicus*, I, p. 397).

325 *Kabbala denudata*, I, Part 1, p. 16.*

creation are brought into being." [326] It is called the "sapphire-stone, because it takes on divers colours from the highest powers, and works in created things now in one wise, now in the contrary, administering at times good, at others evil, now life, now death, now sickness, now healing, now poverty, now riches." [327] The stone appears here as the power of fate; indeed, as the reference to Deuteronomy 32 : 39 shows, it is God himself.[328] Knorr von Rosenroth was himself an alchemist, and his words here are written with deliberate intent.[329] He emphasizes that the stone is the one "which the builders rejected and is become the head of the corner." [330] It occupies a middle position in the Sefiroth system since it unites in itself the powers of the upper world and distributes them to the lower.[331] According to its position, therefore, it would correspond to Tifereth.[332]

---

326 Ibid., p. 16.* *Zohar*, I, 231a (Eng. trans., II, p. 339) says: "The world did not come into being until God took a certain stone, which is called the foundation-stone, and cast it into the abyss so that it held fast there, and from it the world was planted. This is the central point of the universe, and on this point stands the Holy of Holies. This is the stone referred to in the verses, 'Who laid the cornerstone thereof? (Job 38 : 6), 'a tried stone, a precious cornerstone' (Isaiah 28 : 16), and 'The stone which the builders rejected has become the head of the corner' (Psalm 118 : 22). This stone is compounded of fire, water, and air, and rests on the abyss. . . . 'This stone has on it seven eyes' . . . (Zech. 3 : 9). It is the rock Moriah, the place of Isaac's sacrifice. It is also the navel of the world."

327 *Kabbala denudata*, I, Part 1, p. 16.*

328 "See now that I, even I, am he, and there is no god with me; I kill, and I make alive; I wound, and I heal; neither is there any that can deliver out of my hand."

329 He recommends his work to "philosophers, theologians of every religion, and lovers of the chymic art." See title-page of Vol. I, Part 1.

330 Pp. 16 and 18.

331 Pp. 16f.

332 The stone refers not only to the upper world but also to Malchuth: "In this perpetual name the mystery of the letter Yod (י) is involved, and that to the greatest degree in Malchuth, for in her exists the letter Yod. For the shapeless mass and form of the י hath the figure of the stone, and Malchuth is the foundation and the stone on which the whole upper edifice is built. Of her it is said in Zachariah 3 : 9: Upon one stone there are seven eyes" * (p. 17). (Cf. supra, ch. II, "The Scintilla," where I discuss the κεφαία of Monoimos, the iota.) The "lower stone" has an evil significance in the Midrashic legend of Armillus, the "son of the stone." The Midrash of the Ten Kings says: "And Satan will come down and have intercourse with the stone in Rome. The stone will conceive and bear Armillus." "This stone is the wife of Belial, and after he had cohabited with her she became pregnant and gave birth to Armillus." The latter has "squinting red eyes, two heads, green feet." "His hair is red like gold." He is thus a Typhon-like figure,

641   I have found no evidence in the alchemical literature that the sapphire was an arcanum before the time of Paracelsus. It seems as though this author introduced it into alchemy from the Cabala as a synonym for the arcane substance:

> For the virtue which lies in the sapphire is given from heaven by way of solution, coagulation, and fixation. Now, since heaven is created so as to work through these three things until it has achieved this [viz., the production of the sapphire and its virtues], so must the breaking up of the sapphire correspond to the same three procedures. This breaking up is such that the bodies vanish, and the arcanum remains. For before the sapphire existed, there was no arcanum. But subsequently, just as life was given to man, the arcanum was given to this material by heaven.[333]

We can recognize here relationships with Cabalistic ideas. Paracelsus's pupil, Adam von Bodenstein, says in his *Onomasticon:* "The sapphire material: that liquid in which there is no harmful matter." [334] Dorn [335] relates the "sapphirine flower" to the "Arcanum Cheyri" of Paracelsus.[336] The "Epistola ad Hermannum" cites a certain G. Ph. Rodochaeus de Geleinen Husio: [337] "Then arises the sapphirine flower of the hermaphrodite, the wondrous mystery of the Macrocosm, of which one part, if it be poured into a thousand parts of the melted Ophirizum, converts it all into its own nature." [338] This passage is influenced by Paracelsus.

642   The Lapis Sapphireus or Sapphirinus is derived from Ezek-

---

the adversary of the second Adam. "He will come to the Edomites and say to them, I am your saviour." The stone in Rome had "the shape of a beautiful girl, who was made in the first six days of the Creation." Armillus corresponds to the three-headed Azi-Dahaka of Persian legend, who subdued Yima, the Anthropos. See Murmelstein, "Adam," pp. 75ff. Further variants in Hurwitz, *Die Gestalt des sterbenden Messias.*   333 *Das Buch Paragranum* (ed. Strunz), p. 77.
334 P. 64.
335 Cf. "Paracelsus as a Spiritual Phenomenon," par. 234, n. 22.
336 *De vita longa,* p. 72.
337 *Theatr. chem.,* V, p. 899.*
338 "Ophirizum" may be derived from Ophir, whose pure gold was proverbial. (Cf. Job 22 : 24 and Isaiah 13 : 12.) Reusner's *Pandora* (p. 304) gives for "purum aurum, clear gold": "Obrizum aurum." This agrees with Isidore of Seville, *Liber etymologiarum,* lib. XVI, cap. XVII, fol. 84ʳ: "Obrycum aurum." L. *obrussa,* Gk. ὄβρυζον χρυσίον, 'pure gold'. Also mentioned in Pico della Mirandola, "De auro," *Theatr. chem.,* II, p. 392.

448

iel 1 : 22 and 26, where the firmament above the "living creature" was like a "terrible crystal" and a "sapphire stone" (also
10 : 1), and from Exodus 24 : 10: "And they saw the God of
Israel: and under his feet as it were a work of sapphire stone,
and as the heaven, when clear" (DV). In alchemy "our gold" is
"crystalline"; [339] the treasure of the Philosophers is "a certain
glassy heaven, like crystal, and ductile like gold"; [340] the tincture of gold is "transparent as crystal, fragile as glass." [341] The
"Book of the Cave of Treasures" says that Adam's body "shone
like the light of a crystal." [342] The crystal, "which appears
equally pure within and without," refers in ecclesiastical language to the "unimpaired purity" of the Virgin.[343] The throne
in Ezekiel's vision, says Gregory the Great, is rightly likened to
the sapphire, "for this stone has the colour of air." [344] He compares Christ to the crystal in a way that served as a model for the
language and ideas of the alchemists.[345]

643   The combination of water and crystal is found also in the
Cabalistic "Sifra de Zeniutha." § 178 of Luria's commentary
says: "The second form is called crystalline dew, and this is

339 Mylius, *Phil. ref.*, p. 151.

340 *Theatr. chem.*, II, p. 526. Cf. Rev. 21 : 21: "pure gold, as it were transparent
glass."

341 Helvetius, "Vitulus aureus," *Mus. herm.*, p. 826 (Waite, II, p. 280).

342 Bezold, *Die Schatzhöhle*, p. 4.

343 Picinellus, *Mundus symbolicus*, I, p. 690.

344 *In Ezechielem*, I, Hom. viii (Migne, *P.L.*, vol. 76, col. 863). He continues: "The
virtues therefore of the heavens are signified by the sapphire stone, for these spirits
. . . hold the dignity of the highest place in heaven." * Cf. also *Moralia in Job*,
lib. XVIII, cap. XXVII.

345 *In Ezechielem*, lib. I, Hom. vii: "The crystal . . . is congealed from water,
and becomes solid. And we know how great is the mobility of water; but the body
of our Redeemer, because it underwent sufferings even unto death, was in some
respects like unto water; for in being born, growing up, and suffering weariness,
hunger, thirst, and death, he pursued a mobile course moment by moment until
his passion. . . . But because through the glory of his resurrection he was restored
out of that corruptibility into the strength of incorruptibility, he hardened after
the fashion of a crystal from water, so that there was one and the same nature in it
and in him, and the mutability of corruption which had formerly been in him was
no more. Therefore water was changed into crystal when the infirmity of corruptibility was changed into the strength of incorruptibility by his resurrection. But
mark that the crystal is said to be dreadful, that is, to be feared . . . and to all who
know the truth it is manifest that the Redeemer of mankind, when he shall appear
as judge, will be comely to the just, but terrible to the unjust." *

formed of the Severity of the Kingdom [346] of the first Adam,
which entered into the Wisdom of Macroprosopus: [347] hence in
the crystal there appears a distinct red colour. And this [form] is
the Wisdom whereof they said, that Judgments are rooted in
it." [348] Although alchemy was undoubtedly influenced by such
comparisons, the stone cannot be traced back to Christ, despite
all the analogies.[349] It was the mystical property of alchemy, this
"stone that is no stone," or the "stone that hath a spirit" and is
found in the "streamings of the Nile." [350] It is a symbol that
cannot be explained away as yet another supererogatory attempt
to obscure the Christian mystery. On the contrary, it appears as
a new and singular product which in early times gradually crystallized out through the assimilation of Christian ideas into
Gnostic material; later, clear attempts were made in turn to assimilate the alchemical ideas to the Christian, though, as Eleazar's text shows, there was an unbridgeable difference between
them. The reason for this is that the symbol of the stone, despite
the analogy with Christ, contains an element that cannot be reconciled with the purely spiritual assumptions of Christianity.
The very concept of the "stone" indicates the peculiar nature of
this symbol. "Stone" is the essence of everything solid and
earthly. It represents feminine *matter,* and this concept intrudes
into the sphere of "spirit" and its symbolism. The Church's
hermeneutic allegories of the cornerstone and the "stone cut out
of a mountain without hands," [351] which were interpreted as
Christ, were not the source of the lapis symbol, but were used by
the alchemists in order to justify it, for the λίθος οὐ λίθος was not of

---

346 The Kingdom (Basilia) refers to Malchuth.

347 The Macroprosopos corresponds to the first triad of the Aziluth system: Kether
(*corona*), Binah (*intelligentia*), and Hokhmah (*sapientia*). "It is certain that
Macroprosopos, the Father and Mother, are the Crown, Wisdom and Intelligence
of the emanative world after the restitution." * (Ibid., sect. 166, pp. 56f.) This triad
is a real Trinity: "From the first three parts of the world of emptiness are constituted three supreme heads, which are contained in the Most Holy Ancient One.
But all three are counted as one in the emanative world, which is Macroprosopos." *
The λόγος μακρόκοσμος or μακροπρόσωπος occurs in Philo.

348 "Commentarius generalis," *Kabbala denudata,* II, Part 2, Tract. IV, p. 61.*

349 Christ is called lapis in the patristic literature. Cf. for example St. Gregory,
Expos. in I Reg., lib. IV, cap. vii, 12 (Migne, *P.L.,* vol. 79, col. 212): "The stone in
Holy Writ signifies our Lord and Redeemer." *

350 Berthelot, *Alch. grecs,* III, vi, 5. Cf. *Psychology and Alchemy,* par. 405.

351 Daniel 2 : 34 (DV).

Christian origin. The stone was more than an "incarnation" of God, it was a concretization, a "materialization" that reached down into the darkness of the inorganic realm or even arose from it, from that part of the Deity which put itself in opposition to the Creator because, as the Basilidians say, it remained latent in the *panspermia* (universal seed-bed) as the formative principle of crystals, metals, and living organisms. The inorganic realm included regions, like that of hell-fire, which were the dominion of the devil. The three-headed Mercurial serpent was, indeed, a triunity in matter [352]—the "lower triad" [353]—complementing the divine Trinity.

644 We may therefore suppose that in alchemy an attempt was made at a symbolical *integration of evil* by localizing the divine drama of redemption in man himself. This process appears now as an extension of redemption beyond man to matter, now as an ascent of the ἀντίμιμον πνεῦμα, 'spirit of imitation,' or Lucifer, and as a reconciliation of this with the spirit descending from above, both the Above and Below undergoing a process of mutual transformation. It seems to me that Eleazar's text conveys some idea of this, as the transformation of the black Shulamite takes place in three stages, which were mentioned by Dionysius the Areopagite as characterizing the mystical ascent: *emundatio* (κάθαρσις, 'purification'), *illuminatio* (φωτισμός), *perfectio* (τελεσμός). [354] Dionysius refers the purification to Psalm 51 : 7 (AV): "Wash me, and I shall be whiter than snow"; and the illumination to Psalm 13 : 3 (AV): "Lighten mine eyes." (The two heavenly luminaries, sun and moon, correspond on the old view to the two eyes.) The perfection he refers to Matthew 5 : 48: "Be ye therefore perfect, even as your Father which is in heaven is perfect." Here we have one aspect of the approximation to divinity; the other aspect is exemplified by the image of the Apocalyptic Son of Man, described earlier.

645 The transformation of the Shulamite as described in the text can thus be conceived as the preliminary stage of an individuation process, rising unexpectedly out of the unconscious in symbolical form, and comparable to a dream that seeks to outline this process and for that purpose makes use now of religious and

352 Cf. "The Spirit Mercurius," pars. 270ff., 283.
353 Cf. "The Phenomenology of the Spirit in Fairytales," pars. 425f., 436ff.
354 *The Celestial Hierarchies*, III, 3 (Eng. trans., p. 18).

now of "scientific" images. So regarded and looked at from a psychological angle, the following facts emerge.

646   The *nigredo* corresponds to the darkness of the unconscious, which contains in the first place the inferior personality, the shadow. This changes into the feminine figure that stands immediately behind it, as it were, and controls it: the anima, whose typical representative the Shulamite is. "I am black, but comely" —not "hateful," as Eleazar would have us believe, after having reconsidered the matter. For since nature was deformed by the sin of Adam, her blackness must in his view be regarded as ugliness, as the blackness of sin, as the Saturnine initial state, heavy and black as lead. But the Shulamite, the priestess of Ishtar, signifies earth, nature, fertility, everything that flourishes under the damp light of the moon, and also the natural life-urge. The anima is indeed the archetype of life itself, which is beyond all meaning and all moral categories. What at first struck us as incomprehensible, namely that the old Adam should come forth from her again, thus reversing the sequence of Creation, can now be understood, for if anyone knows how to live the natural life it is the old Adam. Here he is not so much the old Adam as an Adam reborn from a daughter of Eve, an Adam restored to his pristine naturalness. The fact that she gives rebirth to Adam and that a black Shulamite produces the original man in his savage, unredeemed state rules out the suspicion that the "old" Adam is a slip of the pen or a misprint. There is a method in it, which allows us to guess what it was that induced the author to adopt a Jewish pseudonym. For the Jew was the handiest example, living under everyone's eyes, of a non-Christian, and therefore a vessel for all those things a Christian could not or did not like to remember. So it was really very natural to put those dark, half-conscious thoughts which began with the Movement of the Free Spirit, the late Christian religion of the Holy Ghost, and which formed the life-blood of the Renaissance, into the mouth of an allegedly Jewish author. Just as the era of the Old Testament prophets began with Hosea, who was commanded by God to marry another Shulamite, so the *cours d'amour* of René d'Anjou, the minnesingers and saints with their passionate love of God, were contemporaneous with the Brethren of the Free Spirit. Eleazar's text is nothing but a late echo of these centuries-old events which changed the face of Christianity. But in any

such echo there is also a premonition of future developments: in the very same century the author of *Faust,* that momentous opus, was born.

647   The Shulamite remains unchanged, as did the old Adam. And yet Adam Kadmon is born, a non-Christian second Adam, just at the moment when the transformation is expected. This extraordinary contradiction seems insoluble at first sight. But it becomes understandable when we consider that the illumination or *solificatio* of the Shulamite is not the first transformation but the second, and takes place within. The subject of transformation is not the empirical man, however much he may identify with the "old Adam," but Adam the Primordial Man, the archetype within us. The black Shulamite herself represents the first transformation: it is the coming to consciousness of the black anima, the Primordial Man's feminine aspect. The second, or *solificatio,* is the conscious differentiation of the masculine aspect—a far more difficult task. Every man feels identical with this, though in reality he is not. There is too much blackness in the archetype for him to put it all down to his own account, and so many good and positive things that he cannot resist the temptation to identify with them. It is therefore much easier to see the blackness in projected form: "The woman whom thou gavest to be with me, she gave me of the tree, and I did eat" holds true even of the most enlightened psychology. But the masculine aspect is as unfathomable as the feminine aspect. It would certainly not be fitting for the empirical man, no matter how swollen his ego-feelings, to appropriate the whole range of Adam's heights and depths. Human being though he is, he has no cause to attribute to himself all the nobility and beauty a man can attain to, just as he would assuredly refuse to accept the guilt for the abjectness and baseness that make man lower than an animal—unless, of course, he were driven by insanity to act out the role of the archetype.

648   But although, when the masculine aspect of the Primordial Man "comes forth again," it is the old Adam, who is black like the Shulamite, it is nevertheless the second Adam, i.e., the still older Adam before the Fall, Adam Kadmon. The ambiguity of this passage is too perfect for the author, who proves himself elsewhere to be a not particularly skilful forger, to have been conscious of it. The coming to consciousness of Adam Kadmon

453

would indeed be a great illumination, for it would be a realization of the inner man or Anthropos, an archetypal totality transcending the sexes. In so far as this Man is divine, we could speak of a theophany. The Shulamite's hope of becoming a "white dove" points to a future, perfect state. The white dove is a hint that the Shulamite will become Sophia,[355] the Holy Ghost, while Adam Kadmon is an obvious parallel of Christ.

649   If the alchemical process of thought corresponded only to the three stages of purification, illumination, perfection, it would be difficult to see the justification for paraphrasing the analogous Christian ideas, which are so patently betrayed, for instance, in the fixing to the "black cross." But the need for a symbolism other than the Christian one is evident from the fact that the transformation process does not culminate in the second Adam and the white dove but in the lapis, which, with God's help, is made by the empirical man. It is a half physical, half metaphysical product, a psychological symbol expressing something created by man and yet supra-ordinate to him. This paradox can only be something like the symbol of the *self*, which likewise can be brought forth, i.e., made conscious, by human effort but is at the same time by definition a pre-existent totality that includes the conscious and the unconscious.

650   This is a thought that goes beyond the Christian world of ideas and involves a mystery consummated in and through man. It is as though the drama of Christ's life were, from now on, located in man as its living carrier. As a result of this shift, the events formulated in dogma are brought within range of psychological experience and become recognizable in the process of individuation.

651   It is naturally not the task of an empirical science to evaluate such spiritual developments from the standpoint of transcendental truth. It must content itself with establishing the existence of these processes and comparing them with parallel observations in modern man. It also has the right to attempt to map out the logical structure of such psychologems. The fact that it must push forward into regions where belief and doubt argue the question of truth does not prove that it has any intention of intervening or presuming to decide what the truth is. Its "truth"

355 The fate of the Shulamite corresponds, in a sense, to that of Sophia among the Gnostics, as reported by Irenaeus. (Cf. *Aion*, pars. 75, n. 23, 118, n. 86, 307, n. 33.)

consists solely in establishing the facts and in explaining them without prejudice within the framework of empirical psychology. Under no circumstances is it entitled to say whether the facts are valid or not, or to try to ascertain their moral or religious value. I must emphasize this so emphatically because my method is constantly suspected of being theology or metaphysics in disguise. The difficulty for my critics seems to be that they are unable to accept the concept of psychic reality. A psychic process is something that really exists, and a psychic content is as real as a plant or an animal. In spite of the fact that the duckbilled platypus, for example, cannot be logically derived from the general premises of zoology, it nevertheless indubitably exists, improbable as this may appear to prejudiced minds. It is not a fantasy and not just somebody's opinion but an immovable fact. It is perfectly true that one can play metaphysics with psychic facts, and particularly with ideas that have always been counted as metaphysical. But the ideas themselves are not metaphysical; they are empirically verifiable phenomena that are the proper subject of the scientific method.

652 With the statements of the Cabala, which as we have seen found their way into alchemy, our interpretation of Adam attains a scope and a depth that can hardly be surpassed. This interpretation includes Eve as the feminine principle itself. She appears chiefly as the "lower," as Malchuth (kingdom), Shekinah (the Indwelling of God), or as Atarah (Crown), the equivalent below of Kether, the upper crown. She is also present in the "hermaphroditic" Sefiroth system, the right half of which is masculine and the left half feminine. Hence Adam Kadmon, as a personification of the whole "inverted tree," is androgynous, but the system itself is a highly differentiated coniunctio symbol, and, as such, divided into three parts (three columns of three Sefiroth each). According to Hippolytus, the Naassenes divided the hermaphroditic Adam into three parts, just as they did Geryon.[356] Geryon was triple-bodied[357] and the possessor of the splendid cattle on the island of Erythia. Heracles slew him with an arrow, on which occasion Hera was wounded in the breast. On the same journey Heracles had threatened to shoot the sun

356 Geryon was the son of Callirhoe and Chrysaor, who sprang from the blood of the Gorgon.
357 *Elenchos,* V, 8, 4.

455

because his rays were too hot. So the slaying of Geryon was the last in a series of three sacrileges.

For they say of this Geryon [continues Hippolytus] that one part is spiritual, one psychic, and one earthly; and they hold that the knowledge of him is the beginning of the capacity to know God, for they say: "The beginning of wholeness is the knowledge of man, but the knowledge of God is perfect wholeness." All this, they say, the spiritual, the psychic, and the earthly, set itself in motion and came down together into one man, Jesus who was born of Mary; and there spoke through it [the spiritual, the psychic, and the earthly] these three men [i.e., the triple-bodied Geryon], each from his own substance to his own. For of all things there are three kinds, the angelic, the psychic, and the earthly; and three Churches, angelic, psychic, and earthly; and their names are the Chosen, the Called, and the Captive.[358]

653   This conception bears a striking resemblance to the Sefiroth system.[359] In particular, Geryon corresponds to the cosmogonic Adam Kadmon. He is the "masculo-feminine Man in all things, [whom] the Greeks call the heavenly horn of the moon.[360] For they say all things were made by him, and without him was not any thing made.[361] That which was made in him is Life. This, they say, is Life—the unutterable generation [γενεά] of perfect men, which to earlier generations was unknown." [362]

[358] Ibid., V, 6, 6f. (Cf. Legge, I, p. 121).
[359] Similar ideas can be found in the *Panarium* of Epiphanius, XXX, 3 (ed. Holl, vol. I, p. 336): The Elkesaites declared that Adam was Christ. He came down into Adam, put on his body and appeared to Abraham, Isaac, and Jacob. Concerning Abraham's grave on Golgotha see ibid., XLVI, 5 (II, pp. 208f).
[360] "Osiris, heavenly horn of the moon" is a cognomen of Attis. (*Elenchos*, V, 9, 8.)
[361] John 1 : 3.
[362] *Elenchos*, V, 8, 4f. (Cf. Legge, I, pp. 131f.).

VI

THE CONJUNCTION

1. THE ALCHEMICAL VIEW OF THE UNION OF OPPOSITES

654   Herbert Silberer rightly called the coniunctio the "central idea" of the alchemical procedure.[1] This author correctly recognized that alchemy was, in the main, symbolical, whereas the historian of alchemy, Eduard von Lippmann, a chemist, did not mention the term "coniunctio" even in his index.[2] Anyone who has but a slight acquaintance with the literature knows that the adepts were ultimately concerned with a union of the substances —by whatever names these may have been called. By means of this union they hoped to attain the goal of the work: the production of the gold or a symbolical equivalent of it. Although the coniunctio is unquestionably the primordial image of what we today would call chemical combination, it is hardly possible to prove beyond a doubt that the adept thought as concretely as the modern chemist. Even when he spoke of a union of the "natures," or of an "amalgam" of iron and copper, or of a compound of sulphur and mercury, he meant it at the same time as a symbol: iron was Mars and copper was Venus, and their fusion was at the same time a love-affair. The union of the "natures" which "embrace one another" was not physical and concrete, for they were "celestial natures" which multiplied "by the command of God." [3] When "red lead" was roasted with gold it produced a "spirit," that is, the compound became "spiritual," [4] and from the "red spirit" proceeded the "principle of the world." [5] The combination of sulphur and mercury was followed by the "bath" and "death." [6] By the combination of copper and the *aqua permanens,* which was usually quicksilver, we

1 *Problems of Mysticism and Its Symbolism,* p. 121.
2 *Entstehung und Ausbreitung der Alchemie.*
3 *Turba Philosophorum* (ed. Ruska), p. 119.
4 Ibid., p. 127.   5 Ibid.   6 P. 126.

think only of an amalgam. But for the alchemists it meant a secret, "philosophical" sea, since for them the *aqua permanens* was primarily a symbol or a philosophical postulate which they hoped to discover—or believed they had discovered—in the various "fluids." The substances they sought to combine in reality always had—on account of their unknown nature—a numinous quality which tended towards phantasmal personification. They were substances which, like living organisms, "fertilized one another and thereby produced the living being [ζῷον] sought by the Philosophers." [7] The substances seemed to them hermaphroditic, and the conjunction they strove for was a philosophical operation, namely the union of form and matter.[8] This inherent duality explains the duplications that so often occur, e.g., two sulphurs, two quicksilvers,[9] *Venus alba et rubea*,[10] *aurum nostrum* and *aurum vulgi*.

655　　It is therefore not surprising that the adepts, as we have seen in the previous chapters, piled up vast numbers of synonyms to express the mysterious nature of the substances—an occupation which, though it must seem utterly futile to the chemist, affords the psychologist a welcome explanation concerning the nature of the projected contents. Like all numinous contents, they have a tendency to self-amplification, that is to say they form the nuclei for an aggregation of synonyms. These synonyms represent the elements to be united as a pair of opposites; [11] for instance as man and woman, god and goddess, son and mother,[12] red and white,[13] active and passive, body and spirit,[14] and so on.

---

[7] Berthelot, *Alch. grecs*, III, xl 2.

[8] Aegidius de Vadis, "Dialogus" (*Theatr. chem.*, II, p. 99): "But minerals and vegetables are of hermaphrodite nature in that they have twofold sex. Nonetheless, there comes about between them a conjunction of form and matter, as with animals." *

[9] "Rosinus ad Sarratantam" (*Art. aurif.*, I, p. 302): "Wherefore there are said to be two sulphurs and two quicksilvers, and they are such that they are called one and one, and they rejoice together, and the one contains the other." *

[10] Ibid.

[11] The mixture and union of the elements is called the "ordo compositionis" ("Liber Plat. quartorum," *Theatr. chem.*, V, p. 182). Wei Po-yang says: "The way is long and obscurely mystical, at the end of which Ch'ien (yang) and K'un (yin) come together" (pp. 210ff).

[12] Maier, *Symbola*, p. 178.

[13] The "red man" and the "white woman," or "Red Sea sand" and "sputum of the moon." *Mus. herm.*, p. 9 (Waite, I, p. 12).　　[14] Ibid., p. 11 (Waite, I, p. 14).

The opposites are usually derived from the quaternio of elements,[15] as we can see very clearly from the anonymous treatise "De sulphure," which says:

Thus the fire began to work upon the air and brought forth Sulphur. Then the air began to work upon the water and brought forth Mercurius. The water began to work upon the earth and brought forth Salt. But the earth, having nothing to work upon, brought forth nothing, so the product remained within it. Therefore only three principles were produced, and the earth became the nurse and matrix of the others.

From these three principles were produced male and female, the male obviously from Sulphur and Mercurius, and the female from Mercurius and Salt.[16] Together they bring forth the "incorruptible One," the *quinta essentia,* "and thus quadrangle will answer to quadrangle." [17]

656   The synthesis of the incorruptible One or quintessence follows the Axiom of Maria, the earth representing the "fourth." The separation of the hostile elements corresponds to the initial state of chaos and darkness. From the successive unions arise an active principle (sulphur) and a passive (salt), as well as a mediating, ambivalent principle, Mercurius. This classical alchemical trinity then produces the relationship of male to female as the supreme and essential opposition. Fire comes at the beginning and is acted on by nothing, and earth at the end acts on nothing. Between fire and earth there is no interaction; hence the four elements do not constitute a circle, i.e., a totality. This is produced only by the synthesis of male and female. Thus the square at the beginning corresponds to the quaternio of elements united in the *quinta essentia* at the end—"quadrangle will answer to quadrangle."

657   The alchemical description of the beginning corresponds psychologically to a primitive consciousness which is constantly liable to break up into individual affective processes—to fall apart, as it were, in four directions. As the four elements repre-

15 As in the *Turba,* p. 117.

16 The "copulatio" takes place in "mercurio menstruali" ("Exercit. in Turbam," *Art. aurif.,* I, p. 161) or in a bath of *aqua permanens,* which again is Mercurius. Mercurius is both masculine and feminine and at the same time the child born of their union.

17 *Mus. herm.,* pp. 622ff. (Waite, II, pp. 142ff.)

sent the whole physical world, their falling apart means dissolution into the constituents of the world, that is, into a purely
inorganic and hence unconscious state. Conversely, the combination of the elements and the final synthesis of male and female
is an achievement of the art and a product of conscious endeavour. The result of the synthesis was consequently conceived
by the adept as self-knowledge,[18] which, like the knowledge of
God, is needed for the preparation of the Philosophers' Stone.[19]
Piety is needed for the work, and this is nothing but knowledge
of oneself.[20] This thought occurs not only in late alchemy but
also in Greek tradition, as in the Alexandrian treatise of Krates
(transmitted by the Arabs), where it is said that a perfect knowledge of the soul enables the adept to understand the many different names which the Philosophers have given to the arcane
substance.[21] The "Liber quartorum" emphasizes that there must
be self-observation in the work as well as of events in due time.[22]
It is evident from this that the chemical process of the coniunctio was at the same time a psychic synthesis. Sometimes it
seems as if self-knowledge brought about the union, sometimes
as if the chemical process were the efficient cause. The latter alternative is decidedly the more frequent: the coniunctio takes
place in the retort [23] or, more indefinitely, in the "natural vessel" or matrix.[24] The vessel is also called the grave, and the
union a "shared death." [25] This state is named the "eclipse of
the sun." [26]

18 See *Aion,* pars. 250ff.
19 "If a man would attain the highest good, he . . . must rightly know first God
and then himself." * *Mus. herm.,* p. 105 (Waite, I, p. 93).
20 Dorn, "Phil. meditativa," *Theatr. chem.,* I, p. 467. "But piety is grace sent down
from God, which teaches every man to know himself as he really is" * ("De
tenebris," *Theatr. chem.,* I, p. 462).
21 Berthelot, *La Chimie au moyen âge,* III, p. 50.
22 *Theatr. chem.,* V, p. 144.
23 ". . . when you see the substances mingle in your distilling vessel." * *Mus. herm.,*
p. 685 (Waite, II, p. 187).
24 "Exercit. in Turbam," *Art. aurif.,* I, p. 159. Also in *Theatr. chem.,* I, p. 180.
25 Ripley, *Opera omnia,* pp. 38 and 81. Cf. also Ventura, *Theatr. chem.,* II, p. 291:
"Let a tomb therefore be dug and the woman buried with the dead man." * This
is a reference to *Turba,* Sermo LIX, but there the woman is buried with the
dragon (supra, par. 15).
26 *Mus. herm.,* p. 686 (Waite, II, p. 188). Cf. "Psychology of the Transference,"
par. 468.

658   The coniunctio does not always take the form of a direct union, since it needs—or occurs in—a medium: "Only through a medium can the transition take place," [27] and, "Mercurius is the medium of conjunction." [28] Mercurius is the soul (anima), which is the "mediator between body and spirit." [29] The same is true of the synonyms for Mercurius, the green lion [30] and the *aqua permanens* or spiritual water,[31] which are likewise media of conjunction. The "Consilium coniugii" mentions as a connective agent the sweet smell or "smoky vapour," [32] recalling Basilides' idea of the sweet smell of the Holy Ghost.[33] Obviously this refers to the "spiritual" nature of Mercurius, just as the spiritual water, also called *aqua aëris* (aerial water or air-water), is a life principle and the "marriage maker" between man and woman.[34] A common synonym for the water is the "sea," as the place where the chymical marriage is celebrated. The "Tractatus Micreris" mentions as further synonyms the "Nile of Egypt," the "Sea of the Indians," and the "Meridian Sea." The "marvels" of this sea are that it mitigates and unites the opposites.[35] An essential feature of the royal marriage is therefore the sea-journey, as described by Christian Rosencreutz.[36] This alchemical motif was taken up by Goethe in *Faust II*, where it underlies the meaning of the Aegean Festival. The archetypal content of this festival has been elaborated by Kerényi in a brilliant amplificatory interpretation. The bands of nereids on Roman sarcophagi reveal the "epithalamic and the sepulchral element," for "basic to the antique mysteries . . . is the identity of marriage and death on the one hand, and of birth and the eternal resurgence of life from death on the other." [37]

[27] Dorn, "Physica Trismegisti," *Theatr. chem.*, I, p. 418.* Cf. his remark "tertium esse necessarium" ("Congeries Paracelsicae," *Theatr. chem.*, I, p. 577).
[28] Ventura, *Theatr. chem.*, II, p. 320.*   [29] Ibid., p. 332.
[30] Ripley, "Axiomata philosophica," *Theatr. chem.*, II, p. 125. Similarly in *Mus. herm.*, p. 39 (Waite, I, p. 42).   [31] *Art. aurif.*, I, p. 281.
[32] *Ars chemica*, p. 74. The counterpart of the "Luna odorifera" mentioned here is the *odor sepulcrorum* (stench of the graves).
[33] Μύρον εὐωδέστατον. Hippolytus, *Elenchos*, VII, 22, 14.
[34] "The aerial water existing between earth and heaven is the life of everything. For that water dissolves the body into spirit, makes the dead to live, and brings about the marriage between man and woman." * (Mylius, *Phil. ref.*, p. 191.)
[35] "[It is able to] moisten what is dry, and to soften what is hard, and to conjoin and weaken bodies" * (*Theatr. chem.*, V, p. 111).   [36] *Chymical Wedding*.
[37] Kerényi, *Das Aegaeische Fest*, p. 55.

659   Mercurius, however, is not just the medium of conjunction but also that which is to be united, since he is the essence or "seminal matter" of both man and woman. *Mercurius masculinus* and *Mercurius foemineus* are united in and through *Mercurius menstrualis,* which is the "aqua." [38] Dorn gives the "philosophical" explanation of this in his "Physica Trismegisti": In the beginning God created *one* world (*unus mundus*).[39] This he divided into two—heaven and earth. "Beneath this spiritual and corporeal binarius lieth hid a third thing, which is the bond of holy matrimony. This same is the medium enduring until now in all things, partaking of both their extremes, without which it cannot be at all, nor they without this medium be what they are, one thing out of three." [40] The division into two was necessary in order to bring the "one" world out of the state of potentiality into reality. Reality consists of a multiplicity of things. But one is not a number; the first number is two, and with it multiplicity and reality begin.

660   It is apparent from this explanation that the desperately evasive and universal Mercurius—that Proteus twinkling in a myriad shapes and colours—is none other than the "unus mundus," the original, non-differentiated unity of the world or of Being; the ἀγνωσία of the Gnostics, the primordial unconsciousness.[41] The Mercurius of the alchemists is a personification and concretization of what we today would call the collective unconscious. While the concept of the *unus mundus* is a metaphysical speculation, the unconscious can be indirectly experienced via its manifestations. Though in itself an hypothesis, it has at least as great a probability as the hypothesis of the atom. It is clear from the empirical material at our disposal today that the contents of the unconscious, unlike conscious contents, are mutually con-

38 "Exercit. in Turbam," *Art. aurif.,* I, pp. 160f.

39 "In a way not unlike that in which God in the beginning created one world by meditation alone, so likewise he created one world, from which all things came into being by adaptation" * (*Theatr. chem.,* I, p. 417).

"Also, as there is only one God and not many, so he willed at first in his mind to create from nothing one world, and then to bring it about that all things which he created should be contained in it, that God in all things might be one" * (ibid., p. 415).

40 Ibid., p. 418.*

41 Cf. the "mountain" in which all knowledge is found, but no distinctions and no opposites. (Abu'l-Qasim Muhammad, *Kitāb al-'ilm al-muktasab,* p. 24.) Further material in *Psychology and Alchemy,* par. 516 and n. 1.

taminated to such a degree that they cannot be distinguished from one another and can therefore easily take one another's place, as can be seen most clearly in dreams. The indistinguishableness of its contents gives one the impression that everything is connected with everything else and therefore, despite their multifarious modes of manifestation, that they are at bottom a unity. The only comparatively clear contents consist of motifs or types round which the individual associations congregate. As the history of the human mind shows, these archetypes are of great stability and so distinct that they allow themselves to be personified and named, even though their boundaries are blurred or cut across those of other archetypes, so that certain of their qualities can be interchanged. In particular, mandala symbolism shows a marked tendency to concentrate all the archetypes on a common centre, comparable to the relationship of all conscious contents to the ego. The analogy is so striking that a layman unfamiliar with this symbolism is easily misled into thinking that the mandala is an artificial product of the conscious mind. Naturally mandalas can be imitated, but this does not prove that all mandalas are imitations. They are produced spontaneously, without external influence, even by children and adults who have never come into contact with any such ideas.[42] One might perhaps regard the mandala as a reflection of the egocentric nature of consciousness, though this view would be justified only if it could be proved that the unconscious is a secondary phenomenon. But the unconscious is undoubtedly older and more original than consciousness, and for this reason one could just as well call the egocentrism of consciousness a reflection or imitation of the "self"-centrism of the unconscious.

661 The mandala symbolizes, by its central point, the ultimate unity of all archetypes as well as of the multiplicity of the phenomenal world, and is therefore the empirical equivalent of the metaphysical concept of a *unus mundus*. The alchemical equivalent is the lapis and its synonyms, in particular the Microcosm.[43]

662 Dorn's explanation is illuminating in that it affords us a deep insight into the alchemical *mysterium coniunctionis*. If this is nothing less than a restoration of the original state of the cosmos and the divine unconsciousness of the world, we can un-

---

[42] See "Concerning Mandala Symbolism," par. 645.
[43] Cf. *Psychology and Alchemy*, par. 426 and n. 2, fig. 195.

derstand the extraordinary fascination emanating from this mystery. It is the Western equivalent of the fundamental principle of classical Chinese philosophy, namely the union of *yang* and *yin* in *tao,* and at the same time a premonition of that "tertium quid" which, on the basis of psychological experience on the one hand and of Rhine's experiments on the other, I have called "synchronicity." [44] If mandala symbolism is the psychological equivalent of the *unus mundus,* then synchronicity is its parapsychological equivalent. Though synchronistic phenomena occur in time and space they manifest a remarkable independence of both these indispensable determinants of physical existence and hence do not conform to the law of causality. The causalism that underlies our scientific view of the world breaks everything down into individual processes which it punctiliously tries to isolate from all other parallel processes. This tendency is absolutely necessary if we are to gain reliable knowledge of the world, but philosophically it has the disadvantage of breaking up, or obscuring, the universal interrelationship of events so that a recognition of the greater relationship, i.e., of the unity of the world, becomes more and more difficult. Everything that happens, however, happens in the same "one world" and is a part of it. For this reason events must possess an *a priori* aspect of unity, though it is difficult to establish this by the statistical method. So far as we can see at present, Rhine seems to have successfully demonstrated this unity by his extrasensory-perception experiments (ESP).[45] Independence of time and space brings about a concurrence or meaningful coincidence of events not causally connected with one another—phenomena which till now were summed under the purely descriptive concepts of telepathy, clairvoyance, and precognition. These concepts naturally have no explanatory value as each of them represents an X which cannot be distinguished from the X of the other. The characteristic feature of all these phenomena, including Rhine's psychokinetic effect and other synchronistic occurrences, is *meaningful coincidence,* and as such I have defined the synchronistic principle. This principle suggests that there is an inter-connection or unity of causally unrelated events, and thus postulates a

[44] Cf. my "Synchronicity: An Acausal Connecting Principle."
[45] Cf. his *New Frontiers of the Mind* and *The Reach of the Mind.* The relevant phenomena are discussed in "Synchronicity," pars. 833ff.

unitary aspect of being which can very well be described as the *unus mundus.*

663   Mercurius usually stands for the arcane substance, whose synonyms are the panacea and the "spagyric medicine." Dorn identifies the latter with the "balsam" [46] of Paracelsus, which is a close analogy of the μύρον of the Basilidians. In the *De vita longa* of Paracelsus, balsam as an *elixir vitae* is associated with the term "gamonymus," which might be rendered "having the name of matrimony." [47] Dorn thinks that the balsam, which "stands higher than nature," is to be found in the human body and is a kind of aetheric substance.[48] He says it is the best medicament not only for the body but also for the mind (*mens*). Though it is a corporeal substance, as a combination of the spirit and soul of the spagyric medicine it is essentially spiritual.[49]

We conclude that meditative philosophy consists in the overcoming of the body by mental union [*unio mentalis*]. This first union does not as yet make the wise man, but only the mental disciple of wisdom. The second union of the mind with the body shows forth the wise man, hoping for and expecting that blessed third union with the first unity [i.e., the *unus mundus*, the latent unity of the world]. May Almighty God grant that all men be made such, and may He be one in All.[50]

*   *   *

664   It is significant for the whole of alchemy that in Dorn's view a mental union was not the culminating point but merely the first stage of the procedure. The second stage is reached when the mental union, that is, the unity of spirit and soul, is conjoined with the body. But a consummation of the *mysterium coniunctionis* can be expected only when the unity of spirit, soul, and body is made one with the original *unus mundus*. This

---

46 Balsam occurs in Zosimos as a synonym for the *aqua permanens.* (Berthelot, *Alch. grecs*, III, xxv, 1.)

47 Cf. "Paracelsus as a Spiritual Phenomenon," par. 171.

48 "For there is in man's body a certain substance conformable to the ethereal, which preserves the other elemental parts in it and causes them to continue" * ("Phil. meditativa," *Theatr. chem.*, I, p. 456).

49 "And we do not deny that our spagyric medicine is corporeal, but we say that it is made spiritual when the spagyric spirit clothes it" * (ibid.). A synonym for balsam is the wine that is "duplex," i.e., both "philosophic" and "common" (ibid., p. 464).   50 Ibid., p. 456.*

third stage of the coniunctio was depicted [51] after the manner of an Assumption and Coronation of Mary, in which the Mother of God represents the body. The Assumption is really a wedding feast, the Christian version of the hierosgamos, whose originally incestuous nature played a great role in alchemy. The traditional incest always indicated that the supreme union of opposites expressed a combination of things which are related but of unlike nature.[52] This may begin with a purely intra-psychic *unio mentalis* of intellect or reason with Eros, representing feeling. Such an interior operation means a great deal, since it brings a considerable increase of self-knowledge as well as of personal maturity, but its reality is merely potential and is validated only by a union with the physical world of the body. The alchemists therefore pictured the *unio mentalis* as Father and Son and their union as the dove (the "spiration" common to both), but the world of the body they represented by the feminine or passive principle, namely Mary. Thus, for more than a thousand years, they prepared the ground for the dogma of the Assumption. It is true that the far-reaching implications of a marriage of the fatherly spiritual principle with the principle of matter, or maternal corporeality, are not to be seen from the dogma at first glance. Nevertheless, it does bridge over a gulf that seems unfathomable: the apparently irremediable separation of spirit from nature and the body. Alchemy throws a bright light on the background of the dogma, for the new article of faith expresses in symbolical form exactly what the adepts recognized as being the secret of their coniunctio. The correspondence is indeed so great that the old Masters could legitimately have declared that the new dogma has written the Hermetic secret in the skies. As against this it will be said that the alchemists smuggled the mystic or theological marriage into their obscure procedures. This is contradicted by the fact that the alchymical marriage is not only older than the corresponding formulation in the liturgy and of the Church Fathers but is

[51] For instance in Reusner's *Pandora*. Cf. *Psychology and Alchemy*, fig. 232.
[52] See "Psychology of the Transference," pars. 419ff. The incest symbolism is due to the intrusion of endogamous libido. The primitive "cross-cousin-marriage" was superseded by a pure exogamy which left the endogamous demands unsatisfied. It is these demands that come to the fore in incest symbolism.

based on classical and pre-Christian tradition.[53] The alchemical tradition cannot be brought into relationship with the Apocalyptic marriage of the Lamb. The highly differentiated symbolism of the latter (lamb and city) is itself an offshoot of the archetypal hierosgamos, just as this is the source for the alchemical idea of the coniunctio.

665 The adepts strove to realize their speculative ideas in the form of a chemical substance which they thought was endowed with all kinds of magical powers. This is the literal meaning of their uniting the *unio mentalis* with the body. For us it is certainly not easy to include moral and philosophical reflections in this amalgamation, as the alchemists obviously did. For one thing we know too much about the real nature of chemical combination, and for another we have a much too abstract conception of the mind to be able to understand how a "truth" can be hidden in matter or what an effective "balsam" must be like. Owing to medieval ignorance both of chemistry and of psychology, and the lack of any epistemological criticism, the two concepts could easily mix, so that things that for us have no recognizable connection with one another could enter into mutual relationship.

666 The dogma of the Assumption and the alchemical *mysterium coniunctionis* express the same fundamental thought even though in very different symbolism. Just as the Church insists on the literal taking up of the physical body into heaven, so the alchemists believed in the possibility, or even in the actual existence, of their stone or of the philosophical gold. In both cases belief was a substitute for the missing empirical reality. Even though alchemy was essentially more materialistic in its procedures than the dogma, both of them remain at the second, anticipatory stage of the coniunctio, the union of the *unio mentalis* with the body. Even Dorn did not venture to assert that he or any other adept had perfected the third stage in his lifetime. Naturally there were as many swindlers and dupes as ever who claimed to possess the lapis or golden tincture, or to be able to

---

[53] This is already the case with the alchemist Democritus, who probably lived at least as early as the 1st cent. A.D. For him it is a marriage of the natures. (Texts in Berthelot, *Alch. grecs*, II, i ff.) Significantly enough, the last and grandest example of an alchemical opus, Goethe's *Faust*, ends with the apotheosis of the Virgin Mother, Mary-Sophia, queen and goddess. The epithet "dea" also occurs in Mechthild of Magdeburg.

make it. But the more honest alchemists readily admitted that they had not yet plumbed the final secret.

667   One should not be put off by the physical impossibilities of dogma or of the coniunctio, for they are symbols in regard to which the allurements of rationalism are entirely out of place and miss the mark. If symbols mean anything at all, they are tendencies which pursue a definite but not yet recognizable goal and consequently can express themselves only in analogies. In this uncertain situation one must be content to leave things as they are, and give up trying to know anything beyond the symbol. In the case of dogma such a renunciation is reinforced by the fear of possibly violating the sanctity of a religious idea, and in the case of alchemy it was until very recently considered not worth while to rack one's brains over medieval absurdities. Today, armed with psychological understanding, we are in a position to penetrate into the meaning of even the most abstruse alchemical symbols, and there is no justifiable reason why we should not apply the same method to dogma. Nobody, after all, can deny that it consists of ideas which are born of man's imagining and thinking. The question of how far this thinking may be inspired by the Holy Ghost is not affected at all, let alone decided, by psychological investigation, nor is the possibility of a metaphysical background denied. Psychology cannot advance any argument either for or against the objective validity of any metaphysical view. I have repeated this statement in various places in order to give the lie to the obstinate and grotesque notion that a psychological explanation must necessarily be either psychologism or its opposite, namely a metaphysical assertion. The psychic is a phenomenal world in itself, which can be reduced neither to the brain nor to metaphysics.

668   I have just said that symbols are tendencies whose goal is as yet unknown.[54] We may assume that the same fundamental rules obtain in the history of the human mind as in the psychology of the individual. In psychotherapy it often happens that, long before they reach consciousness, certain unconscious tendencies betray their presence by symbols, occurring mostly in dreams but also in waking fantasies and symbolic actions. Often we have

[54] This does not contradict the statement that symbols are the best possible formulation of an idea whose referent is not clearly known. Such an idea is always based on a tendency to represent its referent in its own way.

the impression that the unconscious is trying to enter consciousness by means of all sorts of allusions and analogies, or that it is making more or less playful attempts to attract attention to itself. One can observe these phenomena very easily in a dream-series. The series I discussed in *Psychology and Alchemy* offers a good example.[55] Ideas develop from seeds, and we do not know what ideas will develop from what seeds in the course of history. The Assumption of the Virgin, for instance, is vouched for neither in Scripture nor in the tradition of the first five centuries of the Christian Church. For a long time it was officially denied even, but, with the connivance of the whole medieval and modern Church, it gradually developed as a "pious opinion" and gained so much power and influence that it finally succeeded in thrusting aside the necessity for scriptural proof and for a tradition going back to primitive times, and in attaining definition in spite of the fact that the content of the dogma is not even definable.[56] The papal declaration made a reality of what had long been condoned. This irrevocable step beyond the confines of historical Christianity is the strongest proof of the autonomy of archetypal images.

2. STAGES OF THE CONJUNCTION

669   The coniunctio affords another example of the gradual development of an idea in the course of the millennia. Its history flows in two main streams which are largely independent of one another: theology and alchemy. While alchemy has, except for a few traces, been extinct for some two hundred years, theology has put forth a new blossom in the dogma of the Assumption, from which it is evident that the stream of development has by no means come to a standstill. But the differentiation of the two streams has not yet passed beyond the framework of the archetypal hierosgamos, for the coniunctio is still represented as a union of mother and son or of a brother-sister pair. Already in the sixteenth century, however, Gerard Dorn had recognized the psychological aspect of the chymical marriage and clearly understood it as what we today would call the individuation process.

[55] Another example is the series of mandalas in "A Study in the Process of Individuation."
[56] Further material in Heiler, *Das neue Mariendogma im Lichte der Geschichte.*

This is a step beyond the bounds which were set to the coniunctio, both in ecclesiastical doctrine and in alchemy, by its
archetypal symbolism. It seems to me that Dorn's view represents a logical understanding of it in two respects: first because
the discrepancy between the chemical operation and the psychic
events associated with it could not remain permanently hidden
from an attentive and critical observer, and secondly because the
marriage symbolism obviously never quite satisfied the alchemical thinkers themselves, since they constantly felt obliged to
make use of other "uniting symbols," besides the numerous variants of the hierosgamos, to express the all but incomprehensible
nature of the mystery. Thus the coniunctio is represented by the
dragon embracing the woman in the grave,[57] or by two animals
fighting,[58] or by the king dissolving in water,[59] and so on. Similarly, in Chinese philosophy the meaning of *yang* is far from exhausted with its masculine connotation. It also means dry,
bright, and the south side of the mountain, just as the feminine
yin means damp, dark, and the north side of the mountain.

670   Although the esoteric symbolism of the coniunctio occupies
a prominent position, it does not cover all aspects of the mysterium. In addition we have to consider the symbolism of death
and the grave, and the motif of conflict. Obviously, very different if not contradictory symbolisms were needed to give an adequate description of the paradoxical nature of the conjunction.
In such a situation one can conclude with certainty that none of
the symbols employed suffices to express the whole. One therefore feels compelled to seek a formula in which the various aspects can be brought together without contradiction. Dorn attempted to do this with the means that were then at his disposal.
He could do so the more easily as the current idea of correspondentia came to his aid. For a man of those times there was
no intellectual difficulty in postulating a "truth" which was the
same in God, in man, and in matter. With the help of this idea
he could see at once that the reconciliation of hostile elements
and the union of alchemical opposites formed a "correspondence" to the *unio mentalis* which took place simultaneously in

---

[57] Cf. Emblema L in Maier's *Scrutinum chymicum*, p. 148. Cf. also *Turba,* Sermo
LIX.
[58] *Scrut. chymicum,* p. 46, and *Mus. herm.,* pp. 351, 357 (Waite, I, pp. 285, 291).
[59] "Merlini allegoria," *Art. aurif.,* I, p. 393.

the mind of man, and not only in man but in God ("that He may be one in All"). Dorn correctly recognized that the entity in which the union took place is the psychological authority which I have called the self. The *unio mentalis*, the interior oneness which today we call individuation, he conceived as a psychic equilibration of opposites "in the overcoming of the body," a state of equanimity transcending the body's affectivity and instinctuality.[60] The spirit (*animus*), which is to unite with the soul, he called a "spiracle [*spiraculum*] of eternal life," a sort of "window into eternity" (Leibniz), whereas the soul is an organ of the spirit and the body an instrument of the soul. The soul stands between good and evil and has the "option" of both. It animates the body by a "natural union," just as, by a "supernatural union," it is endowed with life by the spirit.[61]

671   But, in order to bring about their subsequent reunion, the mind (*mens*) must be separated from the body—which is equivalent to "voluntary death" [62]—for only separated things can unite. By this separation (*distractio*) Dorn obviously meant a discrimination and dissolution of the "composite," the composite state being one in which the affectivity of the body has a disturbing influence on the rationality of the mind. The aim of this separation was to free the mind from the influence of the "bodily appetites and the heart's affections," and to establish a spiritual position which is supraordinate to the turbulent sphere of the body. This leads at first to a dissociation of the personality and a violation of the merely natural man.

672   This preliminary step, in itself a clear blend of Stoic philosophy and Christian psychology, is indispensable for the differentiation of consciousness.[63] Modern psychotherapy makes use of the same procedure when it objectifies the affects and in-

60 "Therefore the mind is well said to be composed when the spirit and the soul are joined by such a bond that the bodily appetites and the heart's affections are restrained" * ("Phil. medit.," *Theatr. chem.*, I, p. 451).

61 Ibid., pp. 451f.

62 Here Dorn cites the "verbum Dei": "He that loveth his soul shall lose it, and he that hateth his soul preserveth it for ever" * (p. 453). Cf. Matthew 16 : 25, Luke 17 : 33, and John 12 : 25.

63 Cf. the parallel in Wei Po-yang: "Closed on all sides, its interior is made up of intercommunicating labyrinths. The protection is so complete as to turn back all that is devilish and undesirable. . . . Cessation of thought is desirable and worries are preposterous. The divine *ch'i* (air, spirit, ethereal essence) fills the quarters. . . . Whoever retains it will prosper and he who loses it, will perish." (P. 238.)

stincts and confronts consciousness with them. But the separation of the spiritual and the vital spheres, and the subordination of the latter to the rational standpoint, is not satisfactory inasmuch as reason alone cannot do complete or even adequate justice to the irrational facts of the unconscious. In the long run it does not pay to cripple life by insisting on the primacy of the spirit, for which reason the pious man cannot prevent himself from sinning again and again and the rationalist must constantly trip up over his own irrationalities. Only the man who hides the other side in artificial unconsciousness can escape this intolerable conflict. Accordingly, the chronic duel between body and spirit seems a better though by no means ideal solution. The advantage, however, is that both sides remain conscious. Anything conscious can be corrected, but anything that slips away into the unconscious is beyond the reach of correction and, its rank growth undisturbed, is subject to increasing degeneration. Happily, nature sees to it that the unconscious contents will irrupt into consciousness sooner or later and create the necessary confusion. A permanent and uncomplicated state of spiritualization is therefore such a rarity that its possessors are canonized by the Church.

673   Since the soul animates the body, just as the soul is animated by the spirit, she tends to favour the body and everything bodily, sensuous, and emotional. She lies caught in "the chains" of Physis, and she desires "beyond physical necessity." She must be called back by the "counsel of the spirit" from her lostness in matter and the world. This is a relief to the body too, for it not only enjoys the advantage of being animated by the soul but suffers under the disadvantage of having to serve as the instrument of the soul's appetites and desires. Her wish-fantasies impel it to deeds to which it would not rouse itself without this incentive, for the inertia of matter is inborn in it and probably forms its only interest except for the satisfaction of physiological instincts. Hence the separation means withdrawing the soul and her projections from the bodily sphere and from all environmental conditions relating to the body. In modern terms it would be a turning away from sensuous reality, a withdrawal of the fantasy-projections that give "the ten thousand things" their attractive and deceptive glamour. In other words, it means introversion, introspection, meditation, and the careful investiga-

tion of desires and their motives. Since, as Dorn says, the soul "stands between good and evil," the disciple will have every opportunity to discover the dark side of his personality, his inferior wishes and motives, childish fantasies and resentments, etc.; in short, all those traits he habitually hides from himself. He will be confronted with his shadow, but more rarely with the good qualities, of which he is accustomed to make a show anyway. He will learn to know his soul, that is, his anima and Shakti who conjures up a delusory world for him. He attains this knowledge, Dorn supposes, with the help of the spirit, by which are meant all the higher mental faculties such as reason, insight, and moral discrimination. But, in so far as the spirit is also a "window into eternity" and, as the *anima rationalis,* immortal, it conveys to the soul a certain "divine influx" and the knowledge of higher things, wherein consists precisely its supposed animation of the soul. This higher world has an impersonal character and consists on the one hand of all those traditional, intellectual, and moral values which educate and cultivate the individual, and, on the other, of the products of the unconscious, which present themselves to consciousness as archetypal ideas. Usually the former predominate. But when, weakened by age or by criticism, they lose their power of conviction, the archetypal ideas rush in to fill the gap. Freud, correctly recognizing this situation, called the traditional values the "super-ego," but the archetypal ideas remained unknown to him, as the belief in reason and the positivism of the nineteenth century never relaxed their hold. A materialistic view of the world ill accords with the reality and autonomy of the psyche.

674 The arcanum of alchemy is one of these archetypal ideas that fills a gap in the Christian view of the world, namely, the unbridged gulf between the opposites, in particular between good and evil. Only logic knows a *tertium non datur;* nature consists entirely of such "thirds," since she is represented by effects which resolve an opposition—just as a waterfall mediates between "above" and "below." The alchemists sought for that effect which would heal not only the disharmonies of the physical world but the inner psychic conflict as well, the "affliction of the soul"; and they called this effect the lapis Philosophorum. In order to obtain it, they had to loosen the age-old attachment of the soul to the body and thus make conscious the conflict be-

tween the purely natural and the spiritual man. In so doing they rediscovered the old truth that every operation of this kind is a figurative death [64]—which explains the violent aversion everybody feels when he has to see through his projections and recognize the nature of his anima. It requires indeed an unusual degree of self-abnegation to question the fictitious picture of one's own personality. This, nevertheless, is the requirement of any psychotherapy that goes at all deep, and one realizes how oversimplified its procedures are only when the analyst has to try out his own medicine on himself. One can, as experience has often shown, relieve oneself of the difficult act of self-knowledge by shutting out the moral criterion with so-called scientific objectivity or unvarnished cynicism. But this simply means buying a certain amount of insight at the cost of artificially repressing an ethical value. The result of this deception is that the insight is robbed of its efficacy, since the moral reaction is missing. Thus the foundations for a neurotic dissociation are laid, and this in no way corresponds to the psychotherapist's intention. The goal of the procedure is the *unio mentalis,* the attainment of full knowledge of the heights and depths of one's own character.

675   If the demand for self-knowledge is willed by fate and is refused, this negative attitude may end in real death. The demand would not have come to this person had he still been able to strike out on some promising by-path. But he is caught in a blind alley from which only self-knowledge can extricate him. If he refuses this then no other way is open to him. Usually he is not conscious of his situation, either, and the more unconscious he is the more he is at the mercy of unforeseen dangers: he cannot get out of the way of a car quickly enough, in climbing a mountain he misses his foothold somewhere, out skiing he thinks he can just negotiate a tricky slope, and in an illness he suddenly loses the courage to live. The unconscious has a thousand ways of snuffing out a meaningless existence with surprising swiftness. The connection of the *unio mentalis* with the death-motif is therefore obvious, even when death consists only in the cessation of spiritual progress.

676   The alchemists rightly regarded "mental union in the over-

[64] The *distractio* is something that "some call voluntary death." Cf. the death of the royal pair in *Ros. phil.,* discussed in "Psychology of the Transference," pars. 467ff.

474

coming of the body" as only the first stage of conjunction or individuation, in the same way that Khunrath understood Christ as the "Saviour of the Microcosm" but not of the Macrocosm, whose saviour was the lapis.[65] In general, the alchemists strove for a *total* union of opposites in symbolic form, and this they regarded as the indispensable condition for the healing of all ills. Hence they sought to find ways and means to produce that substance in which all opposites were united. It had to be material as well as spiritual, living as well as inert, masculine as well as feminine, old as well as young, and—presumably—morally neutral. It had to be created by man, and at the same time, since it was an "increatum," by God himself, the *Deus terrestris.*

677   The second step on the way to the production of this substance was the reunion of the spirit with the body. For this procedure there were many symbols. One of the most important was the chymical marriage, which took place in the retort. The older alchemists were still so unconscious of the psychological implications of the opus that they understood their own symbols as mere allegories or—semiotically—as secret names for chemical combinations, thus stripping mythology, of which they made such copious use, of its true meaning and using only its terminology. Later this was to change, and already in the fourteenth century it began to dawn on them that the lapis was more than a chemical compound. This realization expressed itself mainly in the Christ-parallel.[66] Dorn was probably the first to recognize the psychological implications for what they were, so far as this was intellectually possible for a man of that age. Proof of this is his demand that the pupil must have a good physical and, more particularly, a good moral constitution.[67] A religious attitude was essential.[68] For in the individual was hidden that "substance of celestial nature known to very few," the "incorrupt medicament" which "can be freed from its fetters, not by its contrary but by its like." The "spagyric medicine" whereby it

65 Cf. supra, par. 355.

66 Early references are given in *Psychology and Alchemy,* pars. 453f.

67 "It is impossible for a man of evil life to possess the treasure that is concealed from the sons of wisdom, and he is unfit to acquire it or to search it out, much less to find it" * ("Phil. medit.," p. 457).

68 "I have thought it right to admonish the disciples to implore the divine aid, and [to remind them] of the need for the most careful diligence in preparing themselves for the reception of this grace" * (ibid.).

is freed must be "conformable to this substance." The medicine "prepares" the body so that the separation can be undertaken. For, when the body is "prepared," it can be separated more easily from "the other parts."

678   Like all alchemists, Dorn naturally did not reveal what the spagyric medicine was. One can only suppose that it was thought of as physical, more or less. At the same time he says that a certain asceticism is desirable, and this may be a reference to the moral nature of the mysterious panacea. At any rate he hastens to add that the "assiduous reader" will thenceforth advance from the meditative philosophy to the spagyric and thence to the true and perfect wisdom. It sounds as if the assiduous reader had been engaged at the outset in reading and meditating, and as if the medicine and the preparation of the body consisted precisely in that.[69] Just as for Paracelsus the right "theoria" was part of the panacea, so for the alchemists was the symbol, which expresses the unconscious projections. Indeed, it is these that make the substance magically effective, and for this reason they cannot be separated from the alchemical procedure whose integral components they are.

679   The second stage of conjunction, the re-uniting of the *unio mentalis* with the body, is particularly important, as only from here can the complete conjunction be attained—union with the *unus mundus*. The reuniting of the spiritual position with the body obviously means that the insights gained should be made real. An insight might just as well remain in abeyance if it is simply not used. The second stage of conjunction therefore consists in making a reality of the man who has acquired some knowledge of his paradoxical wholeness.

680   The great difficulty here, however, is that no one knows how the paradoxical wholeness of man can ever be realized. That is the crux of individuation, though it becomes a problem only when the loophole of "scientific" or other kinds of cynicism is not used. Because the realization of the wholeness that has been made conscious is an apparently insoluble task and faces the psychologist with questions which he can answer only with hesitation and uncertainty, it is of the greatest interest to see how the

---

69 "I am the true medicine [says Wisdom], correcting and transmuting that which *is no longer* into that which it *was before* its corruption, and that which *is not* into that which it *ought to be*." * (Ibid., p. 459).

more unencumbered symbolical thinking of a medieval "philosopher" tackled this problem. The texts that have come down to us do not encourage the supposition that Dorn was conscious of the full range of his undertaking. Although in general he had a clear grasp of the role the adept played in the alchemical process, the problem did not present itself to him in all its acuteness, because only a part of it was enacted in the moral and psychological sphere, while for the rest it was hypostatized in the form of certain magical properties of the living body, or as a magical substance hidden within it. This projection spread over the problem a kind of mist which obscured its sharp edges. The alchemists still believed that metaphysical assertions could be proved (even today we have still not entirely freed ourselves from this somewhat childish assumption), and they could therefore entrench themselves behind seemingly secure positions in the Beyond, which they were confident would not be shaken by any doubts. In this way they were able to procure for themselves considerable alleviations. One has only to think what it means if in the misery and incertitude of a moral or philosophical dilemma one has a *quinta essentia,* a lapis or a panacea so to say in one's pocket! We can understand this *deus ex machina* the more easily when we remember with what passion people today believe that psychological complications can be made magically to disappear by means of hormones, narcotics, insulin shocks, and convulsion therapy. The alchemists were as little able to perceive the symbolical nature of their ideas of the arcanum as we to recognize that the belief in hormones and shocks is a symbol. We would indignantly dismiss such an interpretation as a nonsensical suggestion.

3. THE PRODUCTION OF THE QUINTESSENCE

681   Much of Dorn's argument moves in the sphere of symbols and soars on winged feet into the clouds. But that does not prevent his symbols from having a more mundane meaning which appears more or less accessible to our psychology. Thus, he knew that even the wise man could not reconcile the opposites unless "a certain heavenly substance hidden in the human body" came to his help, namely the "balsam," the quintessence, the "philo-

477

sophic wine," [70] a "virtue and heavenly vigour" [71]—in short, the "truth." [72] This truth was the panacea. It is only indirectly hidden in the body, since in reality it consists in the *imago Dei* imprinted in man. This imago is the true quintessence and the "virtue" of the philosophic wine. The latter is therefore an apt synonym, because wine in the form of a liquid represents the body, but as alcohol it represents spirit, which would seem to correspond with the "heavenly virtue." This, although divided up among individuals, is universal; it is *one,* and when "freed from its fetters in the things of sense" it returns to its original state of unity. "This is one of the secrets of nature, whereby the spagyrics have attained to higher things." [73] The "wine" can be prepared from grain [74] and from all other seeds.[75] The extracted essence is reduced to its "greatest simplicity" by "assiduous rotary movements," [76] whereby the pure is separated from the impure:

Then you will see the pureness floating to the top, transparent, shining, and of the colour of purest air. . . .[77] You will see the heretofore spagyric [i.e., secret] heaven, which you can bedeck with the lower stars, as the upper heaven is bedecked with the upper stars. . . .[78] Will now the unbelievers, who have imitated the Physicists, marvel that we handle in our hands the heaven and the stars? . . . For us, therefore, the lower stars are all individuals produced by nature in this lower world by their conjunction with heaven, like [the conjunction] of the higher with the lower elements.[79] Now I

[70] The vinum philosophicum contains the *essentia caelestis.* ("Phil. medit.," p. 464.)   [71] P. 457.

[72] "But truth is the supreme virtue and an impregnable stronghold" * (p. 458).

[73] P. 464.*   [74] "Grana" can also mean grape-pips.

[75] For details of this procedure see infra.

[76] P. 465.

[77] Cf. Rupescissa, *La Vertu et la propriété de la quinte essence.* The quintessence is the equivalent of heaven (p. 15). It is also called "esprit du vin" and "eau de vie." It is the "ciel humain" (p. 17), "de la couleur du ciel" (p. 19).

[78] Dorn is probably referring here to the magical procedure described in the second part of Artefius, "Clavis maioris sapientiae" (*Bibl. chem.,* I, pp. 503ff., and *Theatr. chem.,* IV, pp. 236ff.), whereby the planetary spirits who are needed in order to unite the spirit or soul with the body, and to transform the latter, are compelled to descend. Cf. the pictures of the coniunctio in the bath in the Ripley Scrowle and its variants, one of which is given in *Psychology and Alchemy,* fig. 257.

[79] "Phil. medit.," p. 466. "Sunt igitur stellae nobis inferiores individua quaevis a natura hoc in mundo inferiori producta coniunctione videlicet earum et caeli tanquam superiorum cum inferioribus elementis" (*Theatr. chem.,* 1602, I, p. 466).

hear the voice of many raging against us, and crying out, Avaunt! let those men be destroyed who say that heaven can conjoin itself to earth . . .

682   The caelum therefore is a heavenly substance and a universal form, containing in itself all forms, distinct from one another, but proceeding from one single universal form. Wherefore, he who knows how individuals can be led on to the most general genus by the spagyric art, and how the special virtues, one or more, can be impressed upon this genus, will easily find the universal medicine. . . . For since there is one single and most general beginning of all corruptions, and one universal fount of regenerating, restoring, and life-giving virtues, who, save a man bereft of his senses, will call such a medicine in doubt? [80]

683   Through the alchemical treatment of the "grana" (or grape-pips),

our Mercurius is concocted by the highest sublimation [*exaltatione*]. The mixture of the new heaven, of honey,[81] Chelidonia,[82]

[80] Ibid., pp. 465f.

[81] "The elixir of honey preserves and cleanses the human body from all imperfections, both within and without" (Penotus, *Theatr. chem.*, I, p. 730). The first chapter of Paracelsus' *Lumen apothecariorum* (Huser, VII, pp. 222ff.; Sudhoff, II, 193ff.) is devoted to honey. In the "third elevation" the honey becomes a "deadly poison," like "Tartarus mortalis." *Von den Tartarischen Krankheiten*, cap. XIV (Huser, II, p. 239; Sudhoff, XI, pp. 88f.). It contains "Tartarum" (Huser, p. 223). It occurs in Zosimos as the *aqua permanens* (Berthelot, *Alch. grecs*, III, xxv, 1). Both here and in the *Turba* (Sermo XXXVII (p. 16) it forms, with vinegar, a pair of opposites.

[82] "Chelidonia" occurs as a secret name in the version of the *Turba* given in *Art. aurif.*, I, pp. 1ff., which does not differ appreciably from Ruska's text: "Some philosophers have named gold Chelidonia, Karnech, Geldum." * Ruska explains "Geldum" as "Chelidonium maius L." (p. 28). Dioscorides (*Materia medica*, II, cap. 176, p. 302) says that with this herb swallows cure blindness in their young. In the Herbal of Tabernaemontanus (I, p. 106) it is cited as an eye-salve (against night-blindness). In Ruland (*Lexicon*, p. 98) Chelidonia is a pseudonym for gold (presumably on account of its yellow flowers). In the maws of young swallows two small stones are found, the "lapides Chelidonii," one of them black, the other red (ibid., pp. 98–99). On account of its colour, the eye-salve (*Succus chelidoniae*) is used to extract the moisture (soul) of Mercurius. (Dorn, "Congeries Paracelsicae," *Theatr. chem.*, I, p. 582). Sal Chelidoniae is mentioned as an "emmenagogue and solvent" (I, p. 759). Chelidonia is a name for the lapis (IV, p. 822) and a cure for insanity (V, p. 432). In Paracelsus there are four Chelidonias synonymous with "anthos" (*Paragranum*, Part II, "De philosophia"; Sudhoff, VIII, pp. 68–90). (Cf. "Cheyri" in "Paracelsus as a Spiritual Phenomenon," par. 171 and n. 7.) Chelidonia is a preservative against thunderstorms (*De phil. occulta*, Huser, IX, p. 361, Sudhoff, XIV, p. 537).

rosemary flowers,[83] Mercurialis,[84] of the red lily[85] and human blood,[86] with the heaven of the red or white wine or of Tartarus, can be undertaken. . . .[87] One can also make another mixture, namely that of heaven and the philosophical key,[88] by the artifice of generation.

684   Here even Dorn remarks that the reader will hold his breath, adding:

It is true that these things are scarcely to be understood [*vix intelligibilia*] unless one has full knowledge of the terms used in the art, and these we consider we have defined in the second stage, treating of meditative knowledge. Meditative knowledge is thus the sure and undoubted resolution by expert certitude, of all manner of opinions concerning the truth. But opinion is an anticipation [*praesumptio*] of the truth, fixed in the mind and doubtful. Experiment, on the other hand, is manifest demonstration of the truth, and resolution the putting away of doubt. We cannot be resolved of any doubt save by experiment, and there is no better way to make it than on ourselves. . . . We have said earlier that piety consists in knowledge of ourselves, and hence we begin to explain meditative knowledge from this also. But no man can truly know himself unless first he

[83] "Ros" (dew) = *aqua permanens*. According to Tabernaemontanus, rosemary is an alexipharmic (p. 312).

[84] Tabernaemontanus (II, pp. 940ff.) says that *Mercurialis testiculata* (Dog's mercury) was found, like moly, by Mercurius, has a divided sex and is an emmenagogue. According to Dioscorides, Mercurialis, inserted into the vagina, determines the sex of the child (*Mat. med.*, lib. IV, cap. 183, p. 559). "Mercurialis saeva: Water of Alum wherein Mercury is generated. It is . . . of a golden colour" (Ruland, *Lexicon*, p. 231).

[85] Lilium = Mercurius and *quinta essentia sulphuris* (Ruland, p. 207). "The Lily of Alchemy and Medicine . . . this is the noblest thing of all the manifestations of the supreme Creator which man may meditate upon." * (Dorn, "Congeries Paracelsicae," p. 608.) *Anthera* (presumably stamen) *liliorum* is given in Paracelsus as an alexipharmic (*Scholia in poëmata Macri*, Huser, VII, p. 268, Sudhoff, III, p. 414). The *succus liliorum* is "mercurial" and "incombustible" (Grasseus, "Arca arcani," *Theatr. chem.*, VI, p. 327). Coniunctio of the white and red lily (ibid., p. 335).

[86] Blood is a synonym for the red tincture (= aqua permanens), a preliminary stage of the lapis (Ruland, p. 286). *Sanguis hominis ruffi* = Sulphur = *Mercurius solis* (ibid.).

[87] Penotus (*Theatr. chem.*, I, p. 749) says of tartar: "It performs wonderful things in the spagyric art, for by its mediation the light of day is turned into the prima materia." * *Saturnus calcinatus* was named by Ripley the "tartar from black grapes" (Orthelius, *Theatr. chem.*, VI, p. 471).

[88] This probably refers to the treatise of Artefius (n. 78).

see and know by zealous meditation . . . *what* rather than *who* he is, on whom he depends, and whose he is, and to what end he was made and created, and by whom and through whom.

685   God made man to partake of his glory and created him in his image. "Even as we were created of the basest and most worthless clay, despised of all, so and no otherwise, by reason of the prime matter whereof we consist, are we more prone to everything vile than to him who out of vile matter created us of old to be most precious creatures, adorned with glory and honour little less than the angels." From the basest matter God created gold and precious stones. Therefore, knowing our nature and our origin, we should abstain from pride, for God looks not upon the person but upon poverty and humility and hates pride. Only he who made the water and the wine can change the one into the other, and so also the earth into a living soul, and he endued it with his image and likeness for the certainty of our salvation. Nevertheless we became rebels through the sin of Adam, but God was reconciled with us. "Who will be so stony [*lapideus*], when he shall revolve in his mind the mystery of the divine goodness, as not to be reconciled with his enemy, however great the injury he received from him?" He who knows God will know his brother also. This is the foundation of the true philosophy. And he who observes all this in himself and frees his mind from all worldly cares and distractions,[89] "little by little and from day to day will perceive with his mental eyes and with the greatest joy some sparks of divine illumination." The soul, moved by this, will unite with the body:

At length the body is compelled to resign itself to, and obey, the union of the two that are united [soul and spirit].[90] That is the wondrous transformation of the Philosophers, of body into spirit, and of the latter into body, of which there has been left to us by the sages the saying, Make the fixed volatile and the volatile fixed,[91] and in this you have our Magistery. Understand this after the following manner: Make the unyielding body tractable, so that by the excellence of the spirit coming together with the soul it becomes a most

89 "Phil. medit.," pp. 470f.

90 "Corpus tandem in amborum iam unitorum unionem condescendere cogitur et obedire."

91 Perhaps this saying lies at the root of the word "spagyric," from σπάειν, 'to rend, tear, stretch out,' ἀγείρειν, 'to bring or collect together.'

stable body ready to endure all trials. For gold is tried in the fire.
. . . Draw near, ye who seek the treasures in such diverse ways, know
the rejected stone which is made the head of the corner. . . . . In
vain do they labour, all searchers after the hidden secrets of nature,
when, looking for another way of ingress, they seek to reveal the virtues of earthly things through earthly things. Learn not heaven
therefore through the earth, but learn the virtues of one by those of
the other. Seek the incorruptible medicine which not only transmutes bodies from corruption to their true disposition [*tempera-
mentum*], but preserves those so disposed [*temperata*] for any length
of time. Such medicine you can find nowhere but in heaven. For
heaven, by virtue of invisible rays coming together from all sides in
the centre of the earth, penetrates, generates, and nourishes all elements, and all things that arise from the elements. This child of the
two parents, of the elements and heaven, has in itself such a nature
that the potentiality and actuality [*potentia et actu*] of both parents
can be found in it. What will remain there till today [i.e., in the
centre of the earth], save the stone in the spagyric generation? [92]
Learn from within thyself to know all that is in heaven and on earth,
and especially that all was created for thy sake. Knowest thou not
that heaven and the elements were formerly one, and were separated
from one another by divine artifice, that they might bring forth thee
and all things? If thou knowest this, the rest cannot escape thee.
Therefore in all generation a separation of this kind is necessary.
. . . Thou wilt never make from others the One which thou seekest,
except first there be made one thing of thyself . . .[93]

4. THE MEANING OF THE ALCHEMICAL PROCEDURE

686   Thus Dorn describes the secret of the second stage of conjunction. To the modern mind such contrivances of thought
will seem like nebulous products of a dreaming fancy. So, in a
sense, they are, and for this reason they lend themselves to de-
cipherment by the method of complex psychology. In his attempt to make the obviously confused situation clearer, Dorn
involved himself in a discussion of the ways and means for producing the quintessence, which was evidently needed for uniting the *unio mentalis* with the body. One naturally asks oneself
how this alchemical procedure enters into it at all. The *unio*

[92] "Quis haerebit adhuc nisi lapis in generatione spagirica?" That is to say, the
centre of the earth and the stone correspond.
[93] Pp. 466ff.

mentalis is so patently a spiritual and moral attitude that one cannot doubt its psychological nature. To our way of thinking, this immediately sets up a dividing wall between the psychic and the chemical process. For us the two things are incommensurable, but they were not so for the medieval mind. It knew nothing of the nature of chemical substances and their combination. It saw only enigmatic substances which, united with one another, inexplicably brought forth equally mysterious new substances. In this profound darkness the alchemist's fantasy had free play and could playfully combine the most inconceivable things. It could act without restraint and, in so doing, portray itself without being aware of what was happening.

687   The free-ranging psyche of the adept used chemical substances and processes as a painter uses colours to shape out the images of his fancy. If Dorn, in order to describe the union of the *unio mentalis* with the body, reaches out for his chemical substances and implements, this only means that he was illustrating his fantasies by chemical procedures. For this purpose he chose the most suitable substances, just as the painter chooses the right colours. Honey, for instance, had to go into the mixture because of its purifying quality. As a Paracelsist, Dorn knew from the writings of the Master what high praises he had heaped upon it, calling it the "sweetness of the earths," the "resin of the earth" which permeates all growing things, the "Indian spirit" which is turned by the "influence of summer" into a "corporeal spirit." [94] Thereby the mixture acquired the property not only of eliminating impurities but of changing spirit into body, and in view of the proposed conjunction of the spirit and the body this seemed a particularly promising sign. To be sure, the "sweetness of the earths" was not without its dangers, for as we have seen (n. 81) the honey could change into a deadly poison. According to Paracelsus it contains "Tartarum," which as its name implies has to do with Hades. Further, Tartarum is a "calcined Saturn" and consequently has affinities with this malefic planet. For another ingredient Dorn takes Chelidonia (*Chelidonium maius,* celandine), which cures eye diseases and is particularly good for night-blindness, and even heals the spiritual "benightedness" (affliction of the soul, melancholy-madness) so much feared by the adepts. It protects against

[94] *Lumen apothecariorum* (Huser, VII, pp. 222ff.).

"thunderstorms," i.e., outbursts of affect. It is a precious ingredient, because its yellow flowers symbolize the philosophical gold, the highest treasure. What is more important here, it draws the humidity, the "soul," [95] out of Mercurius. It therefore assists the "spiritualization" of the body and makes visible the essence of Mercurius, the supreme chthonic spirit. But Mercurius is also the devil.[96] Perhaps that is why the section in which Lagneus defines the nature of Mercurius is entitled "Dominus vobiscum." [97]

688   In addition, the plant Mercurialis (dog's mercury) is indicated. Like the Homeric magic herb Moly, it was found by Hermes himself and must therefore have magical effects. It is particularly favourable to the coniunctio because it occurs in male and female form and thus can determine the sex of a child about to be conceived. Mercurius himself was said to be generated from an extract of it—that spirit which acts as a mediator (because he is *utriusque capax*, "capable of either") and saviour of the Macrocosm, and is therefore best able to unite the above with the below. In his ithyphallic form as Hermes Kyllenios, he contributes the attractive power of sexuality, which plays a great role in the coniunctio symbolism.[98] Like honey, he is dangerous because of his possibly poisonous effect, for which reason it naturally seemed advisable to our author to add rosemary to the mixture as an alexipharmic (antidote) and a synonym for Mercurius (*aqua permanens*), perhaps on the principle that "like cures like." Dorn could hardly resist the temptation to exploit the alchemical allusion to "ros marinus," sea-dew. In agreement with ecclesiastical symbolism there was in alchemy, too, a "dew of grace," the *aqua vitae,* the perpetual, permanent, and two-meaninged ὕδωρ θεῖον, divine water or sulphur water. The water was also called *aqua pontica* (sea-water) or simply "sea." This was the great sea over which the alchemist sailed in his mystic peregrination, guided by the "heart" of Mercurius in the heavenly North Pole, to which nature herself points with the magnetic compass.[99] It was also the bath of regeneration, the spring

95 The essence.
96 Cf. "The Spirit Mercurius," par. 276.
97 "Harmonia chemica," *Theatr. chem.,* IV, p. 820.
98 Cf. "The Spirit Mercurius," par. 278.
99 Cf. *Psychology and Alchemy,* par. 265, also *Aion,* par. 206.

rain which brings forth the vegetation, and the "aqua doctrinae."

689   Another alexipharmic is the lily. But it is much more than that: its juice is "mercurial" and even "incombustible," a sure sign of its incorruptible and "eternal" nature. This is confirmed by the fact that the lily was conceived to be Mercurius and the quintessence itself—the noblest thing that human meditation can reach (see n. 85). The red lily stands for the male and the white for the female in the coniunctio, the divine pair that unite in the hierosgamos. The lily is therefore a true "gamonymus" in the Paracelsan sense.

690   Finally, the mixture must not lack the thing that really keeps body and soul together: human blood, which was regarded as the seat of the soul.[100] It was a synonym for the red tincture, a preliminary stage of the lapis; moreover, it was an old-established magic charm, a "ligament" for binding the soul either to God or the devil, and hence a powerful medicine for uniting the *unio mentalis* with the body. The admixture of human blood seems to me unusual if one assumes that the recipe was meant literally. We move here on uncertain ground. Although the vegetable ingredients are obviously indicated because of their symbolic value, we still do not know exactly how far the symbolism had a magical quality. If it had, then the recipe must be taken literally. In the case of blood, increased doubts arise because either it was simply a synonym for the *aqua permanens* and could then be practically any liquid, or else real blood was meant, and then we must ask where this blood came from. Could it have been the adept's? This problem seems to me not entirely irrelevant, since Dorn, in his "Philosophia meditativa," was greatly influenced, as we shall see, by the Sabaean "Liber quartorum," which he obviously knew although he did not mention it. The Sabaeans were reputed to have sacrificed human victims for magical purposes,[101] and even today human blood is used for signing pacts with the devil. It is also not so long since tramps were made

100 So, too, in Paracelsus, where the soul, Melusine, lives in the blood. Cf. "Paracelsus as a Spiritual Phenomenon," par. 180.

101 Cf. the passage from the Fihrist-el-U'lum of Muhammad ibn Ishak al-Nadim in Chwolsohn, *Die Ssabier und der Ssabismus,* II, pp. 19f., describing the maceration of a man's body in oil and borax. The head of the corpse was then used as an oracle. See also the report by Laurens van der Post in "Transformation Symbolism in the Mass," par. 370.

drunk and quickly immured on a building site in order to make the foundations safe. A magical recipe of the sixteenth century, therefore, might easily have used human blood as a *pars pro toto*.

691   This whole mixture was then joined "with the heaven of the red or white wine or of Tartarus." The *caelum*, as we have seen, was the product of the alchemical procedure, which in this case consisted in first distilling the "philosophic wine." Thereby the soul and spirit were separated from the body and repeatedly sublimated until they were free from all "phlegm," i.e., from all liquid that contained no more "spirit." [102] The residue, called the *corpus* (body), was reduced to ashes in the "most vehement fire" and, hot water being added, was changed into a *lixivium asperrimum*, "very sharp lye," which was then carefully poured off the ashes by tilting the vessel. The residue was treated in the same way again, until in the end no "asperitas" remained in the ashes. The lye was filtered and then evaporated in a glass vessel. What was left over was *tartarum nostrum* ("our winestone," *calculus vini*), the natural "salt of all things." This salt "can be dissolved into tartaric water, in a damp and cool place on a slab of marble." [103] The tartaric water was the quintessence of the philosophic and even of ordinary wine, and was then subjected to the above-mentioned rotation. As in a centrifuge, the pure was separated from the impure, and a liquid "of the colour of the air" floated to the top. This was the *caelum*.

692   I have detailed this process in order to give the reader a direct impression of the alchemical procedure. One can hardly suppose that all this is mere poppycock, for Dorn was a man who obviously took things seriously. So far as one can judge he meant what he said, and he himself worked in the laboratory. Of course

---

[102] Cf. the description of the *caput mortuum* in Christianos: ". . . black and soulless and dead, and so to speak unbreathing." * (Berthelot, *Alch. grecs*, VI, xii, 1.) Phlegm has also a moral connotation: "Sow likewise thy wisdom in our hearts, expel from them the phlegm, the corrupt choler and boiling blood, and lead us in the ways of the blessed" * ("Allegoriae sap.," *Theatr. chem.*, V, p. 66). The residue, the "black earth," is the ash of which the "Tractatus Micreris" says: "Despise not the ashes . . . for in them is the diadem, the ash of the things that endure" * (*Theatr. chem.*, V, p. 104).

[103] There is in man a "marmoreus tartarus," a "very hard stone" (Ruland, p. 220). Bowls of marble or serpentine are said to give protection against poison. (Hellwig, *Lexikon Medico-Chymicum*, p. 162.) "Know also that the spirit is enclosed in a house of marble; open therefore the passages that the dead spirit may come forth" * ("Alleg. sap.," p. 66).

we do not know what success he had chemically, but we are sufficiently informed about the results of his meditative exertions.

693   The *caelum*, for Dorn, was the celestial substance hidden
in man, the secret "truth," the "sum of virtue," the "treasure
which is not eaten into by moths nor dug out by thieves." In the
world's eyes it is the cheapest thing, but "to the wise more
worthy of love than precious stones and gold, a good that passeth
not away, and is taken hence after death." [104] The reader will
gather from this that the adept was describing nothing less than
the kingdom of heaven on earth. I think that Dorn was not exag-
gerating, but that he wanted to communicate to his public something very important to him. He believed in the necessity of the
alchemical operation as well as in its success; he was convinced
that the quintessence was needed for the "preparation" of the
body,[105] and that the body was so much improved by this "universal medicine" that the coniunctio with spirit and soul could
be consummated. If the production of the *caelum* from wine is a
hair-raising chemical fantasy, our understanding ceases altogether when the adept mixes this heaven with his "gamony-
mous" and other magical herbs. But if the one consists mainly
of fantasies so does the other. This makes it interesting. Fantasies always mean something when they are spontaneous. The
question then arises: what is the psychological meaning of the
procedure?

5. THE PSYCHOLOGICAL INTERPRETATION OF THE PROCEDURE

694   The answer to this question concerns us very closely, because
here we come upon something that is of particular interest to
modern psychology: the adept produces a system of fantasies that
has a special meaning for him. Although he keeps within the
general framework of alchemical ideas, he does not repeat a prescribed pattern, but, following his own fancy, devises an individual series of ideas and corresponding actions which it is
evident have a symbolic character. He starts with the production
of the medicine that will unite the *unio mentalis,* his spiritual
position, with the body. The ambiguity already begins here: is

104 Dorn, "Phil. medit.," pp. 457f. Obviously, therefore, the immortal part of man.
105 "Therefore, for the preparation of a good disposition of the body, we make
use of the spagyric medicine" (ibid., p. 457).*

the "corpus" his human body or the chemical substance? Apparently it is, to start off with, his living body, which as everyone knows has different desires from the spirit. But hardly has the chemical process got under way than the "body" is what remains behind in the retort from the distillation of the wine, and this "phlegm" is then treated like the subtle body of the soul in the purgatorial fire. Like it, the residue from the wine must pass through many subliming fires until it is so purified that the "air-coloured" quintessence can be extracted from it.

695   This singular identity, simply postulated and never taken as a problem, is an example of that "participation mystique" which Lévy-Bruhl very rightly stressed as being characteristic of the primitive mentality.[106] The same is true of the unquestionably psychic *unio mentalis,* which is at the same time a substance-like "truth" hidden in the body, which in turn coincides with the quintessence sublimed from the "phlegm." It never occurred to the mind of the alchemists to cast any doubt whatsoever on this intellectual monstrosity. We naturally think that such a thing could happen only in the "dark" Middle Ages. As against this I must emphasize that we too have not quite got out of the woods in this respect, for a philosopher once assured me in all seriousness that "thought could not err," and a very famous professor, whose assertions I had ventured to criticize, came out with the magisterial dictum: "It must be right because I have thought it."

696   All projections are unconscious identifications with the object. Every projection is simply there as an uncriticized datum of experience, and is recognized for what it is only very much later, if ever. Everything that we today would call "mind" and "insight" was, in earlier centuries, projected into things, and even today individual idiosyncrasies are presupposed by many people to be generally valid. The original, half-animal state of unconsciousness was known to the adept as the *nigredo,* the chaos, the *massa confusa,* an inextricable interweaving of the soul with the body, which together formed a dark unity (the *unio naturalis*). From this enchainment he had to free the soul by

---

106 Lévy-Bruhl's view has recently been disputed by ethnologists, not because this phenomenon does not occur among primitives, but because they have not understood it. Like so many other specialists, these critics prefer to know nothing of the psychology of the unconscious.

means of the *separatio,* and establish a spiritual-psychic counter-position—conscious and rational insight—which would prove immune to the influences of the body. But such insight, as we have seen, is possible only if the delusory projections that veil the reality of things can be withdrawn. The unconscious identity with the object then ceases and the soul is "freed from its fetters in the things of sense." The psychologist is well acquainted with this process, for a very important part of his psychotherapeutic work consists in making conscious and dissolving the projections that falsify the patient's view of the world and impede his self-knowledge. He does this in order to bring anomalous psychic states of an affective nature, i.e., neurotic symptoms, under the control of consciousness. The declared aim of the treatment is to set up a rational, spiritual-psychic position over against the turbulence of the emotions.

697   Projections can be withdrawn only when they come within the possible scope of consciousness. Outside that, nothing can be corrected. Thus, in spite of all his efforts, Dorn was unable to recognize the—for us—blatant projection of psychic contents into chemical substances and thereby dissolve it. Evidently his understanding in this respect still moved within the confines of the contemporary consciousness, even though in other respects it plumbed to greater depths than did the collective consciousness of that age. Thus it is that the psychic sphere representing the body miraculously appeared to the adept to be identical with chemical preparation in the retort. Hence he could believe that any changes he effected in the latter would happen to the former as well. Significantly enough, one seldom hears of the panacea or lapis being applied to the human body. As a rule the carrying out of the chemical procedure seemed sufficient in itself. At any rate it was for Dorn, and that is why his chemical *caelum* coincided with the heavenly substance in the body, the "truth." For him this was not a duality but an identity; for us they are incommensurables that cannot be reconciled because, owing to our knowledge of chemical processes, we are able to distinguish them from psychic ones. In other words, our consciousness enables us to withdraw this projection.

698   The list of ingredients to be mixed with the *caelum* gives us a glimpse into the nature of the psychic contents that were pro-

jected. In the honey, the "sweetness of the earths," [107] we can easily recognize the balsam of life that permeates all living, budding, and growing things. It expresses, psychologically, the joy of life and the life urge which overcome and eliminate everything dark and inhibiting. Where spring-like joy and expectation reign, spirit can embrace nature and nature spirit. The Chelidonia, a synonym for the philosophical gold, corresponds to Paracelsus's magic herb Cheyri (Cheiranthus cheiri). Like this, it has four-petalled yellow flowers. Cheyri, too, was related to the gold, since it was called "aurum potabile." It therefore comes into the category of the Paracelsan "Aniada," "perfectors from below upward"—magical plants which are collected in the spring and grant long life.[108] Dorn himself, in his "Congeries Paracelsicae chemicae de transmutatione metallorum," commented on Paracelsus's *De vita longa,* where this information can be found. Celandine was one of the most popular curative and magical herbs in the Middle Ages, chiefly on account of its yellow, milky juice—a remedy for non-lactation. It was also called "enchanter's nightshade." [109] Like the Cheyri, it owes its singular significance to the quaternity of its gold-coloured flowers, as Paracelsus points out.[110] The analogy with gold always signifies an accentuation of value: the addition of Chelidonia projects the highest value, which is identical with the quaternity of the self, into the mixture. If it "draws out the soul of Mercurius," this means psychologically that the image of the self (the golden quaternity) draws a quintessence out of the chthonic spirit.

699   I must agree with Dorn, and no doubt with the reader too, that this statement is "vix intelligibilis." I can explain this only as a result of the extraordinary intellectual difficulties we get into when we have to wrestle seriously with a mind that could make no proper distinction between psyche and matter. The underlying idea here is that of Mercurius, a dual being who was as much spiritual as material. In my special study of that subject I have pointed out that outwardly Mercurius corresponds to quicksilver but inwardly he is a "deus terrenus" and an *anima*

107 Cf. "Thereniabin," manna, etc. Honeydew or "maydew" occurs in Paracelsus. Cf. "Paracelsus as a Spiritual Phenomenon," par. 190 and n. 93.
108 Baechtold-Stäubli, *Handwörterbuch,* s.v. Schellkraut.
109 Ibid., pp. 86f.
110 "And the Spagyric makes of the four a harmonious whole, as the flower Cheyri shows" (*De vita longa,* Book III, cap. I, in Sudhoff, I, 3, p. 301).

490

mundi—in other words, that part of God which, when he "imag-ined" the world, was as it were left behind in his Creation [111] or, like the Sophia of the Gnostics, got lost in Physis. Mercurius has the character which Dorn ascribes to the soul. He is "good with the good, evil with the evil," and thus occupies a middle position morally. Just as the soul inclines to earthly bodies, so Mercurius frequently appears as the spirit in matter, in chthonic or even καταχθόνιος (underworldly) form, as in our text. He is then the (non-human) spirit who holds the soul captive in Physis, for which reason it must be liberated from him.

700   In a psychological sense Mercurius represents the uncon-scious, for this is to all appearances that "spirit" which comes closest to organic matter and has all the paradoxical qualities attributed to Mercurius. In the unconscious are hidden those "sparks of light" (*scintillae*), the archetypes, from which a higher meaning can be "extracted." [112] The "magnet" that attracts the hidden thing is the self, or in this case the "theoria" or the sym-bol representing it, which the adept uses as an instrument.[113] The *extractio* is depicted figuratively in an illustration in Reus-ner's *Pandora:* a crowned figure, with a halo, raising a winged, fish-tailed, snake-armed creature (the spirit), likewise crowned with a halo, out of a lump of earth.[114] This monster represents the *spiritus mercurialis*, the soul of the world or of matter freed from its fetters; the *filius macrocosmi*, the child of sun and moon born in the earth, the hermaphroditic homunculus, etc. Basi-cally all these synonyms describe the inner man as a parallel or complement of Christ. The reader who seeks further informa-tion on this figure should refer to *Psychology and Alchemy* [115] and *Aion*.[116]

701   Let us now turn to another ingredient of the mixture, namely the "rosemary flowers" (*flores rosis marini*). In the old pharmacopeia, rosemary (*Rosmarinus officinalis*) was regarded as an antitoxin, presumably on symbolic grounds which may be connected with its curious name. *Ros marinus* (sea-dew) was for the alchemist a welcome analogy for the *aqua permanens*, which

111 Cf. *Mus. herm.*, p. 112 (Waite, I, p. 98).
112 Cf. "extraction of the cogitation" in "Liber Plat. quartorum," *Theatr. chem.*, V, p. 144.   113 *Aion*, pars. 239ff.
114 *Pandora*, p. 253. Cf. *Psychology and Alchemy*, fig. 232.
115 "The Lapis-Christ Parallel."
116 Ch. v.

in its turn was Mercurius.[117] But what lends rosemary its special significance is its sweet smell and taste. The "sweet odour" of the Holy Ghost occurs not only in Gnosticism but also in ecclesiastical language,[118] and of course in alchemy—though here there are more frequent references to the characteristic stench of the underworld, the *odor sepulchrorum*. Rosemary was often used in marriage customs and as a love philtre, and therefore had—for the alchemist—a binding power, which was of course particularly favourable for the purpose of conjunction.[119] Thus the Holy Ghost is the "spiration" binding Father and Son, just as, in alchemy, he occasionally appears as the "ligament" of body and soul. These different aspects of rosemary signify so many qualities which are imparted to the mixture.

702   Mercurialis is a magic herb too, but unlike rosemary it is connected not with love but with sexuality, and is another "binding" power which, as we have mentioned, can even determine the sex of the child. The red lily, as the quintessence of sulphur (n. 85), represents the male partner in the alchemical marriage, the *servus rubeus* who unites with the *foemina candida*. With this figure the adept mixed himself into the potion, so to speak, and, to make the bond inviolable, he added human blood as a further ingredient. Being a "special juice" with which

---

117 Also called "ros Gideonis" with reference to Judges 6 : 36ff. This is an ancient idea, cf. Macrobius (*Saturnalia*, VII, 16): "There is in its [the moon's] light something that flows down from it, which moistens bodies and soaks them with a kind of hidden dew." * Dew wakens the dead and is the food of the holy (*Zohar*, 128b). Irenaeus speaks of the "dew of light" in Gnosticism (*Adv. haer.*, I, 30, 3, and III, 17, 3). In Rabanus Maurus it is "God's grace" (Migne, *P.L.*, vol. 112, col. 1040). In Romanus it is Christ (Pitra, *Analecta sacra*, I, p. 237). Dew contains the "mellifluous nectar of heaven" (Steeb, *Coel. sephirot.*, p. 139). Hermes Trismegistus meant dew when he said in the "Tabula Smaragdina": "Its father is the sun, its mother the moon." (*De alchimia*, p. 363). Dew is frequently mentioned in the *Turba* (e.g., in Sermo 58).

118 Theodore the Studite (Pitra, I, p. 337): "Thou hast made right faith to give forth an odour above ointment." * "It imbued the whole world with the odour of knowledge" * (ibid., p. 342). The "Great Book of the Mandaeans" speaks of the "odour of almighty life" (Lidzbarski, *Ginza, der Schatz*, p. 110). Compare the sweet odour of Sapientia with the perfume of the mother goddess in and around the temple of Hierapolis (Lucian, "The Syrian Goddess," *Works*, I, p. 261), and with the scent of the Tree of Life in the Book of Enoch (Charles, *Apocrypha and Pseudepigrapha*, II, p. 205). See also Nestle, "Der süsse Geruch als Erweis des Geistes," p. 95, and Lohmeyer, "Vom göttlichen Wohlgeruch," pp. 41ff.

119 Baechtold-Stäubli, *Handwörterbuch*, s.v. Rosmarin.

pacts with the devil are signed, it would magically consolidate the bond of marriage.

703   This peculiar mixture was then to be united with the "heaven of the red or white wine or of Tartarus." The *caelum* or blue tincture, as we have seen, was concocted from the "phlegm" of the wine or sublimated from the "wine-stone." Just as the phlegm is the residue, in the bottom of the vessel, of the evaporated wine, so Tartarus, the underworld and realm of the dead, is the sediment or precipitate of a once living world. In Khunrath, *Sal tartari mundi maioris* is identical with *sal Saturni* and *sal Veneris*.[120] It contains—or is—the "scintilla Animae Mundi."[121] Tartar is the *sal sapientiae*.[122] *Sal saturni* refers to Kronos enchained in Tartarus. Plutarch identifies Typhon with Tartarus.[123] This is in agreement with the malefic nature of Saturn. *Sal tartari* therefore has a sinister, underworldly nuance reminiscent of death and hell. Saturn (lead) is one of the best known synonyms for the prima materia, and hence is the matrix of the filius Philosophorum. This is the sought-for celestial substance, the *caelum*, etc.

704   What are we to think of this most peculiar philtre? Did Dorn really mean that these magic herbs should be mixed together and that the air-coloured quintessence should be distilled from the "Tartarus," or was he using these secret names and procedures to express a moral meaning? My conjecture is that he meant both, for it is clear that the alchemists did in fact operate with such substances and thought-processes, just as, in particular, the Paracelsist physicians used these remedies and reflections in their practical work. But if the adept really concocted such potions in his retort, he must surely have chosen his ingredients on account of their magical significance. He worked, accordingly, with *ideas*, with psychic processes and states, but referred to them under the name of the corresponding substances. With the honey the pleasure of the senses and the joy of life went into the mixture, as well as the secret fear of the "poison," the deadly danger of worldly entanglements. With the Chelidonia the highest meaning and value, the self as the total personality, the healing and "whole-making" medicine which is

---

120 *Von hylealischen Chaos*, pp. 263ff.   121 Ibid., p. 264.
122 P. 260.
123 "Isis and Osiris," cap. 57, *Moralia*, V, p. 137.

recognized even by modern psychotherapy, was combined with spiritual and conjugal love, symbolized by rosemary; and, lest the lower, chthonic element be lacking, Mercurialis added sexuality, together with the red slave moved by passion,[124] symbolized by the red lily, and the addition of blood threw in the whole soul. All this was united with the azure quintessence, the *anima mundi* extracted from inert matter, or the God-image imprinted on the world—a mandala produced by rotation; [125] that is to say the whole of the conscious man is surrendered to the self, to the new centre of personality which replaces the former ego. Just as, for the mystic, Christ takes over the leadership of consciousness and puts an end to a merely ego-bound existence, so the *filius macrocosmi,* the son of the great luminaries and of the dark womb of the earth, enters the realm of the psyche and seizes the human personality, not only in the shining heights of consciousness but in the dark depths which have not yet comprehended the light that appeared in Christ. The alchemist was well aware of the great shadow which Christianity obviously had not assimilated, and he therefore felt impelled to create a saviour from the womb of the earth as an analogy and complement of God's son who came down from above.

705   The production of the *caelum* is a symbolic rite performed in the laboratory. Its purpose was to create, in the form of a substance, that "truth," the celestial balsam or life principle, which is identical with the God-image. Psychologically, it was a representation of the individuation process by means of chemical substances and procedures, or what we today call active imagination. This is a method which is used spontaneously by nature herself or can be taught to the patient by the analyst. As a rule it occurs when the analysis has constellated the opposites so powerfully that a union or synthesis of the personality becomes an imperative necessity. Such a situation is bound to arise when the analysis of the psychic contents, of the patient's attitude and particularly of his dreams, has brought the compensatory or complementary images from the unconscious so insist-

124 Such was the significance of the Rubeus in the art of geomancy, much practised in Dorn's day.

125 Concerning the rotation of the mandala see "Concerning Mandala Symbolism," par. 693 and Fig. 38, also *Aion,* pars. 408ff.

ently before his mind that the conflict between the conscious and the unconscious personality becomes open and critical. When this confrontation is confined to partial aspects of the unconscious the conflict is limited and the solution simple: the patient, with insight and some resignation or a feeling of resentment, places himself on the side of reason and convention. Though the unconscious motifs are repressed again, as before, the unconscious is satisfied to a certain extent, because the patient must now make a conscious effort to live according to its principles and, in addition, is constantly reminded of the existence of the repressed by annoying resentments. But if his recognition of the shadow is as complete as he can make it, then conflict and disorientation ensue, an equally strong Yes and No which he can no longer keep apart by a rational decision. He cannot transform his clinical neurosis into the less conspicuous neurosis of cynicism; in other words, he can no longer hide the conflict behind a mask. It requires a real solution and necessitates a third thing in which the opposites can unite. Here the logic of the intellect usually fails, for in a logical antithesis there is no third. The "solvent" can only be of an irrational nature. In nature the resolution of opposites is always an energic process: she acts *symbolically* in the truest sense of the word,[126] doing something that expresses both sides, just as a waterfall visibly mediates between above and below. The waterfall itself is then the incommensurable third. In an open and unresolved conflict dreams and fantasies occur which, like the waterfall, illustrate the tension and nature of the opposites, and thus prepare the synthesis.

706   This process can, as I have said, take place spontaneously or be artificially induced. In the latter case you choose a dream, or some other fantasy-image, and concentrate on it by simply catching hold of it and looking at it. You can also use a bad mood as a starting-point, and then try to find out what sort of fantasy-image it will produce, or what image expresses this mood. You then fix this image in the mind by concentrating your attention. Usually it will alter, as the mere fact of contemplating it animates it. The alterations must be carefully noted down all the time, for they reflect the psychic processes in the unconscious background, which appear in the form of images consisting of

126 A σύμβολον is a 'throwing together.'

conscious memory material. In this way conscious and unconscious are united, just as a waterfall connects above and below. A chain of fantasy ideas develops and gradually takes on a dramatic character: the passive process becomes an action. At first it consists of projected figures, and these images are observed like scenes in the theatre. In other words, you dream with open eyes. As a rule there is a marked tendency simply to enjoy this interior entertainment and to leave it at that. Then, of course, there is no real progress but only endless variations on the same theme, which is not the point of the exercise at all. What is enacted on the stage still remains a background process; it does not move the observer in any way, and the less it moves him the smaller will be the cathartic effect of this private theatre. The piece that is being played does not want merely to be watched impartially, it wants to compel his participation. If the observer understands that his own drama is being performed on this inner stage, he cannot remain indifferent to the plot and its dénouement. He will notice, as the actors appear one by one and the plot thickens, that they all have some purposeful relationship to his conscious situation, that he is being addressed by the unconscious, and that *it* causes these fantasy-images to appear before him. He therefore feels compelled, or is encouraged by his analyst, to take part in the play and, instead of just sitting in a theatre, really have it out with his alter ego. For nothing in us ever remains quite uncontradicted, and consciousness can take up no position which will not call up, somewhere in the dark corners of the psyche, a negation or a compensatory effect, approval or resentment. This process of coming to terms with the Other in us is well worth while, because in this way we get to know aspects of our nature which we would not allow anybody else to show us and which we ourselves would never have admitted.[127] It is very important to fix this whole procedure in writing at the time of its occurrence, for you then have ocular evidence that will effectively counteract the ever-ready tendency to self-deception. A running commentary is absolutely necessary in dealing with the shadow, because otherwise its actuality cannot be fixed. Only in this painful way is it possible to gain a positive insight into the complex nature of one's own personality.

127 Cf. "Relations between the Ego and the Unconscious," pars. 341ff.

6. SELF-KNOWLEDGE

707   Expressed in the language of Hermetic philosophy, the ego-personality's coming to terms with its own background, the shadow, corresponds to the union of spirit and soul in the *unio mentalis,* which is the first stage of the coniunctio. What I call coming to terms with the unconscious the alchemists called "meditation." Ruland says of this: "Meditation: The name of an Internal Talk of one person with another who is invisible, as in the invocation of the Deity, or communion with one's self, or with one's good angel." [128] This somewhat optimistic definition must immediately be qualified by a reference to the adept's relations with his *spiritus familiaris,* who we can only hope was a good one. In this respect Mercurius is a rather unreliable companion, as the testimony of the alchemists agrees. In order to understand the second stage, the union of the *unio mentalis* with the body, psychologically, we must bear in mind what the psychic state resulting from a fairly complete recognition of the shadow looks like. The shadow, as we know, usually presents a fundamental contrast to the conscious personality. This contrast is the prerequisite for the difference of potential from which psychic energy arises. Without it, the necessary tension would be lacking. Where considerable psychic energy is at work, we must expect a corresponding tension and inner opposition. The opposites are necessarily of a characterological nature: the existence of a positive virtue implies victory over its opposite, the corresponding vice. Without its counterpart virtue would be pale, ineffective, and unreal. The extreme opposition of the shadow to consciousness is mitigated by complementary and compensatory processes in the unconscious. Their impact on consciousness finally produces the uniting symbols.

708   Confrontation with the shadow produces at first a dead balance, a standstill that hampers moral decisions and makes convictions ineffective or even impossible. Everything becomes doubtful, which is why the alchemists called this stage *nigredo, tenebrositas,* chaos, melancholia. It is right that the magnum opus should begin at this point, for it is indeed a well-nigh unanswerable question how one is to confront reality in this torn

128 Cf. *Lexicon,* p. 226.

and divided state. Here I must remind the reader who is acquainted neither with alchemy nor with the psychology of the unconscious that nowadays one very seldom gets into such a situation. Nobody now has any sympathy with the perplexities of an investigator who busies himself with magical substances, and there are relatively few people who have experienced the effects of an analysis of the unconscious on themselves, and almost nobody hits on the idea of using the objective hints given by dreams as a theme for meditation. If the ancient art of meditation is practised at all today, it is practised only in religious or philosophical circles, where a theme is subjectively chosen by the meditant or prescribed by an instructor, as in the Ignatian *Exercitia* or in certain theosophical exercises that developed under Indian influence. These methods are of value only for increasing concentration and consolidating consciousness, but have no significance as regards effecting a synthesis of the personality. On the contrary, their purpose is to shield consciousness from the unconscious and to suppress it. They are therefore of therapeutic value only in cases where the conscious is liable to be overwhelmed by the unconscious and there is the danger of a psychotic interval.

709   In general, meditation and contemplation have a bad reputation in the West. They are regarded as a particularly reprehensible form of idleness or as pathological narcissism. No one has time for self-knowledge or believes that it could serve any sensible purpose. Also, one knows in advance that it is not worth the trouble to know oneself, for any fool can know what he is. We believe exclusively in doing and do not ask about the doer, who is judged only by achievements that have collective value. The general public seems to have taken cognizance of the existence of the unconscious psyche more than the so-called experts, but still nobody has drawn any conclusions from the fact that Western man confronts himself as a stranger and that self-knowledge is one of the most difficult and exacting of the arts.

710   When meditation is concerned with the objective products of the unconscious that reach consciousness spontaneously, it unites the conscious with contents that proceed not from a conscious causal chain but from an essentially unconscious process. We cannot know what the unconscious psyche is, otherwise it would be conscious. We can only conjecture its existence,

though there are good enough grounds for this. Part of the unconscious contents is projected, but the projection as such is not recognized. Meditation or critical introspection and objective investigation of the object are needed in order to establish the existence of projections. If the individual is to take stock of himself it is essential that his projections should be recognized, because they falsify the nature of the object and besides this contain items which belong to his own personality and should be integrated with it. This is one of the most important phases in the wearisome process of self-knowledge. And since projections involve one in an inadmissible way in externalities, Dorn rightly recommends an almost ascetic attitude to the world, so that the soul may be freed from its involvement in the world of the body. Here only the "spirit" can help it, that is, the drive for knowledge of the self, on a plane beyond all the illusion and bemusement caused by projection.

711   The *unio mentalis,* then, in psychological as well as in alchemical language, means knowledge of oneself. In contradistinction to the modern prejudice that self-knowledge is nothing but a knowledge of the ego, the alchemists regarded the self as a substance incommensurable with the ego, hidden in the body, and identical with the image of God.[129] This view fully accords with the Indian idea of *purusha-atman.*[130] The psychic preparation of the magisterium as described by Dorn is therefore an attempt, uninfluenced by the East, to bring about a union of opposites in accordance with the great Eastern philosophies, and to establish for this purpose a principle freed from the opposites and similar to the *atman* or *tao.* Dorn called this the *substantia coelestis,* which today we would describe as a transcendental principle. This "unum" is *nirdvandva* (free from the opposites), like the *atman* (self).

712   Dorn did not invent this idea but merely gave clearer expression to what had long been secret knowledge in alchemy. Thus

---

129 Cf. *Aion,* pars. 70ff.

130 In Chinese alchemy this is *chên-yên,* the true man (τέλειος ἄνθρωπος). "True man is the extreme of excellence. He is and he is not. He resembles a vast pool of water, suddenly sinking and suddenly floating. . . . When first gathered, it may be classified as white. Treat it and it turns red. . . . The white lives inside like a virgin. The squareness, the roundness, the diameter and the dimensions mix and restrain one another. Having been in existence before the beginning of the heavens and the earth: lordly, lordly, high and revered." (Wei Po-yang, pp. 237f.)

we read in the "Liber octo capitulorum de lapide philos-ophorum" of Albertus Magnus,[131] with reference to quicksilver (*Mercurius non vulgi*, the philosophical mercury):

Quicksilver is cold and moist, and God created all minerals with it, and it itself is aerial, and volatile in the fire. But since it withstands the fire for some time, it will do great and wonderful works, and it alone is a living spirit, and in all the world there is nothing like it that can do such things as it can . . . It is the perennial water, the water of life, the virgin's milk, the fount, the alumen,[132] and [who-ever] drinks of it shall not perish. When it is alive it does certain works, and when it is dead it does other and the greatest works. It is the serpent that rejoices in itself, impregnates itself, and gives birth in a single day, and slays all metals with its venom. It flees from the fire, but the sages by their art have caused it to withstand the fire, by nourishing it with its own earth until it endured the fire, and then it performs works and transmutations. As it is transmuted, so it transmutes. . . . It is found in all minerals and has a "sym-bolum" [133] with them all. But it arises midway between the earthly and the watery, or midway between [*mediocriter*] [134] a subtle living oil and a very subtle spirit. From the watery part of the earth it has its weight and motion from above downwards, its brightness, fluidity, and silver hue. . . . But quicksilver is clearly seen to have a gross substance, like the Monocalus,[135] which excels even gold in the heaviness of its immense weight.[136] When it is in its nature [137] it is of

131 *Theatr. chem.*, IV, pp. 948ff.

132 Here a synonym for Mercurius. Cf. Ruland, *Lexicon*, p. 24.

133 In the strictest sense of the word, a "symbolum" is a coin broken into two pieces, so that the halves "tally." Cf. Aegidius de Vadis, "Dialogus" (*Theatr. chem.*, II, p. 107): ". . . concord and discord, which we take to mean symboliza-tion." * The symbolum here means the capacity of elements to combine; it is the "retinaculum elementorum," the rope of the elements. (Lully, "Theorica et prac-tica," *Theatr. chem.*, IV, p. 133.)   134 Instead of *medioxime*.

135 Presumably derived from μονόκαυλος (bot.), 'one-stemmed', but more probably a misprint for *monocolus* (μονόκωλος), 'one-footed', or for the late Latin *monoca-leus*, 'having only one testicle, semi-castrated.' (Cf. Du Cange, *Glossarium*, s.h.v.) Monocaleus might be a reference to the androgynous nature of Mercurius. The conjecture *monocerus* (μονόκερως) is possible, since the unicorn signified Mercurius and was well known in 16th- and especially 17th-cent. alchemy. (Cf. *Psychology and Alchemy*, pars. 518, 547.) According to Horapollo the scarab, which in the Leyden Papyrus is identical with Osiris, is one-horned (ibid., par. 530).

136 The text is not in a good state. I have therefore placed a full point after "praeponderat" and begin a new sentence with "dum in sua natura."

137 Obviously its arcane nature.

the strongest composition [*fortissimae compositionis*] [138] and of uniform nature, since it is not divided [or: is indivisible]. It can in no way be separated into parts, because it either escapes from the fire with its whole substance or endures with it in the fire. For this reason the cause of perfection is necessarily seen in it.

713   Since Mercurius is the soul of the gold and of the silver, the conjunction of these two must be accomplished:

Our final secret consists in this, that one obtains the medicine which flows, before Mercurius evaporates. . . . There is no worthier or purer substance than the sun and its shadow the moon, without which no tincturing quicksilver can be produced. . . . He who understands, therefore, how to unite this with the sun or moon will obtain the arcanum, which is named the sulphur of the art.

714   Mercurius is the prima materia. This must be dissolved at the beginning of the work, and the dissolved bodies then transformed into "spirits." The transformation is effected by putrefaction, which is synonymous with the *nigredo*, the grave, and death. The spirits are joined together as *sponsus* and *sponsa*.

Our stone is of watery nature, because it is cold and moist. For such a disposition of the body is considered obvious or manifest. But breadth is the middle [*media*] disposition whereby depth is attained. This is the medium between depth and breadth, as between two extremes or opposites, and the passage from one opposite to the other or from one extreme to the other is impossible save by a medium disposition. [This is possible] because the stone is by nature cold and moist.

Mercurius is not only the lapis as *prima* materia but the lapis as *ultima* materia, the goal of the opus. Hence Albertus cites Geber: "One is the stone, one the medicine, and therein lies the whole magistery."

715   In these words Albertus Magnus, more than three hundred years earlier than Dorn, describes the celestial substance, the balsam of life, and the hidden truth. His description has roots that go still further back into Greek alchemy, but I cannot discuss this here. His account is sufficient for our purpose: it describes a transcendental substance characterized, as is only to be expected, by a large number of antinomies. Unequivocal statements can be made only in regard to immanent objects; tran-

[138] By which something like "cohesion" is meant.

scendental ones can be expressed only by paradox. Thus, they are and they are not (that is to say, not to be found in our experience). Even the physicist is compelled by experience to make antinomian statements when he wants to give a concrete description of transcendental facts, such as the nature of light or of the smallest particles of matter, which he represents both as corpuscles and as waves. In the same way, the quicksilver is a material substance and at the same time a living spirit whose nature can be expressed by all manner of symbolic synonyms—though only, it is true, when it is made fire-resistant by artificial means. The quicksilver is a substance and yet not a substance, since, as a natural element, it does not resist fire and can do this only through the secret of art, thereby turning into a magical substance so wonderful that there is no prospect of our ever coming across it in reality. This clearly means that quicksilver is the symbol for a transcendental idea which is alleged to become manifest in it when the art has made it capable of resisting fire. It is also assumed that this occult quality is at least potentially present in Mercurius, since he is the prima materia of all metals and is found in all minerals. He is not only the initial material of the process but also its end-product, the lapis Philosophorum. Thus he is at the outset a significant exception among the metals and chemical elements. He is the primordial matter from which God created all material things. The change which the artifex proposes to induce in it consists, among other things, in giving it "immense weight" and indivisible wholeness. This strange statement assumes another aspect when we compare it with the modern view that matter consists of extraordinarily, indeed "immensely" heavy elementary corpuscles which in a certain sense are of "uniform nature" and apparently indivisible. They are the bricks nature builds with and they therefore contain everything that nature contains, so that each of them represents the whole of the universe. From this point of view it almost seems as if Albertus Magnus had anticipated one of the greatest physical discoveries of our time. This, of course, would be to recognize only the physical truth of his intuition, but not the symbolic implications which were bound up with it in the medieval mind.

716   If we have hazarded a parallel between Albertus's views and the discontinuity of protons and energy quanta, we are obliged

to attempt another parallel in regard to the symbolical statements. These, as we have seen from Dorn (supra, sec. 3), refer to the psychological aspect of Mercurius. In order to avoid needless repetition, I must here refer the reader to my earlier investigations of Mercurius and the symbols of the self in alchemy. Anyone who knows the extraordinary importance of the concept of psychic wholeness in the practical as well as theoretical psychology of the unconscious will not be surprised to learn that Hermetic philosophy gave this idea, in the form of the lapis Philosophorum, pre-eminence over all other concepts and symbols. Dorn in particular made this abundantly and unequivocally clear, in which respect he has the authority of the oldest sources. It is not true that alchemy devised such an interpretation of the arcanum only at the end of the sixteenth century; on the contrary, the idea of the self affords the clue to the central symbols of the art in all centuries, in Europe, the Near East, and in China. Here again I must refer the reader to my previous works.[139] Unfortunately it is not possible to exhaust the wealth of alchemical ideas in a single volume.

717   By introducing the modern concept of the self we can explain the paradoxes of Albertus without too much difficulty. Mercurius is matter and spirit; the self, as its symbolism proves, embraces the bodily sphere as well as the psychic. This fact is expressed particularly clearly in mandalas.[140] Mercurius is also the "water," which, as the text emphasizes, occupies a middle position between the volatile (air, fire) and the solid (earth), since it occurs in both liquid and gaseous form, and also as a solid in the form of ice. Mercurius shares his "aquaeositas" with water, since on the one hand he is a metal and amalgamates himself in solid form with other metals, and on the other hand is liquid and evaporable. The deeper reason why he is so frequently compared with water is that he unites in himself all those numinous qualities which water possesses. Thus, as the central arcanum, the ὕδωρ θεῖον or *aqua permanens* dominated alchemy from those remote times when it was still the holy and blessed water of the Nile until well into the eighteenth century. In the course of time, mainly under Gnostic-Hermetic influence, it took on the

139 Particularly *Aion*.
140 Cf. "A Study in the Process of Individuation" and "Concerning Mandala Symbolism."

significance of the Nous, with which the divine *krater* was filled so that those mortals who wished to attain consciousness could renew themselves in this baptismal bath; later it signified the *aqua doctrinae* and a wonder-working magical water. Its very ancient identification with *hydrargyrum*, quicksilver, drew the whole Hermes Trismegistus tradition into the immemorially numinous sphere of the water's significance. This could happen all the more easily since its maternal aspect as the matrix and "nurse of all things" makes it an unsurpassable analogy of the unconscious. In this way the idea of the "water" could gradually develop into the tremendous paradox of Mercurius, who, as the "age-old son of the mother," is the Hermetic spirit, and, as a chemical substance, a magically prepared quicksilver.

718 The "serpent rejoicing in itself" (*luxurians in se ipso*) is the Democritean physis (*natura*) "which embraces itself" [141] and is symbolized by the uroboros of Greek alchemy, a well-known emblem of Mercurius. It is the symbol of the union of opposites *par excellence* and an alchemical version of the proverb: *les extrêmes se touchent*. The uroboros symbolizes the goal of the process but not the beginning, the massa confusa or chaos, for this is characterized not by the union of the elements but by their conflict. The expression "giving birth in a single day" (*in uno die parturiens*) likewise refers to Mercurius, since he (in the form of the lapis) was named the "son of one day." [142] This name refers to the creation of light in Genesis 1 : 5: "And there was evening and morning, one day." As the "son of one day," therefore, Mercurius is light. Hence he is praised as the *lux moderna* and a light above all lights.[143] He is thus Sunday's child (born on the day of the sun), just as the planet Mercury is the nearest to the sun and was accounted its child. St. Bonaventure (1221–74) also speaks of the one day in his *Itinerarium*, where he discusses the three stages of illumination (*triplex illustratio*). The first stage consists in giving up the bodily and the temporal in order to attain the "first principle," which is spiritual and eternal and "above us":

141 Berthelot, *Alch. grecs*, II, i, 3.
142 Khunrath, *Hyl. Chaos*, p. 195. Cf. supra, pars. 472ff.
143 For instance in Mylius, *Phil. ref.*, p. 244, and *Ros. phil., Art. aurif.*, II, p. 381: "And I illumine all luminaries with my light."

We must enter into our mind [*mentem*], which is the eternal spiritual image of God within us, and this is to enter into the truth of the Lord; we must pass beyond ourselves to the eternal and preeminently spiritual, and to that which is above us . . . this is the threefold illumination of the one day.[144]

The "one day" is the day on which light appeared over the darkness. I cite this passage not only for that reason but as a parallel to the three stages of conjunction in Dorn, which obviously originated in the exercises for spiritual contemplation in the early Middle Ages. The parallel is clearly discernible: first the turning away from the world of sense, then the turning towards the inner world of the mind and the hidden celestial substance, the image and truth of God, and finally the contemplation of the transcendental *unus mundus,* the potential world outside time, of which we shall have more to say below. But first we examine more closely Albertus's statements on the nature of the quicksilver.

719   The middle position ascribed to Mercurius provokes Albertus to a remarkable reflection: it seems to him that the concept of breadth (*latitudo*) expresses the "middle disposition" whereby depth can be attained. This disposition is the "medium between depth and breadth" (*media est inter profunditatem et latitudinem*), as between two extremes or opposites (*contraria*). The idea at the back of his mind is obviously that of a cross, for height is the complement of depth.[145] This would indicate the quaternity, a symbol of Mercurius quadratus, who, in the form of the lapis, consists of the four elements.[146] He thus forms the mid-point of the cosmic quaternity and represents the quinta essentia, the oneness and essence of the physical world, i.e., the anima mundi. As I have shown elsewhere, this symbol corresponds to the modern representations of the self.

7. THE MONOCOLUS

720   Evidently in order to emphasize the unity of Mercurius, Albertus makes use of the expression "monocolus" (as is prob-

[144] Cf. *The Franciscan Vision,* pp. 14f. For the "one day" in Epiphanius, see supra, pars. 472ff.

[145] Cf. Ephesians 3 : 18: ". . . so that . . . you may be able to comprehend . . . what is the breadth and length and height and depth . . ."

[146] The alchemical sign for the four elements is a cross.

ably the right reading), or "uniped." It seems to me that this must be an alchemical ἅπαξ λεγόμενον,[147] for I have found it nowhere else in the literature. The alchemist's use of a rare or strange word generally served to emphasize the extraordinary nature of the object expressed by it. (As we know, with this trick one can also make banalities appear unusual.) Even though the word "monocolus" appears to be unique, the image is not, for the uniped occurs in several illustrated alchemical manuscripts, for instance in the aforementioned Paris codex (Fr. 14765) entitled "Abraham le Juif." [148] As the title shows, this presumably purported to be, or was intended to replace, the zealously sought "Rindenbuch" of the same author, of which Nicholas Flamel gives an account in his autobiography and whose loss the alchemists so deeply deplored. Though this mythical work was never found, it was reinvented in Germany;[149] but this forgery has nothing to do with our manuscript. On page 324 of the manuscript we find the first in a series of pictures of unipeds (cf. Pl. 4). On the left there is a crowned man in a yellow robe, and on the right a priest in a white robe with a mitre. Each of them has only one foot. The inscription under the picture begins with the sign for Mercurius (☿) and runs: "There they make but one." This refers to the preceding text, "For there is but one single thing, one medicine, and in it all our magistery consists; there are but two coadjutors who are made perfect here." [150] The subject is obviously Mercurius duplex. In my chapter on Sulphur I have pointed out that it, especially in its red form, is identical with gold, the latter being generally regarded as "rex." The red sceptre of the king might be an allusion to this. There is, as I have shown, a red and a white sulphur, so it too is duplex and identical with Mercurius. Red sulphur stands for the masculine, active principle of the sun, the white for that of the moon. As sulphur is generally masculine by nature and forms the counterpart of the feminine salt, the two figures probably

147 An expression occurring only once.

148 Supra, pars. 634 ff.

149 Eleazar, *Uraltes Chymisches Werck.*

150 The Latin MS. "Figurarum aegyptiorum secretarum" (author's possession) has on fol. 19: "Duo tantum sunt coadjutores qui hic perficiuntur." Pl. 4 is taken not from the Paris Codex but from the above MS., fol. 20. The pictures are similar in both. [Cf. *Psychology and Alchemy,* par. 391, n. 101.]

signify the spirits of the arcane substance, which is often called
rex, as in Bernardus Trevisanus.

721   This curious separation or union of the figures occurs several
times in the manuscript. In the next picture (Pl. 5), on page 331,
the king on the left has a blue robe and a black foot, and the one
on the right a black robe and a blue foot. Both the sceptres are
red. The inscription runs: "Thus is it done, that what was hid
may be revealed." [151] This refers, as the preceding text makes
clear, to the *nigredo* which is about to ensue. The *nigredo* signifies the *mortificatio, putrefactio, solutio, separatio, divisio,*
etc., a state of dissolution and decomposition that precedes the
synthesis. This picture is followed by one showing the two figures separated, each with two feet. The figure on the left wears
the spiritual crown and the one on the right the temporal, corresponding to the occult-spiritual and earthly-corporeal nature
of sulphur. The figure on the left wears a robe whose right half
is blue and the left black, the one on the right the reverse. They
thus complement one another. The text explains: "The colours
of the 9th year and ½ this month of January 1772 are represented by these two figures. Likewise by the mortification of
our natural ☿ and of the dead water reduced to another form."
The inscription under the picture runs: "A very long time, and
by putrefaction, calcination, incineration, fixation, and coagulation the materials become solid, but this comes to pass naturally
after a very long time."

722   This probably refers to the completion of the *nigredo* after
a period of pregnancy, i.e., to the complete separation of Mercurius or the two sulphurs, or of their bodily and spiritual natures, corresponding to Dorn's extraction of the soul from the
body and the production of the *unio mentalis.* According to the
picture, the one figure, as regards its colours, is the mirror-image
of the other. This indicates a relationship of complementarity
between *physis* and spirit, so that the one reflects the other.[152]
That, too, is probably the meaning of the "manifestation of the
hidden": through the *unio mentalis* that which is hidden in

151 The corresponding picture in my MS. (fol. 27) bears the inscription: "Sic fit, ut
quod latuit, pateat."
152 Just as Albertus supposes that gold is silver "inside" and vice versa. Here I
would recall to the reader the dream of the black and white magicians, discussed
supra, pars. 79f.

physis by projection is made conscious. In the *nigredo,* the "dark night of the soul," the psychic contents free themselves from their attachment to the body, and the nature and meaning of this connection are recognized.

723   In the next picture (p. 335) the two figures are united again (Pl. 6). Their colours and other attributes are the same. Each figure has only one blue foot. The inscription runs: "Wherefore saith the Philosopher: He obtaineth the Art who can manifest that which is hidden, and conceal that which is manifest." And underneath: "Hic artem digne est consecutus" (Here is the art worthily followed, or: This man worthily followed the art), and: "The blue colour after the yellow which will lead to the complete blackness or putrefaction after a very long time."

724   On page 337 the (spiritual) king from the previous picture is joined to a similarly crowned queen (Pl. 7). He wears a black upper garment and a blue under garment. His crown has a black rim, but the mitre-like part is gold, as in the previous picture. He has one blue foot tipped with black, as if he had dipped it in black paint. The green-clad queen has her hand in his left sleeve, presumably indicating that she takes the place of the left —worldly or bodily—half of the king and appears as his "better half," so to speak. Her feet are black. The text runs: "There comes about an inconstant fixation, then after a little the soft hardens. The watery becomes earthy and dry; thus a change of nature is made from one to the other; and a single colour in the form of a black Raven, and the ♐ [sulphur] of the male ☿ and of the female, have become of the same nature." The inscription says: "Take therefore in God's almighty name this black earth, reduce it very subtly and it will become like the head of a Raven." As if explaining the *caput corvi* the text remarks that the "Silène endormy" is bound by the shepherds with garlands of flowers in all colours of the rainbow and, after quaffing his wine, says: "I laugh at my bond. So say the philosophers that when the blackness appears one must rejoice." [153] The text adds that Troy was reduced to ashes after ten years of siege.

725   This picture represents the union of the monoculus with the earth (the body). As the sulphur of the male Mercurius he is a

[153] Pernety (*Les Fables égyptiennes et grecques,* I, p. 179) says of the putrefaction: "It uncovers for us the interior of the mixture. . . . It makes . . . the hidden manifest. It is the death of accidentals, the first step to generation."

very active power,[154] for he is the red sulphur of the gold or the active principle of the sun. The king in the saffron-yellow robe was originally gold and the sun but has now become totally black—the *sol niger*—and even his blue robe, signifying heaven, is covered with a black one.[155] Only the top of his crown displays the solar gold. Dame Earth wears the same crown (only it is all gold) and thus reveals that her nature is equivalent to his: both are sulphur. One could call the sulphur of the king the "spirit," which, hiding its light in the darkness, unites with the queen.

726   This earth is of a watery nature, corresponding to Genesis 1 : 2 and 6: "And the earth was without form, and void. . . . And the Spirit of God moved upon the face of the waters. . . . And God said, Let there be a firmament in the midst of the waters . . ." In this way heaven can embrace the sea instead of the earth. We may recall the myth of Isis and Osiris: Isis copulated with the spirit of the dead Osiris, and from this union sprang the god of the mysteries, Harpocrates. Osiris plays a certain role in the ancient alchemical texts: the brother/sister or mother/son pair are sometimes called Isis and Osiris.[156] In Olympiodorus [157] Osiris is lead, as arcane substance, and the principle of moisture; [158] in Firmicus Maternus he is the life-principle.[159] The alchemical interpretation of him as Mercurius has its parallel in the Naassene comparison of Osiris to Hermes.[160] Like the latter, he was represented ithyphallically, and this is significant in regard to the monoculus.[161] He is the dying and resurgent God-man and hence a parallel to Christ. He is of a blackish

---

[154] The king's foot is the right one. This has always been regarded as masculine and luck-bringing. That is why in some countries one starts to march with the right foot. Besides this, the foot in general has a phallic significance. See Aigremont, *Fuss- und Schuhsymbolik und -Erotik.*

[155] He has himself become the "black earth" referred to earlier: "Prenez cette terre noire."

[156] Maier, *Symbola,* pp. 344f.

[157] Berthelot, *Alch. grecs,* II, iv, 42.

[158] Corresponding to the ὑγροποιὸς ἀρχή in Plutarch ("Isis and Osiris," c. 33, *Moralia,* V, pp. 8of.)

[159] ". . . the seeds of fruits are Osiris" (*De errore prof. relig.,* 2, 6).

[160] Osiris is also likened to the Logos, the corpse, and the grave. (Hippolytus, *Elenchos,* V, 8, 10; V, 8, 22; V, 9, 5 and 8.)

[161] Hippolytus, V, 8, 10. Although there are no one-footed heroes in Greek mythology, names like Oedipus and Melampus and ideas such as that of the one tooth and one eye of the Phorcyds suggest something very similar.

colour (μελάγχρους) [162] and was therefore called Aithiops,[163] in Christian usage the devil,[164] and in alchemical language the prima materia.[165] This antithesis is characteristic of Mercurius duplex. Wine as the blood of Osiris occurs in the ancient magical texts.[166] In the Egyptian texts Osiris had a sun-and-moon nature, and was therefore hermaphroditic like Mercurius.[167]

727   Corvus (crow or raven) or caput corvi (raven's head) is the traditional name for the nigredo (nox, melancholia, etc.). It can also, as pars pro toto, mean a "capital" thing or "principle," as for instance the caput mortuum, which originally meant the head of the black Osiris,[168] but later Mercurius philosophorum, who, like him, undergoes death and resurrection and transformation into an incorruptible state. Thus the anonymous author of the "Novum lumen chemicum" exclaims: "O our heaven! O our water and our Mercurius! O dead head or dregs of our sea! . . . And these are the epithets of the bird of Hermes,[169] which never rests." [170] This bird of Hermes is the raven, of which it is said: "And know that the head of the art is the raven, who flies without wings in the blackness of the night and the brightness of the day." [171] He is a restless, unsleeping spirit, "our aerial and volatile stone," a being of contradictory nature.[172] He is the "heaven" and at the same time the "scum of the sea." Since he is also called "water," one thinks of rain-water, which comes from the sea and falls from heaven. As a matter of fact the idea of clouds, rain, and dew is often found in the texts and is extremely ancient.[173] A papyrus text says: "I am the mother of the

---

162 Plutarch, "Isis and Osiris," c. 22, pp. 54f.

163 Doelger, Die Sonne der Gerechtigkeit und der Schwarze, p. 64.

164 Cf. von Franz, "Die Passio Perpetuae," in Aion (Swiss edn.), pp. 467f.

165 Theatr. chem., III, p. 854. In "Super arborem Aristotelis" (Theatr. chem., II, p. 526) the nigredo or caput corvi is termed the "caput nigrum aethiopis."

166 Cf. Reitzenstein, Die hellenistischen Mysterienreligionen, p. 80.

167 Jacobsohn, Die dogmatische Stellung des Königs in der Theologie der alten Aegypter, p. 23: "Hail to thee [Osiris] . . . who risest in the heavens as Ra, renewing thy form as the moon."

168 Cf. Lippmann, Entstehung und Ausbreitung der Alchemie, I, pp. 180, 303, 326.

169 The bird of Hermes is usually the goose.

170 Mus. herm., pp. 581f. (Waite, II, p. 108).*

171 Ros. phil., Art. aurif., II, p. 258.*   172 Ibid., p. 259.

173 "It [the water] is also called a round cloud, death, blackness, darkness, shadow." * Mus. herm., p. 327 (Waite, I, p. 263). Rupescissa speaks of a "dark blue cloud" (La Vertu et la propriété de la quinte essence, p. 29). It is mentioned in the

gods, named heaven; I am Osiris, named water; I am Isis, named dew; . . . I am Eidolos, likened to the true spirits." Thus speaks a magician who wishes to conjure up his familiar: he himself is a spirit and thus akin to the bird of the night. In Christian tradition the raven is an allegory of the devil.[174]

728   Here we encounter the primitive archetypal form of spirit, which, as I have shown,[175] is ambivalent. This ambivalence or antagonism also appears in the ancient Egyptian pair of brothers, Osiris and Set, and in the Ebionite opposition of Christ and Satan. The night raven (*nycticorax*) is an allegory of Christ.[176]

729   Nowadays the *caput mortuum*, or colcothar, denotes "the brownish-red peroxide of iron which remains in the retort after

Turba (ed. Ruska, pp. 120f.) together with the shadow. "That work comes about as suddenly as the clouds from heaven" (Hoghelande, *Theatr. chem.*, I, p. 204).* In Mylius (*Phil. ref.*, pp. 108 and 304) the "water of the cloud" is Mercurius, also in Abu'l-Qasim (p. 420). "Black clouds" are the *nigredo* (Mylius, p. 234, and "Tractatus aureus," *Ars chemica*, p. 15). References to the "cloud rising from the sea," "the new waters," "the life-potion that rouses the sleepers" occur in the very ancient treatise of Komarios (Berthelot, *Alch. grecs*, IV, xx, 8), and in Rabanus Maurus the cloud represents the "comfort of the Holy Ghost and Christ's ascension" (Migne, *P.L.*, vol. 112, col. 1007). This would correspond to the remark in Komarios that "the clouds rising from the sea carry the blessed waters" (Berthelot, IV, xx, 12). Augustine likens the apostles to a cloud, which symbolizes the concealment of the Creator under the flesh (*Expositions of the Book of Psalms*, Ps. 88 (89) : 7, IV, p. 245). Similarly, Christ was prefigured by the pillar of cloud that guided the Jews through the wilderness (Augustine, Ps. 98 (99): 10, p. 456, and Epiphanius, *Ancoratus*). "From thee the clouds flow," says Hildegard of Bingen of the Holy Ghost (Remy de Gourmont, *Le Latin mystique*, p. 157). The alchemical concept of the cloud may have been influenced by the liturgical "Drop down dew, ye heavens, from above, and let the clouds rain down the Just One: let the earth open and bud forth a Saviour" (*Roman Missal*, Introit for 4th Sunday of Advent. Cf. Isaiah 45 : 8). One thinks also of the Eleusinian ὖε κύε, "Let it rain, make fruitful!" (Cf. Kerényi, "Kore," pp. 205f.) In Mandaeism the cloud signifies the feminine. One of the texts says: "Yonder, yonder I stand, I and the cloud that arose with me" (Lidzbarski, *Ginza*, p. 399).

[174] In a lecture at the Eranos Conference of 1945, which was not printed in the *Eranos Jahrbuch*, Rahner discussed the allegory of the devil in patristic literature.

[175] "The Phenomenology of the Spirit in Fairytales," sects. III and IV.

[176] Based on Psalm 102 : 6: "I am like an owl of the desert." Cf. Eucherius, *Liber formularum spiritalis intelligentiae* (Migne, *P.L.*, vol. 50, col. 750), and Rabanus Maurus (Migne, *P.L.*, vol. 112, col. 1006). For the crucifixion of the raven see "Spirit in Fairytales," par. 422. Referring to the story in Aelian, Caussin says: "The raven, overcome with age, offers itself for food to its young; but our phoenix, Christ the Lord . . . offered himself to us as heavenly nourishment" * (*Polyhistor symbolicus*, pp. 308f.). The raven is thus an allegory of Christ, or of the Host.

the distillation of sulphuric acid from iron sulphate," [177] whereas the *caput Osiridis* was black and was therefore called *caput corvi*. The "Aquarium sapientum" compares it with Christ, whose "visage was so marred more than any man" (Isaiah 52 : 14).[178] The blackening usually took forty days, corresponding to the forty days between Easter and Ascension, or Christ's forty days' fast in the wilderness, or the forty-year wanderings of the Jews in the desert.[179] In the heat of the *nigredo* the "*anima media natura* holds dominion." The old philosophers called this blackness the Raven's Head or black sun.[180] The *anima media natura* corresponds to the Platonic world-soul and the Wisdom of the Old Testament.[181] In this state the sun is surrounded by the *anima media natura* and is therefore black. It is a state of incubation or pregnancy. Great importance was attached to the blackness as the starting point of the work.[182] Generally it was called the "Raven." [183] In our context the interpretation of the *nigredo* as *terra* (earth) [184] is significant. Like the *anima media natura* or Wisdom, earth is in principle feminine. It is the earth which, in Genesis, appeared out of the waters,[185] but it is also the "terra damnata." [186]

177 *Oxford English Dictionary*, s.v. colcothar.

178 *Mus. herm.*, p. 117 (Waite, I, p. 102).

179 Ibid., pp. 91 and 117 (Waite, I, pp. 82, 102).

180 "Liber de arte chymica" *(Art. aurif.*, I, p. 610) mentions in this connection a trinitarian image of three suns, black, white, and red. The commentary to "Tractatus Aureus" *(Theatr. chem.*, IV, p. 703) remarks that there are three ravens on the mountain of the Philosophers: "The black which is the head of the art, the white which is the middle, and the red which brings all things to an end." * "Consil. coniugii" *(Ars chemica*, p. 167) even mentions a quaternity of ravens. In the Book of El-Habib (Berthelot, *La Chimie au moyen âge*, III, p. 100), Mary says that the red male (i.e., the Sulphur) should be recognized as the "head of the world."

181 Mylius *(Phil. ref.*, p. 19) comments that if Lucifer had had within him the *anima media natura* or God, he would not have been cast into hell.

182 "When you see your matter going black, rejoice: for that is the beginning of the work." * *(Ros. phil., Art. aurif.*, II, p. 258) "The raven's head is the beginning of the work" * (Hoghelande, *Theatr. chem.*, I, p. 166).

183 "It is called antimony, pitch, coal, the raven, the raven's head, lead, burnt copper, burnt ivory" * *(Theatr. chem.*, I, p. 166).

184 *Ros. phil.*, p. 265.

185 "And thus you have two elements, first water by itself, then earth from water" * (ibid.).

186 Steinerus, *Dissertatio chymico-medica*, p. A 2v.

730   The *caput mortuum* or *caput corvi* is the head of the black
Osiris or Ethiopian, and also of the "Moor" in the *Chymical
Wedding*.[187] The head was boiled in a pot and the broth poured
into a golden ball. This gives us the connection with the "golden
head" of the Greek alchemy, discussed earlier. The Moor in the
Chymical Wedding is probably identical with the black executioner mentioned there, who decapitates the royal personages.
In the end his own head is struck off.[188] In the further course of
events a black bird is beheaded.[189] Beheading is significant symbolically as the separation of the "understanding" from the
"great suffering and grief" which nature inflicts on the soul. It
is an emancipation of the "cogitatio" which is situated in the
head, a freeing of the soul from the "trammels of nature."[190] Its
purpose is to bring about, as in Dorn, a *unio mentalis* "in the
overcoming of the body."

731   The Moor or Ethiopian is the black, sinful man, whom St.
Hilary (d. 367) compared to the raven. ("The raven made in the
form of the sinner."[191]) In the *Chymical Wedding* there is a
black king, and in Schema XXIV Mylius represents the relation
of king and queen under the symbol of two ravens fighting.[192]
Just as the raven symbolizes man's black soul, so the *caput corvi*
represents the head or skull (*testa capitis*), which in Sabaean alchemy served as the vessel of transformation.[193] The Sabaeans
were suspected of magical practices that presupposed the killing
of a man. The "brain-pan or head of the element Man" therefore has a somewhat sinister aspect: they needed a human skull
because it contained the brain and this was the seat of the understanding. "And the understanding exists in that organ, because

[187] Rosencreutz, *Chymical Wedding*, p. 148.

[188] Ibid., p. 123.

[189] P. 159.

[190] Cf. "Liber Plat. quart.," *Theatr. chem.*, V, p. 186. Concerning the Sabaean
magical rite of decapitation see "The Visions of Zosimos," pars. 93f.

[191] * *Tract. super Psalmos*, CXLVI, 12 (Migne, *P.L.*, vol. 9, col. 874).

[192] *Phil. ref.*, p. 190. The ravens are the black souls of the king and queen. Cf. the
story of Aristeas, who saw his soul fly out of his mouth in the shape of a raven.
(Pliny, *Nat. hist.*, lib. VII, cap. LII.) The raven is the black soul-symbol, the dove
is the bright one. There is a battle between raven and dove in *Chymical Wedding*.
p. 24.

[193] "The vessel necessary in this work must be round in shape, that the artifex
may be the transformer of this firmament and of the brainpan" * ("Lib. Plat.
quart.," pp. 150f.).

it rules the soul and assists her liberation." [194] "The corpus rotundum built the skull about itself as a stronghold, girt itself with this armour, and opened windows in it," i.e., the five senses. But the corpus rotundum, "the living being, the form of forms and the genus of genera, is man." [195] The "rotundum" [196] obviously refers not to the empirical but to the "round" or whole man, the τέλειος ἄνθρωπος. "Afterwards he drew the soul to the higher world, that he might give her freedom. The higher world has always an effect in man, which consists in the perfect inspiration of man at his death; nor shall he fail to reach the firmament, until that which proceeded from the higher world returns to its place." [197] The higher world is the "world of worlds," obviously the *mundus potentialis* of Dorn, who was inspired by this text as his use of the ideas of the stronghold (*castrum sapientiae*) [198] and of the "window" (*spiraculum vitae aeternae*) shows.

732   The round vessel or stronghold is the skull. "The divine organ," says the "Liber quartorum," "is the head, for it is the abode of the divine part, namely the soul." That is why the philosopher must "surround this organ with greater care than other organs." Because of its roundness, "it attracts the firmament and is by it attracted; and it is attracted in similar manner by the attracter, until the attraction reaches its end in the understanding. Man is worthier than the beasts and closer to the simple, and this on account of his understanding." The simple (*simplex*

[194] "The upper place is the brain, and that is the seat of the understanding" * (ibid., p. 187).
[195] Ibid., p. 186.*
[196] "The vessel is made round after the fashion of the upper and lower [worlds?]. For it is eminently suited to that [thing] whose generation is sought in it, for a thing is bound by its like" * (p. 150).
[197] P. 186.*
[198] "Seest thou that gleaming and impregnable stronghold?" * ("Spec. phil.," *Theatr. chem.*, I, p. 278). "Truth is . . . an impregnable stronghold. In this citadel is contained that true treasure which is taken hence after death." * ("Phil. medit.," p. 458). The "castle" is an allegory of Mary (Godefridus, *Homiliae Dominicales*, Migne, *P.L.*, vol. 174, col. 32). Dorn distinguishes four strongholds, placed as it were on top of one another. The lowest is of crystal and shelters "philosophical love"; the second is of silver and contains Sophia; the third is of diamond (*adamantina*) and only a few get there, "who are taken up by the will of God"; the fourth is golden but "not perceptible to the senses," "a place of eternal felicity, free from care and filled with every manner of eternal joy" ("Spec. phil.," p. 279). Cf. the four stages of transformation in the "Liber quartorum," discussed in *Psychology and Alchemy*, pars. 366ff.

or *res simplex*) is the One,[199] the *natura caelestis* of Dorn, the round and perfect, the firmament or heaven in man.[200] "Plato is of the opinion that the man whose righteousness is the greatest attains to the bountiful [*largam*] upper substance when he is assimilated by his work to the highest place." [201] This shows us how the production of the *caelum* attracts the starry firmament and the influences (or spirits) of the planets into the Microcosm, just as by the same operation man is likened to the "upper substance," the *anima mundi* or *res simplex* or the "One."

733   In the *nigredo* the brain turns black. Thus a Hermes recipe cited in the *Rosarium* says: "Take the brain . . . grind it up with very strong vinegar, or with boys' urine,[202] until it turns black." [203] The darkening or benightedness is at the same time a psychic state which, as we have seen, was called melancholia. In the "Aurelia occulta" there is a passage where the transformative substance in the *nigredo* state says of itself (cf. Pl. 10):

I am an infirm and weak old man, surnamed the dragon; therefore am I shut up in a cave, that I may be ransomed by the kingly crown. . . . A fiery sword inflicts great torments upon me; death makes weak my flesh and bones. . . . My soul and my spirit depart; a terrible poison, I am likened to the black raven, for that is the wages of sin; in dust and earth I lie, that out of Three may come One. O soul and spirit, leave me not, that I may see again the light of day, and the hero of peace whom the whole world shall behold may arise from me.[204]

* * *

734   What our Abraham le Juif text says about the royal persons sounds like a mythologem: the sun, the king of the blue sky, descends to earth and it becomes night; he then unites with his wife, the earth or sea. The primordial image of Uranos and Gaia may well be the background of this picture. Similarly, in con-

---

[199] Honorius of Autun says in *Liber duodecim quaest.* (Migne, *P.L.*, vol. 172, col. 1179): "The creature as conceived in the divine mind is simple, unchanging, and eternal, but in itself it is multiple, changing, transitory." *

[200] Cf. Reitzenstein, *Poimandres*, p. 16, and the description of the Microcosmus in the *Sacramentarium* of Honorius (Migne, *P.L.*, vol. 172, col. 773): his head is round as heaven and his eyes are the sun and moon.

[201] *Theatr. chem.*, V, p. 189.

[202] Both synonyms for the *aqua permanens*.

[203] *Art. aurif.*, II, p. 264.

[204] *Theatr. chem.*, IV, pp. 569f.

nection with the raven [205] as the name for this situation, we must consider the creative night mentioned in an Orphic hymn, which calls it a bird with black wings that was fertilized by the wind (*pneuma*). The product of this union was the silver egg, which in the Orphic view contained heaven above and earth below, and was therefore a cosmos in itself, i.e., the Microcosm. In alchemy it is the philosophical egg. The French alchemists of the eighteenth century were familiar with the king, the hot, red sulphur of the gold, and called it Osiris; the moist (*aquosum*) they called Isis. Osiris was "the fire hidden in nature, the igneous principle . . . which animates all things"; [206] Isis was "the passive and material principle of all things." The dismemberment of Osiris corresponded to the *solutio, putrefactio,* etc. Of this Dom Pernety,[207] the source for these statements, says: "The solution of the body is the coagulation of the spirit." The blackness pertains to Isis. (Apuleius says she was clad in a "shining robe of the deepest black.") If heaven or the sun incline to her they are covered in her blackness.

735   The relation of alchemical fantasies to the primordial images of Greek mythology is too well known for me to document it. The cosmogonic brother-sister incest,[208] like the Creation itself, had been from ancient times the prototype of the alchemists' great work. Yet we seek the Graeco-Roman tradition in vain for traces of the wonder-working monoculus. We find him, perhaps, in Vedic mythology, and in a form that is highly significant for our context, namely, as an attribute of the sun-god Rohita [209] (red sun), who was called the "one-footed goat" [210] (*agá ékapada*). In Hymn XIII, 1 of the *Atharva-veda* he is praised together with his wife Rohini. Of her it says: "Rise up, O steed, that art within

205 The "Introitus apertus" says: "With the death of the lion the raven is born," * i.e., when desire dies, the blackness of death sets in. "O sad spectacle and image of eternal death, but glad news for the Artificer! . . . For thou knowest that the spirit enclosed within is quickened, which at the time appointed by the Almighty will restore life to these dead bodies." * (*Mus. herm.,* p. 691.)
206 Usually, in better accord with ancient tradition, he is the moist principle.
207 *Les Fables égyptiennes et grecques,* I, p. 179.
208 Cf. Kerényi, *The Gods of the Greeks,* p. 19.
209 Synonymous with Surya, the sun. Cf. *Hymns of the Atharva-Veda,* XIII, 1, 32 (trans. by Bloomfield, p. 211).
210 Like the "high-climbing" goat, the he-goat in general has a sexual significance, as has the foot (see n. 154). In view of the coniunctio situation this aspect is not without importance. (See par. 688, concerning Mercurialis.)

the waters," and "The steed that is within the waters is risen up." [211] The hymn begins with this invocation to Rohini, who is thereby united with Rohita after he has climbed to his highest place in heaven. The parallel with our French text is so striking that one would have to infer its literary dependence if there were any way of proving that the author was acquainted with the *Atharva-veda*. This proof is next to impossible, as Indian literature was not known in the West at all until the turn of the eighteenth century, and then only in the form of the *Oupnek'hat* of Anquetil du Perron,[212] a collection of Upanishads in Persian which he translated into Latin.[213] The *Atharva-veda* was translated only in the second half of the nineteenth century.[214] If we wish to explain the parallel at all we have to infer an archetypal connection.

736   From all this it appears that our picture represents the union of the spirit with material reality. It is not the common gold that enters into combination but the spirit of the gold, only the right half of the king, so to speak. The queen is a sulphur, like him an extract or spirit of earth or water, and therefore a chthonic spirit. The "male" spirit corresponds to Dorn's *substantia coelestis*, that is, to knowledge of the inner light—the self or imago Dei which is here united with its chthonic counterpart, the feminine spirit of the unconscious. Empirically this is personified in the psychological anima figure, who is not to be confused with the "anima" of our mediaeval philosophers, which was merely a philosophical *anima vegetativa*, the "ligament" of body and spirit. It is, rather, the alchemical queen who corresponds to the psychological anima.[215] Accordingly, the coniunctio appears here as the union of a consciousness (spirit), differentiated by self-knowledge, with a spirit abstracted from previously unconscious contents. One could also regard the latter as a quintessence of fantasy-images that enter consciousness either spontaneously or

211 *Hymns of the Atharva-Veda*, p. 207. *Ekapāda* is also a one-foot verse metre (Gk. μονοποδία and μονοποδιαῖος). *Agá ékapād* has the subsidiary meanings of 'herd-driver', 'shepherd', and 'unborn,' 'eternal'. Cf. MacDonell, *Sanskrit-English Dictionary*, s.v., and *Sacred Books of the East*, XLII, p. 664.

212 Floruit 1731 to 1805. The *Oupnek'hat* was published between 1802 and 1804. First German trans. in 1808.

213 It had a great influence on Schopenhauer. In the *Oupnek'hat* there is a section entitled "Oupnek'hat Naraiin," which is an excerpt from the *Atharva-veda*. But there is nothing in it about the *ékapād*.

214 Grill, *Hundert Lieder des Atharva-Veda*.   215 See *Aion*, ch. 3.

through active imagination and, in their totality, represent a moral or intellectual viewpoint contrasting with, or compensating, that of consciousness. To begin with, however, these images are anything but "moral" or "intellectual"; they are more or less concrete visualizations that first have to be interpreted. The alchemist used them more as technical terms for expressing the mysterious properties which he attributed to his chemical substances. The psychologist, on the contrary, regards them not as allegories but as genuine symbols pointing to psychic contents that are not known but are merely suspected in the background, to the impulses and "idées forces" of the unconscious. He starts from the fact that connections which are not based on sense-experience derive from fantasy creations which in turn have psychic causes. These causes cannot be perceived directly but are discovered only by deduction. In this work the psychologist has the support of modern fantasy material. It is produced in abundance in psychoses, dreams, and in active imagination during treatment, and it makes accurate investigation possible because the author of the fantasies can always be questioned. In this way the psychic causes can be established. The images often show such a striking resemblance to mythological motifs that one cannot help regarding the causes of the individual fantasies as identical with those that determined the collective and mythological images. In other words, there is no ground for the assumption that human beings in other epochs produced fantasies for quite different reasons, or that their fantasy images sprang from quite different *idées forces,* from ours. It can be ascertained with reasonable certainty from the literary records of the past that at least the universal human facts were felt and thought about in very much the same way at all times. Were this not so, all intelligent historiography and all understanding of historical texts would be impossible. Naturally there are differences, which make caution necessary in all cases, but these differences are mostly on the surface only and lose their significance the more deeply one penetrates into the meaning of the fundamental motifs.

737   Thus, the language of the alchemists is at first sight very different from our psychological terminology and way of thinking. But if we treat their symbols in the same way as we treat modern fantasies, they yield a meaning such as we have already deduced

from the problematical modern material. The obvious objection that the meaning conveyed by the modern fantasy-material has been uncritically transferred to the historical material, which the alchemists interpreted quite differently, is disproved by the fact that even in the Middle Ages confessed alchemists interpreted their symbols in a moral and philosophical sense. Their "philosophy" was, indeed, nothing but projected psychology. For as we have said, their ignorance of the real nature of chemical matter favoured the tendency to projection. Never do human beings speculate more, or have more opinions, than about things which they do not understand.

8. THE CONTENT AND MEANING OF THE FIRST TWO STAGES

738   I would like to impress on the reader that the following discussion, far from being a digression, is needed in order to bring a little clarity into what seems a very confused situation. This situation arose because, for the purpose of amplification, we commented on three symbolic texts ranging over a period of more than five hundred years, namely those of Albertus Magnus, Gerard Dorn, and an anonymous author of the eighteenth century. These three authors were concerned, each in his own way, with the central events and figures of the magistery. One could, of course, adduce yet other descriptions of the mysterious process of conjunction, but that would only make the confusion worse. For the purpose of disentangling the fine-spun web of alchemical fantasy these three texts are sufficient.

739   If Dorn, then, speaks of freeing the soul from the fetters of the body, he is expressing in rather different language what Albertus Magnus describes as the preparation or transformation of the quicksilver, or what our unknown author depicts as the splitting of the king in the yellow robe. The arcane substance is meant in all three cases. Hence we immediately find ourselves in darkness, in the *nigredo,* for the *arcanum,* the mystery, is dark. If, following Dorn's illuminating hints, we interpret the freeing of the soul from the fetters of the body as a withdrawal of the naïve projections by which we have moulded both the reality around us and the image of our own character, we arrive on the one hand at a *cognitio sui ipsius,* self-knowledge, but on the other hand at a realistic and more or less non-illusory view of

the outside world. This stripping off of the veils of illusion is felt as distressing and even painful. In practical treatment this phase demands much patience and tact, for the unmasking of reality is as a rule not only difficult but very often dangerous. The illusions would not be so common if they did not serve some purpose and occasionally cover up a painful spot with a wholesome darkness which one hopes will never be illuminated. Self-knowledge is not an isolated process; it is possible only if the reality of the world around us is recognized at the same time. Nobody can know himself and differentiate himself from his neighbour if he has a distorted picture of him, just as no one can understand his neighbour if he had no relationship to himself. The one conditions the other and the two processes go hand in hand.

740   I cannot describe the process of self-knowledge here in all its details. But if the reader wishes to form some idea of it, I would draw his attention to the wide variety of infantile assumptions and attachments which play a great role not only in psychopathology but in so-called normal life, and which cause endless complications in every sphere of human existence. Freud's lasting achievement in this field suffers only from the defect that, from the insights gained, a theory was prematurely abstracted which was then used as a criterion of self-knowledge: projections were recognized and corrected only so far as they were assumed to correspond to known infantile fantasies. That there are many other kinds of illusion is mentioned hardly at all in the literature, and for just that reason. As we have seen from Dorn, there are very many important things which are posited as self-evident and which do not exist, such as the alchemist's assumption that certain substances have magical qualities which in fact are projections of fantasy. The progressive correction of these brings us, however, to a frontier which at first cannot be crossed. As a rule it is set up by the spirit of the age with its specific conception of truth, and by the state of scientific knowledge prevailing at the time.

741   Self-knowledge is an adventure that carries us unexpectedly far and deep. Even a moderately comprehensive knowledge of the shadow can cause a good deal of confusion and mental darkness, since it gives rise to personality problems which one had never remotely imagined before. For this reason alone we can

understand why the alchemists called their *nigredo* melancholia, "a black blacker than black," night, an affliction of the soul, confusion, etc., or, more pointedly, the "black raven." For us the raven seems only a funny allegory, but for the medieval adept it was, as we have said, a well-known allegory of the devil.[216] Correctly assessing the psychic danger in which he stood, it was therefore of the utmost importance for him to have a favourable familiar as a helper in his work, and at the same time to devote himself diligently to the spiritual exercise of prayer; all this in order to meet effectively the consequences of the collision between his consciousness and the darkness of the shadow. Even for modern psychology the confrontation with the shadow is not a harmless affair, and for this reason it is often circumvented with cunning and caution. Rather than face one's own darkness, one contents oneself with the illusion of one's civic rectitude. Certainly most of the alchemists handled their *nigredo* in the retort without knowing what it was they were dealing with. But it is equally certain that adepts like Morienus, Dorn, Michael Maier, and others knew in their way what they were doing. It was this knowledge, and not their greed for gold, that kept them labouring at the apparently hopeless opus, for which they sacrificed their money, their goods, and their life.

742   Their "spirit" was their own belief in the light—a spirit which drew the soul to itself from its imprisonment in the body; but the soul brought with it the darkness of the chthonic spirit, the unconscious. The separation was so important because the dark deeds of the soul had to be checked. The *unio mentalis* signified, therefore, an extension of consciousness and the governance of the soul's motions by the spirit of truth. But since the soul made the body to live and was the principle of all realization, the philosophers could not but see that after the separation the body and its world were dead.[217] They therefore called this state the grave, corruption, mortification, and so on, and the problem then arose of reanimation, that is, of reuniting the soul with the "inanimate" body. Had they brought about this reanimation in a direct way, the soul would simply have snapped back

216 The raven is a symbol of the devil in Paulinus of Aquileia, *Liber Exhortationis*, cap. 50 (Migne, *P.L.*, vol. 99, col. 253) and Wolbero, *Commentaria super Cant. Cant.* (ibid., vol. 195, col. 1159).

217 "It is well known that the soul, before it was mingled with its body, was dead, and its body likewise" * ("Tractatus Micreris," *Theatr. chem.*, V, p. 106).

into its former bondage and everything would have been as before. The volatile essence so carefully shut up and preserved in the Hermetic vessel of the *unio mentalis* could not be left to itself for a moment, because this elusive Mercurius would then escape and return to its former nature, as, according to the testimony of the alchemists, not infrequently happened. The direct and natural way would have been to give the soul its head, since we are told that it always inclines to the body. Being more attached to this than to the spirit, it would separate itself from the latter and slip back into its former unconsciousness without taking with it anything of the light of the spirit into the darkness of the body. For this reason the reunion with the body was something of a problem. Psychologically, it would mean that the insight gained by the withdrawal of projections could not stand the clash with reality and, consequently, that its truth could not be realized in fact, at least not to the desired degree or in the desired way. You can, as you know, forcibly apply the ideals you regard as right with an effort of will, and can do so for a certain length of time and up to a certain point, that is, until signs of fatigue appear and the original enthusiasm wanes. Then free will becomes a cramp of the will, and the life that has been suppressed forces its way into the open through all the cracks. That, unfortunately, is the lot of all merely rational resolutions.

743 Since earliest times, therefore, men have had recourse in such situations to artificial aids, ritual actions such as dances, sacrifices, identification with ancestral spirits, etc., in the obvious attempt to conjure up or reawaken those deeper layers of the psyche which the light of reason and the power of the will can never reach, and to bring them back to memory. For this purpose they used mythological or archetypal ideas which expressed the unconscious. So it has remained to the present time, when the day of the believer begins and ends with prayer, that is, with a *rite d'entrée et de sortie*. This exercise fulfils its purpose pretty well. If it did not, it would long since have fallen into disuse. If ever it lost its efficacy to any great extent, it was always in individuals or social groups for whom the archetypal ideas have become ineffective. Though such ideas or "représentations collectives" are always true in so far as they express the unconscious archetype, their verbal and pictorial form is greatly influenced by the spirit of the age. If this changes, whether by contact with

a foreign and possibly more advanced civilization, or through an expansion of consciousness brought about by new discoveries and new knowledge, then the rite loses its meaning and degenerates into mere superstition. Examples of this on a grand scale are the extinction of the ancient Egyptian civilization and the dying out of the gods of Greece and Rome. A similar phenomenon can be observed in China today.

744   The demand that arises under such conditions is for a new interpretation, in accord with the spirit of the age, of the archetypes that compensate the altered situation of consciousness. Christianity, for instance, was a new and more suitable formulation of the archetypal myth, which in its turn gave the rite its vitality. The archetype is a living idea that constantly produces new interpretations through which that idea unfolds. This was correctly recognized by Cardinal Newman in regard to Christianity.[218] Christian doctrine is a new interpretation and development of its earlier stages, as we can see very clearly from the ancient tradition of the God-man. This tradition is continued in the unfolding of ecclesiastical dogma, and it is naturally not only the archetypes mentioned in the canonical writings of the New Testament that develop, but also their near relatives, of which we previously knew only the pagan forerunners. An example of this is the newest dogma concerning the Virgin; it refers unquestionably to the mother goddess who was constantly associated with the young dying son. She is not even purely pagan, since she was very distinctly prefigured in the Sophia of the Old Testament. For this reason the definition of the new dogma does not really go beyond the *depositum fidei,* for the mother goddess is naturally implied in the archetype of the divine son and accordingly underwent a consistent development in the course of the centuries.[219] The *depositum fidei* corresponds in empirical reality to the treasure-house of the archetypes, the "gazophylacium" of the alchemists, and the collective unconscious of modern psychology.

745   The objection raised by theologians that the final state of the dogma in any such development would be necessarily more com-

[218] *Essay on the Development of Christian Doctrine.*
[219] Declaration of the Virgin's right to the title of Theotokos ("God-bearer") at the Council of Ephesus in 431, and definition of the Immaculate Conception by Pope Pius IX in 1854.

plete or perfect than in the apostolic era is untenable. Obviously the later interpretation and formulation of the archetype will be much more differentiated than in the beginning. A glance at the history of dogma is sufficient to confirm this. One has only to think of the Trinity, for which there is no direct evidence in the canonical writings. But it does not follow from this that the primitive Christians had a less complete knowledge of the fundamental truths. Such an assumption borders on pernicious intellectualism, for what counts in religious experience is not how explicitly an archetype can be formulated but how much I am gripped by it. The least important thing is what I think about it.[220]

746 The "living idea" is always perfect and always numinous. Human formulation adds nothing and takes away nothing, for the archetype is autonomous and the only question is whether a man is gripped by it or not. If he can formulate it more or less, then he can more easily integrate it with consciousness, talk about it more reasonably and explain its meaning a bit more rationally. But he does not possess it more or in a more perfect way than the man who cannot formulate his "possession." Intellectual formulation becomes important only when the memory of the original experience threatens to disappear, or when its irrationality seems inapprehensible by consciousness. It is an auxiliary only, not an essential.

747 Christianity, to return to our previous argument, was "a *unio mentalis* in the overcoming of the body." In just this respect the rite fulfilled its purpose, so far as that is possible for fallible human beings. Ancient man's sensuous delight in the body and in nature did not disappear in the process, but found free play in the long list of sins which has never at any time diminished in scope. His knowledge of nature, however, presents a special problem. Ever since antiquity it had flourished only in secret and among the few, but it handed down certain basic conceptions through the centuries and, in the later Middle Ages, fertilized man's reawakened interest in natural bodies. Had the alchemists not had at least a secret premonition that their Christian *unio mentalis* had not yet realized the union with the world of the body, their almost mystical thirst for

220 Cf. I Corinthians 13 : 12: "Now I know in part, but then I shall know even as I am known."

knowledge would scarcely be explicable, let alone the symbolism, rivalling that of Christianity, which began to develop already at the end of the thirteenth century. The Christ-lapis parallel shows more clearly than anything else that the world of natural bodies laid claim to equality and hence to realization in the second stage of the coniunctio.

748   This raised the question of the way in which the coniunctio could be effected. Dorn answered this by proposing, instead of an overcoming of the body, the typical alchemical process of the *separatio, solutio, incineratio, sublimatio,* etc. of the red or white wine, the purpose of this procedure being to produce a physical equivalent of the *substantia coelestis,* recognized by the spirit as the truth and as the image of God innate in man. Whatever names the alchemists gave to the mysterious substance they sought to produce, it was always a celestial substance, i.e., something transcendental, which, in contrast to the perishability of all known matter, was incorruptible, inert as a metal or a stone, and yet alive, like an organic being, and at the same time a universal medicament. Such a "body" was quite obviously not to be met with in experience. The tenacity with which the adepts pursued this goal for at least seventeen hundred years can be explained only by the numinosity of this idea. And we do indeed find, even in the ancient alchemy of Zosimos, clear indications of the archetype of the Anthropos,[221] as I have shown in *Psychology and Alchemy;* an image that pervades the whole of alchemy down to the figure of the homunculus in *Faust.* The idea of the Anthropos springs from the notion of an original state of universal animation, for which reason the old Masters interpreted their Mercurius as the *anima mundi;* and just as the original animation could be found in all matter, so too could the *anima mundi.* It was imprinted on all bodies as their *raison d'être,* as an image of the demiurge who incarnated in his own creation and got caught in it. Nothing was easier than to identify this *anima mundi* with the Biblical *imago Dei,* which represented the truth revealed to the spirit. For the early thinkers the soul was by no means a merely intellectual concept; it was visualized sensuously as a breath-body or a volatile but physical substance which, it was readily supposed, could be chemically extracted

[221] Cf. the *chén-yén* of Wei Po-yang.

and "fixed" by means of a suitable procedure. This intention was served by the preparation of the *phlegma vini*. As I pointed out earlier, this was not the spirit and water of the wine but its solid residue, the chthonic and corporeal part which would not ordinarily be regarded as the essential and valuable thing about the wine.

749   What the alchemist sought, then, to help him out of his dilemma was a chemical operation which we today would describe as a symbol. The procedure he followed was obviously an allegory of his postulated *substantia coelestis* and its chemical equivalent. To that extent the operation was not symbolical for him but purposive and rational. For us, who know that no amount of incineration, sublimation, and centrifuging of the vinous residue can ever produce an "air-coloured" quintessence, the entire procedure is fantastic if taken literally. We can hardly suppose that Dorn, either, meant a real wine but, after the manner of the alchemists, *vinum ardens, acetum, spiritualis sanguis,* etc., in other words *Mercurius non vulgi,* who embodied the *anima mundi.* Just as the air encompasses the earth, so in the old view the soul is wrapped round the world. As I have shown, we can most easily equate the concept of Mercurius with that of the unconscious. If we add this term to the recipe, it would run: Take the unconscious in one of its handiest forms, say a spontaneous fantasy, a dream, an irrational mood, an affect, or something of the kind, and operate with it. Give it your special attention, concentrate on it, and observe its alterations objectively. Spare no effort to devote yourself to this task, follow the subsequent transformations of the spontaneous fantasy attentively and carefully. Above all, don't let anything from outside, that does not belong, get into it, for the fantasy-image has "everything it needs." [222] In this way one is certain of not interfering by conscious caprice and of giving the unconscious a free hand. In short, the alchemical operation seems to us the equivalent of the psychological process of active imagination.

750   Ordinarily, the only thing people know about psychotherapy is that it consists in a certain technique which the analyst applies to his patient. Specialists know how far they can get with it. One can use it to cure the neuroses, and even the milder psychoses, so that nothing more remains of the illness except the general hu-

222 "Omne quo indiget" is frequently said of the lapis.

man problem of how much of yourself you want to forget, how much psychic discomfort you have to take on your shoulders, how much you may forbid or allow yourself, how much or how little you may expect of others, how far you should give up the meaning of your life or what sort of meaning you should give it. The analyst has a right to shut his door when a neurosis no longer produces any clinical symptoms and has debouched into the sphere of general human problems. The less he knows about these the greater his chances are of coming across comparatively reasonable patients who can be weaned from the transference that regularly sets in. But if the patient has even the remotest suspicion that the analyst thinks rather more about these problems than he says, then he will not give up the transference all that quickly but will cling to it in defiance of all reason—which is not so unreasonable after all, indeed quite understandable. Even adult persons often have no idea how to cope with the problem of living, and on top of that are so unconscious in this regard that they succumb in the most uncritical way to the slightest possibility of finding some kind of answer or certainty. Were this not so, the numerous sects and -isms would long since have died out. But, thanks to unconscious, infantile attachments, boundless uncertainty and lack of self-reliance, they all flourish like weeds.

751   The analyst who is himself struggling for all those things which he seeks to inculcate into his patients will not get round the problem of the transference so easily. The more he knows how difficult it is for him to solve the problems of his own life, the less he can overlook the fear and uncertainty or the frivolity and dangerously uncritical attitude of his patients. Even Freud regarded the transference as a neurosis at second hand and treated it as such. He could not simply shut the door, but honestly tried to analyze the transference away. This is not so simple as it sounds when technically formulated. Practice often turns out to be rather different from theory. You want, of course, to put a whole man on his feet and not just a part of him. You soon discover that there is nothing for him to stand on and nothing for him to hold on to. Return to the parents has become impossible, so he hangs on to the analyst. He can go neither backwards nor forwards, for he sees nothing before him that could give him a hold. All so-called reasonable possibilities have been tried out

and have proved useless. Not a few patients then remember the faith in which they were brought up, and some find their way back to it, but not all. They know, perhaps, what their faith ought to mean to them, but they have found to their cost how little can be achieved with will and good intentions if the unconscious does not lend a hand. In order to secure its co-operation the religions have long turned to myths for help, or rather, the myths always flung out bridges between the helpless consciousness and the effective *idées forces* of the unconscious. But you cannot, artificially and with an effort of will, believe the statements of myth if you have not previously been gripped by them. If you are honest, you will doubt the truth of the myth because our present-day consciousness has no means of understanding it. Historical and scientific criteria do not lend themselves to a recognition of mythological truth; it can be grasped only by the intuitions of faith or by psychology, and in the latter case although there may be insight it remains ineffective unless it is backed by experience.

752   Thus the modern man cannot even bring about the *unio mentalis* which would enable him to accomplish the second degree of conjunction. The analyst's guidance in helping him to understand the statements of his unconscious in dreams, etc. may provide the necessary insight, but when it comes to the question of real experience the analyst can no longer help him: he himself must put his hand to the work. He is then in the position of an alchemist's apprentice who is inducted into the teachings by the Master and learns all the tricks of the laboratory. But sometime he must set about the opus himself, for, as the alchemists emphasize, nobody else can do it for him. Like this apprentice, the modern man begins with an unseemly prima materia which presents itself in unexpected form—a contemptible fantasy which, like the stone that the builders rejected, is "flung into the street" and is so "cheap" that people do not even look at it. He will observe it from day to day and note its alterations until his eyes are opened or, as the alchemists say, until the fish's eyes, or the sparks, shine in the dark solution. For the eyes of the fish are always open and therefore must always see, which is why the alchemists used them as a symbol of perpetual attention. (Pls. 8 and 9.)

753   The light that gradually dawns on him consists in his understanding that his fantasy is a real psychic process which is hap-

pening to him personally. Although, to a certain extent, he looks on from outside, impartially, he is also an acting and suffering figure in the drama of the psyche. This recognition is absolutely necessary and marks an important advance. So long as he simply looks at the pictures he is like the foolish Parsifal, who forgot to ask the vital question because he was not aware of his own participation in the action. Then, if the flow of images ceases, next to nothing has happened even though the process is repeated a thousand times. But if you recognize your own involvement you yourself must enter into the process with your personal reactions, just as if you were one of the fantasy figures, or rather, as if the drama being enacted before your eyes were real. It is a psychic fact that this fantasy is happening, and it is as real as you —as a psychic entity—are real. If this crucial operation is not carried out, all the changes are left to the flow of images, and you yourself remain unchanged. As Dorn says, you will never make the One unless you become one yourself. It is, however, possible that if you have a dramatic fantasy you will enter the interior world of images as a *fictitious personality* and thereby prevent any real participation; it may even endanger consciousness because you then become the victim of your own fantasy and succumb to the powers of the unconscious, whose dangers the analyst knows all too well. But if you place yourself in the drama as you really are, not only does it gain in actuality but you also create, by your criticism of the fantasy, an effective counterbalance to its tendency to get out of hand. For what is now happening is the decisive rapprochement with the unconscious. This is where insight, the *unio mentalis,* begins to become real. What you are now creating is the beginning of individuation, whose immediate goal is the experience and production of the symbol of totality.

754   It not infrequently happens that the patient simply continues to observe his images without considering what they mean to him. He can and he should understand their meaning, but this is of practical value only so long as he is not sufficiently convinced that the unconscious can give him valuable insights. But once he has recognized this fact, he should also know that he then has in his hands an opportunity to win, by his knowledge, independence of the analyst. This conclusion is one which he does not like to draw, with the result that he frequently stops

short at the mere observation of his images. The analyst, if he has not tried out the procedure on himself, cannot help him over this stile—assuming, of course, that there are compelling reasons why the procedure should be continued. In these cases there is no medical or ethical imperative but only a command of fate, which is why patients who by no means lack the necessary acumen often come to a standstill at this point. As this experience is not uncommon I can only conclude that the transition from a merely perceptive, i.e., *aesthetic*, attitude to one of *judgment* is far from easy. Indeed, modern psychotherapy has just reached this point and is beginning to recognize the usefulness of perceiving and giving shape to the images, whether by pencil and brush or by modelling. A musical configuration might also be possible provided that it were really composed and written down. Though I have never met a case of this kind, Bach's *Art of Fugue* would seem to offer an example, just as the representation of the archetypes is a basic feature of Wagner's music. (These phenomena, however, arise less from personal necessity than from the unconscious compensations produced by the *Zeitgeist*, though I cannot discuss this here.)

755 The step beyond a merely aesthetic attitude may be unfamiliar to most of my readers. I myself have said little about it and have contented myself with hints.[223] It is not a matter that can be taken lightly. I tried it out on myself and others thirty years ago and must admit that although it is feasible and leads to satisfactory results it is also very difficult. It can be recommended without misgiving if a patient has reached the stage of knowledge described above. If he finds the task too difficult he will usually fail right at the beginning and never get through the dangerous impasse. The danger inherent in analysis is that, in a psychopathically disposed patient, it will unleash a psychosis. This very unpleasant possibility generally presents itself at the beginning of the treatment, when, for instance, dream-analysis has activated the unconscious. But if it has got so far that the patient can do active imagination and shape out his fantasies, and there are no suspicious incidents, then there is as a rule no longer any serious danger. One naturally asks oneself what fear —if fear it is—prevents him from taking the next step, the transi-

223 Cf. "The Transcendent Function," pars. 166ff.

tion to an attitude of judgment. (The judgment of course should be morally and intellectually binding.) There are sufficient reasons for fear and uncertainty because voluntary participation in the fantasy is alarming to a naïve mind and amounts to an anticipated psychosis.

756   Naturally there is an enormous difference between an anticipated psychosis and a real one, but the difference is not always clearly perceived and this gives rise to uncertainty or even a fit of panic. Unlike a real psychosis, which comes on you and inundates you with uncontrollable fantasies irrupting from the unconscious, the judging attitude implies a voluntary involvement in those fantasy-processes which compensate the individual and —in particular—the collective situation of consciousness. The avowed purpose of this involvement is to integrate the statements of the unconscious, to assimilate their compensatory content, and thereby produce a whole meaning which alone makes life worth living and, for not a few people, possible at all. The reason why the involvement looks very like a psychosis is that the patient is integrating the same fantasy-material to which the insane person falls victim because he cannot integrate it but is swallowed up by it. In myths the hero is the one who conquers the dragon, not the one who is devoured by it. And yet both have to deal with the same dragon. Also, he is no hero who never met the dragon, or who, if he once saw it, declared afterwards that he saw nothing. Equally, only one who has risked the fight with the dragon and is not overcome by it wins the hoard, the "treasure hard to attain." He alone has a genuine claim to self-confidence, for he has faced the dark ground of his self and thereby has gained himself. This experience gives him faith and trust, the *pistis* in the ability of the self to sustain him, for everything that menaced him from inside he has made his own. He has acquired the right to believe that he will be able to overcome all future threats by the same means. He has arrived at an inner certainty which makes him capable of self-reliance, and attained what the alchemists called the *unio mentalis*.

757   As a rule this state is represented pictorially by a mandala. Often such drawings contain clear allusions to the sky and the stars and therefore refer to something like the "inner" heaven, the "firmament" or "Olympus" of Paracelsus, the Microcosm.

531

This, too, is that circular product, the *caelum*,[224] which Dorn wanted to produce by "assiduous rotary movements." Because it is not very likely that he ever manufactured this quintessence as a chemical body, and he himself nowhere asserts that he did, one must ask whether he really meant this chemical operation or rather, perhaps, the opus alchymicum in general, that is, the transmutation of Mercurius duplex under the synonym of the red and white wine,[225] thus alluding at the same time to the *opus ad rubeum et ad album*. This seems to me more probable. At any rate some kind of laboratory work was meant. In this way Dorn "shaped out" his intuition of a mysterious centre pre-existent in man, which at the same time represented a cosmos, i.e., a totality, while he himself remained conscious that he was portraying the *self* in matter. He completed the image of wholeness by the admixture of honey, magic herbs, and human blood, or their meaningful equivalents, just as a modern man does when he associates numerous symbolic attributes with his drawing of a mandala. Also, following the old Sabaean and Alexandrian models, Dorn drew the "influence" of the planets (*stellae inferiores*)—or Tartarus and the mythological aspect of the underworld—into his quintessence, just as the patient does today.[226]

758   In this wise Dorn solved the problem of realizing the *unio mentalis*, of effecting its union with the body, thereby completing the second stage of the coniunctio. We would say that with this production of a physical equivalent the idea of the self had taken shape. But the alchemist associated his work with something more potent and more original than our pale abstraction. He felt it as a magically effective action which, like the substance itself, imparted magical qualities. The projection of magical qualities indicates the existence of corresponding effects on consciousness, that is to say the adept felt a numinous effect emanating from the lapis, or whatever he called the arcane substance. We, with our rationalistic minds, would scarcely attribute any such thing to the pictures which the modern man makes of his intuitive vision of unconscious contents. But it

224 Cf. "Concerning Mandala Symbolism," fig. 28 and commentary, par. 682, and the blue centre of Indian mandalas.
225 Red (= sun) and white (= moon) are the alchemical colours.
226 Cf. "A Study in the Process of Individuation," Picture 9.

depends on whether we are dealing with the conscious or with the unconscious. The unconscious does in fact seem to be influenced by these images. One comes to this conclusion when one examines more closely the psychic reactions of the patients to their own drawings: they do have in the end a quietening influence and create something like an inner foundation. While the adept had always looked for the effects of his stone outside, for instance as the panacea or golden tincture or life-prolonging elixir, and only during the sixteenth century pointed with unmistakable clarity to an inner effect, psychological experience emphasizes above all the subjective reaction to the formation of images, and—with a free and open mind—still reserves judgment in regard to possible objective effects.[227]

9. THE THIRD STAGE: THE UNUS MUNDUS

759   The production of the lapis was the goal of alchemy in general. Dorn was a significant exception, because for him this denoted only the completion of the second stage of conjunction. In this he agrees with psychological experience. For us the representation of the idea of the self in actual and visible form is a mere *rite d'entrée*, as it were a propaedeutic action and mere anticipation of its realization. The existence of a sense of inner security by no means proves that the product will be stable enough to withstand the disturbing or hostile influences of the environment. The adept had to experience again and again how unfavourable circumstances or a technical blunder or—as it seemed to him—some devilish accident hindered the completion of his work, so that he was forced to start all over again from the very beginning. Anyone who submits his sense of inner security to analogous psychic tests will have similar experiences. More than once everything he has built will fall to pieces under the impact of reality, and he must not let this discourage him from examining, again and again, where it is that his attitude is still defective, and what are the blind spots in his psychic field of vision. Just as a lapis Philosophorum, with its miraculous powers, was never produced, so psychic wholeness will never be attained empirically, as consciousness is too narrow and too one-sided to comprehend the full inventory of the psyche. Always we

[227] I refer here to the relation between the archetype and the phenomenon of synchronicity.

shall have to begin again from the beginning. From ancient times the adept knew that he was concerned with the "res simplex," and the modern man too will find by experience that the work does not prosper without the greatest simplicity. But simple things are always the most difficult.

760   The One and Simple is what Dorn called the *unus mundus.* This "one world" was the *res simplex.*[228] For him the third and highest degree of conjunction was the union of the whole man with the *unus mundus.* By this he meant, as we have seen, the potential world of the first day of creation, when nothing was yet "in actu," i.e., divided into two and many, but was still one.[229] The creation of unity by a magical procedure meant the possibility of effecting a union with the world—not with the world of multiplicity as we see it but with a potential world, the eternal Ground of all empirical being, just as the self is the ground and origin of the individual personality past, present, and future. On the basis of a self known by meditation and produced by alchemical means, Dorn "hoped and expected" to be united with the *unus mundus.*

761   This potential world is the "mundus archetypus" of the Schoolmen. I conjecture that the immediate model for Dorn's idea is to be found in Philo Judaeus, who, in his treatise *De mundi opificio,*[230] says that the Creator made in the intelligible world an incorporeal heaven, an invisible earth, and the idea of the air and the void. Last of all he created man, a "little heaven" that "bears in itself the reflections of many natures similar to the stars." Here Philo points clearly to the idea of the Microcosm and hence to the unity of the psychic man with the cosmos. According to Philo, the relation of the Creator to the *mundus intelligibilis* is the "imago" or "archetypus" of the relation of the mind to the body. Whether Dorn also knew Plotinus is questionable. In his fourth Ennead (9, 1ff.) Plotinus discusses the problem of whether all individuals are merely one soul, and he believes he has good grounds for affirming this question. I mention Plotinus because he is an earlier witness to the idea of the

228 In the "Liber Platonis quartorum" this is the term for the arcane substance.
229 Similarly, Aquinas conceives the prima materia as "ens in potentia" (*Summa,* Part I, p. 66, Art. 1). Cf. von Franz, *Aurora Consurgens,* Commentary, p. 174, n. 88.
230 Philo's writings were available in the Latin edition of Petronillus (Lyons, 1561) and may have been known to Dorn, who wrote ca. 1590.

unus mundus. The "unity of the soul" rests empirically on the basic psychic structure common to all souls, which, though not visible and tangible like the anatomical structure, is just as evident as it.

762 The thought Dorn expresses by the third degree of conjunction is universal: it is the relation or identity of the personal with the suprapersonal atman, and of the individual tao with the universal tao. To the Westerner this view appears not at all realistic and all too mystic; above all he cannot see why a self should become a reality when it enters into relationship with the world of the first day of creation. He has no knowledge of any world other than the empirical one. Strictly speaking, his puzzlement does not begin here; it began already with the production of the *caelum,* the inner unity. Such thoughts are unpopular and distressingly nebulous. He does not know where they belong or on what they could be based. They might be true or again they might not—in short, his experience stops here and with it as a rule his understanding, and, unfortunately, only too often his willingness to learn more. I would therefore counsel the critical reader to put aside his prejudices and for once try to experience on himself the effects of the process I have described, or else to suspend judgment and admit that he understands nothing. For thirty years I have studied these psychic processes under all possible conditions and have assured myself that the alchemists as well as the great philosophies of the East are referring to just such experiences, and that it is chiefly our ignorance of the psyche if these experiences appear "mystic."

763 We should at all events be able to understand that the visualization of the self is a "window" into eternity, which gave the medieval man, like the Oriental, an opportunity to escape from the stifling grip of a one-sided view of the world or to hold out against it. Though the goal of the opus alchymicum was indubitably the production of the lapis or *caelum,* there can be no doubt about its tendency to spiritualize the "body." This is expressed by the symbol of the "air-coloured" liquid that floats to the surface. It represents nothing less than a *corpus glorificationis,* the resurrected body whose relation to eternity is self-evident.

764 Now just as it seems self-evident to the naïve-minded person that an apple falls from the tree to the earth, but absurd to say

that the earth rises up to meet the apple, so he can believe without difficulty that the mind is able to spiritualize the body without being affected by its inertia and grossness. But all effects are mutual, and nothing changes anything else without itself being changed. Although the alchemist thought he knew better than anyone else that, at the Creation, at least a little bit of the divinity, the *anima mundi,* entered into material things and was caught there, he nevertheless believed in the possibility of a one-sided spiritualization, without considering that the precondition for this is a materialization of the spirit in the form of the blue quintessence. In reality his labours elevated the body into proximity with the spirit while at the same time drawing the spirit down into matter. By sublimating matter he concretized spirit.

765 This self-evident truth was still strange to medieval man and it has been only partially digested even by the man of today. But if a union is to take place between opposites like spirit and matter, conscious and unconscious, bright and dark, and so on, it will happen in a third thing, which represents not a compromise but something new, just as for the alchemists the cosmic strife of the elements was composed by the λίθος οὐ λίθος (stone that is no stone), by a transcendental entity that could be described only in paradoxes.[231] Dorn's *caelum,* which corresponded to the stone, was on the one hand a liquid that could be poured out of a bottle and on the other the Microcosm itself. For the psychologist it is the self—man as he is, and the indescribable and super-empirical totality of that same man. This totality is a mere postulate, but a necessary one, because no one can assert that he has complete knowledge of man as he is. Not only in the psychic man is there something unknown, but also in the physical. We should be able to include this unknown quantity in a total picture of man, but we cannot. Man himself is partly empirical,

---

[231] The antiquity of the stone symbolism is shown by the fact that it occurs not only among primitives living today but in the documents of ancient cultures as well, as for instance in the Hurrian texts of Boghazköy, where the son of the father-god Kumarbi is the stone Ullikummi, a "terrible" diorite stone that "grew in the water." This stone parallels the Greek myth of the stone which Kronos swallowed and spat out again when Zeus compelled him to yield up the children he had devoured. Zeus then set it up as a cult-object in Pytho. Ullikummi is a Titanic being and, interestingly enough, an implacable enemy of the gods. (Cf. Güterbock, "Kumarbi," *Istanbuler Schriften,* No. 16; Gurney, *The Hittites,* pp. 190ff.)

partly transcendental; he too is a λίθος οὐ λίθος. Also, we do not know whether what we on the empirical plane regard as physical may not, in the Unknown beyond our experience, be identical with what on this side of the border we distinguish from the physical as psychic. Though we know from experience that psychic processes are related to material ones, we are not in a position to say in what this relationship consists or how it is possible at all. Precisely because the psychic and the physical are mutually dependent it has often been conjectured that they may be identical somewhere beyond our present experience, though this certainly does not justify the arbitrary hypothesis of either materialism or spiritualism.

766　　With this conjecture of the identity of the psychic and the physical we approach the alchemical view of the *unus mundus,* the potential world of the first day of creation, when there was as yet "no second." Before the time of Paracelsus the alchemists believed in *creatio ex nihilo.* For them, therefore, God himself was the principle of matter. But Paracelsus and his school assumed that matter was an "increatum," and hence coexistent and coeternal with God. Whether they considered this view monistic or dualistic I am unable to discover. The only certain thing is that for all the alchemists matter had a divine aspect, whether on the ground that God was imprisoned in it in the form of the *anima mundi* or *anima media natura,* or that matter represented God's "reality." In no case was matter de-deified, and certainly not the potential matter of the first day of creation. It seems that only the Paracelsists were influenced by the dualistic words of Genesis.[232]

767　　If Dorn, then, saw the consummation of the mysterium coniunctionis in the union of the alchemically produced *caelum* with the *unus mundus,* he expressly meant not a fusion of the individual with his environment, or even his adaptation to it, but a *unio mystica* with the potential world. Such a view indeed seems to us "mystical," if we misuse this word in its pejorative modern sense. It is not, however, a question of thoughtlessly used words but of a view which can be translated from medieval language into modern concepts. Undoubtedly the idea of the *unus mundus* is founded on the assumption that the multiplicity

232 Genesis 1 : 2: "The earth was without form and void, and the Spirit of God brooded over the deep." (Author's trans.)

of the empirical world rests on an underlying unity, and that not two or more fundamentally different worlds exist side by side or are mingled with one another. Rather, everything divided and different belongs to one and the same world, which is not the world of sense but a postulate whose probability is vouched for by the fact that until now no one has been able to discover a world in which the known laws of nature are invalid. That even the psychic world, which is so extraordinarily different from the physical world, does not have its roots outside the one cosmos is evident from the undeniable fact that causal connections exist between the psyche and the body which point to their underlying unitary nature.

768   All that *is* is not encompassed by our knowledge, so that we are not in a position to make any statements about its total nature. Microphysics is feeling its way into the unknown side of matter, just as complex psychology is pushing forward into the unknown side of the psyche. Both lines of investigation have yielded findings which can be conceived only by means of antinomies, and both have developed concepts which display remarkable analogies. If this trend should become more pronounced in the future, the hypothesis of the unity of their subject-matters would gain in probability. Of course there is little or no hope that the unitary Being can ever be conceived, since our powers of thought and language permit only of antinomian statements. But this much we do know beyond all doubt, that empirical reality has a transcendental background—a fact which, as Sir James Jeans has shown, can be expressed by Plato's parable of the cave. The common background of microphysics and depth-psychology is as much physical as psychic and therefore neither, but rather a third thing, a neutral nature which can at most be grasped in hints since in essence it is transcendental.

769   The background of our empirical world thus appears to be in fact a *unus mundus*. This is at least a probable hypothesis which satisfies the fundamental tenet of scientific theory: "Explanatory principles are not to be multiplied beyond the necessary." The transcendental psychophysical background corresponds to a "potential world" in so far as all those conditions which determine the form of empirical phenomena are inherent in it. This obviously holds good as much for physics as for psy-

chology, or, to be more precise, for macrophysics as much as for the psychology of consciousness.

770   So if Dorn sees the third and highest degree of conjunction in a union or relationship of the adept, who has produced the *caelum*, with the *unus mundus*, this would consist, psychologically, in a synthesis of the conscious with the unconscious. The result of this conjunction or equation is theoretically inconceivable, since a known quantity is combined with an unknown one; but in practice as many far-reaching changes of consciousness result from it as atomic physics has produced in classical physics. The nature of the changes which Dorn expects from the third stage of the coniunctio can be established only indirectly from the symbolism used by the adepts. What he called *caelum* is, as we have seen, a symbolic prefiguration of the self. We can conclude from this that the desired realization of the whole man was conceived as a healing of organic and psychic ills, since the *caelum* was described as a universal medicine (the panacea, alexipharmic, *medicina catholica,* etc.). It was regarded also as the balsam and elixir of life, as a life-prolonging, strengthening, and rejuvenating magical potion. It was a "living stone," a λίθος ἔμψυχος (*baetylus*), a "stone that hath a spirit," [233] and the "living stone" mentioned in the New Testament,[234] which in the *Shepherd of Hermas* is the living man who adds himself as a brick to the tower of the Church. Above all, its incorruptibility is stressed: it lasts a long time, or for all eternity; though alive, it is unmoved; it radiates magic power and transforms the perishable into the imperishable and the impure into the pure; it multiplies itself indefinitely; it is simple and therefore universal, the union of all opposites; it is the parallel of Christ and is called the Saviour of the Macrocosm. But the *caelum* also signifies man's likeness to God (*imago Dei*), the *anima mundi* in matter, and the truth itself. It "has a thousand names." It is also the Microcosm, the whole man (τέλειος ἄνθρωπος), *chên-yên,* a homunculus and a hermaphrodite. These designations and significations are but a small selection from the plethora of names mentioned in the literature.

771   Not unnaturally, we are at a loss to see how a psychic expe-

233 Berthelot, *Alch. grecs,* III, vi, 5.
234 I Peter 2 : 5: ". . . like living stones be yourselves built into a spiritual edifice" (RSV, mod.). Cf. Ephesians 2 : 20.

rience of this kind—for such it evidently was—can be formulated as a rational concept. Undoubtedly it was meant as the essence of perfection and universality, and, as such, it characterized an experience of similar proportions. We could compare this only with the ineffable mystery of the *unio mystica,* or *tao,* or the content of *samadhi,* or the experience of *satori* in Zen, which would bring us to the realm of the ineffable and of extreme subjectivity where all the criteria of reason fail. Remarkably enough this experience is an empirical one in so far as there are unanimous testimonies from the East and West alike, both from the present and from the distant past, which confirm its unsurpassable subjective significance. Our knowledge of physical nature gives us no *point d'appui* that would enable us to put the experience on any generally valid basis. It is and remains a secret of the world of psychic experience and can be understood only as a numinous event, whose actuality, nevertheless, cannot be doubted any more than the fact that light of a certain wave-length is perceived as "red"—a fact which remains incomprehensible only to a man suffering from red-green blindness.

772   What, then, do the statements of the alchemists concerning their arcanum mean, looked at psychologically? In order to answer this question we must remember the working hypothesis we have used for the interpretation of dreams: the images in dreams and spontaneous fantasies are symbols, that is, the best possible formulation for still unknown or unconscious facts, which generally compensate the content of consciousness or the conscious attitude. If we apply this basic rule to the alchemical arcanum, we come to the conclusion that its most conspicuous quality, namely, *its unity and uniqueness*—one is the stone, one the medicine, one the vessel, one the procedure, and one the disposition [235]—presupposes a *dissociated consciousness.* For no one who is one himself needs oneness as a medicine—nor, we might add, does anyone who is unconscious of his dissociation, for a *conscious* situation of distress is needed in order to activate the archetype of unity. From this we may conclude that the more philosophically minded alchemists were people who did not feel satisfied with the then prevailing view of the world, that is, with the Christian faith, although they were convinced of its truth. In this latter respect we find in the classical Latin

[235] *Ros. phil., Art. aurif.,* II, p. 206.

and Greek literature of alchemy no evidences to the contrary, but rather, so far as Christian treatises are concerned, abundant testimony to the firmness of their Christian convictions. Since Christianity is expressly a system of "salvation," founded moreover on God's "plan of redemption," and God is unity *par excellence,* one must ask oneself why the alchemists still felt a disunity in themselves, or not at one with themselves, when their faith, so it would appear, gave them every opportunity for unity and unison. (This question has lost nothing of its topicality today, on the contrary!) The question answers itself when we examine more closely the other attributes that are predicated of the arcanum.

773   The next quality, therefore, which we have to consider is its *physical* nature. Although the alchemists attached the greatest importance to this, and the "stone" was the whole *raison d'être* of their art, yet it cannot be regarded as merely physical since it is stressed that the stone was alive and possessed a soul and spirit, or even that it was a man or some creature like a man. And although it was also said of God that the world is his physical manifestation, this pantheistic view was rejected by the Church, for "God is Spirit" and the very reverse of matter. In that case the Christian standpoint would correspond to the *"unio mentalis* in the overcoming of the body." So far as the alchemist professed the Christian faith, he knew that according to his own lights he was still at the second stage of conjunction, and that the Christian "truth" was not yet "realized." The soul was drawn up by the spirit to the lofty regions of abstraction; but the body was de-souled, and since it also had claims to live the unsatisfactoriness of the situation could not remain hidden from him. He was unable to feel himself a whole, and whatever the spiritualization of his existence may have meant to him he could not get beyond the Here and Now of his bodily life in the physical world. The spirit precluded his orientation to physis and vice versa. Despite all assurances to the contrary Christ is not a unifying factor but a dividing "sword" which sunders the spiritual man from the physical. The alchemists, who, unlike certain moderns, were clever enough to see the necessity and fitness of a further development of consciousness, held fast to their Christian convictions and did not slip back to a more unconscious level. They could not and would not deny the truth of Chris-

tianity, and for this reason it would be wrong to accuse them of heresy. On the contrary, they wanted to "realize" the unity foreshadowed in the idea of God by struggling to unite the *unio mentalis* with the body.

774 The mainspring of this endeavour was the conviction that this world was in a morbid condition and that everything was corrupted by original sin. They saw that the soul could be redeemed only if it was freed by the spirit from its natural attachment to the body, though this neither altered nor in any way improved the status of physical life. The Microcosm, i.e., the inner man, was capable of redemption but not the corrupt body. This insight was reason enough for a dissociation of consciousness into a spiritual and a physical personality. They could all declare with St. Paul: "O wretched man that I am, who shall deliver me from the body of this death?" [236] They therefore strove to find the medicine that would heal all the sufferings of the body and the disunion of the soul, the φάρμακον ἀθανασίας which frees the body of its corruptibility, and the elixir vitae which grants the long life of the Biblical aforetime, or even immortality. Since most of them were physicians, they had plenty of opportunities to form an overwhelming impression of the transitoriness of human existence, and to develop that kind of impatience which refuses to wait till Kingdom come for more endurable conditions better in accord with the message of salvation. It is precisely the claims of the physical man and the unendurability of his dissociation that are expressed in this gnawing discontent. The alchemists, consequently, saw themselves faced with the extremely difficult task of uniting the wayward physical man with his spiritual truth. As they were neither unbelievers nor heretics, they could not and would not alter this truth in order to make it more favourably disposed to the body. Besides, the body was in the wrong anyway since it had succumbed to original sin by its moral weakness. It was therefore the body with its darkness that had to be "prepared." This, as we have seen, was done by extracting a quintessence which was the physical equivalent of heaven, of the potential world, and on that account was named "caelum." It was the very essence of the body, an incorruptible and therefore pure and eternal substance, a *corpus glorificatum*, capable and worthy of being united with the *unio*

236 Romans 7 : 24.

mentalis. What was left over from the body was a "terra damnata," a dross that had to be abandoned to its fate. The quintessence, the *caelum,* on the other hand, corresponded to the pure, incorrupt, original stuff of the world, God's adequate and perfectly obedient instrument, whose production, therefore, permitted the alchemist to "hope and expect" the conjunction with the *unus mundus.*

775 This solution was a compromise to the disadvantage of physis, but it was nevertheless a noteworthy attempt to bridge the dissociation between spirit and matter. It was not a solution of principle, for the very reason that the procedure did not take place in the real object at all but was a fruitless projection, since the *caelum* could never be fabricated in reality. It was a hope that was extinguished with alchemy and then, it seems, was struck off the agenda for ever. But the dissociation remained, and, in quite the contrary sense, brought about a far better knowledge of nature and a sounder medicine, while on the other hand it deposed the spirit in a manner that would paralyse Dorn with horror could he see it today. The elixir vitae of modern science has already increased the expectation of life very considerably and hopes for still better results in the future. The *unio mentalis,* on the other hand, has become a pale phantom, and the *veritas christiana* feels itself on the defensive. As for a truth that is hidden in the human body, there is no longer any talk of that. History has remorselessly made good what the alchemical compromise left unfinished: the physical man has been unexpectedly thrust into the foreground and has conquered nature in an undreamt-of way. At the same time he has become conscious of his *empirical* psyche, which has loosened itself from the embrace of the spirit and begun to take on so concrete a form that its individual features are now the object of clinical observation. It has long ceased to be a life-principle or some kind of philosophical abstraction; on the contrary, it is suspected of being a mere epiphenomenon of the chemistry of the brain. Nor does the spirit any longer give it life; rather is it conjectured that the spirit owes its existence to psychic activity. Today psychology can call itself a science, and this is a big concession on the part of the spirit. What demands psychology will make on the other natural sciences, and on physics in particular, only the future can tell.

10. THE SELF AND THE BOUNDS OF KNOWLEDGE

776   As I have repeatedly pointed out, the alchemist's statements about the lapis, considered psychologically, describe the archetype of the self. Its phenomenology is exemplified in mandala symbolism, which portrays the self as a concentric structure, often in the form of a squaring of the circle. Co-ordinated with this are all kinds of secondary symbols, most of them expressing the nature of the opposites to be united. The structure is invariably felt as the representation of a central state or of a centre of personality essentially different from the ego. It is of numinous nature, as is clearly indicated by the mandalas themselves and by the symbols used (sun, star, light, fire, flower, precious stone, etc.). All degrees of emotional evaluation are found, from abstract, colourless, indifferent drawings of circles to an extremely intense experience of illumination. These aspects all appear in alchemy, the only difference being that there they are projected into matter, whereas here they are understood as symbols. The arcanum chymicum has therefore changed into a psychic event without having lost any of its original numinosity.

777   If we now recall to what a degree the soul has humanized and realized itself, we can judge very much it today expresses the body also, with which it is coexistent. Here is a coniunctio of the second degree, such as the alchemists at most dreamed of but could not realize. Thus far the transformation into the psychological is a notable advance, *but only if the centre experienced proves to be a spiritus rector of daily life.* Obviously, it was clear even to the alchemists that one could have a lapis in one's pocket without ever making gold with it, or the *aurum potabile* in a bottle without ever having tasted that bittersweet drink—hypothetically speaking, of course, for they never succumbed to the temptation to use their stone in reality because they never succeeded in making one. The psychological significance of this misfortune should not be overestimated, however. It takes second place in comparison with the fascination which emanated from the sensed and intuited archetype of wholeness. In this respect alchemy fared no worse than Christianity, which in its turn was not fatally disturbed by the continuing nonappearance of the Lord at the Second Coming. The intense emo-

tion that is always associated with the vitality an archetypal idea conveys—even though only a minimum of rational understanding may be present—a premonitory experience of wholeness to which a subsequently differentiated understanding can add nothing essential, at least as regards the totality of the experience. A better developed understanding can, however, constantly renew the vitality of the original experience. In view of the inexhaustibility of the archetype the rational understanding derived from it means relatively little, and it would be an unjustifiable overestimation of reason to assume that, as a result of understanding, the illumination in the final state is a higher one than in the initial state of numinous experience. The same objection, as we have seen, was made to Cardinal Newman's view concerning the development of dogma, but it was overlooked that rational understanding or intellectual formulation adds nothing to the experience of wholeness, and at best only facilitates its repetition. The experience itself is the important thing, not its intellectual representation or clarification, which proves meaningful and helpful only when the road to original experience is blocked. The differentiation of dogma not only expresses its vitality but is needed in order to preserve its vitality. Similarly, the archetype at the basis of alchemy needs interpreting if we are to form any conception of its vitality and numinosity and thereby preserve it at least for our science. The alchemist likewise interpreted his experience as best he could, though without ever understanding it to the degree that psychological explanation makes possible today. But his inadequate understanding did not detract from the totality of his archetypal experience any more than our wider and more differentiated understanding adds anything to it.

778   With the advance towards the psychological a great change sets in, for self-knowledge has certain ethical consequences which are not just impassively recognized but demand to be carried out in practice. This depends of course on one's moral endowment, on which as we know one should not place too much reliance. The self, in its efforts at self-realization, reaches out beyond the ego-personality on all sides; because of its all-encompassing nature it is brighter and darker than the ego, and accordingly confronts it with problems which it would like to avoid. Either one's moral courage fails, or one's insight, or both, until in the end

fate decides. The ego never lacks moral and rational counter-arguments, which one cannot and should not set aside so long as it is possible to hold on to them. For you only feel yourself on the right road when the conflicts of duty seem to have resolved themselves, and you have become the victim of a decision made over your head or in defiance of the heart. From this we can see the numinous power of the self, which can hardly be experienced in any other way. For this reason *the experience of the self is always a defeat for the ego.* The extraordinary difficulty in this experience is that the self can be distinguished only conceptually from what has always been referred to as "God," but not practically. Both concepts apparently rest on an identical numinous factor which is a condition of reality. The ego enters into the picture only so far as it can offer resistance, defend itself, and in the event of defeat still affirm its existence. The prototype of this situation is Job's encounter with Yahweh. This hint is intended only to give some indication of the nature of the problems involved. From this general statement one should not draw the overhasty conclusion that in every case there is a hybris of ego-consciousness which fully deserves to be overpowered by the unconscious. That is not so at all, because it very often happens that ego-consciousness and the ego's sense of responsibility are too weak and need, if anything, strengthening. But these are questions of practical psychotherapy, and I mention them here only because I have been accused of underestimating the importance of the ego and giving undue prominence to the unconscious. This strange insinuation emanates from a theological quarter. Obviously my critic has failed to realize that the mystical experiences of the saints are no different from other effects of the unconscious.

779   In contrast to the ideal of alchemy, which consisted in the production of a mysterious substance, a man, an *anima mundi* or a *deus terrenus* who was expected to be a saviour from all human ills, the psychological interpretation (foreshadowed by the alchemists) points to the concept of human wholeness. This concept has primarily a therapeutic significance in that it attempts to portray the psychic state which results from bridging over a dissociation between conscious and unconscious. The alchemical compensation corresponds to the integration of the unconscious with consciousness, whereby both are altered.

Above all, consciousness experiences a widening of its horizon. This certainly brings about a considerable improvement of the whole psychic situation, since the disturbance of consciousness by the counteraction of the unconscious is eliminated. But, because all good things must be paid for dearly, the previously unconscious conflict is brought to the surface instead and imposes on consciousness a heavy responsibility, as *it* is now expected to solve the conflict. But it seems as badly equipped and prepared for this as was the consciousness of the medieval alchemist. Like him, the modern man needs a special method for investigating and giving shape to the unconscious contents in order to get consciousness out of its fix. As I have shown elsewhere, an experience of the self may be expected as a result of these psychotherapeutic endeavours, and quite often these experiences are numinous. It is not worth the effort to try to describe their totality character. Anyone who has experienced anything of the sort will know what I mean, and anyone who has not had the experience will not be satisfied by any amount of descriptions. Moreover there are countless descriptions of it in world literature. But I know of no case in which the bare description conveyed the experience.

780   It is not in the least astonishing that numinous experiences should occur in the course of psychological treatment and that they may even be expected with some regularity, for they also occur very frequently in exceptional psychic states that are not treated and may even cause them. They do not belong exclusively to the domain of psychopathology but can be observed in normal people as well. Naturally, modern ignorance of and prejudice against intimate psychic experiences dismiss them as psychic anomalies and put them in psychiatric pigeon-holes without making the least attempt to understand them. But that neither gets rid of the fact of their occurrence nor explains it.

781   Nor is it astonishing that in every attempt to gain an adequate understanding of the numinous experience use must be made of certain parallel religious or metaphysical ideas which have not only been associated with it from ancient times but are constantly used to formulate and elucidate it. The consequence, however, is that any attempt at scientific explanation gets into the grotesque situation of being accused in its turn of offering a metaphysical explanation. It is true that this objection will be

547

raised only by one who imagines himself to be in possession of metaphysical truths, and assumes that they posit or give valid expression to metaphysical facts corresponding to them. It seems to me at least highly improbable that when a man says "God" there must in consequence exist a God such as he imagines, or that he necessarily speaks of a real being. At any rate he can never prove that there is something to correspond with his statement on the metaphysical side, just as it can never be proved to him that he is wrong. Thus it is at best a question of *non liquet,* and it seems to me advisable under these circumstances and in view of the limitations of human knowledge to assume from the start that our metaphysical concepts are simply anthropomorphic images and opinions which express transcendental facts either not at all or only in a very hypothetical manner. Indeed we know already from the physical world around us that in itself it does not necessarily agree in the least with the world as we perceive it. The physical world and the perceptual world are two very different things. Knowing this we have no encouragement whatever to think that our metaphysical picture of the world corresponds to the transcendental reality. Moreover, the statements made about the latter are so boundlessly varied that with the best of intentions we cannot know who is right. The denominational religions recognized this long ago and in consequence each of them claims that it is the only true one and, on top of this, that it is not merely a human truth but the truth directly inspired and revealed by God. Every theologian speaks simply of "God," by which he intends it to be understood that his "god" is *the* God. But one speaks of the paradoxical God of the Old Testament, another of the incarnate God of Love, a third of the God who has a heavenly bride, and so on, and each criticizes the other but never himself.

782   Nothing provides a better demonstration of the extreme uncertainty of metaphysical assertions than their diversity. But it would be completely wrong to assume that they are altogether worthless. For in the end it has to be explained why such assertions are made at all. There must be some reason for this. Somehow men feel impelled to make transcendental statements. Why this should be so is a matter for dispute. We only know that in genuine cases it is not a question of arbitrary inventions but of involuntary numinous experiences which happen to a man and

provide the basis for religious assertions and convictions. Therefore, at the source of the great confessional religions as well as of many smaller mystical movements we find individual historical personalities whose lives were distinguished by numinous experiences. Numerous investigations of such experiences have convinced me that previously unconscious contents then break through into consciousness and overwhelm it in the same way as do the invasions of the unconscious in pathological cases accessible to psychiatric observation. Even Jesus, according to Mark 3 : 21,[237] appeared to his followers in that light. The significant difference, however, between merely pathological cases and "inspired" personalities is that sooner or later the latter find an extensive following and can therefore transmit their effect down the centuries. The fact that the long-lasting effect exerted by the founders of the great religions is due quite as much to their overwhelming spiritual personality, their exemplary life, and their ethical self-commitment does not affect the present discussion. Personality is only one root of success, and there were and always will be genuine religious personalities to whom success is denied. One has only to think of Meister Eckhart. But, if they do meet with success, this only proves that the "truth" they utter hits on a consensus of opinion, that they are talking of something that is "in the air" and is "spoken from the heart" for their followers too. This, as we know to our cost, applies to good and evil alike, to the true as well as the untrue.

783   The wise man who is not heeded is counted a fool, and the fool who proclaims the general folly first and loudest passes for a prophet and Führer, and sometimes it is luckily the other way round as well, or else mankind would long since have perished of stupidity.

784   The insane person, whose distinguishing mark is his mental sterility, expresses no "truth" not only because he is not a personality but because he meets with no consensus of opinion. But anyone who does, has to that extent expressed the "truth." In metaphysical matters what is "authoritative" is "true," hence metaphysical assertions are invariably bound up with an unusually strong claim to recognition and authority, because authority is for them the only possible proof of their truth, and by this

237 "And when his friends heard of it, they went out to lay hold on him: for they said, He is beside himself."

proof they stand or fall. All metaphysical claims in this respect inevitably beg the question, as is obvious to any reasonable person in the case of the proofs of God.

785   The claim to authority is naturally not in itself sufficient to establish a metaphysical truth. Its authority must also be backed by the equally vehement need of the multitude. As this need always arises from a condition of distress, any attempt at explanation will have to examine the psychic situation of those who allow themselves to be convinced by a metaphysical assertion. It will then turn out that the statements of the inspired personality have made conscious just those images and ideas which compensate the general psychic distress. These images and ideas were not thought up or invented by the inspired personality but "happened" to him as experiences, and he became, as it were, their willing or unwilling victim. A will transcending his consciousness seized hold of him, which he was quite unable to resist. Naturally enough he feels this overwhelming power as "divine." I have nothing against this word, but with the best will in the world I cannot see that it proves the existence of a transcendent God. Suppose a benevolent Deity did in fact inspire a salutary truth, what about all those cases where a half-truth or unholy nonsense was inspired and accepted by an eager following? Here the devil would be a better bet or—on the principle "omne malum ab homine"—man himself. This metaphysical either-or explanation is rather difficult to apply in practice because most inspirations fall between the two extremes, being neither wholly true nor wholly false. In theory, therefore, they owe their existence to the co-operation of a good and a bad power. We would also have to suppose a common plan of work aiming at an only tolerably good goal, so to speak, or make the assumption that one power bungles the handiwork of the other or—a third possibility—that man is capable of thwarting God's intention to inspire a perfect truth (the inspiration of a half-truth is naturally out of the question) with an almost daemonic energy. What, in any of these cases, would have happened to God's omnipotence?

786   It therefore seems to me, on the most conservative estimate, to be wiser not to drag the supreme metaphysical factor into our calculations, at all events not at once, but, more modestly, to

make an unknown psychic or perhaps psychoid [238] factor in the human realm responsible for inspirations and suchlike happenings. This would make better allowance not only for the abysmal mixture of truth and error in the great majority of inspirations but also for the numerous contradictions in Holy Writ. The psychoid aura that surrounds consciousness furnishes us with better and less controversial possibilities of explanation and moreover can be investigated empirically. It presents a world of relatively autonomous "images," including the manifold God-images, which whenever they appear are called "God" by naïve people and, because of their numinosity (the equivalent of autonomy!), are taken to be such. The various religious denominations support this traditional viewpoint, and their respective theologians believe themselves, inspired by God's word, to be in a position to make valid statements about him. Such statements always claim to be final and indisputable. The slightest deviation from the dominant assumption provokes an unbridgeable schism. One cannot and may not think about an object held to be indisputable. One can only assert it, and for this reason there can be no reconciliation between the divergent assertions. Thus Christianity, the religion of brotherly love, offers the lamentable spectacle of one great and many small schisms, each faction helplessly caught in the toils of its own unique rightness.

787   We believe that we can make assertions about God, define him, form an opinion about him, differentiate him as the only true one amongst other gods. The realization might by this time be dawning that when we talk of God or gods we are speaking of debatable images from the psychoid realm. The existence of a transcendental reality is indeed evident in itself, but it is uncommonly difficult for our consciousness to construct intellectual models which would give a graphic description of the reality we have perceived. Our hypotheses are uncertain and groping, and nothing offers us the assurance that they may ultimately prove correct. That the world inside and outside ourselves rests on a transcendental background is as certain as our own existence, but it is equally certain that the direct perception of the archetypal world inside us is just as doubtfully correct as that of the physical world outside us. If we are convinced that we know the ultimate truth concerning metaphysical things, this means noth-

238 Cf. "On the Nature of the Psyche," par. 368.

ing more than that archetypal images have taken possession of our powers of thought and feeling, so that these lose their quality as functions at our disposal. The loss shows itself in the fact that the object of perception then becomes absolute and indisputable and surrounds itself with such an emotional taboo that anyone who presumes to reflect on it is automatically branded a heretic and blasphemer. In all other matters everyone would think it reasonable to submit to objective criticism the subjective image he has devised for himself of some object. But in the face of possession or violent emotion reason is abrogated; the numinous archetype proves on occasion to be the stronger because it can appeal to a vital necessity. This is regularly the case when it compensates a situation of distress which no amount of reasoning can abolish. We know that an archetype can break with shattering force into an individual human life and into the life of a nation. It is therefore not surprising that it is called "God." But as men do not always find themselves in immediate situations of distress, or do not always feel them to be such, there are also calmer moments in which reflection is possible. If one then examines a state of possession or an emotional seizure without prejudice, one will have to admit that the possession in itself yields nothing that would clearly and reliably characterize the nature of the "possessing" factor, although it is an essential part of the phenomenon that the "possessed" always feels compelled to make definite assertions. Truth and error lie so close together and often look so confusingly alike that nobody in his right senses could afford *not* to doubt the things that happen to him in the possessed state. I John 4 : 1 admonishes us: "Beloved, believe not every spirit, but try the spirits whether they are of God; because many false prophets are gone out into the world." This warning was uttered at a time when there was plenty of opportunity to observe exceptional psychic states. Although, as then, we think we possess sure criteria of distinction, the rightness of this conviction must nevertheless be called in question, for no human judgment can claim to be infallible.

788   In view of this extremely uncertain situation it seems to me very much more cautious and reasonable to take cognizance of the fact that there is not only a psychic but also a psychoid unconscious, before presuming to pronounce metaphysical judgments which are incommensurable with human reason. There is

no need to fear that the inner experience will thereby be deprived of its reality and vitality. No experience is prevented from happening by a somewhat more cautious and modest attitude—on the contrary.

789   That a psychological approach to these matters draws man more into the centre of the picture as the measure of all things cannot be denied. But this gives him a significance which is not without justification. The two great world-religions, Buddhism and Christianity, have, each in its own way, accorded man a central place, and Christianity has stressed this tendency still further by the dogma that God became very man. No psychology in the world could vie with the dignity that God himself has accorded to him.

790   Alchemy, with its wealth of symbols, gives us an insight into an endeavour of the human mind which could be compared with a religious rite, an *opus divinum*. The difference between them is that the alchemical opus was not a collective activity rigorously defined as to its form and content, but rather, despite the similarity of their fundamental principles, an individual undertaking on which the adept staked his whole soul for the transcendental purpose of producing a *unity*. It was a work of reconciliation between apparently incompatible opposites, which, characteristically, were understood not merely as the natural hostility of the physical elements but at the same time as a moral conflict. Since the object of this endeavour was seen outside as well as inside, as both physical and psychic, the work extended as it were through the whole of nature, and its goal consisted in a symbol which had an empirical and at the same time a transcendental aspect.

791   Just as alchemy, tapping its way in the dark, groped through the endless mazes of its theoretical assumptions and practical experiments over a course of many centuries, so the psychology of the unconscious that began with C. G. Carus took up the trail that had been lost by the alchemists. This happened, remarkably enough, at a moment in history when the aspirations of the alchemists had found their highest poetic expression in Goethe's *Faust*. At the time Carus wrote, he certainly could not have guessed that he was building the philosophical bridge to an empirical psychology of the future, which would take quite literally the old alchemical dictum: *in stercore invenitur*—"it is found in filth." Not, this time, in the cheap, unseemly substance, which, rejected by all, could be picked up anywhere in the street, but rather in the distressing darkness of the human psyche, which meanwhile had become accessible to clinical observation. There alone could be found all those contradictions, those grotesque phantasms and scurrilous symbols which had fascinated the mind of the alchemists and confused them as

much as illuminated them. And the same problem presented itself to the psychologist that had kept the alchemists in suspense for seventeen hundred years: What was he to do with these antagonistic forces? Could he throw them out and get rid of them? Or had he to admit their existence, and is it our task to bring them into harmony and, out of the multitude of contradictions, produce a unity, which naturally will not come of itself, though it may—*Deo concedente*—with human effort?

792　　Herbert Silberer has the merit of being the first to discover the secret threads that lead from alchemy to the psychology of the unconscious. The state of psychological knowledge at that time was still too primitive and still too much wrapped up in personalistic assumptions for the whole problem of alchemy to be understood psychologically. The conventional devaluation of alchemy on the one hand and of the psyche on the other had first to be cleared away. Today we can see how effectively alchemy prepared the ground for the psychology of the unconscious, firstly by leaving behind, in its treasury of symbols, illustrative material of the utmost value for modern interpretations in this field, and secondly by indicating symbolical procedures for synthesis which we can rediscover in the dreams of our patients. We can see today that the entire alchemical procedure for uniting the opposites, which I have described in the foregoing, could just as well represent the individuation process of a single individual, though with the not unimportant difference that no single individual ever attains to the richness and scope of the alchemical symbolism. This has the advantage of having been built up through the centuries, whereas the individual in his short life has at his disposal only a limited amount of experience and limited powers of portrayal. It is therefore a difficult and thankless task to try to describe the nature of the individuation process from case-material. Since one aspect tends to predominate in one case and another in another, and one case begins earlier and another later, and the psychic conditions vary without limit, only one or the other version or phase of the process can be demonstrated in any given instance. No case in my experience is comprehensive enough to show all the aspects in such detail that it could be regarded as paradigmatic. Anyone who attempted to describe the individuation process with the help of case-material would have to remain content with a mosaic of bits and pieces without beginning or end, and if he wanted to be understood he would have to count on a reader whose experience in the same field was equal to his own. Alchemy, therefore, has performed for me the great and invaluable service of providing material in which my experience could find sufficient room, and has thereby made it possible for me to describe the individuation process at least in its essential aspects.

APPENDIX

LATIN AND GREEK TEXTS

The asterisks (*) in the footnotes refer to the following passages quoted by the author in Latin or Greek. In general, only translations are given in the body of the book. The entries below carry the pertinent footnote numbers.

I. THE COMPONENTS OF THE CONIUNCTIO

3. In hoc lapide sunt quatuor elementa et assimulatur mundo et mundi compositioni. / Natura, inquam, dum circumgyravit aureum circulum, in ipso motu qualitates quatuor in eo aequavit, hoc est, homogeneam illam simplicitatem in sese redeuntem quadravit, sive in quadrangulum duxit aequilaterum, hac ratione, ut contraria a contrariis et hostes ab hostibus aeternis quasi vinculis colligentur, et invicem teneantur. / In circulo sunt elementa coniuncta vera amicitia.

8. aquila volans per aerem et bufo gradiens per terram.

12. Desponsavi ego duo luminaria in actu, et facta est illa quasi aqua in actu habens duo lumina.

18. Hermes: Necesse est ut in fine mundi coelum et terra coniungantur, quod verbum est philosophicum.

20. Sic absconditur altitudo et manifestatur profunditas.

21. de mortuo facit vivum.

23. . . . consurgit aequalitas . . . ex quatuor repugnantibus, in natura communicantibus. / καὶ Ὀρφεὺς οἶδε μὲν καὶ τὸν τοῦ Διονύσου χρατῆρα, πολλούς δὲ καὶ ἄλλους ἱδρύει περὶ τὴν ἡλιαχὴν τράπεζαν.

26. *Erat vir unus.* Nos, qui adhuc peccatores sumus, non possumus istum titulum laudis acquirere, quia unus quisque nostrum non est 'unus', sed multi. . . . Vides, quomodo ille qui putatur 'unus' esse, non est 'unus', sed tot in eo personae videntur esse, quot mores, quia et secundum scripturas 'insipiens sicut luna mutatur'. / Ubi peccata sunt, ibi est multitudo . . . ubi autem virtus, ibi singularitas, ibi unio. / Intellige te habere intra temet ipsum greges boum. . . . Intellige habere te et greges ovium et greges caprarum. . . . Intellige esse intra te etiam

aves coeli. Nec mireris quod haec intra te esse dicimus; intellige te et alium mundum esse in parvo et esse intra te solem, esse lunam, esse etiam stellas. . . . Videas habere te omnia, quae mundus habet. / Quatuor in caelo planetis imperfectioribus, quatuor in corpore nostro correspondere volunt elementa, ut Saturno, Mercurio, Veneri, et Marti, terra, aqua, aer, et ignis, ex quibus conflatum est, et infirmum propter partium imperfectionem. Plantetur itaque arbor ex eis, cuius radix adscribitur Saturno . . .

33. combinationes duarum contrarietatum, frigidum et humidum, quae . . . non sunt amicabilia caliditati et siccitati.

34. Puerulus tuus senex est, o virgo, ipse est Antiquus dierum et omnia praecessit tempora.

40. Dum enim rostrum applicat pectori, totum collum cum rostro flectitur in circularem formam. . . . Sanguis effluens e pectore mortuis pullis reddit vitam.

41. Tanquam principium et fons, a quo . . . defluunt; et simul etiam finis ultimus.

44. Omnem rem solidam penetrabit.

48. Talis est amor philosophicus, inter inanimatorum partes, et inimicitia, *qualis in partibus hominis.* Verum in illis, non magis quam in his, unio vera fieri non potest, corruptione dictarum partium non ablata prius ante coniunctionem: qua propter pacem inter inimicos est quod facias, ut amici conveniant in unum. In omnibus corporibus imperfectis, et ab ultimata sua perfectione deficientibus, sunt amicitia et inimicitia simul innatae; haec si tollatur hominis ingenio vel industria, necesse est alteram ad perfectionem suam ultimatam redire per artem, quam in hominis unione declaravimus.

49. Fertur etiam quod pellicanus in tantum pullos suos diligat, ut eos unguibus interimat. Tertia vero die prae dolore se ipsum lacerat, et sanguis de latere eius super pullos distillans eos a morte excitat. Pellicanus significat Dominum qui sic dilexit mundum ut pro eo daret Filium suum unigenitum, quem tercia die victorem mortis excitavit et super omne nomen exaltavit.

52. cuius vis est spiritualis sanguis id est tinctura. . . . Nam corpus incorporat spiritum per sanguinis tincturam; quia omne quod habet Spiritum, habet et sanguinem. / Sensibilis autem et vitalis (spiritus) sanguis est essentia; dicit enim alibi, omni spiritui carnis sanguis est.

53. Fili, accipere debes de pinguiori carne. / crescit ex carne et sanguine. / Ovum in carne capere. / Elige carnem teneram et habebis rem optimam. / An forte carnibus ad vesperam . . . ille significatur, qui traditus est propter delicta nostra.

54. Et tunc accipe vitrum cum sponso et sponsa, et proiice eos in fornacem, et fac assare per tres dies, et tunc erunt duo in carne una.

55. Quemadmodum Christus. . . . Lapis angularis ab aedificatoribus reiectus in sacra scriptura vocatur; ita quoque Lapidi Sophorum idem accidit . . .

64. Recipit vim superiorum et inferiorum. Sic habebis gloriam totius mundi.

66. Mercurius Trismegistus . . . lapidem vocavit orphanum. / Hic lapis Orphanus proprio nomine caret.

78. Ποίησον τὸ δεῖνα πρᾶγμα ἐμοὶ τῷ τῆς χήρας ὀρφανῷ κατατετιμημένης.

79. Ipsa maritali dum nato foedere mater
     Jungitur, incestum ne videatur opus.
     Sic etenim natura iubet, sic alma requirit
     Lex fati, nec ea est res male grata Deo.

83. Ἐγώ εἰμι Ἶσις ἡ καλουμένη δρόσος·

95. Ἴσιδος σῶμα γῆν·

109. Omnis Ecclesia una vidua est, deserta in hoc saeculo.

111. (Almana) Vidua. Est Malchuth, quando Tiphereth non est cum ipsa.

116. Luna, terra, sponsa, matrona, regina coeli, piscina, mare, puteus, arbor scientiae boni et mali, cerva amorum (ita vocatur Malchuth potissimum ob mysterium novilunii), venter.

120. . . . quod Malchuth vocetur hortus irriguus Jesch. 58, 11 quando Jesod in Ipsa est, eamque adimplet, atque irrigat aquis supernis. / cum Malchuth influxum accipit a 50 portis per Jesod, tunc vocatur sponsa.

136. Anima quippe humana recedens a sole iustitiae, ab illa scl. interna contemplatione incommutabilis veritatis, omnes vires suas in terrena convertit et eo magis magisque obscuratur in interioribus ac superioribus suis; sed cum redire coeperit ad illam incommutabilem sapientiam, quanto magis ei propinquat affectu pietatis, tanto magis exterior homo corrumpitur, sed interior renovatur de die in diem omnisque lux illa ingenii, quae ad inferiora vergebat, ad superiora convertitur et a terrenis quodam modo aufertur, ut magis magisque huic saeculo moriatur et vita eius abscondatur cum Christo in Deo.

145. die enim quarto in quartum, quartanam naturaliter patitur.

150. Hoc itaque completo scias quod habes corpus corpora perforans et naturam naturam continentem et naturam natura laetantem, quod profecto tyriaca philosophorum vocatur et dicitur vipera, quia sicut vipera, concipiendo prae libidinis ardore, caput secat masculi et pariendo moritur et per medium secatur. Sic lunaris humor, concipiens lucem Solarem sibi con-

venientem, Solem necat et pariendo progeniem Philosophorum, ipsa similiter moritur et uterque parens moriendo animas filio tradunt et moriuntur et pereunt. Et parentes sunt cibus filii.

151. ... incineretur corpus residuum, quod vocatur terra, a qua est extracta tinctura per aquam ... Deinde capiti suo iunge et caudae.

152. ἡ φύσις τῇ φύσει τέρπεται, καὶ ἡ φύσις τὴν φύσιν νικᾷ, καὶ ἡ φύσις τὴν φύσιν κρατεῖ.

153. Sic tyrium nostrum (colorem) in unoquoque regiminis gradu sui coloris nomine nuncupamus. / Hoc est sulphur rubeum, luminosum in tenebris: et est hyacinthus rubeus, et toxicum igneum, et interficiens, et Leo victor, et malefactor, et ensis scindens, et Tyriaca sanans omnem infirmitatem.

161. Qui me Miserculam i.e. me habentem materiam Mercurialem et Lunarem ... ac dilectum meum i.e. pinguedinem solarem mecum i.e. (c)um humiditate Lunari vinculaverit i.e. in unum corpus coniunxerit, Sagitta Ex Pharetra nostra.

164. Παρθένος ἡ γῆ εὑρίσκεται ἐν τῇ οὐρᾷ τῆς παρθένου.

170. Pulchra es amica mea, suavis et decora sicut Jerusalem: Terribilis ut castrorum acies ordinata. 4: Averte oculos tuos a me quia ipsi me avolare fecerunt ... 9: Quae est ista, quae progreditur quasi aurora consurgens pulchra ut luna, electa ut sol, terribilis ut castrorum acies ordinata?

176. Procedit Christus quasi sponsus de thalamo suo, praesagio nuptiarum exiit ad campum saeculi ... pervenit usque ad crucis torum et ibi firmavit ascendendo coniugium; ubi eum sentiret anhelantem in suspiriis creaturam, commercio pietatis se pro coniuge dedit ad poenam ... et copulavit sibi perpetuo iure matronam.

178. Per cor amor intelligitur, qui in corde esse dicitur, et continens pro contento ponitur, et est similitudo, ab illo qui nimirum aliquam amat, et eius cor amore vulneratur. Ita Christus amore Ecclesiae vulneratus est in cruce. Prius vulnerasti cor meum, quando causa amoris tui flagellatus sum, ut te facerem mihi sororem ... iterum vulnerasti cor meum, quando amore tui in cruce pendens vulneratus sum, ut te sponsam mihi facerem gloriae participem, et hoc in uno oculorum tuorum.

181. ... illo vulnerato, neci dato ros iungitur.

185. Hic est infans Hermaphroditus, qui a primis suis incunabulis per Canem Corascenum rabidum morsu infectus est, unde perpetua hydrophobia stultescit insanitque. / vilescit per ca[r]nem infirmatus Leo.

186. Naturae siquidem per serpentem introducto morbo, lethalique inflicto vulneri quaerendum est remedium.

188. Mundi vitam enim . . . esse naturae lucem atque caeleste sulphur, cuius subiectum est firmamentalis humor aethereus et calor, ut sol et luna.

190. Alcumistas omnium hominum esse perversissimos.

193. Minuitur Luna, ut elementa repleat.
Hoc est vere grande mysterium.
Donavit hoc ei qui omnibus donavit gratiam.
Exinanivit eam, ut repleat,
Qui etiam se exinanivit, ut omnes repleret.
Exinanivit enim se ut descenderet nobis,
Descendit nobis, ut ascenderet omnibus . . .
Ergo annuntiavit Luna mysterium Christi.

196. Ut cum Deus homo, cum immortalis mortuus, cum aeternus sepultus est, non sit intelligentiae ratio, sed potestatis exceptio; ita rursum e contrario non sensus, sed virtutis modus sit, ut Deus ex homine, ut immortalis ex mortuo, ut aeternus sit ex sepulto.

197. Quia lassae erant creaturae ferendo figuras maiestatis eius, eas suis figuris exoneravit sicut exoneravit ventrem qui eum gestavit.

218. . . . umbra mortis, quoniam tempestas dimersit me; tunc coram me procident Aethiopes et inimici mei terram meam lingent / . . . at qui de dracone comedit non alius est, quam spiritualis Aethiops per draconis laqueos mutatus et ipse in serpentem.

221. Τὸν θεὸν ἐξ ὕλης συγχρόνου καὶ ἀγενήτου πάντα πεποιηκέναι.

227. Lapis . . . incipit propter angustiam carceris sudare.

228. Hic princeps sudat ex tribulatione sua cuius sudor pluviae sunt. / In postremis suis operationibus . . . liquor obscurus ac rubens instar sanguinis, ex sua materia suoque vase guttatim exudat; inde praesagium protulerunt, postremis temporibus hominem purissimum in terras venturum, per quem liberatio mundi fieret, hunc ipsum guttas rosei rubeive coloris et sanguineas emissurum, quo mundus a labe redimeretur.

229. Et Marcus dicit, concipiunt in balneis, significat calorem lentum et humidum balneorum, in quibus sudat lapis in principio dissolutionis suae. / Tunc accipitur corpus perfectissimum, et ponitur ad ignem Philosophorum; tunc . . . illud corpus humectatur, et emittit sudorem quendam sanguineum post putrefactionem et mortificationem, Rorem dico Coelicum, qui quidem Ros dicitur Mercurius Philosophorum sive Aqua permanens.

232. Quae cum adparuerit, maribus femina decora adparet, feminis vero adolescentem speciosum et concupiscibilem demonstrat.

563

II. THE PARADOXA

1. Antiquissimi philosophorum viderunt hunc lapidem in ortu et sublimatione sua . . . omnibus rebus mundi tam realibus quam intellectualibus . . . posse in similitudinibus convenire. Unde quaecumque dici et tractari possunt de virtutibus et vitiis, de coelo et omnibus tam corporeis quam incorporeis, de mundi creatione . . . et de Elementis omnibus . . . et de corruptibilibus et incorruptibilibus et visibilibus et invisibilibus et de spiritu et anima et corpore . . . et de vita et morte, et bono et malo, de veritate et falsitate, de unitate et multitudine, de paupertate et divitiis, de volante et non volante, de bello et pace, de victore et victo et labore et requie, de somno et vigilia, de conceptione et partu, de puero et sene, de masculo et foemina, de forti et debili, de albis et rubeis et quibuslibet coloratis, de inferno et abysso et eorum tenebris, ac etiam ignibus sulphureis, et de paradiso et eius celsitudine, et claritate ac etiam pulchritudine et gloria eius inaestimabili. Et breviter de iis, quae sunt et de iis quae non sunt et de iis quae loqui licet et quae loqui non licet possunt omnia dici de hoc lapide venerando.

6. (illa res) vilis et pretiosa, obscura celata et a quolibet nota, unius nominis et multorum nominum.

8. Τί ὑμῖν καὶ τῇ πολλῇ ὕλῃ ἑνὸς ὄντος τοῦ φυσικοῦ καὶ μιᾶς φύσεως νικώσης τὸ πᾶν:

16. Currens sine cursu, movens sine motu.

17. Fac Mercurium per Mercurium.

21. Tot haec nostra materia habet nomina, quod res sunt in mundo.

24. εὐκοπώτερον δέ ἐστιν τὸν οὐρανὸν καὶ τὴν γῆν παρελθεῖν ἢ τοῦ νόμου μίαν κεραίαν πεσεῖν.

27. Iste enim spiritus generatur ex rebus ponticis et ipse vocat ipsum humidum siccum igneum.

30. Puncti proinde, monadisque ratione, res et esse coeperunt primo.

33. Punctum solis id est germen ovi quod est in vitello, quod germen movetur calore gallinae.

34. O admiranda sapientia, quae ex punctulo vix intelligibili, quicquid unquam ingentis machinae huius, vastae ponderosaeque molis a creatione factum est, solo verbo potuit excitare.

37. Ego ducam te ad aeternam mortem, ad inferos et ad domum tenebrosam. Cui anima: Anime mi spiritus. Quare ad eum sinum non reducis, a quo me adulando exceperis? credebam te

564

mihi deuinctum necessitudine. Ego quidem sum amica tua, ducamque te ad aeternam gloriam. / Sed miser ego abire cogor, cum te super omnes lapides preciosos constituero beatamque fecero. Quare te obsecro, cum ad regni solium deveneris, mei aliquando memor existes. / Quod si is spiritus apud animam et corpus manserit, perpetua ibidem esse corruptio.

42. Deus est figura intellectualis, cuius centrum est ubique, circumferentia vero nusquam.

49. triplici muro Castrum aureum circumdatum.

50. aeternitatis imago visibilis.

51. unus in essentia / una substantia homogenea.

59. Ἵνα ἔχῃ τὸν σπινθῆρα δουλεύοντα.

60. Rex natans in mari, clamans alta voce: Qui me eripiet, ingens praemium habebit. / . . . quis est homo qui vivit sciens et intelligens eruens animam meam de manu inferi?

72. Fuit quidam homo, qui nihil quidquam profuit nec detineri potuit: omnes enim carceres confregit, imo et poenas omnes parvi fecit, interea quidam simplex vel humilis et sincerus repertus est vir, qui hujus naturam bene noverat, et consilium tale dederat, ut is omnibus vestibus exutus denudetur. / Vestes abiectae illius ad pedes illius iacebant erantque nimis rancidae, foetidae, venenosae etc. atque tandem hunc in modum loqui incipiebat: 'Stolam meam exui, quomodo eandem iterum induam?'

76. Quousque terra lucescat veluti oculi piscium.

77. Grana instar piscium oculorum. / In principio . . . quasi grana rubea et in coagulatione velut oculi piscium. / Quando veluti oculi piscium in eo elucescunt.

79. Hic lapis est subtus te, supra te, et ergo a te, et circa te.

80. Cuius pulli rostro eruunt matri oculos.

86. Alterius profani sacramenti signum est θεὸς ἐκ πέτρας . . . alius est lapis, quem deus in confirmandis fundamentis promissae Hierusalem missurum se esse promisit: Christus nobis venerandi lapidis significatione monstratur.

91. Ἔτι τὴν Αἴγυπτον ἐν ταῖς μάλιστα μελάγγειον οὖσαν ὥσπερ τὸ μέλαν τοῦ ὀφθαλμοῦ χημίαν καλοῦσιν καὶ καρδίᾳ παρεικάζουσιν·

92. Est quasi oculus quidam visusque animae, quo saepe affectus animae nobis et consilium indicatur, cuius radiis et intuitu omnia coalescunt.

97. Ὄσιριν πολυόφθαλμον . . . πανταχῇ γὰρ ἐπιβάλλοντα τὰς ἀκτῖνας ὥσπερ ὀφθαλμοῖς πολλοῖς κτλ.

101. Ἐκ δὲ τῶν ἀτόμων συνελθουσῶν γενέσθαι καὶ τὸν θεὸν καὶ τὰ στοιχεῖα καὶ τὰ ἐν αὐτοῖς πάντα καὶ Ζῷα καὶ ἄλλα κτλ.

104. Si homo res in maiori mundo transmutare novit . . . quanto

magis id in microcosmo, hoc est, in se ipso noverit, quod extra se potest, modo cognoscat hominis in homine thesaurum existere maximum et non extra ipsum.

107. Chemicam artem naturaliter exercet Archeus in homine.

108. Quia homo est in corruptione generatus, odio prosequitur eum sua propria substantia.

109. Armoniac sal id est stella. / Ista est optima, quae extrahitur vi chalybis nostri qui invenitur in ventre Arietis . . . ante debitam coctionem est summum venenum.

110. Homo quidam est esca, in qua[m] per cotem scl. Mercurium, et chalybem (scl.) Caelum, ignis huiusmodi scintillae excussae, fomentum accipiunt, viresque suas exserunt.

112. Nam in rerum natura nihil est, quod non in se mali tantum quantum boni contineat.

133. Matrimonium enim quasi pallium hoc quicquid est vitii, tegit et abscondit.

134. Scorpio i.e. venenum. Quia mortificat seipsum et seipsum vivificat. / Εὐοῖ, δίκερως δίμορφε! deus iste vester non biformis est, sed multiformis . . . ipse est basiliscus et scorpio . . . ipse malitiosus anguis . . . ipse tortuosus draco, qui hamo ducitur . . . iste deus vester Lernaei anguis crinibus adornatur.

135. . . . ἀνάστηθι ἐκ τοῦ τάφου . . . καὶ τὸ φάρμακον τῆς ζωῆς εἰσῆλθεν πρὸς σέ . . . / Spiritus tingens et aqua metallina perfundens se in corpus ipsum vivificando.

137. Hanc Omnia esse, Omnia in se habere, quibus indiget ad sui perfectionem, Omnia de ipsa praedicari posse et ipsam vicissim de omnibus.

138. Unum enim est totum, ut ait maximus Chimes, ob quod Χύμης δὲ καλῶς ἀπεφήνατο· "Εν γὰρ τὸ πᾶν· καὶ δι' αὐτοῦ τὸ πᾶν sunt omnia, et si totum non haberet totum nihil totum esset. / γέγονεν. ἐν τὸ πᾶν. καὶ εἰ μὴ πᾶν ἔχοι τὸ πᾶν οὐ γέγονε τὸ πᾶν.

140. materiam nostram simul esse in caelo, terris et aquis, tanquam totam, in toto, et totam in qualibet parte: adeo ut partes illae, alioquin separabiles, nusquam ab invicem separari possint, postquam unum facta sunt: hinc tota Lex et Prophetia chemica pendere videtur.

144. Quisnam igitur liber? Sapiens, sibi qui imperiosus, quem neque pauperies neque mors neque vincula terrent, responsare cupidinibus, contemnere honores fortis, et in se ipso totus teres atque rotundus.

146. Nam ipsa est continens contentum in se convertens, atque sic est sepulchrum seu continens, non habens in se cadaver seu contentum, veluti Lothi coniunx ipsa sibi sepulchrum fuisse dicitur absque cadavere et cadaver absque sepulchro.

148. crassities aëris et omnia membra in atomos divellantur. / ποτὲ δὲ νέκυν ἢ θεὸν ἢ τὸν ἄκαρπον / Et sicut sol a principio occultatur in lunam, ita in fine occultatus extrahitur a luna.

150. Nam et eius (corporis mortui) odor est malus, et odori sepulchrorum assimilatur.

151. Purus laton tamdiu decoquitur, donec veluti oculi piscium elucescat.

152. Posito hoc Uno in suo sepulcro sphaerico. / (Vas) dicitur etiam sepulcrum.

157. Tumulus ergo in quo Rex noster sepelitur Saturnus . . . dicitur.

158. In adytis habent idolum Osiridis sepultum.

159. Hinc dicit Avicenna: Quamdiu apparuerit nigredo, dominatur obscura foemina, et ipsa est prior vis nostri lapidis.

162. Extat epitaphium antiquum Bononiae quod multorum fatigavit ingenia . . . Sunt qui hoc aenigma interpretentur animum hominis, alii nubium aquam, alii Nioben in Saxum mutatam, alii alia.

166. (Epitaphium) loquitur nempe . . . de filia Laelio nascitura, eademque sponsa Agathoni designata, sed non filia, sed non sponsa, quia concepta, non edita; quia non orta, sed aborta; qua propter tali ac tanta spe frustratus Agatho, jam pridem delectus in coniugem, et a sorte elusus, hac Aenigmatica Inscriptione iuremerito sic et ipse lusit, vel ludentis speciem praebuit.

169. Itaque vocatus sum Hermes Trismegistus, habens tres partes philosophiae totius mundi.

170. Numero Deus impari gaudet.

174. Hic serpens est calidus, quaerens exitum ante ortum, perdere volens foetum, cupiens abortum.

175. Naturae subtilitas . . . causam dedit augmentationis et vitae, et se in naturas perfectissimas reduxit. / Hic Serpens . . . tanquam Bufo nigerrimus tumescit et . . . petit a sua tristitia liberari.

179. Dico Aeliam Laeliam Crispem ex Hamadryadibus unam fuisse . . . i.e. Quercui in Suburbano agro Bononiensi applicitam, seu inclusam, quae mollissima simul et asperrima apparens jam a bis mille forsitan annis inconstantissimos Protei in morem tenens vultus Lucii Agathonis Prisci civis tunc Bononiensis Amores ex Chao certe, i.e. confusione Agathonia . . . elicitos anxiis curis et solicitudinibus implevit.

182. Tertium tandem aenigma erit de Quercu, mundum elementarem repraesentantem in caelesti quodammodo viridario plantata, ubi Sol et Luna duo veluti flores circumferuntur.

567

189. Induxit quercum veterem fissam per medium, (qui) tuetur a solis radiis, umbram faciens.

190. Primo duro lapide et claro clauditur, tum demum cava quercu.

193. Τὸ σωτήριον ἐκεῖνο ὕδωρ, καὶ τάφος ὑμῖν ἐγένετο καὶ μήτηρ·

195. Per matricem, intendit fundum cucurbitae. / Vas spagiricum ad similitudinem vasis naturalis esse construendum.

196. Locus generationis, licet sit artificialis, tamen imitatur naturalem, quia est *concavus, conclusus.*

198. Quod enim est matrix embrioni, hoc est aqua fideli. In aqua enim fingitur et formatur. Primum dicebatur: Producant aquae reptile animae viventis. Ex quo autem Jordanis fluenta ingressus est Dominus non amplius reptilia animarum viventium, sed animas rationales Spiritum Sanctum ferentes aqua producit.

199. Arbores quae in ipso (paradiso) sunt, concupiscentiae sunt et ceterae seductiones corrumpentes cogitationes hominum. Illa autem arbor quae est in paradiso, ex qua agnoscitur bonum, ipse est Jesus et scientia eius quae est in mundo; quam qui acceperit, discernit bonum a malo.

204. Item dixit Marchos et est tempus in isto genito quod nascitur de quo facit talem similitudinem. Tunc aedificabimus sibi talem domum, quae dicitur monumentum Sihoka. Dixit, terra est apud nos quae dicitur tormos, in qua sunt reptilia comedentes opaca ex lapidibus adurentibus, et bibunt super eis sanguinem hircorum nigrorum, manentes in umbra, concipiunt in balneis, et (pariunt) in aëre et gradiuntur supra mare et manent in monumentis et etiam manent in sepulchris, et pugnat reptile contra masculum suum, et in sepulchro manet masculus eius 40 noctibus . . .

215. Christus in deserto quadraginta diebus totidemque noctibus ieiunavit, quemadmodum etiam per quadraginta menses in terra concionatus est, et miracula edidit, per quadraginta horas in sepulcro iacuit: quadraginta dies, inter resurrectionem a mortuis et ascensionem suam ad coelos, cum discipulis conversatus vivum esse ipsis repraesentavit.

219. Marmor coruscans est elixir ad album. / Et proiicient semen super marmore simulachrorum et in aqua sibi simili deifica, et venient corvi volantes, et cadunt super illud simulacrum. Intendit nigredinem . . . per corvos. / Maximum quidem mysterium est creare animas, atque corpus inanime in statuam viventem confingere. / Tunc autem haec fient, cum statua venerit. / Semper extrahis oleum (= anima) a corde statuarum: quia anima est ignis in similitudine, et ignis occultatus. / Calefacimus eius aquam extractam a cordibus statuarum ex

568

lapidibus. / Animas venerari in lapidibus: est enim mansio eorum in ipsis.

236. Cum mea me mater gravida gestaret in alvo,
Quid pareret fertur consuluisse deos.
Phoebus ait: Puer est; Mars: Femina; Juno: Neutrum.
Jam qui sum natus Hermaphroditus eram.
Quaerenti letum dea sic ait: Occidet armis;
Mars: Cruce; Phoebus: Àqua. Sors rata quaeque fuit.
Arbor obumbrat aquas; conscendo, labitur ensis
Quem tuleram casu, labor et ipse super;
Pes haesit ramis, caput incidit amne, tulique
—Vir, mulier, neutrum—flumina, tela, crucem.

237. Vir non vir, videns non videns, in arbore non in arbore, sedentem non sedentem, volucrem non volucrem, percussit non percussit, lapide non lapide.

238. ὅτι βάλοι ξύλῳ τε καὶ οὐ ξύλῳ καθημένην ὄρνιθα καὶ οὐκ ὄρνιθα ἀνήρ τε κ᾽ οὐκ ἀνὴρ λίθῳ τε καὶ οὐ λίθῳ · τούτων γάρ ἐστι τὸ μὲν νάρθηξ, τὸ δὲ νυκτηρίς, τὸ δὲ εὐνοῦχος, τὸ δὲ κίσηρις.

242. Ὁ τύμβος οὗτος ἔνδον οὐκ ἔχει νεκρὸν [or νέκυν],
ὁ νεκρὸς οὗτος ἐκτὸς οὐκ ἔχει τάφον
ἀλλ᾽ αὐτὸς αὑτοῦ νεκρός ἐστι καὶ τάφος·

243. Igneus est illi vigor et coelestis origo, a qua nunc hic Haelia nominatur.

245. Habet in se . . . totius Humanitatis quasi dicerem αὐτότητα.

246. Sic si seipsam volet anima cognoscere, in animam debet intueri, inque eum praecipue locum, in quo inest virtus animae, sapientia.

247. Nihil aliud esse hominem quam animam ipsius.

248. Animamque ut ideam hoc Epitaphio notari.

249. Prima materia cum nihil sit, sed imaginatione sola comprehendatur, nullo istorum locorum contineri potest.

251. Scopum Autoris esse mirifice complecti Generationis, Amicitiae ac Privationis attributa.

255. Crispulus ille, quis est, uxori semper adhaeret?
Qui Mariane tuae? Crispulus iste quis est?

260. (Anima) quae extra corpus multa profundissima imaginatur et hisce assimilatur Deo.

III. THE PERSONIFICATION OF THE OPPOSITES

4. Domine, quamvis rex sis, male tamen imperas et regis.

5. Aurum nostrum non est aurum vulgi.

6. Aurum et argentum in metallina sua forma lapidis nostri materiam non esse.

7. Substantia aequalis, permanens, fixa, longitudine aeternitatis. / Est enim Sol radix incorruptibilis. / Immo non est aliud fundamentum artis quam sol et eius umbra.

9. Scias igitur quod ignis sulphur est, id est Sol.

10. Sol noster est rubeus et ardens. / Sol nihil aliud est, quam sulphur et argentum vivum.

15. (Tractans de quadam virtute invisibili) vocat eam balsamum, omnem corporis naturam excèdentem, qui duo corpora coniunctione conservat, et coeleste corpus una cum quatuor elementis sustentat.

18. Fatuum esset cum plurimis credere, solem esse duntaxat ignem caelestem.

20. Ut fons vitae corporis humani, centrum est cordis eius, vel id potius quod in eo delitescit arcanum, in quo viget calor naturalis.

21. ῾Ήλιος ὁ πάντα ποιῶν.

22. quorumvis seminaria virtus atque formalis delitescit. / Punctum solis i. e. germen ovi, quod est in vitello.

23. Masculinum et universale semen primum et potissimum est eius naturae sulphur, generationum prima pars omnium, ac potissima causa. Proinde a Paracelso prolatum est, sol et homo per hominem, generant hominem.

24. Terra fecit Lunam . . . deinde ortus est sol . . . post tenebras quas posuisti ante ortum solis in ipsa.

27. Et hoc modo Alchemia est supra naturam et est divina. Et in hoc lapide est tota difficultas istius artis, neque potest assignari sufficiens ratio naturalis, quare hoc ita esse possit. Et sic cum intellectus non possit hoc comprehendere, nec satisfacere sibi, sed oportet ipsum credere, sicut in miraculosis rebus divinis, ita ut fundamentum fidei Christianae, quod supra naturam existit, a non credentibus primo existimetur verum omnino, quoniam finis eius miraculose et supra naturam completur. Ideo tunc solus Deus est operator, quiescente natura artifice.

29. Cum non suffecissem mirari de tanta rei virtute sibi coelitus indita et infusa.

30. Porro in humano corpore latet quaedam substantia caelestis naturae paucissimis nota, quae nullo penitus indiget medicamento, sed ipsamet est sibi medicamentum incorruptum.

33. Non intelligit animalis homo . . . facti sumus sicut lapides oculos habentes et non videntes.

37. Cum Solem . . . Plato visibilem filium Dei appellet, cur non intelligamus nos imaginem esse invisibilis filii. Qui si lux vera est illuminans omnem *mentem* expressissimum habet simu-

lachrum hunc Solem, qui est lux imaginaria illuminans omne corpus.

38. Qui autem sapientum venenum sole et eius umbra tinxit, ad maximum pervenit arcanum. / In umbra solis est calor Lunae.

39. Fili, extrahe a radio umbram suam.

40. terra auri suo proprio spiritu solvitur. / . . . obscuratus est Sol in ortu suo. Et haec denigratio est operis initium, putrefactionis indicium, certumque commixtionis principium.

41. In manifesto sunt corporalia et in occulto spiritualia.

42. Sicut sol a principio occultatur in Lunam, ita in fine occultatus extrahitur a Luna.

45. quae ex radiis Solis vel Lunae vi magnetis extracta est.

46. Sine sole terreno opus Philosophicum non perficitur.

50. Sicut enim sol sub nube, sic sol iustitiae latuit sub humana carne.

81. Sulphur est omne id quod incenditur, nequicquam concipit flammam nisi ratione sulphuris. / Sulphur enim aliud nihil est quam purus ignis occultus in mercurio. / simplex ignis vivus, alia corpora mortua vivificans.

97. Sulfura sunt animae, quae in quatuor fuerant occultae corporibus.

101. quousque natus viridis tibi appareat, qui eius est anima, quam viridem avem et aes et sulphur philosophi nuncupaverunt.

104. Pater et semen virile. / Substantia sulphuris quasi semen paternum, activum et formativum.

108. Sed quod maius est, in Regno eius est speculum in quo totus Mundus videtur. Quicunque in hoc speculum inspicit, partes sapientiae totius Mundi in illo videre et addiscere potest, atque ita sapientissimus in hisce Tribus Regnis evadet.

109. Domine, scitne etiam Sulphur aliquid in metallis? Vox: Dixi tibi, quod omnia scit et in metallis multo melius quam alibi. / est cor omnium rerum.

116. candelulae, quas vetulae ad accendendum ignem vulgo vendunt. / elychnia ex sulphure, quo subducuntur fila aut ligna.

130. In Sulphure Philosophorum totum hoc arcanum latet, quod etiam in penetralibus Mercurii continetur.

133. Caput eius vivit in aeternum et ideo caput denominatur vita gloriosa, et angeli serviunt ei.

140. Animans autem vis, tanquam mundi glutinum, inter spiritum atque corpus medium est, atque utriusque vinculum, in Sulphure nimirum rubentis atque transparentis olei cuiusdam, veluti Sol in Majore Mundo, et cor Microcosmi.

141. ab omni feculentia terrestri, et cadit Lucifer: hoc est, immunditia et terra maledicta e coelo aureo.

143. pinguedo in cavernis terrae.

146. Res ex qua sunt res est Deus invisibilis et immobilis, cuius voluntate intelligentia condita est, et voluntate et intelligentia est anima simplex, per animam sunt naturae discretae, ex quibus generatae sunt compositae.

149. Non habet in actu suo finem, quia tingit in infinitum.

170. Idque Philosophi diversimodo indigitarunt, atque Sponso et Sponsae (quemadmodum etiam Salomon in Cantico Canticorum suo ait) compararunt.

177. Verum Luna, cum infimus sit planetarum, ut matrix concipere fertur virtutes astrorum omnium, rebusque inferioribus deinceps impartiri . . . Luna universas siderum vires . . . gignendis rebus cunctis et potissimum earum seminibus infert inseritque. / . . . etiam in interraneis eiusdem (scl. terrae) visceribus lapidum, metallorum, imo animantium species excitando condendoque.

180. Iste vult concumbere cum matre sua in medio terrae. / Et coelum corporum incorruptibilium et inalterabilium sedes et vas est Luna, quae humiditati praesidet, aquam et terram repraesentat.

181. Cum autem videris terram sicut nivem albissimam . . . est cinis a cinere et terra extractus, sublimatus, honoratus . . . est quaesitum bonum, terra alba foliata.

182. Primum enim opus ad Album in Domo Lunae.

188. Sed nescio quae proprietas . . . et quaedam natura inest lumini, quod de ea defluit, quae humectet corpora et velut occulto rore madefaciat.

191. πηγὴ ἀέναος τοῦ παραδείσου. / mortalium corporum autor et conditrix / φυσικὸν autem, id est crescendi natura, de lunari ad nos globositate perveniunt.

192. τὴν δὲ ψυχὴν ἡ σελήνη . . . παρέσχεν εἰς τὴν γένεσιν.

197. Forsitan vultis videre sacratissimas arbores Solis et Lunae, quae annuntient vobis futura.

204. In maris Luna est spongia plantata.

205. Illud vero quod est vapor, vel in eis partibus subtilitas non retinetur nisi a corpore duro . . . et quandoque est lapis qui circundat substantias velut spongia. / Sol et Luna cum prima aqua calcinantur philosophice, ut corpora aperiantur, et fiant spongiosa et subtilia, ut aqua secunda melius possit ingredi. / Pars superior est anima, quae totum lapidem vivificat et reviviscere facit. / Zoophyton, neque animal, neque frutex, sed tertiam habet quandam naturam.

208. quod radices suarum minerarum sunt in aëre, et summitates in terra. Et quando evelluntur a suis locis, auditur sonus terribilis,

et sequitur timor magnus. Quare vade cito, quia cito evanescunt.

219. Et sicut omnes res fuerunt ab uno, meditatione unius: sic omnes res natae fuerunt ab hac una re, adaptatione. / Pater eius est Sol, mater eius Luna; portavit illud ventus in ventre suo. / Aër mediator inter ignem (= Sol) et aquam (= Luna) per calorem et humiditatem suam. / Aër est vita uniuscuiusque rei. / Natus sapientiae in aëre nascitur.

220. . . . spiritus et anima quando decocti fuerint, in iteratione destillationis, et tunc permiscentur permixtione universali, et unus retinebit alterum et fient unum. Unum in subtilitate et spiritualitate . . .

227. Dixit magister noster Belenius Philosophus, ponas lumen tuum in vase vitreo claro et nota quod omnis sapientia mundi huius circa ista tria versatur.

228. Una vero die vocavit me magister meus Bolemus Philosophus et dixit mihi: eja fili, spero te esse hominem *spiritualis intellectus,* et quod poteris pertingere ad gradum supremum sapientiae.

234. Ἑρμῆ κοσμοκράτωρ, ἐγκάρδιε, κύκλε σελήνης, στρογγύλε καὶ τετράγωνε.

239. Ciconia serpentes devorat, carnes eius contra omnia venena valent.

243. Natus est draco in nigredine, et . . . interficit seipsum.

244. Mundi animam praecipue in Sole collocamus.

248. Draco non moritur nisi cum fratre suo et sorore sua.

253. intellectum qui actu est, Lunam eum, qui est potentia.

258. Hinc illud Chaldaeorum: Vas tuum inhabitant bestiae terrae, et apud Platonem in republica discimus habere nos domi diversa genera brutorum.

260. Et lunari certe semicirculo (☽) ad solare (☉) complementum perducto: Factum est vespere et mane dies unus. Sit ergo primus, quo lux est facta Philosophorum.

261. Lunam terram statuimus infimam ignobilissimamque omnium siderum, uti est terra omnium elementorum opacitate, itidem substantiae et maculis illi persimilem.

262. Lunam quidem scimus omnibus inferiorem.

270. Luna enim est umbra Solis, et cum corporibus corruptibilibus consumitur et per ipsius corruptionem . . . Leo eclipsatur.

271. Et sicut aetheris et aëris: ita divinorum et caducorum luna confinium est.

272. A luna deorsum natura incipit caducorum, ab hac animae sub numerum dierum cadere et sub tempus incipiunt. . . . Nec dubium est, quin ipsa sit mortalium corporum et autor et conditrix.

573

274. Secunda empirica (metodica) i.e. experientissima inventa est ab Esculapio.

276. . . . quod fieri dicunt, cum Lunae lumen incipit crescere, usque ad quintam decimam Lunam, et rursus ad tricesimam minui, et redire ad cornua, donec nihil penitus lucis in ea appareat. Secundum hanc opinionem Luna in allegoria . . . significat ecclesiam, quod ex parte quidem spirituali lucet ecclesia, ex parte autem carnali obscura est.

280. mitis electis, terribilis reprobis, pastor verus. / vel qui alii hujus gregis canes vocantur, nisi doctores sancti?

283. [Hermes] dixit: Fili, accipe canem masculum Corascenen et caniculam Armeniae, et iunge in simul, et parient canem coloris coeli, et imbibe ipsum una siti ex aqua maris: quia ipse custodiet tuum amicum et custodiet te ab inimico tuo et adiuvabit te ubicunque sis, semper tecum existendo in hoc mundo et in alio. Et voluit dicere Hermes, pro cane et canicula, res quae conservant corpora a combustione ignis et eius caliditate.

285. Hali, Philosophus et Rex Arabiae in suo Secreto dicit: Accipe canem coëtaneum, et catulam Armeniae, iunge simul, et hi duo parient tibi filium canem, coloris coelici: et iste filius servabit te in domo tua ab initio in hoc Mundo et in alio.

299. Rumpe ergo domum, frange parietes, purissimum inde extrahe succum cum sanguine; coque ut edere possis. Unde dicit Arnaldus in libro Secretorum: Purga lapidem: tere portam: frange caniculam: elige carnem teneram, et habebis rem optimam. In una ergo re omnia membra latent, omnia metalla lucent. Horum duo sunt artifices, duo vasa, duo tempora, duo fructus, duo fines, una salus.

305. Utraque avis volans ad regum mensas et capita salit. / Et venient corvi volantes et cadunt supra illud.

306. Recipe Gallum, crista rubea coronatum et vivum plumis priva.

311. Aquae . . . , quae Canis Balsami dicitur, sive lac virginis, aut argentum vivum nostrum, seu anima, aut ventus aut cauda draconis.

315. . . . recipit ille globus carnem, id est coagulationem, et sanguinem, id est tincturam. / Ex his possunt philosophicae transmutationes intelligi: nonne scimus et panis et vini puriorem substantiam in carnem et sanguinem transmutari? / Iam suam carnem sanguineam et rubeam tradit omnibus manducandam. / habere scientiam corporis, grossi, turbidi, carnei, quod est pondus naturarum, et pervenit ad animam simplicem.

316. Est enim lapis unus, una medicina, cui nil extranei additur, nec diminuitur, nisi quod superflua removentur. / Unus est

lapis, una medicina, unum vas, unum regimen, unaque dispositio.

319. Primum enim opus ad Album in domo Lunae, secundum in secunda Mercurii domo terminari debet. Primum autem opus ad rubeum in secundo Veneris domicilio; postremum vero in altero regali Jovis solio desinet, a quo Rex noster potentissimus coronam pretiosissimis Rubinis contextam suscipiet. / Albus (lapis) in occasu Solis incipit apparere super facies aquarum, abscondens se usque ad mediam noctem et postea vergit in profundum. Rubeus vero ex opposito operatur, quia incipit ascendere super aquas in ortu Solis usque ad meridiem et postea descendit in profundum.

320. Et opus secundum est albificatio et rubificatio, et sapientes haec duo opera in unum contraxerunt. Nam quando loquuntur de uno, loquuntur etiam et de alio, unde diversificantur legentibus eorum scripta.

321. Cur arborem dimisisti narrare, cuius fructum qui comedit, non esuriet unquam? / Dico quod ille senex de fructibus illius arboris comedere non cessat ad numeri perfectionem, quousque senex ille iuvenis fiat. . . . Pater filius factus est.

322. Tibimet, Dei vates, in visione visus es tanquam vitis ampla, universum orbem implens divinis verbis, quasi fructibus. / An ignoratis quod tota divina pagina parabolice procedit? Nam Christus . . . modum servavit eundem et dixit: Ego sum vitis vera.

324. Spagyri . . . ex ipsa Luna oleum eliciunt . . . adversus morbum caducum, omnesque cerebri affectus.

326. Μανίας περιπίπτουσιν ἀλλ' οὐ νοῖ.

329. In philosophica Mercurii sublimatione sive praeparatione prima Herculeus labor operanti incumbit . . . limen enim a cornutis belluis custoditur . . . earum ferocitatem sola Dianae insignia et Veneris columbae mulcebunt, si te fata vocant.

335. Claves habet ad carceres infernales, ubi sulphur ligatum iacet.

337. Ψυχὴ . . . ἔλαφον (ἐλάφου Miller) μορφὴν περικειμένη κοπιᾷ θανάτῳ μελέτημα (θανάτου μελέτῃσι Diels) κρατουμένη.

350. Columba fuit Dominus Jesus . . . dicens Pax Vobis . . . En Columba, en oliva virens in ore. / Unde Propheta exclamat: Quis dabit mihi pennas [sic]ut columbae, videlicet cogitationes contemplationesque immaculatas ac simplices.

358. Ego sum illuminans omnia mea et facio lunam apparere patenter de interiore de patri meo Saturno et etiam de matre dominante, quae mihi inimicatur.

360. matrem et uxorem solis, quae foetum spagiricum a sole conceptum in sua matrice uteroque vento gestat in aëre.

369. . . . cum hac tinctura vivificantur omnes mortui, ut semper vivant, et hoc est fermentum primum elementatum, et est ad Lunam, et hoc est lumen omnium luminum, et est flos et fructus omnium luminum, quod illuminat omnia.

370. Primum namque aqua destillata pro Luna aestumatur: Sol enim, tamquam ignis, in ea occultatus est.

379. Quartus est Infernalis intelligibili oppositus, ardoris et incendii absque ullo lumine.

383. Sal autem reperitur in nobili quodam Sale et in rebus omnibus; quo circa veteres Philosophi illud vulgarem Lunam appellarunt.

384. (Deum habere) circa se ipsum amorem. Quem alii spiritum intellectualem asseruere et igneum, non habentem formam, sed transformantem se in quaecumque voluerit, et coaequantem se universis. . . . Unde rite per quandam similitudinem animae naturae Deum aut Dei virtutem, quae omnes res sustinet, Animam mediam naturam, aut animam Mundi appellamus.

397. Primo fit cinis, postea sal, et de illo sale per diversas operationes Mercurius Philosophorum.

404. Qui non gustaverit saporem salium, nunquam veniet ad optatum fermentum fermenti.

410. Alexander Magnus, Macedoniae Rex, ad nos, in Philosophia sua ita ait: Benedictus Deus in coelo siet, qui artem hanc in Sale creavit.

425. (In initio) Sal est nigrum ferme ac foetidum.

441. Est lapis occultus, et in imo fonte sepultus,
Vilis et eiectus, fimo vel stercore tectus . . .
Et lapis hic avis, et non lapis, aut avis hic est . . .
. . . nunc spuma maris vel acetum,
. . . .
Nunc quoque gemma salis, Almisadir sal generalis
. . . .
Nunc mare purgatum cum sulphure purificatum . . .

445. . . . cuius collum aureus fulgor, reliquum corpus purpureus color in pennis cinxit.

451. Ad hoc, scl. (corpus) spirituale, ignis, ad illud vero scl. corruptibile Sal refertur.

453. Profundum maris sedem intelligamus inferni.

462. Diabolus maria undique circumdat et undique pontum.

463. (imaginationis) res amaras ut lachrymas, tristitiam et vermem conscientiae.

464. Gustus torquebitur perpetua fame sitique rabiosa, in quarum levamen dabitur miseris Damnatis pro cybo absynthium, pro potu autem aqua fellis.

466. Mare Rubrum significat Baptismum.

467. Mare rubrum est baptismus sanguine Christi rubicundus, in quo hostes scl. peccata, merguntur.

479. Melius est gaudere in opere, quam laetari in divitiis sive virtuoso labore.

509. Ibi Oryx in summo aestu sitibunda lachrymis quasi effusis et gemitibus iteratis ardorem solis detestari traditur.

510. Res, cuius caput est rubeum, oculi nigri et pedes albi, est magisterium.

516. Tum tua res agitur, paries cum proximus ardet.

518. Fenix arabie avis dicta quod colorem fenicium habeat et quod sit in toto orbe singularis et unica.

519. Quem tu hic quaeris, inquit, peregrine? Ad virginem non licitum est viro appropinquare.

529. Doceat nos haec avis vel exemplo sui resurrectionem credere. / Cur igitur Judaei iniqui, Domini nostri Jesu Christi triduanam resurrectionem non crediderunt, cum avis trium dierum spatio seipsam suscitet?

532. Sapiens, pennas cui dabis, oro, tuas.

533. Divitiae cedant et opes, huic cedat et aurum, cui mens non eadem, non homo, sed pecus est.

540. Pater ejus est Sol, mater ejus Luna; portavit illud ventus in ventre suo; nutrix ejus terra est.
Vis ejus integra est, si versa fuerit in terram.
Ascendit a terra in coelum, iterumque descendit in terram et recipit vim superiorum et inferiorum. Sic habebis gloriam totius mundi.

550. Draco mulierem et haec illum interimit, simulque sanguine perfunduntur.

552. Aenigmate hoc olim involutum est a Philosophis: fac fixum, inquiunt, volatile, et rursus volatile fixum, et totum habebis magisterium.

553. Nemo enim ascendit in caelum, quod quaeritis, nisi qui de caelo (quod non quaeritis) descendit, illuminet eum.

555. Disce ex te ipso, quicquid est et in caelo et in terra, cognoscere, ut sapiens fias in omnibus. Ignoras caelum et elementa prius unum fuisse, divino quoque ab invicem artificio separata, ut et te et omnia generare possent? Si hoc nosti, reliquum et te fugere non potest, aut ingenio cares omni. Rursus in omni generatione, separatio talis est necessaria, qualem de te supra dixi fiendam, antequam ad verae philosophiae studia velum applices. Ex aliis nunquam unum facies quod quaeris, nisi prius ex te ipso fiat unum.

556. Simul descensus in quatuor et ascensus ad monadem. / De-

coquendus igitur, assandus, et fundendus: ascendit atque descendit, quae quidem operationes omnes unica sunt igne solo facta (operatio).

557. Lapis noster transit in terram, terra in aquam, aqua in aerem, aer in ignem, ibi est status, sed descendetur e converso.

559. Hac similitudine tibi satisfaciam: Filius Dei delapsus in virginem ibique caro figuratus homo nascitur, qui cum nobis propter nostram salutem veritatis viam demonstrasset, pro nobis passus et mortuus, post resurrectionem in coelos remeat. Ubi terra, hoc est humanitas, exaltata est, super omnes circulos mundi, et in coelo intellectuali sanctissimae Trinitatis est collocata.

570. Dehinc (animam) descendentem per quosdam circulos a principatibus malignis capi et secundum voluntatem victoris principis in corpora diversa contrudi eisque adscribi chirographum.

578. Itaque vocatus sum Hermes Trismegistus, habens tres partes Philosophiae totius mundi.

580. Vis eius integra est, . . . si versa fuerit in terram.

584. Nam serpentes ideo introrsum spectantia capita habent ut significent inter se legatos colloqui et convenire debere . . . Unde enim . . . legati pacis caduceatores dicuntur . . . Quibus caduceis duo mala adduntur unum Solis aliud Lunae . . . Mercurius haec tam fera animalia concordat, nos quoque concordare debere certum est. / Alii Mercurium quasi medicurrium a latinis dictum volunt, quod inter coelum et inferos semper incurrat . . . Caduceus illi adeo adsignatur, quod fide media hostes in amicitiam conducat. / Perfacile is discordes animos in concordiam trahet, duosque angues, hoc est odia mutua, doctrinae suae virgâ in unum obligabit.

585. Primo regnat Saturnus in nigredine.

587. Ut per solutionem corpora solvuntur, ita per cognitionem resolvuntur philosophorum dubia.

595. Laton autem est immundum corpus.

597. Laton est ex Sole et Luna compositum corpus imperfectum citrinum; quod cum dealbaveris et . . . ad pristinam citrinitatem perduxeris, habes iterum Latonem . . . , tunc intrasti ostium, et habes artis principium.

600. Azoth et ignis latonem abluunt, et nigredinem ab eo auferunt.

601. Ignis et aqua latonem abluunt et eius nigredinem abstergunt.

602.
$$\theta\epsilon\omega\rho\tilde{\omega}\nu\ \grave{\epsilon}\nu\ \mu\acute{\epsilon}\sigma\omega\ \tau\tilde{\omega}\nu\ \acute{\rho}\epsilon\acute{\iota}\theta\rho\omega\nu\ \tau\acute{o}\nu\ \pi\sigma\tau\epsilon$$
$$\pi\alpha\acute{\iota}\delta\omega\nu\ \tau\rho\iota\tilde{\omega}\nu\ \mu\acute{\epsilon}\sigma\sigma\nu\ \theta\alpha\nu\acute{\epsilon}\nu\tau\alpha\ \delta\rho\acute{o}\sigma\sigma\nu\ \grave{\epsilon}\nu$$
$$\pi\nu\rho\grave{\iota}\ \nu\tilde{\nu}\nu\ \pi\tilde{\nu}\rho\ \grave{\epsilon}\nu\ \tau\tilde{\omega}\ \text{'}I\sigma\rho\delta\acute{\alpha}\nu\eta\ \lambda\acute{\alpha}\mu\pi\sigma\nu\ \kappa\tau\lambda.$$

603. Et si in fonte auri et argenti *baptisati* fuerimus et spiritus corporis nostri cum patre et filio in coelum ascenderit, et de-

scenderit, animae nostrae reviviscent, et corpus meum animale candidum permanebit, scl. Lunae.

604. Quando autem baptizat tunc infundit animam.

608. Ἐν γὰρ τῷ Ἅδῃ κατάκλεισον αὐτά / ἐν τῷ Ἅδῃ κλείσατε αὐτά / τιτρώσκουσιν αὐτὴν κλύδωνες . . . ἐν τῷ Ἅδει καὶ ἐν τῷ τάφῳ ἐν ᾧ κατάκεινται. Ὅταν δὲ ἀνεωχθῇ ἡ τάφος, ἀναβήσονται αὐτὰ ἐξ Ἅδου ὡς οἷα βρέφος ἐκ γαστρός.

609. Τὸ σωτήριον ἐκεῖνο ὕδωρ καὶ τάφος ὑμῖν ἐγένετο καὶ μήτηρ.

610. Aqua velut morientem deducit in tumulum: spiritus sanctus velut resurgentem perducit ad caelum.

615. ἀετὸς χαλκοῦς κατερχόμενος ἐν πηγῇ καθαρᾷ καὶ λουόμενος καθ' ἡμέραν ἐντεῦθεν ἀνανεούμενος.

616. ἐγὼ φυτὸν ὄνομα βαΐς, ἐγὼ ἀπόρροια αἵματος . . . ὁ ἐκπεφυκὼς ἐκ τοῦ Βυθοῦ . . . , ἐγώ εἰμι τὸ ἱερὸν ὄρνεον Φοῖνιξ . . . , ἐγώ εἰμι ὁ Ἥλιος . . . ἐγώ εἰμι Ἀφροδείτη . . . ἐγώ εἰμι Κρόνος, ὁ δεδειχὼς φῶς . . . ἐγώ εἰμι Ὄσιρις ὁ καλούμενος ὕδωρ, ἐγώ εἰμι Ἶσις ἡ καλουμένη δρόσος, ἐγώ εἰμι Ἡσενεφυς ἡ καλουμένη ἔαρ.

619. Terra alba foliata est corona victoriae, quae est cinis extractus a cinere, et corpus eorum secundum.

626. lapis albus, sol albus, Luna plena, terra alba fructuosa, mundificata et calcinata.

633. σώματα ὄντα πνεύματα γίνονται, ἵνα ἐν τῇ καταβαφῇ τοῦ πνεύματος βάψει.

640. Sale et facetiis Caesar . . . vicit omnes.

642. Sal est in se uno continens aquae et ignis elementum; et hoc ex duobus est unum.

661. Τοσαύτη κλεῖς λόγου τῆς ἐγκυκλίου τέχνης ἡ σύνοψις. / Quanto magis libros legebam, tanto magis mihi illuminabatur.

680. O aquam in acerba specie, quae tu elementa conservas! o naturam vicinitatis, quae tu naturam solvis! o naturam optumam, quae tu naturam ipsam superas! . . cum lumine coronata et nata es . . . et quinta essentia ex te orta est.

682. O aquam in amara acerbaque specie! Durum enim difficileque cui vis, ut fontem illum inveniat.

688. Quae cum ita sint, satis erit humano ingenio post lucem fidei, Divinae maiestatis veluti refractos radios in mundo, et rebus creatis agnoscere.

689. Esse in Chemia nobile aliquod corpus . . . in cuius initio sit miseria cum aceto, in fine vero gaudium cum laeticia, ita et mihi eventurum praesupposui, ut primo multa aspera, amara, tristia, taediosa gustarem, perferrem et experirer, tandem omnia laetiora et faciliora visurus essem.

691. ὁ καθολικὸς ὄφις, φησίν, οὗτός ἐστι ὁ σοφὸς τῆς Εὔας λόγος.

692. Pater omnis telesmi est hic.

IV. REX AND REGINA

5. . . . occidit Osirim artuatimque laceravit et per omnes Nili fluminis ripas miseri corporis palpitantia membra proiecit. / Nam Liberum ad Solem volunt referre commenta Graecorum etc. . . . qui vidit puerum solem? quis fefellit? quis occidit? quis laceravit? quis divisit? quis membris ejus epulatus est? . . . sed et errorem istum physica rursum volunt ratione protegere: indivisam mentem et divisam, id est τόν ἀμέριστον καὶ τόν μεμερισμένον νοῦν, hac se putant posse ratione venerari.

13. Εἷς Βάϊτ, εἷς ῾Αθώρ μία τῶν βία, εἷς δὲ ᾿Ακῶρι, χαῖρε πάτερ κόσμου, χαῖρε τρίμορφε θεός.

17. Βίβλος ἀληθὴς Σοφε Αἰγυπτίου καὶ θείου ῾Εβραίων κυρίου τῶν δυναμέων Σαβαωθ.

21.   Hostes meos omnes superavi et vici,
    Venenosumque draconem pedibus meis subegi,
    Sum Rex eximius et dives in terris
    . . . .
    Hinc mihi Hermes nomen *sylvarum domini* tribuit.

25. Inquiunt quidam, venerare humiditates, reges namque sunt magnanimi iniuriam non patientes, parce ergo eis et eorum capta benevolentiam, et suis oculis tibi dabunt, ut quodvis ab eis habebis.

27. Denique . . . videbis Lapidem Philosophicum Regem nostrum et Dominum Dominantium, prodire ex sepulchri vitrei sui thalamo ac throno in scenam mundanam hanc . . . clamantem: Ecce, Renovabo omnia.

28. Ihsuh Christi crucifixi, Salvatoris totius generis humani, id est Mundi minoris, in Naturae libro, et ceu Speculo, typus est, Lapis Philosophorum, Servator Mundi maioris.

37. Et scito quod aqua est quae occultum extrahit.

41. Cave ab hydropisi et diluvio Noe.

42. Equorum venter secretum est maximum: in hoc se abscondit noster hydropicus, ut sanitatem recuperet et ab omni aqua ad solem se exoneret.

43. Ita senex in balneo sedet, quem in vase optime sigillato et clauso contine, quoad Mercurius visibilis invisibilis fiat et occultetur.

45. Et ad Naaman dictum est: Vade et lavare septies in Jordano et mundaberis. Nam ipse est unum baptisma in absolutionem peccatorum.

46. O benedicta aquina forma pontica, quae elementa dissolvis.

50. . . . igitur homo, caelum, et terra unum sunt, etiam aer et

aqua. Si homo res in maiori mundo transmutare novit . . . quanto magis id in microcosmo, hoc est in se ipso noverit, quod extra se potest, modo cognoscat hominis in homine thesaurum existere maximum, et non extra ipsum.

53. Nemo creatorem poterit melius cognoscere quam ex opere noscitur artifex.

69. Masculus autem est, qui sine alis existit sub foemina, foemina vero habet alas. Propterea dixerunt: Proiicite foeminam super masculum et ascendet masculus super foeminam.

73. Haec petra nisi fuerit percussa aquas non dabit.

74. Sonora vox, suavis et grata philosophantium auribus. O fons divitiarum inexhaustibilis veritatem et iustitiam sitientibus! O desolatorum imperfectioni solatium! Quid ultra quaeritis mortales anxii? cur infinitis animos vestros curis exagitatis miseri? quae vestra vos excaecat dementia quaeso? cum in vobis, non ex vobis sit omne quod extra vos, non apud vos quaeritis.

75. Paradisum ipsum non terrenum videri posse, non in solo aliquo, sed in nostro principali, quod animatur et vivificatur animae virtutibus, et infusione spiritus Dei.

84. Antiquus dierum cum sua celsitate habitavit, ut infans, in utero.

85. Puerulus tuus senex est, o virgo, ipse est Antiquus dierum et omnia praecessit tempora.

95. assimilavit subtilitatem caloris ignis, gressui piae matris super ventrem filii sui.

102. Illa res . . . passim apparere colores facit. / hic est igitur lapis, quem omnibus nuncupavimus nominibus, qui opus recipit et bibit, et ex quo omnis color apparet. / Omnes Mundi colores manifestabuntur.

104. Dum autem Quinta Essentia in terra est, id in multiplicibus coloribus contrarii splendoris Solis cognoscis, quemadmodum cernis in Iride dum Sol per pluviam splendet.

105. Τὴν κόρην τοῦ ὀφθαλμοῦ παραφέρει καὶ τὴν ἴριν τὴν οὐρανίαν.

112. Qui animam meam levaverit, eius colores videbit.

116. Oro ex toto corde Misericordiam tuam, ut mittas mihi de caelis sanctis tuis Ruach Hhochmah-El, Spiritum Sapientiae tuae, qui mihi familiaris semper adsistat, me dextre regat, sapienter moneat, doceat; mecum sit, Oret, Laboret; mihi det bene velle, nosse, esse et posse in Physicis, Physicomedicis.

122. Hic sigillata mater in infantis sui ventre surgit et depuratur, ut ob tantam . . . puritatem putredo hinc exulet . . . Jam scias Virginem nostram terram ultimam subire cultivationem, ut in ea fructus Solis seminetur ac maturetur . . .

125. Quae tamen omnia bonum praenunciant indicium: quod videlicet tam bene vexatus homo tandem aliquando beatum exopta-
tumque exitum consecuturus siet: quemadmodum etiam et
ipsa SS. scriptura testis est, in qua (2 Tim. 3, Act. 4) legitur,
quod videlicet omneis, qui beate in Christo Jesu vivere velint,
persequutionem pati cogantur, quodque nos, per multas tribu-
lationes et angustias, regnum coelorum ingredi necessum
habeamus.

128. Foenix dicitur rubeus, et est Christus, de quo dicitur: Quis
est iste, qui venit de Edom tinctis vestibus de Bosra. / Quare
ergo rubrum est indumentum tuum et vestimenta tua sicut
calcantium in torculari? / Edom quod dicitur rufus, est Esau
appellatus, propter rufum pulmentum quo a fratre suo Jacob
est cibatus. / Tertia die avis reparatur, quia Christus tertia die
suscitatur a Patre.

129. Ἡ ὡς ᾠὸν ταοῦ ἔχον ἐν ἑαυτῷ τὴν τῶν χρωμάτων ποικίλην πληθύν.

131. Et certe solitudo, unicum conservandi spiritualis animi remedium amplissimam internae felicitatis occasionem praebet.

134. Si autem mortuus fuerit pavo, non marcescit eius caro nec
foetidum dat odorem, sed manet tamquam condita aromatibus.

136. Hermes Princeps.—Post tot illata generi humano damna, Dei
consilio: Artisque adminiculo, medicina salubris factus heic
fluo.—Bibat ex me qui potest; lavet qui vult; turbet qui audet;
bibite fratres et vivite.

138. totum elixir albedinis et rubedinis, et est aqua permanens,
et aqua vitae et mortis, et lac virginis, herba ablutionis—et est
fons animalis: de quo qui bibit, non moritur, et est suscep-
tivum coloris et medicina eorum, et faciens acquirere colores,
et est illud quod mortificat, siccat et humectat, calefacit et
infrigidat et facit contraria. / Et ipse est Draco, qui maritat se
ipsum et impraegnat seipsum et parit in die suo, et interficit
ex veneno suo omnia animalia. / Accede Corpus ad fontem
hunc, ut cum tua Mente bibas ad satietatem et in posterum
non sitias amplius vanitates. O admiranda fontis efficacia, quae
de duobus unum, et pacem inter inimicos facit! Potest amoris
fons de spiritu et anima mentem facere, sed hic de mente et
corpore *virum unum* efficit. Gratias agimus tibi Pater, quod
filios tuos inexhausti virtutum fontis tui participes facere
dignatus sis. Amen.

148. Alii appellaverunt hanc terram Leonem viridem fortem in
praelio; Alii draconem devorantem, congelantem vel mortifi-
cantem caudam suam.

150. Sed nullum corpus immundum ingreditur, excepto uno, quod
vulgariter vocatur a philosophis Leo viridis.

151. quia depopulata (terra) est a suis spiritibus.

155. Qui sui ipsius spiritus tam multa devorat.

156. In Leone nostro viridi vera materia . . . et vocatur Adrop, Azoth, aut Duenech viride.

173. . . . lapidem, quem qui cognoscit, ponit illum super oculos suos.

178. Dixit enim ei mater sua: O Marchos, oportet ne hunc ignem esse leviorem calore febris? Dixit ei Marchos, o mater, fiat in statu febris. Revertor et accendo illum ignem.

189. Venus autem, cum sit orientalis, Solem praecedit.

193. Igneque debito videbis Emblema Operis magni, nempe nigrum, caudam pavonis, album, citrinum, rubeumque.

204. Et nota quod natura in principio suae originis intendit facere Solem vel Lunam, sed non potest propter Venerem, corruptum argentum vivum, commistum, vel propter terram foetidam, quare sicut puer in ventre matris suae ex corruptione matricis contrahit infirmitatem et corruptionem causa loci per accidens, quamvis sperma fuerit mundum, tamen puer sit leprosus et immundus causa matricis corruptae, et sic est de omnibus metallis imperfectis, quae corrumpuntur ex Venere, et terra foetida.

205. Leonem tuum in oriente quaeras, et aquilam ad meridiem in assumptum hoc opus nostrum . . . tuum iter ad meridiem dirigas oportet; sic in Cypro votum consequeris, de quo latius minime loquendum.

210. Completur rosa alba tempore aestivali in Oriente.

213. . . . quomodo hortus aperiendus, et rosae nobiles in agro suo conspiciendae sient.

218. Antichristus in magna Babylonia de meretrice generis Dan nascetur. In matris utero diabolo replebitur et in Corozaim a maleficis nutrietur.

219.   Ut rosa per medias effloret roscida spinas,
         sic Veneris nunquam gaudia felle carent.

220. Et ita tandem, in unum contentum corruat imbibendo cum uno fermento, id est aqua una, quia aqua est fermentum aquae.

221. Πρῶτος αὐτὸς τοῦτο ἐποίησεν ἐνάγων αὐτοὺς ἀταράχως εἰς τὴν κοινωνίαν τῶν μυστηρίων· Διὰ τοῦτο τὸ ἑαυτοῦ αἷμα αὐτὸς ἔπιεν.

222. Sic et duas Graeciae litteras, summam et ultimam, sibi induit Dominus, initii et finis concurrentium in se figuras uti quemadmodum A ad Ω usque volvitur (Apoc. I, 8) et rursus Ω ad A replicatur, ita ostenderent in se esse et initii decursum ad finem et finis recursum ad initium, ut omnis dispositio in eum desinens per quem coepta est.

224. Quicunque Chemicam artem addiscere vult, philosophiam,

non Aristotelicam, sed eam quae veritatem docet, addiscat . . .
nam eius doctrina tota consistit in amphibologia, quae men-
daciorum optimum est pallium. Cum ipse Platonem, et reliquos
reprehendisset, quaerendae famae gratia, nullum potuit commodius instrumentum reperisse, quam idem, quo in reprehen-
dendo fuerat usus, amphibologico sermone scilicet, scripta sua
contra sinistram oppugnantem, dextro subterfugio salvans, et
e contra; quod Sophismatis genus in omnibus eius scriptis
videre licet.

250. Quod cum cognovisset bonus pater tenebras ad terram suam
supervenisse, produxit ex se virtutem, quae dicitur mater vitae,
qua circumdedit primum hominem, quae sunt quinque elementa, id est ventus, lux, aqua, ignis et materia, quibus in-
dutus, tamquam ad adparatum belli, descendit deorsum pug-
nare adversum tenebras.

263. Deinde fermentum tangit cum corpore imperfecto praeparato,
ut dictum est, quousque fiant unum corpore, specie et aspectu
et tunc dicitur Ortus; quia tunc natus est lapis noster, qui
vocatus est rex a Philosophis, ut in Turba dicitur: Honorate
regem nostrum ab igne venientem, diademate coronatum.

264. . . . quare signo illum notabili notavit Omnipotens, cuius
nativitas per Orientem in Horizonte Hemisphaerii sui philosophicum annunciatur. Viderunt Sapientes in Evo Magi et
obstupuerunt statimque agnoverunt Regem serenissimum in
mundo natum. Tu, cum eius Astra conspexeris, sequere ad
usque cunabula, ibi videbis infantem pulcrum, sordes semo-
vendo, regium puellum honora, gazam aperi, auri donum
offeras, sic tandem post mortem tibi carnem sanguinemque
dabit, summam in tribus Terrae Monarchiis medicinam.

265. Et videatis iksir vestitum regni vestimento.

266. Lapis Philosophorum est rex de coelo descendens, cuius montes
sunt argentei rivuli aurei et terra lapides et gemmae pretiosae.

268. Quod infunditur anima corpori, et nascitur Rex coronatus. /
Ego coronor, et diademate ornor, et regiis vestibus induor:
quia corporibus laetitiam ingredi facio. / Cinerem ne vilipendas, quia Deus reddet ei liquefactionem et tunc ultimo
Rex diademate rubeo divino nutu coronatur. Oportet te ergo
hoc magisterium tentare.

272. Proiice ergo supra quodvis corpus, et ex eo tantum quantum
vis, quoniam in duplo multiplicabitur Tinctura eius. Et si
una pars sui primo convertit cum suis corporibus centum
partes; secundo convertit mille. Tertio decem millia, quarto
centum millia; quinto mille millia in solificum et lunificum
verum.

277. Et quamvis exanimis ipse philosophicorum Rex videatur, tamen vivit et ex profundo clamat: Qui me liberabit ex aquis et in siccum reducet, hunc ego divitiis beabo perpetius. Hic clamor etsi audiatur a multis, nulli tamen eius commiseratione ducti, quaerere regem subeunt. Quis enim, inquiunt, se demerget in aequor? Quis suo praesentaneo periculo alterius periculum levabit? Pauci sunt eius lamentationi creduli et putant vocem auditam esse Scillae et Charybdis resonos fragores et boatus. Hinc ociosi sedent domi nec regiam gazam, ut nec salutem curant.

280. Verum philosophorum antimonium in mari profundo, ut regius ille filius demersum delitescit.

289. Plumbum vexationes et molestias significat, per quas Deus nos visitat et ad resipiscentiam reducit. Quemadmodum enim plumbum omnes metallorum imperfectiones comburit et exterminat, unde Boethus Arabs illud aquam sulphuris vocat, ita quoque tribulatio in haec vita multas maculas, quas contraximus, a nobis abstergit: unde S. Ambrosius illam clavem coeli appellat.

291. Ex ossibus deinde et medullis eius nasci primo ceu vermiculum, inde fieri pullum.

301. Hic enim dum nascitur, rerum vicissitudo fit et innovatio.

306. Phoenix avis pavone pulchrior est; pavo enim aureas argenteasque habet alas; Phoenix vero hyacinthinas et smaragdinas, preciosorumque lapidum coloribus distinctas; coronam habet in capite.

316. Ascendit per se, nigrescit, descendit et albescit, crescit et decrescit . . . nascitur, moritur, resurgit, postea in aeternum vivit.

319. Eptacephalus draco, princeps tenebrarum, traxit de coelo cauda sua partem stellarum et nebula peccatorum eas obtexit, atque mortis tenebris obduxit.

335. σκώληξ καὶ οὐκ ἄνθρωπος, ὄνειδος ἀνθρώπου καὶ ἐξουθένημα λαοῦ· αὐτός ἐστιν ὁ βασιλεὺς τῆς δόξης, ὁ ἐν πολέμῳ δυνατός.

351. Nam requiei aditus nimis est coarctatus, neque ad illam quisquam potest ingredi, nisi per animae afflictionem.

352. Esse in Chemia nobile aliquod corpus, quod de domino ad dominum movetur.

361. quod vocat Plato intelligibile non sensibile. / Simplex est pars inopinabilis / est unius essentiae / Opus non perficitur nisi vertatur in simplex. / Conversio elementorum ad simplex. / Homo est dignior animalium et propinquior simplici et hoc propter intelligentiam.

362. Eiusque (veritatis) talem esse virtutem compererunt, ut miracula fecerit.

366. . . . ad amussim studeat centrum cognoscere ac scire, eoque se totum conferat, et centrum liberabitur ab omnibus imperfectionibus et morbis, ut ad prioris monarchiae statum restituatur.

367a. Accipite spiritum nigrum veterem, et eo corpora diruite et cruciate, quousque alterantur.

368. Irritate bellum inter aes et argentum vivum, quoniam peritum tendunt et corrumpuntur prius. / Inter ea pugnam irritate aerisque corpus diruite, donec pulvis fiat.

369. Diabolum ista in caelum erexisse decidens ac deiectus ab eo, nec non illa postmodum in mentem humanam infigere conatum fuisse, videlicet ambitionem, brutalitatem, calumniam, et divortium.

370. Homo a Deo in fornacem tribulationis collocatur et ad instar compositi Hermetici tamdiu omnis generis angustiis, diversimodisque calamitatibus et anxietatibus premitur, donec veteri Adamo et carni (Ephes. 4) siet mortuus et tamquam vere novus homo . . . iterum resurgat.

373. Per spiritualem istam suam mortem, anima sua omnino eximitur.

380. Postremum vero (opus) in altero regali Jovis solio desinet, a quo Rex noster potentissimus coronam pretiosissimis Rubinis contextam suscipiet, "sic in se sua per vestigia volvitur annus."

383. Ciconia ibi sedebat, quasi se appellans circulum lunarem.

384. Rex ortus est, id est anima . . . lapidi mortuo infusa est.

395. Haec enim res a te extrahitur; cuius etiam minera tu existis; apud te namque illam inveniunt, et, ut verius confitear, a te accipiunt; quod cum probaveris, amor eius et dilectio in te augebitur. Et scias hoc verum et indubitabile permanere.

411. ὅταν τὸ τῆς αἰσχύνης ἔνδυμα πατήσητε, καὶ ὅταν γένηται τὰ δύο ἓν καὶ τὸ ἄρρεν μετὰ τῆς θηλείας οὔτε ἄρρεν οὔτε θῆλυ.

412. Confert enim Deus hanc divinam et puram scientiam suis fidelibus et servis illis scilicet quibus eam a primaeva rerum natura conferre disposuit . . . Nam haec res nihil nisi donum Dei altissimi (esse) potest; qui prout vult, et etiam cui vult, ex suis servis et fidelibus illud committit, et monstrat . . . Praeponit enim Dominus ex suis servis quos vult et eligit, ut hanc scientiam divinam homini celatam quaerant, et quaesitam secum retineant.

413. Dicit enim primus spagirorum Dux: Pulsate et aperietur vobis.

414. Nam evenire quandoque solet, ut post multos annos, labores

586

et studia . . . nonnulli sint electi, multis pulsationibus, orationibus et investigatione sedula praemissis.

416. Sic etiam lapidis compositum Rex et Regina dicuntur . . . Sic vir et mulier dicuntur Masculus et femina propter copulam videlicet et actionem et passionem. Rosinus: Artis auri arcanum et mare et femina consistit.

420. Quem divus Plato in ignea substantia habitare posuit: intelligens videlicet inenarrabilem Dei in seipso splendorem et circa seipsum amorem.

429. Qui per alienum ingenium et manum mercenariam operatur, aliena a veritate opera videbit. Et vice versa, qui alteri servilem praestat operam, uti servus in arte, nunquam ad Reginae mysteria admittetur.

V. ADAM AND EVE

1. Iste est Philosophorum Mercurius, ille celeberrimus Microcosmus et Adam.

3. Accipe Adam et quod assimilatur Adam, nominasti hic Adam et tacuisti nomen foeminae seu Evae, et non nominans eam, quia scis quod homines qui sunt tui similes in mundo, sciunt quod illud, quod tibi assimilatur, est Eva.

4. Qua propter ingenio et intellectu validissimis adseverarunt suum lapidem esse animalem, quem etiam vocaverunt suum Adamum, qui suam invisibilem Evam occultam in suo corpore gestaret ab eo momento, quo virtute summi conditoris omnium unita sunt. Ea de causa merito dici potest, Mercurium philosophorum nihil aliud esse, quam compositum eorum abstrusissimum Mercurium et non vulgarem illum . . . est in Mercurio quicquid quaerunt sapientes . . . lapidis philosophorum materia, nihil aliud est, quam . . . verus hermaphroditus Adam atque microcosmus. / Natura in primis requirit ab artifice, ut philosophicus Adam in Mercurialem substantiam adducatur. / . . . compositio huius sacratissimi lapidis Adamici, fit ex sapientum Adamico Mercurio.

6. Ecce Adam heic duo sunt, fixatum et constans unum, fugax alterum.

7. Et Adamus erat Dominus, Rex et Imperator.

8.   Adam in balneo residebat,
         In quo Venus sui similem reperiebat,
         Quod praeparaverat senex Draco.

18. Secundus Adam qui dicitur homo philosophicus.

587

19. Ex quatuor autem elementis pater noster Adam et filii eius
. . . creati sunt.

26. (Deus) incepit autem colligere pulverem primi hominis e
quatuor terrae angulis, videlicet rubrum, nigrum, album et
viridem. Ruber pulvis factus est sanguis, niger fuit pro visceribus, albus pro ossibus et nervis, viridis factus est corpus.

33. Scivit enim per ternarium Adami non patere potuisse aditum
unario protegente ternarium, binarium igitur Evae tentavit
ingredi.

34. . . . item non ignoravit Evam a viro suo divisam tanquam
naturalem binarium ab unario sui ternarii.

36. Nam Elementa circularia sunt, ut Hermes sentit, quodlibet a
duobus aliis circumdatur, cum quibus convenit in una quali-
tatum ipsorum sibi appropriata, uti est terra inter ignem et
aquam, participans de igne in siccitate, et de aqua in frigiditate.
Et sic de caeteris.

37. Homo igitur, qui magni mundi est imago, et hinc microcosmus
seu parvus mundus vocatus (sicut mundus ad archetypi sui
similitudinem factus, et ex quatuor elementis compositus, magnus homo appellatur) etiam suum coelum et terram habet.
Nam anima et intellectus sunt ejus coelum; corpus vero et
sensualitas ejus terra. Adeo ut coelum et terram hominis
cognoscere, idem sit quod plenam et integram totius mundi et
rerum naturalium cognitionem habere.

47. In Adamo ergo protoplaste . . . continebantur omnes illae
notiones sive Species supradictae a Psyche factiva usque ad
singularitatem emanativam.

50. Deinde caput, manus et pedes (leonis) colligo, et calefacio eis
aquam extractam a cordibus statuarum ex lapidibus albis et
citrinis, quae cadit de coelo tempore pluviae.

52. Laudanum autem barbae eius, i.e. mumia vel ysopos aut sudor.

53. Universae creaturae fundamenta . . . contineantur in . . .
Radicali humido, Mundi semine, Mumia, Materia prima.

55. Et ideo per ablutionem aquae et desiccationem ignis semper
extrahis oleum a corde statuarum. / Hoc oleum est tinctura,
aurum et anima, ac philosophorum unguentum. / Illud oleum
seu aqua divina . . . et vocatur *Mediator*.

61. Faciebant autem in iis (statuis) cum ostia, tum concavitates,
quibus deorum quos colebant, simulacra imponebant. Appare-
bant itaque viles eiuscemodi statuae Mercuriales, sed intra se
deorum ornamenta (καλλωπισμούς) continebant.

65. proiiciet semen suum supra marmorem in simulachrum.

67. Duo Adam efficiuntur: unus, pater noster, in mortem, quia
mortalis factus est, peccans: secundus, pater noster, in resur-

rectionem, quoniam immortalis cum esset, per mortem devicit mortem atque peccatum. Primus Adam, hic, pater: posterior illic, etiam primi Adam est pater.

68. Restat nunc pars altera philosophicae praxeos, longe quidem difficilior, longe sublimior. In quo omnes ingenii neruos, omnia denique mentis curricula multorum philosophorum elanguisse legimus. Difficilius et enim hominem faceres reviviscere, quam mortem oppetere. Hic Dei petitur opus: Maximum quidem mysterium est creare animas, atque corpus inanime in statuam viventem confingere.

70. . . . et ita dimittitur magnus ille ignis qui mundum consumat universum; deinde iterum demittunt animam, quae obicitur inter medium novi saeculi, ut omnes animae peccatorum vinciantur in aeternum. Tunc autem haec fient, cum statua venerit.

78. Nunc de igne terreno ad coelestem ut ascendamus, qui est sol, mundi sensibilis oculus et cor, et Dei invisibilis imago. S. Dionysius manifestam et claram Dei statuam illum vocat.

79. (ἥλιος) ἡ τῆς θείας ἀγαθότητος ἐμφανὴς εἰκών. / Ἥλιος ἐν τύπῳ θεοῦ ἐστιν ἡ δὲ σελήνη ἀνθρώπου.

82. (filius) Clarissimum est, quod ad Tiphereth pertineat.

83. Matris quoque nomine appellatur Malchuth, quia mater est omnium sub ipsa existentium usque ad finem totius Abyssi.

84. Pulchritudo eius (solis) cum sponso ex camera sua nuptiali prodeunte comparata. Et ipse tanquam sponsus procedens de thalamo suo.

85. Procedit Christus quasi sponsus de thalamo suo; praesagio nuptiarum exiit ad campum saeculi; cucurrit sicut gigas exsultando per viam: pervenit usque ad crucis thorum, et ibi firmavit ascendendo conjugium; ubi cum sentiret anhelantem in suspiriis creaturam, commercio pietatis se pro conjuge dedit ad poenam. Tradidit quoque carbunculum, tanquam sui sanguinis gemmam, et copulavit sibi perpetuo jure matronam. 'Aptavi vos,' inquit Apostolus, 'uni viro virginem castam exhibere Christo.'

88. Latere in antimonio plus virtutis medicinalis quam in ullo alio simplici ideoque etiam plus virtutis tingentis seu tincturae.

89. Et ideo dicitur quod lapis in quolibet homine. Et Adam portavit secum de paradiso, ex qua materia in quolibet homine lapis noster vel Elixir eliciatur.

100. Adam tradidit Enocho, qui introductus in mysterium embolysmi intercalavit annum.

101. Dixit Adam: hae sunt tabulae, quibus inscripturus est Sanctus benedictus digito suo.

103. Mundum per aquam esse renovandum vel potius castigandum, pauloque minus quam delendum.

119. Decem circulos a se invicem disiunctos complectebatur alter circulus, qui huius universitatis anima esse ferebatur, et cuius nomen erat Leviathan.

120. In eodem (diagrammate) reperi eum, qui vocatur Beemoth sub infimo circulo collocatum. Leviathanis nomen ab impii diagrammatis auctore bis erat scriptum, in superficia scl. et in centro circuli.

121. Animam tamen omnia permeantem impium hoc diagramma esse ponit.

124. Nunc autem angelum leoni similem aiunt habere cum astro Saturni necessitudinem.

125. Tibi, prime et septime . . . opus filio et patri perfectum.

130. Τῷ μὲν Κρόνῳ προσήκει ἡ ἑβδομὰς μάλιστα καὶ πρῶτως . . . τῇ δέ ʿΡέᾳ ἡ ὀγδοάς.

131. Isti autem aliis alia addunt, Prophetarum dicta, circulos circulis inclusos . . . virtutum ex quadam Prunico virgine manantem, viventem animam.

135. Quia Solis et Lunae colores haec duo metalla referunt.

136. Redemptor autem noster in carne veniens, pleiades iunxit, quia operationes septiformis spiritus simul in se et cunctas et manentes habuit.

153. Habet in se unusquisque Adam et Evam. Sicut enim in illa prima hominis transgressione suggessit serpens, delectata est Eva, consensit Adam: sic et quotidie fieri videmus, dum suggerit diabolus, delectatur caro, consentit spiritus.

158. 'Plasmavit Deus hominem', id est finxit de terrae limo. Is autem qui ad imaginem Dei factus est et ad similitudinem, interior homo noster est, invisibilis et incorporalis et incorruptus atque immortalis.

159. Ὁ δὲ κατὰ τὴν εἰκόνα ἰδέα τις ἢ γένος, ἢ σφραγίς, νοητός, ἀσώματος οὔτε ἄρρεν οὔτε θῆλυ, ἄφθαρτος φύσει.

187. Esse in Chemia nobile aliquod corpus, quod de domino ad dominum movetur, in cuius initio sit miseria cum aceto, in fine vero gaudium cum laeticia.

193. Psyche, quae ipsis nephesch dicitur, sit spiritus vitalis, non quatenus plane corporeus sed insitus ille atque primitivus et seminalis, quem recentiores *Archeum* vocant, cum quo correspondet Philosophorum anima vegetativa seu plastica, et Platonicorum τὸ ἐπιθυμητικὸν seu concupiscible.

193a. Mater enim nil est nisi propensio Patris ad inferiora.

195. (Adam) a Cabbalistis Adam Kadmon dicitur, ad differentiam Adami Protoplastae . . . eo quod inter omnia a Deo emanata

primum occupet locum, prout protoplastes in specie hominum: ita ut per illum nihil commodius intelligi queat, quam anima Messiae, quem et Paulus ad I Corinth. 15, vers. 45–49 indigitat.

201. . . . inquit Ezechiel 34, v. 31: Vos Adam estis. Id est, vos merito vocamini Adami nomine. Sensus enim est: si literaliter textus intelligendus esset, objectio merito fieret, omnes etiam populos mundi sive gentiles eodem modo esse homines, quo Israelitae; statura nempe erecta. Ubi porro quoque dicendum fuisset, vos homines estis. Verum enim vero (sensus hic est, ex animabus vestris consistebat microcosmus Adami) . . . § 11: Vos estis Adam. (Quasi diceret omnes Israelitarum animas nihil aliud fuisse quam Adamum nimirum protoplasten:) Et vos scintillae illius atque membra ejus extitistis.

203. Hinc quoque dixerunt Magistri nostri: Non veniet filius David, donec plene exiverint omnes animae, quae fuerunt in corpore (nimirum protoplastae).

204. Differentias autem numericas referri ad dispositionem bilanci-formem ubi facies faciei obvertitur, et duo vel plura ejusdem perfectionis, et speciei, tantum distinguuntur, ut mas et foemina. Quae differentiae numericae etiam denotantur per id, quod dicitur anterius, et posterius.

218. Τὸ ἓν γίνεται δύο, καὶ τὰ δύο γ΄, καὶ τοῦ γ^{του} τὸ ἓν τέταρτον.

219. Jam Adam Kadmon emanavit ab uno simplici, adeoque est unitas: sed et descendit, et delapsus est in ipsam naturam suam, adeoque est duo. Iterumque reducitur ad unum, quod in se habet, et ad summum; adeoque est tria et quatuor.

220. Et haec est causa, quod nomen essentiale habeat quatuor literas, tres diversas, et unam bis sumptam: quoniam He primum est uxor τοῦ Jod; et alterum, uxor τοῦ Vav. Primum emanavit a Jod, via directa, et alterum a Vav, via conversa et reflexa.

222. Jod, quia simplex, est unum et primum quid, et simile uni, quod numeris; et puncto, quod corporibus omnibus prius est. Punctum autem, secundum longitudinem motum producit lineam, nempe Vav. / Litera Jod quae punctum ipsum, facta est principium, medium et finis; imo ipsa etiam principium Decadum et finis unitatum atque ideo redit in unum. / Quoniam Sapientia Benedicti videbat, quod etiam in splendore hoc non possent manifestari mundi, cum Lux ibi adhuc nimis magna esset atque tenuis; hinc iterum innuit literae huic Jod, ut denuo descenderet et perrumperet sphaeram splendoris atque emitteret lucem suam, quae paulo crassior erat. / Lucem atque Influentiam insignem vibrabat in illam Sapientiam.

223. Vav denotat vitam, quae est emanatio et motus essentiae, quae

in se ipsa manifestatur: estque medium uniendi, et connexionis, inter essentiam et intellectum.

225. *He* designat ens, quod est compositum ex essentia et existentia. / *He* ultimum est imago et similitudo intellectus vel mentis.

228. Viriditate enim videtur praefigurari virginitas.

229. O benedicta viriditas, quae cunctas res generas!

230. Nonne spiritus Domini, qui est amor igneus, quum ferebatur super aquas, edidit eisdem igneum quendam vigorem, cum nihil sine calore generari possit? Inspiravit Deus rebus creatis . . . quandam germinationem, hoc est viriditatem, qua sese cunctae res multiplicarent . . . Omnes res dicebant esse virides, cum esse viride crescere dicatur . . . Hanc ergo generandi virtutem rerumque conservationem Animam Mundi vocare libuit.

231. Unde Aristoteles ait in libro suo: Aurum nostrum, non aurum vulgi: quia illa viriditas, quae est in eo corpore, est tota perfectio eius. Quia illa viriditas, per nostrum magisterium cito vertitur in aurum verissimum.

238.   Lapis candens fit ex tribus;
              Nulli datur nisi quibus
              Dei fit spiramine.

248. Vas . . . oportet esse rotundae figurae: Ut sit artifex huius mutator firmamenti et testae capitis. / Caput eius vivit in aeternum et ideo caput denominatur vita gloriosa et angeli serviunt ei. Et hanc imaginem posuit Deus in paradiso deliciarum, et in ea posuit suam imaginem et similitudinem. / . . . quousque caput nigrum aethiopis portans similitudinem fuerit bene lavatum.

249. Accipe cerebrum eius, aceto acerrimo terite . . . quousque obscuretur.

250. Cum igitur spiritus ille aquarum supracoelestium in cerebro sedem et locum acquisierit.

253. . . . oportet nos vertere membrum (scl. cerebri s. cordis) in principio operis, in id ex quo generatum est, et tunc convertimus ipsum per spiritum in id quod volumus. / . . . nam est triangulus compositione et est propinquius omnibus membris corporis ad similitudinem simplicis.

254. Maxima virtus mineralis est in quolibet homine, et maxime in capite inter dentes, ut suo tempore inventum est aurum in granis minutis et oblongis . . . propter hoc dicitur quod lapis est in quolibet homine.

263. τὸ σχῆμα τῆς ταρεγκεφαλίδος ἐοικὸς κεφαλῇ δράκοντος.

270. Similiter nominant hanc aquam Nubem vivificantem, mundum inferiorem et per haec omnia intelligunt Aquam foliatam,

quae est aurum Philosophorum, quod vocavit dominus Hermes Ovum, habens multa nomina. Mundus inferior est corpus et cinis combustus, ad quem reducunt Animam honoratam. Et cinis combustus, et anima, sunt aurum sapientum, quod seminant in terra sua alba, et terra margaritarum stellata, foliata, benedicta, sitiente, quam nominavit terram foliorum, et terram argenti, et terram auri. / In quo dixit Hermes: Seminate aurum in terram albam foliatam. Terra alba foliata est Corona victoriae, qua est cinis extractus a cinere . . .

271. Ergo Luna mater et ager in quo solare seminarique debet semen . . . / (ait sol) Ego enim sum sicut semen seminatum in terram bonam . . . / Jam scias Virginem nostram terram, ultimam subire cultivationem, ut in ea fructus Solis seminetur ac maturetur. / Recipiam a te animam adulando. / Aqua supra terram incidente, creatus est Adam, qui et mundus est minor. / Terra dicitur mater elementorum, quia portat filium in ventre suo. / Quamvis in primo suo partu per Solem et Lunam generatus, et de terra in accretione sua postulatus siet. / Pater suscipit filium, hoc est, terra retinet spiritum. / Quia totius mundi ima pars terra est, aetheris autem ima pars luna est: Lunam quoque terram, sed aetheream, vocaverunt.

275. Accipe itaque tu, charissime, verborum meorum legitimum sensum, et intellige, quia philosophi similes sunt hortulanis et agricolis, qui primum quidem semina deligunt, et delecta non in vulgarem terram, sed in excultos agros, aut hortorum iugera seminant . . . / Habito autem Sole et Luna philosophorum tanquam semine bono, terra ipsa ab omnibus suis immunditiis et herbis inutilibus expurganda est et diligenti cultura elaboranda, in eamque sic elaboratam Solis et Lunae praedicta semina mittenda sunt . . .

276. Ubi terra, hoc est humanitas, exaltata est super omnes circulos Mundi, et in caelo intellectuali sanctissimae Trinitatis est collocata. / Donum namque Dei est, habens mysterium individuae unionis sanctae Trinitatis. O scientiam praeclarissimam, quae est theatrum universae naturae, eiusque anatomia, astrologia terrestris, argumentum omnipotentiae Dei, testimonium resurrectionis mortuorum, exemplum remissionis peccatorum, infallibile futuri iudicii experimentum et speculum aeternae beatitudinis!

278. Quamobrem in centro terrae ignis est copiosissimus aestuantissimusque (ex radiis solaribus ibidem collectus), qui barathrum sive orcus nuncupatur, neque alius est ignis sublunaris: faeces enim sive terrestres reliquiae principiorum praedictorum,

videlicet caloris solaris et aquae, sunt ignis et terra: damnatis destinata.

279. Ipsum enim est, quod ignem superat, et ab igne non superatur: sed in illo amicabiliter requiescit, eo gaudens.

285. Ad dextram vocatur Sol justitiae Mal. 4, 2, sed ad sinistram (Sol) a calore Ignis Gebhurae.

288. In naturalibus Jesod sub se continet argentum vivum; quia hoc est fundamentum totius artis transmutatoriae.

290. (Jessod) in personis denotat membrum genitale utriusque sexus. / Quapropter pervolare semper Adonai ad Mensuram El-chai continua aestuat cupidine. / Ipse autem hic gradus firmus est inter Illum et Illam, ut natura seminis subtilissima e supernis demissa non dimoveatur. / . . . angelus redemtor, fons aquarum viventium, arbor scientiae boni et mali, Leviathan, Salomon, Messias filius Joseph.

291. Iste enim est effusorium aquarum supernarum: Et duae olivae super illud, sunt Nezach et Hod, duo testiculi masculini.

295. Foedus Pacis autem, seu perfectionis propterea dicitur, quia iste modus pacis et perfectionis autor est inter Tiphereth et Malchuth, ita ut de eo dicitur, I Par. 29, 11, quia modus ille, qui vocatur Col, est in coelo et in terra, ubi Targum hac utitur paraphrasi, quod uniatur cum coelo et cum terra.

298. Propinquus . . . et melior quam frater e longinquo, qui est Tiphereth.

299. . . . quod robustus Jisrael sit nomen medium inter Nezach et Hod.

301. In Sohar, in historia illius Puelli, dicitur, quod Justus (Jessod) vocetur Amicus fidelis ad locum Cant. 7. 10. Vadens ad dilectum meum. Et hinc Jesod dicitur Amicus, quia unit duos dilectos et amicos: quia per ipsum fit unio Tiphereth et Malchuth.

308. Hoc est illud quod non sine mysterio vocatur stella . . . / Aquae El boni, seu Argenti vivi . . . Hoc argentum vivum . . . vocatur Aqua Sphaerica.

309. Haec (aqua) dicitur filia Matredi, i.e. . . . . Viri aurificis laborantis cum assidua defatigatione; nam haec aqua non fluit e terra, nec effoditur in mineris, sed magno labore et multa assiduitate elicitur et perficitur. Huius uxor appellatur Aqua auri sive talis Aqua, quae aurum emittit. Cum hac si desponsatur artifex, filiam generabit, quae erit Aqua balnei regii.

314. In Sohar haec litera dicitur scaturigo vitae.

315. אפרח Pullus avis cujusque. Deut. 22, 6. Psalm. 84, 4. In Raja Mehimna R. Schimeon ben Jochai tradit per hoc nomen intelligi Gradum Tiphereth, quatenus constat e sex membris

594

suis, quae sunt sex alae, quibus sursum volat et deorsum. Sed in Tikkunim sub initium Libri R. Bar, Bar Channa; haec appellatio dicitur referenda ad Justum sub mysterio Lucis reflexae ab imo ad summum. Verba sunt haec: Aephrochim sunt flores, qui fructum nondum praebent perfectum. Suntque Sephiroth sub notione arboris, quae ab imo sursum conversa est, et quidem circa Jesod.

316. Penna, ala: it. membrum, et quidem genitale . . . hoc nomen exponit de Jesod, cui cognomen Justi tribuitur.

318. Phoenix . . . ex cuius pennis circa collum aureolis . . . Medicina ad omnes affectiones humanae naturae contrarias in temperiem sanitatis optatam reducendas utilissima . . . inventa et usurpata est.

322. Sic vocatur Malchuth . . . estque locus destinatus ad coctionem et elixationem influentiae, a marito ad ipsam demissae ad nutritionem catervarum. Sicut notum est: foeminam calore suo excoquere semen ad generandum.

324. De Dei filio intelligit, qui in castigandis mundi sceleribus formidandum Leonem sat diu imitatus paulo post, morte propinquante, dum SS. Eucharistiae Sacramentum instituit, in melleos favos longe suavissimos se ipsum convertit.

325. Saepius Adonai nomen Sephirae ultimae, et ipsa Malchuth, Regnum, ita dicitur; quoniam ipsum totius mundanae fabricae fundamentum extat.

326. . . . lapis capitalis, a quo omnes catervae superiores et inferiores in opere creationis promuntur in esse.

327. Sapphireus, quia varium a supernis gradibus colorem trahit, et in creatis mox hoc, mox contrario modo operatur: nam bonum nonnunquam, quandoque malum, nunc vitam, nunc interitum, nunc languorem, nunc medelam, nunc egestatem, nunc divitias ministrat.

332. In hoc nomine perpetuo mysterium literae ‎י (Jod) involvitur, et quidem ut plurimum in Malchuth, quatenus in ista existit litera Jod. Informis enim massa et figura τοῦ ‎י figuram habet lapidis; et Malchuth est fundamentum et lapis cui totum aedificium superius superstruitur. De ea dicitur Zach. 3, 9: Lapis unus septem oculorum.

337. Tunc exsurgit Hermaphroditi flos Saphyricus, admirandum Maioris Mundi Mysterium. Cuius pars, si in mille liquati Ophirizi partes infundatur, id omne in sui naturam convertit.

344. . . . quoniam lapis sapphirus aereum habet colorem. Virtutes ergo coelestium lapide sapphiro designantur, quia hi spiritus . . . superioris loci in coelestibus dignitatem tenent.

345. Crystallum . . . ex aqua congelascit, et robustum fit. Scimus

vero quanta sit aquae mobilitas. Corpus autem redemptoris nostri, quia usque ad mortem passionibus subiacuit, aquae simile iuxta aliquid fuit: quia nascendo, crescendo, lassescendo, esuriendo, sitiendo, moriendo usque ad passionem suam per momenta temporum mobiliter decucurrit . . . Sed quia per resurrectionis suae gloriam ex ipsa sua corruptione in incorruptionis virtutem convaluit, quasi crystalli more ex aqua duruit, ut in illo et haec eadem natura esset, et in ipsa quae jam fuerat corruptionis mutabilitas non esset. Aqua ergo in crystallum versa est, quando corruptionis eius infirmitas per resurrectionem suam ad incorruptionis est firmitatem mutata. Sed notandum quod hoc crystallum horribile, id est, pavendum, dicitur . . . omnibus vera scientibus constat quia redemptor humani generis cum iudex apparuerit, et speciosus iustis, et terribilis erit iniustis.

347. Certum quidem est, quod macroprosopus, Pater et Mater, sint Corona, Sapientia et Intelligentia mundi Emanativi post restitutionem. / . . . e tribus punctis primis mundi inanitionis constituta sint tria capita superna, quae continentur in Sene Sanctissimo. Omnia autem tria numerantur pro uno in mundo Emanativo, qui est macroprosopus.

348. Forma secunda vocatur Ros crystallinus; et haec formatur a Severitate Basiliae Adami primi, quae intrabat intra Sapientiam Macroprosopi: hinc in crystallo color quidam emphaticus rubor apparet. Et haec est Sapientia illa, de qua dixerunt, quod in illa radicentur Iudicia.

349. Lapis in sacro eloquio Dominum et redemptorem nostrum significat.

VI. THE CONJUNCTION

8. Mineralia tamen atque vegetabilia Hermaphroditae sunt naturae, eo quod utrumque sexum habeant. Nihilominus fit ex seipsis coniunctio formae et materiae, quemadmodum fit de animalibus.

9. Unde duo sulphura et duo argent[a] viv[a] dicuntur et sunt talia, quod unum et unum dixerunt, et sibi congaudent, et unum alterum continet.

19. Si enim homo ad summum bonum pervenire cupit, tunc . . . primo Deum, dein seipsum . . . agnoscere illum oportet.

20. Pietas autem est gratia divinitus prolapsa, quae docet unumquemque seipsum, vere ut est, cognoscere.

23. . . . cum in vitro tuo conspexeris naturas insimul misceri . . .

25. Effodiatur ergo sepulcrum et sepeliatur mulier cum viro mortuo . . .
27. Non fieri transitum nisi per medium.
28. Mercurius est medium coniungendi.
34. Aqua aeris inter caelum et terram existens, est vita uniuscuiusque rei. Ipsa enim aqua solvit corpus in spiritum, et de mortuo facit vivum, et facit matrimonium inter virum et mulierem.
35. Siccum humectare, et durum lenificare, et corpora coniungere et attenuare.
39. Non absimili modo quo Deus primo creavit unum mundum sola meditatione, pariformiter creavit unum mundum, ex quo quidem res omnes natae fuerunt adaptatione. / Item ut unus Deus tantum est non plures unum etiam per unum ex nihilo mundum in mente sua prius creare voluit ut subinde in effectum producere quo continerentur omnia quae crearet in ipso: Deus ut esset in omnibus unus.
40. Sub isto binario spirituali et corporeo, tertium quid latuit, quod vinculum est sacrati matrimonii. Hoc ipsum est medium usque huc in omnibus perdurans, ac suorum amborum extremorum particeps, sine quibus ipsum minime, nec ipsa sine hoc suo medio esse possunt, quod sunt, ex tribus unum.
48. Est enim in humano corpore quaedam substantia conformis aethereae, quae reliquas elementares partes in eo praeservat, et continuare facit.
49. Spagiricam autem nostram medicinam esse corpoream non negamus, sed spiritalem dicimus esse factam, quam spiritus spagiricus induit.
50. Concludimus meditativam philosophiam in superatione corporis unione mentali facta, consistere. Sed prior haec unio nondum sophum efficit, nec nisi mentalem sophiae discipulum: unio vero mentis cum corpore secunda sophum exhibet, completam illam et beatam unionem tertiam cum unitate prima sperantem et expectantem. Faxit omnipotens Deus ut tales efficiamur omnes et ipse sit in omnibus unus.
60. Mens igitur bene dicitur esse composita, quoties animus cum anima tali vinculo iunctus est, ut corporis appetitus et cordis affectus fraenare valeat.
62. Qui diligit animam suam, perdet eam, et qui odit animam suam, in aeternum custodit eam.
67. Impossibile est enim vitae malae hominem possidere thesaurum sapientiae filiis reconditum, et male sanum ad eum acquirendum vel inquirendum, multo minus ad inveniendum aptum esse.

68. Admonendos esse discipulos putavi auxilii divini implorationis, deinceps accuratissimae diligentiae in disponendo se ad eiusmodi gratiam recipiendam.

69. Ego sum . . . vera medicina, corrigens ac transmutans, id quod non est amplius, in id quod fuit ante corruptionem, et in multo melius, item id quod non est, in id quod esse debet.

72. At veritas est summa virtus et inexpugnabile castrum.

73. Libera tamen ad suam unitatem redit. Hoc est unum ex arcanis naturae, per quod ad altiora pertigerunt spagiri.

82. Quidam Philosophi nominaverunt aurum Chelidoniam, Karnech, Geldum.

85. Lili Alchemiae et Medicinae . . . nobilissimum hoc omne quod ex altissimi conditoris manifestatione meditationibus hominum obtingere potest.

87. Miranda praestat in spagyrica arte, nam eo mediante lux diei in primam materiam reducitur.

102. μέλαν καὶ ἄψυχον καὶ νεκρὰ καὶ ὡς εἰπεῖν ἄπνους. / Item sapientiam tuam semina in cordibus nostris, et ab eis phlegma, choleram corruptam, et sanguinem bulientem expelle, ac per vias beatorum perducas. / Ne cinerem vilipendas . . . in eo enim est Diadema quod permanentium cinis est.

103. Item scitote, quod spiritus est in domo marmore circundata, aperite igitur foramina, ut spiritus mortuus exeat.

105. Ad corporis igitur bonam dispositionem artificiatam, utimur spagirico medicamento.

117. . . . quaedam inest lumini (lunae), quod de ea defluit, quae humectet corpora et velut occulto rore madefaciat.

118. Rectam fidem super unguentem olere fecisti. / Odore scientiae totum perfudit orbem.

133. . . . concordantia et . . . discordantia, quam symbolizationem intelligimus.

170. O coelum nostrum! o aqua nostra et Mercurius noster! . . . o caput mortuum seu faeces maris nostri . . . Et haec sunt aviculae Hermetis epitheta, quae nunquam quiescit.

171. Et scitote quod caput artis est corvus, qui in nigredine noctis et diei claritate sine alis volat.

173. Vocatur quoque rotunda aliqua nubes, mors itidem, nigredo, utpote tenebrae et umbra. / Istud opus fit ita subito sicut veniunt nubes de caelo.

176. Corvus se pullis senio confectum praebet in pabulum: at Phoenix noster Christus Dominus . . . se nobis in coelestem alimoniam praebuit.

180. Niger qui caput est artis, albus qui medium et rubeus qui finem rerum omnium imponit.

182. Cum videris materiam tuam denigrari, gaude: quia principium est operis. / Caput corvi artis est origo.

183. Antimonium, pix, carbo, corvus, caput corvi, plumbum, aes ustum, ebur ustum dicitur.

185. Et sic habes duo elementa, primo aquam per se, dehinc terram ex aqua.

191. corvus in formam peccatoris constitutus.

193. Vas autem necessarium in hoc opere oportet esse rotundae figurae: ut sit artifex huius mutator firmamenti et testae capitis.

194. Locus superior est cerebrum, et est sedes intelligentiae.

195. Et animal forma formarum et genus generum est homo.

196. Vas autem factum est rotundum ad imitationem superius et inferius. Est namque aptius rerum ad id cuius generatio quaeritur in eo, res enim ligatur per suum simile.

197. Mundus superior habet semper effectum in homine, et perfecta inspiratio eius scilicet hominis in morte sua, usque ad firmamentum, nec deest perventio, donec revertatur, quod egressum est de mundo superiori, ad locum suum.

198. Videtisne relucens illud et inexpugnabile castrum? / Veritas est . . . inexpugnabile castrum. Hac in arce verus . . . continetur ille thesaurus, qui . . . asportatur hinc post mortem.

199. Creatura in divina mente concepta est simplex, invariabilis et aeterna, in se ipsa autem multiplex, variabilis, transitoria.

205. Moriente leone nascitur corvus. / O triste spectaculum et mortis aeternae imago: at artifici dulce nuntium! . . . Nam spiritum intus clausum vivificum scias, qui statuto tempore ab Omnipotente vitam hisce cadaveribus reddet.

217. Notum est, quod anima antequam suo corpori misceretur, mortua fuerat, et eius corpus similiter.

BIBLIOGRAPHY

BIBLIOGRAPHY

The items of the bibliography are arranged alphabetically under two headings: *A*. Volumes containing collections of alchemical tracts by various authors; *B*. General bibliography, including cross-references to the material in section *A*. Short titles of the alchemical volumes are printed in capital letters.

A. VOLUMES CONTAINING COLLECTIONS OF ALCHEMICAL TRACTS BY VARIOUS AUTHORS

ARS CHEMICA, quod sit licita recte exercentibus, probationes doctissimorum iurisconsultorum. . . . Strasbourg, 1566.

Contents quoted in this volume:

i   Septem tractatus seu capitula Hermetis Trismegisti aurei [pp. 7–31; usually referred to as "Tractatus aureus"]

ii   Studium Consilii coniugii de massa solis et lunae [pp. 48–263; usually referred to as "Consilium coniugii"]

ARTIS AURIFERAE quam chemiam vocant. . . . Basel, 1593. 2 vols.*

Contents quoted in this volume:

VOLUME I

i   Turba philosophorum [two versions: pp. 1–64, 65–139]

ii   Allegoriae super librum Turbae [pp. 139–45]

iii   Aenigmata ex visione Arislei et allegoriis sapientum [pp. 146–54; usually referred to as "Visio Arislei"]

iv   In Turbam philosophorum exercitationes [pp. 154–82]

v   Aurora consurgens, quae dicitur Aurea hora [pp. 185–246]

vi   Rosinus ad Euthiciam [pp. 246–77]

vii   Rosinus ad Sarratantam episcopum [pp. 277–319]

* Other editions of the *Artis auriferae* include one in 1572 (from which the "Visio Arislei" is sometimes quoted in this volume) and one in 1610 (3 vols.; from which "Rosinus ad Euthiciam" [I, pp. 158–78] is quoted in this volume).

MANGETUS, JOANNES JACOBUS (ed.). *BIBLIOTHECA CHEMICA CURIOSA, seu Rerum ad alchemiam pertinentium thesaurus instructissimus*. . . . Geneva, 1702. 2 vols.

Contents quoted in this volume:

viii [d'Espagnet:] Arcanum hermeticae philosophiae opus [pp. 649–61]

ix Barnaud: In aenygmaticum quoddam Epitaphium Bononiae . . . Commentariolus [pp. 713–16]

In hoc volumine DE ALCHEMIA continentur haec: . . . Nuremberg, 1541.

Contents quoted in this volume:

i Geber: Summa perfectionis [pp. 20–205]

ii Tabula smaragdina Hermetis Trismegisti [p. 363]

MUSAEUM HERMETICUM reformatum et amplificatum . . . , continens tractatus chimicos XXI praestantissimos . . . Frankfurt a. M., 1678. For translation, see: (*B*) WAITE, *The Hermetic Museum.*

Contents quoted in this volume:

i [Hermes Trismegistus:] Tractatus aureus de lapide philosophorum [pp. 1–52]

ii Madathanus: Aureum saeculum redivivum [pp. 53–72]

iii [Siebmacher:] Hydrolithus sophicus, seu Aquarium sapientum [pp. 73–144]

iv Mehung: Demonstratio naturae [pp. 145–71]

v Flamel: Tractatus brevis seu Summarium philosophicum [pp. 172–79]

vi [Barcius (F. von Sternberg)]: Gloria mundi, alias Paradisi tabula [pp. 203–304]

vii Liber Alze [pp. 325–35]

viii Lambspringk: De lapide philosophico figurae et emblemata [pp. 337–72]

ix Valentinus: De prima materia [pp. 424–25]

x Sendivogius: Novum lumen chemicum e naturae fonte et manuali experientia depromptum [pp. 545–600; Parabola, seu Aenigma philosophicum Coronidis . . . , pp. 585–90]

xi [Sendivogius:] Novi luminis chemici Tractatus alter de sulphure [pp. 601–46]

xii Philalethes: Introitus apertus ad occlusum regis palatium [pp. 601–46]

xiii Philalethes: Fons chymicae veritatis [pp. 799–814]

xiv Helvetius: Vitulus aureus [pp. 815–63]

THEATRUM CHEMICUM, praecipuos selectorum auctorum tractatus . . . continens. Vols. I–III, Ursel, 1602. Vols. IV–VI, Strasbourg, 1613, 1622, 1661.

Contents quoted in this volume:

VOLUME I

xx   Ventura: De ratione conficiendi lapidis [pp. 244–356]

xxi   Joannes Pico Mirandola: De auro [pp. 357–432]

xxii   Albertus Magnus: Super arborem Aristotelis [pp. 524–27]

VOLUME III

xxiii   De magni lapidis compositione et operatione [pp. 1–56]

xxiv   Rupescissa: Liber de confectione veri lapidis philosophorum [pp. 191–200]

xxv   Hollandus: Opera mineralia, seu de lapide philosophico
omnia [pp. 320–564]

xxvi   Greverus: Secretum [pp. 783–810]

xxvii   Alani philosophi dicta de lapide philosophico [pp. 811–20]

xxviii   Barnaud: Commentarium in quoddam Epitaphium Bononiae . . . [pp. 836–48]

xxix   Delphinas: Liber secreti maximi [pp. 871–78]

VOLUME IV

xxx   Lully: Theorica et practica [pp. 1–191]

xxxi   Artefius: Clavis majoris sapientiae [pp. 221–40]

xxxii   Aphorismi Basiliani sive Canones Hermetici [pp. 368–71]

xxxiii   Beatus: Aurelia occulta philosophorum [pp. 525–81]

xxxiv   Arnold of Villanova: Speculum alchimiae [pp. 583–613]

xxxv   Hermes Trismegistus: Tractatus aureus . . . cum scholiis
Dominici Gnosii [pp. 672–797]

xxxvi   Lagneus: Harmonia chemica [pp. 813–903]

xxxvii   Albertus: Liber octo capitulorum de lapide philosophorum
[pp. 948–71]

xxxviii   Valentinus: Opus praeclarum ad utrumque [pp. 1061–75]

xxxix   Petrus de Silento: Opus [pp. 1113–27]

VOLUME V

xl   Allegoriae sapientum . . . supra librum Turbae [pp. 64–
100]

xli   Tractatus Micreris suo discipulo Mirnefindo [pp. 101–13]

xlii   Liber Platonis quartorum . . . [pp. 114–208]

xliii   Senior: De chemia [pp. 219–66]

xliv   Mennens: Aureum vellus [pp. 267–470]

xlv   Consilium coniugii [pp. 479–566]

xlvi   Bonus: Pretiosa margarita novella correctissima [pp. 589–
794]

xlvii   Tractatus Aristotelis alchymistae ad Alexandrum Magnum
de lapide philosophico [pp. 880–92]

607

B. GENERAL BIBLIOGRAPHY

ABEGG, EMIL. *Der Messiasglaube in Indien und Iran.* Berlin and Leipzig, 1928.

ABRAHAM ELEAZAR. See ELEAZAR.

ABT, ADAM. *Die Apologie des Apuleius von Madaura und die antike Zauberei.* (Religionsgeschichtliche Versuche und Vorarbeiten, vol. 4, part 2, pages 75–345.) Giessen, 1908.

ABU 'L-QĀSIM MUHAMMAD IBN AHMAD AL-'IRĀQĪ. *Kitāb al-'ilm al-muktasab* (Book of Knowledge acquired concerning the cultivation of gold). Edited and translated by E. J. Holmyard. Paris, 1923.

Acta Archelai. See Hegemonius.

Acta Joannis (Acts of John). See JAMES.

Acta Thomae (Acts of Thomas). See JAMES.

AEGIDIUS DE VADIS. "Dialogus inter naturam et filium philosophiae." See *(A) Theatrum chemicum,* **xiv.**

AELIAN (Claudius Aelianus). *De natura animalium.* Edited by Rudolph Hercher. Leipzig, 1864–66. 2 vols.

"Aenigmata ex visione Arislei philosophi, et allegoriis sapientum" ("Aenigmata philosophorum"). See *(A) Artis auriferae,* **iii** and **xxi.**

AGNOSTUS, IRENAEUS, pseud. (Friedrich Grick). *Prodromus Fr. R. C.* [*Rhodostauroticus*]. Segoduni (Rodez), 1620.

608

AGRIPPA VON NETTESHEIM, CORNELIUS. *De incertitudine et vanitate scientiarum.* Cologne, 1585. English translation: *The Vanity of Arts and Sciences.* London, 1676.

AIGREMONT, DR., pseud. (Siegmar Baron von Schultze-Galléra). *Fuss- und Schuhsymbolik und -Erotik.* Leipzig, 1909.

[ALANUS.] "Dicta Alani." See *(A) Theatrum chemicum,* xxvii.

ALBERTUS MAGNUS (Albert the Great, Saint). "Liber octo capitulorum de lapide philosophorum." See *(A) Theatrum chemicum,* xxxvii.

———. "Scriptum super arborem Aristotelis." See *(A) Theatrum chemicum,* xxii.

ALDROVANDUS, ULYSSES. *Dendrologiae libri duo.* Bologna [1667.] 2 vols.

'ALĪ, M. TURĀB (ed.). "Three Arabic Treatises on Alchemy by Muhammad bin Umail," *Memoirs of the Asiatic Society of Bengal* (Calcutta), XII (1933), 1–116.

"Allegoria Merlini." See *(A) Artis auriferae,* xiii.

"Allegoriae sapientum supra librum Turbae XXIX distinctiones." See *(A) Theatrum chemicum,* xl.

"Allegoriae super librum Turbae." See *(A) Artis auriferae,* ii.

[ALTUS, pseud.] *Mutus Liber.* La Rochelle, 1677. See also *(A)* MANGETUS, *Bibliotheca chemica curiosa,* iv.

AMBROSE, SAINT. *Commentarius in Cantica Canticorum e scriptis S. Ambrosii a Guillelmo, quondam Abbate S. Theodorici, collectus.* See Migne, *P.L.,* vol. 15, cols. 1851–1962.

———. *De excessu fratris.* See: *S. Ambrosii Opera,* Pars VII. Edited by Otto Faller. (Corpus Scriptorum Ecclesiasticorum Latinorum, 73.) Vienna, 1955. (pp. 209–35.)

———. *Epistolae.* See Migne, *P.L.,* vol. 16, cols. 875–1286.

———. *Explanatio Psalmorum XII.* See: *S. Ambrosii Opera,* Pars VI. Edited by M. Petschenig. (Corpus Scriptorum Ecclesiasticorum Latinorum, 64.) Vienna and Leipzig, 1919.

———. *Hexaemeron.* See Migne, *P.L.,* vol. 14, cols. 123–274.

ANGELUS SILESIUS (Johann Scheffler). *Sämtliche Poetische Werke.* Edited by Hans Ludwig Held. Munich, 1949–52. 3 vols. ("Der Cherubinische Wandersmann," Vol. III, pp. 7–218.) For translations of certain parts of the "Cherubinische Wandersmann," see:

FLITCH, J. E. CRAWFORD. *Angelus Silesius: Selections from the Cherubinic Wanderer*. London, 1932.

ANTONY OF PADUA, SAINT. *Sermones*. Padua, 1895–1913. 3 vols.

"Aphorismi Basiliani sive Canones Hermetici." See *(A) Theatrum chemicum*, **xxxii.**

APTOWITZER, VIKTOR (AVIGDOR). "Arabisch-jüdische Schöpfungstheorien," *Hebrew Union College Annual* (Cincinnati), VI (1929), 205–46.

APULEIUS, LUCIUS. *Metamorphoses*. See: *The Golden Ass*. With an English translation by Richard Adlington. Revised by Stephen Gaselee. (Loeb Classical Library.) London and Cambridge, Mass., 1947.

"Aquarium sapientum." See *(A) Musaeum hermeticum*, **iii.**

"Arcanum Hermeticae philosophiae opus." Geneva, 1653. See also D'ESPAGNET.

[ARISLEUS.] "Visio Arislei." See *(A) Artis auriferae*, **iii** and **xxi.**

ARISTOTLE. [*De Anima.*] *On the Soul; Parva Naturalia; On Breath*. With an English translation by W. S. Hett. (Loeb Classical Library.) London and Cambridge, Mass., 1935.

[ARISTOTLE, pseud.] "Tractatus Aristotelis Alchymistae ad Alexandrum Magnum, de Lapide philosophico." See *(A) Theatrum chemicum*, **xlvii.** Another version in *(A) Artis auriferae*, **xi.**

ARNALDUS DE VILLA NOVA (Arnold of Villanova). "Speculum alchimiae." See *(A) Theatrum chemicum*, **xxxiv.**

———. "Thesaurus Thesaurorum" and "Rosarius." See *(A) Artis auriferae*, **xxii.**

ARTEFIUS. "Clavis maioris sapientiae." See *(A) Theatrum chemicum*, **xxxi.** Another version in *(A)* MANGETUS, *Bibliotheca chemica curiosa*, **iii.**

ARTEMIDORUS DALDIANUS. *Onirocriticon Libri V*. Edited by Rudolf Hercher. Leipzig, 1864.

Atharvaveda. *Hymns of the Atharva-Veda*. Translated by Maurice Bloomfield. (Sacred Books of the East, 42.) Oxford, 1897.

———. See also GRILL.

ATHENAEUS, ALEXIS. *The Deipnosophists*. With an English translation by Charles Burton Gulick. (Loeb Classical Library.) London and New York, 1927–41. 7 vols.

ATHENAGORAS. *Legatio pro Christianis.* See Migne, *P.G.,* vol. 6, cols. 889–972.

ATWOOD, MARY ANNE. *A Suggestive Enquiry into the Hermetic Mystery.* Revised edn., Belfast, 1920. (Contains translation of Hermes Trismegistus, "Tractatus aureus.")

AUGUSTINE, SAINT. *The City of God.* Translated by John Healey. Edited by R. V. G. Tasker. (Everyman's Library.) London and New York, 1945. 2 vols.

——. *The Confessions.* Translated by Francis J. Sheed. London and New York, 1951.

——. *Contra Faustum* (Reply to Faustus the Manichean). In *St. Augustine: The Writings against the Manichaeans and against the Donatists.* Translated by Richard Stothert and others. (Select Library of Nicene and Post-Nicene Fathers, 4.) Grand Rapids, 1956. (pp. 155–345.)

——. *De actis cum Felice Manichaeo.* See Migne, *P.L.,* vol. 42, cols. 519–52.

——. *De Natura Boni* (On the Nature of the Good). See *Augustine: Earlier Writings.* Selected and translated by John H. S. Burleigh. (Library of Christian Classics, 6.) London, 1953. (pp. 326–48.)

——. [*Enarrationes in Psalmos.*] *Expositions of the Book of Psalms.* [Translated by J. Tweed, T. Scratton, and others.] (Library of Fathers of the Holy Catholic Church.) Oxford, 1847–57. 6 vols.

——. *Epistola 55.* See *S. Aurelii Augustini Epistolae Pars I.* Edited by A. Goldbacher. (Corpus Scriptorum Ecclesiasticorum Latinorum, 34.) Vienna, Prague, Leipzig, 1895. (pp. 169–213.)

——. *Quaestiones in Heptateuchum.* See Migne, *P.L.,* vol. 34, cols. 547–824.

——. *Sermo Suppositus 120 (In Natali Domini IV. 8).* See Migne, *P.L.,* vol. 39, cols. 1984–87.

——. [*Tractatus in Joannis Evangelium.*] *Lectures or Tractates on the Gospel according to St. John.* Translated by James Innes. (*Works of Aurelius Augustinus,* edited by Marcus Dods.) Edinburgh, 1874. 2 vols.

"Aurelia occulta philosophorum." See *(A) Theatrum chemicum,* **xxxiii.**

"Aureum vellus." See *(A) Theatrum chemicum,* **xliv.**

611

"Aurora consurgens" [Part II]. See (A) *Artis auriferae*, v. For Part I, see FRANZ.

"Authoris ignoti, philosophici lapidis secreta metaphorice describentis." See (A) *Artis auriferae*, **xii.**

[AVALON, ARTHUR, pseud.] (Sir John Woodroffe) (ed. and trans.). *The Serpent Power. Being the Shat-Chakra-Nirupana and Paduka-Panchaka.* 2nd rev. edn., Madras, 1924.

[AVICENNA.] *Tractatulus Avicennae.* See (A) *Artis auriferae*, **xv.**

BAADER, BENEDICT FRANZ XAVER VON. *Sämmtliche Werke.* Leipzig, 1851–60. 10 vols.

BAECHTOLD-STÄUBLI, HANNS. *Handwörterbuch des deutschen Aberglaubens.* Berlin and Leipzig, 1927–42. 10 vols.

BARNAUD, NICOLAS. "Commentarium in quoddam epitaphium Bononiae . . ." See (A) *Theatrum chemicum*, **xxviii.** Also in (A) MANGETUS, *Bibliotheca chemica curiosa*, **ix.**

BAUDIUS, DOMINICUS. *Amores.* Edited by Petrus Scriverius. Leyden, 1638. (For "Epitaphium Amoris ex Casperii Gevartii Electorum Libri III," see pp. 497–518.)

BAYNES, H. G. "On the Psychological Origins of Divine Kingship," *Folklore* (London), XLVII (1936), 74–104.

BECKER, FERDINAND. *Die Darstellung Jesu Christi unter dem Bilde des Fisches.* Breslau, 1866.

BEER, PETER. *Geschichte, Lehren und Meinungen aller bestandenen und noch bestehenden religiösen Sekten der Juden und der Geheimlehre oder Cabbalah.* Brunn, 1822–23. 2 vols.

[BELINUS.] "Dicta Belini." Included in "Allegoriae sapientum super Turbae." See (A) *Theatrum chemicum*, **xl.**

BERNARD OF TREVISO (Bernardus Trevisanus.) "Liber de alchemia" ("De chemico miraculo, quod lapidem philosophiae appellant"). See (A) *Theatrum chemicum*, **xii.**

[BERNARDINO DE SAHAGÚN.] *Einige Kapitel aus dem Geschichtswerk des Fray Bernardino de Sahagun aus dem Aztekischen übersetzt von Eduard Seler.* Edited by Cäcilie Seler-Sachs and others. Stuttgart, 1927.

———. *General History of the Things of New Spain (Florentine Codex).* Book III: The Origin of the Gods. Translated by Arthur J. C. Anderson and Charles E. Dibble. (Monographs of the School of American Research, 14, Part IV.) Santa Fe, 1952.

BERNOULLI, RUDOLF. "Spiritual Disciplines as Reflected in Alchemy and Related Disciplines." In *Spiritual Disciplines* (q.v.), pp. 305–40.

BÉROALDE DE VERVILLE, FRANÇOIS (trans.). *Le Tableau des riches inventions . . . qui sont représentées dans le Songe de Poliphile.* Paris, 1600. (Contains the "Recueil sténographique.")

BERTHELOT, MARCELLIN. *La Chimie au moyen âge.* Paris, 1893. 3 vols.

——. *Collection des anciens alchimistes grecs.* Paris, 1887–88. 3 vols.

——. *Les Origines de l'alchimie.* Paris, 1885.

BEZOLD, CARL (ed. and trans.). *Mě'arrath Gazzē. Die Schatzhöhle.* Leipzig, 1883–88. 2 parts.

BISCHOFF, ERICH. *Die Elemente der Kabbalah.* Berlin, 1913. 2 vols.

BOEHME, JAKOB. [*Zweyte Apologie wieder Balthazar Tilken.*] *The Second Apologie to Balthazar Tylcken.* See: *The Remainder of Books written by Jacob Behmen.* Englished by John Sparrow. London, 1662. See also below.

——. *Des gottseligen, hocherleuchteten Jacob Böhmen Teutonici Philosophi alle Theosophische Schrifften.* Amsterdam, 1682. (This edition of Boehme's Works consists of a number of parts, each separately paginated and variously bound up. The parts are not numbered. It includes, inter alia, the following works referred to in the present volume. The bracketed English titles and volume references, following the German title of each work, refer to the 1764–81 London translation of the *Works,* cited below.)

——. *Aurora. Morgenröte im Ausgang . . .* [*Aurora.* Vol. I.]

——. [*Drey principia.*] *Beschreibung der drey Principien Göttliches Wesens.* [*Three Principles of the Divine Essence.* Vol. I.]

——. *Hohe und tiefe Gründe von dem dreyfachen Leben des Menschen.* [*A High and Deep Search concerning the Threefold Life of Man.* Vol. II.]

——. *Mysterium magnum.* [*Mysterium magnum.* Vol. III.]

——. [*Quaestiones theosophicae.*] *Theosophische Fragen in Betrachtung Göttlicher Offenbahrung . . .* [Not in English collection.]

——. "Tabula Principiorum." See *De signatura rerum* in this edition, pp. 269–87.

BOEHME, JAKOB. *Von der Menschwerdung Jesu Christi.* [Not in English collection.]

———. *The Works of Jacob Behmen.* [Edited by G. Ward and T. Langcake.] London, 1764–81. 4 vols.

———. *Zweyte Apologia wieder Balthazar Tilken.* [Not in English collection; see above.]

BONAVENTURE, SAINT. [*Itinerarium mentis in Deum.*] *The Franciscan Vision.* Translated by Fr. James, O.M.Cap. London, 1937.

BONUS, PETRUS. "Pretiosa margarita novella." See *(A)* MANGETUS, *Bibliotheca chemica curiosa,* v. Another version in *(A) Theatrum chemicum,* xlvi. Another version, edited by Janus Lacinius, Venice, 1546.

BOUCHÉ-LECLERCQ, AUGUSTE. *L'Astrologie grecque.* Paris, 1899.

BOUSSET, WILHELM. [*Der Antichrist.*] *The Antichrist Legend.* Translated by A. H. Keane. London, 1896.

———. *Hauptprobleme der Gnosis.* Göttingen, 1907.

———. "Die Himmelsreise der Seele," *Archiv für Religionswissenschaft* (Tübingen and Leipzig), IV (1901), 136–69.

BRANT, SEBASTIAN. *Hexastichon . . . in memorabiles Evangelistarum figuras.* Pforzheim, 1502.

BREASTED, JAMES HENRY. *Development of Religion and Thought in Ancient Egypt.* New York and London, 1912.

BRENTANO, CLEMENS. *Gesammelte Schriften.* Edited by Christian Brentano. Frankfurt a. M., 1852–55. 9 vols.

Brihadaranyaka Upanishad. See *Upanishads.*

BRUCHMANN, C. F. H. *Epitheta Deorum quae apud Poetas Graecos leguntur. (Ausführliches Lexikon der griechischen und römischen Mythologie,* Supplement.) Leipzig, 1893.

BRUGSCH, HEINRICH. *Religion und Mythologie der alten Ägypter.* Leipzig, 1885.

BUDGE, ERNEST ALFRED WALLIS. *Coptic Apocrypha in the Dialect of Upper Egypt.* London, 1913.

———. *The Egyptian Heaven and Hell.* London, 1905–6. 2 vols.

———. *The Gods of the Egyptians.* London, 1904. 2 vols.

———. *Osiris and the Egyptian Resurrection.* London, 1911. 2 vols.

[*Bundahisn.*] *Der Bundehesh.* Edited by Ferdinand Justi. Leipzig, 1868.

614

BURNET, JOHN. *Early Greek Philosophy.* London, 1892; 4th edn., 1930.

BURY, ROBERT GREGG. See PLATO.

CAESARIUS OF HEISTERBACH. *Dialogue on Miracles.* Translated by H. von E. Scott and C. C. Swinton Bland. London, 1929. 2 vols.

CALID. See KALID.

CAMPBELL, COLIN. *The Miraculous Birth of King Amon-Hotep III.* Edinburgh and London, 1912.

CAPELLE, PAUL. *De luna stellis lacteo orbe animarum sedibus.* Halle. 1927.

CARDANUS, HIERONYMUS (Jerome Cardan). *De subtilitate.* Basel, 1611.

CASSEL, PAULUS STEPHANUS (previously Selig). *Aus Literatur und Symbolik.* Leipzig, 1884.

CASSIODORUS, M. AURELIUS. *Expositio in Cantica Canticorum.* See Migne, *P.L.,* vol. 70, cols. 1055–1106.

——. *Expositio in Psalterium.* See Migne, *P.L.,* vol. 70, cols. 25–1056.

CAUSSIN, NICHOLAS. *De symbolica Aegyptiorum sapientia.* Paris, 1618.

——. *Polyhistor symbolicus.* Paris, 1618.

CEDRENUS, GEORGIUS. *Historiarum compendium.* See Migne, *P.G.,* vols. 121 (whole) and 122, cols. 9–368.

CHARLES, R. H. (ed.). *Apocrypha and Pseudepigrapha of the Old Testament.* Oxford, 1913. 2 vols.

CHRISTENSEN, ARTHUR E. "Les Types du premier homme et du premier roi dans l'histoire légendaire des Iraniens," *Archives d'Études orientales* (Stockholm), XIV (1917).

CHRISTOPHER OF PARIS. "Elucidarius artis transmutatoriae metallorum summa major." See *(A) Theatrum chemicum,* 1.

CHWOLSOHN, D. *Die Ssabier.* St. Petersburg, 1856. 2 vols.

CICERO. *De natura Deorum: Academica.* With a translation by H. Rackham. (Loeb Classical Library.) London and New York, 1933.

——. *De officiis.* With an English translation by Walter Miller. (Loeb Classical Library.) London and Cambridge, Mass., 1938.

"Clangor buccinae." See *(A) Artis auriferae,* xvi.

615

CLEMENT OF ALEXANDRIA. *Stromata* (Miscellanies). In: *Clement of Alexandria* [*Works*]. Edited by Otto Stählin. Leipzig, 1906–9. 3 vols. (Vol. II, and Vol. III, pp. 3–102.) For translation, see: *The Writings of Clement of Alexandria*. Translated by William Wilson. (Ante-Nicene Christian Library, 4, 12. Edinburgh, 1867–69. 2 vols. Vol. I, pp. 349–470, and the whole of Vol. II.)

CLEMENT OF ROME. *The Apostolical Constitutions*. See next entry.

———. *The Clementine Homilies and the Apostolical Constitutions*. Translated by Thomas Smith, Peter Peterson, and James Donaldson. (Ante-Nicene Christian Library, 17.) Edinburgh, 1870. (The two works have separate pagination.)

———. *Recognitiones*. See Migne, *P.G.*, vol. 1, cols. 1207–1474. For translation, see THEOPHILUS OF ANTIOCH.

———. *Second Epistle to the Corinthians*. See: LAKE, KIRSOPP (ed. and trans.). *The Apostolic Fathers* (Loeb Classical Library.) London and New York, 1914. 2 vols. (Vol. I, pp. 128–63.)

Codices and Manuscripts.

Berlin. Cod. Berolinensis Latinus 532. (Folios 147^v–164^v, "Commentum beati Thomae de Aquino super . . . codice[m] qui et Turba dicitur Phylosophorum.")

Florence. Biblioteca Medicea-Laurenziana. MS. (Ashburnham 1166). "Miscellanea d'alchimia." 14th cent.

London. British Museum. MS. Add. 5025. Four rolls drawn in Lübeck. 1588. (The "Ripley Scrowle.")

Munich. Staatsbibliothek. Codex Germanicus 598. "Das Buch der heiligen Dreifaltigkeit. . . ." 1420.

Munich. Codex Latinus 4453. Gospels from Cathedral Treasury at Bamberg. 10th cent.

Oxford. Bodleian Library. MS. Ashmole 1394. Contains two versions of Ripley's "Cantilena," pp. 67–74, 75–82. 17th cent.

Oxford. Bodleian Library. MS. Ashmole 1445. Contains two English versions of Ripley's "Cantilena," fols. 2–12, 41–44.

Oxford. Bodleian Library. MS. Ashmole 1479. Contains Ripley's "Cantilena," fols. 223^v–225^v.

Oxford. Bodleian Library. MS. Bruce 96 (Codex Brucianus). See: BAYNES, CHARLOTTE AUGUSTA. *A Coptic Gnostic Treatise Contained in the Codex Brucianus*. Cambridge, 1933.

Oxford. Bodleian Library. MS. Digby 83. 12th cent. Contains at folio 24 "Epistola Ethelwoldi ad Gerbertum papam, de circuli quadratura."

Paris. Bibliothèque de l'Arsenal. MS. 3022. "Vision advenue en songeant à Ben Adam. . . ."

Paris. Bibliothèque Nationale. MS. 2327. "Livre sur l'art de faire l'or." 1478.

Paris. Bibliothèque Nationale. MS. français 14765. Abraham le Juif. "Livre des figures hiéroglifiques."

St. Gall. Codex Germanicus Alchemicus Vadiensis. 16th cent.

In possession of author. "Figurarum Aegyptiorum secretarum." 18th cent.

COLONNA, FRANCESCO. See BÉROALDE DE VERVILLE.

"Consilium coniugii." See *(A) Ars chemica*, ii; *(A)* MANGETUS, *Bibliotheca chemica curiosa*, vii; and *(A) Theatrum chemicum*, xlv.

CORDOVERO, MOSE. *Pardes Rimmonim.* Cracow, 1592. Other editions: Mantua, 1623; Amsterdam, 1708; Munkacs, 1906.

CORNFORD, FRANCIS MACDONALD (trans.). *Plato's Cosmology. The Timaeus of Plato translated with a running commentary.* London, 1937.

Corpus Hermeticum. See SCOTT, WALTER: *Hermetica;* also MEAD.

Corpus Inscriptionum Latinarum. Consilio et auctoritate Academiae Litterarum regiae Borussicae editum. Berlin, 1863ff. 15 vols.

CRASSELAME, MARCANTONIO. See TACHENIUS.

CRAWFORD, J. P. WICKERSHAM. "El Horóscopo del Hijo del Rey Alcaraz en el 'Libro de buen Amor,'" *Revista de filologia española* (Madrid), XII (1925), 184–90.

CRAWLEY, ALFRED ERNEST. *The Idea of the Soul.* London, 1909.

CUMONT, FRANZ. *Textes et monuments figurés relatifs aux mystères de Mithra.* Brussels, 1894–99. 2 vols.

CURTIUS, ERNST ROBERT. *European Literature and the Latin Middle Ages.* Translated by Willard R. Trask. New York (Bollingen Series XXXVI) and London, 1953.

——. *James Joyce und sein Ulysses.* Zurich, 1929.

CYRIL OF JERUSALEM, SAINT. *Catecheses mystagogicae.* See Migne, *P.L.,* vol. 33, cols. 1066–1128. Another edition: *Opera.* Edited by Wilhelm Karl Reischl and Joseph Rupp. Munich, 1848–60. 2 vols. (Vol. I, p. 29 – Vol. II, p. 343.)

DALE, ANTHONY VAN. *Dissertationes de origine ac progressu idololatriae et superstitionum.* Amsterdam. 1696.

DAMASCIUS DIADOCHUS. *Damascii Successoris Dubitationes et Solutiones de Primis Principiis in Platonis Parmenidem.* Edited by C. Emil Ruelle. Paris, 1889. 2 vols.

"De arte chymica." See *(A) Artis auriferae,* **xvii.**

DEE, JOHN. "Monas hieroglyphica." See *(A) Theatrum chemicum,* **xix.**

DE GUBERNATIS, ANGELO. *Zoological Mythology.* London, 1872. 2 vols.

DELATTE, LOUIS. *Textes latins et vieux français relatifs aux Cyranides.* (Bulletin de la faculté de philosophie et lettres de l'Université de Liége, fasc. 93.) Liége and Paris, 1942.

DELPHINAS. "Liber secreti maximi." See *(A) Theatrum chemicum,* **xxix.**

"De magni lapidis compositione et operatione." See *(A) Theatrum chemicum,* **xxiii.**

"De promissionibus et praedictionibus Dei." Attributed by some to St. Prosper (of Aquitaine). See Migne, *P.L.,* vol. 51, cols. 733–858.

D'ESPAGNET. "Arcanum Hermeticae philosophiae opus." See *(A)* MANGETUS, *Bibliotheca chemica curiosa,* **viii.** See also above, s.v. "Arcanum. . . ."

DEUSSEN, PAUL. *Allgemeine Geschichte der Philosophie.* Leipzig, 1894–1917. 2 vols. (each comprising 3 Abteilungen.)

———. *Geheimlehre des Veda.* Leipzig, 1907.

DIELS, HERMANN. *Fragmente der Vorsokratiker.* Berlin, 1934–37. 3 vols.

DIODORUS OF SICILY. *Bibliotheke Historike.* Translated by C. H. Oldfather, C. L. Sherman, and R. M. Gerr. (Loeb Classical Library.) London and New York, 1933– (in progress). 12 vols.

DIONYSIUS THE AREOPAGITE, pseud. *De coelesti hierarchia.* See Migne, *P.G.,* vol. 3, cols. 119–370. (The commentary of George Pachymeres is here printed with the text.) For translation, see: *The Celestial Hierarchies.* Translated by the Editors of the Shrine of Wisdom. (Shrine of Wisdom Manual 15.) London, 1935.

———. *De divinis nominibus.* See Migne, *P.L.,* vol. 3, cols. 585–996.

For translation, see: *On the Divine Names and the Mystical Theology*. Translated by C. E. Rolt. London and New York, 1920.

[Dioscorides.] *Petri Andreae Matthioli Medici Senensis Commentarii in libros sex Pedacii Dioscoridis Anazarbei de Medica Materia*. Venice, 1554.

Dirr, Adolf (ed. and trans.). *Kaukasische Märchen. (Die Märchen der Weltliteratur*, ed. Fr. von der Leyen and P. Zaunert, 12.) Jena, 1920.

Doelger, Franz Josef. *Antike und Christentum*. Münster, 1929–36. 5 vols.

———. *Die Sonne der Gerechtigkeit und der Schwarze*. Münster, 1918.

Dorn, Gerard. "Congeries Paracelsicae chemicae de transmutatione metallorum." See *(A) Theatrum chemicum*, x.

———. "De tenebris contra naturam et vita brevi." See *(A) Theatrum chemicum*, viii.

———. "Duellum animi cum corpore." See *(A) Theatrum chemicum*, ix.

———. "Philosophia chemica." See *(A) Theatrum chemicum*, vii.

———. "Philosophia meditativa." See *(A) Theatrum chemicum*, vi.

———. "Physica genesis." See *(A) Theatrum chemicum*, iii.

———. "Physica Trismegisti." See *(A) Theatrum chemicum*, iv.

———. "Physica Trithemii." See *(A) Theatrum chemicum*, v.

———. "Speculativa philosophia." See *(A) Theatrum chemicum*, ii.

———. (ed.). *Theophrasti Paracelsi Libri V de Vita longa*. Frankfurt a. M., 1583.

Drexelius, Hieremias. *Opera*. Antwerp, 1643. 2 vols.

Du Cange, Charles du Fresne. *Glossarium ad scriptores mediae et infimae Graecitatis*. Breslau, 1891.

———. *Glossarium ad Scriptores mediae et infimae Latinitatis*. 1733–36. 6 vols. New edn., Graz, 1954. 10 vols. in 5.

du Perron, Anquetil. *Oupnek'hat (id est, Secretum tegendum)* . . . *in Latinum conversum*. Strasbourg, 1801–2. 2 vols.

Eckert, Eduard Emil. *Die Mysterien der Heldenkirche, erhalten und fortgebildet im Bunde der alten und der neuen Kinder der Wittwe*. Schaffhausen, 1860.

[ECKHART, MEISTER.] [*Works of*] *Meister Eckhart.* Translated by C. de B. Evans. London, 1924–52. 2 vols.

EIRENAEUS ORANDUS. See FLAMEL.

EISLER, ROBERT. *Weltenmantel und Himmelszelt.* Munich, 1910. 2 vols.

——. "Zur Terminologie und Geschichte der jüdischen Alchemie," *Monatsschrift für Geschichte und Wissenschaft des Judentums* (Dresden), LXX (n.s., 34), (1926), 194–201.

ELEAZAR, ABRAHAM. *Uraltes Chymisches Werck.* Leipzig, 1760. (Part II has separate pagination.)

ELIADE, MIRCEA. *Shamanism: Archaic Techniques of Ecstasy.* Translated by Willard R. Trask. New York (Bollingen Series) and London, 1964. (Orig.: *Le Chamanisme et les techniques archaïques de l'extase.* Paris, 1951.)

[ELIEZER BEN HYRCANUS.] *Pirkê de Rabbi Eliezer.* Translated and edited by Gerald Friedlander. London and New York, 1916.

Encyclopaedia Judaica. Edited by Jacob Klatzkin. Berlin, 1928– (publication suspended).

Enoch, Book of. See CHARLES, R. H.

[EPHRAEM SYRUS, SAINT.] *Sancti Ephraemi Syri Hymni et Sermones.* Edited by Joseph Lamy. Mechlin, 1882–1902. 4 vols. (Numbered in columns, not pages.)

——. *Opera omnia.* Translated (into Latin) and edited by Gerard Voss. 3rd edn., Cologne, 1616. ("De paenitentia," pp. 561–84.)

EPIPHANIUS. *Ancoratus* and *Panarium.* Edited by Karl Holl. (Griechische christliche Schriftsteller.) Leipzig, 1915–33. 3 vols. (*Ancoratus,* Vol. I, pp. 1–149; *Panarium,* Vol. I, p. 169–Vol. III, p. 496.)

"Epistola ad Hermannum archiepiscopum Coloniensem de lapide philosophorum." See *(A) Theatrum chemicum,* **xlviii.**

ERMAN, ADOLF. *Die Religion der Ägypter.* Berlin and Leipzig, 1934.

EUCHERIUS, BISHOP OF LYONS. *Liber Formularum Spiritalis Intelligentiae.* See Migne, *P.L.,* vol. 50, cols. 727–72.

EUSEBIUS. *Constantini Oratio ad Sanctorum Coetum.* In Migne, *P.G.,* vol. 20, cols. 1233–1316.

EUSTATHIUS MACREMBOLITES. *De Hysmines et Hysminiae Amoribus Libri XI.* Edited by Isidore Hilberg. Vienna, 1876.

EUTHYMIOS ZIGABENOS. *Panoplia Dogmatica.* See Migne, *P.G.,* vol. 130 (whole vol.)

EVANS. See ECKHART.

"Exercitationes in Turbam." See *(A) Artis auriferae,* **iv.**

FERGUSON, JOHN. *Bibliotheca chemica.* Glasgow, 1906, 2 vols.

FICINO, MARSIGLIO (Marsilius Ficinus). *Opera.* Basel, 1576. 2 vols.

FIERZ-DAVID, LINDA (ed.). *The Dream of Poliphilo.* Translated by Mary Hottinger. (Bollingen Series XXV.) New York, 1950.

FIGULUS, BENEDICTUS (Benedict Torpfer). *Rosarium novum olympicum et benedictum.* Basel, 1608. 2 parts, separately paginated, but second part has no separate title-page.

FIRMICUS MATERNUS, JULIUS. *Liber de errore profanarum religionum.* See: *M. Minucii Felicis Octavius et Julii Firmici Materni Liber de errore profanarum religionum.* Edited by Karl Halm. (Corpus Scriptorum Ecclesiasticorum Latinorum, 2.) Vienna, 1867.

——. *Matheseos Libri VIII.* Edited by W. Kroll, F. Skutsch, and K. Ziegler. Leipzig, 1897–1913. 2 vols.

[FLAMEL, NICOLAS.] "Annotata quaedam ex Nicolao Flamelo." See ZACHARIAS.

——. *His Exposition of the Hieroglyphicall Figures, etc.* By Eirenaeus Orandus. London, 1624.

——. "Summarium philosophicum." See *(A) Musaeum hermeticum,* **v.**

FLITCH, J. E. CRAWFORD. See ANGELUS SILESIUS.

"Fons chymicae veritatis." See PHILALETHES.

FRANCE, ANATOLE. *Penguin Island.* Translated by E. W. Evans. (Penguin Books.) West Drayton, 1948.

FRANZ, MARIE-LOUISE VON. *Aurora Consurgens; Ein dem Thomas von Aquin zugeschriebenes Dokument der alchemistischen Gegensatzproblematik.* (Part III of C. G. JUNG: *Mysterium Coniunctionis.*) Zurich, 1957. (English edn.: *Aurora Consurgens; A Document Attributed to Thomas Aquinas on the Problem of Opposites in Alchemy.* Translated by R. F. C. Hull and A. S. B. Glover. (New York [Bollingen Series] and London, 1966.)

——. "Die Passio Perpetuae." In: JUNG, C. G. *Aion: Untersuch-*

ungen zur Symbolgeschichte. (Psychologische Abhandlungen, VIII.) Zurich, 1951.

FRAZER, SIR JAMES G. *The Golden Bough.* London, 1911–15. 12 vols. (Part II: *Taboo and the Perils of the Soul,* Vol. III. Part III: *The Dying God,* Vol. IV. Part IV: *Adonis, Attis, Osiris,* Vols. V and VI. Part VII: *Balder the Beautiful,* Vols. X and XI.)

FRESNOY. See LENGLET DU FRESNOY.

FROBENIUS, LEO. *Das Zeitalter des Sonnengottes.* Vol. I (no more published), Berlin, 1904.

GALEN(US), CLAUDIUS. *De simplicium medicamentorum facultatibus libri XI.* Translated (into Latin) by Theodoricus Gerardus Gaudenus. Lyons, 1561.

GARNERUS DE SANCTO VICTORE. *Gregorianum.* See Migne, *P.L.,* vol. 193, cols. 9–462.

GEBER (JABIR.) "Summa perfectionis." See *(A) De alchemia,* i.

———. *Works.* Englished by Richard Russell (1678). Edited by Eric J. Holmyard. London, 1928.

GEFFCKEN, JOANNF? (ed.). *Die Oracula Sibyllina.* (Griechische christliche Schriftsteller.) Leipzig, 1902.

[Gemma Gemmarum.] *Dictionarium quod Gemma Gemmarum vocant, nuper castigatum.* Hagenau, 1518.

GEOFFREY OF MONMOUTH. *Histories of the Kings of Britain.* Translated by Sebastian Evans. London, 1904. (Book VII, pp. 170–188, contains the "Prophecies of Merlin.")

GEVARTIUS, JOANNES CASPARIUS. *Electorum Libri III.* Paris, 1619.

GHAZÂLI, AL-. *Die kostbare Perle im Wissen des Jenseits.* Edited by Mohammed Brugsch. Hanover, 1924.

GIKATILA, JOSEPH. *Shaare ora.* Offenbach, 1715.

GLAUBER, JOHANN RUDOLPH. *Tractatus de natura salium.* Amsterdam, 1658.

———. *Tractatus de signatura salium, metallorum, et planetarum.* Amsterdam, 1658.

"Gloria mundi." See *(A) Musaeum hermeticum,* vi.

GNOSIUS, DOMINICUS. See HERMES TRISMEGISTUS.

GODEFRIDUS (GODFREY), ABBOT OF ADMONT. *Homiliae Dominicales.* See Migne, *P.L.,* vol. 174, cols. 21–632. (*Homilia III in Dominica*

III Adventus, cols. 32–36; *Homilia IV in Dominica IV Adventus,* cols. 36–42.)

GOETHE, JOHANN WOLFGANG VON. *Faust.* Translated by Philip Wayne. Harmondsworth, 1949, 1959. 2 vols.

———. *Faust. An abridged version.* Translated by Louis MacNeice. London, 1951.

———. *Die Geheimnisse.* In *Werke* (Gedenkausgabe), edited by Ernst Beutler. Zurich, 1948–54. 24 vols. (Vol. III, pp. 273–83.)

———. *West-östlicher Diwan.* In *Werke,* ed. Beutler. (Vol. III, pp. 285–412.)

GOETZ, BRUNO. *Das Reich ohne Raum.* Potsdam, 1919. 2nd rev. and enlarged edn., Constance, 1925.

GOLDSCHMIDT, ADOLPH. *German Illumination.* Florence and Paris, 1928. 2 vols.

GOLDSCHMIDT, GUENTHER (ed.). *Heliodori Carmina Quattuor ad fidem Codicis Casselani* (Religionsgeschichtliche Versuche und Vorarbeiten, 19, part 2.) Giessen, 1923.

GOODENOUGH, ERWIN R. "The Crown of Victory in Judaism," *Art Bulletin* (New York), XXVIII (1926), 139–59.

GOURMONT, RÉMY DE. *Le Latin mystique.* Paris, 1930.

GRASSEUS, JOHANNES. "Arca arcani." See *(A) Theatrum chemicum,* li.

GRATAROLUS, GULIELMUS. *Verae alchimiae artisque metallicae, citra aenigmata . . .* Basel, 1561. 1 vol. in 2 parts, separately paginated. (*Rosarium philosophorum,* pp. 35–59 of Part II.)

GREGORY THE GREAT, SAINT. *Homiliae in Evangelia.* See Migne, *P.L.,* vol. 76, cols. 1075–1312.

———. *Homiliae in Ezechielem.* See Migne, *P.L.,* vol. 76, cols. 786–1072.

———. *In Librum Primum Regum Expositiones.* See Migne, *P.L.,* vol. 79, cols. 17–468.

———. *In Septem Psalmos Poenitentiales.* See Migne, *P.L.,* vol. 79, cols. 549–658.

———. *Moralia in Job.* See Migne, *P.L.,* vol. 75, col. 509–vol. 76, col. 782.

———. *Super Cantica Canticorum Expositio.* See Migne, *P.L.,* vol. 79, cols. 471–548.

623

GRENFELL, BERNARD P., and HUNT, ARTHUR S. *New Sayings of Jesus and Fragment of a Lost Gospel*. Oxford, 1904.

GREVERUS, JODOCUS. "Secretum." See *(A) Theatrum chemicum*, **xxvi.**

GRILL, JULIUS (ed.). *Hundert Lieder des Atharva-Veda*. 2nd edn., Stuttgart, 1888.

GRIMM, JACOB. *Teutonic Mythology*. Translated by James Steven Stallybrass. London, 1880–88. 4 vols.

—— AND WILHELM. *Fairy Tales*. Translated by Margaret Hunt and James Stern. New York, 1944.

GRUENBAUM, MAX. *Jüdisch-deutsche Chrestomathie*. Leipzig, 1882.

GRUNWALD, MAX. "Neue Spuk- und Zauberliteratur," *Monatsschrift für Geschichte und Wissenschaft des Judentums* (Dresden), LXXVII (n.s., XLI), (1933), 161–72.

GÜTERBOCK, HANS GUSTAV. "Kumarbi," *Istanbuler Schriften* (Zurich and New York), XVI (1946).

GURNEY, O. R. *The Hittites*. (Pelican Books.) Harmondsworth, 1952.

HALLER, MAX. "Das Hohe Lied." In: *Handbuch zum Alten Testament*. Edited by Otto von Eissfeldt. First Series, 18: *Die Fünf Megilloth*. Tübingen, 1940.

HAMBURGER, JACOB (ed.). *Encyclopädie des Judentums*. Leipzig, 1896–1901. 3 vols.

HARDING, M. ESTHER. *Woman's Mysteries*. 2nd edn., New York, 1955.

HARNACK, ADOLF VON. *Lehrbuch der Dogmengeschichte*. 5th edn., Tübingen, 1931.

HASTINGS, JAMES (ed.). *Encyclopedia of Religion and Ethics*. Edinburgh and New York, 1908–27. 13 vols.

HEGEMONIUS. *Acta Archelai*. Edited by Charles Henry Beeson. (Griechische christliche Schriftsteller.) Leipzig, 1906.

HEILER, FRIEDRICH. *Das neue Mariendogma im Lichte der Geschichte und im Urteil der Ökumene*. (Ökumenische Einheit, Heft 2.) Munich and Basel, 1951.

HELD, HANS LUDWIG. See ANGELUS SILESIUS.

HELIODORUS. See GOLDSCHMIDT.

HELLWIG, CHRISTOPH VON. *Neu eingerichtetes Lexicon Medico-Chymicum, oder Chymisches Lexicon*. Frankfort and Leipzig, 1711.

624

HELVETIUS, JOHANN FRIEDRICH. "Vitulus aureus." See *(A) Musaeum hermeticum,* xiv.

HERMAS. *The Shepherd.* In: LAKE, KIRSOPP (ed. and trans.). *The Apostolic Fathers.* (Loeb Classical Library.) London and New York, 1912–13. 2 vols. (Vol. II, pp. 6–305.)

[HERMES TRISMEGISTUS.] "Tractatus aureus." See *(A)* MANGETUS, *Bibliotheca chemica curiosa,* ii. For other versions, see: *(A) Theatrum chemicum,* xxxv; *(A) Musaeum hermeticum,* i; ATWOOD; *(A) Ars chemica,* i. Also: *Tractatus vere aureus de lapidis philosophici secreto. Cum scholiis Dominici Gnosii.* Leipzig, 1610.

HERODOTUS. *The Histories.* Translated by Aubrey de Selincourt. Harmondsworth, 1959.

HERZOG, J. J., and HAUCK, ALBERT (eds.). *Realencyklopädie für protestantische Theologie und Kirche.* Leipzig, 1896–1913. 24 vols.

HILARIUS (Hilary of Poitiers, Saint). *Commentarium in Matthaei Evangelium.* See Migne, *P.L.,* vol. 9, cols. 917–1078.

———. *Tractatus super Psalmos.* See Migne, *P.L.,* vol. 9, cols. 231–908.

———. *De Trinitate Libri XII.* See Migne, *P.L.,* vol. 10, cols. 25–472.

HILKA, ALFONS. *Der altfranzösische Prosa-Alexanderroman nach der Berliner Bildenhandschrift.* Halle, 1920.

HIPPOLYTUS. *Elenchos (Refutatio omnium haeresium). (Werke,* Vol. III.) Edited by Paul Wendland. (Griechische christliche Schriftsteller.) Leipzig, 1916. For translation, see: *Philosophumena, or The Refutation of all Heresies.* Translated by Francis Legge. London and New York, 1921. 2 vols.

HOCART, ARTHUR MAURICE. *Kings and Councillors.* (Egyptian University: Collection of Works published by the Faculty of Arts, 12.) Cairo, 1936.

HOFFMANN, ERNST THEODORE WILHELM (AMADEUS). *The Devil's Elixir.* (Trans. anon.) Edinburgh, 1824. 2 vols.

HOGHELANDE, THEOBALD DE. "De alchemiae difficultatibus" ("Liber de alchemia"). See *(A) Theatrum chemicum,* i. Another version in *(A)* MANGETUS, *Bibliotheca chemica curiosa,* i.

HOLLANDUS, JOANNES ISAACUS. "Fragmentum de opere philosophorum." See *(A) Theatrum chemicum,* xvii.

———. "Operum mineralium liber." See *(A) Theatrum chemicum,* xxv.

HOLMYARD, ERIC J. (ed. and trans.). "Abu 'l-Qāsim al-'Irāqī," *Isis* (Brussels), VIII (1926), 403–26.

———. See also ABU 'L-QĀSIM; GEBER.

HOMER. *The Iliad*. Translated by E. V. Rieu. Harmondsworth, 1958.

———. *The Odyssey*. Translated by E. V. Rieu. Harmondsworth, 1958.

HONORIUS OF AUTUN. *Elucidarium*. See Migne, *P.L.*, vol. 172, cols. 1109–76.

———. *Expositio in Cantica Canticorum*. See Migne, *P.L.*, vol. 172, cols. 347–496.

———. *Liber duodecim quaestionum*. See Migne, *P.L.*, vol. 172, cols. 1177–86.

———. *Sacramentarium*. See Migne, *P.L.*, vol. 172, cols. 737–806.

———. *Sermo in Dominica in Palmis*. See Migne, *P.L.*, vol. 172, cols. 913–922.

———. *Sermo in Epiphania Domini*. See Migne, *P.L.*, vol. 172, cols. 843–50.

———. *Speculum de mysteriis Ecclesiae*. See Migne, *P.L.*, vol. 172, cols. 813–1108.

HORACE (Quintus Horatius Flaccus.) *Satires, Epistles, and Ars Poetica*. With an English translation by H. Rushton Fairclough. (Loeb Classical Library.) London and New York, 1929.

HORAPOLLO NILIACUS. *The Hieroglyphics*. Translated by George Boas. (Bollingen Series XXIII.) New York, 1950.

HORNEFFER, ERNST. *Nietzsches Lehre von der ewigen Wiederkunft*. Leipzig, 1900.

HUGH OF ST. VICTOR. *De laude charitatis*. See Migne, *P.L.*, vol. 176, cols. 969–76.

HURWITZ, S. "Archetypische Motive in der chassidischen Mystik." In: *Zeitlose Dokumente der Seele*. (Studien aus dem C. G. Jung-Institut, 13.) Zurich, 1952.

———. *Die Gestalt des sterbenden Messias*. (Studien aus dem C. G. Jung-Institut, 8.) Zurich, 1958.

HUXLEY, ALDOUS. *Grey Eminence*. London, 1956.

I Ching, or the Book of Changes. The German translation by Richard Wilhelm rendered into English by Cary F. Baynes. New York (Bollingen Series XIX) and London, 1950. 2 vols. 3rd edn., 1 vol., 1967.

IGNATIUS LOYOLA, SAINT. *The Spiritual Exercises.* Translated with a commentary by Joseph Rickaby. London, 1923.

IRENAEUS. *Adversus Haereses.* See: *The Writings of Irenaeus.* Translated by Alexander Roberts and W. H. Rambaut. (Ante-Nicene Christian Library, vols. 5, 9.) Edinburgh, 1868–9. 2 vols.

ISIDORE OF SEVILLE, SAINT. *De natura rerum.* Edited by Gustav Becker. Berlin, 1857.

———. *Liber etymologiarum.* Basel, 1489.

IZQUIERDO, SEBASTIANO. *Practica di alcuni esercitij spirituali di S. Ignatio.* Rome, 1686.

JABIR. See GEBER.

JACOBSOHN, HELMUTH. "Die dogmatische Stellung des Königs in der Theologie der alten Ägypter," *Ägyptologische Forschungen,* ed. by Alexander Scharff (Gluckstadt, Hamburg, and New York), VIII (1939).

JAFFÉ, ANIELA. "Bilder und Symbole aus E. T. A. Hoffmanns Märchen 'Der Goldene Topf.'" In: JUNG, C. G. *Gestaltungen des Unbewussten.* Zurich, 1950.

JAMES, MONTAGUE RHODES (ed. and trans.). *The Apocryphal New Testament.* Oxford, 1924. (Contains "Acts of Thomas," pp. 364–438; "Acts of John," pp. 228–70.)

JASTROW, MORRIS. *Die Religion Babyloniens und Assyriens.* Giessen, 1912. 2 vols.

JEROME, SAINT. *Epistola II ad Theodosium et caeteros Anachoretas.* In: (*Opera* Sec. I, Part I), *Epistolarum,* Pars I. Edited by Isidore Hilberg. (Corpus Scriptorum Ecclesiasticorum Latinorum, 54.) Vienna and Leipzig, 1910.

Jewish Encyclopaedia, The. Edited by Isidore Singer. New York and London, 1925. 12 vols.

JOEL, DAVID HEYMANN. *Die Religionsphilosophie des Sohar.* Leipzig, 1849.

JOHN CHRYSOSTOM, SAINT. *Homiliae in Joannem.* See Migne, *P.G.,* vol. 59, cols. 23–482. (*Homilia XXVI, alias XXV,* cols. 153–58.)

———. *Homiliae in Matthaeum.* See Migne, *P.G.,* vol. 57, col. 13–vol. 58, col. 794.

JOHN OF RUYSBROECK. See RUYSBROECK.

JOHN OF THE CROSS, SAINT. *Works.* Translated by E. Allison Peers.

London, 1934–35. 3 vols. ("The Dark Night of the Soul," Vol. I, pp. 335–486.)

JOYCE, JAMES. *Ulysses.* Hamburg, Paris, Bologna, 1932.

JUNG, CARL GUSTAV.* *Aion. Coll. Works,* 9, ii. 1959; 2nd edn., 1968.

———. *Alchemical Studies. Coll. Works,* 13. 1967.

———. "An Analysis of the Associations of an Epileptic." In *Coll. Works,* 2. 1973.

———. "Analytical Psychology and Education." In *Coll. Works,* 17.

———. "Answer to Job." In *Coll. Works,* 11.

———. "Archetypes of the Collective Unconscious." In *Coll. Works,* 9, i.

———. "Brother Klaus." In *Coll. Works,* 11.

———. "Commentary on *The Secret of the Golden Flower.*" In *Alchemical Studies.*

———. "Concerning the Archetypes, with Special Reference to the Anima Concept." In *Coll. Works,* 9, i.

———. "Concerning Mandala Symbolism." In *Coll. Works,* 9, i.

———. "Concerning Rebirth." In *Coll. Works,* 9, i.

———. *The Development of Personality. Coll. Works,* 17. 1954.

———. "Instinct and the Unconscious." In *Coll. Works,* 8.

———. "The Interpretation of Visions." Seminar reports, multigraphed for private circulation. Zurich, 1939.

———. "On the Nature of Dreams." In *Coll. Works,* 8.

———. "On the Nature of the Psyche." In *Coll. Works,* 8.

———. "On Psychic Energy." In *Coll. Works,* 8.

———. "Paracelsus the Physician." In *Coll. Works,* 15.

———. "Paracelsus as a Spiritual Phenomenon." In *Alchemical Studies.*

———. "The Phenomenology of the Spirit in Fairytales." In *Coll. Works,* 9, 1.

———. "The Philosophical Tree." In *Alchemical Studies.*

———. "A Psychological Approach to the Dogma of the Trinity." In *Coll. Works,* 11.

* For details of the Collected Works of C. G. Jung, see list at end of this volume.

JUNG, CARL GUSTAV. "The Psychological Aspects of the Kore." In *Coll. Works*, 9, i.

———. *Psychological Types. Coll. Works*, 6. 1971.

———. *Psychology and Alchemy. Coll. Works*, 12. 1953; rev. edn., 1968.

———. "The Psychology of the Child Archetype." In *Coll. Works*, 9, i.

———. "The Psychology of Eastern Meditation." In *Coll. Works*, 11.

———. "Psychology and Religion." In *Coll. Works*, 11.

———. "The Psychology of the Transference." In *Coll. Works*, 16.

———. "The Relations between the Ego and the Unconscious." In *Coll. Works*, 7.

———. "A Review of the Complex Theory." In *Coll. Works*, 8.

———. "Spirit and Life." In *Coll. Works*, 8.

———. "The Spirit Mercurius." In *Alchemical Studies*.

———. "A Study in the Process of Individuation." In *Coll. Works*, 9, i.

———. *Symbols of Transformation. Coll. Works*, 5. 1956; rev. edn., 1967.

———. "Synchronicity: An Acausal Connecting Principle." In *Coll. Works*, 8.

———. "The Transcendent Function." In *Coll. Works*, 8.

———. "Transformation Symbolism in the Mass." In *Coll. Works*, 11.

———. *Two Essays on Analytical Psychology. Coll. Works*, 7. 1953; rev. edn., 1966.

———. "Ulysses: A Monologue." In *Coll. Works*, 15.

———. "The Visions of Zosimos." In *Alchemical Studies*.

———. See also WILHELM.

*

*

*

*

629

*

*

*

*

KALID. "Liber secretorum." See *(A) Artis auriferae,* **ix.**

———. "Liber trium verborum." See *(A) Artis auriferae,* **x.**

Katha Upanishad. See *Upanishads.*

KEES, HERMANN. *Der Götterglaube im alten Ägypten.* (Mitteilungen der Vorderasiatisch-ägyptischen Gesellschaft, 45.) Leipzig, 1941.

KERÉNYI, C. (OR KARL). *Das Ägäische Fest.* (Albae Vigiliae, XI.) Zurich, 1941; 3rd edn., Wiesbaden, 1950.

———. *Asklepios: Archetypal Image of the Physician's Existence.* Translated by Ralph Manheim. New York (Bollingen Series XV; 3) and London, 1959.

———. *The Gods of the Greeks.* Translated by Norman Cameron. (Pelican Books.) Harmondsworth, 1958.

———. "Kore." In: KERÉNYI and JUNG, C. G. *Essays on a Science of Mythology.* (Bollingen Series XXII.) New York, 1949. Also published as *Introduction to a Science of Mythology,* London, 1950.)

———. *Töchter der Sonne.* Zurich, 1944.

KHUNRATH, HEINRICH. *Amphitheatrum sapientiae.* Hanau, 1609.

———. *Von hylealischen Chaos.* Magdeburg, 1597.

KIRCHER, ATHANASIUS. *Oedipus Aegyptiacus.* Rome, 1652–54. 3 vols.

KNORR VON ROSENROTH, CHRISTIAN. *Kabbala Denudata.* Sulzbach and Frankfurt a. M., 1677–84. 2 vols.

KOEHLER, REINHOLD. *Kleinere Schriften zur erzählenden Dichtung des Mittelalters.* Berlin, 1898–1900. 3 vols.

KOEPGEN, GEORG. *Die Gnosis des Christentums.* Salzburg, 1939.

KOHUT, ALEXANDER. "Die talmudisch-midraschische Adamssage in ihrer Rückbeziehung auf die persische Yima- und Meshiasage," *Zeitschrift der deutschen Morgenländischen Gesellschaft* (Leipzig), XXV (1871), 59–94.

KOPP, HERMANN. *Die Alchemie in älterer und neuerer Zeit.* Heidelberg, 1886. 2 vols.

Koran, The. Translated by N. J. Dawood. (Penguin Books.) Harmondsworth, 1956.

KRIEG, CLAUS W. *Chinesische Mythen und Legenden.* Zurich, 1946.

LACINIUS, JANUS. See BONUS.

LAGNEUS, DAVID. "Harmonia chemica." See *(A) Theatrum chemicum*, xxxvi.

LAJARD, FELIX. "Mémoire sur une représentation figurée de la Vénus orientale androgyne," *Nouvelles annales de l'Institut archéologique, Section française* (Paris), I (1836), 161–212.

———. *Recherches sur le culte de Vénus.* Paris, 1849.

LAKE, KIRSOPP (ed. and trans.). *The Apostolic Fathers.* (Loeb Classical Library.) London and New York, 1914. 2 vols.

LAMBSPRINGK. "De lapide philosophico figurae et emblemata." See *(A) Musaeum hermeticum*, viii.

LARGUIER, LEO. *Le Faiseur d'or Nicolas Flamel.* (L'Histoire inconnue, 4.) Paris, 1936.

LEISEGANG, HANS. *Die Gnosis.* Leipzig, 1924.

———. *Der heilige Geist.* Vol. I, part 1 (no more published). Leipzig and Berlin, 1919.

LENGLET DU FRESNOY, PIERRE NICOLAS. *Histoire de la philosophie hermétique.* Paris and The Hague, 1742. 3 vols.

LEO HEBRAEUS (Leone Ebreo). *Philosophy of Love.* Translated by F. Friedeberg-Seeley and Jean H. Barnes. London, 1937.

LESSER, FRIEDRICH CHRISTIAN. *Lithotheologie.* Hamburg, 1735.

"Liber Alze." See *(A) Musaeum hermeticum*, vii.

"Liber de arte chymica." See *(A) Artis auriferae*, xvii.

"Liber de magni lapidis compositione." See *(A) Theatrum chemicum*, xxiii.

LICETUS, FORTUNIUS. *Allegoria peripatetica de generatione amicitia* etc. Padua, 1630.

LIDZBARSKI, MARK. *Das Johannesbuch der Mandäer.* Giessen, 1915.

LIDZBARSKI, MARK (ed. and trans.). *Ginza: der Schatz oder das grosse Buch der Mandäer.* (Quellen der Religionsgeschichte, Group 4, vol. 13.) Göttingen and Leipzig, 1925.

LIPPMANN, EDUARD O. VON. *Entstehung und Ausbreitung der Alchemie.* Berlin, 1919–54. 3 vols.

LOHMEYER, ERNST. "Vom göttlichen Wohlgeruch," *Sitzungsberichte der Heidelberger Akademie der Wissenschaften, Phil.-hist. Kl.,* IX. Abhandlung (1919).

LORICHIUS, JOHANNES. *Aenigmatum Libri III.* Frankfurt a. M., 1545.

LU CH'IANG-WU. See WEI PO-YANG.

[LUCIAN.] *Scholia in Lucianum.* Edited by Hugh Kabe. Leipzig, 1906.

LUCIAN. "Pseudomantis." See: "Alexander; or, The False Prophet." In: *Works.* Translated from the Greek by Several Eminent Hands [Walter Moyle and others]. London, 1711. 2 vols. (Vol. I, pp. 144–181.)

———. "The Syrian Goddess" (De Dea Syria). In *Works* (as above). (Vol. I, pp. 241–271.)

"Ludus puerorum." See *(A) Artis auriferae,* **xx.**

LULLY, RAYMUND. *Codicillus.* Rouen, 1651.

———. "Theorica et practica." See *(A) Theatrum chemicum,* **xxx.**

Mabinogion, The. Translated by Gwyn Jones and Thomas Jones. (Everyman's Library.) London, 1949. ("Peredur son of Efrawg," pp. 183ff.)

MACDONELL, ARTHUR ANTHONY. *A Sanskrit-English Dictionary.* London, 1893.

[MACROBIUS.] *Macrobii Ambrosii Theodosii Opera.* Edited by Ludovicus Janus. Quedlinburg and Leipzig, 1848–52. 2 vols. ("Commentarium in Somnium Scipionis," Vol. I, pp. 13–215; "Saturnalia," Vol. II, pp. 3–647.) For translation of former, see: *Commentary on the Dream of Scipio.* Translated by William Harris Stahl. (Records of Civilization, Sources and Studies, 48.) New York, 1952.

MADATHANUS, HENRICUS. "Aureum saeculum redivivum." See *(A) Musaeum hermeticum,* **ii.**

MAIER, MICHAEL. *Atalanta fugiens, hoc est, emblemata nova de secretis naturae chymica.* Oppenheim, 1618.

——. *De circulo physico quadrato.* Oppenheim, 1616.

——. *Jocus severus.* Frankfurt a. M., 1617.

——. *Secretioris naturae secretorum Scrutinium chymicum.* Franfurt a. M., 1687.

——. *Symbola aureae mensae duodecim nationum.* Frankfurt a. M., 1617.

MAITLAND, EDWARD. *Anna Kingsford: Her Life, Letters, Diary, and Work.* London, 1896. 2 vols.

MÂLE, EMILE. *L'Art religieux du XIIe siècle en France.* 2nd edn., Paris, 1924.

MALVASIUS, CAESAR (Carlo Cesare Malvasio). *Aelia Laelia Crispis non nata resurgens.* Bologna, 1683.

MARIA PROPHETISSA. "Practica . . . in artem alchimicam." See *(A) Artis auriferae,* **viii.**

MARSILIUS FICINUS. See FICINO.

MARTIAL. *Epigrams,* with an English translation by Walter C. A. Ker. (Loeb Classical Library.) London and New York, 1920–25. 2 vols.

MEAD, GEORGE ROBERT STOW (ed. and trans.). *Thrice Greatest Hermes.* London, 1949. 3 vols.

MEERPOHL, FRANZ. "Meister Eckharts Lehre vom Seelenfünklein," *Abhandlungen zur Philosophie und Psychologie der Religion* (Würzburg), Heft 10 (1926).

ME(H)UNG, JEAN DE. "Demonstratio naturae." See *(A) Musaeum hermeticum,* **iv.**

MEIER, C. A. *Antike Inkubation und moderne Psychotherapie.* (Studien aus dem C. G. Jung-Institut, 1.) Zurich, 1949.

MENNENS, WILLIAM. "Aurei velleris sive sacrae philosophiae vatum selectae et unicae Libri tres." See *(A) Theatrum chemicum,* **xliv.**

Merlin. Edited by Gaston Paris and Jacob Ulrich. (Société des anciens textes français.) Paris, 1886. For translation, see: *Merlin, or the Early History of King Arthur.* Edited by Henry B. Wheatley. (Early English Text Society, Original Series, nos. 10, 21, 36, 112.) London, 1899. 2 vols. See also GEOFFREY OF MONMOUTH.

MERLINUS. "Allegoria de arcano lapidis." See *(A) Artis auriferae,* **xiii.**

MICRERIS. "Tractatus Micreris suo discipulo Mirnefindo." See *(A) Theatrum chemicum*, xli.

Midrash Rabbah. Edited by W. Freedman and Maurice Simon. London and Bournemouth, 1951. 10 vols.

MIGNE, JACQUES PAUL (ed.) *Patrologiae cursus completus.*

[*P.L.*] Latin Series. Paris, 1844–64, 221 vols.

[*P.G.*] Greek Series. Paris, 1857–66. 166 vols.

(These works are referred to in the text and in this bibliography as "Migne, *P.L.*" and "Migne, *P.G.*" respectively. References are to columns, not to pages.)

MORET, ALEXANDRE. *Du caractère religieux de la royauté pharaonique.* (Annales du Musée Guimet, 15.) Paris, 1922.

———. *Mystères égyptiens.* Paris, 1922.

MORIENUS ROMANUS. "De transmutatione metallica." See *(A) Artis auriferae*, xviii.

MORRIS, RICHARD. *Legends of the Holy Rood.* London, 1871.

MUELLER, ERNST (trans.). *Der Sohar. Das heilige Buch der Kabbala. Ausgewählte Texte.* Vienna, 1932.

———. *Der Sohar und seine Lehre.* Vienna and Berlin, 1920.

MURMELSTEIN, BENJAMIN. "Adam: ein Beitrag zur Messiaslehre," *Wiener Zeitschrift für die Kunde des Morgenlandes* (Vienna), XXXV (1928), 242–75, and XXXVI (1929), 51–86.

"Mutus liber." See ALTUS.

MYLIUS, JOHANN DANIEL. *Philosophia reformata.* Frankfurt a.M., 1622.

NEIHARDT, JOHN G. *Black Elk Speaks. Being the Life Story of a Holy Man of the Og[a]lala Sioux.* New York, 1932.

NELKEN, JAN. "Analytische Beobachtungen über Phantasien eines Schizophrenen," *Jahrbuch für psychoanalytische und psychopathologische Forschungen* (Leipzig and Vienna), IV (1912), 504–62.

NESTLE, E. "Der süsse Geruch als Erweis des Geistes," *Zeitschrift für die neutestamentliche Wissenschaft* (Giessen), VII (1906), 95–96.

NEUMANN, ERICH. *The Origins and History of Consciousness.* Translated by R. F. C. Hull. New York (Bollingen Series XLII) and London, 1954.

634

NEWMAN, JOHN HENRY. *An Essay on the Development of Christian Doctrine*. London, 1845.

NIEDNER, FELIX. "Edda: Götterdichtung und Spruchdichtung." *Thule* (Jena), II (1920).

NIETZSCHE, FRIEDRICH WILHELM. *Thus Spake Zarathustra*. Translated by Thomas Common; revised by Oscar Levy and John L. Beevers. London, 1932.

NORTON, THOMAS. "The Ordinall of Alchimy." See *(A) Theatrum chemicum Britannicum*, i.

Nova Acta Paracelsica. (V. Jahrbuch der Schweizerischen Paracelsus-Gesellschaft, 1948.) Einsiedeln, 1949.

"Occulta Chemicorum Philosophia." See: VALENTINUS, BASILIUS. *Triumphwagen Antimonii*. Leipzig, 1604. (pp. 579–694.)

ORANDUS, EIRENAEUS. See FLAMEL.

ORIGEN. *Contra Celsum*. Translated by Henry Chadwick. Cambridge, 1953.

———. *De Oratione*. See Migne, *P.G.*, vol. 11, cols. 415–562. For translation, see: *Alexandrian Christianity. Selected Translations of Clement and Origen*. Edited and translated by John Ernest Leonard Oulton and Henry Chadwick. (Library of Christian Classics, 2.) London, 1954. (pp. 238–329.)

———. *In Cantica Canticorum Homiliae*. See Migne, *P.G.*, vol. 13, cols. 37–58.

———. *In Exodum Homiliae*. See Migne, *P.G.*, vol. 12, cols. 297–396.

———. *In Ezechielem Homiliae*. See Migne, *P.G.*, vol. 13, cols. 665–768.

———. *In Genesim Homiliae*. See Migne, *P.G.*, vol. 12, cols. 145–262.

———. *In Leviticum Homiliae*. See Migne, *P.G.*, vol. 12, cols. 405–574.

———. *In Numeros Homiliae*. See Migne, *P.G.*, vol. 12, cols. 585–806.

———. *In Librum Regnorum Homiliae*. See Migne, *P.G.*, vol. 12, cols. 995–1027.

———. *Peri Archon Libri IV*. See Migne, *P.G.*, vol. 11, cols. 115–414.

OROSIUS, PAULUS. *Ad Aurelium Augustinum Commonitorium*. In: *Priscilliani quae supersunt . . . accedit Orosii Commentarium de Errore Priscillianistarum et Origenistarum*. (Corpus Scriptorum Ecclesiasticorum Latinorum.) Prague, Leipzig, Vienna, 1889.

Orphic Fragments. See: *Orphica.* Edited by Eugen Abel. Leipzig and Prague, 1885.

ORTHELIUS. "Discursus de praecedente epistola" (i.e., Epistola Andreae de Blawen). See *(A) Theatrum chemicum,* **liii.**

———. "Epilogus et recapitulatio . . . in Novum lumen chymicum Sendivogii." See *(A) Theatrum chemicum,* **lii.**

OVID. *Metamorphoses.* With an English translation by Frank Justus Miller. (Loeb Classical Library.) London and Cambridge, Mass., 1946. 2 vols.

PACHYMERES, GEORGE. See DIONYSIUS, *De coelesti hierarchia.*

PARACELSUS (Theophrastus Bombastus of Hohenheim). See: SUDHOFF, KARL (ed.), *Theophrast von Hohenheim genannt Paracelsus Sämtliche Werke.* First section: *Medizinische Schriften.* 14 vols. Munich and Berlin, 1922–35. See also: HUSER, JOHANN (ed.) *Aureoli Philippi Theophrasti Bombasts von Hohenheim Paracelsi . . . Philosophi und Medici Opera Bücher und Schrifften.* Strasbourg, 1589–90. 10 parts. Reprinted 1603, 1616, 2 vols.

———. *Liber Azoth.* In Sudhoff, Vol. XIV, pp. 547–595; in Huser (1616), Vol. II, pp. 519–43.

———. *Deutsche Fragmente zu den Fünf Büchern der Vita Longa.* In Sudhoff, Vol. III, pp. 293–308.

———. *De generatione rerum naturalium* (Book I of "De natura rerum"). In Sudhoff, Vol. XI, pp. 307–403.

———. *Von dem Hönig.* In Sudhoff, Vol. II, pp. 193–204.

———. *Labyrinthus Medicorum.* In Sudhoff, Vol. XI, pp. 161–220.

———. *Lumen Apothecariorum Spagyrorum.* In Sudhoff, Vol. II, pp. 193ff.

———. *De natura rerum.* In Sudhoff, Vol. XI, pp. 307–403; in Huser (1590), Vol. I, pp. 881ff.

———. *Das Buch Paragranum.* In Sudhoff, Vol. VIII. Another edition, edited by Franz Strunz, Leipzig, 1903.

———. *Vorrede und erste beide Bücher des Paragranum.* In Sudhoff, Vol. II, pp. 33–113.

———. *De pestilitate.* In Sudhoff, Vol. XIV, pp. 597–661; in Huser (1599), Part III.

636

——. *De philosophia occulta.* In Sudhoff, Vol. XIV, pp. 513–42.

——. *Philosophia ad Athenienses.* In Sudhoff, Vol. XIII, pp. 390–423; in Huser (1616), Vol. II, pp. 1–63.

——. *Scholia in poemata Macri.* In Sudhoff, Vol. III, pp. 383–424; in Huser (1616), Vol. I, pp. 1070–88.

——. *Von den dreyen ersten Principiis oder essentiis.* In Sudhoff, Vol. III, pp. 3–11.

——. *Von den tartarischen Krankheiten.* In Sudhoff, Vol. XI, pp. 15–121; in Huser (1599), Part II.

——. *De vita longa.* In Sudhoff, Vol. III, pp. 247–90. Another edition, edited by Adam von Bodenstein, Basel, 1562. See also DORN.

PAULINUS OF AQUILEIA, SAINT. *Liber exhortationis ad Henricum Forojuliensem.* See Migne, *P.L.,* vol. 99, cols. 197–282.

PAULINUS OF NOLA, SAINT. *Poema 25.* In Migne, *P.L.,* vol. 61, cols. 633–38.

PAULY, AUGUST FRIEDRICH VON. *Paulys Realencyclopädie der classischen Altertumswissenschaft.* Neue Bearbeitung . . . , edited by Georg Wissowa. Stuttgart, 1893– (in progress).

PAUSANIAS. *Description of Greece.* With a translation by W. H. S. Jones. (Loeb Classical Library.) London and New York, 1926–35. 5 vols.

PENOTUS. "Characteres secretorum celandorum" ("Philosophi potius occultare artem conati sunt quam patefacere"). ⌜A table.⌝ See *(A) Theatrum chemicum,* **xv.**

——. "De medicamentis chemicis" ("De vera praeparatione et usu medicamentorum chemicorum"). See *(A) Theatrum chemicum,* **xi.**

——. "Quinquagintaseptem canones de opere physico" ("Regulae et canones"). See *(A) Theatrum chemicum,* **xviii.**

PERNETY, ANTOINE JOSEPH. *Dictionnaire mytho-hermétique.* Paris, 1758 [1787].

——. *Les Fables égyptiennes et grecques.* Paris, 1758. 2 vols.

PETRUS DE SILENTO. "Opus." See *(A) Theatrum chemicum,* **xxxix.**

PHILALETHES, EIRENAEUS. "Introitus apertus ad occlusum regis palatium." See *(A) Musaeum hermeticum,* **xii.**

——. "Fons chymicae veritatis." See *(A) Musaeum hermeticum,* **xiii.**

——. See also VAUGHAN.

PHILO. *De opificio mundi* (On the Account of the World's Creation Given by Moses). In *Works,* Loeb edition, Vol. I, pp. 6–137.

———. *Quaestiones in Genesim* (Questions and Answers on Genesis). Translated by Ralph Marcus. *Philo, Supplement.* (Loeb Classical Library.) London and Cambridge, Mass., 1953. 2 vols.

———. *Quis rerum divinarum haeres?* (Who is the Heir of Divine Things?). In *Works,* Loeb edition, Vol. IV, pp. 284–447.

———. [*Works.*] Translated by F. H. Colson and G. H. Whitaker. (Loeb Classical Library.) New York and London, 1929– . 10 vols. (in progress).

PICINELLUS, PHILIPPUS (Filippo Picinello). *Mundus Symbolicus.* Cologne, 1687. 2 vols.

PICO DELLA MIRANDOLA, GIOVANNI. *Opera.* Venice, 1557. (Contains: *Heptaplus,* fols. 1ʳ–13ʳ; *Apologia tredecim quaestionum,* fols. 13ᵛ–40ʳ; *Disputationes adversus Astrologos,* fols. 75ʳ–150ʳ.)

———. *Opera omnia.* Basel, 1572–73. 2 vols. (Contains *Heptaplus,* Vol. I, pp. 11–62; *In Astrologiam,* Vol. I, pp. 411–732.)

———. "De auro." See *(A) Theatrum chemicum,* **xxi.**

Pistis Sophia. Edited and translated by G. R. S. Mead. London, 1955. Another version: translated (into German) by Carl Schmidt. Leipzig, 1925.

PITRA, JOHN BAPTIST (ed.). *Analecta sacra Spicilegio Solesmensi praeparata.* Paris, 1876–91. 8 vols.

PIUS XII, POPE. *Apostolic Constitution "Munificentissimus Deus."* Translated into English. Dublin (Irish Messenger Office), 1950.

PLATO. *The Republic.* Translated by R. D. P. Lee. (Penguin Books.) Harmondsworth and Baltimore, 1958.

———. *The Symposium.* Translated by W. Hamilton. (Penguin Books.) Harmondsworth and Baltimore, 1959.

———. *The Symposium of Plato.* Translated and edited by R. G. Bury. Cambridge, 1909.

———. See also CORNFORD.

"Platonis Liber Quartorum." See *(A) Theatrum chemicum,* **xlii.**

PLINY. *Natural History.* With an English translation by H. Rackham. (Loeb Classical Library.) London and Cambridge, Mass., 1938. 10 vols.

PLOTINUS. *The Enneads.* Translated by Stephen MacKenna. 2nd edn., revised by B. S. Page. London and New York, 1956.

PLUTARCH. *Moralia.* Translated by F. C. Babbitt. (Loeb Classical Library.) London and Cambridge, Mass., 1927ff. 14 vols. ("De defectu oraculorum" [The Obsolescence of Oracles], Vol. V, pp. 401ff.; "De facie in orbe lunae" [The Face on the Moon], Vol. XII, pp. 34–223; "De Iside et Osiride" [Isis and Osiris], Vol. V, pp. 6–191; "Quaestiones Romanae" [Roman Questions], Vol. IV, pp. 6–171.)

PORDAGE, JOHN. *Sophia.* Amsterdam, 1699.

[PORPHYRY.] *Porphyry the Philosopher to his Wife Marcella.* Translated by Alice Zimmern. London, 1896.

PREISENDANZ, KARL. *Papyri Graecae Magicae: Die griechischen Zauberpapyrien.* Berlin, 1928–31. 2 vols.

PREUSCHEN, ERWIN. *Antilegomena.* Giessen, 1901; rev. edn., 1905.

PROCLUS. *Commentaries on the Timaeus of Plato.* Translated by Thomas Taylor. London, 1820. 2 vols.

RABANUS MAURUS. *Allegoriae in Sacram Scripturam.* See Migne, *P.L.,* vol. 112, cols. 849–1088.

"Rachaidibi . . . Fragmentum." See *(A) Artis auriferae,* **xiv.**

RADHAKRISHNAN, SARVAPALLI. *Indian Philosophy.* London, 1923–27; rev. edn., 1929–31. 2 vols.

RAHNER, HUGO. "Antenna Crucis II—Das Meer der Welt," *Zeitschrift für katholische Theologie* (Innsbruck), LXVI (1942), 89–118.

———. "Das christliche Mysterium von Sonne und Mond." In *Eranos-Jahrbuch X: 1943.* Zurich, 1944. (pp. 305–404.)

———. "Flumina de ventre Christi." *Biblica* (Rome), XXII (1941), 269–302, 367–403.

———. "Die Gottesgeburt," *Zeitschrift für katholische Theologie* (Innsbruck), LIX (1935), 333–418.

———. "Mysterium Lunae," *Zeitschrift für katholische Theologie* (Innsbruck), LXIII (1939), 311–49, 428–42; LXIV (1940), 61–80, 121–131.

———. "Die seelenheilende Blume," in *Eranos-Jahrbuch XII: Festgabe für C. G. Jung.* Zurich, 1945. (pp. 117–239.)

[RAMANUJA.] *The Vedanta-Sutras with the Commentary of Rama-nuja.* Translated by George Thibaut. (Sacred Books of the East, 34, 38, 48.) Oxford, 1890–1904. 3 volumes.

READ, JOHN. *Prelude to Chemistry.* 2nd edn., London, 1939.

Realencyklopädie für protestantische Theologie. See HERZOG.

"Regulae et canones de opere physico." See PENOTUS.

REITZENSTEIN, RICHARD. *Die hellenistischen Mysterienreligionen.* Leipzig, 1910. 2nd edn., 1923; 3rd edn., 1927.

——. "Himmelswanderung und Drachenkampf." In: *Friedrich Karl Andreas Festschrift zur Vollendung des siebzigsten Lebens-jahres.* Leipzig, 1916. (pp. 33–50.)

——. *Poimandres.* Leipzig, 1904.

——. *Zwei religionsgeschichtliche Fragen.* Berlin, 1926.

—— and SCHAEDER, H. *Studien zum antiken Synkretismus aus Iran und Griechenland.* (Studien der Bibliothek Warburg, 7.) Berlin, 1926.

REUCHLIN, JOHANNES. *De arte cabbalistica.* Hagenau, 1517.

——. *De verbo mirifico.* Lyons, 1552.

REUSNER, H. (ed.). *Pandora.* Basel, 1588.

RHINE, J. B. *New Frontiers of the Mind.* London, 1937.

——. *The Reach of the Mind.* New York, 1947; London, 1948.

RIESSLER, PAUL (ed.). *Altjüdisches Schrifttum ausserhalb der Bibel.* Augsburg, 1928.

Rigveda. See: *The Hymns of the Rig-Veda.* Translated by Ralph T. H. Griffith. 2nd edn., Benares, 1896–97. 2 vols.

RIPLEY, SIR GEORGE. *Chymische Schrifften.* Erfurt, 1624.

——. *Omnia opera chemica.* Cassel, 1649.

——. "Duodecim portarum axiomata philosophica." See *(A) Theatrum chemicum,* **xvi.**

ROHDE, ERWIN. *Psyche.* Translated by W. B. Hillis. London, 1925.

Rosarium philosophorum. See *(A) Artis auriferae,* **xxi**; see also GRATAROLUS.

ROSCHER, W. H. (ed.). *Ausführliches Lexikon der griechischen und römischen Mythologie.* Leipzig and Berlin, 1884–1937. 6 vols.

ROSENCREUTZ, CHRISTIAN (pseud. of Johann Valentin Andreae). *Chymische Hochzeit.* Strasbourg, 1616. For translation, see: *The*

Hermetick Romance, or The Chymical Wedding. Translated by E. Foxcroft. London, 1690.

"Rosinus ad Euthiciam." See *(A) Artis auriferae,* vi; also ibid., 1610 edn., pp. 158–78.

"Rosinus ad Sarratantam Episcopum." See *(A) Artis auriferae,* vii.

ROTH-SCHOLTZ, FRIEDRICH. *Deutsches Theatrum Chemicum.* Nürnberg, 1728–32. 3 vols.

ROUSSELLE, ERWIN. "Drache und Stute, Gestalten der mythischen Welt Chinesischer Urzeit," in *Eranos-Jahrbuch 1934.* Zurich, 1935. (pp. 11–33.)

RULAND(US), MARTIN. *Lexicon Alchemiae sive Dictionarium alchemisticum.* Frankfurt a. M., 1622. For translation, see: *A Lexicon of Alchemy.* London, 1892.

RUPESCISSA, JOANNES DE. "De confectione veri lapidis." See *(A) Theatrum chemicum,* xxiv.

——. *La Vertu et la propriété de la quinte essence.* Lyons, 1581.

RUSKA, JULIUS (ed.). *Buch der Alaune und Salze (De speciebus salium).* Berlin, 1905.

——. "Die Vision des Arisleus." In: *Georg Sticker Festschrift: Historische Studien und Skizzen zur Natur- und Heilwissenschaft.* Berlin, 1930.

——. "Studien zu Muhammad ibn Umail," *Isis* (Bruges), XXIV (1935–36), 310–42.

——. *Tabula Smaragdina.* (Heidelberger Akten der von-Portheim-Stiftung, 16.) Heidelberg, 1926.

——. *Turba Philosophorum.* Berlin, 1931.

RUYSBROECK, JOHN OF. *The Adornment of the Spiritual Marriage* [etc.]. Translated by C. A. Wynschenk Dom. London, 1916.

Saint-Graal, Le. Le Mans (published by Eugene Bucher), 1875–78. 3 vols.

"Scala philosophorum." See *(A) Artis auriferae,* xix.

SCHAEDER, HANS HEINRICH. *Urform und Fortbildungen des manichäischen Systems.* (Vorträge der Bibliothek Warburg.) Leipzig and Berlin, 1924–25. (pp. 65–157.)

SCHEFFLER, JOHANN. See ANGELUS SILESIUS.

SCHEFTELOWITZ, ISIDOR. *Die altpersische Religion und das Judentum.* Giessen, 1920.

SCHEFTELOWITZ, ISIDOR. "Das Fischsymbol in Judentum und Christentum," *Archiv für Religionswissenschaft* (Leipzig), XIV (1911), 321–85.

SCHMIDT, CARL (ed.). *Manichäische Handschriften der Staatlichen Museen, Berlin.* Stuttgart, 1935–39. Vol. I (no more published).

SCHMIEDER, KARL CHRISTOPH. *Geschichte der Alchemie.* Halle, 1832.

SCHOLEM, GERHARD (Gershom G.) *Das Buch Bahir.* (Quellen und Forschungen zur Geschichte der jüdischen Mystik, 1.) Leipzig, 1923.

——. *Major Trends in Jewish Mysticism.* London, 1955.

——. "Zu Abraham Eleazars Buch und dem Esch Mazareph." *Monatsschrift für Geschichte und Wissenschaft des Judentums* (Dresden), LXX (n. s., XXXIV; 1926), 202–209.

SCHREBER, DANIEL PAUL. *Memoirs of My Nervous Illness.* Translated by Ida Macalpine and Richard A. Hunter. (Psychiatric Monograph Series, 1.) London, 1955. (Original, *Denkwürdigkeiten eines Nervenkranken,* 1903.)

SCHULTZ, WOLFGANG. *Dokumente der Gnosis.* Jena, 1910.

SCHULTZE, FRITZ. *Psychologie der Naturvölker.* Leipzig, 1900.

SCHWARTZ, C. "Explanatio Inscriptionis cujusdam veteris." *Acta Eruditorum* (Leipzig), 1727, pp. 332–35.

SCHWEITZER, ALBERT. *Geschichte der Leben-Jesu-Forschung.* Tübingen, 1921.

SCOTT, WALTER. *Hermetica.* Oxford, 1924–36. 4 vols.

SELLIN, ERNST. *Introduction to the Old Testament.* Translated by W. Montgomery. London, 1923.

SENDIVOGIUS, MICHAEL. "Parabola, seu Aenigma Philosophicum, Coronidis et super additamenti loco adjunctum." See *(A) Musaeum hermeticum,* x.

——. "Novum lumen chemicum." See *(A) Musaeum hermeticum,* x.

——. "Tractatus de Sulphure." See *(A) Musaeum hermeticum,* xi.

[SENIOR.] *De Chemia Senioris antiquissimi philosophi libellus.* Strasbourg, 1566. (Includes "Epistola Solis ad Lunam crescentem," pp. 7–10.) Other versions in *(A)* MANGETUS, *Bibliotheca chemica curiosa,* vi, and in *(A) Theatrum chemicum,* xliii.

"Septem tractatus Hermetis." See HERMES TRISMEGISTUS.

SERVIUS. *Servii Grammatici qui feruntur in Vergilii Carmina commentarii.* Edited by Georg Thilo and Hermann Hagen. Leipzig, 1878–1902. 3 vols.

[Sibylline Oracles.] See GEFFCKEN.

SIECKE, ERNST. *Beiträge zur genauen Kenntnis der Mondgottheit bei den Griechen.* Berlin, 1885.

SILBERER, HERBERT. *Problems of Mysticism and Its Symbolism.* Translated by Smith Ely Jelliffe. New York, 1917.

SOCRATES SCHOLASTICUS. [*Historia ecclesiastica.*] *The Ecclesiastical History.* In: *Socrates, Sozomenus, Church Histories.* Translation (anon.) revised by A. C. Zenos. (Select Library of Nicene and Post-Nicene Fathers, Second Series, 2.) Oxford and New York, 1891. (pp. 1–178.)

SPIEGELBERG, W. "Der Gott Bait in dem Trinitätsamulett des Britischen Museums," *Archiv für Religionswissenschaft* (Leipzig and Berlin), XXI (1922), 225–27.

Spiritual Disciplines. Translated by Ralph Manheim and R. F. C. Hull. (Papers from the Eranos Yearbooks, 4.) New York (Bollingen Series XXX: 4) and London, 1960.

SPITTELER, CARL. *Olympischer Frühling.* Leipzig, 1900–1905. 4 parts.

"Splendor solis." See TRISMOSIN.

SPON, JACOB, and WHELER, GEORGE. *Voyage d'Italie, de Dalmatie, de Grèce et du Levant fait aux années 1675 et 1676.* Amsterdam, 1679. 2 vols.

STADTMULLER, HUGO (ed.). *Anthologia Graeca Epigrammatum.* Leipzig, 1894–1906. 2 vols.

STAPLETON, H. E., and HUSAIN, M. HIDAYAT. "Muhammad bin Umail: His Date, Writings, and Place in Alchemical History," *Memoirs of the Asiatic Society of Bengal* (Calcutta), XII (1933).

STEEB, JOHANN CHRISTOPH. *Coelum Sephiroticum Hebraeorum.* Mainz, 1679.

STEINERUS, HENRICUS. *Dissertatio chymico-medica inauguralis de Antimonio.* Basel, [1699].

STOLCIUS DE STOLCENBERG, DANIEL. *Viridarium Chymicum.* Frankfurt a. M., 1624.

[SUIDAS.] *Suidae Lexicon.* Edited by Ada Adler. (Lexicographi Graeci, 1.) Leipzig, 1928–38. 5 parts.

643

TABERNAEMONTANUS, JACOBUS THEODORUS. *Kräuterbuch.* Basel, 1731. 2 vols. (pagination continuous throughout).

"Tabula smaragdina." See *(A) De alchemia, ii.* See also RUSKA.

TACHENIUS, OTTO (pseud. of Marcantonio Crasselame). *Lux obnubilata suapte natura refulgens. Vera de lapide philosophico theorica metro italico descripta.* . . . Venice, 1666. French translation: *La Lumière sortant par soi-mesme des ténèbres.* Paris, 1687. Another edn., 1693.

[Talmud.] *The Babylonian Talmud.* Edited by I. Epstein. London, 1935–52. 35 vols. (*Seder Nezikin,* Vols. III and IV, being Baba Bathra, Vols. I and II, translated by Israel W. Slotki; *Seder Nezikin,* Vols. V and VI, being Sanhedrin, Vols. I and II, translated by Jacob Schachter and H. Freedman.)

Tao Teh Ching. See WALEY.

TERESA, SAINT. *Works.* Translated by E. Allison Peers. London, 1946. 3 vols.

TERSTEEGEN, GERHART. *Geistliches Blumengärtlein inniger Seelen.* Frankfurt a. M. and Leipzig, 1778.

TERTULLIAN. *De Monogamia. Treatises on Marriage and Remarriage.* Translated by William P. LeSaint. (Ancient Christian Writers, 13.) Westminster (Maryland) and London, 1951.

TETZEN, JOHANNES DE (JOHANNES TICINENSIS). *Processus de Lapide Philosophorum.* In: *Johannis Ticinensis, Anthonii de Abbatia, Edoardi Kellaei Drey Chymische Bücher.* Hamburg. 1670.

THEODORET OF CYRUS. *Haereticarum fabularum compendium.* See Migne, *P.G.,* vol. 83, cols. 335–556.

THEOPHILUS OF ANTIOCH. *Three Books to Autolycus.* In: *The Writings of Tatian and Theophilus, and the Clementine Recognitions.* Translated by B. P. Pratten, Marcus Dods, and Thomas Smith. (Ante-Nicene Christian Library, 3.) Edinburgh, 1867. (pp. 53–133.)

THOMAS AQUINAS, SAINT. *Summa theologica.* Translated by the Fathers of the English Dominican Province. New York, 1947–48. 3 vols.

THORNDIKE, LYNN. *A History of Magic and Experimental Science.* New York, 1923–58. 8 vols.

THORPE, BENJAMIN. "A Dialogue between Saturn and Solomon." In: *Analecta Anglo-Saxonica.* London, 1834. (pp. 95–100.)

TONIOLA, JOHANNES. *Basilea sepulta retecta continuata.* Basel, 1661.

"Tractatulus Aristotelis." See ARISTOTLE, pseud.

"Tractatulus Avicennae." See AVICENNA.

"Tractatus aureus de lapide philosophorum." See HERMES TRISMEGISTUS.

"Tractaus Micreris." See MICRERIS.

TRAUBE, LUDWIG. "O Roma nobilis. Philologische Untersuchungen aus dem Mittelalter," *Abhandlungen der philosophisch-philologischen Classe der Königlich Bayerischen Akademie der Wissenschaften* (Munich), XIX (1892), 299–392.

TRISMOSIN, SALOMON. *Aureum vellus, oder Guldin Schatz und Kunstkammer.* Rorschach, 1598. ("Splendor solis" is Tractatus Tertius. There are several tractates each separately paginated. For translation of "Splendor solis," see: *Splendor Solis: Alchemical Treatises.* Edited by J. K. London [1920].)

TSCHARNER, EDUARD HORST VON. "Das Vermächtnis des Laotse," *Bund,* 13 and 20 June, 1934.

"Turba philosophorum." See RUSKA; also *(A) Artis auriferae,* i.

TYLOR, EDWARD B. *Primitive Culture.* London, 1871. 2 vols.

Upanishads. See MAX MÜLLER, FRIEDRICH (trans.). *The Upanishads.* Parts I and II. (Sacred Books of the East, 1, 15.) Oxford, 1879, 1884.

USENER, HERMANN. *Das Weihnachtsfest.* Bonn, 1911.

Vajasaneyi-samhita. See: *The Texts of the White Yajurveda.* Translated with commentary by Ralph T. H. Griffith. Benares, 1899.

VALENTINUS, BASILIUS. *Chymische Schrifften.* Hamburg, 1677.

———. "De prima materia lapidis philosophici." See *(A) Musaeum hermeticum,* ix.

———. "Opus praeclarum ad utrumque." See *(A) Theatrum chemicum,* xxxviii.

———. *Triumphwagen Antimonii.* Leipzig, 1611. For translation, see: *The Triumphal Chariot of Antimony.* With the commentary of Theodore Kerckringius. Edited by A. E. Waite. London, 1893.

VAN BEEK, CORNELIUS JOANNES M. J. (ed.). *Passio SS Perpetuae et Felicitatis.* Nymwegen, 1936.

[VAUGHAN, THOMAS.] *The Works of Thomas Vaughan: Eugenius Philaletha.* Edited by A. E. Waite. London, 1919.

VENTURA, LAURENTIUS. "De ratione conficiendi lapidis philosophici." See *(A) Theatrum chemicum*, xx.

VERANIUS, CAIETANUS FELIX. *Pantheon argenteae elocutionis.* Frankfurt a.M., 1712.

Verus Hermes. [Untraceable.]

VIGENÈRE, BLAISE DE (Vigenerus). "De igne et sale." See *(A) Theatrum chemicum*, xlix.

VIGNON, PAUL. *The Shroud of Christ.* Translated from the French. Westminster, 1902.

VITUS, RICHARDUS. See WHITE, RICHARD.

WAITE, ARTHUR EDWARD. *The Holy Kabbalah.* London, 1929.

——. *The Real History of the Rosicrucians.* London, 1887.

——. (ed. and trans.). *The Hermetic Museum Restored and Enlarged.* London, 1893. 2 vols.

——. See also VAUGHAN.

WALCH, CHRISTIAN WILHELM FRANZ. *Entwurf einer vollständigen Historie der Ketzereien.* Leipzig, 1762–83. 11 parts.

WALEY, ARTHUR (trans.). *The Way and Its Power.* London, 1934.

WEGMANN, HANS. *Das Rätsel der Sünde.* (Gottesglaube und Welterlebnis, 3.) Leipzig, 1937.

WEIL, GUSTAV. *Biblische Legenden der Musulmänner.* Frankfurt a. M., 1845.

WEI PO-YANG. "An Ancient Chinese Treatise on Alchemy, entitled Ts'an t'ung ch'i. Written by Wei Po-yang," translated by Lu-ch'iang Wu with introduction and notes by Tenney L. Davis, *Isis* (Bruges), XVIII (1932), 210–85.

WELLING, GEORG VON. *Opus Mago-Cabbalisticum et Theosophicum.* Hamburg, 1735.

WERNER, EDWARD THEODORE CHALMERS. *Myths and Legends of China.* London, 1922.

WHITE, RICHARD, OF BASINGSTOKE (Richardus Vitus Basinstochius). *Aelia Laelia Crispis Epitaphium.* Dordrecht, 1618.

WHITE, VICTOR. "The Scandal of the Assumption," *Life of the Spirit* (Oxford), V (1950), 199–212.

WICKES, FRANCES G. *The Inner World of Man.* New York and London, 1950.

WIELAND, C. MARTIN. *Dschinistan, oder ausleserne Feen- und Geistermärchen.* Winterthur, 1786–89. 3 vols. ("Der Stein der Weisen," Vol. I, pp. 218–79.)

WILAMOWITZ-MOELLENDORFF, U. VON. "Isyllos von Epidauros," *Philologische Untersuchungen* (Berlin), Heft 9 (1886).

WILHELM, RICHARD (ed.). *The Chinese Fairy Book.* Translated by Frederick H. Martens. London, 1922.

——— (trans.). *The Secret of the Golden Flower.* With a Commentary and Memorial by C. G. Jung. Translated by Cary F. Baynes. London and New York, 1931. (New edn., 1962.)

WINTER, J., and WÜNSCHE, AUGUST. *Die Jüdische Literatur seit Abschluss des Kanons.* Trier, 1894–96. 3 vols.

WITTEKINDT, W. *Das Hohe Lied und seine Beziehungen zum Ištarkult.* Hanover, 1925.

WOLBERO, ABBOT OF ST. PANTALEON, COLOGNE. *Commentaria super Canticum Canticorum.* See Migne, *P.L.,* vol. 195, cols. 1001–1278.

WÜNSCHE, AUGUST. "Die Sagen vom Lebensbaum und Lebenswasser," *Ex Oriente Lux* (Leipzig), I, parts 2 and 3 (1905).

———. "Salomos Thron und Hippodrom. Abbilder des Babylonischen Himmelsbildes," *Ex Oriente Lux* (Leipzig), II, part 3 (1906).

———. "Schöpfung und Sündenfall des ersten Menschenpaares im jüdischen und moslemischen Sagenkreise," *Ex Oriente Lux* (Leipzig), II, part 4 (1906).

ZACHARIUS, DIONYSIUS. "Opusculum philosophiae naturalis metallorum, cum annotationibus Nicolai Flamelli." See *(A) Theatrum chemicum,* xiii.

ZIMMER, HEINRICH. *Der Weg zum Selbst.* Edited by C. G. Jung. Zurich, 1944.

Zohar, The. Translated by Harry Sperling and Maurice Simon. London, 1931–34. 5 vols. See also MUELLER.

"Zosimus ad Theosebeiam." See "Rosinus ad Euthiciam."

INDEX

When cross reference is made to the "names of individual authors or treatises" in alchemical compilations, see the Bibliography, above, pp. 601 ff, where the names are listed.

A

orphan, 17, 37, 41; as panacea, 318,
477, 533; paradox of, 42ff, 452; as
quaternity of elements, 188; quartered, 422; and resurrection, 158n;
sand as, 204; as saviour, 39, 124,
281, 317f, 475; secret of, 172, 398;
as self, *see* self; as "son of man,"
222f; spirit, soul and body of, 372,
541; as symbol, 216n, 372, 454;
synonyms of, 4n, 118, 262f, 290,
371, 423, 463; as tincture/medi-
cine, 485; triunity of, 265; as union
of opposites, 118, 396; unity of, 79,
153n, 222, 272, 342n, 371, 385,
540; as *unum/unus mundus*, 385,
463; volatile, 510; white stone,
239; as youth, 10, 166; *see also*
stone
Larguier, Leo, 153n
Last Supper, 307, 364
lato, 235
Lauterburg, M., 337n
Lavoisier, Antoine Laurent, 124
law, tables of, 398
lead, 156, 225, 227, 335n, 351, 382,
428
Leah, 389
leap-year, 398
Lebhûdhâ, 388
Lehmann, F. R., 95n
Leibniz, G. W. von, 471
Leisegang, Hans, 15n, 348n, 402n,
403n
Lemures, 175, 236
Lenglet du Fresnoy, *see* Du Fresnoy
Leo, *see* lion
Leone Ebreo, 53n
Lesser, F. C., 18n
Leto, 71n, 205
Leviathan, 198, 210, 251, 401, 445
Leviticus, Book of, 15n, 242n, 411n
Lévy-Bruhl, L., 250n, 488
*Libellus Desideriorum Joannis
Amati*, 33n
"Liber Alze," 64n, 193
"Liber Azoth," *see* Paracelsus
"Liber de arte chymica," *see* "De arte
chymica"

"Liber de magni lapidis compositione," 438n
Liber mutus, see Mutus liber
"Liber Quartorum," *see* "Platonis
Liber Quartorum"
Libra, 7, 176
Licetus, Fortunatus, 85
Lidzbarski, Mark, 409n, 410n, 492n,
511n
life-style, 365n
light, 47, 139, 338; Christ as, 338;
crown of, 9; in Adam's nature,
406; Mercurius as, 504
Lilith, 122, 408
lily, 480, 485, 492
lion/Leo, 5, 28n, 32, 112n, 125, 141,
144, 147, 148, 176, 210, 297, 301ff,
332, 360n, 364, 365, 400n, 446; as
allegory of Christ, 311, 324, 345n;
—, of the devil, 298, 332; *antiquus*,
297; as arcane substance, 125, 295;
in astrology, 350n; blood of, *see*
blood; corruption of, 28; and dog,
297; dung of, 294n; and eagle,
323n; as evil, 117, 298; as evil
passions, 160, 295; erotic aspect of,
298, 304, 310; green, 293f, 296,
304f, 323, 335, 461, 473; and lioness, 5, 295, 298; "lion-hunt" of
Marchos, 284, 298f; mutilation of,
142, 350, 364n; queen and, 311;
red, 296, 335, 473; and sun, 144,
147, 297f; as synonym for Mercurius, 117, 295, 338, 461
Lippmann, Eduard von, 10n, 72n,
80n, 235n, 268n, 385n, 457, 510n
"Livre des Balances," 406n
"Livre des Secrez de Nature," 159n
Logos, 104, 179f; Christ as, 142, 290,
338, 361; as dog, 147n, 148, 149;
ibis and, 195
Lohmeyer, Ernst, 492n
Lorichius, Johannes, 65, 82n
Lot's wife, 83n
love, and the unconscious, 86
Loyola, *see* Ignatius
Lucian, 342n, 409n, 492n
Lucifer, 118f, 170, 436n, 441, 512n

Typhon, 21–22*n*, 52*n*, 63*n*, 93, 175*n*, 193, 251*f*, 260*n*, 272*n*, 493
Tyre, 20
Tyriac, 29
Tyrian dye, 201

U

ὕδωρ θεῖον, 484, 503
"ugliest man," 247
Ullikummi, 536*n*
unarius, 48, 352
Unas, 30
unconscious(ness), 58, 81, 128, 181, 199*f*, 202, 210, 248, 253, 295, 368, 437*n*, 495, 522, 526, 527; Africa as, 211; ambivalence of, 197; archetypal structure of, 390; artificial, 472; attention to, 152, 163, 232; autonomy of, 254; birth of self in, 384; collective, 81, 84, 87, 91, 104, 106, 122*f*, 199, 258, 278, 280, 300, 523; —, personal and, 199*f*; compensatory character of, 103, 126, 156*f*, 162, 178*f*, 217, 232, 310, 333*f*, 346, 349, 366, 494, 497, 518, 531, 540; contamination of, 274, 293, 462*f*; counterposition in, 200; dangers of, 156*f*; destructive tendency of, 126, 184*f*, 200*f*; ego and, *see* ego; hermaphroditism of, 177; *idées forces* of, 528; illumination/ making conscious of, 172, 201, 229, 311, 320, 356; increase of potential of, 363; integration of, 257, 546; irrational contents of, 229, 471; irruption of, 98*n*, 121*n*, 157, 208, 530, 549; longing of, for consciousness, 437; luminosity, multiple/ scintillae of, 55*n*, 207, 491; lunar/ feminine/maternal character of, 103*n*, 135, 144, 154, 175*f*, 178, 184, 241, 272, 356, 379, 517; Mercurius as, *see* Mercurius; as nigredo, see *nigredo;* opposites and, 79, 81; personification of, 106; physical symptoms and, 238; primordial, 462;

projection of, 126, 196, 253, 299, 361; psychoid, 552; sea as, *see* sea; theriomorphic symbols of, 210*ff*; transformation of, 77; treatment of, 209; unknowable, 498*ff*; water as, 272*f*, 504
underworld, imprisonment in, 236
unicorn, 5, 281, 400, 423*n*, 500*n*
unio mentalis/mental union, 465*ff*, 470*f*, 474, 476, 482*f*, 485, 487*ff*, 497, 499, 507, 513, 521*f*, 524, 528, 531*f*, 541
unio mystica, 443, 537, 540
unio naturalis, 488
uniped(s), Pl. 4; *see also* Monocolus
unity: of arcanum, 540; creation of, 534
universals, 439*n*
unus mundus, see world
Upanishads, 135*n*, 136*n*, 517
Uranos, 515
uroboros, 79, 102*n*, 115*n*, 116, 223, 251, 294, 295*f*, 307*f*, 311, 340, 342*n*; Agathodaimon as, 9*n*; aqua divina as, 112; as arcane substance, 29*n*, 60; as goal of opus, 504; as the One, 365; as self-devouring, 60, 144*n*, 285, 445; as symbol of self-origination / immortality, 293*n*, 365; *see also* dragon; snake
Ursa Major, 205*n*
Usener, Hermann, 71*n*

V

Vajasaneyi-samhita, 109*n*
Valentinus/Valentinians, 282, 338*n*, 383, 403*n*, 417*n*
Valentinus, Basilius, 5*n*, 116*n*, 152*n*, 190, 296, 302, 303, 304, 332*n*, 383
value, in psychology, 426*f*
van der Post, Laurens, 485*n*
vas, see vessel
vau (Hebrew letter), 430
Vaughan, Thomas, 33*n*; *see also* Philaletha
Vedas, *see* Atharva-veda; Rig-veda

CORRELATION OF PARAGRAPH NUMBERS

As the Gesammelte Werke edition of *Mysterium Coniunctionis* (2 vols., 1968) retains the textual arrangement and paragraph numbering of the first Swiss edition (1955/1956) and therefore varies in these respects from the Collected Works edition, the following table gives the equivalents between the two. The principal changes of arrangement, approved by Professor Jung, are explained in footnotes in the Collected Works edition. Paragraphs 1–30 are numbered alike in both editions.

Collected Works	Gesammelte Werke	Collected Works	Gesammelte Werke	Collected Works	Gesammelte Werke
[Band I]		54	49	82	79
		55	50	83	80
CHAPTER I		56	51	84	81
1	1	57	52/53	85	82
......	......	58	53	86	83
31/32	31	59	54	87	84
33	32	60	55	88	85
34	33	61	56	89	86
35	34	62	57/58	90	87
		63	59	91	88
CHAPTER II		64	60	92	89
36	35	65	63	93	90
37	36	66	64	94	91
38	37	67	65	95	92
39	38	68	66	96	93
40	39	69	67	97	94
41	40	70	68	98	95
42	41	71	69	99	96
43	42	72	70	100	97
44	43	73	71	101	98
45	44/60	74	72	102	99
46	61	75	73	103	100
47	62	76	37 [Bd. II]	CHAPTER III	
48/49	44	77	74		
50	45	78	75	104	101
51	46	79	76	105	102
52	47	80	77	106	103
53	48	81	78	107	104

Collected Works	Gesammelte Werke	Collected Works	Gesammelte Werke	Collected Works	Gesammelte Werke
108	105	159	154	210	204
109	106	160	155	211	205
110	107	161	156	212	206
111	108	162	157	213	207
112	109	163	158	214	208
113	110	164	159	215	209
114	111	165	160	216	210
115	112	166	161	217	211
116	113	167	162	218	212
117	114	168	163	219	213
118	115	169	164	220	214
119	116	170	165	221	215
120	117	171	166	222	216
121	118	172	167	223	217
122	119	173	168	224	218
123	120	174	169	225	219
124/125	121	175	170	226	220
126	122	176	171	227	221
127	123	177	172	228	222
128	124	178	173	229	223
129	125	179	174	230	224
130	126	180/181	175	231	225
131	127	182	176	232	226
132	128	183	177	233	227
133	129	184	178	234	228
134	130	185	179	235	229
135	131	186	180	236	230
136	132	187	181	237	231
137	133	188	182	238	232
138	134	189	183	239	233
139	135	190	184	240	234
140	136	191	185	241	235
141	137	192/193	186	242	236
142	138	194	187	243	237
143	139	195	188	244	238
144	140	196	189	245	239
145/146	141	197	190	246	240
147	142	198	191	247	241
148	143	199	192	248	242
149	144	200	193	249	243
150	145	201	194	250	244
151	146	202	195	251	245
152	147	203	196/197	252	246
153	148	204	198	253	247
154	149	205	199	254	248
155	150	206	200	255	249
156	151	207	201	256	250
157	152	208	202	257	251
158	153	209	203	258	252

Collected Works	Gesammelte Werke	Collected Works	Gesammelte Werke	Collected Works	Gesammelte Werke
259	253	308	302	356	8/9
260	254	309	303	357	10
261	255	310	304	358	11
262	256	311	305	359	12
263	257	312	306	360	13
264	258	313	307	361	14
265	259	314	308	362	15
266	260	315	309	363	16
267	278	316	310	364	17
268	261	317	311	365	18
269	262	318	312	366	19
270	263	319	313	367	20
271	264	320	314	368	21
272	265	321	315	369	22
273	266	322	316	370	23
274	267	323	317	371	24
275	268	324	318	372	25
276	269	325	319	373	26/27
277	270	326	320	374	28/29
278	271	327	321	375	30
279	272	328	322	376	31
280	273	329	323	377	32
281	274	330	324	378	33
282	275	331	325	379	34
283	276	332	326	380	35/40
284	277	333	327	381	41
285	278/279	334	328	382	42
286	280	335	329	383	43
287	281	336	330	384	44
288	282	337	331	385	45
289	283	338	332	386	46
290	284	339	333	387	47
291	285	340	334	388	48
292	286	341–343	335	389	49
293	287	344	336	390	50
294	288	345	337	391	51
295	289	346/347	338	392	52
296	290	347	339	393	53
297	291	348	340	394	54
298	292			395	55
299	293		[Band II]	396	56
300	294	CHAPTER IV		397	57
301	295	349	1	398	58
302	296	350	2	399	59
303	297	351	3	400	60
304	298	352	4	401	61
305	299	353	5	402	62
306	300	354	6	403	63
307	301	355	7	404	64

Collected Works	Gesammelte Werke	Collected Works	Gesammelte Werke	Collected Works	Gesammelte Werke
405	65	455	121	504	169
406	66	456	122	505/506	170
407	67	457	123	507	171
408	68	458	124	508	172
409	69	459	125/126	509	173
410	70	460	127	510	174
411	71	461	128	511	175
412/413	72	462	129	512	176
414	73	463	130	513	177
415	74	464/465	131	514	178
416	75	466	132	515	179
417/418	76	467/468	133	516	180
419	77	469	134	517	181
420	78	470	135	518	182
421	79	471	136	518a*	183
422	81	472	137	519	184
423	82	473	138	520	185
424/425	83	474	139	521	186
426	84	475	140	522	187
427	85	476	141	523	188
428	86	477	142	524	189
429	87	478	143	525	190
430	88	479	144	526	191
431	89	480	145	527	192
432	90	481	146	528	193
433	91	482	147	529	194
434	93/92/94	483	148	530	195
435	95	484	149	531	196
436	96	485	150	532	197
437	97	486	151	533	198
438	98/99	487	152	534	199
439	100	488	153	535	200
440	101	489	154	536	201
441	102	490	155	537	202
442	103	491	156	538	203
443	104	492	157	539	204
444	105	493	158	540	205
445	106	494	159	541	206
446	107	495	160	542	207
447	108	496	161	543	208
448	109/110	497	162		
449	111	498	163	CHAPTER V	
450	112	499	164	544	209
451	113	500	165	545	210
452	114	501	166	546	211
453	115–119	502	167	547	212
454	120	503	168	548	213

* For par. 518a, inadvertently omitted in the first edition, see supra, p. vii.

Collected Works	Gesammelte Werke	Collected Works	Gesammelte Werke	Collected Works	Gesammelte Werke
549	214	598	262	647	313
550	215	599	263	648	314
551	216	600	264	649	315
552	217	601	269	650	316
553	218	602	270	651	317
554	219	603	271	652	318
555	220	604	272	653	319
556	221	605	273		
557	222	606	265	CHAPTER VI	
558	223	607	274	654/655	320
559	224	608	275	656	321
560	225	609	276	657	322
561	226	610	277	658	323
562	227	611	278	659	324
563	228	612	279	660	325
564	229	613	280	661	326
565	230	614	281	662	327
566	231	615	282	663	328
567	232	616	283	664	329
568	233	617	284	665	330
569	234	618	285	666	331
570	235/248	619	267	667	332
571	235/248	620	286	668	333
572	236	621	287	669	334
573	237	622	288	670–672	335
574	238	623	289	673	338
575	239	624	290	674	339
576	240	625	291	675	340
577	241	626	292	676	336
578	242	627	293	677/678	337
579	243/246	628	294	679	341
580	244	629	295	680	342
581	245	630	296	681	343
582	246	631	297	682	344
583	249	632	298	683	345
584	250	633	299	684/685	346
585	251	634	300/274/303	686/687	347
586	252	635	300	688	348
587	253	636	301	689	349
588	254	637	302	690	350
589	255	638	304	691	351
590	256	639	305	692	352
591	257	640	306	693	353
592	258	641	307	694	354
593	266	642	308	695	355
594	268	643	309	696	356
595	259	644	310	697	357
596	260	645	311	698	358
597	261	646	312	699	359

Collected Works	Gesammelte Werke	Collected Works	Gesammelte Werke	Collected Works	Gesammelte Werke
700	360	733	390	766	421
701	361	734	391	767	422
702	362	735	392	768	423
703	363	736	393	769	424
704	364	737	394	770	425
705/706	365	738	395	771	426
707	366	739	396	772	427
708	367	740	397	773	428
709	368	741–743	398	774	429
710	369	744	399	775	430
711	370	745	400	776	431
712–714	371	746	401	777	432
715	372	747	402	778	433
716	373	748	403	779	434
717	374	749	404	780	435
718	375	750	405	781	436
719	376	751/752	406	782	437
720	377	753	407	783	438
721	378	754	408	784	439
722	379	755	409	785	440
723	380	756	410	786	441
724	381	757	411	787	442
725	382	758	412	788	443
726	383	759	413	789	444
727	384	760	414		
728	385	761	415/416	EPILOGUE	
729	386	762	417		
730	387	763	418	790	445
731	388	764	419	791	446
732	389	765	420	792	447

THE COLLECTED WORKS OF
C. G. JUNG

THE PUBLICATION of the first complete edition, in English, of the works of C. G. Jung was undertaken by Routledge and Kegan Paul, Ltd., in England and by Bollingen Foundation in the United States. The American edition is number XX in Bollingen Series, which since 1967 has been published by Princeton University Press. The edition contains revised versions of works previously published, such as *Psychology of the Unconscious*, which is now entitled *Symbols of Transformation*; works originally written in English, such as *Psychology and Religion*; works not previously translated, such as *Aion*; and, in general, new translations of virtually all of Professor Jung's writings. Prior to his death, in 1961, the author supervised the textual revision, which in some cases is extensive. Sir Herbert Read (d. 1968), Dr. Michael Fordham, and Dr. Gerhard Adler compose the Editorial Committee; the translator is R. F. C. Hull (except for Volume 2) and William McGuire is executive editor.

The price of the volumes varies according to size; they are sold separately, and may also be obtained on standing order. Several of the volumes are extensively illustrated. Each volume contains an index and in most a bibliography; the final volume will contain a complete bibliography of Professor Jung's writings and a general index to the entire edition.

In the following list, dates of original publication are given in parentheses (of original composition, in brackets). Multiple dates indicate revisions.

---

* Published 1971.   † Published 1953; 2nd edn., 1966.
‡ Published 1960; 2nd edn., 1969.

* Published 1959; 2nd edn., 1968. (Part I: 79 plates, with 29 in colour.)

* Published 1964; 2nd edn., 1970. (8 plates.)
† Published 1958; 2nd edn., 1969.

* Published 1953; 2nd edn., completely revised, 1968. (270 illustrations.)
† Published 1968. (50 plates, 4 text figures.)
‡ Published 1963; 2nd edn., 1970. (10 plates.)

* Published 1966.
† Published 1954; 2nd edn., revised and augmented, 1966. (13 illustrations.)
‡ Published 1954.

The Development of Personality (1934)
Marriage as a Psychological Relationship (1925)

18. THE SYMBOLIC LIFE
Miscellaneous Writings

19. BIBLIOGRAPHY OF C. G. JUNG'S WRITINGS

20. GENERAL INDEX TO THE COLLECTED WORKS

See also:

C. G. JUNG: LETTERS
Selected and edited by Gerhard Adler, in collaboration with Aniela Jaffé.
Translations from the German by R.F.C. Hull.
VOL. 1: 1906–1950
VOL. 2: 1951–1961

THE FREUD/JUNG LETTERS
The Correspondence between Sigmund Freud and C. G. Jung
Translated by Ralph Manheim and R.F.C. Hull
Edited by William McGuire